An Introduction to the History of Israel and Judah

J. Alberto Soggin

AN INTRODUCTION TO THE HISTORY OF ISRAEL AND JUDAH

Second, completely revised and updated edition

Trinity Press International
Valley Forge, PA

First U.S. Edition
Trinity Press International
P.O. Box 851
Valley Forge, PA 19482-0851

Translated by John Bowden from *Introduzione alla Storia d'Israele e di Giuda*,
to be published by Paideia Editrice, Brescia

© Paideia Editrice 1993

Translation © John Bowden 1993

Library of Congress Cataloging-in-Publication
Data available.

1-56338-073-0
First British edition published 1993 by SCM Press Ltd,
26-30 Tottenham Road, London N1 4BZ

Printed in the U.S.A.

93 94 95 96 97 98   6 5 4 3 2 1

לאוניברסיטה העברית בירושלים,
שבמכון ללימודים מתקדמים שלה,
בשנת תשמ"ג, העניקה לי זמן ומקום, עזרה ושלוה;
בלעדיהם מחקר זה לא היה בא לעולם.

To the Hebrew University of Jerusalem which,
in its 'Institute of Advanced Studies',
during the academic year 1982-83
provided me with quiet, space, time and
co-operation, without which this book
would never have been written.

Contents

Plates

Contents

From the Preface to the First Edition

This book could never have been written without a series of circumstances which helped it in a number of ways:

1. The invitation I received from the Institute of Advanced Studies in the Hebrew University of Jerusalem to be Fellow at the Institute for the academic year 1982-83 and the many facilities put at my disposal and at that of my colleagues.

2. The study leave which was immediately granted by the Rector of the University of Rome on the recommendation of the Faculty of Arts and Philosophy, and the readiness of my colleagues in the Institute of Near Eastern Studies to support me.

3. The brotherly welcome from the École biblique et archéologique française of the Dominican Convent of St Stephen in Jerusalem, whose superb library I could enjoy at my leisure.

4. The collaboration of my colleagues in the Waldensian Faculty in Rome.

Many colleagues, in Italy and abroad, have discussed with me important parts of this work and I have profited enormously from the time that I have spent with them. I cannot even list their names. However, in particular I would like to recall the staff of the Hebrew University in Jerusalem, some of whom continued to discuss issues with me while making no bones about their disagreement over a number of the positions put forward here. 'The zeal (and sometimes indeed the jealousy) of scholars increases wisdom', as the ancient 'father' of the Talmud remarked.

The reader will often notice, here and there in this book, a certain disproportion between the attention given to some features which are clearly not of primary importance and the lesser attention given to others which are obviously more important. I offer no excuses for this in advance; things sometimes work out like this, and only constant refinement can remedy the proportions or eliminate the disproportions.

In the course of this work I have not spent time discussing the books of the Bible. For this I would refer the reader to my *Introduction to the Old Testament*, London and Philadelphia ³1989. I should also point out that the bibliographies are almost always select ones. To provide complete bibliographies would not only be to embark on pointless toil but would also turn an attempt at a history into a bibliographical manual which would have virtually nothing to do with a history.

This book ends with the events of 74 and 135 CE, which led to the destruction of Judaism in Judaea and the dispersion of the survivors; after the destruction of the temple (which has never been rebuilt) by Titus and the failure of the Bar Kochba revolt, the cultural and religious centre of Judaism in Palestine ceased to exist, and it was the Diaspora, which from now on even included some parts of the Holy Land, which was to be the determinative element. Here we find ourselves confronted with one of those breaks in history which in all respects can be compared with the 'official' end of the Roman empire as marked by the deposition of Romulus Augustulus in 476. Therefore it seems to me legitimate to break off the investigation at this point.

The reader will note that from the period of the Maccabees onwards the account becomes more synthetic, more sparse. The truth of the matter is that after the discovery of the Qumran manuscripts in 1947, little or nothing new can be said in this field. So for a detailed account the reader should refer to the various *Histories of Israel* which deal with it, sometimes at length: Ricciotti, Noth, Gunneweg, Hayes and Miller, Bright (see below, 3.5), and all the monographs listed in the bibliographies. For two highly specialized themes, the chronology of the period of the monarchy and Palestinian archaeology, I have felt it necessary to make use of the works of particularly competent scholars, D.Conrad of the University of Marburg and H.Tadmor of the Hebrew University of Jerusalem. While the contribution by the former was written specially for this work, the latter's study is a reprint of a chapter of the *World History of the Jewish People*, by kind permission of the publisher, Massada Press in Jerusalem.

I would like to thank those who have put photographs, diagrams and other materials at my disposal, some of them unpublished:

The Department of Antiquities of the State of Israel, Jerusalem;

The Hebrew Union College of Jerusalem (Professor A.Biran);

The Israel Exploration Society of Jerusalem (Professor N.Avigad);

The Institute of Archaeology of the University of Tel Aviv (Professor R.Gophan).

One last word. It is clear that this history, like all histories, is no more than an attempt. The traditions which Israel handed down about itself are also no more than an attempt, even if, in Christian doctrine, they are regarded as an inspired attempt. And that is the limit of this work, which is now open to discussion.

Jerusalem, summer 1983
Rome, autumn 1983

Preface to the Second Edition

This second edition of my *History* is in fact a total reworking of the first edition. After only a few years, some proposals have had to be changed and other, new, ones proposed. As a result, on almost every page this is a completely revised edition.

A German edition, *Einführung in die Geschichte Israels und Judah*, Wissenschaftliche Buchgesellschaft, Darmstadt 1991, has recently appeared, abbreviated in some sections; it contains some of the new features of the present work.

This new edition was completed during a year of sabbatical leave which I spent at Christ Church, Oxford, as Hugh Pilkington Scholar. I would like here to express my gratitude to the college for its generous and warm hospitality, which even included the use of a personal computer, and which made my stay in Oxford pleasant in every way. I am also grateful to my wife, who has read through the text and indicated a number of inconsistencies. Richard Coggins, of King's College, London, has again provided invaluable help in checking the bibliographies.

Last but not least, John Bowden of the SCM Press in London has been not only a friend, but as always the best of translators.

Christ Church, Oxford, summer 1992

Abbreviations

AASOR	Annual of the American Schools of Oriental Research
AB	The Anchor Bible
ABLAK	M.Noth, *Abhandlungen zur biblischen Landes- und Altertumskunde*, Neukirchen 1974
ADPV	*Abhandlungen des Deutschen Palästinavereins*
AfO	Archiv für Orientforschung
AGWG.PH	Abhandlungen der Gesellschaft der Wissenschaft zu Göttingen
AHw	W.von Soden, *Akkadisches Handwörterbuch*, Wiesbaden 1965-1981
AION	*Annali dell Instituto Orientale di Napoli*
AJBI	*Annual of the Japanese Biblical Institute*
AnBibl	Analecta Biblica
ANET	J.B.Pritchard (ed.), *Ancient Near Eastern Texts relating to the Old Testament*, Princeton ³1969
ANEP	J.B.Pritchard (ed.), *The Ancient Near East in Pictures*, Princeton ³1969
ANL-M/R	Atti dell'Accademia nazionale dei Lincei – Memorie/Resconti
AOAT	Alter Orient und Altes Testament
AOF	*Altorientalische Forschungen*
ARM	Archives royales de Mari
ASNSP	*Annali della Scuola Normale Superiore di Pisa*
ASOR	The American Schools of Oriental Research
ASTI	*Annual of the Swedish Theological Institute*
ATANT	Abhandlungen zur Theologie des Alten und Neuen Testaments
ATD	Das Alte Testament Deutsch
AUSS	Andrews University Seminary Studies
AustBR	*Australian Biblical Review*
BA	*The Biblical Archaeologist*
Bab	Babylonian Talmud
BAR	*Biblical Archaeology Review*
BASOR	*Bulletin of the ASOR*

BBB	Bonner biblische Beiträge
BeO	*Bibbia e Oriente*
BHH	*Biblisch-historisches Handwörterbuch*, 4 vols., Göttingen 1962-1975
BHK	*Biblia Hebraica*, ed. R.Kittel
BHS	*Biblia Hebraica Stuttgartensia* (= *BHK⁴*)
Bib	*Biblica*
BiblOr	Biblica et Orientalia
BiblRes	*Biblical Research*
BJRL	*Bulletin of the John Rylands Library*
BK	Biblischer Kommentar zum AT
BN	*Biblische Notizen*
BO	*Bibliotheca Orientalis*
BTB	*Biblical Theology Bulletin*
BWANT	Beiträge zur Wissenschaft vom Alten und Neuen Testament
BZ	*Biblische Zeitschrift*
BZAW	Beihefte zur *ZAW*
CAH	*Cambridge Ancient History*
CB-OTS	Coniectanea Biblica – Old Testament Series
CBQ	*Catholic Biblical Quarterly*
CHJ	*The Cambridge History of Judaism*
CTA	A.Herdner, *Corpus des tablettes alphabétiques découvertes à Ras-Shamra-Ugarit 1929-39*, Paris 1963
DBAT	*Dielheimer Blätter zum Alten Testament*
DOTT	*Documents from Old Testament Times*, ed. D.Winton Thomas, London and New York 1958
EI	*'Ereṣ Isra'el*
EncBibl	*Encyclopaedia Biblica* (in Hebrew)
EncJud	*Encyclopedia Judaica*
ETL	*Ephemerides Theologicae Lovaniensis*
EvTh	*Evangelische Theologie*
ExpT	*Expository Times*
FRLANT	Forschungen zur Religion und Literatur vom Alten und Neuen Testament
FS	Festschrift
GA	Gesammelte Aufsätze
Gr	*Gregorianum*
GS	Gesammelte Schriften
GThT	*Gereformeerd theologisch tijdschrift*
HAT	Handbuch zum Alten Testament
Hen	*Henoch*
HorBibTh	*Horizons in Biblical Theology*
HKAT	Handkommentar zum Alten Testament

HSM	Harvard Semitic Monographs
HTR	*Harvard Theological Review*
HUCA	*Hebrew Union College Annual*
IASHP	*Israel Academy of Sciences and Humanities – Proceedings*
ICC	International Critical Commentary
IDB-SV	Interpreter's Dictionary of the Bible – Supplementary Volume
IEJ	*The Israel Exploration Journal*
Int	*Interpretation*
JANESCU	*Journal of the Ancient Near Eastern Society*, Columbia University
JAOS	*Journal of the American Oriental Society*
JBL	*Journal of Biblical Literature*
JCS	*Journal of Cuneiform Studies*
JEA	*Journal of Egyptian Archaeology*
JESHO	*Journal of the Economic and Social History of the Orient*
JJS	*Journal of Jewish Studies*
JNES	*Journal of Near Eastern Studies*
JNWSL	*Journal of North Western Semitic Literature*
JPOS	*Journal of the Palestine Oriental Society*
JQR	*Jewish Quarterly Review*
JSOT	*Journal for the Study of the Old Testament*
JSOT-SS	*Journal for the Study of the Old Testament – Supplement Series*
JSS	*Journal of Semitic Studies*
JTS	*Journal of Theological Studies*
KAI	W.Donner and W.Röllig, *Kanaanäische und Aramäische Inschriften*, Wiesbaden ²1966-70
KB	L.Köhler and W.Baumgartner, *Lexicon in Veteris Testamenti Libros*, Leiden ³1967-83
KS	Kleine Schriften
KuD	*Kerygma und Dogma*
LA-SBF	*Liber Annuus- Studii Biblici Franciscani*
LXX	Septuagint: Greek translation of the Hebrew Bible
NKZ	*Neue Kirchliche Zeitschrift*
OA	*Oriens Antiquus*
ÖAW-Sitzb	Österreichische Akademie der Wissenschaften – Sitzungsberichte
OBO	Orbis Biblicus et Orientalis
OLZ	*Orientalische Literaturzeitung*
Or	*Orientalia*
OTL	Old Testament Library
OTOS	J.A.Soggin, *Old Testament and Oriental Studies*, BibOr, Rome 1975

OTS	*Oudtestamentische Studiën*
OTW	M.Noth, *The Old Testament World*, ET London 1966
PEQ	*Palestine Exploration Quarterly*
PJB	Palästina-Jahrbuch
PL	Patrologia Latina, ed. J.P.Migne
PP	*La Parola del Passato*
Prot	*Protestantesimo*
RA	*Revue d'Assyriologie*
RB	*Revue Biblique*
RGG	*Die Religion in Geschichte und Gegenwart*
RHPR	*Revue d'Histoire et de philosophie religieuse*
RHR	*Revue d'histoire des religions*
RiBib	*Rivista biblica*
RIDA	*Revue internationale des droits de l'antiquité*
RSF	*Rivista di studi fenici*
RSLR	*Rivista di storia e di letteratura religiosa*
RSO	*Rivista di studi orientali*
RTP	*Revue de théologie et de philosophie*
SBL DS/MS	Society of Biblical Literature – Dissertation Series/ Monograph Series
SBS	Stuttgarter Bibelstudien
SBT	Studies in Biblical Theology
ScandJOT	*Scandinavian Journal of Theology*
ScrHier	*Scripta Hierosolymitana*
SDB	*Supplément au Dictionnaire de la Bible*
SEÅ	*Svensk Exegetisk Årsbok*
Sem	*Semitica*
SJT	*Scottish Journal of Theology*
SMSR	*Studi e materiali di storia delle religioni*
SNTS-MS	Society for New Testament Studies – Monograph Series
SOTS-MS	Society for Old Testament Study – Monograph Series
SSI	J.C.L.Gibson, *Textbook of Syrian Semitic Inscriptions*, Oxford I, 1971; II, 1975; III, 1982
SSR	*Studi di Storia delle Religioni*
ST	*Studia Theologica*
StSem	Studi semitici
SVT	Supplements to *Vetus Testamentum*
TA	*Tel Aviv*
Targ	Targum: Aramaic translation of the Hebrew Bible
TDOT	*Theological Dictionary of the Old Testament*
TheolVers	*Theologische Versuche*
ThRev	*Theologische Revue*
TLZ	*Theologische Literaturzeitung*

TR	*Theologische Rundschau*
TRE	*Theologische Realenzyklopädie*
TS	*Theological Studies*
TUAT	O.Kaiser, *Texte aus der Umwelt des Alten Testaments*, Gütersloh 1982ff.
TynB	*Tyndale Bulletin*
TZ	*Theologische Zeitschrift*
VuF	*Verkündigung und Forschung*
WHJP	B.Mazar (ed.), *The World History of the Jewish People*, Jerusalem 1964ff. (cf. 3.5.2.10)
WMANT	Wissenschaftliche Monographien zum Alten und Neuen Testament
WuD	*Wort und Dienst*
WUS	J.Aistleitner, *Wörterbuch der ugaritischen Sprache*, Berlin 1963
ZA	*Zeitschrift für Assyriologie*
ZAW	*Zeitschrift für die Alttestamentliche Wissenschaft*
ZDMG	*Zeitschrift der Deutschen Morgenländischen Gesellschaft*
ZDPV	*Zeitschrift der Deutschen Palästinavereins*
ZNW	*Zeitschrift für die Neutestamentliche Wissenschaft*
ZTK	*Zeitschrift für Theologie und Kirche*

Works quoted frequently
in abbreviated form

* = History of Israel

Y.Aharoni, *The Land of the Bible*, London and Philadelphia ²1979 (cf. 2.10.2)

W.F.Albright*, *From the Stone Age to Christianity*, Baltimore 1940, ²1957 (cf. 3.5.2.1); unless indicated otherwise, quotations come from the second edition

J.Bright*, *A History of Israel*, Philadelphia and London ³1981 (cf.3.5.2.3)

G.Buccellati, *Cities and Nations of Ancient Syria*, StSem 26, Rome 1967

W.M.Clark*, cf. Hayes-Miller*

R. de Vaux*, *The Early History of Israel*, London 1978 (cf. 3.5.2.4)

W.G.Dever*, cf. Hayes-Miller*

H.Donner*, cf. Hayes-Miller*

G.Fohrer*, *Geschichte Israels*, Heidelberg ³1982 (cf. 3.5.2.7)

G.Garbini, *I Fenici – Storia e religione*, Naples 1980

– *, *History and Ideology in Ancient Israel*, London and New York 1988 (cf. 3.5.2.16)

N.K.Gottwald, *The Tribes of Yahweh*, Maryknoll 1979 - London 1980

A.H.J.Gunneweg*, *Geschichte Israels bis Bar Kochba*, Stuttgart ³1979 (cf. 3.5.2.5)

J.H.Hayes and J.M.Miller (eds.)*, *Israelite and Judaean History*, London and Philadelphia 1977 (cf. 3.5.2.8)

S.Herrmann*, *A History of Israel in Old Testament Times*, London and Philadelphia ²1981 (cf. 3.5.2.6)

T.Ishida (ed.), *Studies in the Period of David and Solomon*, Tokyo 1982

H.Jagersma*, *A History of Israel in the Old Testament Period*, London and Philadelphia 1982 (cf. 3.5.2.9)

– , *A History of Israel from Alexander the Great to Bar Kochba*, London and Philadelphia 1985 (cf. 3.5.2.9)

K.A.Kitchen, *The First Intermediate Period in Egypt*, Warminster 1973

A.R.C.Leaney*, cf. Hayes-Miller*

A.Lemaire*, *Histoire du peuple hébreu*, Paris 1981 (cf. 3.5.3.4)

A.D.H.Mayes*, cf. Hayes-Miller*

J.Neusner*, cf. Hayes-Miller*

M.Noth, *The History of Israel*, London ²1959 (cf. 3.5.2.2)

– , *A History of Pentateuchal Traditions*, Englewood Cliffs, NJ 1972, reprinted Chico, Ca 1982

G.Ricciotti*, *The History of Israel* (1932), ET Milwaukee 1955 (cf. 3.5.1.4)

P.Schäfer, cf. Hayes-Miller*

P.Sacchi*, *Storia del mondo giudaico*, Turin 1965 (cf. 3.5.2.19)

J.A.Soggin, *Das Königtum in Israel – Ursprung, Spannungen, Entwicklung*, BZAW 104, Berlin 1967
– , *Introduction to the Old Testament*, London and Philadelphia ³1989
– , *Joshua – A Commentary*, OTL, London and Philadelphia 1972
– , *Judges – A Commentary*, OTL, London and Philadelphia 1981
– *, cf. Hayes-Miller*
M. Stern, *Greek and Latin Authors on Jews and Judaism*, Jerusalem I, 1974; II, 1980; III, 1984
T.L.Thompson*, cf. Hayes-Miller*
M.Weippert, *The Settlement of the Israelite Tribes in Palestine*, SBT II 21, London 1971
G.Widengren*, cf. Hayes-Miller*

PART ONE

Introductory Problems

1

Prolegomena

1.1 The title of this work, which differs from that of my 1984 *History of Israel*, is the result of deep reflection on the subject. The results of this reflection can be summed up in three points.

1.1.1 First of all, 'Israel' and 'Judah' seem always to have been two independent and autonomous ethnic and political entities (cf. below, 4.1.1). Only under David and Solomon, in the few decades during which it was possible for the empire to be maintained, do we find the two entities united, though not without frequent tensions. Otherwise, 'Israel' generally refers to the North and it was only the Deuteronomistic history work (Dtr) which attempted to fuse the two groups (cf. below, 3.1.7.4). However, this did not correspond to any historical reality; it was intended in a theological and thus in an ideological sense. To the present day, the Samaritan traditions which have come down to us have tended to affirm that the name Israel refers only to the North.

1.1.2 Secondly, the sources at our disposal, for the most part contained in the Hebrew Bible and the writings of Flavius Josephus, are essentially religious and apologetic, and therefore offer an idealized and partial framework of events. The term 'Introduction' thus indicates that the reader will often only be introduced to the various problems, with no attempt at a reconstruction of events where such a reconstruction seems impossible.

1.1.3 A third point relates to the religion of Israel: as described in the sources mentioned below, this appears as a religion revealed directly by God to Moses as mediator and transmitted by him to the people, and therefore pure and uncorrupted in origin; later, because of the sins of the people and its contacts with the Canaanites, the religion is said to have been corrupted, despite the attempts at reform by the prophets and some pious and zealous kings like Hezekiah and Josiah. I think it unnecessary to emphasize that this concept, too, especially in its version in the Deuteronomistic history, is purely theological, part of the ideology of the post-exilic Judahite community; at the historical-critical level such a theory seems impossible to maintain: again as we shall see, the reality is much more complex.

1.2 The history of Israel mostly takes place in the small territory situated on the coast of the eastern Mediterranean, south of Lebanon and Syria, west of the Jordan and north-east of Egypt. Here and there Israelite or Judahite settlements are attested east of the Jordan, and parts of the region were under the rule of Israel and Judah from the beginning of the first millennium BCE onwards, though only at intervals.

1.3 So the scene of the history of Israel and Judah is for the most part the land of Canaan, also called Palestine because of the settlement of the Philistines. It is therefore logical to make this phase of history end with the destruction or expulsion of the greater part of Palestinian Judaism. The Samaritans were able to remain there for some centuries, and a remnant survives down to the present day; this is relatively small.

1.4 After the failure of the two revolts, that of 67 and 74 CE and that of 132-134, the centre of Judaism henceforth moved outside the Holy Land, into the Diaspora, though there was always an Israelite presence in the region, as is demonstrated by the remains of synagogues in the plain of Jezreel, in Galilee, in the southern hill-country and even in Transjordan, all dating from the Roman and Byzantine periods (see below, 13.7 and 15.10). Moreover the importance of the Diaspora is already clear at the time of Ezra and Nehemiah (see also 13.7).

1.5 At this point a problem arises which is difficult to solve in the present state of research and with our present sources: that of the relationship between Israel and Judah and Egypt during the first half of the first millennium BCE. All the indications in fact are that the two Hebrew kingdoms were dependencies of Egypt. It is clear that for the most part this dependency was purely nominal, in the sense that the legal sovereignty of Egypt over the region was recognized in a purely theoretical form, with no consequences at a practical level. That would explain how the two kingdoms kept turning to Egypt in situations of danger or to take refuge there, constantly to be disappointed, like their predecessors in the el-ʿAmarna period (2.8 below).

1.5.1 We know of the following direct interventions by Egypt in the region:

1. The invasion of Shishak/Shoshenk I at the end of the tenth century BCE;

2. The expedition against Sennacherib in 701 BCE;

3. Another expedition, around 609, under Pharaoh Necho II;

4. An expedition around 601;

and finally, 5. an expedition asked for by Judah during the last years before its exile – we do not know whether this last expedition ever took place.

In cases 1., 3., and 4. it is not surprising that Egypt should have sought to impose its own sovereignty not only theoretically but also *de facto*, an enterprise which may at least partially have succeeded.

1.5.2 In cases 2. and 5. Egyptian intervention was directly requested by Judah, whether or not it in fact took place. And the ostraca of *tell ʿArad* speak of troops called by the title *kittīm* (below, 12.4.1.2), probably Greek mercenaries in the pay of Egypt, to whose maintenance Judah seems to have had to make a major contribution (G.Garbini, oral communication).

2

The Country

2.1 Characteristics

As I have just indicated, the greater part of the history of Israel and
Judah took place in the region to the west of Jordan and the Dead Sea,
though Israelite and Judahite settlements are attested here and there
in Transjordan during the first half of the first millennium BCE. Here
they necessarily came into conflict with the indigenous populations:
the Edomites, the Moabites and the Ammonites. The situation during
the second half of the millennium proved substantially different,
because Israel and Judah lost their political independence, except for
around a century under Hasmonaean sovereignty (below, 14.11).

Bibliography

G.Dalman, *Arbeit und Sitte in Palästina*, Gütersloh I, 1928 – VII, 1942
and reprint (the classic work of the great German philologist and
ethnologist which records the agricultural techniques, crafts, products
and foods to be found in Palestine before Zionism introduced modern
techniques); A.Moscati, *I predecessori d'Israele*, Rome 1957; M.Noth,
The Old Testament World, London and Philadelphia 1966; H.Donner,
Einführung in die biblische Landes- und Altertumskunde, Darmstadt 1976;
Y.Aharoni, *The Land of the Bible*, London and Philadelphia ²1979. For
the geographical and climatic problems cf. J.Sapin, 'La géographie
humaine de la Syrie-Palestine au deuxième millénaire avant Jésus
Christ', *JESHO* 24, 1981, 1-62; 25, 1982, 1-49, 114-86. For the complex
ethnic and sociological problems cf. the studies by D.C.Hopkins, *The
Highlands of Canaan*, Sheffield 1985; O.Borowski, *Agriculture in Iron Age
Israel*, Winona Lake, Ind. 1987 (cf. the very critical review of this by
M.Liverani, *OA* 27, 1987, 145-7, and of Hopkins and Borowski by H.
and M.Weippert, *ZDPV* 104, 1987, 163-7); L.E.Stager, 'The First Fruits
of Civilization', in *Palestine in the Bronze and Iron Ages. FS Olga Tufnell*,
London 1985, 172-88; G.W.Ahlström, *Who Were the Israelites?*, Winona

Lake, Ind. 1986; F.S.Frick, *The Formation of the State in Ancient Israel*, Sheffield 1985, Ch.IV (cf. the critical review by M.Liverani, *OA* 27, 1988, 148-50); J.W.Flanagan, *David's Social Drama*, Sheffield 1988, 119-36; R.B.Coote and K.W.Whitelam, *The Emergence of Early Israel in Historical Perspective*, Sheffield 1987 (reviewed by E.Otto in *TR* 85, 1989, 3-10, and, critically, by G.Garbini, *JSS* 35, 1990, 131-3); N.P.Lemche, *The Canaanites and Their Land*, Sheffield 1991.

2.1.1 The territory is ecologically, ethnically and linguistically part of Syria, so that we can distinguish between a 'Syria major', which also includes the present-day territories of Lebanon, Israel and Jordan, and a Syria in the narrower sense, comprising only present-day Syria together with the sanjak of Alexandretta, ceded to Turkey in the 1920s because most of the population were Turks.

2.1.2 'Syria major' in turn is part of the region which we call the 'Near East' (a more appropriate designation than the usual 'Middle East', which should be kept for Iran, Afghanistan and Pakistan). It is also known by the more colourful title the 'Fertile Crescent', a term often used in the Anglo-Saxon world, arising from the fact that pictorially it can be depicted as enclosed within two arcs, one broader than the other, and joined at the end to produce the shape of a crescent moon, arcs which include Egypt.

2.2 The name

The region is given many names; here we shall be occupied only with the most frequent ones.

2.2.1 The first, most ancient and most authentic name is Canaan, written consonantally *kn'n*, vocalized in Hebrew as *k^{e}na'an*.[1] It probably already appears in the cuneiform texts at Ebla (end of the third millennium BCE) in the form *kinaḫḫu* and orthographic variants,[2] and was in use in Roman North Africa among the population of Punic origin as late as the fourth and fifth centuries CE, as is attested by St Augustine.[3]

2.2.2 The origins of this name are connected with the production of purple dye,[4] in antiquity one of the main sources of income in the region. However, this took place in Phoenicia, and the Greek word φοῖνιξ and its derivatives, already attested in the tablets of Mycenae as *po-ni-ki-yo*, refer to Phoenicia in the narrower sense rather than to the region in general. If we keep to the use of the term Canaan in the biblical texts and other ancient Near Eastern texts, it becomes probable that at least originally the name could denote the whole region and not just the small part known as Phoenicia.[5] Moreover, in Isa.19.18, part of a late eschatological addition to the chapter, meant to provide information about eighth-century events, Hebrew is rightly called *šᵉpat kᵉnaʿan*, 'the language of Canaan'.

2.2.3 Another very frequent name, 'Palestine',[6] goes back to the settlement in the region of an alien population whose origins are still a matter of controversy, the Philistines: these settled principally on the southern coast of the region around the twelfth century BCE. The term appears for the first time in Herodotus (fifth century BCE) as an adjective (ἐν τῇ Παλαιστίνῃ Συρίᾳ, I, 105) and as a noun (ἡ Παλαιστίνη, III, 91 and elsewhere), to distinguish the region from Phoenicia, properly so-called, with which the term Canaan could have been confused. Today the term is used to indicate the region in a generic sense, regardless of whoever exercised sovereignty there, as distinct from Syria and Lebanon. However, since the official name of the region, *Palaestina*, was introduced by the Romans after the revolt of 132-134 CE in place of the traditional *Iudaea* (cf. below 15.9.2), it is usually rejected in Hebrew circles, which use the following terms.

2.2.4 Another name, rare in the Bible (I Sam.13.19; II Kings 6.23; Ezek.27.27, where, however, the expression refers to the North [above, 1.1.1]), is 'land of Israel', in Hebrew *'ereṣ iśrā'ēl*. It is attested many times in rabbinic literature and today is used as the official name of the country within the Zionist movement and by the State of Israel.[7]

2.2.5 Given the perceived character of the region, there is no lack of names of a theological type, 'Promised Land', 'Holy Land', and so on.

2.3 Geography and orography

A first characteristic of the region is its extremely small size: the country is roughly equivalent to Belgium or the state of Vermont in length and breadth. In antiquity, it extended 'from Dan to Beersheba (in the northern Negeb)', i.e. a distance of a little less than 150 miles as the crow flies; its breadth from the Mediterranean to the Jordan in a straight line is not more than 36 miles. This makes its orographic structure all the more remarkable, producing a series of regions with very different climates and therefore very different ecologies. I shall list these from east to west.

2.3.1 The plateau of Transjordan, which on average is about 2300 feet above sea level, is furrowed by rivers and streams which flow westwards and drop down into the Jordan or the Dead Sea. To the east the region loses itself in the desert of northern Arabia. As one gradually moves westwards, however, it becomes increasingly fertile because it is favoured by the winter rains: in antiquity it was regarded as the granary of the region. A kind of continental climate predominates, hot and dry in the summer though tempered by the altitude, and cold and rainy in the winter, with frequent and heavy falls of snow. Today it comprises the greater part of the Hashemite kingdom of Jordan whose capital, Amman, has retained the second part of the name used in antiquity by the Ammonites and the Hebrews, Rabbath-(beth)-ammon. As I mentioned earlier (above 2.1), the region was the scene of Israelite and Judahite settlements from the time of the empire of David and Solomon onwards, sometimes under the sovereignty of one of the two kingdoms.

2.3.2 The depression formed by the Jordan is part of a geological or perhaps tectonic rift which runs from north to south. It begins in the *beqa'a* of Syria and Lebanon at around 3300 feet above sea level and reaches its greatest depth below sea level in the region of the Dead Sea; it then continues through the *'ᵃrābāh* and again reaches sea level in the Gulf of Aqaba. The fault or rift continues through the Red Sea, to become the Rift Valley in East Africa (Ethiopia, Kenya and Tanzania), and beyond. Its origins are to be sought in a prehistoric seismic cataclysm; even today the whole of the region is sensitive to earthquakes.

2.3.3 From a height still above sea level at the border between Israel and Lebanon the Jordan valley soon reaches Lake Huleh, a marsh not more than ten or twelve feet deep and about eight square miles in surface area; it was partly drained during the 1950s and all that is left of it is a pool in a national park. From there, after a few miles the valley descends to Lake Tiberias, something over 650 feet below sea level, and then, at the depth of the Dead Sea, reaches the lowest point of the land: more than 1300 feet below sea level. Throughout the depression the climate is tropical and humid, springlike and gentle in winter, oppressive in summer. About twelve miles south of Lake Tiberias the rains tend to become increasingly sparse and then cease almost completely: there is thus a desert zone which can only be cultivated where there are oases (Jericho, *'ain-fašḥa*, *'ēn gᵉdī*), or where it is possible to supply water in other ways.

2.3.4 The river Jordan, closely confined between banks which are often prone to landslides a few miles south of Lake Tiberias, cannot be used for agriculture without the installation of irrigation systems which would be so expensive as to make the produce uneconomical; furthermore the river is not navigable and has hardly any fish in it. It is therefore of little benefit to the economy of the region and divides rather than unites those who live on its banks. However, where there is water, or it is possible to convey the water needed for irrigation, the Jordan valley is very fertile; it produces early crops on the stretch around Lake Tiberias and tropical fruit along its southern reaches.

2.3.5 The plateau on the west bank of the Jordan was the main theatre of the history of Israel and Judah. From north to south it is divided successively into the mountain chains of upper Galilee and the hill-country of the northern centre and the south, separated by the plain of Jezreel. The mountains of upper Galilee reach a maximum height of just under 4000 feet above sea level and have fertile valleys. They are covered with woods, some of which are still original. The hill-country of the north and centre extends from the plain of Jezreel up to the northern limits of Jerusalem; its maximum height is 3200 feet above sea level. Today the region seems relatively barren; the vegetation is sparse: only part of it is original, and the rest is the result of modern afforestation; only around the Arab villages are there signs of intensive cultivation even of fruit trees, in part made possible by the use of terraces. The southern hill-country begins south of Jerusalem and reaches its greatest height near Hebron (Arabic *el-ḥalīl*), at about 3500 feet above sea level; it then merges into the Negeb, the southern steppe, with a northern part which can be cultivated after particularly wet winters and now with modern systems of irrigation. Here too the woods are for the most part the product of afforestation; around the Arab villages the soil is intensively cultivated, again also with fruit trees.

2.3.6 The western part of the mountains of Galilee and the two plateaux, exposed to the winds from the Mediterranean, has a moderate mountain climate: healthy, cold in winter and moderately warm in summer, with abundant falls of rain and even snow in the winter. The eastern area, however, tends to become increasingly dry the further east one goes.

2.3.7 Between Galilee and the hill-country of the centre and north lies the fertile plain of Jezreel and its surroundings; to the east this drops towards the Jordan valley and to the west extends as far as the Mount Carmel chain, which runs from south-east to north-west, maintaining an average height of around 1000 feet, with a summit 1500 feet above sea level. It ends at the city and port of Haifa, Hebrew *ḥēpāh*, Arabic *ḥayfāh*. However, the port was largely constructed in the present century.

2.3.8 Between the plateaux and the Mediterranean coast is an intermediate hilly zone, called *šᵉpēlāh* in Hebrew; this, too, is fertile where it has not been eroded and it is possible to supply water.

2.3.9 The coasts are generally sandy and little suited either to agriculture or to the construction of ports. This last feature could explain why the ancient Israelites always mistrusted the sea, which they considered a relic of ancient chaos: unlike their neighbours the Phoenicians, they were no sailors.

2.4 Climate

The orography of the region makes it very varied in climate, even over a relatively short distance. However, all the regions (with the exception of Transjordan) lie in an area which has a sub-tropical Mediterranean climate. There is a regular sea breeze from the south-west, which brings coolness in the summer and rain in the winter. More rarely, in spring and in autumn a wind comes off the eastern desert, a kind of dry sirocco, called *ḥamsīn* in Arabic and *šārāb* in Hebrew. This causes trouble both for human beings and domestic animals, and its ruinous consequences for agriculture are also noted in the Bible (Isa.40.7). The north wind, which blows especially in the winter and tends to bring rain, is also more rare.

2.4.1 Despite all the local variations, one of the main characteristics of the climate in the region is the division of the year into two main seasons: the winter, with abundant though intermittent rain, which can often turn into cloudbursts and snow on the high ground, followed by many calm days; and the summer, a completely dry season. The spring and the autumn tend to be very brief and are almost unnoticed.

2.4.2 It is the occurrence of rain, in particular, that is one of the fundamental differences between Canaan and the other civilizations in the region, Mesopotamia and Egypt. These two latter civilizations, which came into being in areas lacking rain, were aware of the benefits of irrigation from time immemorial. This irrigation was carried out by making canals for water from rivers which could be exploited by the techniques of construction and maintenance available at the time. By contrast, in Canaan, which was a mountainous region with sparse and meagre watercourses, until only a few decades ago agriculture was dependent on the volume of the winter rains, which were preceded in the autumn by the 'first rains' (Hebrew *yōreh*) and followed by the 'latter rains' (Hebrew *malqōš*). A dry winter or a winter with insufficient rain could easily lead to ecological catastrophe: the springs and the wells dried up, and the cisterns emptied. It was asking a lot for domestic animals, who were also deprived of fodder, to survive in such conditions; sometimes even the very survival of human beings was in danger. There is a reference to a particularly serious drought, lasting for three years, in I Kings 17.1ff. (see below 10.10.8.1). Today, with a centralized plan for the use of water and the possibility of constructing canals on a national scale, such catastrophes can be avoided, though a prolonged drought can still have serious consequences for agriculture.

2.4.3 On the plateaus and in the valleys of the mountain chains, however, the rain was never enough to ensure the permanent settlement of human beings and animals, except of course where there were springs. So it was necessary to be able to save water from the winter rains for use during the dry season. This was made possible through the discovery of a special mortar for coating cisterns, thus making them impermeable. Hence the settling of regions of the hill-country, which took place in the first Bronze Age as a result of the demographic explosion and again in the transition from the Bronze Age to the Iron Age in the last centuries of the second millennium BCE, as a result of the dominant insecurity in the plains. For tables relating to the situation of the land and the rainfall see Frick 1985, ch.IV.

2.4.4 This dependence on factors beyond human control explains why agriculture has always been so precarious in the region until recent decades. As J.Sapin pointed out in his basic study (1981-82, I, 13), 'It is a marginal world without defences or autonomy', an easy prey either for the ambitions of the city or for the rapacious depredations of the nomads.

2.4.5 The further east we go, especially east of the watershed in the hill-country, the more the rains, which average about 15-19 inches in the west, diminish, and then cease almost completely in the Jordan valley and the region of the Dead Sea.

2.4.6 With the onset of the rainy season in the autumn the vegetation grows again and the cycle of agricultural work begins once more with ploughing and sowing. The end of the rains in the spring leads to the death of all the vegetation other than trees and bushes, though the seed germinates again in the autumn. The trees and bushes generally manage to survive the burning heat of summer, provided that they have received enough water during the winter.

2.4.7 This natural cycle also explains what little we know of Canaanite religion. Ba'al, the god of the fertility of the soil and the flocks, dies in spring and is buried: now Lord Mot reigns, the god of death and the underworld. In autumn Ba'al rises again; first he fertilizes the soil with the rain (the classical authors called this τὸ σπῆρμα τοῦ βααλ, 'the seed of Ba'al'), and then, at the end of the winter, he fertilizes the flocks and the herds, again dying in the spring. So this religion, with its contrast between the creative principle of fertility and the chaotic principle of death, seems to be a mythical reproduction of the natural cycle and is aimed at guaranteeing its regular occurrence. It has often been argued that it had an orgiastic character, but this has never been proved.

2.5 Flora

Bibliography

Fauna and Flora of the Bible (Helps for Translators), The United Bible Societies, London and New York ²1980 (this book provides a complete general bibliography on the subject); M.Zohary, *Plants of the Bible*,

Cambridge 1982. Cf. also B.S.J.Isserlin, 'Ancient Forests in Palestine: Some Archaeological Indications', *PEQ* 86, 1955, 87f.; F.S.Bodenheimer, *Animal and Man in Bible Lands* (two vols.), Leiden 1960; J.V.Thirgood, *Man and the Mediterranean Forest*, London 1981, 107-22.

2.5.1 Remains of the original flora can still be found today in the woods and scrubland. In ancient times a good deal of the hill-country and the mountains seems to have been wooded, though we should never imagine ancient Canaan as a great forest, as was the case with, for example, central and northern Europe, Siberia and North America. At all events the progressive exploitation of the hill-country and the mountains for agriculture and pasturage, along with a rapacious use of the resources provided by the forest, soon led to a marked reduction in the ancient woodland, and now it can be found in its original form only over a limited area of Upper Galilee and on Carmel. This original woodland has now become rare, and the Mediterranean scrub mixed with some trees with tall trunks seems more common. The work of deforestation still continued throughout the period of Turkish domination until 1917-1918.

2.5.2 Among the original trees of the region one might mention some types of oak, the most widespread of which are the *quercus coccifera* and the *quercus aegilops*; the terebinth, *pistacia terebinthus*, and a local type of conifer, *pinus halepensis*. In the steppes we still find the tamarisk, *tamarix*, and various kinds of shrubs.

2.5.3 In the course of the last half-century enormous work has been done on reforestation, sponsored first by the British under the mandate and then by the Jewish National Fund; it has made a remarkable difference in the appearance of many areas and in the number of trees in them. One has only to travel from Jerusalem to Tel Aviv one way in the bus and the other in the train: in the bus one goes through an area which has been completely reforested, as far as the entry into the mountains through the *bab el-wād* (Arabic) or *šaʿar haggay* (Hebrew, coord.136-152; for an explanation of this reference see below); in the train one follows the picturesque and winding course of the Ottoman railway, finished in 1892, which goes through areas which have not been reforested. The difference is striking.

As a result of these works species have been introduced into the region which are more resistant to drought and economically more useful: other types of conifer and cypress, and in the marshy regions eucalyptus trees, imported from Australia. The original flora of the region have therefore necessarily been changed.

2.5.4 Again, various kinds of shrubs and grasses are indigenous. The shrubs, which are often spiny (the so-called 'thorns' of the Bible), flower at the end of the rainy season and then dry out again in the summer; the grass begins to shoot during the rain and then finally dries up during the course of the last siroccos, at the end of the spring.

2.5.5 As was attested by agricultural discoveries made during the excavations at Jericho in the 1950s, the region has been cultivated at least from the eighth millennium BCE. Although it is not particularly fertile (there is nothing to match the 'black earth' of the Ukraine or the plains of North and South America), it has always produced what was needed to sustain its inhabitants when the winter rains have been sufficient. In some cases it has provided an abundance of crops. However, to produce particularly good results in this field substantial investment has always proved necessary, often coming from abroad; this situation has lasted in part right down to the present day. It is understandable that this happens only when particular interests militate in their favour (Coote and Whitelam 1987).

2.5.6 Fruit trees include the classical olive, fig, almond and vine, this last being hung between other trees or cultivated on the ground. Nowadays wine is produced by Arab Christians and Israelis, since, like all alcoholic drinks, it is forbidden to Muslims. There are also sycamores, pistachios and nuts. Quite recently apples, pears and citrus fruits (oranges, lemons, mandarins and grapefruit) have been introduced; legend has it that citrus fruits were introduced into the country, along with the tomato, by Franciscans in the seventeenth century. Bananas and avocados are cultivated in regions with a tropical climate. The date palm, *phoenix dactylifera L*, no longer attested after Roman times (Jericho was also called the 'City of Palms', Deut.34.3; Judg.3.13; I Chron.28.15), has also been recently introduced. The prickly pear, used by the Arabs and in southern Italy for fencing, also seems to be relatively late. Its fruit is eaten and the 'peel', treated properly, can be used as fodder for livestock in time of drought.

2.5.7 We also find various types of cereals, principally barley and wheat, which are cultivated almost everywhere. As I have indicated, in ancient times Transjordan was considered the granary of the region. The harvest takes place between March and May, the threshing at the beginning of the summer, a little later in the hill-country.

2.5.8 Agriculture has been radically transformed over the last half-century, first in the Jewish agricultural colonies and then in the State of Israel. The small-holdings, usually consisting of farms run by families, have disappeared, giving place to large-scale enterprises which were granted land at one time by the Jewish National Fund and later by the state: this has produced large co-operatives (Hebrew *mōšāb*), some of which have a socialist structure (Hebrew *qibbūṣ*). However, ancient farms once run by a family or the property of the village, which assigned land in turn to those who had a right to it, have remained in areas where the population is predominantly Arab.

2.5.9 On the Jewish co-operative farms the traditional crops have partly been replaced by crops which on the one hand resemble those in central and southern Europe, and on the other resist the heat and can be harvested mechanically. On the Arab farms, however, the traditional crops are still produced on a large scale. The techniques in question have brought considerable changes to agriculture on the Hebrew farms; similar modifications are also in progress on the Arab farms.

2.6 Fauna

The differences in climate favour a difference in fauna, as they do in flora.

2.6.1 The marked increase in the Israeli and Arab population over the last half-century and the intensification of agriculture and pasturage has had serious consequences for wild animals, restricting or even destroying their habitat and leading to increased difficulties, if not extinction. That is the case, for example, with the wolf, the hyena, the wild dog and the wild cat, the fox, the wild boar, the hare, the wild goat and the badger. Other animals of the Bible are now extinct, like the bear and the Asiatic lion; a few bears still survive in the scant protection of the Syrian and Lebanese mountains. In Israel the threatened species are now adequately protected, but little can be done about conserving their habitat, a situation similar to that in other industrialized countries.

2.6.2 The birds have also suffered from the reduction of their natural habitat and from atmospheric pollution. Among the birds of prey there are the falcon, the vulture and, very rarely, the eagle, while the others include the quail, the guinea fowl and some game birds: the fact that Muslims and Jews only eat meat which has been ritually slaughtered much reduces the effect of hunting and favours the preservation of the species.

2.6.3 There are abundant reptiles: snakes, lizards and tortoises. Down to the end of the last century there was even evidence of crocodiles on the tributaries to the east of the Jordan.

2.6.4 From time immemorial fish have been the main wealth of Lake Tiberias. Today, on ground which is not really suitable for agriculture, artificial pools have been made and stocked with fresh-water (or, rarely, with salt-water) fish. As is well known, the Dead Sea does not allow any form of animal life because of the high level of its salinity.

2.6.5 Among the insects, the best known is the locust (*oedipoda migratoria, locusta viridissima*, cf. Joel 1.1ff.) because of the damage to agriculture which it has caused over the centuries. Today it is possible to take effective measures against it, neutralizing or at least containing the damage it causes. However, even at the beginning of the First World War a particularly serious plague of locusts reduced Syria Major to famine, contributing not a little to the success of the English expedition on the Turkish front in 1917-1918. (For this occurrence see the classic article, with copious documentation, by J.D.Whiting, *National Geographic Magazine* 28, 1915, 511-50.)

2.6.6 Until very recently the ox and the ass were the main domestic animals; the horse appears more rarely, being considered a luxury. In biblical times the ox and the ass were the working animals, as they often still are today for the Arab peasant (*fellah*). Nowadays they are essentially limited to regions which are hardly accessible to motorized vehicles. Otherwise, these traditional friends and collaborators of humankind are being condemned to progressive extinction as mechanized agriculture is also spreading among the Arabs.

2.6.7 The camel, too, *camelus dromedarius*, the Western Asian species with a single hump, is now used mainly in the steppes and in the desert, where it is reared by the Bedouin; hence it is possible to come across herds of camels in the central and southern Negeb. However, in those regions where agriculture is intensive, while the camel appeared frequently in the 1960s, it is becoming increasingly rare: it too tends to be replaced, where possible, with motorized vehicles. It was domesticated during the course of the second millennium BCE, so that it has been possible to use it only in a relatively late historical period.

2.6.8 Other domestic animals are the cow, the sheep and the goat, all reared for milk, meat and hides; the sheep and the goat are also kept for their wool. The cow is now almost always reared on mechanized modern farms so as to increase productivity; however, sheep and goats have to be put out to pasture if they are to produce good-quality wool, so Arab and Israeli shepherds can often be found in the scrubland. In the biblical period the cow was a luxury and the beasts usually found west of the Jordan were the 'small cattle', Hebrew ṣō'n; however, in Basan, present-day Hauran, in northern Transjordan, the rearing of cattle was common and their quality was proverbial (cf. Amos 4.1).

2.6.9 Among domestic animals which have recently been imported, mention might be made of various kinds of poultry, ducks, geese and turkeys. Here, too, breeding has been rationalized among the Israelis; it takes a more traditional form among the Arabs, though there too modern techniques are making increasing strides.

2.7 The ancient populations

The Hebrew Bible provides a good deal of information about the peoples living in Canaan at the time of the Israelite settlement: their number is fixed at a conventional maximum of seven. Furthermore the whole concept is based on the notion that 'Israel' will have been a group coming from outside and therefore different from these populations (see 8.8 below).

2.7.1 Of these seven, however, three are generic designations for the inhabitants of the whole region. i.e. 'Canaanites', 'Amorites' and 'Hittites', the last two probably deriving from names used in Mesopotamia, where the populations of Syria Major were called *amurru, ḫatti* and derivatives at different times (see nos.5 above and 8 below):

2.7.2 There remain the names of four other populations, listed in varying order: Hivites, Perizzites, Girgashites and Jebusites.[8] Of these only the Hivites and the Jebusites are connected with particular cities, the former with Shechem and the latter with Jerusalem (below, 8.2.4); however, these are associations which appear only in the Hebrew Bible and not in other texts. In the numerous extra-biblical texts which have come down to us, the two places are never associated with these peoples.[9] The Hivites have sometimes been connected with the Hurrians, a population from Asia Minor whose language is not Semitic; of the others we know nothing as research now stands. We do not even know whether the names are real and therefore recall peoples which actually existed, or whether they are fabulous, mythical designations, as is the case, for example, with the Rephaim, whom we shall discuss below (8.2.11.5), or even the fruit of fantasy.

2.7.3 One alien people, the Philistines, is said to have been hostile to 'Israel' from the start. We shall discuss them below (4.4).

2.7.4 Around Israel and Judah there is evidence of people with whom the two nations had reciprocal dealings over the centuries: to the north the maritime city-states of Phoenicia; to the east, in Transjordan, the Ammonites, the Edomites and the Moabites, all together with Israel and Judah speaking variants of the same language. The peoples of Transjordan settled in the region rather later than Israel and Judah. In Syria, however, we find the Aramaeans, who spoke a different language, Aramaic, even if they too were part of the Western Semitic group.

2.8 Internal politics

Given the present state of research it is impossible to reconstruct with even a minimum of certainty the ethnic composition of the region at the time of the Israelite settlement; however, we do have important first-hand information about its political structure and economy, in sources which are a little earlier.

2.8.1 This appears first of all in the archives of el-ʿAmarna, a place in Egypt about half-way between Cairo and Luxor. The archive contains the correspondence which came to the court of the Pharaohs Amenophis III and IV (Akhenaten), between the end of the fifteenth and the middle of the fourteenth century BCE from Egyptian vassals in the Near East: a large number of them were Canaanite.

Bibliography

J.A.Knudtzon, *Die El-Amarna Tafeln*, Leipzig 1908-15; A.F.Rainey, *The El-Amarna Tablets*, Neukirchen/Vluyn-Kevelaer ²1978; the important texts have been reproduced in *ANET*, 483-90, and *TUAT* I, 512-20. A new critical edition is being edited by W.L.Moran of Harvard University; for the present see a French translation: W.L.Moran, *Les lettres de El-Amarna: correspondence politique du Pharaon*, Paris 1987; cf. also M.Liverani, 'Political Lexicon and Political Ideology in the Amarna Letters', *Berytus* 31, 1983, 41-56.

2.8.2 The texts from the Syrian city-state of Ugarit, just north of Laodicea, which was destroyed in the twelfth century, are still important. Its ruins were excavated by a French expedition from the time of their discovery in 1928; the expedition also produced an edition of the texts.

Bibliography

Critical editions: A.Herdner, *Corpus des tablettes cunéiformes alphabétiques découvertes à Ras Shamra-Ugarit de 1929 à 1939*, Paris 1963, and E.Dietrich, O.Loretz and J.Sanmartin, *Die keilalphabetischen Texte aus Ugarit*, Neukirchen/Vluyn-Kevelaer I, 1976; II, 1992. Translations: C.H.Gordon, *Ugaritic Literature*, Rome 1949; U.Cassuto, *The Goddess Anat*, Jerusalem 1951 (in Hebrew) and 1971 (in English); A.Jirku, *Kanaanäische Mythen und Epen aus Ras Schamra-Ugarit*, Gütersloh 1962; J.Aistleitner, *Die mythologischen und kultischen Texte aus Ras Schamra*, Budapest 1964; *ANET*, 129-55 (not yet in *TUAT*); J.C.L.Gibson, *Canaanite Myths and Legends*, Edinburgh ²1978; G.del Olmo Lete, *Mitos y leyendas de Canaan*, Madrid 1981. Material relevant to the present work is discussed by M.Heltzer, *The Rural Community in Ancient Ugarit*, Wiesbaden 1976; id., *The Internal Organization of the Kingdom of Ugarit*, Wiesbaden 1982; M.Liverani, 'Ras Shamra-Ugarit: territoire et population 2', *SDB* IX, 1979, 1316-23; W.R.G.Harr, 'Population in Ancient Ugarit', *BASOR* 266, 1987, 31-43; P.Vargya, 'Stratification sociale á Ugarit', in M.Heltzer and É.Lipiński (eds.), *Society and Economy in the Eastern Mediterranean (c.1500-1000 BC)*, Louvain 1988, 111-23; M.Heltzer, 'Die Entwicklung des Handwerks vom Dienstsystem zum selbständigen Produzenten im östlichen Mittelmeergebiet', *AOF* 15, 1988, 124-32.

2.8.3 The social and political picture which emerges from the el-

'Amarna letters is particularly interesting. It shows various city-states, all governed by a ruler who is often a foreigner, though he never bears the title king (perhaps out of respect for the Pharaoh). From Ugarit, where that title does, however, occur, we have economic texts which provide information on the internal social and economic situation.

2.8.3.1 Below the person of the monarch, around the palace, we have a structure rather like a pyramid: there are the noblemen, who constitute an assembly, an institution which seems to have had considerable power even over against the crown; then there are landowners, merchants and craftsmen (organized into 'guilds'), manual workers and unskilled labourers, and finally slaves. There seems to have been a similar structure around the temple, which thus formed a real alternative centre of power.

2.8.3.2 We also know from the el-'Amarna archive in Canaan that the city-states were for the most part located in the plains and commanded only very small territories (the size of these cities was also very small compared with modern urban centres: Hazor, regarded as one of the greatest, measured less than thirty-five acres at its widest extent); however, they were densely populated and intensively cultivated.

2.8.3.3 In the hill-country the city-states could be counted on the fingers of one hand: we know of the existence only of Hebron, Jerusalem and Shechem and, in Galilee, Hazor.

2.8.4 The capital was surrounded by countryside in which there could be lesser centres. A characteristic of the countryside seems to have been that on the one hand there was an absence of any effective power to counter the actions of the state, and that on the other hand it was the major producer of goods in the principal areas of the economy, namely agriculture and cattle. In other words, the capital of the city-state monopolized economic and political power through the palace, the temple and the army (usually made up of mercenaries), and its riches were based on developing and trading in the produce of the countryside. The inhabitants of the countryside themselves do not seem to have had any power in decision-making worth noting.[10]

2.8.5 A situation of this kind might suggest a vigorous and continuous conflict between the city, which did the exploiting, and the countryside, the productive region which was exploited. However, this does not seem to have happened. In the el-'Amarna texts, although we find accounts of rebellions and of kings forced to flee, none of these movements arises in the country, in an attempt to throw off the yoke of the city; they occur actually within the city, usually between the assembly of the nobility and the monarch, i.e. between groups which already held power in one way or another, or as a result of intrigues on the part of refugees who had sought haven there.

2.8.6 Such refugees, often called *ḫapiru* or *ʿprm* (logogram SA-GAZ) were one of the major problems of the city state, as we shall see in greater detail below (6.6.3). Those exiled from one city-state (for political or economic reasons) would take refuge in another nearby and with their intrigues endanger not only the place from which they had fled but often also the place which had taken them in; as a result this would be involved against its will in conflicts which originally had nothing to do with it.

2.8.7 It is not surprising that the combination of these factors – fragmentation and often conflict at a political level, hostilities within the city-state, the remarkable economic prosperity and the presence of sparsely populated and cultivated territories in the hill-country and the steppes – encouraged the settlement of those groups which formed the ancestors of Israel, and, in the neighbouring regions, of those from whom the peoples of Syria and Jordan descended.

2.9 International politics

One thing must always be remembered in this connection: Canaan has almost always been a region whose destiny has been decided elsewhere, by the great powers and their politics. 'The domination of this area by non-Palestinian political powers is one of the most important constants of Palestinian history, which has had a profound effect upon settlement patterns' (Coote and Whitelam 1987, 21). One of the rare exceptions is perhaps the history of Israel and Judah during the first half of the first millennium BCE, though, as I indicated earlier (1.5), if we leave out the brief empire of David and Solomon, this independence does not seem to have been total and unconditional.

This situation arises from the fact that the region has always been the bridge between Africa and Asia, and therefore between Egypt on the one side and the Hittite and Mesopotamian empires on the other. All the great powers were therefore ambitious to control it. So from the end of the second millennium BCE to the middle of the first millennium we find constant conflict between Egypt on the one hand and the Hittites, Assyrians and Babylonians on the other; later, in the second half of the millennium, first between Egypt and Persia, and then between the Hellenistic kingdoms. This, too, is one of the objective elements which have characterized the region and still do so down to the present day.

2.10 Working tools

Maps and other geographical tools are indispensable for anyone who wants more than a superficial knowledge of the region.

2.10.1 The most practical and complete map is that made by the

Survey of Israel, which goes back to the British Mandate. It is published in two forms: in two sheets on a scale of 1:250,000 with two additional sheets for Sinai, and on a scale of 1:100,000 in twenty-two sheets. These exist in Hebrew and English; the physical map is preferable.[11] There are also maps on a scale of 1:25,000 which are particularly useful for archaeology and topography even if they have not been updated; however, they have to be consulted in libraries since they are not available commercially.

There is another superb map by E.Höhne to a scale of 1:300,000 which appears as a supplement to *BHH* IV, 1979.

The maps made by the Survey of Israel are printed with a precise system of co-ordinates, which are repeated in the best works; I have used them here.

2.10.2 The various geographies of the Bible are other indispensable working tools for the student. However, not all give the co-ordinates of the *Survey*, which reduces their usefulness.

Bibliography

F.-M.Abel, *Géographie de la Palestine*, Paris I, 1933; II, 1938, reprinted 1967; M.du Buit, *Géographie de la Terre Sainte*, Paris I-II, 1958; J.Simons, *The Geographical and Topographical Texts of the Old Testament*, Leiden 1959; D.Baly, *The Geography of the Bible*, New York ²1974; Y.Aharoni, *The Land of the Bible*, Philadelphia ²1979; Y.Karmon, *Israel. Eine geographische Landeskunde*, Darmstadt 1983; O.Keel and H.Küchler, *Orte und Landschaften der Bibel*, Zurich and Göttingen I, 1985; II, 1982; III, IV in preparation (this is the most complete guide, and is up-to-date on geography, climate, topography and archaeology); E.K.Vogel and B.Holtzclaw, 'Bibliography of Holy Land Sites', *HUCA* 42, 1971, 1-98 and 52, 1981, 1-92; E.K.Vogel, *HUCA* 58, 1987, 1-63.

2.10.3 Of the various archaeologies, cf. Y.Aharoni, *The Archaeology of the Land of Israel*, Philadelphia and London 1982; H.Weippert, *Palästina in vorhellenistischer Zeit*, Munich 1988; I.Finkelstein, *The Archaeology of the Israelite Settlement*, Jerusalem 1988. These are abbreviated in the text by **. The collection of German aerial photographs from the First World War, G.Dalman, *Hundert deutsche Flugbilder aus Palästina*, Gütersloh 1925, is also important.

2.10.4 In this book I have largely followed the details given by Aharoni 1979.

3

Problems, Methodology, Bibliography and Sources

3.1 Problems

There are now many histories of Israel and Judah, scientific and critical in approach, up-to-date in method and bibliographies (3.6 below). Many biblical scholars have produced such works from the Second World War onwards and, as one might expect, few Near Eastern scholars have failed to incorporate the history of Israel and Judah into their works. To judge from the number of histories of Israel which have been published, the years between 1940 and 1990 have been the most productive. However, in most of the histories published during this period it is not easy to find any advance on the positions arrived at at the end of the last century. Important exceptions are the works of Alt and Noth and, more recently, those of Donner 1984-86, Jagersma 1981-85, Miller and Hayes 1987, and Lemche 1988. Important contributions have been made by the works of the Dielheim group, by Thompson, Van Seters 1975 and Liverani (especially 1980). However, it is clear that all these recent authors relate back to the works of Kuenen 1869 and Stade 1885[1] and not to those of their immediate predecessors, which makes it difficult to speak of real progress in historiography in this area.

Bibliography

M.Weippert, 'Fragen des israelitischen Geschichtsbewusstseins', *VT* 23, 1973, 415-42; T.L.Thompson, *The Historicity of the Patriarchal Narratives*, Berlin 1974; J.Van Seters, *Abraham in History and Tradition*, New Haven and London 1975; J.M.Miller, *The Old Testament and the Historian*, Philadelphia 1976; M.Metzger, 'Probleme der Frühgeschichte Israels', *VuF* 22.1, 1977, 30-43; J.A.Soggin, 'The Davidic-Solomonic Kingdom', in Hayes and Miller* 1977, ch.VI; id., 'The History of Israel – A Study of Some Questions of Method', *EI* 14, 1978, 44*-51*; M.Liverani, 'Le "origini" d'Israele – progetto irrealizzabile di ricerca etnogenetica', *RiBib* 28, 1980, 9-32; J.M.Sasson, 'On Choosing Models for Recreating Pre-Monarchical Israel', *JSOT* 21, 1981, 3-24; A.Malamat, 'Die Frühgeschichte Israels', *TZ* 39, 1983, 1-16; B.J.Diebner, 'Kultus, Sakralrecht und die Anfänge des Geschichtsdenkens', *DBAT* 17, 1983, 1-20; E.Hobsbawm and T.Ranger (eds.), *The Invention of Tradition*, Cambridge 1983; J.A.Soggin, 'Geschichte als Glaubenbekenntnis – Geschichte als Gegenstand wissenschaftlicher Forschung', *TLZ* 110, 1985, 161-72; id., 'Probleme einer Vor- und Frühgeschichte Israels', *ZAW* 100 (1988 Suppl.), 255-67; R.B.Coote and K.W.Whitelam, *The Emergence of Early Israel in Historical Perspective*, Sheffield 1987; T.L.Thompson, *The Original Tradition of Ancient Israel*, Sheffield 1987; E.Otto, 'Israels Wurzeln in Kanaan. Auf dem Wege zu einer neuen Kultur- und Sozialgeschichte des antiken Israels', *ThRev* 85, 1989, 3-10; U.Becker, *Richterzeit und Königtum*, Diss.theol. Bonn 1989; K.W.Whitelam, 'Israel's Traditions of Origin: Reclaiming the Land', *JSOT* 44, 1989, 19-42; S.Kreuzer, *Die Frühgeschichte Israels*, Berlin 1989; T.L.Thompson, *Early History of the Israelite People*, Leiden 1992, which I have been able to use only in part.

3.1.1 One thing seems certain: at the time of the letters contained in the el-'Amarna archives (above 2.8), not only is there no reference to groups which bear the name of Israel and Judah, but there is not even a place for them in the region. Then, in the course of the last centuries of the second millennium BCE, 'Israel' and probably also 'Judah' unexpectedly exist and rapidly develop into an empire; Israel is explicitly mentioned on the stele of Pharaoh Merenptah from the end of the thirteenth century (below, 3.6.7.5). These are the accredited facts in the present state of research. Moreover, the silence of the ancient Near Eastern sources lasts down to the last years of the ninth century BCE, to the stele of Mesha king of Moab. In these conditions we must ask whether it is still possible to discover anything at all about the origins of Israel and Judah, and if so what. According to the biblical texts, the two entities appear first as groups ('tribes') and then, after the brief period of the reign of Saul (which probably covered only the North, i.e. Israel), as a united kingdom first under David and then under Solomon. However, these are notes which inform us only partly about what happened at this period.

3.1.2 Yet as Liverani showed in 1980, the problem of the birth of a people does not have a solution from within, in Israel and in Judah or anywhere else, and that complicates the situation considerably. Only when there are external sources is it possible to make any statements in this connection. What have been noted as traditions of individual peoples have practically always been the product of later considerations. Moreover, it is only when a people already exists that it begins to ask questions about its origins. To answer these questions it makes use of its own traditions, traditions which are of course selected according to criteria the original scope of which had nothing to do with this; nor can we always rule out the possibility that this is material created *de novo*. In the case of Israel and Judah such a choice of material took place at the earliest during the Babylonian exile, 587-586 to 539 BCE (12.6.3 below, Coote and Whitelam 1987, 15). Clearly this does not exclude the possibility that very old material may have been preserved; however, in any case this has happened outside its original context and the material now therefore serves different purposes (Soggin 1988, 265f.). Moreover, this happens not only in the case of Israel and Judah but throughout the ancient Near East and also in the West, as is demonstrated by the histories of Greece and Rome. In this connection see the two recent works by M.Liverani, *Antico Oriente. Storia, società, economia*, Bari 1988 (where there is relatively little talk of history, but much of societies and the economy), and *Prestige and Interest*, Padua 1990. In short, it is only from outside that the problem can validly be raised and hence also resolved.

3.1.3 As I have said, we cannot rule out *a priori* the possibility that in the historical period traditions may exist, whether oral or written, which take the reader directly to particular phases of this process of the birth of a nation and which therefore allow us to reconstruct part of the development, even if only in outline and in particular areas. However, the actual facts in attempts of this kind tend to be very few. At the beginning of his career, the great American archaeologist and philologist W.F.Albright gave a warning: 'The long memory possessed by semi-civilized peoples for historical fact is a pious fiction of over-zealous apologists...'[2] – a view which, however, was soon to be replaced by other much more optimistic ones.

3.1.4 In this connection it is worth recalling a famous phrase of R.G.Collingwood from 1956. He thought it useful to compare the work of the historian with that of the detective. From 1984 onwards I have tried to develop this concept, applying it to the court in a criminal trial. The court cross-examines the witnesses, examines the evidence, and evaluates the circumstances, and finally, on the basis of its findings, arrives at a verdict based on what is considered an authentic and normative reconstruction of events. However, we should also recall that while the traditions were being handed down, whether orally or in writing, they were often subject, like the evidence in a trial, to the phenomenon which in legal jargon is called 'contamination'. That happens quite simply because, even leaving aside errors or omissions, carelessness or forgetfulness, different interests can come into play from the ones which motivated those who originally handed down the traditions, and it was as a result of these original interests that certain data came to be collected and handed down, and other data were discarded. Added to that, it may well be that some statements are the product of later theological, philosophical or psychological reflections or, in quite a few cases, the products of fantasy for apologetic or polemical ends. Cases of this kind, not for the Bible, have been noted by Hobsbawm and Ranger 1983, and for the Bible by Coote and Whitelam 1987, 13ff.

3.1.5 Rome under Augustus is a good example, because it is much less controversial. Livy and Tacitus as historians, and Virgil as an epic poet, have handed on information about the migration of Aeneas from Troy to Italy, about the foundation of Rome, the monarchy and then the birth of the Republic, and the Punic wars. Often, as is well known, we are confronted with legendary material: the migration of Aeneas, the stories of Romulus and Remus, the rape of the Sabine women; at other times we find elements which are historically at least probable, even if as things are there is no way of trying to prove their truth: for example in the case of relations between Rome and Alba Longa in the early days (Liverani 1980). In the work of the two historians I have mentioned there is also more concrete material, but it is essentially concerned with famous men and women with whom readers are to identify and therefore whom they are to imitate; there are also negative examples, arousing aversion and therefore not to be imitated in any way. Now without *a priori* denying the possibility that this material goes back to real experience and to individuals who really existed and that it can therefore reflect actual facts, the problem seems to me rather different, at any rate for the historian, whose view here is quite distinct from that of the pedagogue: what possible importance could stories of heroes like Horatius Coclites and Mucius Scaevola, of virtuous women like Cornelia and Lucretia, or politicians of integrity like Cincinnatus the dictator, ultimately have? Or the heroic death of the consul Attilius Regulus for keeping his word in the interest of the Republic (truth and state interest proving to be in irreconcilable conflict) as it were on the purely historical level? These stories have had their place in pedagogy from time immemorial as edifying episodes, but what importance could they have for a reconstruction of the functions and *modus operandi* of the dictatorship at the beginning of the Republic, or for a study of the duties of the consuls during the Punic wars? The same goes for the virtuous women whom I have mentioned: can these stories offer the student an analysis of social ethics at the time to which they refer?

3.1.6 What we have here, then, are positive heroes and heroines, examples to imitate, to inspire later generations (and they have performed these functions admirably, right down to the present day); they are also perhaps embodiments of the hope of the more enlightened members of the court at the time of Augustus that, for his greater glory, the ancient virtues, the *pietas* of days gone by, might be reborn in a return of conditions not dissimilar from those of the golden age: Virgil's Fourth Eclogue is explicit in this respect. If, however, we want to establish what were the relations between Rome and the Etruscans at the end of the monarchy and the beginning of the Republic, it will be necessary to make use of a variety of materials, materials which, fortunately for scholars, exist. So it is nevertheless possible to arrive at a relatively faithful framework for these two periods.[3]

3.1.7 For these reasons it seems vital that the historian of Israel and Judah, too, should be able to establish when and for what reasons certain traditions emerged and when and for what reasons they were handed down, and also whether they have any historical foundation. The discipline which we call 'Introduction to the Old Testament'[4] is concerned with this. Its scope is that of tracing, again within the limits of possibility, a history of biblical literature, in an attempt to discover the ideological preconceptions of the tradents and hence their aims.

3.1.7.1 Nowadays, for example, it seems fairly clear that the horizon of the 'ancient' traditions of the Pentateuch, and also that of the so-called Former Prophets and of the major prophets, was determined by the extremely traumatic experience of the exile. The deportation of elements first of the Northern Kingdom and then of the Southern Kingdom, the fall of the Davidic monarchy, the eternity of which seems to have been proclaimed by ancient oracles, and the loss of political independence, had to be 'explained' and developed in a theological framework.

3.1.7.2 So to take another example, the migrations of the patriarchs towards the promised land reflect some features from the time of the empire of David and Solomon; however, for those who handed down these stories the main interest was now in the possession of the land and in ancestral descent, as is shown by the various divine promises made specially to Abraham and to Jacob. The migration of Abraham from Ur in Chaldaea to Haran and from there to Canaan becomes perfectly logical once it is accepted that this was the customary route which linked the southern Babylonian Diaspora with the homeland.

3.1.7.3 The exodus from Egypt and what has been presented as a conquest but what we more appropriately call the 'settlement', accompanied by the foundation of the 'league of the twelve tribes', with the emphasis on the religious unity of 'Israel' around the common sanctuary, are features which fit splendidly into the ideology of the restoration among the exiles who returned home; it is no coincidence that Second Isaiah (Isa.41.18ff.; 43.1ff., 16ff.; 48.20ff.) speaks of a 'second exodus'. Moreover it is only from that time that Egypt, at first the country to which people turned for aid or political asylum, received those negative attributes which soon made it the country of oppression,[5] independently of the age of these traditions. The same thing happens with passages like Ex.19.1ff. (v.6!): here the concepts of the 'kingdom of priests' and the 'holy nation' are presented as clear alternatives to the fallen monarchy; there is no need to point out that the two expressions cannot be applied to the pre-exilic period!

3.1.7.4 The situation over the monarchy seems to be the same. Again according to the biblical traditions, there was a relatively long period during which the people was ruled over by what was basically an eminently religious structure, the tribal league. The monarchy, which the latest stratum of the Deuteronomic history interpreted as a blasphemous choice on the part of the people, that of an earthly king in place of the heavenly King (I Sam.8.1ff.), was then introduced only because of external pressures, despite the fact that, again according to this stratum, the tribal league was quite adequate both for coping with foreign dangers (I Sam.7.1ff.) and for maintaining internal law and order (Judg.19-21). It was from this basic, primordial breach of trust that the disastrous effects arose which centuries later led to national catastrophe. However, this theory of the ancient historian clearly compounds erroneous choices made in matters of foreign politics especially during the sixth century BCE (in a situation which moreover left very little space for manoeuvre, cf. also 12.6) with something like a kind of original sin committed in prehistoric times.

3.1.7.5 Moreover that also emerges from the little that we can still reconstruct of the religion of Israel and Judah in prehistoric times. The few data available to us show a religion which differed hardly, if at all, from that of Canaan, the one chief dissimilarity being that the national deity worshipped was called YHWH. If the traditions are not completely misleading, it was the great prophets of the ninth, eighth and seventh century BCE who proposed an alternative to this religious form by proclaiming a monotheism which in some cases was also to become intolerant. There are no clear historical traces of a tribal league with an essentially religious character of Yahwistic monotheism, but only legends with a highly ideological content.

3.1.8 To sum up, we can claim that here in any case we are confronted with highly ideologized attempts at reconstructing the past, the aim of which was not (indeed was probably not even meant to be) to transmit a precise framework, even in part, for the pre-exilic history, far less for the pre-monarchical history of Israel and Judah. The intention was in fact to cope with a past which came to a tragic conclusion with the exile, the legitimation of the present domination of the priesthood of Jerusalem and an explanation of the present wretchedness (before the exile the situation was far better, as was known) as the product of divine judgment, though mitigated by grace.[6] What has recently been asserted by K.A.D.Smelik is also increasingly clear:[7] that the biblical narratives were much more free with the tradition than is commonly thought: that historical fidelity was not part of their operating criteria. So it was possible to adapt or even invent historical 'facts' depending on the needs of the moment; many hands worked on the complex from Genesis to Kings over a long period, some from positions which are illogical to us, given that, for example, they often inserted different versions of the same event into their narratives. This brings us to another topic.

3.2 Historiography in the ancient Near East

This is a topic which can only be touched on here; it merits a monograph in itself. Furthermore it is possible to establish with certainty that, contrary to a widespread opinion, the historiography of Judah in the exilic and post-exilic period (we know nothing of anything earlier like that of Israel) was not substantially different from that of the ancient Near East.

Bibliography

J.Oberman (ed.), *The Idea of History in the Ancient Near East*, New Haven and London 1955; H.Gese, 'Geschichtliches Denken im alten Orient und im Alten Testament', *ZTK* 55, 1958, 127-45 = *Vom Sinai zum Zion*, Munich 1974, 81-98; J.J.Finkelstein, 'Mesopotamian Historiography', in *Proceedings of the American Philosophical Society* 107, 1963, 461ff.; B.Albrektson, *History and the Gods*, Lund 1967; H.A.Hoffner, 'Propaganda and Political Justification in Hittite Historiography', in H.Goedicke and J.J.M.Roberts (ed.), *Unity and Diversity*, Baltimore 1975, 49-62; id., *Or* 49, 1980, 283-32; M.Liverani, 'Memorandum on the Approach to Historiographical Texts', *Or* 42, 1973, 178-84; P.Machinist, 'Literature as Politics: The Tukulti-Ninurta Epic and the Bible', *CBQ* 38, 1976, 455-82; H.Tadmor, 'History and Ideology in the Assyrian Royal Inscriptions', in F.M.Fales (ed.), *Assyrian Royal Inscriptions*, Rome 1981, 13-33; J.W.Wevers, 'Histories and Historians of the Ancient Near East. Preface', *Or* 49, 1980, 137-9; J.van Seters, 'History and Historians of the Ancient Near East. The Israelites', *Or* 50, 1981, 137-93; id., *In Search of History*, New Haven and London 1982; H.Tadmor and M.Weinfeld (ed.), *History, Historiography and Interpretation*, Jerusalem 1983; O.Carena, *History of Near Eastern Historiography and its Problems, 1852-1985*, Neukirchen-Vluyn/Kevelaer 1981, Vol.1; H.Cazelles, 'Die biblische Geschichtsschreibung im Licht der altorientalischen Geschichtsschreibung', in *XXIII. Deutscher Orientalistentag... Würzburg 1986*, Wiesbaden 1989, 38-49; A.Roccati, *La littérature historique sous l'ancien empire égyptien*,

Paris 1982; H.Fahr, *Herodot und das Alte Testament*, Frankfurt 1985; V.Fritz, 'Mythische Elemente in der Geschichtsschreibung Israels und bei Hesiod', *ZTK* 87, 1990, 145-62; H.C.Schmitt, 'Die Geschichte vom Sieg über die Amalekiter Ex 17: theologische Lehrerzählung', *ZAW* 102, 1990, 335-44; H.Cazelles, 'Historiographies bibliques et pré-bibliques', *RB* 98, 1991, 481-512; D.V.Edelman (ed.), *The Fabric of History*, Sheffield 1991.

The widespread thesis, which in some quarters has almost become an axiom, according to which the faith of Israel (and only this faith) is based on history and for that reason produced a historiography qualitatively superior to that of the other peoples of the region, cannot be proved in critical terms, as was exhaustively demonstrated by B.Albrektson 1967 and by various scholars after him. However, just one difference should be noted: the monotheistic basis that we should presuppose in the period when Israelite historiography reached its apogee. Thanks to monotheism, any divine intervention whatsoever is presented in the Hebrew scriptures in a different way from that in other civilizations. However, this diversity does not in any way denote superiority.

3.2.1 Ancient Near Eastern historiography set itself many aims, but they can perhaps be reduced to a common denominator: propaganda. The ruling house was glorified, in a way which brought out the monuments that it built, especially the temples; its military campaigns, which were always victorious; and its good government (plenty of cheap consumer goods, social and forensic justice). Attempts were made to legitimate usurpers, a feature which is also attested in the Hebrew Bible, to the degree that such a figure presented himself either as a legitimate aspirant to the throne who had initially gone unrecognized (thus e.g. the inscription on the statue of Idrimi, king of Alalakh, *ANET*, 557, and *TUAT* I, 501-4, cf. Lemche* 1988, 54), or according to the theme of the child who is hidden and thus escapes the massacre (cf. II Kings 11.2; II Chron.22.11). It is also claimed that the monarch was called directly by the deity, in place of others reigning at the time (for the Bible cf. I Sam.16.1-16 [Dtr] and II Kings 9.1-10). Ancient Near Eastern historiography often justifies a vassal relationship by a description of the gifts with which the great king has abundantly blessed the vassal, so that a relationship which was originally enforced is no longer presented as such, but as an expression of the gratitude of the lesser towards the greater. Finally, this historiography has royal lists and inscriptions, chronicles and annals. In all these works the intervention of the gods in the destinies of human beings depending on their behaviour is a fundamental element: this is always a historiography conceived of theologically, contrary to what happens in modern historiography. That was true for the Hittite empire, for Mesopotamia and for Syria, cf. the inscription on the statue of Idrimi cited above, and also the texts of Karatepe and Sefîre. It was true to a lesser degree for Egypt, whose texts many scholars would therefore like to exclude.

3.2.2 These literary genres are not frequent in the Hebrew Bible; no royal inscriptions exist any longer (and there must have been such inscriptions, just as we have the stele of Mesha king of Moab),[8] and not even the texts of vassal treaties have been handed down. I have already referred to the theme of the legitimation of a usurper. Nor has anything come down to us of the chronicles and the annals: it is said only that once there was a *sēper dibrē (hayyāmīm) (li-)šᵉlōmōh* (I Kings 11.41), a *sēper dibrē hayyāmīm lᵉmalᵉkē yiśrā'ēl* (I Kings 14.19), and a *sēper...* *lᵉmalᵉkē yᵉhūdāh* (I Kings 14.29), books on which the Deuteronomistic author will have composed a kind of commentary. Today it is difficult to say what really existed.[9] However, in the Hebrew Bible we can note the tendency to regroup the material in historiographical works on a large scale: the Deuteronomistic history and Chronicles. We also find reflections of a historiographical kind in the prophets, that is, unless these are Deuteronomistic elaborations (see below 3.6.1).

3.2.3 The main difference between the biblical historiography (only that of Judah, since we have nothing from the North) and that of the Near East, in addition to its monotheism, lies in the difference of literary genre. In Judah we find later works of synthesis, which also contain elaborations of earlier texts. But in Judah there was also a major work of legitimation, as I have already indicated: that of the post-exilic priesthood, which obtains its own definitive redaction in the Deuteronomistic history work. This is because the priesthood saw itself as the legitimate successor to the fallen monarchy, over against any attempt at restoration. Indeed, this legitimation was even transferred to the prehistory, a period which was considered normative, when the people, imagined as a substantial unity, was thought to have been governed by a tribal league which also included the tribes of the north. And the sin of the people was to have replaced this divinely willed order with a secular form of government!

3.3 The beginnings of historiography in Israel and Judah

Where, then, does a history of Israel and Judah begin? In other words, is there a time after which the material in the tradition begins to offer verifiable accounts, information about individuals who existed and events which happened (or at least which are probable, given the state of our present knowledge), relevant facts in the economic and political sphere?

3.3.1 Such questions are not new; they have been asked for more than a century now. In 1869 the Dutchman Abraham Kuenen and in 1885 the German Bernhard Stade put them in exactly the same terms,[10] and each gave his own answer; the former suggested the eighth century BCE, the latter the empire of David and Solomon. The legitimacy of such questions is now generally recognized, and even the North American Sumeriologist and Assyriologist W.W.Hallo, who is very critical of the answer I shall be giving later, accepts them fully. In the last decade I have felt that the answer should be the empire of David and Solomon, an empire which, according to the sources, would have also included, in one way or another, a large part of the neighbouring nations (cf. also 4.1, and Soggin in Hayes and Miller* 1977, 1978 and 1984). This theory was put forward earlier, as we saw, by Stade. And in fact from that time on Israel and Judah began to exist not only as ethnic entities (as the tribes would have been when they had settled on their own territories, as Malamat 1983 would have it), but also as political entities, in that they constituted themselves as a state; and it is only from that time onwards that reflection on the past not only began to have some significance but also became possible. By contrast, Noth would prefer to go back to the period of the twelve-tribe league. However, the problems which have emerged in recent decades in connection with the existence of this organization, which seems rather to be an ideological reconstruction of prehistory in the post-exilic period, made in an attempt to see Israel and Judah as a substantive unity, have removed the ground from under what in any case was never more than a hypothesis.

3.3.2 It is only with the formation of the state, first national and then territorial, that the problem of their own national identity, their own legitimacy, arose for Israel and Judah, precariously united into an empire. It does not seem to be coincidence that it is at precisely that point that we find the first political information and the first administrative and economic texts (see further at 4.7 below). To go back to the time of the exodus from Egypt, as is proposed by W.W.Hallo, who has already been cited above, as the moment when 'Israel' acquired its own 'group identity', 'the awareness of a collective destiny', is to use these somewhat rhetorical formulations to cloak a degree of naivety, if we look at the proposal in the light of what is being said here.

3.3.3 For the moment I feel it necessary to maintain this position, despite the objections which have been made to it. For example E.Meyer and similarly already J.A.Montgomery and H.S.Gehman identify the north-western frontier of the empire with that of the Persian satrapy of Transeuphrates, and J.M.Sasson and M.C.Astour have recently supported this suggestion.[11] They do so for the following reasons. I Kings 5.1,4 speaks of the frontiers of the empire 'from the river Euphrates [to the] Philistines' (the text is not all there) and 'in all the region beyond the Euphrates'. However, the Hebrew expressions *min hannāhār* and *bᵉkol ʿeber hannāhār* are identical to those attested in Assyria from Assurbanipal (668-627) onwards and are regularly used in the Persian administration for the territories situated west of the river (*ʿeber nāri*). So it is clear that the text uses a terminology not attested before the seventh century BCE and current only in the sixth and fifth centuries. Furthermore – and this is disconcerting, even if well known – there are no traces of the empire of David and Solomon in Near Eastern texts, which is all the more remarkable considering the importance that the empire assumes within the Hebrew Bible.

So is it possible that the reference to David and Solomon and to their empire is simply a later, artificial construction, tending to glorify a past which never existed to compensate for a present which is dull and gray?[12] Must we, in other words, return to Kuenen's theory and begin with the eighth century or perhaps even only with the Deuteronomistic work?[13] These are theories which recently have had the support of a number of often distinguished authors: among others, Garbini* argues that on the best of hypotheses, David and Solomon will have reigned over a territory which was much smaller than that described, including Judah, Israel and the Philistine and Moabite territories, and that much information will not be earlier than the eighth century BCE. Questions arise here which are neither absurd nor wrong-headed, and they show our obvious limits when we seek to study a period the sources for which present so many difficulties.

3.3.3.1 Despite this, I think that it is possible to obtain historical data relating to the empire, even if so far no evidence for it has emerged in the writings of the ancient Near East. It is simply a matter of examining and interrogating the sources at our disposal adequately. Certainly we should be careful to avoid simply paraphrasing the biblical texts, a danger which is always present, as Coote and Whitelam indicate; what we need to do is to extrapolate from their present context those sources from that time which have been handed down, using them for the purpose of reconstruction, even if the change of context means that their functions have now become different. In other words, exegesis must seek to recover the original meaning and function of these texts. To give an example: the information that the texts provide about the administration, its officials and governors, about taxation, about constructions, about commercial enterprises, about oppressive and exploitative systems of government imposed on the North, especially when these considerations are critical and not triumphalistic, have a presumption of authenticity which it is difficult (though not completely impossible) to deny: they would not have any function as products of a later period.

3.3.3.2 So perhaps it will be necessary to follow Garbini*'s proposal and reduce the traditional dimensions of the empire, if with him we accept the antiquity of the text II Sam.23.8-39 (cf. below 4.1.4), regarding the rest of the information (for example about conquests in Syria and Transjordan, which are also attributed to Saul in I Sam.14.47-52) as triumphalistic reconstructions of the past. Another of Garbini*'s proposals, that the north-eastern frontiers might be described in terms of the situation of Israel and Judah in the eighth century (below, 10.15.2-3) under king Jeroboam II and Uzziah, is interesting and will be discussed in due course. In this way it should be possible to reduce the actual frontiers of the empire to their precise dimensions.

3.3.4 These are the reasons why I prefer to begin with the empire of David and Solomon, even if there are quite a number of factors in favour of beginning at the end of the ninth century BCE (when Israel is mentioned on the stele of Mesha king of Moab, a text which Kuenen did not yet know), or with the eighth century (when it appears in the Assyrian annals), and again, more radically, only with the Deutero-nomistic work.[14]

3.3.5 Of the period before the formation of the state we therefore know little (if anything), so that it would seem impossible to verify the validity of the biblical thesis according to which 'Israel' will have gone through a relatively long period, up to the end of the second millennium, in which it was not governed by any central power; in the light of what has been said it seems all the more improbable, and Coote and Whitelam 1987, 74ff., produce evidence of considerable value to support the thesis that the 'analysis of the origins of Israel' cannot be separated 'from the concerns of the monarchic state'. In the present state of Near Eastern studies the study of the period before the monarchy in Israel and Judah therefore remains 'a project of ethnogenetic research which is impossible to realize', to take up the evocative title of Liverani's basic study of 1980.

3.4. *Questions of method*

From what I have said it is clear that a history of Israel and Judah which seeks to limit itself to a paraphrase of the biblical texts, where possible supplementing them with texts from the ancient Near East, is not only following a wrong method, which would moreover emerge from a comparison with the traditions of other peoples, but presents a misleading picture of what happened, in that it takes over in an uncritical and therefore illegitimate form the image which Judah made of itself and of Israel in later times.

3.4.1 Furthermore, that is true not only of the prehistory but often also of the later period, for which the Deuteronomistic history work has handed down various pieces of data. Here, too, there are many shady areas, sometimes of complete obscurity. And here too we must never lose sight of the fact that even where it is possible to demonstrate the antiquity of particular traditions, as I have indicated, the contexts in which they are to be found are not the original ones, and as a result they have taken on different functions and therefore other meanings. In any case, where we know little or nothing it is better to keep silent than to paraphrase.

3.4.2 What I have said clearly also obliges me to reshape considerably what I stated in my writings of the 1960s and the 1970s.[15] But that does not mean that I disown these studies: their results represent an attempt to reconstruct not so much ancient periods as what later redactors and tradents affirmed at times subsequent to such periods.

3.5 The histories of Israel and Judah today

For just over a century there has been a discipline called 'history of Israel' (which is taken to mean the history of Israel, Judah and neighbouring countries). Up to the second half of the nineteenth century this history was written essentially as a paraphrase of the biblical books. A critical historiography came into being in the second half of the last century, under the shadow of German historicism: however, the results were not always equally valid. Clearly there can be no question here of reviewing all the histories published over this century and more; here I shall limit myself to indicating the most important of them to have appeared before the Second World War. I shall, however, comment in more detail on those which appeared during and after this period.

3.5.1 After the works of Kuenen 1869 and Stade 1885 (see above, 3.3.1), I would list the following:

3.5.1.1 J.Wellhausen, *Israelitische und jüdische Geschichte*, Berlin 1894, [7]1914 and reprints. This work uses for historical purposes the information derived from the division of the Pentateuch into sources and the various works of the author. For Wellhausen the history begins with the second millennium BCE, and 'Israel' and 'Judah' here stand for the pre-exilic and post-exilic periods respectively.

3.5.1.2 R.Kittel, *Geschichte der Hebräer*, Gotha 1888 (ET *A History of the Hebrews*, London, Edinburgh and New York 1889),[2]1909, as *Geschichte des Volkes Israel*, Stuttgart [7]1932. Despite his essentially conservative approach, from the second edition onwards Kittel makes systematic use of the information coming from the archaeological discoveries and texts of the ancient Near East. So we can regard him as the inaugurator of the comparative historical method.

3.5.1.3 M.Weber, *Ancient Judaism* (1921, ET Glencoe 1952) is the first attempt at a sociological and historical analysis of pre-exilic Israel and is still largely valid.[16] Weber was neither an orientalist nor a biblical scholar, and had to use the works of other authors as a basis, so his material is second-hand. He is regarded as the first to have worked with the concept of the twelve-tribe league.

3.5.1.4 G.Ricciotti, *The History of Israel* (1932), two vols, ET Milwaukee 1955. This is a very conservative work which is almost 'fundamentalist' in its approach and largely uncritical; however, it becomes good in the section dealing with the Maccabean period. Still, as in other works by this author, the main problems are generally ignored.

3.5.1.5 W.O.E.Oesterley and T.H.Robinson, *A History of Israel*, two vols, London 1932 and reprints, is a solid work, constructed in the best British humanistic tradition; it is still useful for those interested in the problems perceived in the 1920s and 1930s.

3.5.2 The period from the Second World War to our day has produced a particularly large number of histories of Israel. I list the following works:

3.5.2.1 W.F.Albright, *From the Stone Age to Christianity*, Baltimore 1940, [2]1957. In a bold historical, philosophical and theological synthesis (though in fact he was neither a historian, a philosopher nor a theologian), the author sees the history of Israel as the model for the evolution of humanity towards monotheism, following the Hegelian pattern of thesis, antithesis and synthesis. There is a summary of the author's position in *The Biblical Period – From Abraham to Ezra*, New York 1949, [3]1963. His work fundamentally shaped one or two generations of archaeologists and philologists in the United States and in Israel.

3.5.2.2 One of the best-known and most influential works in this area is certainly that of M.Noth, *The History of Israel* (1950, [2]1954), ET [2]1959. As I have indicated (above 3.3.1), Noth's starting point is a supposed league of twelve tribes formed in the last centuries of the second millennium BCE, which he erroneously calls an 'amphictyony'. He has a contemporary follower in M.Metzger, *Grundriss der Geschichte Israels*, Neukirchen 1963, [6]1985.

3.5.2.3 J.Bright, *A History of Israel*, Philadelphia and London 1959, [3]1981, follows in the wake of W.F.Albright; his approach is conservative, but the history is particularly useful for the amount of archaeological and ancient Near Eastern material that it contains. Without being 'fundamentalist', it considers the biblical texts, which moreover it treats with moderation, as important sources which are sufficient for historians provided that what they say is confirmed by archaeology.

3.5.2.4 R.de Vaux, *The Early History of Israel* (two vols 1971, 1974), ET London 1978, was to have been a work in three volumes; Vol.I is complete and only some fragments of Vol.II have been published, which were already available at the author's death. Volume I is probably the most complete work on the patriarchs, the exodus, the journey through the wilderness and the settlement in Canaan. There is a critical review in M.Liverani, *OA* 15, 1976, 145-9.

3.5.2.5 A.H.J.Gunneweg, *Geschichte Israels bis Bar Kochba*, Stuttgart 1973, ⁶1989, offers a good presentation of present-day views with original proposals. However, the bibliographies have not always been brought up to date. In the latest (sixth) edition a new final chapter deals with the history of Zionism from the foundation of the State in 1948.

3.5.2.6 S.Herrmann, *A History of Israel in Old Testament Times* (1973, ²1980), ET London and Philadelphia 1975, ²1981, is a solidly conservative work which is particularly important for its Egyptological contributions. The first edition ended with Ezra/Nehemiah; the second goes down to the Roman occupation. A third edition is in preparation.

3.5.2.7 G.Fohrer, *Geschichte Israels*, Heidelberg 1977, ³1982, provides a good synthesis of present-day problems, even if it has not always been brought up to date. A last chapter deals, somewhat sketchily, with the history of Israel from the events of 70-134 CE to our days.

3.5.2.8 J.H.Hayes and J.M.Miller (eds.), *Israelite and Judaean History*, Philadelphia and London 1977, is a work by various specialists. The presentation of the problems and possible solutions is virtually complete and up-to-date throughout. It is a particularly important work.

3.5.2.9 H.Jagersma, *A History of Israel in the Old Testament Period* (1979), London and Philadelphia 1982; *A History of Israel from Alexander the Great to Bar Kochba* (1985), London and Philadelphia 1985. These are succinct works, full of original ideas. For Jagersma, too, there is no certain information prior to the formation of the state.

3.5.2.10 B.Mazar (ed.), *The World History of the Jewish People*, first series, 8 vols., Jerusalem 1964ff. This is a detailed national history which is to be completed in three series. The approach is generally conservative. A similar work in approach, but on a much smaller scale, is H.H.Ben-Sasson (ed.), *History of the Jewish People*, London and Cambridge, Mass. 1976.

3.5.2.11 H.Cazelles, *Histoire politique d'Israël*, Paris 1982. As might be expected of a 'political' history, this begins with the foundation of the state.

3.5.2.12 F.Castel, *Histoire d'Israël et de Juda, dès les origines au IIᵉ siècle après Jésus-Christ*, Paris 1982. This is a gifted popular work, original and useful for its illustrations, diagrams, geographical maps and reproductions of ancient Near Eastern texts.

3.5.2.13 H.Donner, *Geschichte des Volkes Israel und seiner Nachbarn*, Göttingen I, 1984, II 1986. This follows the traditional order, though it is doubtful about the possibility of reconstructing a history of the premonarchical period. It is a particularly important work.

3.5.2.14 J.M.Miller and J.H.Hayes, *A History of Ancient Israel and Judah*, Philadelphia and London 1986. The two scholars, this time authors and not just editors (above, 3.5.2.8), regard the traditions which speak of the period before the formation of the state as valueless for the period that they set out to describe. The book reproduces many Near Eastern texts which are important for the history of Israel and Judah. An important work.

3.5.2.15 N.P.Lemche, *Ancient Israel*, Sheffield 1988: this is probably the most up-to-date work available today, though it is too short for the importance of the themes. It argues that we know very little, if anything, about the period before the foundation of the state; of the monarchical period only the little that the Deuteronomistic history work and later Chronicles have wanted to hand down: something can still be deduced from the prophetic books and the ancient Near Eastern texts, but again very little. This is a particularly important work for the new starting point.

3.5.2.16 G.Garbini, *History and Ideology in Ancient Israel* (1986), London and New York 1988, is a very original work, even if it is not always precise in detail. The Hebrew Bible is assessed as an ideological document from the late post-exilic period. At all events this important work should not be ignored, even if its reflections in Chapter 1 on Old Testament scholars, particularly German Protestant scholars, are out of place. Cf. the reviews by J.A.Soggin, *Paideia* 42, 1987, 334-40; M.Liverani, *OA* 27, 1988, 301-9; H.Engel, *Bibl* 69, 1988, 126-9 (very critical); and P.R.Davies, *JTS* 40, 1990, 121-8.

3.5.2.17 H.Shanks (ed.), *Ancient Israel. A Short History from Abraham to the Roman Destruction of the Temple*, Washington DC 1988. This is a work by various scholars of different orientations, which explains the different approaches and solutions to problems.

3.5.2.18 J.Vermeylen, *Un peuple passioné de Dieu*, Brussels 1988, is based on university lectures and provides a useful attempt at a synthesis.

3.5.2.19 P.Sacchi, *Storia del mondo giudaico*, Turin 1976: a basic work on the post-exilic period.

3.5.3 Among the shorter works which are critical in approach, see:

3.5.3.1 H.M.Orlinsky, *Ancient Israel*, Ithaca, NY ²1960;

3.5.3.2 M.A.Beek, *Geschiedenis van Israël*, Zeist 1957, ⁵1983;

3.5.3.3 E.L.Ehrlich, *A Concise History of Israel*, ET London and New York 1963;

3.5.3.4 A.Lemaire, *Histoire du peuple hébreu*, Paris 1981;

3.5.3.5 R.Rendtorff, *The Old Testament: An Introduction* (1983), ET London and Philadelphia 1985, 1-76: this has a synthesis of the history of Israel which precedes rather than follows the study of the texts;

3.5.3.6 S.Beck, *Kleine Geschichte Israels*, Freiburg im Breisgau 1989.

3.5.4 Now whereas, as I commented, Kuenen and Stade doubted the possibility of going back, the former beyond the eighth century (like Sasson today) and the latter beyond the tenth century, thanks to Wellhausen* and Kittel*, though each for different reasons, the habit became established again in the second half of the last century of beginning with the second millennium BCE. This tendency was taken up and developed by the American school after the Second World War (Albright* and Bright*), who spoke consistently of a patriarchal age, and in this they were followed by some Israeli scholars who had studied under them. By contrast, Weber* and Noth* thought in terms of the last centuries of the second millennium, when the tribal league which they postulate would have existed. This was an institution whose existence is still maintained by Donner*, who regards it as a political and not a religious factor; similarly Buccellati in 1967 and Malamat in 1983. Albright*, Bright*, Aharoni** and H.Weippert**. However, Coote and Whitelam begin with the Stone Age, regarding the history of Israel and Judah as an integral part of the history of Palestine generally.

3.6 Sources

From what has been said so far it should have become clear that the sources for a history of Israel and Judah down to the end of the ninth century BCE consist almost exclusively of the biblical texts. I have tried to point out the problems associated with them at the historical level, albeit only synthetically. At a later stage the Bible is supplemented by other sources, from Israel and the ancient Near East, which give us a more complete framework of the events and persons involved, though despite everything there are many notably shady zones. And if the biblical texts are numerous, their quantity is as it were negatively counterbalanced by their dubious value as history, if only because they are presented in terms of problems which are very often centuries away from the events that they seek to describe.

3.6.1 In the first place we have a historical collection which has the lion's share of material, the 'Deuteronomistic history' (Dtr), so called because it gathers together its own traditions according to criteria inspired by the fifth book of the Bible. To this we owe the redaction of at least two, probably three, phases of Deuteronomy (with the exception of chs.32, 33 and 34), and of the so-called historical books (the Former Prophets): Joshua, Judges, I and II Samuel and I and II Kings.[17] For the patriarchal narratives and the accounts of the exodus and the journey through the wilderness we have the J and E sources of the first four books of the Pentateuch; the source E is not often attested, indeed so rarely that some scholars have questioned its existence. After the book of Genesis it is in any case difficult to distinguish between the two earliest sources, so that the majority of analyses of these sources are made on the basis of the first book of the Bible alone. There is much controversy today over whether, as was at first generally believed, these sources are very ancient, whether they are to be dated to a period shortly before the exile, or indeed whether they exist at all; some scholars would prefer to replace the documentary hypothesis with traditio-historical or redaction-historical schemes. Some laws contained in the so-called Book of the Covenant (Ex.20.22-23.33) are probably earlier than the seventh century (the date of the reform of king Josiah, cf. below, 12.4) along with poems like Gen.49.1ff.; Deut 33.1ff.; Judg.5.1ff., even if, contrary to widespread views, it is impossible to date them to the period before the formation of the state. It is possible to deduce interesting information about the rural community in Israel and Judah from the first complex, though use of this material is made difficult by the impossibility of dating the texts with even a minimum of certainty. The epic and heroic songs only rarely provide features which the historian can use, not least because they too are difficult to date and their references are not always clear.

3.6.2 J and E seem to have been combined shortly before the exile; however, they too have been subjected to a revision of a Deuteronomic or Deuteronomistic kind: this has introduced, always at key points (e.g. Gen.15; Ex.13.1-10; 19.3-8; 34.10-13 and others) factors which are clearly intended to provide the key to reading the whole of the section. A Deuteronomic redaction is now generally accepted for the prophets Hosea, Jeremiah and Ezekiel, and it has recently also been proposed for Proto-Isaiah by Kaiser; a redaction of this kind also seems possible for passages from the prophet Amos.[18] Very sparse information about the end of the pre-exilic period is given by the prophets mentioned above (in those passages which we can extract from the Deuteronomistic redaction) and from Nahum, Habakkuk and Zephaniah.

The books of Haggai and Proto-Zechariah provide information on the period immediately after the exile. The prophets Trito-Isaiah, Obadiah and Malachi provide information about the end of the sixth and the beginning of the fifth century BCE. The first four books of the Pentateuch then received a final redaction in the early post-exilic period at the hand of P, the last source of the Pentateuch. In all these cases it is clear that we have reached a period not earlier than the second half of the sixth century BCE.

3.6.3 A second complex of history writing is that of Chronicles, to which until recently it was usual to add the books of Ezra and Nehemiah. Whereas in the Deuteronomistic history work a semblance of secular history has been maintained, in Chronicles sacred history clearly gains the upper hand, so that for most of the time the reader is confronted with hagiography pure and simple; the historical information is therefore, with exceptions, very limited. The historical information that can be deduced from the Book of Psalms is minute, while the book of Lamentations gives us information about the situation immediately after the destruction of Jerusalem in 587 or 586.[19]

3.6.4 The deutero-canonical books of I-II Maccabees and Baruch and the deutero-canonical additions to the books of Daniel and Esther are important for the Hellenistic period. So too, finally, is a pseudepigraphical book, III Ezra (I Esdras), a work parallel to Chronicles, Ezra and Nehemiah and containing some original material which some scholars consider more reliable than that of the canonical works.

3.6.5 Outside the Bible but still within the Jewish tradition we have the works of the historian Josephus, son of Mattathias, who later took the name Flavius: he was a Jewish priest who at first commanded the rebel Jewish troops in Galilee, in 67-70 CE, but then went over to the Romans, so that he was regarded as a traitor in Israel.

3.6.5.1 His works are the *Antiquities* (*Antt.*), an important source partly parallel to the Hebrew Bible; the *Jewish War* (*War*), a chronicle of the revolt of 67-70 CE; an apologetic work, *Contra Apionem*; and a *Vita*, an autobiographical work. There is a useful edition of Josephus edited by H.St-J.Thackeray and R.Marcus, in the Loeb Classical Library, nine volumes, London and Cambridge, Mass. 1926-65, which has a Greek critical text with an English translation opposite.

3.6.5.2 Josephus' work, which is strongly apologetic in orientation, should be used with great caution, as moreover should the majority of other classical histories. He often cites Phoenician and Greek authors whose works have been lost, so that it is no longer possible to verify his statements; some scholars today doubt whether Josephus ever had access to authentic and first-hand sources.[20] The sources cited by Josephus have recently been collected, along with other Greek and Latin works, by M.Stern, *Greek and Latin Authors on Jews and Judaism*, Jerusalem I, 1974; II, 1980; III, 1982.

3.6.6 We find other information in Philo of Alexandria and, later, in Eusebius of Caesarea; also among other ancient authors, pagan and Christian, all collected by Stern. This material is often very interesting, but at other times it is not very valuable because of its polemical or apologetic character; the polemical works often reflect a remarkable ignorance of the subject, even if they do show us what were already the prejudices against Judaism at that time.

3.6.7 Finally, as I have already indicated, Israel and Judah are mentioned in ancient Near Eastern sources from the end of the ninth century BCE. Mention should be made of:

3.6.7.1 The stele of Mesha, king of Moab, *KAI*, 1,68; *SSI* I, 71-83; *ANET*, 320f.; and *TUAT* I, 646-50 (cf. below, 12.6.6).

3.6.7.2 The Assyrian royal inscriptions and annals and, later, the Babylonian chronicles. D.D.Luckenbill (ed.), *Ancient Records of Assyria and Babylonia*, Chicago 1926-27, is an old collection which is still useful, as is D.J.Wiseman, *Chronicles of the Chaldaean Kings (625-556) in the British Museum*, London 1961; a selection of the material can also be found in *ANET* and *TUAT*.

3.6.7.3 The Western Semitic texts are published in a critical edition by H.Donner and W.Röllig, *Kanaanäische und aramäische Inschriften*, three vols, Wiesbaden [3]1968ff., and J.C.L.Gibson, *A Textbook of Syrian Semitic Inscriptions*, three vols., Oxford 1971-82.

3.6.7.4 Non-specialists will find the following works useful: J.B.Pritchard (ed.), *Ancient Near Eastern Texts Relating to the Old Testament*, Princeton [3]1969; id., *The Ancient Near East in Pictures*, Princeton 1969; O.Kaiser (ed.), *Texte aus der Umwelt des Alten Testaments*, Gütersloh 1982 (= *TUAT*); and, on a smaller scale: K.Galling (ed.), *Textbuch zur Geschichte Israels*, Tübingen [2]1968; A.Jepsen (ed.), *Von Sinuhe bis Nebukadnezar*, Leipzig 1975; W.Beyerlin (ed.), *Near Eastern Religious Texts Relating to the Old Testament*, London and Philadelphia 1978; K.A.D.Smelik, *Writings from Ancient Israel* (1984), Edinburgh 1991.

3.6.7.5 The earliest Near Eastern text which makes explicit mention of 'Israel' is the stele of Pharaoh Merenptah, c.1212-1202 BCE, dated to the fifth year of his reign, i.e. around 1207. It was found at Thebes and there is a copy at Karnak. Thanks to this double transmission and fragments of other copies, we can be certain about the text.

3.6.7.5.1 The text reads (on the basis of the translation by S.Moscati):[21]

The princes lie prostate, saying 'Salaam!'
No one lifts his head among the 'nine bows'
Tehenu is destroyed, Hatti pacified,
Canaan is plundered with every evil.
Ashkelon is deported, Gezer captured,
Yanoam is annihilated, Israel is devastated, its seed is no more!
Hurru has become a widow for Egypt.

The 'nine bows' is an expression which denotes people allied to Egypt in a vassal relationship, here evidently rebels who have been tamed. 'Tehenu' is a name for Libya; 'Ashkelon', Hebrew *'ašqᵉlōn* (coord.107-118) is in the south-west of Canaan and soon afterwards was to become a Philistine city; 'Gezer' is in the centre, to the west (coord.142-140); according to the convincing proposal by Alt, Yanoam is probably to be identified with *tell en na'am*, situated a few miles southwest of the Sea of Galilee (coord.197-237; H.Engel). 'Hurru' is a play on words between the name for the Hurrites and the Egyptian term for 'widow'; 'Israel' has the prefix for a 'non-sedentary population', and in any case is in Canaan.[22]

3.6.7.5.2 However, the present text presents more difficulties than can be resolved. First of all, it primarily refers to a campaign by the

Pharaoh against Libya ('Tehenu'), i.e. to the west; so how can this unexpected move of the Egyptian army towards the north-east, followed by a campaign in Canaan, have taken place? Consequently a number of Egyptologists (for example J.A.Wilson, who edited the text for *ANET*) doubt the historicity of the Canaanite campaign; the end of the stele could have been composed out of a love of symmetry, in an attempt to show the Pharaoh as a victor everywhere, and have been added to the text at a secondary stage.

3.6.7.5.3 The text says absolutely nothing about the character of Israel. How was it made up? What was its ethnic composition and its political and economic situation? Precisely where was it? The last question could be answered, even if only hypothetically: since the places mentioned on the stele are listed from south-west to north-east, one might think of central or upper Galilee; however, other scholars have suggested the central hill-country, in the vicinity of Shechem, putting Yanoam more to the south-west, on the plateau. We shall examine other features below, 8.4.2.

3.6.7.6 A little earlier I mentioned the stele of Mesha, king of Moab. This gives an account which is partly parallel to, and partly differs from, II Kings 1.1 and 3.4-27, of course from a Moabite perspective. We shall be concerned with this in due course (cf. 10.10.12).

3.7 Chronology

Bibliography

A.Momigliano, 'Time in Ancient Historiography', *History and Theory* 6, 1966, 1-23; H.Tadmor, 'Kronologia', in *EBB* IV, 1962, 261-4 (in Hebrew); id., 'The Chronology of the First Temple Period', in *WHJP* IV.1, Jerusalem 1979, 44-60, 318-20, which I have included in the Appendix to this book; K.T.Andersen, 'Die Chronologie der Könige von Israel und Juda', *ST* 29, 1969, 69-114; P.Daffinà, 'Senso del tempo e senso della storia', *RSO* 61, 1987 [1988], 1-71: 6-13; K.Matthiae and W.Thiel, *Biblische Zeittafeln*, Neukirchen/Vluyn 1985; P.J.James, 'Syria-Palestine: Conflicting Chronologies', in *Studies in Ancient Chronology*, ed. P.J.James, London 1987, I, 58-67; J.H.Hayes and P.K.Hooker, *A New Chronology for the Kings of Israel and Judah and its Implications for Biblical History and Literature*, Atlanta 1988; J.Hughes, *Secrets of the Times*, Sheffield 1990.

For the chronology of Egypt see K.A.Kitchen, *The Third Intermediate Period in Egypt(1100-850)*, Warminster 1975; id., 'Egypt and Israel during the First Millennium BC', *SVT* 40, 1988, 107-23; E.F.Wente and C.C.van Siclen III, 'A Chronology of the New Kingdom', in *Studies in Honor of George R.Hughes*, Chicago 1976, 216-61; E.Hornung, 'Chronologie in Bewegung', in *FS E.Edel zum 12. März 1979*, Bamberg 1979, 247-52;

D.B.Redford, *Pharaonic King Lists, Annals and Day Books: A Contribution to the Study of the Egyptian Sense of History*, Missonga, Ont. 1986.

The ancient world, in both east and west, seems to have been little interested in chronological problems, as Momigliano pointed out around twenty years ago and Daffinà has recently remarked yet again. Today the link between history and chronology is felt to be fundamental, so that dating becomes an indispensable element for the historian (Daffinà 1987, 71); however, in the ancient world this was not the case, and that also explains the existence of marked vagueness in this area. Only in the early church does a marked interest in chronology seem to have arisen.

3.7.1 Throughout the ancient Near East, i.e. in Egypt, Assyria, Babylon and Syria, it was the custom to date events from the year of the ruler's enthronement (H.Tadmor). So it is probable that there was also a similar system in Israel and Judah from the beginning of the empire of David and Solomon. However, this immediately poses two difficulties to the scholar: 1. the chronological information specified for the individuals and the events of prehistory; 2. the differences which exist between various systems of calculation within a particular text and between different texts. Thus there are already marked tensions within the Hebrew Massoretic text: one need only think, for example, of an event of fundamental importance like the fall of Jerusalem in 587 or 586; according to II Kings 25.8 and other texts this was in the nineteenth year of Nebuchadnezzar (586), but Jer.52.29 speaks of the eighteenth year (587, below, 12.6.6). Tensions were already noted by the authors of the *Seder 'Olam Rabbah*,[23] a rabbinic tractate, and by mediaeval Jewish exegetes. Moreover, it is a well known fact that the Greek translation of the Hebrew Bible (the Septuagint), the Vulgate and other traditions (e.g. Flavius Josephus) have other, divergent chronologies.

3.7.2 So we should not be surprised that in the course of this study we shall constantly be faced with insoluble chronological problems: for the problem in general I would refer readers to what is so far the best study of the subject, that of Tadmor 1979. In some cases it is clear that the Hebrew text is in disorder and can no longer be reconstructed. However, in the second part of his study Tadmor offers a series of assured chronological data through which it is possible to construct at least an approximate calendar. As for the prehistory, I would refer readers to the comments in my Judges commentary.[24] As is generally accepted today, these dates are artificial, calculated by criteria which are unknown to us, but not necessarily arbitrary ones.

4

David and His Empire

4.1 The tradition

The biblical tradition is unanimous in asserting that in the last years of the second millennium BCE and the first years of the first millennium a single monarchical state was formed in Canaan and the surrounding territories, modelled on the great empires of the ancient Near East. However, this very model has caused perplexity among some scholars: B.J.Diebner, one of the first to review the 1984 edition of this *History*,[1] rightly pointed out that this very similarity contains a disconcerting element. Does the tradition, instead of bringing out the specific characteristics and hence the distinctiveness of the Davidic empire (an aspect which in other cases is brought out even when it is somewhat dubious), show it as being modelled on patterns common in the region?

Be this as it may, the origins of the empire were modest: the original nucleus was formed of the tribe of Judah and groups affilliated to it; a few years later they were joined by Israel in the strict sense of the term, the northern tribes (Ephraim and Manasseh from the central hill-country and those of Galilee). Benjamin, a very small tribe with few economic resources (though it had some renown for its products in the military sphere), wedged between the borders of Judah and Ephraim, belonged sometimes to the South and sometimes to the North, as often happens to regions in such a situation. The kingdom expanded essentially as a result of military campaigns and treaties with neighbouring nations.

It is also surprising that the biblical tradition knows a relatively long period in which a centralized state did not exist: for a short time this was followed by the purely local reign of Abimelech at Shechem and that of Saul (below 4.3; 9.6).

Bibliography

A.Alt, 'The Formation of the Israelite State in Palestine' (1930), *Essays on Old Testament History and Religion*, Oxford 1966, 171-237; H.U.Nübel, *Davids Aufstieg in der Frühe israelitischer Geschichtsschreibung*, Diss.theol.-Bonn 1959; R.A.Carlson, *David the Chosen King*, Stockholm 1964; A.Weiser, 'Die Legitimation des Königs David', *VT* 16, 1966, 325-54; J.A.Soggin, *Das Königtum in Israel*, BZAW 104, Berlin 1967, 53ff. (with bibliography); J.H.Grønbaek, *Die Geschichte von Davids Aufstieg (1 Sam.15-2.Sam.5)*, Copenhagen 1971; J.Conrad, 'Zum geschichtlichen Hintergrund von Davids Aufstieg', *TLZ* 97, 1972, 321-32; T.D.N.Mettinger, *King and Messiah*, CB-OTS 8, Lund 1976; F.Langlamet, 'Pro ou contre Salomon? La rédaction pro-salomonienne de I Rois I-II', *RB* 83, 1976, 321-9; J.Van Seters, 'Problems in the Literary Analysis of the Court History of David', *JSOT* 1, 1976, 22-9; T.Ishida, *The Royal Dynasties in Ancient Israel*, Berlin 1977; W.Dietrich, 'David in Überlieferung und Geschichte', *VuF* 22, 1977, 44-64 (with a long annotated bibliography); H.Donner, 'Israel und Tyrus im Zeitalter Davids und Salomos', *JNWSL* 10, 1982, 43-52; G.W.Ahlström, *Royal Administration and National Religion in Ancient Palestine*, Leiden 1982; J.Conrad, 'Der Gegenstand und die Intention der Geschichte von der Thronnachfolge Davids', *TLZ* 108, 1983, 161-76; A.Malamat, *Das davidische und salomonische Königreich und seine Beziehungen zu Ägypten und Syrien*, Vienna 1983; Garbini* 1986, ch.2; A.van der Lingen, *David en Saul in I Samuel 16 – II Samuel 6*, Den Haag 1983; S.Herrmann, 'King David's State', in *In the Shelter of Elyon – FS G.W.Ahlström*, Sheffield 1984, 261-75; T.S.Im, *Das Davidsbild der Chronikbücher*, Diss.Theol.Bonn 1985; É.Lipiński, 'Juda et "tout Israël". Analogies et contrastes', in id. (ed.), *The Land of Israel – Cross-Road of Civilization*, Louvain 1985, 93-112; F.S.Frick, *The Formation of the State in Ancient Israel*, Sheffield 1985; M.L.Chaney, 'Systematic Study of the Israelite Monarchy', *Semeia* 37, 1986, 53-76; J.P.Floss, *David und Jerusalem*, St Ottilien 1987; L.E.Axelson, *The Lord Rose from Seir*, Lund 1987, ch.7; I.W.Provan, *Hezekiah and the Book of Kings*, Berlin 1988, ch.4; J.W.Flanagan, *David's Social Drama*, Sheffield 1988; J.Vermeylen, *David*, Brussels 1988; F.Finkelstein, 'The Emergence of the Monarchy in Israel. The Environmental and Socio-Economic Aspects', *JSOT* 44, 1989, 43-74; A.Leonard Jr, 'Archaeological Sources for the History of Palestine: The Late Bronze Age', *BA* 52, 1989, 4-39; E.H.Merrill, ' "Accession Year" and Davidic Chronology', *JANESCU* 19, 1981, 101-12; T.Ishida, 'The Role of Nathan the Prophet in the Episode of Solomon's Birth', in *Near Eastern Studies. Dedicated to...Takahito Mikasa*, Wiesbaden 1991, 133-8.

4.1.1 Now the time has come to deal in much more depth with a fact

I have already pointed out many times: the division between North and South (i.e. Israel in the strict sense, also called 'house of Joseph' and 'Ephraim', and Judah) is an original division on an ethnic and political level, and probably also (as far as we can establish) on the religious level, in that it already existed before the dissolution of the empire of David and Solomon (below 4.1.5.2), though in the present state of the sources it is not possible to discover much of the detail. There is no doubt that the two groups were ethnically and religiously akin: but there was also separation.[2] The tendency of the biblical tradition is, however, to show the two groups as being fundamentally united if not in fact identical, at least on the religious level, and in intent heirs, as they are shown to be, of the pre-historical tribal league formed of the two tribes of Judah and the ten tribes of Israel. This essential unity is then said to have been broken as a result of human inadequacy and sin, especially on the part of the North.

However, the reality is different: only with the empire, through the institution of the personal union (a concept which we shall examine later, 4.6.7), were the two groups united under the same king; but they were never completely amalgamated, and the assertion that they were in reality a single group is to be taken as a religious rather than a political statement, just as today Christians in the ecumenical movement talk of the unity of the church despite its manifest divisions. Only with the emergence of the Samaritan community (below 14.4) at a point in the Hellenistic period which cannot be identified, does it seem that this unity, hitherto confessed against all appearances, gave place to the awareness that there were now two groups in the region which defined themselves as 'Israel', both of which appealed to the *tōrāh* of Moses, even if in the South the hope of some form of reunion was never dropped completely.

4.1.2 At a time which it is no longer possible to determine precisely, but almost certainly under the reign of David, Israel and Judah succeeded in subjecting the Canaanite city-states in the North (Judg.1.27ff.).[3] All the indications are that this happened in a preeminently peaceful form, probably through treaties (a better translation than the 'subject to tribute' which is usually proposed). In this way they entered the united kingdom to become entities which were politically, though not ethnically, different; even the city-state of Jerusalem, well known from the correspondence from el-ʿAmarna, was incorporated into the kingdom and declared its capital. Later, with the division of the kingdom, it passed to Judah. So for the first and last time in its ancient history, though only briefly, the region was unified under a single sceptre, instead of being divided into many more or less autonomous entities.

4.1.3 Again according to the biblical tradition, the united kingdom very rapidly grew beyond the frontiers of Canaan; indeed, this expansionist dynamic seems to have constituted its original power. So in a short time we see under the crown of David (either by conquest or by spontaneous submission), again according to the biblical tradition, the whole of Transjordan (Ammon, Edom and Moab) and the major part of Syria (the various Aramaean kingdoms); these were peoples which, like Israel and Judah, had recently been formed. The north-eastern frontier is said to have reached to the Euphrates. But with the decline of this expansionist dynamic (a process which already began with Solomon, below 5.6), the fate of the sovereignty of Israel and Judah was sealed.

4.1.4 Thus far the biblical tradition. But I have already pointed out several times that the empire is not mentioned in any ancient Near Eastern source (above 4.1), and a number of scholars have recently argued independently of each other that this information has to be substantially reshaped (Garbini*, on the basis of the text II Sam.23.8-39, which he thinks to be ancient: the united kingdom will have comprised only Judah, Israel, Moab and some Philistine cities; similarly Donner*, 1984, 199ff.; Miller and Hayes*, 1987, 180ff.; and Vermeylen*, 1988, 65; Diebner 1975 even speaks of a national 'myth of unity'). Nevertheless the formation of an empire does not appear manifestly absurd, if we take into account the setting in which it is said to have come about; there were objective conditions favourable to its formation. The Assyrian empire was still far from the region and Egypt was going through one of its many periods of eclipse;[4] on the other hand, it is also clear in the biblical tradition that many regions were not conquered by force of arms but associated, as it were, with the empire by treaties of more or less close vassalage. So even according to the Hebrew text the territories administered directly by the crown at the greatest extension of the empire were considerably fewer. Furthermore, we may ask how it is that the texts speak of rebellions in those very regions whose incorporation into the kingdom is said to have been the product of later glorification (cf. I Kings 11.13, which mentions Edom, Zobah and Damascus). These are problems which need to be resolved before a reductive approach is developed further.

4.1.5 As soon as the other great kingdoms moved to play their traditional parts in the Near Eastern scene, the dominion of Israel and Judah came to an end; however, again according to the sources, the united kingdom succeeded in maintaining itself for around seventy years.

4.1.5.1 Again according to the tradition, David was first crowned at Hebron 'by the men of Judah' while he was still a vassal of the Philistines (below, 4.4, II Sam.2.4).

4.1.5.2 At the same time Israel, the North, was laboriously recovering from the defeat which had been inflicted shortly beforehand by the Philistines near Mount Gilboa, in which king Saul and three of his sons had fallen. According to the tradition, it seems that in Israel there were then five years of disorders, until an uncle of Saul, Abner, who commanded the army, had Saul's surviving son Eshbaal (for the exact name cf. I Chron.8.33; 9.39) crowned, transferring the capital of the kingdom to Mahanaim in Transjordan (probably present-day *tell el-ḫaǧǧaǧ*, coord.214-177), out of range of Philistine incursions. Again according to the tradition, there will have been periods of struggle between Israel and Judah (II Sam.2.12-3.1). But Eshbaal, whom the texts describe as a weak, incapable and irresolute figure, soon found himself in conflict with Abner, who then went over to David. Eshbaal was deposed and killed (II Sam.3.7ff.). And after reigning seven and a half years in Hebron, David was also crowned king of the north by 'all the elders of Israel' (II Sam.5.1-4).

4.2 David's origins

A series of narratives tell us about the origins of David, a man of Judah of modest birth, though his family was not without means (it had its own flocks); for the most part these are legendary, partly novellistic and often contradictory.[5] All these accounts are unanimous in affirming that David began his own career as a follower of Saul and continued it in a sense at Saul's expense.

4.2.1 In the absence of Near Eastern texts on the matter, we are forced to follow the biblical traditions, the problems posed by which we considered earlier (above 3.1.3). For details see an Introduction to the Old Testament (15.3 of mine). The following texts are relevant:

4.2.1.1 The 'history of the accession of David to the throne', I Sam.16 – II Sam.4, an account which we shall be considering in detail shortly in connection with relations between David and Saul (below 4.3).

4.2.1.2 The 'narrative of the ark', which we shall be examining below (4.4.2.2). It begins in I Sam.4 with the capture of the ark by the Philistines after the defeat of Israel at Eben-ezer. Chapter 5 relates the plagues produced among the Philistines by rash treatment of the ark, and in ch.6 we are told how the Philistines, not knowing how to avoid other plagues, sent it back. In this way the ark first reached Beth-shemesh (coord.147-128) and then Kiriath-jearim (coord.159-135), where it remained until David had it brought to Jerusalem, his new capital, a generation later (II Sam.6). The complex is not easy to date but is probably quite late, and is interwoven with legendary and even humorous features.

4.2.1.3 The 'history of the succession to the throne of David' (II Sam.9-20; I Kings 1-2, perhaps preceded by II Sam.21.1-14)[6] is very important. It presents a series of accounts connected with the work of David as a military commander, as a politician and also as the head of a family. However, the importance of this text is reduced by a series of factors: first of all the difficulty of establishing its literary genre and hence its scope, features on which scholars still disagree today; then the fact that whereas up until a few decades ago the 'History' was celebrated as a prime example of ancient Israelite historiography, perhaps the earliest example of historiography ever produced,[7] today we have become much more prudent, if not more knowledgeable: the study by Whybray cited in n.6 rightly speaks of a 'historical novel', indicating that the scenes which take place in the bedroom (e.g. II Sam.13) are clearly romanticized, whereas the narrative (in family rather than political terms) is also more typical of the romance. The imperessive scene in II Sam.12, in the face of which political events almost seem to take second place, is also legendary. However, among the various arguments about the scope of the 'History', one seems to me to have a degree of probability, that proposed independently by Langlamet in 1976 and Ishida (cf. n.6): it aimed at legitimizing Solomon's accession to the throne, scorning the natural line of succession through which the throne would have been expected to go to David's oldest son, Adonijah. In this situation David appears as a very aged figure, in complete physical and moral decline, the toy of his wife Bathsheba and the general Joab; hence the intervention of Solomon, though dynastically irregular and accompanied by proscriptions and political assassinations, must have represented the lesser evil. In this phase the political element thus seems to have unexpectedly prevailed over the family element.

4.2.1.4 In II Sam.5; 8 we have a summary account of the military campaigns of David, which we can add, as many scholars do, to the 'History of the Succession'. Originally the account will also have contained a report of the capture of the Ammonite capital, which is now inserted into the story of David's adultery (II Sam.10-12).

4.2.1.5 In Chronicles David appears as a stained-glass-window saint, when the texts are not simply parallel to II Samuel and I Kings; its statements are only rarely a source for the historian.

4.2.1.6 On an archaeological level, the discoveries which can certainly be attributed to the time of David are few and controversial. We shall be considering them in the next chapter along with those from the time of Solomon (5.1.3).

4.3 Saul

Since the sources are almost all slanted in David's favour, the figure of Saul as a military leader and politician has clearly slipped to a secondary position, even if the sources are unanimous in stating that he was the one who started the revolt against the Philistines.

Bibliography

J.A.Soggin, *Das Königtum in Israel*, Berlin 1967, 22ff. (with bibliography); F.Langlamet, 'Les récits de l'institution de la royauté (I Sam.VII-XIII)', *RB* 77, 1970, 161-200; J.M.Miller, 'Saul's Rise to Power', *CBQ* 36, 1974, 157-74; V.Fritz, 'Die Deutungen des Königtums Sauls in den Überlieferungen von seiner Entstehung: I Sam.9.11', *ZAW* 88, 1976, 346-62; C.Grottanelli, 'Possessione carismatica e razionalizzazione statale nella Bibbia ebraica', *SSR* 1, 1977, 263-88; D.M.Gunn, *The Fate of King Saul*, JSOT-SS, Sheffield 1980; H.Donner, 'Basic Elements of Old Testament Historiography. Illustrated by the Saul Tradition', *OTWGSA* 24, 1982, 40-54; id., *Die Verwerfung des Königs Saul*, Wiesbaden 1983; E.Fretheim, 'Divine Foreknowledge, Divine Constancy and the Rejection of Saul's Kingship', *BQ* 47, 1985, 595-602; B.Peckham, 'The Dtr History of Saul', *ZAW* 97, 1985, 190-210; T.Seidl, 'David statt Saul. Göttliche Legitimation und menschliche Kompetenz des Königs als Motive der Redaktion von I Sam 16-18', *ZAW* 98, 1986, 39-56; G.Bettenzoli, 'Samuel und das Problem des Königtums', *BZ* NF 30, 1986, 222-36; id., 'Samuel und Saul in geschichtlicher und theologischer Auffassung', *ZAW* 98, 1986, 338-51; K.-D.Schunck, 'König Saul – Etappen seines Weges zum Aufbau eines israelitisches Staates', *BZ* 36, 1992, 175-206; A.G.Auld and C.Y.S.Ho, 'The Making of David and Goliath', *JSOT* 56, 1992, 19-39.

4.3.1 Very little can be established about Saul with any degree of certainty; if at all, the sources are interested in the first king of Israel only as an antagonist of David. The latest phase of Dtr (DtrN) even goes so far as to assert that the very institution of the monarchy and the establishment of Saul in this function were blasphemous actions and marked the beginning of the process which some centuries later was to lead to the loss of the independence of the two kingdoms and the deportation of some of their inhabitants (cf. I Sam.8.1ff.; 10.17-27). It is interesting that nothing similar is said about the monarchy of David and the other kings generally. As is well known, the other sources which narrate the institution of the monarchy (9.1-10.16; 11.1ff.) are more favourable to the institution; the latter makes Saul the victorious leader, elected by the people by acclamation after his liberation of the city of Jabesh in Transjordan from siege.

4.3.2 In the 'history of David's accession to the throne' the merits of the first king in the military and political sphere appear clearly, even if because of insertions here and there (for example in the ancient texts I

Sam.13-14 and in the later ch.15), any undertaking by Saul and
Jonathan, however heroic, is always frustrated by some impious action
or attitude, although for the modern reader, and perhaps already for
the ancient reader, the seriousness of such actions seems anything but
obvious! Moreover the bias towards David tends to present the final
phase of Saul's reign as characterized by a series of wrong choices: the
reader is meant to be given the impression that the ruler was now
politically incompetent, religiously unworthy and lacking in the necessary psychological equilibrium, so that he was afflicted with persecution
mania and often fell into states of depression, alternating with homi-
cidal moods, conditions which only the young David, who had been
brought to court, could cure with a kind of melotherapy (I Sam.16.14ff.).
The reader is led to infer that there is nothing more logical than that
others more capable and more worthy should rob him of his position;
and who was more qualified than his able and always victorious
general? The fact that David went over to the Philistines shortly
afterwards (I Sam.23.1-5; 28.1-2; 29.1-11), a move which was certainly
disconcerting for both contemporaries and posterity, could thus easily
be justified as caused by the undeserved persecutions to which he had
been subjected.

4.3.3 It is these considerations, moreover, which serve to give
legitimation to David, a legitimation which the texts present with a
series of arguments through which David is meant to appear as the
man for whom the kingdom now waited. In the Deuteronomistic text
I Sam.16.1-13, David is directly designated by God and 'anointed' king
by the prophet Samuel, to replace Saul, who is now rejected.[8] No one
but Kessler 1970 now regards this passage as ancient. In 18.17-27 David
marries Michal, Saul's daughter, after being subjected to romantic trials
of valour, all of which he surmounts. The possibility that the whole
passage is an artificial construction is by no means to be ruled out: in I
Sam.25.44 the woman is given as wife to a certain Palti(el) who is later
forced to suffer what seems to him to be an intolerable slight, to 'give
back' his wife to David (II Sam.3.15). But the theory that the woman
was first given as David's wife and then, while David still alive, to
another, does not fit at all well with what we know to have been the
law and the practice later in Israel and in Judah (cf. Deut.24.1-4; Jer.3.1);
moreover even in II Sam.12 David, now king, is forced to have
Bathsheba's husband killed in order to be able to marry her. In any
case, regardless of the historical value of the account, there is no doubt
about its aim: once Saul has fallen in battle with three of his sons and
only Meribbaal (another name which Chronicles reports exactly) is left
as Saul's sole successor, though unsuited to kingship because he was
lame as the result of a fall when he was young (II Sam.4.4), marriage
to Saul's daughter could automatically put David in the line of suc-

cession to the throne, for want of other heirs. The attribution to David of extraordinary prowess in battle (I Sam.17; the 'giant' Goliath, a text which is probably from the Persian period,[9] which on some points contradicts the information given in 16.17ff.; 18.20-27 and elsewhere), as a result of which it is said that people maliciously sang under Saul's window the refrain

'Saul has slain his thousands
and David his ten thousands' (I Sam.18.7; cf. 22.12; 29.5),

and later the phrase pronounced by the elders of the north who came to crown David, 'In times past, when Saul was king over us, it was you that led out and brought in Israel...' (II Sam.5.2, a statement which does not in fact correspond with the sources), are all well-known elements in the popular traditions which illustrate the thesis of the account: Saul could not remain king and this function was better taken over by David. So it is no surprise to find at one point that the assembly of the elders of the North offer the crown to David with a procedure which we could call democratic (II Sam.5.3).

For the Deuteronomistic history, the element of divine designation (ch.16) seems to have been the most important and decisive one. It is interesting to note that this is a theme which is also attested elsewhere in the ancient Near East (cf. above 3.2): the direct divine designation as a legitimation of someone who ascended the throne outside the direct succession. In the Hebrew Bible we have the case of Jehu, already cited, who was designated and 'anointed' by a prophet (II Kings 9); in the ancient Aramaean world we have the case of Zakkur (or Zakkir), king of Hamath, whose stele says: 'I am Zakkur..., a man of humble birth [...] Ba'al SMYN: and he has raised me up to him... and has made me king over Hazrak...'[10] (*KAI*, 202; *SSI* II, 5 line 2). Similar examples are also attested in Assyrian inscriptions.[11]

The frequent offers of friendship and loyalty to the house of Saul and the remarks which seek to dissociate David from any responsibility for its extinction or even for the death of Abner (II Sam.1.13-16; 4.9-12; 9.1ff.; cf. the poems 1.19-27; 3.33-34, regardless of whether or not David wrote them) serve to provide legitimation. That accusations of this kind were made against David is explicitly stated in II Sam.16.5-14.[12]

4.3.4 That Saul had already come to power as the victorious commander of the army is not only possible but follows a pattern frequently attested in the ancient Near East and the Hebrew Bible. It is also probable that his reign did not last long: according to I Sam.13.1, a text which is very obscure, he reigned for only two years, something which cannot be ruled out *a priori*. The text also attributes to him a series of expeditions against neighbouring peoples (I Sam.14.47ff.: Moab,

Ammon, Edom, two Aramaean city-states, the Philistines and the Amalekites). According to the texts, he either committed suicide or was killed at his request by a follower, at the end of the battle which he lost near Mount Gilboa (I Sam.31; II Sam.1).

4.3.5 If there ever was a chronicle of Saul, it must therefore have presented him as a kind of soldier king without any great intellectual aspirations; but it was then revised primarily to serve to legitimate David's assumption of the throne. As Lemche rightly comments:[13] David wins the victory and as victor 'writes the history'! In fact the thesis of the account, that a madman, a maniac, a prey to deep psychological crises and thus basically incompetent, could have gained supreme power at a particularly difficult time, appears highly improbable, even if history does record cases of this kind from time to time. To this revision were then added other elements of a literary and theological kind which have made it a kind of tragedy: they present the figure of an honest man, struggling not just with an inscrutable fate but with a deity, YHWH, who behaves in a not dissimilar way; it is from this situation that the tragedy arises, a feature which moreover has been taken up by modern writers from V.Alfieri to André Gide. Into this have been woven noble and beautiful episodes: the improbable friendship (given the circumstances) between David and Jonathan (chs.19ff.) and the faithfulness and loyalty of his wife Michal (18.10b-17); these are elements in which a love of story-telling clearly gains the upper hand. Saul's death in battle appears as the resolution of a situation from which not even the author-playwright saw a way out.

4.4 David and the Philistines

It is difficult to accept that David could have assumed the kingship over Judah without the consent of the Philistines whose vassal he was, having gone over to them, as the tradition tells us, following Saul's unjust persecution. On the other hand it is easy to imagine that the Philistines would have been pleased for the southern hill-country, which was of fundamental strategic importance to them, to be put under the control of someone who was favourable to them, instead of their occupying the region directly. The same considerations will have applied when David was crowned king of Israel a few years later: the new situation allowed the Philistines control of all the hill country through someone who was loyal to them, without having to strike a blow or invest manpower and means.

4.4.1 We also need to dwell, if briefly, on the Philistines, a people who from the start seem to have been the enemy of Israel *par excellence* and who were subjected only for a short time. This is because, as was acutely observed about twenty-five years ago, they 'constituted so to speak a dialectical element in the history of Israel. Indeed it could be said that had there not been such a strong adversary against which they had to defend themselves, the Hebrews might perhaps never have succeeded in achieving political unity.'[14]

Bibliography

G.A.Wainwright, 'Some Sea Peoples', *JEA* 47, 1961, 71-90; B.Hrouda, 'Die Einwanderung der Philister in Palästina', in *Studien und Aufsätze...Anton Moortgat*, Berlin 1965, 126-35; F.S.Donadoni, 'Testi egizi sui "popoli del mare" ', *RSIt* 77, 1965, 130-14; M.-L. and U.Erlenmeyer, M.Delcor, 'Philistins', *SDB* VII, 1966, 1233-88; K.A.Kitchen, 'The Philistines', in D.J.Wiseman (ed.), *Peoples from Old Testament Times*, Oxford 1973, 53-78; A.Strobel, *Der spätbronzezeitliche Seevölkersturm*, Berlin 1976; T.Dothan, 'The Philistine Settlement in Canaan and the Northern Border of Philistia', *TA* 12, 1985, 109-22; A.Mazar, 'The Emergence of Philistine Material Culture', *IEJ* 35, 1985, 97-107; I.Singer, 'The Origin of the Sea People and Their Settlement on the Coast of Canaan'; A.Mazar, 'Some Aspects of the "Sea People" Settlement', both in M.Heltzer and É.Lipiński (eds.), *Society and Economy in the Eastern Mediterranean (c.1500-1000 BC)*, Louvain 1988, 238-50, 251-60; B.Cifola, 'Ramses III and the Sea Peoples: A Structural Analysis of the Medinet Habu Inscription', *OR* 57, 1988, 275-306; C.Vandersleyen, 'Le dossier égyptien des Philistins', in É.Lipiński (ed.), *The Land of Israel – Crossroad of Civilization*, Louvain 1985, 39-54; T.Dothan, 'Aspects of Egyptian and Philistine Presence in Canaan during the Late Bronze – Early Iron', ibid., 55-75: G.A.Rendsburg, 'Genesis 10.13-14: An Authentic Hebrew Tradition concerning the Origin of the Philistines', *JNWSL* 13, 1987, 89-96.

4.4.1.1 One thing needs to be said in advance: we do not have any written documents going back directly to the Philistines, but only mention of them by Egyptian texts and the Hebrew Bible and, later, in Assyrian and Babylonian texts. It is only in the last few years that archaeological excavations have begun to provide first-hand discoveries; so far, however, these are only objects and there are no inscriptions. Here I should mention the excavations at Ashdod (Azotus, coord.117-129, from the 1960s onwards); Ekron (probably Hebrew *tell miqneh*, Arabic *ḫirbet el-muqanna'*, coord.136-131), and *tell qaṣīle* (coord.131-168), now on the northern periphery of Tel Aviv (we do not know to what Philistine locality this corresponds).

4.4.1.2 According to the biblical tradition, in a period conventionally identified, for lack of any objective chronological information, with the last centuries of the second millennium BCE and especially with the period of the reign of Saul during the last decades of the millennium, the Philistines in fact seem to have been assimilated to the Western Semitic world: I Sam.5-6 presents them as worshippers of the Canaanite deity Dagon or Dagan, one of the various forms of *ba'al*, as whose son he sometimes appears. The various narratives never speak of differences and hence of difficulties in the linguistic sphere (we have just the term *s^erānīm* – plural, we do not know the singular – for their leaders: it is of unknown origin, perhaps Illyrian, though some connect it with the Greek τύραννος). However, all this could also indicate the probability that the information in question does not go back to the second millennium but comes from much later, when the assimilation of the Philistines to the Canaanite world had already come about.

4.4.1.3 Egyptian texts (*ANET*, 262ff.; not yet in *TUAT*) give us information about the settlement of the Philistines, which is considered part of the migration of the 'sea peoples', on the south-western coast of Canaan. Until recently it was thought that these texts had to be interpreted to mean that throughout the second half of the second millennium BCE, with a high point under Pharaohs Merenptah (c.1212-1202) and Ramses III (c. 1182-1151), groups commonly called 'sea peoples' came by land and sea first to Egypt and Libya, thence to be settled by the Egyptians in the south-west part of Canaan. Today, however, scholars tend to think (cf. Singer 1985) that these migrations took place later: there will not have been settlements proper prior to Ramses III, but only groups of mercenaries on the move here and there. Only towards the end of the thirteenth and the beginning of the twelfth century BCE did the groups which went by land succeed in destroying Ugarit and Alalakh; after that, having been settled by Ramses III in the south-west of Canaan, they became nominal vassals of Egypt. The precise knowledge of the 'Sea Peoples' which emerges from the Egyptian texts – their composition, the names of various groups and similar information – suggests that there was a long and always peaceful co-existence between these groups and Egypt: in the present state of research it is impossible to discover how conflict ever arose (G.Garbini, orally).

4.4.1.4 According to the late text Josh.13.3 the Philistines had a coalition of five cities in the south-west of the country: Ashdod and Ekron mentioned above (4.4.1.1); and also Ashkelon (coord.107-118); Gath, perhaps *tell es-ṣ afī(t)* (coord.135-123) and Gaza (*'azzah*, coord.099-101); and each of these places will have been ruled over by one of the *s^erānīm*.

4.4.1.5 Another group of 'sea peoples' settled at Dor (present-day *ḥirbet el-burj*, coord.142-224); their presence there is attested by the account of the Egyptian official Wen Amon (end of the twelfth century BCE, *ANET*, 25-9, not yet in *TUAT*).

4.4.1.6 The influence of the 'sea peoples' seems to have extended as far as Beth-shean (present-day *tell el-ḥuṣn*, coord.198-213, a few yards to the north of the old railway station). This was originally an Egyptian stronghold on the eastern edge of the plain of Jezreel. Near to it the Philistines defeated Saul and three of his sons, on Mount Gilboa (I Sam.31.1ff.; II Sam.1.1ff.); among other things this presupposes the existence of good relations with the Canaanite city-states of the region, on whom they depended for supplies. Moreover Mycenaean pottery, often called 'Philistine', was spread throughout the eastern coast of the Mediterranean. However, this does not tell us anything about the diffusion of the Philistines, since the manufacture and users of a product are now separated (G.Garbini, orally); but that does not mean that smaller groups could not have existed here and there.

4.4.1.7 Finally, in I Sam.13.20-22 the Hebrew Bible attributes to them something like a monopoly in the working of iron: the information is not easy to interpret historically; the account suffers from 'having had read into it information which it does not contain in and of itself' (Frick 1985, 180).

4.4.1.8 Although the Philistines proved victorious over Israel and were spread throughout the region, their strategic position remained weak. They did not have control over the hill-country, which according to the biblical tradition they lost after the first Israelite victories in the time of Saul and did not reconquer. However, with the coronation of their vassal David first in the South and then in the North, this last problem too seemed to have been resolved in the most favourable way.

4.4.2 First enterprises

According to the biblical sources (II Sam.5; 8), David soon sought to liberate himself from the position of being a Philistine vassal, an undertaking which was crowned with success. He is said to have done this by following an independent foreign policy and making a series of military expeditions on his own account, thus provoking Philistine intervention which led to their defeat.

4.4.2.1 If we accept the sequence of events and the description of the facts presented in II Sam.5, we have a picture of the situation which is not manifestly improbable, though as we shall see (below 4.4.2.3) there are scholars who would want to change the order of the events. The first enterprise after David's coronation over Israel seems to have been the conquest of the city-state of Jerusalem, whose territory, wedged between Judah and Benjamin, made communications difficult between the south and the centre. According to the sources, it is not clear how this proved possible: II Sam.5.8 could speak of a group of volunteers who crept in by the water conduit (Hebrew *ṣinnōr*), but there is dispute over the precise meaning of the term in ancient Hebrew; other scholars,[15] however, argue that the group will have interrupted the water supply, thus forcing the city to surrender; a third theory[16] argues that the city was never conquered, but given to David following a treaty, something which also seems to have happened, as we shall see (below 4.6.3), with the city states of the North.

4.4.2.2 David is then said to have settled in Jerusalem and to have brought there the ark, which the Philistines had captured before the time of Saul and then abandoned (I Sam.4-6; II Sam.6). He is also said to have restored the walls and other buildings, making Jerusalem from then on the capital of the kingdom: this despite the fact that it did not belong to any of the tribes – indeed perhaps for this very reason. Consequently an exclusively Canaanite population was incorporated into the kingdom, something which also happened with the city states of the North. With the bringing of the ark to Jerusalem the biblical tradition seeks to stress the continuity with the past and at the same time the new beginning. In fact, at this point a new era did begin, which came to an end only with the fall of Jerusalem in 587 or 586 (below, 12.6.6). However, the ark does not seem to have had any function in the cult in the monarchical period, so we might ask what function it had before the constitution of the state. In any case, in the time of Solomon it seems to have been one of the sacred furnishings (below 5.5.2), though it is not mentioned again.[17]

4.4.2.3 Mazar 1963 differs. In his view the order of events will have been the following: (a) David crowned at Hebron; (b) conquest of Jerusalem; (c) struggles in the North and the death of Eshbaal (above, 4.1.5.2); (d) building works at Jerusalem; (e) David king of Israel; (f) restoration and building work at Jerusalem; (g) Jerusalem proclaimed capital of the united kingdom. In the present state of research a decision is not easy: however, one can point out that the proclamation of the city as capital makes sense only when David had become king over the two groups and not before.

4.4.2.4 Again according to the biblical tradition, in this period David will have initiated dealings with the Phoenician city of Tyre, even if on a closer reading of the texts things do not seem as clear as they might at first sight. The materials we have speak explicitly of a king of Tyre named Hiram (II Sam.5.11, etc.), probably the Ahiram I mentioned by Josephus who, again according to Josephus, is supposed to have reigned from around 970/69 to 936 or 926. However, this note comes up against chronological difficulties, as Garbini* 1988, 22f., rightly points out: the ruler in fact appears almost certainly as a contemporary of Solomon, with whom he had frequent dealings, so that, if his reign coincides with that of David at all, it coincides with its end and not its beginning, and the biblical text does not indicate any dealings with

Hiram's father 'Abiba'al. Is it possible that there were two rulers of the same name, one a contemporary of David, the other of Solomon? We do not know, but it seems improbable; it is more likely that here there is a significant confusion over the chronology, in the case of both the Bible and of Josephus (to whom we owe the details, *c.Ap.* I, 108; *Antt.* VIII, 62ff.). That explains Garbini's scepticism about the historicity of these reports, even about that relating to Solomon. Moreover, we know little about Phoenicia at this time: our scant information is based on extracts from the list of the kings of Tyre in a work by a certain Menander of Ephesus who lived in the second century BCE. He is said to have seen Phoenician sources and is quoted by Josephus (cf. Stern I, 199).[18]

4.4.2.5 No matter in what circumstances they began, relations between the city-state of Tyre and first the empire, then the kingdom of Israel, proved lasting. It was only after Jehu's *coup d'état* in Israel and the overthrow of the dynasty of Omri at the end of the ninth century BCE (during which the ruling house was exterminated and the queen mother, a princess of Tyre, was killed, cf. below, 10.11) that relations between Israel and Tyre were broken off. The lasting nature of these relationships is well explained by the fact that the two nations had complementary economies: Phoenicia helped Israel, which in antiquity was never a sea-faring people, in its overseas enterprises.

4.4.2.6 By making a treaty with Tyre without Philistine permission David had violated one of the fundamental norms of the vassal treaties of the time. We know in fact from texts of such treaties which have come down to us[19] that in no case was the vassal allowed an autonomous foreign policy, so David's action was an evident *casus belli*. In other words, the hope of the Philistines of dominating the hill-country through an intermediary proved impossible, and the problems which decades earlier had led to conflict between the Philistines and Israel broke out again, accentuated by the fact that now Judah and Israel were united in a single kingdom. Here we have a series of elements in favour of the credibility of the tradition.

4.4.2.7 The biblical sources indicate two campaigns by the Philistines against David, the first in II Sam.5.17-21 and the second in 5.23-25. Both took the form of an attack against Jerusalem through the valley of the Rephaim, generally identified with the present-day *baqʿa* (coord.127-167) through which the railway now runs. Both times the attackers are said to have been defeated. In this way relations between David and the Philistines seem to have been turned upside down: the vassal had become the great king. However, this does not seem to have caused notable resentment among the Philistines, if the argument is correct that the contingents which the text calls 'Cherethites and Pelethites' (8.18; 15.18) and 'Hittites' (15.18)[20] were composed of Philistine mercenaries. David's relations with Achish of Gath, whose vassal he had originally been, seem to have remained good until the era of Solomon (I Kings 2.29).

4.5 Foreign campaigns

After the unification of Judah and Israel in one kingdom, the conquest of Jerusalem and the neutralization of the Philistines, David went on, again according to the biblical tradition, to a series of military campaigns which led in succession to the conquest of Transjordan and a large part of Syria. Of course in evaluating this information we must also take account of the perplexity of a number of scholars about its credibility (cf. above 3.3.3). Be this as it may, according to the tradition, which is contained in chs.5 and 8, to which we should probably add chs.10-12 which speak of a campaign against Ammon, now moreover disfigured by the episode of Uriah the Hittite, David undertook a series of campaigns. This is information which for some scholars has clear annalistic characteristics at a literary level, so they would prefer to attribute it to an ancient source. However, the imprecision at a chronological level seems to be an obstacle here: the reader is left with the figure forty both for the years of David's reign and for those of Solomon.

4.5.1 Bibliography

M.F.Unger, *Israel and the Aramaeans of Damascus*, London 1957 and reprints; B.Mazar, 'Geshur and Maacah', *JBL* 80, 1961, 16-28; id., 'The Military Elite of King David', *VT* 13, 1963, 310-20 (both in *The Early Biblical Period*, Jerusalem 1986, 113ff., 83ff.); A.Malamat 1983 (cited at 4.1); H.S.Sader, *Les états araméens de Syrie depuis leur fondation jusqu'à leur transformation en provinces assyriennes*, Wiesbaden 1987.

According to II Sam.8, David defeated the Philistines again, and then the Moabites, the Aramaean kingdoms of Zobah and Damascus, and finally the Edomites, while Hamath submitted of its own accord. II Samuel 10-12 reports the defeat of the Ammonites and the Aramaeans of Beth-rehob, Ma'acah and Tob.

4.5.2 It was probably at this time that the city states of the northern plains were incorporated into the empire: this probably happened before the expeditions to Transjordan and Aram, since it is reasonable to suppose that control of them was indispensable if David was to be able to leave tribal territory with his flanks protected. The places are explicitly indicated in Judg.1.27ff.; cf. Josh.17.11ff. as territories which had not been conquered, information which is followed by the comment that they were 'subjected to tribute' (according to the current translation) or better 'by means of a treaty', 'when Israel became powerful' (Josh.17.13; Judg.1.18); this is a piece of information which can only be connected with the Davidic empire. Some decades later Solomon then incorporated them into the new system of districts into which the North was divided (I Kings 4.7-19, below 5.8). On the other hand, today it is far from clear whether the text Judg.1.27ff. is to be regarded as being as old as was once thought;[21] if it is not (as would seem probable), the text would have arisen to explain the reasons for the continuous 'synoecism' (a term going back to Mommsen and quoted by Smend 1983) and hence the co-existence between Israelites and Canaanites, an element rejected by DtrN.

4.5.3 In II Sam.3.3 it is said that David had married a daughter of the king of Geshur, another Aramaean kingdom of Syria, so that for many years there was a close alliance between this city-state and the empire. And it is in fact to Geshur, to his maternal grandmother, that the tradition makes Absalom flee after the facts narrated in II Sam.13.37-39 (cf. 14.23, 32). This must originally have been an alliance between equals, as in the case of Tyre.

4.6 Constitutional problems

The modern expression is probably not at all appropriate, since at that time what we now call a constitution did not exist. However, it is an adequate expression for what I want to say: that the composition of the empire was very complex, and gave rise to a number of problems.

4.6.1 First of all we have the traditional territories, to begin with that of Judah and then that of Israel, over which David reigned by the decision of the respective popular assemblies. To what point these can be called 'democratic' in the modern sense of the term is something that cannot be examined here.

4.6.2 Two places seem to have belonged to the royal family personally and therefore to have enjoyed a special status: Ziklag, a place which the Philistines had given to David when he was their vassal (I Sam.27.5-6), and the territory of the city-state of Jerusalem, over which David was a ruler by right of conquest (but cf. above 4.4.2.1).

4.6.3 The Canaanite city-states in the northern plains, which, for want of direct information, we may take to have been incorporated peacefully into the empire.

4.6.4 The territories of the Transjordanian kingdoms of Ammon, Edom and Moab, which correspond roughly to the present-day Hashemite Kingdom of Jordan. According to II Sam.8.13f. Edom was annexed, while the other states became vassals.

4.6.5 Finally, the various Aramaean city states in present-day Syria and eastern Lebanon.

4.6.6 Such a complex structure evidently gave rise to equally complex and often contradictory situations, which could therefore lead to conflict at a legal level. In fact substantially different and partly almost incompatible institutions had come together and been superimposed: the personal union between the two Hebrew groups, a problem to which we shall return (below 4.6.7); the special status of certain city states; the position of the nations in Transjordan and Syria, some annexed and some allies. This is confirmed in broad outline by the account of the census carried out by David (II Sam.24/I Chron.21, a text of uncertain date but certainly a different tradition from the other sources). It will have extended from the *wādī el-'arīš*, the border with Egypt down to the present day (the so-called 'brook of Egypt'), to the Euphrates in the north-east, even if, as we have seen (above 3.3.3), some scholars doubt this information. This is a structure which, as I have already commented (above 4.1), was not unusual in the ancient Near East; indeed, it is very reminiscent first of the neo-Assyrian empire and then of the Neo-Babylonian and Persian empires. Like these, it incorporated territories occupied by foreign populations (all of which evidently aimed at achieving their own autonomy) and far exceeded the original frontiers of the homeland; like these, too, it needed a complex public administration which was difficult to achieve with the methods and techniques of the time. Thus already during the last years of the reign of Solomon this prompted a generalized centrifugal process which accelerated and became irreversible after the separation of the North from the South on the death of Solomon.

4.6.7 In 1930 Alt called this structure a 'personal union' as far as relations between Judah and Israel were concerned. This is a political form in which two or more nations have the same head of state but autonomous and different governments; a modern example is that of Denmark and Iceland up to the Second World War: the king of Denmark was the head of state of the two nations, each of which, however, had its own legislative and executive organs. But two scholars, Buccellati in 1967 and recently Schäfer-Lichtenberger,[22] have questioned this theory of Alt's.

4.6.7.1 For Buccellati the concept is not applicable to Ziklag, a place which can no longer be identified with certainty. For Buccellati the situation of this place seems simply to be governed by the fact that David received it from the Philistines (I Sam.27.6: 'So that day Achish gave him [David] Ziklag; therefore Ziklag has belonged to the kings of Judah to this day'; the implications of the formula are not completely clear), but without ever giving it back once the relationship ended. Another difficulty lies in the fact, to which I have alluded, that the place has yet to be identified precisely. According to current opinion, as stated by Simons,[23] it is the present *tell el-ḥuweilife* (coord.136-088, about nine miles north-north-east of Beersheba); in that case the place will not have belonged to the Philistines but will have been occupied by them only at the time of their greatest expansion. At one of such periods it will have been assigned to David; thus the Philistines had it under their control without extending their lines of communication too far, an attempt similar to that made in the hill-country (above 4.4). Were that so, however, it is not clear why David should have given the place back to the Philistines after defeating them. Another authoritative attempt to identify the place has been made by Y.Aharoni; he wants to connect it with *tell eš-šarī'ah* (coord.119-088), about nine miles north-north-west of Beersheba. In that case it will be a typical frontier locality, subject to changes of sovereignty depending on the different political conditions. Here too it seems that we should not speak of restitution once David became independent. A third proposal has recently been made by V.Fritz; the place could be identified with *tell eš-šeba'*, the *tell* of Beersheba. In any case the redactors of the texts, which are certainly later than the period of Solomon, can only note that the place belongs to the royal house – we could say by virtue of ancient state possession, independently of any sovereignty of the house of David over Judah and its ordering. However, where Buccellati is evidently right is in stating that we have nothing to indicate that before being assigned to David the place was a city state governed by a hereditary monarchy, and was then taken over by David and his successors: the text simply says that 'it belonged' to the dynasty, without specifying how, and under what legal régime.

4.6.7.2 The question of Jerusalem seems much more complicated, not least because of the infinitely greater importance of the capital, whether on the political level or the historical and religious level. Here, as we saw above (4.4.2.1 and 4.6.2), its character as a city-state ruled by a monarch who was a vassal of Egypt is solidly attested in the pre-Israelite period and there is no reason to doubt that this was its condition at the time when it was incorporated into the empire. So the question arises: did Jerusalem continue to retain this status even after the Israelite conquest with David as king? For lack of any direct evidence, here too we must rely on indirect and implicit evidence, which is all we have to go on. David and his successors never bore the title 'king of Jerusalem' (unlike the Crusader kings and their successors), but we have seen that in the el-'Amarna letters the rulers never had this title either (above, 2.8.3). On the other hand, the texts never speak of Jerusalem as an ancient administrative or topographical entity belonging to Judah, or of Judah as including the city; that would have been obvious had the city been incorporated into the administrative structure of Judah. The phrase used is always 'Judah and Jerusalem', which suggests a special administrative situation, autonomous over against both the tribal institutions and those of the state, and governed directly by the crown. Indirect confirmation of this state of things appears in Josh.15.7b-19, where the unexpected wealth of frontier points as soon as we reach the area of the capital seems meant to indicate the separation between Judah and the territory of the ex-city-state.[24] In my contribution to Hayes-Miller* 1977 I have therefore suggested as a possible parallel the federal districts and the 'federal capitals' of Australia and America. This would indicate that, apart of course from the republican form of government in the modern parallels, Jerusalem was, like these, both united and yet separate from the kingdom at the same time.

4.6.7.3 Again according to Alt,[25] the status of Samaria in the North, founded towards the end of the ninth century BCE (see also 10.10.5.1-2; also cf. there the objections to this theory), was not dissimilar. The sole difference was that Samaria was a new foundation and never had the tradition of a city-state behind it; the similarity lay essentially in the fact that the model for the status of Samaria will have been that of Jerusalem. So in the present state of research it would seem logical to maintain Alt's thesis for Jerusalem.

4.6.7.4 However, Buccellati has put in question the very concept of a personal union, while recognizing that it has many elements in its favour. In his view the concept is not really compatible with that of a highly centralized administration based on the capital. In this connection, however, it should be recalled that the biblical tradition is almost unanimous in affirming (and I see no reasons for doubting it at this point) that David was crowned first over Judah and then over Israel; it thus seems clear that these were two distinct administrative entities, and on the death of Solomon Israel left the union after laborious negotiations (below 10.1). Furthermore, as we shall consider in the next chapter (5.8.3), only the North (and not also the South) was divided into administrative districts by Solomon, a feature which can only be interpreted as a fiscal discrimination against the North. Moreover it is not difficult to see the existence of marked centrifugal tendencies, especially in the North, which would contrast with the centripetal ones supported by the court; in periods of crisis this would lead to real rebellions (below 4.8).

4.7 The public administration

As we saw, a complex structure like that of the empire needed a differentiated administration (above 4.6). That explains why it is only with David that we can really talk of a true public administration, a bureaucracy with trained officials for the various and mostly new tasks that had to be performed.

Bibliography

H.Donner, 'Der "Freund des Königs" ', *ZAW* 73, 1961, 269-77; A.Cody, 'Le titre égyptien et le nom propre du scribe de David', *RB* 72, 1965, 381-9; A.Penna, 'Amico del re', *RiBib* 14, 1966, 459-66; M.Mazar, '*Sōfēr hammelek ūbᵉʿayat happᵉqīdūt haggᵉbōhāh bᵉmalkūt iśrāʾēl*', in *Canaan and Israel. Historical Essays*, Jerusalem 1980, 208-21 (in Hebrew); T.N.D.Mettinger, *Solomonic State Officials*, CB-OTS 5, Lund 1971; G.J.Wenham, 'Were David's Sons Priests?', *ZAW* 87, 1975, 79-82; J.A.Soggin, in Hayes and Miller* 1977, 336ff.; U.Rüterswörden, *Die Beamten der israelitischen Königszeit*, Stuttgart 1985; Donner* I, 1984, 203-7; Miller and Hayes* 1987, 186-8, 205-7.

4.7.1 Three texts give us information about various government officials of David and Solomon; the first is II Sam.8.15-18//I Chron.18.14-17; the second is II Sam.20.23-26 (with no parallel in Chronicles), probably a little later; the third is I Kings 4.1-6 (again without a parallel in Chronicles). These are texts which are generally regarded as ancient. In the first of these lists, v.17//16 should probably read, '...and Zadok, and Abiathar, son of Ahimelech, son of Ahitub...' These are in fact the names of the father and the grandfather of Abiathar (I Sam.22.20), whereas originally Zadok appears without a genealogy; only in I Chron.6.34ff. is he given one.

4.7.1.1 The following officials appear in the lists:

4.7.1.1.1 Joab, commander of the army (8.16; 20.24); he no longer appears in the list from the time of Solomon, having been killed in the meantime. However, one of his sons appears in I Kings 4.6, again as a commander.

4.7.1.1.2 Jehoshaphat, who has the title *mazkīr* (8.16; 20.24).

4.7.1.1.3 Zadok and Abiathar, priests (8.17; 20.25).

4.7.1.1.4 Seraiah, who has the title *sōfēr* (8.17); however, in 20.26 he appears as *šᵉyāʾ* in the Kethib and *šᵉwāʿ* in the Qere; in I Chronicles he appears as *šawšāʾ*, whereas in I Kings 4.6 he appears as *šīšā*. It is generally thought that this is a corruption of the original title of an Egyptian official: *sš.sʿt* or *šḥšʿt*, 'scribe + letter'.

4.7.1.1.5 Benaiah, commander of the 'Cherethites and Pelethites' (8.18; 20.23, cf. above 4.4.2.7).

4.7.1.1.6 The 'sons of David' as priests (8.18); but I Chron. 18.17 has 'the first beside the king', probably a deliberate correction at a time which could not accept priests who were not Levites.

4.7.1.1.7 Adoniram, in charge of forced labour (only 20.24 and I Kings 4.6); cf 5.9 below.

4.7.1.1.8 'Ira, 'priest for David' (only 20.25), whatever this expression is meant to indicate.

4.7.1.1.9 A 'prefect of the palace' (*[ᵃšer] ᶜal habbayit*) called Ahishar (with variants in LXX) appears in I Kings 4.6.

4.7.2 Other texts tell us about other officials:

4.7.2.1 A counsellor of the king, *yōᶜēṣ*, named Ahithophel, appears in II Sam.15.12/I Chron 27.33, whereas

4.7.2.2 II Sam.15.37; 16.16; I Kings 4.5; I Chron.27.33 speak of a 'king's friend', *rēᶜēh hammelek*, called Hushai). This is an originally Egyptian title (*śmr wᶜty* and *rḥ nśwt*), very widespread and attested from the el-ᶜAmarna correspondence down to the imperial Roman house (Donner* 1984).

4.7.2.3 It is probable that the framework for all these bureaucratic functions was predominantly drawn from Canaanite elements; it is certain that some of the titles are Egyptian in origin. Today only Kitchen 1988 (above 3.7) questions this theory, though he recognizes that we have to take Egyptian influence into account.

4.7.2.4 The titles *sōpēr* and *mazkīr* are translated by the LXX γραμματεύς and ὑπομνηματόγραφος respectively; in some modern translations they appear as 'scribe' and 'secretary'; in reality the title 'secretary' seems to refer to the first of the two, contrary to later Hebrew usage; his office is the one which is in fact referred to by the Egyptian title which is usually associated with it. We know virtually nothing of the latter and there are those who think that he had a representative function.

4.8 Internal tensions

As I have already pointed out, the complex structure of the Davidic empire and the institutions of what was evidently a real centralized public administration, especially as far as taxation was concerned, inevitably led here and there to tensions, if not to real conflicts, at a local level. This happened especially when it was involved in struggles with the Israelite tribal institutions and those of the city state and other groups incorporated into the empire. These in fact forced otherwise autonomous groups to limit their own freedom for reasons which in no case could appear connected with the common good or public order, in allowing themselves to be conscripted for works whose utility was either misunderstood or was in effect non-existent (we shall be concerned with this in more detail below, 5.9). Even today, in the so-called 'segmentary' societies of non-Muslim Africa, a parallel which is often adduced despite the chronological and geographical distances, there are similar conflicts in analogous situations. We shall be dealing with this last problem in due course (below 8.9.7.2).

4.8.1 The sources have handed down information about at least two rebellions, the first probably involving Judah and Israel, the second essentially limited to the North.

4.8.1.1 The texts of II Sam.15-19 mention a first rebellion which produced a real crisis for the empire. David had to abandon the capital and flee, along with all the state apparatus, abandoning everything, even his harem. The rebellion was led by Absalom, the crown prince, and according to the practice of the 'succession narrative', the affair is presented in predominantly family terms (cf. above 4.2.1.3). The prince, it is said, had avenged the honour of his sister Tamar who had been enticed, raped and then rejected and insulted by her half-brother Amnon. Absalom had killed the guilty party and then had to flee abroad, to Geshur, to his mother's family (above 4.5.3). Then, however, having obtained pardon from his father, he had returned home. The texts (cf. II Sam.15.2-6) present him as being endowed with remarkable personal gifts, capable of skilfully exploiting to his own advantage the popular discontent which the sources claim to have been quite widespread. After spending some time making preparations, he is said to have gone to Hebron, where he had himself proclaimed king, immediately obtaining the support of 'all the tribes of Israel', to whom he had sent messengers. The text does not, however, say whether by 'Israel' it means the North, as usual, or also Judah; the latter seems probable, given that there is mention of 'all' the tribes (this goes counter to what I have affirmed previously). The meeting place was the capital of the southern hill-country, which had seen David's coronation in II Sam.2.4; furthermore the almost catastrophic dimensions of the event suggest an action which must have involved almost everyone. Be this as it may, according to the sources David will then have succeeded in gaining the upper hand over Absalom's popular militia, especially thanks to his own personal army; the prince was also killed during the flight.

4.8.1.2 A second rebellion, this time of more modest proportions, involved only the North and does not seem to have constituted a real danger. There was a rebellion among the Benjaminites, soon joined by Ephraim and Manasseh. It is reported that the rebels had as their war-cry:

'We have no portion in David,
and we have no inheritance in the son of Jesse;
every man to his tents, O Israel!' (II Sam.20.1).

The phrase is also attributed to the secessionists of the North a generation later, with the addition of a fourth line: 'Look now to your own house, David!' (I Kings 12.16).

This shows a North which had spontaneously entered the empire through the personal union and decided to leave when the original reasons no longer existed.

This time, too, David succeeded in gaining the upper hand: the chief of the rebels, a certain Sheba, was killed in the place where he had taken refuge, and the rebels were pardoned by David.

4.8.2 The 'succession narrative' ends with the accession of Solomon to the throne on the death of David (I Kings 1-2). In this conclusion David appears totally senile, incapable of taking decisions and hence of governing, completely at the mercy of the intrigues of the harem and the court. The real ruler was Joab, the commander of the popular militia. The crown prince Adonijah tried to secure the succession for himself, which moreover he expected by right, making use of the help of Joab and Abiathar the priest. Solomon, however, the second in line, was designated by David himself on the instigation of Solomon's mother Bathsheba; he was supported by David's private army, which once again proved its efficiency, and by Zadok the priest (above 4.7.1.1.3). Solomon managed to get the better of his opponents and used the first period of his new power to proscribe or even eliminate physically on various pretexts all those who might have been a danger to him. So this is a real *coup d'état*, though the author of the 'succession narrative' describes the political ability and wisdom of the new ruler in laudatory terms. Evidently he regarded Solomon's seizure of power as the lesser evil, if not actually a good thing. With this approach to the problem he clearly abandoned any pretence at objectivity, seeking to disqualify (apparently with some reason) both the old dying ruler and his successor in the dynastic line, and legitimating the second in line to the succession and his seizure of power. Thus, *mutatis mutandis*, what happened to David was very similar to what had once happened to Saul, a feature which we can perhaps also see as a didactic aim of the 'succession narrative'.

4.9 Religion

One of the most complex problems in the study of this period, which is virtually insoluble in the present state of research, is that of the content and development of the religion of Israel and Judah from this time onwards, down to Josiah's reform (below 12.4.2). In this case, too, in fact the sources report only what the post-exilic Judahite community wanted to hand down. The result is the following framework: little by little, a religion which was revealed and thus originally pure and incorrupt, became contaminated because of the sin of the people and forbidden contacts with the Canaanite population. However, years afterwards, following the work of just and pious monarchs, the greatest of whom was Josiah, and later under the governorship of Ezra and Nehemiah, this was restored to its original purity. This is a framework which is clearly not that of a modern historico-critical reconstruction,

but is only the ideological and theological attempt to legitimate the
post-exilic hierocracy.

4.9.1 According to this framework, which we can call official, a
process began under David which decades ago I called 'state syncretism'.[26] This will have consisted of deliberate measures, planned
from above, with the aim of providing a common religion for all the
peoples living within the empire, a unification which was impossible
to obtain on the ethnic and political levels. To this end David is said to
have had recourse to a series of syncretistic religious measures, which
were taken over and completed by his successor Solomon.

4.9.2 It is in this context that the moving of the ark to Jerusalem and
Solomon's building of the temple are to be seen. With the acceptance
of the royal Canaanite ideology, a series of polytheistic elements will
have entered into the state cult: the prophecy of the eternal duration of
the dynasty (II Sam.7.15; Ps.2.7; 110.4; Isa.9.6 and yet other passages).
Also in Israel, as in Ugarit (*CTA* 15.II, 25-27; *ANET*, 146, not yet in
TUAT; and 16.10f.) the person of the king appears as being endowed
with a divinity which put him in a sphere which was at least partially
divine. In Ps.45.7 the king is even addressed as 'God' (cf. II Kings 21.11-
14, where anyone who blasphemes 'God and the king' is put to death),
while Ps.21.5 promises the king 'eternal life', a divine prerogative; in
II Sam.23.1 (in the emended text) *'elyōn* (a Canaanite divinity, also
attested in the Hebrew Bible, later identified with YHWH) elevates him
above all men. His presence encourages the development of communal
life and the fertility of the soil and the flocks (II Sam.21.17; Lam.4.20;
Ps.72.6-7,16). As high priest (below, 5.5) the king acts just like the priest-
king in the Phoenician city states,[27] and according to Deuteronomy and
the Deuteronomist, the laws of reform in matters relating to the cult
are within his competence, and remain so down to the end of the
seventh century BCE.

4.9.3 This is the view of the Deuteronomic thesis according to which
we have a process of progressive corruption; however, the reality is
certainly different: in fact everything indicates that in these elements
we find at least fragments of what must have been the religion in Judah
and Israel before the exile:[28] a basically polytheistic religion of a
Canaanite type, even if the person of YHWH must be assigned a
position of pre-eminence as a national deity. These are features about
which later history believed it had to be severely critical, presenting
them as degenerations and one of the main causes of the divine
judgment. Certainly, even before the exile there were individuals and
groups who argued the need for Israel and Judah to worship a single
God, YHWH, without accepting others, and aspects of this can be
found among the prophets and their disciples. It seems only reasonable
to suppose that the authors of Deuteronomy and the Deuteronomistic

history could draw abundantly on the sources, and that they will have had their spiritual roots there.

4.9.4 Particularly revealing information appears from Hebrew nomenclature. Tradition attributes a second name, Jerubbaal, to Gideon; a son of Saul is called Eshbaal and one of his grandsons Meribbaal or Mephibaal; a son of David bears the name Ba'alyada (II Sam.5.16). These are names which indicate some kind of devotion to this Canaanite deity or his identification with the God of Israel; later, when this deity had become the opponent of YHWH *par excellence*, the redactors sometimes distorted the name to *bōšet*, 'shame' (in II Sam.11.21, Jerubbaal has become Jerubbesheth). And we can also ask whether many names beginning or ending in *'el* did not originally refer to the supreme deity of the Canaanite pantheon before he was identified with YHWH. That must be stated, given that the opposite theory is still so often put forward.

4.9.5 What seems to have happened, then, is that increasingly influential groups, for the most part led by the prophets, struggled down the centuries to impose on the religion of Israel and Judah that form of monotheism which was to become its main characteristic: and that these struggles crystallized in the various religious reforms, first that of king Hezekiah (below 12.2.1) and then that of king Josiah (below 12.4.3).

4.10 The economic and political problems which arose with the emergence of the new form of government, with its demands in the form of personal and collective taxation, claims for contributions in kind and for compulsory, sometimes forced, labour, are also particularly complex. We shall be dealing with them in the next chapter (5.9), in the context of the reign of Solomon, for whom the sources are clearer. I have already alluded to them above (4.8).

5

The Empire under Solomon

5.1 The sources

As we have seen, the texts which give us information about Solomon
begin with the conclusion of the 'succession narrative' (I Kings 1-2);
they continue as far as I Kings 11. Again we principally have biblical
material which, as I have already pointed out (above 3.2.2), refers to a
'Chronicle of Solomon' (I Kings 11.41). However, we know absolutely
nothing of works of this kind: for some scholars this is an official
chronicle of the court; for others, given the lack of any element of proof,
this is one of the many references to documents with which all literature,
including classical literature, is abundantly furnished.[1] The same thing
also happens in relatively recent times as literary fiction. We find other
material in Flavius Josephus, whose works we have already considered
(above 3.6.5.1). All these references and the information in question
need to be treated with caution, and examined carefully, all the more
so since where the biblical text is concerned we never have real extracts,
but only general references. So it is not surprising that the figure of
Solomon is sometimes thought to be purely fictitious, perhaps a
mythical monarch from a happy past.[2]

But here too some caution is called for: the many criticisms which
the texts make of Solomon, as already of David, seem to exclude any
hagiographical exaltation of this past.

5.1.1 If we are to accept the existence of a court chronicle of this kind
from which the author of Kings abstracted material (and we can do that
in a purely hypothetical form), we should try to identify what material
could go back to it. I repeat that this is a purely conjectural operation.
In other words, we should try to isolate that material which seems
to contain relevant information on the political, administrative and
economic level, in which family elements, anecdotes or purely narrative
material is lacking, or at least secondary. It is also important that this

was of little or no interest to the exilic and post-exilic period and that possibly their approach was critical of the past. Such material is in fact present in the sources; it is:

5.1.1.1 The list of state officials in I Kings 4.1-6, which we discussed earlier (4.7.1).

5.1.1.2 The list of districts and the governors appointed over them (I Kings 4.7-19).

5.1.1.3 The brief note on forced labour (below, 5.9) in I Kings 5.27, which contrasts with what is said in the Deuteronomistic note in 9.15-22 (with an interesting addition in the LXX text).

5.1.1.4 Sparse references to commercial enterprises launched by Solomon (10.11ff., 22, 28ff.).

5.1.2 In Chronicles.

Bibliography

H.G.M.Williamson 'The Accession of Solomon in the Books of Chronicles', *VT* 26, 1976, 351-61; R.B.Dillard, 'The Literary Structures of the Chronicler's Solomon Narrative', *JSOT* 30, 1984, 85-93.

In Chronicles Solomon, like David, has become a kind of hero/national saint, without a blemish. As sources for the historian, most of the material relating to him is therefore to be discarded.

5.1.3 In terms of archaeology we are slightly better informed than about the time of David (above 4.2.1.6), even if quite a lot of the data previously considered certain seems to be in need of revision (Wightman 1990). So what I wrote in 1977*, 340ff., still applies: the data at our disposal are 'deceptively scarce'.

Bibliography

G.E.Wright, *Biblical Archaeology*, Philadelphia and London ²1962; K.M.Kenyon, *Digging up Jerusalem*, London 1974, 99-106; and the reports by Y.Shiloh, *BA* 42, 1979, 165-78; 44, 1981, 161-70. See also G.W.Ahlström, *Royal Administration and National Religion in Ancient Palestine*, Leiden 1982; W.G.Dever, 'Monumental Architecture in Ancient Israel in the Period of the United Monarchy', in T.Ishida (ed.), *Studies in the Period of David and Solomon and Other Essays*, Tokyo 1982, 269-306; H.Weippert** 1989, 449ff.; G.J.Wightman, 'The Myth of Solomon', *BASOR* 277-8, 1990, 5-22 (but cf. the criticism by W.G.Dever, 'Of Myths and Methods', ibid., 121-30); J.D.Currid, 'The Re-Stratification of Megiddo during the United Monarchy', *ZDPV* 107, 1991 [1992], 28-38.

5.1.3.1 At the beginning of 1960 the North American archaeologist G.E.Wright pointed out: 'No discovery has been made in Jerusalem which can be dated with a minimum of certainty to the time of David and Solomon.' Today this situation has partly changed, but only in certain sectors, after about thirty years of excavations, especially in the Jewish quarter of the city and in the zone of Silwan, published first by the English expeditions led by K.M.Kenyon (1964, 1974) and then by the Israeli one led by Y.Shilo, and on his death by his successors.

5.1.3.2 This situation is not difficult to explain; to carry out archaeological explorations and especially excavations under an inhabited centre has always been an extremely complex undertaking. Only in very special cases like the restoration of the Jewish Quarter in the Old City of Jerusalem or the building of the Seminary of the Armenian Patriarchate south of the Jaffa Gate has it become possible, and then only in limited sectors. The same goes for the eastern Arab suburb of Silwān, ancient Siloah, almost certainly the old 'City of David' and densely populated.

5.1.3.3 At all events, the two English expeditions thought that they could identify an old earth rampart with an ancient filling of ground with man-made objects that the texts call *millō'* (literally 'filling up'). David is said to have extended and restored this (II Sam.5.9), and Solomon is said to have reinforced it and strengthened it (I Kings 9.24; 11.27). A wall from the time of Solomon has also been identified under the Herodian walls which supported the old Temple court, now the Muslim sanctuary *ḥarām eš-šarīf* (Dever 1982).

5.1.3.4 The situation for ancient Megiddo, *tell el-mutesellim* (coord.167-221), is more favourable, even if some statements from the past have meanwhile been revised. It was excavated at the beginning of the century and during the 1920s. Among the information to be revised is the claim to have discovered 'Solomon's stables' (below, figs.3-4, cf. I Kings 9.15ff.), which closer checking has proved to be one or two centuries later and which then are perhaps not even stables at all![3]

5.1.3.5 The situation seems to be similar with ancient Hazor (*tell el-qedaḥ* or *tell el-waqqaṣ*, coord. 203-269) and Gezer (below, fig.8, coord. 142-140), the former excavated in the 1950s, the latter at the beginning of the century and in the 1960s and 1970s. I Kings 9.15 states that Solomon 'built' them (root *bānāh*), probably here to be translated 'restored' or 'rebuilt' (cf. also 13.5.1).

5.1.3.6 In these places, among other things the remains have been discovered of a city gate with some characteristics typical of this period: beside the passage-way we find three rectangular niches; these are usually taken to be guard rooms (see below, figs.12-13). At Megiddo, the excavations show that this kind of gate is to be found at the end of the development of a particular technique, attested in Canaan some centuries earlier. However, the gates of Dan (*tell el-qādī* in the extreme north, coord. 211-294, see below, fig.2) and Beersheba (*tell eś-śaba'*, coord. 134-072), in the Negeb, show a similar construction, but one that is later and considerably simplified, but with only two spaces, one on each side of the passage. [4]

5.1.3.7 Little is known about Solomon's port on the Red Sea, Eziongeber. It is now stated that this cannot be *tell el-ḥeleife* (coord.147-884), situated between present-day Aqaba and Eilat, since there is no trace of any port installations: so the locality is sought further south, perhaps in the bay ('the fiord') south of the 'Isle of Corals' or 'of the Pharaoh' (Arabic *jazīrat al-far'ūn*, Hebrew *hā'almōgīm*, coord. 133-871), the ancient Egyptian port for the transport of copper ore. What are known as 'Solomon's Pillars' or 'Solomon's Mines' at Timnah, north of Eilat (coord.145-909), were abandoned between the twelfth and the tenth century BCE, so they can hardly have been used in the time of Solomon.

5.2 Legitimacy

At the end of the 'succession narrative', then, Solomon appears firmly seated on his throne, now with no enemies who could have thwarted the operation. And as we have seen (above 4.2.1.3 and 4.8.2), for the author of the 'history' it was good that things worked out like this: only the priest Abiathar, who had sided with his enemies, is not physically eliminated but sent to imprisonment in Anathoth, near to the present Arab village of *'anāta* which has kept the name, but to be identified with *raś el-ḥarrūbe* (coord. 174-135), around five miles north of the city. So the texts do not conceal the fact that this was a *coup d'état*, a palace revolt.

5.2.1 According to I Kings 3.4-15, Solomon was confirmed in his functions and endowed with particular wisdom by a divine oracle which he received in the sanctuary of Gibeon. The information, the content of which contrasts with the tendency in Dtr to centralize the cult, could be prior to this redaction. The information provides the basis for the later legend of the monarch's wisdom, but in addition to this there are some elements of even greater importance: the phrase which YHWH addresses to the king is remarkably identical semantically to the formula for the ritual of the coronation of the ruler, attested in Ps.2.8, as is clear from the following table:

I Kings 3.5 : *š'l   mh w'tn lk*
Ps.2.8   : *š'l mmny w'tn*
Ps.2.8 LXX: *š'l mmny w'tn lk*

In the first case we have 'Ask what [you will] and I will give (it)' to you; in the second (and the third), 'Ask me [what you will] and I will give [it] to you'.

In other words, Solomon received from the oracle not only the promise of wisdom but also the necessary legitimation, since he had ascended the throne after a *coup d'état* (above 3.2.1). As I wrote in 1977*, 367: 'In other words, Solomon tried to keep the shell of ancient institutions, making things look as much as possible as they were before. At the same time, however, he substantially modified their institutional content': there is in fact no mention of any approval by popular assemblies (at least for Judah and Israel).

5.2.2 Solomon is mentioned in the texts for two reasons: his construction of the temple at Jerusalem, the building which through changing circumstances was the spiritual centre of Judaism for about a thousand years, down to its destruction by Titus' soldiers in 70 CE; and for his wisdom, which became proverbial.

5.2.2.1 The fact that three and a half chapters out of a total of nine which speak of the reign of Solomon are devoted to the construction and inauguration of the temple is a sign of the importance which the whole narrative attributes to the event and therefore of the orientation of all these texts.

Today it is almost impossible, in the present state of research and on the basis of the biblical texts (cf. I Kings 6), to reconstruct the appearance of the outside and inside of the temple, the way in which it was built and its structure. Evidence of this is the fact that authors who have tackled the problem have usually arrived at different results, none of which can be considered certain. That is also the case even if its topography is sufficiently known as a result of other discoveries in the region. The legitimacy of this comparison with other analogous constructions in the region rests on the fact that these same texts explicitly affirm that Solomon made use˙of Phoenician craftsmen (I Kings 5.15-31; 7.13-14), while Israel merely provided the unskilled manual labourers. That allows only one interpretation: that also according to the biblical sources Solomon's intention was to build a Canaanite temple, so that we have to look for models for his work in the region, and not elsewhere. Finally, the procedure followed is that attested also in Mesopotamia from Gudea king of Lagash onwards: decision by the king followed by a divine confirmation (I Kings 5.17-18), preparation of material and engagement of the labour force (5.20-23), description of the building (chs.6-7), inauguration (8.1-11, 62-66), the king's prayer (8.12-61). All this leads us to an examination of possible models.

5.2.2.2 The 'Syrian' temple. The best known model is that of *tell tayīnat*, near Alexandretta on the Orontes, around twelve miles north, opposite *tell alalakh* in present-day Turkey. Meanwhile similar buildings have been discovered near Hamath and on the *tell* of Hazor (Wright 1971, 1985). Furthermore it seems that Solomon built other sanctuaries outside Jerusalem: that of Megiddo (Ussishkin 1989, above n.3, see also fig.3) and the little temple on *tell 'ārād* in the eastern Negeb (coord. 162-076, below fig.7).[5]

Bibliography

A.Alt, 'Verbreitung und Herkunft des syrischen Tempeltypus' (1939), *KS* II, 100-15; T.A.Busink, *Der Tempel von Jerusalem*, Leiden I, 1970; II, 1980; D.Ussishkin, 'Building IV in Hamat and the Temple of Solomon and Tell Tayinat', *IEJ* 16, 1966, 104-10; A.Kuschke, 'Der Tempel Salomos und der "syrischen Tempeltypus" ', in *Das ferne und nahe Wort – FS L.Rost*, Berlin 1967, 124-32; id., 'Tempel', *BRL*[2], 1977, 333-42 (with thirty-four plans of various temples: a basic study); G.R.H.Wright, 'Pre-Israelite Temples in the Land of Canaan', *PEQ* 103, 1971, 17-32; H.-D.Hoffman, *Reform und Reformen*, Zurich 1980, 47ff.; A.V.Hurowitz, *Temple Building in the Bible, in the Light of Mesopotamian and North-East Semitic Writing*, Diss.Hebrew University Jerusalem 1983 (in Hebrew with an English summary); G.R.H.Wright, *Ancient Building in South Syria and Palestine*, Leiden 1985, 215-63, esp.264ff.; H.Weippert** 1989, 461ff.; D.Milson, 'Megiddo, Alalakh and Troy: A Design Analogy between the Bronze Age Temples', *PEQ* 121, 1989, 64-8. For the problem of royal patronage over the Jerusalem cult see the basic study by K.Galling, 'Königliche und nichtkönigliche Stifter beim Tempel von Jerusalem', *ZDPV* 68, 1949-51, 134-42.

5.2.2.3 Characteristically, the covered Syro-Canaanite sanctuary (the open-air one clearly takes a different form) has a basically tripartite structure: a vestibule surrounded by a covered verandah but otherwise open; the building proper, and within it the holy of holies, the place for the statue of the deity who was worshipped (below, plates 10-11). In Jerusalem, as the sources tell us, because the cult was aniconic, the ark took the place of the statue and then, when the ark disappeared (Jer.3.16),[6] there was nothing at all, a feature which always caused amazement and perplexity to foreign invaders (below 14.11.9).

5.2.2.4 According to I Kings 6.1, 35f.; 8.2, the construction of the temple took seven years. The two months, called by their ancient Canaanite names (*ziw* = *iyyār*, April-May, the month of Pentecost, and *'ētannīm* = *tišrī*, September-October, the month of the feast of Tabernacles), coincide not only with the two main agricultural feasts in Israel but also with the Canaanite festivities in honour of Ba'al; in particular the autumn festival is connected at least chronologically with the resurrection of Ba'al (above 2.4.6) and with the building of his heavenly temple;[7] it even seems that the inauguration after the completion of the building was put back some months, perhaps so that it could coincide with the festivities for Baʿal!

5.2.2.5 As in Mesopotamia, so too in Jerusalem a characteristic feature of the work seems to have been the continual intervention of the king in cultic and technical questions; this made him, if not *de iure* than at least *de facto*, the one who exercised functions similar to those of the high priest.

5.2.2.5.1 Solomon also intervenes directly in the internal affairs of the priesthood in that he has Abiathar exiled (I Kings 2.26) and entrusts all power to Zadok (2.35). This is taken to be normal and he was never reproved for it.

5.2.2.5.2 Also in the course of the consecration of the temple Solomon exercises functions which are clearly sacerdotal: he leads the ark into the holy of holies (8.1-13), blesses 'all the congregation of Israel' (*'et kol qᵉhal iśrā'ēl* – *qāhāl*, which LXX does not translate, is later the technical term for the cultic community, 8.14); he pronounces a first short prayer, markedly developed by Dtr (8.15-21), while in 8.22-52, before the altar, he pronounces a longer complex one. In 8.54-61 he blesses the community and finally (8.62) he sacrifices along with the people. These are functions which correspond to the phrase, all the details of which are not clear, attested in Ps.110.4, where the king is called 'priest for ever'.

5.2.2.5.3 Now if we recall what was said above (4.9.2), namely that in all probability the Phoenician kings also seem to have been priests in the state cult, the picture becomes clearer, particularly in the light of the close relationship existing between Israel and the Phoenicians of the time: Solomon did not simply assume priestly functions *ad hoc*, during the building of the temple, but will have had the title priest legitimately and expressed it effectively.

5.3 Enemies

Only towards the end of the reign of Solomon do the texts speak of problems: 11.14-25 mentions enemies abroad, 11.26-40 enemies at home. The Deuteronomistic historian connects these events with what he regards as Solomon's syncretism in cultic matters, and in this connection formulates a kind of doctrine of retaliation, of retribution for the sinner, in which cultic sin is punished in the political sphere. Here too we have an artificial system (cf. above Chapter 4, n.26) of events under the theme of 'under the blessing – under the curse', which appears especially where the curse is said to have been the result of syncretism.

5.3.1 In 11.14-25 Solomon's foreign enemies are the Edomites and the Aramaeans, i.e. groups which belonged to the empire in one way or another. The position of Egypt is not always clear here, in that it offers political sanctuary to Solomon's enemies.

5.3.2 However, the text 11.26-40 speaks of an attempt at rebellion on the part of Jeroboam, who was in charge of forced labour and later became king of Israel (cf. above 4.7.1.1.7; below 10.3.7); he too is said to have been offered political sanctuary in Egypt.

5.4 Solomon's wisdom

Solomon has also gone down in history or, better, in legend for his wisdom, which soon became proverbial: so much so that traditionally the majority of the wisdom literature, from the book of Proverbs to the deutero-canonical Wisdom of Solomon, has been attributed to him.

5.4.1 In what did this wisdom consist? The texts describe it in terms of anecdote and folk-lore, as millennia later the *Thousand and One Nights* describes the wisdom of Harun-el Rashid and Saladin. In the Near East, ancient and modern, the tradition of the wise and benevolent sovereign is ancient and constant and contrasts pleasantly with the character of the modern politician, in the region and elsewhere, who is lacking in such virtues.

5.4.2 Wisdom and ability in the political sphere, albeit totally unscrupulous, appear in I Kings 2 where, as I have indicated, the king succeeds in ridding himself of his opponents, both potential and real, by skilful pretexts which absolve him of all blame.

5.4.3 In 3.16-28, as a direct consequence of the wisdom which he chose and obtained in his vision at Gibeon, we have the famous episode of the 'judgment of Solomon', which is more a proof of astuteness and good sense than of wisdom in our sense of the term.

5.4.4 In 4.29-39 [Hebrew 5.9-14], Solomon is said to have had a remarkable capacity for composing proverbs and riddles and discourses on subjects of various kinds, mainly relating to the plant and animal world. We shall not go far wrong in thinking that the authors had in mind the literary genre of the fable, which had plants and animals as its subjects. However, no examples of such work by Solomon have ben handed down: there is no mention in the wisdom writings attributed to him by tradition of 'trees, from the cedar that is in Lebanon to the hyssop that grows out of the wall', nor of 'beasts, and of birds, and of reptiles, and of fish' (4.33f. [5.13]).

5.4.5 The wisdom discussions with the solving of riddles which Solomon is said to have had with the Queen of Sheba (10.1-13, a kingdom which did not yet exist in the tenth century, Lemche* 1988, 143f.) belong to the same literary genre. These are narrative embellishments to the life of a legendary ruler of the past.

5.5 Cult, temple and palace

The tradition also reports that Solomon saw to the building not only of the temple but also of the royal palace, thus carrying forward a line begun by David. The palace stood right beside the temple, so near that some centuries later, in the sixth century BCE, Ezek.43.6-9 harshly criticizes the fact that the two stood as close as a pair of feet. This made the temple in effect something like a Palatine chapel. In I Kings 9.10 we are told that the building of the temple and the palace took about twenty years, and 7.1ff. calculates the time needed to build the place at thirteen years. So it seems clear that the time taken to build the palace was markedly longer than that devoted to building the temple; the subordinate function of the latter could hardly be better expressed.

5.5.1 However, the basis that the tradition attributes to Solomon for the organization of the cult, the temple and the palace – in other words, if one can use a modern expression, the relations between church and state – proved to be very solid: it survived in Judah down to the events of 587/586.

5.5.2 In Judah, while the monarchy existed, people looked to the sovereign as the head of the state cult, with the right to intervene directly in its performance and its organization. Thus we shall see (below, 12.2.1) first king Hezekiah and then king Josiah (below, 12.4.2) acting as genuine reforming sovereigns (and it is no coincidence that in the late Renaissance Philip II of Spain put their statues among the others which adorned the front of the Escorial, north of Madrid). Little or nothing seems to have distinguished the functions exercised by the king of Judah in the cult from those exercised by the Phoenician rulers.

5.5.3 However, in the post-exilic period we see the high priest taking over all these prerogatives (13.11 below), and also assuming what remained in Judah of political autonomy.

5.6 Politics

The biblical tradition which presents David, at least to begin with, as a skilful military leader also stresses the skill of Solomon in the political sphere, especially in the sphere of international relationships. This is considered part of his wisdom and is something that can be accepted as a working hypothesis. Such a development is by no means obvious: in the previous chapter (4.1.3) I pointed out the expansionist dynamic (one could call it imperialistic, without giving this term a pejorative sense) inherent in the Davidic empire; the shift towards more complex and subtle international political relationships, with a resultant need for negotiations, could also have been alien to the very character of the empire and therefore could have contributed to its break-up. However, it could also have been that Solomon, to turn Clausewitz's dictum upside down, instead of waging war, succeeded in international politics by other means, obtaining more than war could have brought him by means of treaties, contracts and commercial enterprises. This latter view seems to be the one supported by the biblical sources, although these are often formulated in triumphalistic tones when they refer to the king's commercial enterprises. However, these theses of the tradition, which are clearly too laudatory by far, need to be put to the test.

5.6.1 Among other things, Solomon is presented as a shipowner,[8] albeit not directly (ancient Israel was never a seafaring people, above 2.3.9; among other things it lacked natural ports from which to sail), but in conjunction with Hiram of Tyre, who has already been mentioned. In 9.26f. it is stated that 'he built a fleet at Ezion-geber' (above, 5.1.3.7) on the Red Sea. Hiram sent his subjects (literally 'servants') with the fleet, seamen who were familiar with the sea, together with the servants of Solomon. We are not in a position to specify precisely where these expeditions in the Red Sea went. The texts (9.28; 10.11) refer to Ophir,[9] a place or region which has not been identified; however, we cannot rule out the possibilty that Ophir and Tarshish (like the earthly paradise and Atlantis) formed part of a purely mythical and symbolic geography with no bearing on reality, as M.Görg recently argued.

5.6.2 Another text (10.22) states that 'a fleet of Tarshish' (a place which some scholars locate on the eastern coast of Spain and others in Cilicia, while yet others suppose it to be part of the mythical and symbolic geography just mentioned) joined the fleet of Hiram of Tyre in making voyages lasting for three years. The dealings with the Queen of Sheba (above 5.4.5) which are mentioned could be a recollection of such voyages.

5.6.3 Again, I Kings 9.28; 10.11,22 report that such enterprises were crowned with remarkable success: the ships brought back gold, precious stones and precious wood (of *'almuggīm*, in Chronicles always *'algummīm*, an unknown wood; the traditional translation 'sandal wood' is unsatisfactory – even more so the modern Hebrew rendering, where the term means 'coral'), a curiosity like apes and peacocks.[10] So this was presumably merchandise obtained through trading.

In any case, if we consider that the seafaring techniques of the period allowed only short coastal voyages, it is impossible that the ships would have gone far from the African or Asiatic coasts of the Red Sea or much beyond the *bab el-mandāb*, the strait which separates Eritrea from Arabia, even if the figure of 'three years' suggests rather longer voyages.

5.6.4 Another text (10.28f.) shows Solomon as a trader in war chariots and horses betwen Egypt and Cilicia (the region of Que). It now seems certain that the first place mentioned is Egypt and not the region of Musri in the Taurus, which has sometimes been suggested.[11] To judge from the texts, this trade will also have involved some minor sovereigns in the north-north east: 'Hittites (the term usually applied to Syria and Canaan, from the Neo-Assyrian texts onwards, above 2.7.1) and the king of Aram.' The position of Canaan as a bridge nation (above 2.9) between Asia and Africa evidently favoured these commercial operations.

5.6.5 The texts for the most part present all these enterprises as having been crowned with success, which clearly suggests that there was a significant influx of capital into the royal coffers. 9.28 and 10.25-27 explicitly speak of the riches which flowed into the royal treasury under Solomon. However, a close examination of the facts indicated here necessarily leads us to an initially more sober, less optimistic and largely negative evaluation of the situation.

5.6.5.1 What is now a marginal note in fact reports that at one time the good relations between Hiram and Solomon were disrupted by the inability of Solomon to pay or at least to give adequate collateral for his debts to Hiram, who, it appears, had allowed him unlimited credit (9.10-14). So, unable to do either, Solomon is said to have found himself forced to cede to Hiram about twenty places, probably situated in Western Galilee (their exact location is not clear), in a region which was later called the 'country of Kabul'. However, Hiram considered this action inadequate to pay or at least guarantee the debts that Solomon had contracted.

5.6.5.2 This must have seemed scandalous, and later II Chron. 8.1-5 reverses the terms of the arrangement: it was Hiram who assigned the places to Solomon. Still, the thesis in I Kings seems the most probable; it fits in well with what we shall discover soon (below 5.6.5.3); here, unless the sources deceive us, we shall be faced with the problem of the financial resources of a nation exploited to the limit.[12]

5.6.5.3 If Solomon thus proved so heavily in debt that he had to cede part of what was originally the territory of his nation in payment of or at least as a guarantee for the debts that he had contracted, we clearly have to ask whether his commercial enterprises, unconditionally praised in the texts, were really crowned with success and therefore contributed actively to the revenue, or whether they were not purely prestige operations or, even worse, a form of crown monopoly of trade, appropriating the practice of trade to himself – of course the two are not exclusive.[13] At all events, the impression given is that of an economy tried to the extreme, which sooner or later was bound to be in crisis, if not bankrupt.

5.6.6 However, the marriage of Solomon to a daughter of a Pharaoh who remains anonymous (I Kings 3.1; 7.8; 9.16, 24; 11.1) must be considered a success of international politics. The alliance is said to have brought with it as a dowry the city of Gezer, conquered and destroyed by the Pharaoh and rebuilt by Solomon. Most scholars identify the Pharaoh with either Siamun (c.978-959) or his successor Psausennes II (c.959-945);[14] according to Kitchen 1973 and 1988 (above 3.7), the Pharaoh will have been Siamun. He also cites some cases in which Egyptian princesses were married to commoners and even to foreigners, especially under the Twenty-Fifth and Twenty-Sixth Dynasties. Despite this, the information presents considerable difficulties which cannot be resolved, and therefore many scholars consider this detail part of the legendary embellishment of the reign of Solomon by the tradition.

5.6.6.1 First of all, there is a degree of unanimity on the fact that, contrary to what Kitchen states, the Pharaohs were *not* accustomed to marry their daughters to foreign rulers. So this case would be exceptional and the silence of the non-biblical sources would be difficult to explain.

5.6.6.2 Again, one has only to consider the sarcastic comment of G.Garbini,[15] who points out that it would be unworthy of a royal marriage for a father-in-law to offer as a dowry a destroyed city for the bridegroom to rebuild at his own expense.

5.6.6.3 Finally, it is often said that at the beginning of the First Intermediate Period Egypt was in a period of decadence; however, Garbini challenges this statement, pointing out that Egypt nevertheless had some power, as is confirmed by its expedition into Canaan: moreover, this was always the decadence of a great power, so that total humiliation is to be excluded.

5.6.6.4 In conclusion, we can also note that the information does not fit with other information that we shall examine later, according to which the Pharaoh offered political sanctuary to those rebelling against Solomon's empire.

5.6.7 The information that Solomon married princesses of allied or subject countries (11.3) also fits the same literary genre. In this way women from Moab, Ammon, Edom, Syria ('Hittite') and Sidon are said to have entered the royal harem. If the information is historically usable, it will indicate only that Solomon continued his own policy of alliances; this has nothing to do with the problem of syncretism, indicated by the texts.

5.7 Territorial development

The worsening of relations with Hiram of Tyre led to a first encroachment on the territory of the empire. This was followed by rebellions, especially in peripheral regions.

5.7.1 Edom very soon succeeded in recovering its own independence (11.14-22) – as it would seem, not without Egyptian help.

5.7.2 There also seem to have been secessionist tendencies in various city-states in Syria.

Bibliography

A.Malamat, *Das Königreich ...*, 1983 (above 4.1), 26 and 31ff.; S.Abramski, 'The Resurrection of the Kingdom of Damascus and its Historiographical Record', in *FS S.E.Loewenstamm*, Jerusalem 1978, I, 189ff. (in Hebrew, with an English summary).

In this way Damascus regained its own independence (11.23-25), and part of the conquest achieved by David (II Sam.8.3ff., 13ff.) was reversed. The text tells us that this came about through a certain Rezon, an ex-official of the king of Zobah, who was also (according to a probable addition by the LXX) active in his own country.

5.7.3 However, even in the North, in Israel in the strict sense, the situation was anything but quiet, as was already the case in the time of David (above 4.8.1). 11.26-40 speaks of a rebellion organized by Jeroboam, a senior official in the state bureaucracy; he too found political sanctuary in Egypt. According to Dtr he was given a divine oracle by a prophet who offered him rule over the ten tribes of the North, a kind of legitimation of the future kingdom of Israel: how this ever came to be inserted into the Deuteronomistic history work is inexplicable.

5.7.4 So a particularly dangerous political situation was in the making, along with what was clearly an economic crisis: also, it is to be assumed that the two elements were not separate: the empire, having become insolvent, was slowly falling apart, especially in the peripheral regions.

5.8 The system of taxation

An element worth noting and one about which the texts inform us with sufficient detail is a complex system of taxation: on the basis of the tradition it is now possible to reconstruct its main features with some precision. Such a possibility of reconstruction is quite rare and, as I have already said several times, that makes it difficult to produce a history of Israel and Judah.

5.8.1 A first text to which I have already referred briefly (above 5.1.1.3) speaks of the division of the North into twelve districts or provinces (but cf. below), each with a governor or a superintendent (Hebrew *nᵉṣîb*, I Kings 4.7-19; 5.2-4,7).[16] The text explicitly states that the aim of this operation was to make each unit responsible for providing provisions for 'the king and his house' (v.7) for one month in each year, a phrase which indicates that the expenses of public administration and the state cult fell in equal parts on the twelve districts in question. One reasonable explanation of this system, which is also attested in Egypt, has been proposed by D.B.Redford.[17]

5.8.1.1 The most obvious parallel to the institution is to be found in Egypt at the time of Pharaoh Shoshenk I (c.945-24, in the Bible he appears as Shishak), who was a younger contemporary of Solomon (below 10.6). In Redford's Egyptian parallel we have the names of places and officials whose task it was to provide a certain type of provisions for the court for each month of the year and also for those days needed for the completion of the solar year. Another purpose of the system was to provide provisions for the frontier garrisons.

5.8.1.2 As in Israel, the accent falls more on the governors than their districts, so that Redford prefers not to speak of districts, whose existence can only be deduced from the texts but cannot be demonstrated.

5.8.1.3 Solomon will also have used the system, as happened in Egypt, for provisioning the garrisons situated in border areas.

5.8.2 Redford's study here clearly takes us a good way further forward; however, for the present discussion it seems unimportant whether we speak of districts, provinces, territories or regions: what is important is that the functions of the system were eminently fiscal.

5.8.3 It should be emphasized that the sources indicate that this division into districts applied only to the North: there is no information about the existence of an analogous institution for the South (cf. below 5.8.3.1-2).

5.8.3.1 It is true that the sources speak in Josh.15.21-61 of a system of twelve districts for the South,[18] which some scholars would prefer to connect with a similar form of taxation, perhaps in connection with the census ordered by David in II Sam.14//I Chron.21 (an action which in the ancient world was always connected with taxation). In other words, there are indications that the taxation in question will not have been limited to the North, but will also have included the South.

5.8.3.2 However, this argument cannot be sustained. Though some scholars preferred to date the earliest part of the list of southern districts to the first period of the kings, this suggestion had to be abandoned after the studies of Alt (1913, 1925, 1927): the list cannot be earlier than the time of king Josiah, so it cannot have been compiled before the last quarter of the seventh century BCE.

5.8.3.3 Finally, what has been said so far would be a good explanation for the marked resentment of the North about the house of David and the very concept of empire, even if it is recognized that the texts do not explicitly say that the South regarded the North as conquered land, to be exploited.

In conclusion, then, if it can be said that there is evidence for the division of the North into administrative districts for the purpose of taxation, nothing of this kind is reported directly of the South.

5.9 Forced labour

A characteristic element of the way in which the tribute was collected by the administrations of David and Solomon is that communities and individuals were conscripted for forced labour. There are parallels to this among all the states in the region, but in Israel under Solomon it must have assumed abnormal and thus intolerable proportions.

Bibliography

J.A.Soggin, 'Compulsory Labor under David and Solomon', in T.Ishida (ed.), *Studies in the Period of David and Solomon and Other Essays*, Tokyo 1982, 259-67 (and bibliography).

5.9.1 At that time a system of labour required of communities and individuals was a substitute for the payment of tax in money or in kind; even today, moreover, such work can be called for in cases of public utility, especially in emergencies.

5.9.2 In Hebrew the term *mas*, of Canaanite origin, was used for work generally: later, however (and down to the present day in modern Hebrew), the term increasingly took on the meaning of 'tax' generally, so that the participle *'ōbēd* was added to it, thus providing the meaning 'tax paid by means of manual labour' (Soggin 1982).

5.9.2.1 Its characteristic was that the work exacted was *imposed* on the community and individuals, a factor which, given its spread, did not necessarily mean that it came up against preconceived hostility. In Israel something evidently happened to make this form of taxation unacceptable; there may have been at least two reasons for this which are not mutually exclusive: people did not see the use of it, and the labour demanded became so onerous that it jeopardized the income of the family and the community.

5.9.2.2 Some observations on the text will help to clarify the matter. I Kings 5.27f. states without a shadow of doubt that 'all Israel' was conscripted for the forced labour, something which is not stated by the parallel text (II Chron.2.16). Josephus, *Antt.* VIII, 58, confirms the text of I Kings 5. However, the information in I Kings 9.15a, 20-22 (LXX 10.22a-c)//I Chron 8.8-10 (and 2.16 quoted above) differs: here only the Canaanites who had been subjected were conscripted for the work.

Moreover this last version of events is either Deuteronomistic or even later and belongs to the hagiographical tradition. The first text gives the information which is closest to reality, and in it 'Israel' probably stands only for the North and not for the whole empire.

5.9.2.3 It is no longer possible to establish when the system was introduced: the fact that it is attested amost everywhere would seem to favour the theory that it was introduced with the foundation of the state. According to II Sam.12.31, David conscripted some of the populations of Transjordan for the labour – the best explanation of this otherwise obscure text. For the pre-Israelite evidence cf. the el-ʿAmarna archive (above 2.8) and the texts of Alalakh and Ugarit. There is even the Canaanism *massu* in the el-ʿAmarna texts.[19]

5.9.2.4 It is reasonable to conclude that this practice, especially if taken to extremes, was one of the main reasons for the frequent disorders which afflicted particularly the North and peripheral regions.

5.10 Enlightenment

A last feature. During recent years the wisdom traditionally attributed to Solomon (above 5.2.1) has often been spoken of in terms of the somewhat infelicitous expression 'the enlightenment' of the Solomonic period.[20] Already at that time Eastern wisdom is said to have made its entry into Israel, and especially into Judah, in particular in the reign of a ruler who has gone down in history and legend for his wisdom; the country is said to have been open to international culture, to the great wisdom currents of the period. The foundations for works like the J source of the Pentateuch, the Joseph story and the 'succession narrative' have been related to this movement.

5.10.1 The thesis was authoritatively proposed some decades ago by G.von Rad, but since there is no concrete information relating to it, this is no more than speculation with no foundation for conclusions.[21]

5.10.2 That seems even clearer in the case of a hypothesis which has often been repeated over recent years. It argues that wisdom schools will have appeared in this period, schools in which future officials will have received the training that they needed for their work in public administration. But given the silence of the sources (nothing is said, for example, about these schools or whether the officials in question bore the title of sages, Hebrew *ḥᵃkāmīm*), it can only be supposed that David and Solomon made use of the existing bureaucratic structures, Canaanite and Egyptian, incorporated in the various city-states, without too many problems.[22]

5.10.3 Of course it is possible that the period of the empire of David and Solomon was a period of cultural openness; however, we have no certain information about this, and the fact that the texts which report Solomon's wisdom are mostly legendary counsels the utmost prudence.

PART TWO

The Traditions about the Origins of the People

6

The Patriarchs

Like so many other peoples, Israel and Judah too had traditions which spoke of their own prehistory. Various narrative cycles fall under this theme: the migration of the patriarchs, the slavery in Egypt and the exodus, the migrations through the desert, the 'conquest', the time of the Judges. The difficulty for a historical evaluation of this material does not lie in its scarcity: it is in fact possible to affirm that there are many traditions of this type; the difficulty is of a qualitative kind, in that all these traditions were set down at a relatively late period, often more than five hundred years after the events to which they refer, and it is difficult if not impossible today to establish whether material from ancient tradition has in fact been preserved and handed down and if so to what degree. Moreover, in the few cases in which the antiquity can be taken to be certain, it is no longer possible to establish how far the material has been corrupted (above 3.1.4).

Bibliography

P.W.Lapp, *The Dhahr Merzabāneh Tombs*, New Haven, Conn. 1966, 86ff.; J.Scharbert, 'Patriarchentradition und Patriarchenreligion', *VuF* 19.1, 1974, 2-22 (bibl.); T.L.Thompson, *The Historicity of the Patriarchal Narratives*, Berlin 1974; J.Van Seters, *Abraham in History and Tradition*, New Haven and London 1976; W.McKane, *Studies in the Patriarchal Narratives*, Edinburgh 1977; M.Weippert, 'The Israelite "Conquest" and the Evidence from Transjordan', in F.M.Cross (ed.), *Symposium Celebrating the Seventy-Fifth Anniversary of the Foundation of the American Schools of Oriental Research, 1900-1975*, Cambridge, Mass 1979, 15-34; M.Liverani, 'Un'ipotesi sul nome di Abramo', *Hen* 1, 1979, 9-18; A.R.Millard and D.J.Wiseman (eds.), *Essays on the Patriarchal Narratives*, Leicester 1980; J.J.Scullion, 'Some Reflections on the Present State of Patriarchal Studies', *AbrN* 21, 1982-83, 50-65; H.Seebass, 'Gehörten Verheissungen zum älteren Bestandteil der Väter-Erzählungen?', *Bib*

64, 1983, 189-210; W.Thiel, 'Geschichtliche und soziale Probleme der Erzväter-Überlieferungen in der Genesis', *TheolVers* 14, 1985, 11-27; A.Lemaire, 'La Haute Mésopotamie et l'origine des Benē Jacob', *VT* 34, 1984, 95-101; Donner* 1984, I, ch.5; Miller and Hayes* 1987, ch.2; P.K.McCarter, 'The Historical Abraham', *Int* 42, 1988, 341-52; M.Weinfeld, 'The Promise to the Patriarchs and its Realization: An Analysis of Foundation Stories', in M.Heltser and É.Lipiński (ed.), *Society and Economy in the Eastern Mediterranean (c.1500-1000 BC)*, Louvain 1988, 353-69; J.Pons, 'Confrontation et dialogue en Genèse 12-36', *ETL* 65, 1990, 15-26; L.Schmidt, 'Väterverheissung und Pentateuchfrage', *ZAW* 104, 1992, 1-27. The volume *Die Väter Israels – FS Joseph Scharbert*, ed. M.Görg, Stuttgart 1989, is devoted to all the patriarchal traditions.

6.1 Problems. Abraham

There is an evident relationship between some of the texts in the patriarchal narratives, especially those transmitted by the J source, and texts which refer to the kingdom of David and Solomon. In fact it seems clear that J, which brought together the majority of the material that might be pre-exilic, saw some texts – we do not know whether this was at a possible earlier stage of the collection – functioning as 'divine promise' and 'fulfilment'; in them the empire of David and Solomon was the fulfilment of ancient promises. That is particularly evident where the patriarchal texts refer to the possession of the land of Canaan and to numerous descendants, and also to the descendants of the patriarchs as a great nation, Hebrew *gōy gādōl*, in contrast to the term 'people', Hebrew *'am*, which is regularly used (cf. Gen.12.2; 18.18 and Num.14.12 with II Sam.7.9b); it is clear that there is a manifest relationship between the promises to the patriarchs and those to David and that David is understood as in some way an antitype to Abraham.[1]

6.1.1 Of course, even if the reference exists, such considerations can relate to an earlier phase of the collection of the traditions; on the other hand it is clear that they fit admirably into a much later period, exilic or early post-exilic, in which the memory of happier times, lost for ever, lived on, and contrasted with a grey present in which the nation no longer existed, the people had been reduced to the minimum, the possession of the country had become doubtful and the monarchy had fallen for ever. The prophecies of the possession of the land and a great posterity were set against a reality which seemed to threaten precisely the opposite.

6.1.2 Now it is to the credit of Thompson 1974 and Van Seters 1975 that they established independently of each other[2] that the mention of ethnic groups, places and individuals in the patriarchal narratives makes sense only during and after the time of the united monarchy, and not before. So if ancient material has been handed down in these narratives, in no case whatsoever does it go back before the empire (Donner* I, 1984, 76ff.). It certainly does not give information about the migrations or relationships of peoples in the course of the second millennium BCE.

6.1.3 The biblical texts which relate to the patriarchs are concentrated in that section of the Pentateuch which runs from Gen.11.10ff. to the end of ch.50. As is well known, in Genesis the patriarchs appear in a genealogical sequence: Abraham, Isaac, Jacob and the eponymous heroes of the twelve tribes; chs. 37; 39-49, on the other hand, are devoted to the figure of Joseph. 11.10-27, 30-31 reports the genealogy of Shem according to P, followed by a note according to which Abraham's ancestors emigrated from 'Ur of the Chaldaeans' in south-eastern Mesopotamia to Harran in north-western Mesopotamia (cf. also Gen.11.28, generally attributed to J). The information also appears in the late texts Gen.15.7[3] and Neh.9.7. The place was an important caravan centre, attested as such from the beginning of the second millennium BCE.

6.1.4 At the beginning of Gen.12.1ff. Abraham obeys the divine call which bids him leave Harran, regarded as his homeland, to go to an unknown country which God will show him in due time; later (12.5) this proves to be Canaan. According to 11.31, Canaan as the goal of the journey was known from the beginning, but this is probably one of the many anticipations which are a typical element of the biblical narrative style.[4] We find that once Abraham has arrived at his destination he moves essentially in the southern part of the country: Hebron and the northern Negeb. Because of a famine (a favourite theme with the biblical writers), we see him making a short stay in Egypt (12.10-20): the narrative gives the picture of a well-ordered country, without famine (since the water is assured by the flooding of the Nile), and a safe refuge for anyone in difficulty. This description of Egypt is to last down to the New Testament (Matt.2.13-23), where the infancy narratives of the Gospels even speak of the 'flight into Egypt'. However, this description is soon joined by another, attested from the exodus narrative onwards: that of Egypt as a land of slavery and oppression, from which only the powerful hand of the God of Israel can free his people.[5] This theme then seems to have been developed fully by Deuteronomy and the Deuteronomist, who made it one of the central elements of Jewish piety down the millennia: from time immemorial it has been the foundation for the celebration of the Passover.

6.1.5 Some scholars have tried to connect Abraham's migration to Canaan with a hypothetical 'Amorite migration', said to have taken place in the same direction at the beginning of the second millennium BCE;[6] in this way they have hoped to be able to rediscover the presumed historical context of the narrative. But this theory can no longer be sustained in the light of the most recent research, in that it is based too much on doubtful interpretations of archaeological discoveries, whereas there are no consistent traces of new arrivals in Canaan at this period. There is also uncertainty at the chronological level (Lapp, Thompson). Hence the statement by Bright, still repeated in the last edition of his *History* (1981), seems all the more rash: 'We conclude, then, that the patriarchs were historical figures, a part of that movement of Northwest-Semitic (Amorite) people which brought a new infusion to the population of Palestine toward the beginning of the second millenium BC' (95).

6.1.6 The patriarchal narratives lack any specific details connected with the journey to Canaan, and the same goes for their account of the brief stay in Egypt: there are no itineraries, nor stopping places, nor is there any overall duration. The journey from 'Ur of the Chaldaeans' seems even more problematical, since the term 'Chaldaeans' is not used as early as the second millennium BCE but only in the first, when the Chaldaeans had settled in the region. However, as I have indicated above (3.1.7.2), the mention both of Ur and of the Chaldaean populations becomes perfectly probable once it is accepted that the patriarchal traditions were re-read at the end of the exile and in the period immediately after the exile: Abraham's route from Ur to Harran and from Harran to the land of Canaan then becomes the itinerary of those who returned home from the deportation and later the regular route between the southern Mesopotamian Diaspora and the homeland. The connection with the last king of Babylon, Nabonidus, at the end of the exile (below 13.1.1), seems less probable, though chronologically it is little earlier; were it accepted the exiles would have brought out a common origin, in a concern to show solidarity (this is the argument of Garbini* 1988, 78f.).[7]

6.1.7 Abraham's stay among the Philistines at Gerar (Gen.20.1-18) evidently also presupposes their settlement in the region, something which in any case could not have happened before the twelfth century (above 4.4.1.3).

Furthermore the name of their ruler, Abimelech, is a good Western Semitic name, already attested in the texts of el-ʿAmarna and Ugarit and also for four other figures in the Hebrew Bible, so that these Philistines now seem perfectly assimilated. Again, for millennia it was a regular phenomenon for 'Asiatic' groups to cross the isthmus of Suez and settle in Egypt; there is an illustration of a typical instance in the well-known frescoes on the tomb of Ḥnum Hotep at Beni Hassan (*ANEP*, no.3) from the nineteenth century BCE. The texts do not give the name of the Pharaoh with whom Abraham is said to have had dealings (and the same thing is true in the case of Joseph, the exodus narratives and Solomon's father-in-law, above 5.5.6) nor is there any mention of places which he visited;[8] this is evidently information which was of little or no interest to those who handed down the material in antiquity, or they simply lacked it altogether. To use a modern expression, their historical interest must have been virtually nil. Some scholars (Weippert, 1979; Liverani 1979; Lemaire 1984; McCarter 1988) have recently tried to identify a historical nucleus in the Abraham traditions: his group is said to have belonged to the semi-nomads which were on the move in the region between the Bronze Age and the Iron Age: these are hypotheses which take the discussion forward but which cannot resolve an insoluble problem in the present state of research.

All these features clearly make it very doubtful whether the narrative corresponds to historically ascertainable facts.

6.2 Isaac

The figure of Isaac appears with similar characteristics to those of Abraham though on a smaller scale; he has 'been put completely in the shade'[9] by Abraham. Original features are the theme of the promise endangered first by the barrenness of Sarah, then by the divine demand to Abraham to sacrifice his only son (Gen.22.1ff.), and finally by his relations with Sarah's handmaid Hagar. The other information is modelled on that in the Abraham cycle: Isaac is born, marries, begets children, grows old and dies. Shortly before his death we have another original element: he is deceived by his wife Rebecca and his son Jacob. Also in Gerar, Isaac is involved in an incident similar to one in which Abraham was involved, with the same local ruler (Gen.26.1-11). It is easy to deduce from these few facts that the figure of Isaac has been played down in favour of that of his father Abraham and his son Jacob, who were evidently thought more important. It is impossible to demonstrate more, nor does it seem probable that this tells in favour 'of his priority'.[10]

6.3 Jacob

The information about Jacob is more complex, although in his case, too, it does not go beyond the characteristic of family detail and anecdotal folk-lore. Here, too, theological reflection plays an important part, in that it shows how the unscrupulous young man, capable of manipulating everything skilfully to his own advantage (often to the limits of what is acceptable and beyond), in the end becomes a pious patriarch.

6.3.1 Jacob is presented as the man who, to escape the understandable anger of his cheated brother, makes something like the reverse of

Abraham's journey, a journey which takes him back to his own Aramaean kinsfolk in the region of Harran (Gen.28.10ff.; 31.20,24). Only after many years does he return to Canaan. The region is called Aram Naharaim (Gen.24.10, a late text,[11] even if it is often attributed to J), whereas in P we often find the term *paddan 'ārām*, an Aramaic expression corresponding to the Hebrew *śᵉdeh 'ārām* (Hos.12.13). This is the region which appears in the cuneiform and Egyptian texts as *naḥ(a)rina* (or even, at the beginning of the millennium, *bīrīt narīm*, 'between the rivers', and from the middle of the millennium *naḥrīma*, *na'rīma* or *narīna*), the region between the Euphrates and the Balikh. The stress on the Aramaean character of the kinsfolk of Isaac and Jacob presupposes the settlement of this population in the region, which did not happen before the twelfth century BCE.[12]

6.3.2 The figure of Jacob has more concrete characteristics than those of his forebears and could at least partially go back to ancient traditions. The texts do not always present him with the same characteristics: first he is is a somewhat timid intriguer dependent on his mother; then he appears gifted with Herculean strength (29.1-14; 32.23-33); in the end he proves to be a skilful breeder of animals, but also a devout and pious man. There are also indications that he was active essentially in Transjordan.[13] From all this it is possible to deduce that various traditions were in circulation about Jacob, and this is also evident from the text cited in Hosea; however, it is impossible to affirm anything with certainty about the age of this material. Finally, in the Hebrew Bible Jacob often stands for 'Israel', the North, a development encouraged by the identity of the name.

6.4 Joseph

The cycle of patriarchal narratives ends with the Joseph story. It now serves to connect the patriarchal cycle with that of the oppression and the exodus. Unless all the signs are misleading, this is a late story, rightly called a 'Diaspora romance'.[14] Here too the theme of famine and seeking help in Egypt is important. The story illustrates the spiritual journey of a young man who is originally not very congenial and an idler, who matures through suffering and faith and becomes a pious patriarch, a blessing to those who have contact with him.

6.5 Characteristics of the narratives

The patriarchal narratives, with the exception of the Joseph story, have some characteristic features: a large number of the themes attested in them are the same and make exhaustive use of a variety of migrations; they also include plots against the tribal mother, who is portrayed as being very beautiful, by a foreign king who introduces her into his harem (increasing levity can be seen in these stories: Gen.12.10-20; 20.1-18; 26.1-11). There are also the constant relations between Syria in the north-east or Mesopotamia in the north-west, the region from which Abraham comes, and from which Isaac and Jacob take their wives (note the preoccupation, a reflection of later times, that these wives should not be chosen from among the women of Canaan, 'Hittites', 24.1ff.; 27.46; 28.1), the stress being on the Aramaean character of their kindred in Mesopotamia. And the ancestor of the person making the offering in Deut 26.3bff., a kind of confession of faith to be recited at the time of the offering of the first fruits, is called a 'wandering...' or 'lost Aramaean'.

6.5.1 So it seems clear that, even if the biblical tradition means to put the patriarchs a long time before the institution of the monarchy (the figures given in Gen.15.13 and I Kings 6.1 are 400 and 480 years respectively, making a total of around 880 years between the patriarchal period and the beginning of the monarchy), the model that the authors or those who handed down the tradition offer is not that of the semi-nomads attested, for example, in central-northern Mesopotamia at the end of the first half of the second millenium BCE, although a comparison on the sociological and economic plane could be valid up to a certain point.[15] The biblical authors do not present the patriarchs as semi-nomads at all, but as migrants from one region to another.[16] It is no longer possible to establish whether or not the model goes back to an ancient tradition, but it is evident that it expresses perfectly the situation of the many deportees who prepared to go home on the fall of the Babylonian empire and, in the case of the people of Judah, the constant relations with the Mesopotamian Diaspora.

6.5.2 The genealogical line which now connects the patriarchs appears to be anything but original.

6.5.2.1 In the ancient Near Eastern world and in the classical world the genealogy appears as the most adequate instrument for explaining the origins of a people or a nuclear family. Both are seen as the product of the natural increase, in varying circumstances, of the progenitor, the patriarch, the eponymous hero. For the West it is enough to recall the relations between the *gens Iulia* and Aeneas; for the modern Arab world the descent in some form from the Prophet or at least from his tribe (for example the kings of Jordan and Morocco), a matchless and legitimizing status symbol, especially when combined with political power.

6.5.2.2 However, this approach to the problem seems totally inadequate on a historical level: Gottwald[17] shows convincingly that it presents a series of insoluble problems, as soon as it moves away from the protagonists to become occupied with secondary figures: wives, concubines, sisters, daughters, handmaids. However, it appears more than adequate for its intended purposes, whether political, religious, or otherwise with a view to legitimization,[18] though not at the level of history and ethnology.

6.5.3 Again, the sparseness of the information and its stereotyped character, connected with differing topographical locations (Abraham in the region of Hebron, Isaac usually in the northern Negeb, Jacob in the central hill-country in the region of Shechem),[19] make it quite possible, as indeed has long been recognized, that the three figures all existed at the same time, or even (if one wants to be even more critical) that they did not exist at all.[20] M.Weinfeld 1988 rightly works here with the category of 'foundation legend'.

6.5.4 In other words, perhaps already in the monarchical period, but certainly at the end of the exile and in the first part of the restoration, Judah confessed that there was a special relationship between it and its land, the 'holy land', which we can well call 'theological'; this land had been granted to it freely by God to enjoy, though God continued to be its absolute sovereign. This relationship between Judah and its land could always be put in doubt and jeopardy by events ranging from the expeditions of foreign kings (for example that of Pharaoh Shoshenk/Shishak I at the end of the tenth century BCE, I Kings 14.25-28// II Chron.12.8-11, cf. below 10.6) to the deportations first by Assyria and then by Babylon, up to the return to the homeland in conditions of extreme hardship and the loss of political independence (below, 13.3).

6.5.5 However, one can hardly call this discourse on its own past 'history', regardless of whether it refers to real historical or supposedly historical figures; rather, it is a theology of history, an attempt to explain, to motivate by means of a confession of faith, what had in fact been a catastrophe on the ethnic and political plane. To the inescapable reality of the political and economic disaster is opposed the confession of faith in the God who guides history; through this confession of the sovereignty of the Creator and the Lord of the universe and of history, to whom the future belongs, the sufferings of the present will (if one can put it that way) be compensated, a basic albeit relatively late feature of the faith of Israel.

6.5.6 As has already been indicated elsewhere, these observations are not new: they have been made many times from the end of the last century onwards (above 3.1); then, some decades afterwards, by Gunkel, by his pupil Gressmann and even later by Galling.[21] Like Thompson, I would like to quote the following conclusive phrase from Gressmann on the Abraham traditions: 'The migration or, as one should say, the nomadism of this patriarch is not therefore based on any historical remembrance but is an artificial composition by the narrator of legends (*Sagen*), intended to hold different traditions together. This observation, an elementary one in connection with the study of legends, *a priori* rules out any modern attempt to argue that the "migration of Abraham from Ur in Chaldaea to Hebron" is something that happened in real life even with the support of the imagination.'[22]

6.5.7 So it cannot fail to cause surprise that during and after the Second World War there was a new apologetic development, especially in the United States, which aimed rather to demonstrate that the biblical traditions about the prehistory of Israel have a credible historical background despite the substantial objections made decades before. The North American archaeologist and explorer Nelson Glueck often mentions in his writings what he calls 'the astonishing historical memory of the Bible',[23] and a similar view has been put forward by some North American and Israeli scholars, usually archaeologists and philologists, shaped by the teaching of W.F.Albright (for whom cf. above 3.5.2.1).[24] However, shortly before Albright's death, one of the most distinguished of his pupils, the archaeologist G.E.Wright, tried to revise such positions considerably.[25] For scholars in the Albright school, the difference between the history of Israel as confessed by the people of God and that reconstructed by historical criticism over the last century is only an apparent one, and is supposed to be bridged by the progressive convergence of the two histories as a result of new archaeological discoveries. Consequently these scholars do not dramatize the problem in any way (cf. below 8.7). By contrast, on the continent of Europe the majority of scholars have tended to indicate the depth of the difference, and some even see it as a serious problem for biblical scholarship.[26] However, this divergence is only natural and typical in the circumstances, as I have tried to demonstrate elsewhere.[27]

6.5.8 Over the years, then, what we might call the 'Albright school' has tried to argue for the substantial historical authenticity of the narratives about the patriarchs and about the exodus, the 'conquest' and the period of the Judges, while not excluding the existence of dubious features in matters of detail. So until very recently we find frequent references to 'the patriarchal age' or equivalent expressions, as if we had to do with a clearly defined and delimited historical period like that of Ur III or Hammurabi in Mesopotamia. However, the reality is very different, as even a superficial look at the works which argue for the essential authenticity of the traditions will show: the various scholars put the patriarchs in periods which range from the beginning of the second millennium (very rarely at the end of the third millennium) to the end of the first half or soon after the first half or even the end of the second millennium; and it is precisely this vagueness on a chronological level (a vagueness which arises exclusively from the inadequacy of the sources) that is the best proof of the historically elusive character of the material at our disposal. Therefore even without *a priori* adopting a sceptical attitude towards this material, we need to take the utmost possible care in evaluating it or using it. Sometimes we have to be so careful that it seems doubtful whether the sources are of any value to the historian. So while Bright* 1981, 69, may call for 'a new and more sympathetic evaluation of the traditions', it must also be pointed out that what might seem a lack of sympathy is not due so much to preconceptions, far less to cynicism or even 'nihilism' (as one sometimes hears), as to the very nature of the sources at our disposal. On the European continent the German scholars Alt and Noth have certainly shown more than 'sympathetic' (to use Bright's term) attitudes to the material (even if these attitudes are not always evaluated as such); for example the latter[28] was ready to admit in broad outline that in the context of the patriarchal narratives '...there are real and manifest features, and, moreover, of such a specific kind that it is necessary to connect them with some historical element' (here the author is thinking of the semi-nomads attested around the Mesopotamian city-state of Mari, above 6.5.1, especially in connection with nomenclature and customs) and their relationship to the patriarchs. And that is certainly much more than we are prepared to admit today, about thirty years after the publication of these remarks.

6.5.9 Finally, the parallels which seemed to exist betwen the customs attested among the patriarchs and those found in other legal texts[29] (and which do not appear later in other texts of the Bible) have meanwhile proved for the most part untenable, based as they were on inadequate interpretations of the texts or on impossible parallels between substantially different sociological and legal situations. As for patriarchal nomenclature, here again all we can say is that the names of the patriarchs, or names with a similar formation, are widespread throughout the ancient Near East, from the Ebla texts (at the end of the third millennium BCE) to the beginning of the first millennium BCE. So when we take into account that names tend to persist down the generations within a constant linguistic context, it seems impossible to use them as a criterion for dating; there is in fact a span of more than a thousand years.[30] Other names belonging to the patriarchal entourage, like Terah, Nahor, Serug, are all place-names attested around Harran, the contemporaneous existence of which has been proved only for the period spanning the end of the second and the beginning of the first millennium BCE. This, moreover, is a period in which the references to the Aramaeans also make sense.[31]

6.5.10 So the problem seems to have remained the same, and decades of studies with an apologetic slant, based on archaeolgoical discoveries, have failed to resolve it. Of course I do not mean to deny the possibility that individual traditions may be unique and in some way go back to actual memories about people who existed and to facts which happened; however, what is lacking in the present state of research is any possibility of even comparative, let alone historical, corroboration. What we can affirm, though, is what Judah confessed many centuries later to have been its own prehistory, a prehistory which was so interesting because in it the people of God saw a foreshadowing, an explanation of, and sometimes even a reason, a legitimation, for its own present existence. And at this point, of course, the problem remains whether these last factors were not the ones which more often than not determined the tradition! It seems difficult to say much more.

6.6 Traditions and context

That having been said, I now want to move on to a detailed analysis of individual traditions, seeking to show how they have been inserted into their new contexts.[32]

6.6.1 The itinerary of the migration of Abraham's ancestors from 'Ur of the Chaldaeans' (Gen.11.28, 31; 15.7; Neh.9.7) to Harran does not present any difficulties: the two points are well known and the itinerary must have followed one of the two banks of the Euphrates.

Ur is usually identified with *tell el-muqáyyar*, the site of ancient Sumerian Ur, today about half-way between Baghdad and the Persian Gulf.[33] Of course it is impossible to demonstrate that the biblical author identified his Ur with Sumerian Ur,[34] so it is not surprising that modern scholars have again directed their researches towards another location, in the north-north-west of Mesopotamia, near to Harran.[35] In this case, however, the mention of the Chaldaeans seems completely out of place, since they lived in the southern region. In any case the very reference to this people presents difficulties: the Hebrew Bible itself mentions them only from Hab.1.6 and Jer.21.14 onwards, i.e. not before the second half of the seventh century BCE! It so happens, however, that the LXX has an interesting variant: in v.11 it reads ἐκ τῆς χώρας τῶν Χαλδαίων, and in v.28 ἐν τῇ χώρᾳ τῶν Χαλδαίων. The variant presupposes the Hebrew *mē'ereṣ* and *bᵉ'ereṣ* instead of *mē'ūr* and *bᵉ'ūr*, i.e. with an extra ṣ in the consonantal text; this is then a general reference to a region which could also be situated towards the north. Albright[36] proposed an original reading *mē'ūr, bᵉ'ereṣ kaśdīm*, of which the Hebrew text will have omitted the second word and the LXX the first, but this proposal does not seem to have found much of a following.

6.6.1.1 But why migrate from Ur to Harran? One might recall the suggestion by Garbini (above 6.1.6) which I regarded as inadequate. Others believe[37] that a reasonable explanation of the journey is the fact that both places were the sites of an important sanctuary dedicated to

Sin, the moon god to which Nabonidus, the last king of Babylon, w is devoted; and some names in Abraham's group seem to refer to a lunar cult: Terah and Laban are both certainly lunar names, while Sarah and Milcah probably are too. And that would lend probability to a journey of this kind by some of Abraham's ancestors.[38]

6.6.1.2 However, a careful examination of the question produces a different result: the note was constructed first by J in its late phase and then by P; conditions in Judah in the second half of the sixth century BCE would seem very appropriate to the time of the Priestly writing, and the mention of the Chaldaeans is relevant then.[39] The itinerary from the south-east of Mesopotamia to the north-west, and then on to the Promised Land, is then the itinerary of the exiles in the course of their journey home, and later the line of communication between the Babylonian Diaspora and the mother country. The position of Harran, apparently too far north, could be explained by the fact that it was an important caravan centre. From there the route went westwards, and then turned south after reaching Syria. In this case the mention of 'the Chaldaeans' unexpectedly becomes logical, serving to distinguish the place from others of the same name; it also explains why, if we leave out Gen.11.31, the theme appears always and only in late texts. Finally it should be noted that Gen.12.1ff. and the traditions of Isaac and Jacob regard Harran, and not Ur, as the home of the patriarchs.

6.6.1.3 Explanations of this kind become even more probable if we suppose that the Deuteronomistic History wanted not only to retell the history of the people but also to lay the foundations for its restoration;[40] however, Deutero-Isaiah (below 13.1.4) sees the return of those who had been deported as a second exodus, a feature which Isa. 41.8-10 specifically connects with the election of the patriarchs.

6.6.2 Genesis 14 is the only text which connects the person of Abraham with events which are said to have thrown Syria and Cannan or at least a good part of them into confusion: the expedition of the four eastern kings against the five city-states situated in the region of the Dead Sea (the 'Valley of Siddim').

Bibliography

The commentaries on Genesis and especially E.A.Speiser, *Genesis*, AB, Garden City, NY 1965; C.Westermann, *Genesis* II, Minneapolis 1985 and London 1986; J.A.Soggin, *Genesi* II, Genoa (in preparation), all *ad loc.*; M.Weippert, *The Settlement of the Israelite Tribes in Palestine*, SBT II 21, London 1971, 93-8; J.A.Emerton, 'Some False Clues in the Study of Gen.XIV', *VT* 21, 1971, 24-47; and 'The Riddle of Gen. XIV', ibid., 403-39; W.Schatz, *Genesis 14, eine Untersuchung*, Bern 1972; Thompson, *Historicity*, ch.IX; Van Seters, *Abraham in History and Tradition*, 112-20;

Y.Muffs, 'Abraham the Noble Warrior', *JJS* 33, 1982, 81-107; J.Ha, *Genesis 15*, Berlin 1989, 201-4.

6.6.2.1 Of the four countries mentioned in connection with the eastern kings, only two can be identified, Mesopotamia and Elam; the identity of the other two is doubtful: what Elassar is is disputed, whereas the second name, *gōyīm* ('of the nations'), is generic. The five city-states of the valley have yet to be identified, and the note that the region of the Dead Sea was very fertile and densely populated (a note which also appears independently in Gen.13.10) before the region was destroyed by a vast cataclysm (Gen.19.24ff.) seems doubtful. The note savours of myth: we do not in fact have any evidence whatsoever for affirming that the region will once have been fertile and densely populated, and then destroyed by a combination of earthquakes and volcanic eruptions, even if such phenomena have been repeated from time to time.[41]

6.6.6.2 Innumerable studies on the chapter have all led to essentially negative results. In the case of the eastern nations and kings we either have too many figures and countries for possible identifications or not enough, while we know nothing at all about the kings of the cities of the valley.[42] The results of the proposal by E.A.Speiser, that the text is founded on an unknown cuneiform document, are no better. In the most favourable case the framework which we have is completely confused and therefore cannot be used by the historian. Finally, as Van Seters relevantly observes, there was only one period in which Mesopotamia and Elam were united and could have undertaken an expedition together – the Persian period!

6.6.2.3 The aim of the texts seems, rather, to be the legitimation of the paying of tithes to the temple of Jerusalem, which happens in vv.17-24 (cf. also Ps.110.4, an archaic or archaizing text).

6.6.2.4 The expedition of the four kings is said to have involved Abraham through his nephew Lot, who had come with him from Harran and parted company with him to go and live at Sodom. The kings take Lot prisoner, but Abraham succeeds in catching up with the rearguard of the four kings and freeing his own kinsfolk and the other prisoners, following the enemy as far as Dan (14.14) – a gross anachronism if we compare the note with Judg. 18.29 (below 8.2.7). On Abraham's return the king of Salem (usually identified with Jerusalem) offers him provisions, receiving from him in exchange a tithe of the booty.

6.6.3 In Gen.14.13 Abraham is called *hā'ibrī*, the Hebrew, a designation which from the 1930s onwards has often been connected with the ethnic-political entity that the Egyptian texts call *'prw*, the Ugaritic texts *'prm* and the Accadian *ḫabīrū* (sometimes a transcription of the logogram SA-GAZ).The Accadian term has often been translated 'brigand', 'criminal' or 'bandit' (figures for whom Accadian, however, normally uses the term *ḫabatu(m)*). So the term was for a while confused with some form of brigandage, and its real nature was only discovered recently.

Bibliography

The texts were brought together by J.Bottéro, *Le problème des Habiru*, Paris 1954, and M.Greenberg, *The Hab/piru*, New Haven 1955. Cf. also B.Landsberger, 'Ḫabiru and Lulaḫḫu', *Kleinasiatische Forschungen* 1, 1930, 321-34; R.Borger, 'Das Problem der ʿApiru (Ḫabiru)', *ZDPV* 72, 1958, 121-32; M.P.Gray, 'The Habiru-Hebrew Problem in the Light of the Source Material Available at Present', *HUCA* 29, 1958, 135-202; M.Liverani, 'Il fuoruscitismo in Siria nella tarda età el bronzo', *RSIt* 77, 1965, 315-36; M.B.Rowton, 'The Topological Factor in the Ḫapiru Problem', in *Studies in Honor of Benno Landsberger*, Chicago 1965, 375-87; N.A.van Uchelen, *Abraham der Hebreeër*, Assen 1965, 71-105; M.Weippert, *The Settlement*, 63-102; R.de Vaux, 'Le problème des Hapiru après quinze années', *JNES* 27, 1968, 221-8; M.Weippert, 'Abraham der Hebräer?', *Bib* 52, 1972, 407-32; H.Schult, 'Eine einheitliche Erklärung des Ausdrucks "Hebräer" in der israelitischen Literatur', *DBAT* 10, 1975, 22-40; N.P.Lemche, ' "Hebrew" as National Name for Israel', *ST* 33, 1979, 1-23; W.Thiel, *Die soziale Entwicklung Israels in vorstaatlicher Zeit*, Berlin 1980 (Neukrichen ²1985), 76-9; O.Loretz, *Habiru-Hebräer*, Berlin 1984; Jagersma* 1982, 1-13; N.P.Lemche, *Early Israel*, Leiden 1985; N. Naʾaman, 'Habiru and Hebrews: The Transfer of a Social Term to the Literary Sphere', *JNES* 45, 1986, 217-88; Lemche* 1988, 85ff., 89f. and 133.

6.6.3.1 In Accadian, *ḫ* usually transcribes the semitic ʿ, while in all the Semitic languages, as in some Indo-European languages, the change between *b* and *p* is frequent.[43] So it seems evident that the various designations that I have cited relate, etymologically speaking, to a single root. Moreover, it has often been suggested that when the Hebrew term *ʿibrī* is not just a synonym for 'Israelite', but indicates some form of social stratification, it should be connected with these groups and located in the context of the disturbances which they caused to the life of the Canaanite city-states, especially in the late Bronze Age. This could be a confirmation of, or at least an allusion to, what the biblical texts present as the Israelite 'conquest' in the same period (below, 8.1ff.). Thus this event would at least be touched on in the extra-biblical documentation of the period, especially in what is said in the el-ʿAmarna letters, even if it is not directly mentioned. This is not the place for summarizing the whole discussion; it should be enough to have indicated the dimensions of the problem.

6.6.3.2 Now the studies of these last decades, and especially the basic article by Liverani 1965, have established beyond a shadow of doubt that the term in no instance denotes an ethnic entity or criminal group, but a sociological element. This is characterized by its lack of any rights in its place of residence; this is the typical fate of the 'outlaw', the refugee sometimes for political or more often for economic reasons, a figure like that found in Anglo-Saxon jurisprudence. Reduction to this state (because we clearly must speak of reduction) could come about at the will of the interested party, but could also come about quite independently of his own free will (cf. below, 6.6.3.4).

6.6.3.3 Their condition made the *ḫapiru* seem a disturbing, destabilizing element in the place in which they came to live, and in the most serious cases they even threatened or caused a crisis for the established order. That also explains the frequent charges of brigandry, which is also supported by the transcription of the logogram SA-GAZ. The case of David fleeing from Saul (cf. above, 4.3) is a valid example within the Hebrew Bible: in fact 'everyone who was in distress, and everyone who was in debt and everyone who was discontented' came to join the future king (I Sam.22.1f.).[44] Thus the theory of Rowton 1965, who seeks to divide the *ḫapīrū* 'ecologically', putting them in particularly suitable territories, does not seem tenable.

6.6.3.4 This element could explain the use of the term *ʿibrī* in the Hebrew Bible, where it is not the ethnic designation of an Israelite, but denotes a particular social condition. Thus for example we have the case of the 'Hebrew' slave (Ex.21.2-6; Deut.15.12-18; cf. also Jer.34.9-14), a category in need of particular protection because it was probably composed of individuals who had entered into slavery voluntarily, thus being guaranteed a roof and food. A parallel, this time a real one, comes from the legal texts of the north-eastern Mesopotamian city state of Nuzi, where we have the case of people who voluntarily go into slavery because they are *ḫapīrū*, and this is the only way in which they can keep alive.

6.6.3.5 Here was clearly an institution which lent itself to a variety of abuses, in Israel as elsewhere, hence the need for it to be regulated adequately.[45] Later, however, first the Egyptians and then the Philistines use the term *ʿibrī* with disparaging connotations, with that derogatory attitude which many people have towards the poor stranger. Then the term went on to denote, in Israel, the condition of people under foreign oppression, while at a late stage (cf. Jonah 1.9; Gen.14.13) it simply became synonymous with 'Israelite', a meaning which it has kept down to the present day. For all the relevant passages the reader must be referred to a concordance and to the study by Loretz, which needs to be examined critically. However, these considerations would prove useless if the proposal of Schult 1975 proved correct. She argues that all the texts in question are post-exilic (a proposal rejected by Loretz 1984, 12ff. and passim, but not always with convincing arguments): in that case *'ibrī* is simply synonymous with Jewish or Judahite.

6.6.3.6 There can only be one conclusion: despite some statements to the contrary,[46] the *'prm/ḫapīrū* have nothing in common with Israel and Judah in prehistory, even if it is possible, as seems likely, to establish an etymological connection.

6.7 Religion

In his 1929 study, which rightly remained famous and normative for decades, Alt affirmed that it is possible to establish the type of religion practised by the patriarchs on the basis of certain statements made by the texts and a kind of religion attested in the ancient Near East, especially among non-sedentary peoples.

Bibliography

A.Alt, 'The God of the Fathers' (1929), in *Essays on Old Testament History and Religion*, Oxford 1966, 3-77; J.Lewy, 'Les textes paléo-assyriens et l'Ancien Testament', *RHR* 110, 1934, 26-54: 50-9; H.S.Nyberg, 'Studien zum Religionskampf im Alten Testament', *AfR* 75, 1938, 329-87; A.Alt, 'Zum "Gott der Väter" ', *PJB* 36, 1940, 93-104; J.P.Hyatt, 'Yahweh as "The God of My Father" ', *VT* 5, 1955, 130-6; J.Hoftijzer, *Die Verheissungen an die drei Erzväter*, Leiden 1956, 84-96 (important for the bibliography, with comments on earlier studies); F.M.Cross, 'Yahweh and the God of the Patriarchs', *HTR* 55, 1962, 225-59; id., *Canaanite Myth and Hebrew Epic*, Cambridge, Mass. 1973, chs. 1-2; K.T.Andersen, 'Der Gott meines Vaters', *ST* 16, 1962, 170-88; M.Haran, 'The Religion of the Patriarchs', *ASTI* 4, 1965, 30-55: 51f.; O.Eissfeldt, 'El and Yahweh', *JSS* 1, 1956, 25-37; H.Seebass, *Der Erzvater Israel*, Berlin 1966, 49-55; H.Cazelles, 'La religion des Patriarches', *SDB* VII, 1966, 141-55; H.Weidmann, *Die Patriarchen und ihre Religion*, FRLANT 94, Göttingen 1968; R.de Vaux, 'El et Baal, le Dieu des pères et Yahweh', *Ugaritica* 6, 1959, 501-17, and *Early History* I, 267-82; G.Fohrer, *History of Israelite Religion*, London and Nashville 1973, 27-42; H.Vorländer, *Mein Gott*, AOAT 23, Kevelaer 1975, 184-215: 224ff.; B.Diebner, 'Die Götter der Väter – eine Kritik der "Vatergott-Hypothese', *DBAT* 9, 1975, 21-51; R.Albertz, *Persönliche Frömmigkeit und offizielle Religion*, Stuttgart 1978, 77-81; N.Wyatt, 'The Problem of the "God of the Fathers" ', *ZAW* 90, 1978, 101-4: J.Van Seters, 'The Religion of the Patriarchs in Genesis',

Bibl 61, 1980, 220-33; Bright*, 95f.; Donner* I, 1984, 79ff.; M.Kockert, *Vätergott und Väterverheissungen*, Göttingen 1987; L.Schmidt, 'Eine radikale Kritik an der Hypothese von Vätergott und Väterverheiss-ungen', *TR* 84, 1989, 415-21.

6.7.1 The sources of the Pentateuch and especially J present the religion of Israel as having been continuous from the time of the patriarchs to that of Moses, though they use different and sometimes contradictory arguments. J makes the worship of YHWH begin even before the flood (Gen.4.26), whereas E and P (Ex.3 and 6 respectively) by contrast argue that the revelation of the Name took place in the time of Moses, though this is only the finalization of a pre-existing relationship. However, the assertion of Josh.24.2, 14, a text which is apparently independent of the Pentateuchal sources, differs: the patriarchs are said to have 'served' other gods beyond the Euphrates and Egypt, and this is a form of cult which their descendants are invited to eliminate, and to be converted to YHWH alone. It is obviously difficult to say how the ancient writers will have imagined such a conversion, which the descendants are also called on to bring about: for Gottwald,[47] this will have been a conversion in the more or less modern sense of the term: as we shall see later in more detail (below 8.5), the rebel rural masses will have accepted belief in YHWH, the liberator God, brought to them by a group coming from the eastern desert.

6.7.2 Now on the basis of the scant conclusions that can be drawn from the biblical tradition, in his pioneer work Alt tried to study the religion practised by the patriarchs, those groups from which Israel confessed that it was descended. These are the premises of his study:

6.7.2.1 'The origin of the people of Israel is based, historically speaking, on the union of its tribes in the common worship of the God YHWH', a development which does not seem to have taken place before their settlement in Canaan. Of course it is no longer possible to deduce from the traditions and legends an adequate picture of this process, which on the one hand was very complex, and on the other has been considerably simplified and schematized by the tradition.

6.7.2.2 The main discovery on which Alt based his own conclusions was that the patriarchs are never presented in the act of worshipping deities connected with the fertility of the soil or their flocks, or with the cycles of nature, nor do they appear in any way associated with the sanctuaries near which they settle or which belong to the region in which they live: Shechem, Bethel, Hebron (Mamre). The deity or deities which they worship (in the texts these are now identified with YHWH on the basis of the concept of continuity to which I referred above, 6.7.1) are given titles and designations indissolubly bound up with the person of the patriarchal head of the family who offers worship to them. So these are authentic personal deities, in the sense that they are identified through the person who is their follower.

6.7.2.3 The most important titles are:

'The God of my father' (Gen.31.5b; Ex.15.2; in the second case in parallelism with 'my God');

'The God of your father' (Gen.31.29b, with Sam. and LXX, the Hebrew text has the plural; 46.1; 50.17);

'Your God and the God of your father' (Gen.43.33);

'The God of Abraham' (Gen.31.53); however, it should be noted that he is called on together with the deity of the other partner to the alliance;

'The God of your father Abraham and your father Isaac' (Gen.28.13; the same in 32.10 but with the first-person suffix);

'The God of your father Abraham' (Gen.26.24).

Again, in the passage cited above, Gen.31.42, 53, we read that Jacob swore by 'the terror of Isaac his father' (Hebrew $b^e pahad$ '$\bar{a}b\bar{i}$...); such an unusual expression was explained by Albright in 1940,[48] followed by various other distinguished scholars,[49] as 'kinsman of Isaac', on the basis of the Palmyrene Aramaic $pahd\bar{a}$, 'family', 'tribe', cf. the Arabic $fahd$ or $f\bar{a}hid$, 'femur', 'loin', hence 'tribal branch from which a family originates'. However, this is a meaning which the term never has: the proposal by Müller 1976, 1980, to understand the term here as 'patron' (deity) seems better. The title attested in Gen.49.24, '$^a bir\ ya^{\cdot a}q\bar{o}b$, literally 'the mighty one of Jacob' (but perhaps we should read '$abb\bar{i}r$, 'the bull of Jacob'), is a parallel expression to 'the God of your father'. In the same archaic passage we find, again in parallelism, 'of the shepherd of the rock of Israel', $r\bar{o}'eh$ '$eben\ yi\acute{s}r\bar{a}'\bar{e}l$, but the text is corrupt and theerefore difficult to use. In the same phrase we find a reference to '$\bar{e}l$ $\check{s}adday$, an expression typical of P, but here in an earlier context.

6.7.2.4 For Alt these expressions are a sign that here we have that particular form of the deity which in the history of religion is called θεὸς πατρῷος: he is not connected either to the agricultural cycle of the seasons or to a sanctuary, but seems closely connected with the group of his own worshippers. He is usually anonymous and is named through the person of the patriarch. In Genesis he often appears with the title '$\bar{e}l$ rather than $^e l\bar{o}h\bar{i}m$, which suggested to Alt that he was originally connected with the sovereign of the Western Semitic pantheon called el or ilu, in Israel later assimilated to YHWH. In 1929 Alt had only a few parallel texts at his disposal, usually late; in fact he had to limit himself to the Nabataeans, who lived more than a millennium after the patriarchs, in southern Transjordan. However, in 1934 J.Lewy, setting out with the intention of criticizing Alt's theory, instead provided a series of ancient Assyrian texts coming from Caesarea in

Cappadocia (present-day Kültepe).[50] In them there appear not only the national deity Assur but also a deity called 'god of your father', often without any other designation or specification. Other examples have been discovered at Mari, where Aplaḥanda, king of Carchemish, writes to Ismaḥ Addu, viceroy of Mari, saying such things as: 'If you have not sent me anything because of the god of my father, my heart will be afflicted' (lines 15ff.).[51] Another later example (second half of the ninth century BCE) is that of *rakīb-'ēl*, patron (*b'l byt*) of the reigning house of *sam'al* in northern Syria.[52]

6.7.3 Perhaps I have devoted a disproportionate space to this problem, but that is because here we could perhaps have a surviving recollection of what might have been the type of religion professed by the ancestors of Israel and Judah before the settlement. Of course it is uncertain, because it is remote and dim. In fact the texts connect this form of religion with the non-sedentary stay of the patriarchs in Canaan, or at least what was later thought to have been such a stay; the numerous parallels in the ancient Near East are evidently a feature in favour of the thesis. But here, too, one can never be too careful: more than thirty years ago the Dutch scholar J.Hoftijzer pointed out that in the Hebrew Bible the mention of the God of the fathers is not limited to the period before the revelation of the name of YHWH (cf. Ex.18.4; I Chron.28.9; II Chron.17.4), so that it cannot serve to identify pre-Yahwistic religion. And in his 1975 study Diebner pointed out polemically that the excavations made at Mamre show that this sanctuary did not yet exist in the pre-exilic period. Finally, Van Seters 1980 would prefer to date the concept about the time of the exile, when in Judah, as we know, there was a debate on the problem of individual responsibility and the relationship of the individual to God.

6.7.4 The patriarchs are also said to have worshipped deities localized at particular sanctuaries, all now identified wtih YHWH, even if their names always appear with *'ēl*: Gen.31.13 and 35.7 mention an *'ēl-bēt'ēl*, probably to be connected with that sanctuary; Gen.21.33 attests worship of an *'ēl 'ōlām* at Beersheba (Gen.16.13) and *'ēl ro'ī* in an unspecified place in the Negeb. Then we have *'ēl 'elyōn*, whom Gen.14.18 (above 6.6.2) associates with the pre-Israelite cult of Jerusalem, but who is probably a late combination of two different deities who were then combined in YHWH, since ἐλιοῦν is also attested in classical texts in Syria; mention of him tends to give Gen.14 an archaic flavour. *El šadday*, with no location, appears essentially in P; the second element now appears in the inscription of Balaam in the text of *tell deir 'alla*. In Judg.9.4,46, outside the patriarchal context,[53] there then appear an *'el bᵉrīt* and a *ba'al bᵉrīt*, both connected with the sacred places of Shechem. Cross 1962 makes the interesting comment that the 'God of the fathers' has the same attributes as *'ēl*: bull, eternal, etc.

7

Slavery in Egypt and Exodus. Moses

7.1 'Israel' in Egypt

In the chronology of the Pentateuch, the migrations of the patriarchs are followed by the stay in Egypt, and this in turn is followed by the oppression and slavery, the exodus and the journey through the desert to the Promised Land. The Joseph story now serves as the connecting link between the two cycles, but, as we shall see in more detail shortly (below, 7.2), there are traditions which seem to be unaware of it. From time immemorial the material connected with the exodus from Egypt has been of central importance for Jewish faith and piety, and it is certainly no coincidence that the Christian tradition also makes a close connection between the redemptive death and resurrection of Jesus and the Passover.

Bibliography

H.H.Rowley, *From Joseph to Joshua*, Oxford [2]1951; S.Herrmann, *Israel in Egypt*, SBT II 27, London 1973: de Vaux, *Early History**, I-II; P.Weimar and E.Zenger, *Exodus – Geschichten und Geschichte der Befreiung Israels*, SBS 75, Stuttgart 1975; H.Engel, *Die Vorfahren Israels in Ägypten*, Frankfurt am Main 1979; T.N.D.Mettinger, *The Dethronement of Sabaoth*, CB – OTS 18, Lund 1982, 72-9; W.H.Schmidt, *Exodus, Sinai und Moses*, Darmstadt 1983, esp. 24ff.; for the popular traditions cf. D.Irvin, *Mytharion*, AOAT 32, Kevelaer 1978.

7.1.1 Given the importance of the events narrated in the exodus for Judaism and through that for Christianity, it is not surprising that over the past century research into their possible historicity has been constant and zealous. This is demonstrated by Hellmut Engel's learned and useful dissertation (1979). Studies of this kind have often concluded that the traditions are substantially historical.[1] John Bright*'s exclamation is famous because it is often quoted with approval:[2] 'It is not the sort of tradition any people would invent! Here is no heroic epic of migration, but the recollection of shameful servitude from which only the power of God brought deliverance.' The argument sounds fine; but can it be maintained in the light of what we know of people in similar conditions? The Roman tradition also has its recollection, of Aeneas, who emigrated after a defeat, with his old father on his shoulders and holding the hand of his little son: these are certainly moving figures, evoking our tenderness (even prompting memories from our school-days), but they are in no way glorious. Moreover, no people willingly mentions its own defeats, whether distant or recent, and when it cannot avoid doing this, the mention is usually made to show how much the heroism and constancy of those who were defeated helped to gain a new victory. The tradition that Rome had barely been founded when it became a city of refuge for all kinds of doubtful people, so that no one wanted to give their daughters to the Romans in marriage, hardly seems to compliment the protagonists, and it is clearly in this kind of narrative that we find mention of the slavery in Egypt or at least of conscription to forced labour. The problem is at the same time different and more complex; it is not in fact about what people invented or did not invent, but about what the tradition reports and its credibility in a historical setting. And in this task of verification we find some points worth noting, which initially seem to support the tradition.

7.1.2 The Israelite traditions about the settlement in Canaan stress that the invaders did not arrive from the north, which was the normal route followed by anyone invading the region and which was also used with variants by Abraham and Jacob, but certainly from the east and perhaps also from the south (below 8.2.1 and 8.2.5). This makes it at least probable that they had started from Egypt.[3]

7.1.3 Other features are less important, but also contribute towards reinforcing the tradition, postulating a stay in Egypt on the part of at least the ancestors of particular groups: in the milieu of the priestly class we find a number of names of Egyptian origin. So we have Hophni and Phinehas, the unworthy sons of the priest Eli, the teacher of the boy Samuel at the end of the second millennium BCE; much later, in the time of Jeremiah, we have Assir and Pashur: the first name has probably been vocalized wrongly and should be pronounced *'ōsīr, 'Osiris'.[4] Moses' own name (Hebrew *mōšeh*) is evidently Egyptian, though in Egyptian it is always combined with the name of a deity: *ah-, ka-. ra`-, tut*, i.e. 'son of NN'. That is the case for Moses despite the attempt to give a Hebrew etymology to the name in Ex.2.10, rather a clumsy attempt from a philological point of view. On the other hand, it fits well in the kind of popular tradition with which it is associated. However, the argument from nomenclature is not conclusive, as we have already seen on other occasions (above, 6.5.9): down to the rise of the Davidic monarchy, the region of Canaan and southern Syria was at least nominally under the rule of Egypt, and, as we saw at the beginning of this study (above 1.5), the two Hebrew states probably remained in this position down to the exile. This emerges clearly from the El-ʿAmarna letters; we know from other sources that Egypt had a garrison at Beth-shean (present-day *tell el-ḥuṣn*, coord. 198-213, a few hundred yards north of the modern place), while under David and Solomon relations seem to have been frequent and cordial, though with exceptions (above 4.7.1.1.4; 5.6.6). In these conditions the presence of foreign linguistic islands is quite likely, and it is not surprising that there are foreign influences on the language and the names.

7.1.4 But in the case of the sojourn in Egypt, too, the biblical material is such that it cannot be verified in any way, a fact which is moreover generally accepted. The only reliable feature seems to be the brief note according to which the 'Israelites' were employed on the building of the places Pithom and Raamses (Ex.1.11).[5] The first place probably corresponds to the Egyptian *pr.'tm*, 'house (= temple) of Atum' (with the omission of the *r* typical of the pronunciation of the New Kingdom) and is certainly in the region of *wādī et-tumeilat*, probably either *tell er-retābeh* or *tell el-mašḥūtā*. *ṭkw* was a few miles to the east; it is probably the Succoth of Ex.12.37. The site of Ramses is none other than the old Hyksos capital Avaris, rebuilt in the reigns of Sethos I (c.1291-1279) and especially Ramses II (c.1279-1212); the second of these rulers, under whom the building work was finished, gave his name to the city. It became *pr.r'mśśw*, 'house of Ramses'; later it was called Tanis, though we cannot discover whether here we have the same place under different names or two different places.

7.1.5 This identification is now usually accepted and would put the date of the slavery towards the beginning or the middle of the thirteenth century BCE.[6] In Hebrew the cities, whether built or rebuilt, have the title *ʿārē miškᵉnōt*, a term probably to be connected with the Accadian *maškantu* or *maškattu*, 'store', 'provision' (*AHw* II, 627),[7] so that it is often translated as 'store cities' or 'warehouse cities'. This is confirmed by Aquila and Symmachus, while LXX has πόλεις ὀχυράς, 'fortified cities'.[8] In any case it is noted that this is a term which was originally Accadian and not Egyptian or Western Semitic in origin; moreover, it is used rarely. It appears only in I Kings 9.19; II Chron.8.6, cf. also II Chron.16.4; 32.28.

7.2 Arrival in Egypt

The end of the Joseph story in Genesis connects the arrival of the patriarchs in Egypt with an invitation sent to them by the reigning Pharaoh (chs.46ff.). What had made this possible was the career of

Jacob's penultimate son, who had risen from being a slave to being prime minister. Ex.1.8 (J) also refers explicitly to the figure of Joseph: here, however, there is a reference to a Pharaoh, also not mentioned by name, who did not know Joseph and his debt of gratitude towards him and his descendants.

7.2.1 However, this is a tradition which is not without internal tension. In Gen.35.16-20 Jacob's youngest son is Benjamin, born some years after Joseph to the same mother Rachel, who died bringing him to birth; in 37.3f. Joseph appears as the 'son of Jacob's old age' and is therefore the favourite; then, however, the presence of Benjamin, who is still a youth, seems indispensable for the development of the story (Gen.43ff.); again in 37.2b; 39.1b (J) Joseph is sold to the Ishmaelites, whereas in 37.28, 36 these are Midianites: this is one of the classic passages for source analysis. The story is well known and here we can only dwell on the essentials. Having arrived in Egypt in a state of extreme wretchedness, Joseph is sold to an Egyptian nobleman. At first his fortunes go from bad to worse, but ultimately he succeeds in becoming the vizier of the kingdom, the highest post open to anyone who is not a member of the royal family. The narrators see in his spectacular career the well-deserved reward for his piety, his honesty and integrity, and his hard work, cf. Gen.39.7ff. and especially 45.5b, where after the dramatic recognition scene he declares to his brothers: 'God sent me before you to preserve life…: it was not you who sent me here but God; and he has made me a father to Pharaoh, and lord of all his house and ruler over all the land of Egypt.' As I pointed out, Exodus 1.8ff.(J) makes explicit reference to Joseph: 'Now there arose a new king over Egypt, who did not know Joseph…', thus implying that the Egyptians owed a debt of recognition to Joseph, a debt which the new Pharaoh chose to ignore.

7.2.2 However, there is another tradition about the migration of the patriarchs to Egypt, much terser, which is contained in what since von Rad has been called the 'confession of faith'; I have already mentioned it in connection with the religion of the patriarchs (above, 6.7.1). Deuteronomy 26.5b affirms: 'A wandering Aramaean was my father; and he went down into Egypt and sojourned there, few in number…', while in Josh.24.4 we read: '… but Jacob and his children went down to Egypt.' This version of the origin of the stay of 'Israel' in Egypt is not aware of any of the Joseph story; this is simply assimilated to 'Jacob and his sons'. The first is of course best known because it takes place on the narrative plane, the second sees only Jacob as the protagonist; the first is rich in details from folklore, topography and in part also chronology, and forms an organic and complete text, the second is completely lacking in these elements and simply notes the fact of the migration. If only the second version existed, one would not be able to see why a Pharaoh should have remembered Joseph, far less have been grateful to him. Now given that, as I have indicated (above 6.4), the Joseph story is almost certainly of late origin, it follows that the note Ex.1.8 must also be, since it presupposes it.

7.2.3 Against this duplication of versions and the internal tensions within the Joseph story we have to set a negative factor: the silence, in the present state of research, of the Egyptian sources. There is no information which could be connected with the migration of the patriarchs, nor do we know anything about an Asiatic vizier who could be associated with the figure and the work of Joseph. And since, as always happens, moreover, down to the death of Solomon, the Pharaoh remains anonymous (the title, cited without the article, is treated almost as if it were his proper name) either with Joseph or with the Pharaoh of the oppression and the exodus, scholars find themselves in the same situation as with the patriarchal traditions, because of the inadequacy and vagueness of the otherwise abundant sources at our disposal.

Bibliography

J.Vergote, *Joseph en Égypte*, Louvain 1959 (cf. the review by S.Morenz, *TLZ* 84, 1959, 401-16); G.von Rad, 'The Joseph Narrative and Ancient Wisdom', in *The Problem of the Hexateuch*, 292-300; id., *Die Josephgeschichte*, Neukirchen 1956: O.Eissfeldt, *Stammessage und Menschheitserzählung in der Genesis*, Berlin 1965; L.Ruppert, *Die Josepherzählung*, Munich 1965; R.N.Whybray, 'The Joseph Story and Pentateuchal Criticism', *VT* 18, 1968, 512-28; D.B.Redford, *A Study of the Biblical Story of Joseph (Genesis 37-50)*, SVT 20, Leiden 1970 (cf. the review by K.A.Kitchen, *OrAnt* 12, 1973, 233-42); G.W.Coats, 'The Joseph Story and Ancient Wisdom: An Appraisal', *CBQ* 35, 1973, 285-97; A.Meinhold, 'Die Gattung der Josephsgeschichte' (above, Chapter 6, n.13); H.Donner, *Die literarische Gestalt der alttestamentlichen Josephsgeschichte*, Heidelberg 1976; H.-P.Müller, 'Die weisheitliche Lehrerzählung im Alten Testament und seiner Umwelt', *WO* 9, 1977-78, 77-98; J.Scharbert, 'Joseph als Sklave', *BN* 37, 1978, 104-28; I.Willi-Plein, 'Historiographische Aspekte der Josephsgeschichte', *Hen* 1, 1979, 305-31; B.Geyer, 'The Joseph and Moses Narratives: Folk Tale and History', *JSOT* 15, 1980, 51-6; T.L.Thompson, 'History and Tradition', ibid., 57-61; H.C.Schmitt, *Die nichtpriesterliche Josephsgeschichte*, Berlin 1980; E.Blum, 'The Joseph Story and Divine Politics', *JBL* 106, 1987, 577-94; L.Ruppert, 'Zur neuen Diskussion um die Josephsgeschichte der Genesis', *BZ* NF 33, 1989, 92-7; C.Zaccagnini, 'Note sulla distribuzioni dei cereali nel Vicino Oriente del II e del I millennio', in R.Dolce and C.Zaccagnini (eds.), *Il pane del re*, Bologna 1989, 101-16; C.Grottanelli, 'Da re al profeta: distribuzione dei cereali ideale religioso nella bibbia ebraica', ibid., 117-

35; H.-J.Zobel, ' "Israel" in Ägypten?', in *Zur Aktualität des Alten Testaments – FS Georg Sauer zum 65.Geburtstag*, Frankfurt-Main 1992, 109-17; J.A.Soggin, 'Notes on the Joseph Story', in *Studies... G.W.Anderson*, Edinburgh 1993.

7.2.4 Martin Noth and Gerhard von Rad always expressed their scepticism about the historicity of the Joseph story. It never aims to relate history but has always had an eminently narrative and edifying function; it served first of all as a connecting link between the patriarchal cycle and that of the exodus.[9] Backwards, the connection with the patriarchal narratives is genealogical (but we have seen, above 6.5.2, that historical value is to be attributed to the genealogies); the connection forwards, however, proves generic. So on a formal level the narrative appears to be a self-sufficient literary unity which does not presuppose either what goes before or what comes afterwards; it is not, therefore, surprising that an increasing number of scholars today want to study it leaving aside the question of the Pentateuchal sources. Noth regarded it essentially as a novellistic amplification of a predetermined theme: the migration of Jacob and his sons to Egypt. The amplification is achieved by means of the insertion of a narrative theme, the elements of which are taken here and there from the rich arsenal of popular tradition and fable: the theme of the younger brother who is privileged and therefore envied; of Joseph as a 'teacher's pet' but also unsympathetic because he 'tells tales' (Gen.37.2b); of the man fallen on hard times who ends up by triumphing over adversity because he is pious and virtuous; of the unfaithful wife who accuses the honest young man who has spurned her advances (there is a very similar Egyptian narrative, that of the 'two brothers', *ANET*, 23ff.); and of the hostility of the brothers and their reconciliation after the triumph of the hero (a theme which also appears in the text of the statue of Idrimi, king of Alalakh, *ANET*, 557ff.). Von Rad again notes[10] that Joseph, his brothers and their father are given such individual characteristics that it is impossible to begin to think of them as eponymous heroes or heads of tribes. The atmosphere of the narrative is totally domestic (while that may be said of a large number of the patriarchal stories, here it seems to be taken to the limit). Moreover, here the family nucleus 'is' all Israel, so that the narrative element, the delight in story-telling, takes on clear paradigmatic functions. The theological dimension of the narrative is also important: the idle and unsympathetic boy is purified by suffering and rediscovers himself and God, and from God he receives wisdom accompanied by the capacity to interpret dreams; from God he also receives the gift of good government; and it is God finally who appears as the one behind the whole framework, turning it to good despite the human intervention. So if we leave aside the initial unsympathetic note (though this is indispensable in providing a rational motivation for the violent reaction of the brothers), Joseph appears as a hero without fault or blemish, rather like David and Solomon in Chronicles. There are none of those cynical or even brutal notes which form part of political life at all times and which are well represented both in the narratives of the first kings and in part in the patriarchal narratives reported by J, and it is precisely this approach of a 'hagiographical kind which is one more element in favour of a late dating. However, the narrative is exhausted in all this without preoccupying itself in the least with whether the information that it offers is real, if indeed information of this kind was available to the authors and interested them. Finally, it is not at all clear what are the relationships with the northern tribes (often called 'Joseph') and especially with Ephraim and Manasseh, assuming of course that such relationships were present in the mind of the author.

7.2.5 Von Rad also seeks to connect the interests of the narrative with what he calls its wisdom orientation. Here he refers to the interest of the story in the court and its ceremonial, the embalming of corpses, the buying of corn by the crown cheaply in times of plenty and its sale at an advantageous price in times of famine. This is the wisdom the principle of which is the fear of God (cf. Gen.39.9; 42.18b with Prov.1.7a), and Eissfeldt sees indirect confirmation of this aspect in the use made of the story in children's catechisms down the centuries. However, von Rad's study leaves a number of problems open.

7.2.5.1 The connection with wisdom which he claims seems very tenuous: what he regards as wisdom features could easily be connected with the narrator's interest in unusual, original features by which he can capture the attention of the reader or the hearer;[11] this has nothing to do with wisdom.

7.2.5.2 At this point, by way of a partial conclusion, we can be sure of at least one thing: clearly this is a historical romance, a novella which is probably post-exilic and which was probably written in the Diaspora (Meinhold 1975-76); it is not a work composed for historiographical purposes. It is no part of the aims of the writers to provide in their text information about Egypt at a particular period, about its form of government, its economy or its administration.

7.3 The settlement of 'Israel' in Egypt

Because of the preponderance in the Joseph story of narrative elements typical of folklore, and for want of any comparative Egyptian historical material, it proves to be an inadequate source for a reconstruction of the events which are supposed to have led the ancestors of Israel and Judah to Egypt and which a number of years later were the cause of the exodus. Despite this an attempt has often been made to connect the migration of Jacob and his sons to Egypt with other popular migrations attested in the ancient Near East in the second millennium BCE.

7.3.1 In 1939, Alt thought that he could connect the migration of Jacob and his sons with the seizure of power in Egypt by a group called Hyksos, who were thought to have come from northern Mesopotamia and to have been made up of Semitic and Indo-European elements.[12] However, a few years later, in 1954,[13] he came to almost opposite conclusions: the rise to power of this group (whose name had first been translated as 'shepherd kings' but which probably means something like 'foreign rulers') had not been the result of migrations, nor even of an invasion. The origins of the group are still largely obscure, but it seems increasingly probable that these were Semitic and Hurrian nuclei which had already been settled for some time in the eastern part of the Delta. At the end of the first quarter of the second millennium BCE they will have succeeded in seizing power, profiting from the disorders of the so-called 'Second Intermediate Period', and in holding it for around 200 years.

7.3.2 So just as the theory of an 'Amorite' migration in the wake of which according to some scholars the patriarchs will have arrived in Canaan (above 6.1.5) from north-western Mesopotamia has proved to be unfounded, so too the similar theory of a migration from Canaan, Syria and northern Mesopotamia to Egypt by the Hyksos, a migration with which Jacob and his sons could be associated, proves to rest on fragile foundations. Of course, in the absence of a migration of the Hyksos to Egypt it is also difficult to assume that they were expelled, though this expression still appears today among scholars;[14] until a few decades ago some of them wanted to connect this event with the figure of the Pharaoh 'who did not know Joseph' (below, 7.6.4.1).[15]

7.3.3 To give some idea of the complexity of the problems associated with the text of the story of Jacob it is enough to recall that the Belgian Egyptologist J. Vergote in his important 1959 study succeeded in bringing together a remarkable series of parallels and agreements in the linguistic field between the Joseph story and Egyptian texts dating from the Nineteenth Dynasty (c.1306-1200). Moreover, not only did Vergote see nothing against putting the story in this period; he found much in favour of such a dating.[16] The German Egyptologist Siegfried Morenz, in his review of Vergote's work, seemed more prudent and less enthusiastic, yet he too was extremely favourable to Vergote's theory. The same can be said of the review of D.B.Redford's book by the English Egyptologist K.A.Kitchen (Redford himself was sceptical). In support of these optimistic theories, the authors refer to various cases of foreigners who rose to 'positions of great power',[17] something which does not seem to have been unusual in the second half of the second millennium BCE. Nor does the motive of famine seem improbable; a prolonged and severe drought at the source of the Nile was enough to lower the level of the waters, thus restricting considerably the possibility of using them for irrigation.

7.3.4 On the other hand there are scholars who would prefer to date the account round about the age of Solomon,[18] i.e. towards the middle of the tenth century BCE, and therefore later than the date proposed by Vergote. They claim that Joseph's Egyptian name *ṣapᵉnat pan ᶜēᵃḥ* in Gen.41.45 would fit at the beginning of the first millennium, being a possible Hebrew transcription of the Egyptian *ḏd NN iw.f'nḫ*: 'NN has declared: "May he live"!'[19] However, the expression with which the Egyptians are said to have saluted Joseph's carriage as he went by would seem to have been very different, *'abrēk* (Gen.41.43): this was first connected with the root *berek* I, 'kneel', and felt to be an invitation to pay homage (Vergote suggests 'Attention').[20] However, the proposal by Friedrich Delitzsch in 1881, taken up by J.C.Croatto and É.Lipiński,[21] seems more probable. They think of a connection with the Accadian *abarakku*, the title of a 'high official',[22] cf. the analogous Phoenician *hbrk b'l* in the first inscription of Karatepe (*KAI*, 26), probably to be understood as: 'I am Azitawadda, the vizier of Baʿal...' This is perhaps an allusion to the priesthood of the king or more simply to his devotion to this god. In this case the term used, along with the designation of the two cities in Ex.1.11 (above 7.1.5), points to the Eastern Semitic language area and would also be relatively late. Little or nothing can be discovered about the other Egyptian names.

7.4 The residence of 'Israel'

The texts tell us that Jacob and his sons were assigned a residence in what is called the 'land of Goshen'.

7.4.1 The practice of assigning land to Asiatic peoples like the patriarchs is well attested in Egypt. Papyrus Anastasi VI (end of the thirteenth century BCE, *ANET*, 259f., not yet in *TUAT*) gives us important information;[23] it contains the report of an official appointed to a post on the eastern frontier. Among other things, it says: '...we have finished passing the tribes of the shepherds[24] through the fortress... which is near *ṯkw* (probably the Succoth of Ex.12.37) to the cisterns of *pr.'tm* (Pithom?, cf. above 7.1.4) which are near *ṯkw*, to keep them and their animals alive by means of the *ka* of the Pharaoh...' There are other texts of this kind, but not as explicit.

7.4.2 So it seems that we should look for the country of Goshen, otherwise unknown, in this frontier area; it is a region which from time immemorial down to the beginning of major reclamation work in modern times to make it suitable for intensive agriculture has been used for the extensive rearing of cattle. Genesis 46.28ff. again tells us that Joseph, travelling in a carriage, could cover the distance between this region and the capital in a relatively short time; this is a sign that the tradition does not locate the capital at Memphis but at Avaris-Tanis (above 7.1.4), which was the capital first under the Hyksos and then during the Nineteenth Dynasty, which rebuilt it.[25]

7.5 The chronology

So we come to the problem of the chronology of the narrative, which like so many others is insoluble in the present state of research. In Gen.15.13ff. (a Deuteronomistic text) and in Ex.12.40ff. (P) there is mention of 400 and 430 years respectively between the time of Abraham and that of the Exodus, but Gen.15.16 mentions only four generations, i.e. a period of at most between 60 and 120 years.[26] The chronology of I Kings 6.1 then takes up the first two figures (400 and 430 years); here the date of the beginning of the work on the building of the temple is put at 480 years after the exodus (above 5.2.2.4). However, all these figures seem problematical on the historical level and they cannot be used to reconstruct a chronology of the prehistory of Israel and Judah. Moreover I pointed out earlier (above 3.7) how little the ancient world was interested in problems of chronology. But the 480 years can be explained from other perspectives, which are ideological and theological rather than historical,[27] whereas the first two figures do not as yet seem to have any certain meaning. So it would be better to give up any chronology and accept that the information at our disposal is not enough to calculate one. We can, however, argue that during the period of the early monarchy Israel (and the reference is probably to the tribes of the north) handed down the memory of its own direct relationships with those groups which, at the beginning of the thirteenth century, under the Nineteenth Egyptian Dynasty, will have rebuilt the two cities of the Delta and will have been conscripted for forced labour to do this by the very authority which at one time will have settled them there. So there is no point in asking what this relationship was: not only do we have no plausible information, but we also know (below 8.8) that the tribes of Israel and Judah were formed in Canaan and not before they got there, as the tradition maintains. So we shall never know which of the ancestors of Israel and Judah, if any, had been slaves in Egypt, nor can we even confirm the intrinsic likelihood of the information, even if, as we have seen, some passages do not seem manifestly absurd. At all events, the information is not necessary to explain the origins of Israel and Judah.

7.6 Forced labour

We have seen (7.3.2 above) that at the beginning of the book of Exodus the slavery of the ancestors of Israel in Egypt is connected with a change at the highest levels of Egyptian power: a Pharaoh ascended the throne who no longer felt bound to the person and work of Joseph and who was also afraid that the people, who had meanwhile become numerous and therefore powerful, might be a danger to Egypt in case of war (1.8-10 J). However, there is no rational reason for such a suspicion, which is the only explanation for a whole series of hostile acts on the part of the Egyptians and the whole exodus, if it is put in the second millennium: according to the tradition, 'Israel' had been in Egypt for centuries and must have been largely assimilated there; moreover the direct dominion of Egypt extended as far as southern Syria, so that an invasion by hostile Canaanite elements is not a viable hypothesis. However, the suspicion seems perfectly well founded in the first decades of the second century BCE during the war between the Seleucids and the Ptolemies, when the Jewish Diaspora in Alexandria had been cut off from the mother country.

7.6.1 This fear was soon translated into hostile acts: forced labour was imposed upon the people, the making of crude bricks: to begin with the administration provided the workers with the necesssary material (1.31ff.); at a later stage, however, the workers had to get hold of the material themselves without the quotas being reduced (5.6-23). In 1.15-23, perhaps E, a third element appears: the order given by the king to the midwives to kill all the newborn males so as to cause a dramatic drop in the growth of the population. However, the attempt failed because of the piety and the religious feeling of the two midwives assigned to Israel, whose names have a sound Western Semitic etymology.[28] Here too, though, the probability of the character of the names cannot constitute a proof of the authenticity of the tradition, but is at most an indication, as we have seen in the case of the patriarchal narratives (above 6.6.1.1). And again, there is a motive characteristic of the fable: that of the malevolent ruler whose plans are thwarted by the attitude of simple but pious and decisive people.

7.6.2 Anyone who wants to be very precise could then point out that there is a certain tension, perhaps even incompatibility, between the two types of persecution. The forced labour in fact has a twofold aim: surveillance of the suspects and at the same time intensive economic exploitation of them. There is no mention of any kind of genocide; indeed, again given the logic of the narrative, one might suppose that they would be freed once the building work was finished and the danger had passed. By contrast, killing the newborn males and thus condemning the active Hebrew population to progressive aging and extinction would in time obviously affect the second of the two aims of the forced labour, its productivity. On the other hand, we can hardly see the theme of genocide as a secondary addition: it now introduces the birth of Moses, who will soon be the main character in the majority of the stories which follow.

7.6.3 However, even the story of the birth of Moses, to which the note about the attempted extermination of the children forms a kind of prologue, is not without its problems. It has an obvious parallel in the 'autobiography' of Sargon I, king of Accad (c.2234-2270 BCE). He too was conceived and borne by his mother in secret; she then 'put him in a basket of reeds, with the covering sealed with pitch', and abandoned him to the river. But the basket, made and treated in a skilful way, did not sink and was rescued by a water-carrier who brought up and educated the child (*ANET*, 119, not yet in *TUAT*). In the biblical narrative, too, we are told that the basket is made watertight, an apparently otiose detail because it is not meant to float, but is abandoned among the reeds (Ex.2.2-3). So on the one hand the story of Moses fits in with the attempt at genocide, and on the other it is a narrative with features which are well attested in the ancient Near East and which was therefore probably well known.

7.6.4 The comment that the anonymous Pharaoh of the oppression 'did not know Joseph' shows that the tradition thought in terms of a substantially different dynasty, characterized by a marked lack of confidence on the part of those who had come to power in those who had been favoured by the previous dynasty, especially as they were foreigners. We have seen (above 6.4.and 7.6) that the note is late because it depends on the Joseph story, which is also late, and moreover that it makes no sense in the second millennium BCE, whereas it would fit well in the situation of the second century BCE. Despite that, attempts have been made to identify the change in dynasty. For this only the following two factors are to be taken into account.

7.6.4.1 The change which took place at the time of the 'expulsion' of the Hyksos around 1550 by the Pharaohs of the Eighteenth Dynasty and especially by Ah-mose (c.1570-1546). That could seem probable: nothing in fact is more obvious than that a new dynasty, taking the place of an earlier one which had been felt to be foreign, should have sought to put a brake on what could have appeared as an abuse on the part of the previous government, namely the settling of friendly allogenous populations in peripheral regions, which could lead to danger in case of conflict. However, anyone who accepts this proposal has also to accept that 'Israel' will have been subjected to forced labour for about 250 years, an improbably long period, and the building of the two cities mentioned in Ex.1.11 will have taken place only at the end of this period.

7.6.4.2 A second change of this kind took place at the beginning of the Nineteenth Dynasty with Sethos I (c.1291-1279); at a chronological level we are much closer to events here. But here too there are notable problems: how could there have been this unexpected mistrust of a population which had now been settled in the region for some time, and which had not caused any trouble but was on the contrary a notable producer of goods in a region which was otherwise unpopulated and unproductive? So there seems to be no rational basis to the change of attitude.

7.6.4.3 To that must be added a factor that I have already alluded to elsewhere in this study: the total silence of the Egyptian sources of the period. On one occasion, Papyrus Anastasi V (end of the thirteenth century, *ANET*, 259b, not in *TUAT*) mentions the pursuit of two (n.b. two!) fugitive slaves beyond the frontier; but we hear nothing of any conscription to forced labour of entire foreign groups living the region.[29] So it is not the case that the Egyptian sources are not concerned with a theme like the one with which we are concerned; they do not know of ours, but they do record other similar instances.

7.7 The oppression and announcements of the exodus

So the study of the oppression and slavery of 'Israel' in Egypt and of the exodus confronts the historian with a series of basic difficulties not unlike those encountered in the study of the patriarchal traditions.

Bibliography

B.S.Childs, 'The Birth of Moses', *JBL* 84, 1965, 109-22; D.B.Redford, 'The Literary Motif of the Exposed Child', *Numen* 14, 1967, 209-28; O.Eissfeldt, in *CAH* II.2, [3]1975, 318ff.; W.H.Schmidt, 'Jahwe in Ägypten', in *Sēfer Rendtorff*, Dielheim 1975, 94-112; de Vaux, *Early History* I, 324ff.; G.von Rad, 'Beobachtungen an der Moseerzählung Exodus 1-14', *EvTh* 31, 1971, 579-88, *GS* II, 189-98; R.J.Williams, ' "A People Come Out of Egpyt''. An Egyptologist Looks at the Old Testament', SVT 28, 1975, 321-52; H.J.-L.Ska, 'La sortie d'Egypte (Ex.7-13) dans le récit sacerdotal (P[g]) et la tradition prophétique', *Bib* 70, 1979, 171-215; G.W.Ramsey, *Reconsidering Israel's Early History*, Atlanta 1981 = *The Quest for the Historical Israel*, London 1982, ch.3; G.W.Coats, *Moses, Heroic Man, Man of God*, Sheffield 1988; A.Nicacci, 'Sullo sfondo egiziano di Esodo 1-15', *LA-SBF* 36, 1986, 7-43.

7.7.1 The biblical sources are rich in anecdotes, popular traditions and elements of folklore; however, as with other cases, they lack information which is capable of verification by historical investigation:

the Pharaohs or other important officials are never named, and the chronological information is imprecise. To this must be added the almost complete silence of the Egyptian sources.

7.7.2 To explain this situation there is always the argument that the Egyptian annals will not have been occupied with minutiae of this kind; however, that does not seem plausible in the light of what we have seen so far (cf. above 7.4.1). Another argument also appears from time to time: that the Pharaohs, and especially the nationalistic Pharaohs of the Nineteenth Dynasty, were not accustomed to record their own defeats. In this connection the example of the battle of Kadesh on the Orontes (in present-day Lebanon), about 1285, is quoted; this resulted in a Hittite victory. The Hittites succeeded in occupying the whole of the northern part of Syria, but the battle was presented by Ramses II as an Egyptian victory. What actually happened, however, was that the Pharaoh managed with some difficulty to avoid being encircled and therefore losing his own troops by beating a hasty retreat; so on the most favourable of readings we have a tactical success, and certainly not a victory.[30] Now it is said that the whole story of the exodus appears as a great Egyptian defeat and therefore was not recorded. However, to note that some Pharaohs kept quiet about certain data or even lied about their defeats in their propaganda or in their war bulletins clearly does not amount to a proof, far less is it a valid alternative to the silence of the Egyptian sources about the facts in which we are interested.

7.7.3 There is more to come. Even the non-specialist reader cannot fail to marvel at the wealth of detail provided in the texts, a wealth which can readily appear suspect, especially when there are references to improbable events.

7.7.3.1 First of all the texts refer to a series of formal encounters between the Pharaoh, surrounded by his own dignitaries and 'magi', and Moses, accompanied by his brother Aaron and possibly by the elders of the people. Now the improbable character of these encounters has often been noted. It seems quite improbable that the Pharaoh, the god-king, should have met on equal terms representatives of a group of foreign cattle-breeders suspected of being a potential fifth column and therefore conscripted to forced labour, even if according to the tradition Moses had been educated at court.

7.7.3.2 Furthermore the narrative seems to be too schematic, too well constructed, to be a record of real events, though one with all the necessary modifications to meet the demands of a narrative. To begin with, Pharaoh grants the requests of Moses, then his heart is 'hardened' by God himself and he goes back on everything. Time and again, under the impact of the successive 'plagues', he yields, and then, once the plague has passed, he has second thoughts. Only with the last plague does he finally yield once and for all, and when yet again he has second thoughts it is too late: 'Israel' has already gone.

7.7.3.3 At all events, it seems difficult to establish whether the narratives contain material which goes back to ancient traditions, and if so, what these are; we cannot tell how much belongs to the purely narrative phase of the discourse and how much again proves to be reflections of an ethical and religious kind. For example, this last category might include the concept that God might deprive the sinner even of the possibility of repenting of his guilt if in his action he went beyond a certain limit. Finally, we do not know how much is purely part of the liturgy for the celebration of the Jewish passover.

7.7.3.4 The theory that in the final analysis Exodus 1-15 belong to the passover liturgy and that they can therefore only be explained in this context was authoritatively put forward in the 1930s by the Danish scholar J.Pedersen,[31] who for precisely this reason stresses that the account is substantially a unity.

7.7.4 *The 'plagues'*. This leads us almost automatically to consider the account of what are called in the translations the 'plagues' of Egypt, plagues which struck the Pharaoh and Egypt as they rebelled against the divine order to let the people of God go. The texts appear in Ex.7.14-11.10 and 12.29-34, and all present serious problems. I shall devote perhaps a disproportionate space to them, but it does seem to me to be worth the trouble, because they show how the Israelite tradition functioned.

Bibliography

G.Hort, 'The Plagues of Egypt', *ZAW* 69, 1957, 84-103; 70, 1958, 498-59; G.Fohrer, *Überlieferung und Geschichte des Exodus*, Berlin 1964, 60-97; M.Greenberg, 'The Redaction of the Plagues Narrative in Exodus', in *Near Eastern Studies in Honor of W.F.Albright*, Baltimore and London 1971, 243-52; S.E.Loewenstamm, 'An Observation on Source Criticism of the Plague Pericope', *VT* 24, 1974, 374-8; E.Otto, 'Erwägungen zum überlieferungsgeschichtlichen Ursprung und "Sitz im Leben" des jahwistischen Plagenzyklus', *VT* 26, 1976, 3-27; A.Ademollo, 'I morbi nel racconto biblico delle piaghe d'Egitto e nella loro rispondenza scientifica', *Rivista di storia della medicina* 20, 2, 1976, 137-67; M.Gilula, 'The Smiting of the First Born – An Egyptian Myth?', *TA* 4, 1976, 94f.; S.I.L.Norin, *Er spaltete das Meer*, Lund 1977, 13ff.; J.-L.Ska, 'La sortie d'Égypte' (7.7 above); J. Van Seters, 'The Plagues of Egypt: Ancient Tradition or Literary Invention?', *ZAW* 98, 1986, 31-9; L.Schmidt, *Beobachtungen zu der Plagenerzählung in Exodus VII 14 – XI 10*, Leiden 1990.

7.7.4.1 Hebrew has five terms for what the translations usually render 'plagues': *niplā'ōt*, 'wonders'; *'ōt*, 'sign (natural)'; *mōpet*, 'sign (miraculous)'; *nega'*, 'blow'; and *negep*, 'affliction'. Furthermore it is possible to divide the plagues into two categories, depending on their character: the first nine belong in the sphere of natural phenomena and the miraculous elements consist only in the fact that they coincide and are of such severity; by contrast the last clearly transcends the natural order of events and is definitive and irreversible.

7.7.4.2 Moreover, despite the apparent unity and schematic character of the narrative, a remarkable amount of editorial and redactional activity has led up to its present form. Greenberg 1971 has seen two strata in the narrative, one JE and the other P, partly overlapping and partly diverging, while Loewenstamm 1974 sees two traditions within J. As if that were not enough, two mentions outside Exodus, Ps.78.43-51 and 105.27-36, list individual plagues in a different order. De Vaux reasonably remarks:[32] 'It would appear, then, that a great deal was said about these "plagues", and that only one tradition, providing one selection, is contained in Exodus.'

7.7.4.3 Not all the sources have all the plagues.

7.7.4.3.1 The first, the pollution of the water, appears in the three sources (7.14-25), but only J connects the water with the death of the fish, whereas E and P have the water turned into blood, probably a variant of the theme of pollution.

7.7.4.3.2 The second plague, the frogs, appears only in J and P (7.26-8.11).

7.7.4.3.3 The third plague, the mosquitoes, appears only in P (8.12-15).

7.7.4.3.4 The fourth plague, the flies (probably the *musca canina*, an insect which attacks domestic animals more than human beings, cf. Zorrell's Lexicon s.v. *'ārōb*), appears only in J (8.16-28).

7.7.4.3.5 The fifth plague, the death of the livestock, is attested only in J (9.1-7).

7.7.4.3.6 The sixth plague, the ulcers, appears only in P (9.8-12).

7.7.4.3.7 The seventh plague, the hailstorm, appears in JE (9.13-35).

7.7.4.3.8 The eighth plague, the locusts, appears in JE (10.12-20).

7.7.4.3.9 The ninth plague, the darkness, appears only in E (10.21-27).

7.7.4.3.10 The tenth plague, the killing of the firstborn of human beings and animals, appears in all three sources (12.39-44).

7.7.4.3.11 Therefore in J we have seven plagues, and in E and P only five each.

7.7.4.4 So we could also take into account that some of the plagues are simply variants or even duplicates of others (nos.3-4, 5-6, 7-8 – these last in the sense that the hail and the locusts are both visitations from the heavens which destroy the crops). That could give us something like seven specific plagues, of which the first five are probably the earliest in terms of tradition.[33]

7.7.4.5 This analysis, which perhaps seems rather extensive given the overall framework of the present work, as I have indicated, allows of only one conclusion. As de Vaux points out, the tradition is a literary composition, not a historical or legendary text; it is a work conceived at the writing desk, not a collection of ancient traditions.

7.7.4.6 Given the precision of the descriptions, it is not surprising that attempts are regularly made to connect the plagues (except the last one) with natural phenomena in the region. The results of such parallels are very modest compared with the resources used and the profound knowledge of those who engage in them. So far, the most interesting argument is that of Hort in 1957-58, and for details I refer the reader to it. For Hort, the only inexplicable element is the hailstorm, the seventh plague, since hail is unknown in Egypt, whereas it is frequent in Palestine during the winter. The last plague, the killing of the first born, would be based on an early error: the *bikkūrīm* will not have been the 'firstborn' but the firstfruits of the produce of the soil, which had been destroyed as a result of the other, earlier plagues; later the term was misunderstood, resulting in the killing of human and animal 'firstborn'. The explanation by Gilula 1977 is different but also not very convincing: the detail is supposed to derive from an ancient Egyptian myth on a similar theme, incorporated into the passover narrative and inserted among the others as the last plague.

7.7.4.7 Now however probable these arguments may be in individual details (and we have seen how rarely this is in fact the case), they do not note how in the narrative the effect is cumulative; it does not depend on individual plagues but on the whole series of them. It is only this last feature which makes the first nine a series of divine signs, miracles. Obviously it is useless to seek to rationalize and explain something which is not rational, and the story loses its point here, without the doubters being convinced.[34] What the text confesses (because this is a confession of faith, as the passover context indicates) is the divine intervention on the side of the humble and the oppressed and their triumph over the greatest power of the time along with its ruler, who was considered a divine being.

7.8 The 'Red' Sea

Chapters 12-14, followed by the epic song in ch.15, narrate the central event of the exodus: the miraculous departure from Egypt through the stretch of water which in Hebrew is called *yam sūp*.

Bibliography

G.R.H.Wright, 'The Passage of the Sea', *Göttinger Miscellen* 33, 1979, 55-68; J.Scharbert, 'Das "Schilfmeerwunder" in den Texten des Alten Testaments', in *Mélanges... H.Cazelles*, Kevelaer and Neukirchen/Vluyn 1981, 295-417; B.F.Batto, 'The Reed Sea: Requiescat in pace', *JBL* 102, 1983, 27-35; J.A.Soggin, 'Das Wunder am Meer und in der Wüste, Exodus cc.14-15', in *D'Ugarit à Qumran. Mélanges... M.Delcor*, Kevelaer and Neukirchen/Vluyn 1985, 379-85; P.Weimar, *Die Meereswundererzählung*, Wiesbaden 1985; J.-L.Ska, *Le passage de la mer*, Rome 1986.

7.8.1 The translation of the Hebrew expression *yam sūp* as 'Red Sea' is conventional and dates from the time of the LXX, which has ἐρυθρὰ θάλασσα (cf. the Vulgate which has *Mare Rubrum*); however, it is wrong, since *sūp* means 'rush' or 'reed' (cf. Ex.2.3,5, where the two ancient translations are in fact correct). The rendering 'Red Sea' probably arises from the fact that in at least two certain texts, I Kings 9.26 and Jer.49.21, the expression refers to the eastern arm of the Red Sea, the present-day Gulf of Aqaba.

So 'Israel' arrived at the Sea of Reeds or Sea of Rushes, having finally succeeded in leaving Egypt, and found itself caught between the waters in front and the pursuing army behind. This is clearly the high point of the narrative: Pharaoh has gone back on his word for the umpteenth time and has begun pursuit with his troops. But as we know, the moment the fugitives arrive the waters open, allowing 'Israel' to pass through, and then close again on the pursuers.

7.8.2 However, the narrative is not so much a unity as might appear at first sight: it is possible to recognize at least three and perhaps four strata in the account, strata which we could, if we wished, identify with the sources of the Pentateuch.[35]

7.8.2.1 What is evidently the earliest stratum, which we could attribute to J, appears in 14.21 aβbα: 'The Lord made the sea withdraw (*wayyōlek*, hiphil) by a strong east wind all night, and made the sea dry land.' This version of the facts is evidently meant to present a natural phenomenon, in which the miraculous element consists exclusively in the perfect synchronization of the event, which helped 'Israel' and hindered the pursuers. For Noth the phenomenon could have historical roots.[36] At the end of the second millennium BCE the Gulf of Suez was still partially connected with the Bitter Lakes; the link was broken only by a narrow tongue of land and, depending on the tide and the wind, this could either be above the water or submerged. In that case, of course, the crossing would have had to have taken place in the southern part of the isthmus of Suez.

7.8.2.2 A later stratum, which we could attribute to P, occurs in 14.21

aαbβ-22 and runs: 'Then Moses stretched out his hand over the sea; and the waters were divided. And the people of Israel went into the midst of the sea on dry ground, the waters being a wall to them on their right hand and on their left...' The waters then closed in on the Egyptians (vv.23, 26ff.). Here we have a miracle pure and simple, and any part of the Mediterranean or the Red Sea could fit the phenomenon; it becomes impossible and indeed unnecessary to provide a topographical location. To try to connect the event with some kind of natural phenomenon (for example it has been suggested that the eruption of the volcano on the island of Santorini in the Aegean during the fourteenth century BCE could have caused a form of tidal wave) does not fit in with the essence of what is meant to be a miracle and nothing else.

7.8.2.3 However, there is a third version of events which is difficult to harmonize with the other two; so much so that the redactors have preferred to indicate this as a later event, independent of the other two (Ex.14.24-25, a text which we could attribute to E): 'And in the morning watch the Lord in the pillar of fire and of cloud looked down upon the host of the Egyptians, and discomfited the host of Egyptians, braking (read *wayye'esor*, root *'āsar*, with Sam, LXX and Syr for the Massoretic *wayyāsar*, root *swr*, 'remove' or 'upset') their chariot wheels so that they drove heavily; and the Egyptians said: "Let us flee from before Israel; for the Lord fights for them against the Egyptians." ' In the narrative style peculiar to E (if we can attribute this section to that source), the Egyptians see the miracle and note that something is going radically wrong, so they decide to retreat. In this version of events the waters do not even appear, thus presupposing a tradition substantially different from the other two. Moreover it is impossible to harmonize this with the other two, especially with the second: in v.23 the Egyptians have already rashly begun the pursuit through the two walls of water, but in vv.24-25 they are still within the camp at the time of the reveille and, having seen that things are taking a turn for the worse, break off the pursuit and return to their bases. For the first two versions the catastrophe is caused by the continuation of the pursuit; in the third, a prudent retreat enables the Egyptians to avoid it.

7.8.2.4 However, perhaps there is even a fourth version, this time an epic poem, that of the song in Ex.15. This is a composition which until recently the majority of scholars thought to be very old, even if vv.13b and 17 suggest the existence of the temple in Jerusalem and 14-15 seem to presuppose the wars of David. There is now a tendency to postdate this composition too.[37] According to this version, YHWH 'cast into the sea Pharaoh's chariots and his host; and his picked officers are sunk (LXX has 'YHWH has sunk') in the Sea of Reeds' (v.4). This could be a simple poetic variant of the second version 7.8.2.2, possibly enriched with the insertion of mythical elements like the 'abysses' (*t^ehōmōt*, v.5) and the 'depths of the sea' (*m^esōlōt*, v.8).

7.9 Itineraries in the desert

However, the three or four descriptions of the phenomenon given by the tradition do not say anything about its topography. As we have seen (above 7.8.2.1), Noth sought to locate it in the region of the Bitter Lakes, on the isthmus of Suez.

Bibliography

O.Eissfeldt, *Baal Zaphon, Zeus Kasios und der Durchzug der Israeliten durch das Meer*, Halle 1932 (a basic study); M.Noth, 'Der Schauplatz des Meereswunders', in *FS O.Eissfeldt zum 70.Geburtstag*, Halle 1947, 181-90, *ABLAK*, 102-10; W.F.Albright, 'Baal Zephon', in *FS Alfred Bertholet*, Tübingen 1950, 1-14; H.Cazelles, 'Les localisations de l'Exode et la critique littéraire', *RB* 62, 1955, 321-63; M.Mazar, 'The Exodus and the Conquest', *WHJP* III, 1971, 69-79; M.Haran, 'Exodus', *IDB-SV*, 1976, 308-10; Y.Aharoni**, 195ff. and map 13; G.I.Davies, *The Way of the Wilderness*, SOTS-MS 5, Cambridge 1979, 70ff.; M.Har-El, *The Sinay Journeys*, San Diego, Ca 1983, 169-71 (against O.Eissfeldt); and the works by Scharbert, Soggin and Ska, cited above, 7.8; M.Görg, 'Pi-Hahirot', *BN* 50, 1989, 7f.

7.9.1 A reconstruction of at least the first part of the itinerary of the exodus is a necessary preliminary to any attempt to locate the miracle at the Sea of Reeds. But is such a reconstruction possible? And if it is, is this an ancient tradition or merely a later attempt to locate the event and thus to rationalize it?

7.9.1.1 The texts begin by stating that 'Israel' did not take the 'Way of the Philistines' (13.17). Apart from the obvious anachronism, which presupposes at least a later redaction, this is the coastal route which under the Romans was called the *via maris*. However, what we can reconstruct of the first part of the journey does seem to indicate that the fugitives chose to follow the coastal route and not a route more to the interior of the peninsula.[38] Moreover, the designation 'Sea of Reeds' or 'rushes' refers to the northern coast; only along the Mediterranean coast, either in the eastern part of the Delta or further east in Lake Sirbonis (present-day *sabḥat el-bardawīl*) are there the stretches of fresh water which are essential for the growth of reeds and rushes. That would seem to exclude the region of the Bitter Lakes, now incorporated into the Suez Canal system, and the coast of the Gulf of Suez.[39] On the other hand, one fact has to be accepted: any on-the-spot investigations in the region of the Canal are now pointless. The topography has been irremediably changed by the building of the waterway, and also, though to a much lesser extent, by the wars fought there in recent years.

7.9.1.2 The stages between the departure from Egypt and the scene of the miracle are given in 13.17-14.9 (cf. also Num.33.5-8). From Raamses (above 7.1.4) the first stopping place is Succoth (12.13), perhaps the *tkw* which I have already mentioned. This could have been the meeting place with the group from further south, from Pithom. From Succoth the group went by Etam (13.20), a place which has still not been identified, then arriving 'in front of Pi-ha-hiroth, between Migdol and the sea, in front of Ba'al-Zephon' (14.2.9). It was here that the pursuing army caught up with them. Now the last two places have been identified thanks to the studies by Eissfeldt 1932, even if the identification is not universally accepted (Haran 1976 and Har-el 1983, and also Noth 1947 and Albright 1950 cited above). As the name indicates, Migdol, 'tower', is a fortress (probably on the frontier) and is usually identified with the Egyptian *mktr*, present-day *el-ḥēr* (coord.912-048). Ba'al-zephon has been identified by Eissfeldt with a well-known seafarers' sanctuary, a place of worship for the deity of that name, for whom there is also evidence at Ugarit. It was on the central part of the western end of the tongue of land which shuts off Lake Sirbonis (*sabḥat el-bardawīl*, coord.967-072). The area was carefully explored by M.Dothan[40] after the Six Day War at the end of the 1960s. Finally, according to Görg 1989, Pi-ha-hirot would not even be a local name.

7.9.1.3 From there, according to some scholars,[41] the fugitives would have made a turn of about 150 degrees, moving south and following more or less the present-day eastern bank of the Suez Canal (13.18; cf. 14.2). However, the expression used by the first of these two texts is not clear because in its present construction it is incorrect: it reads *derek hammidbār yam sūp*, and it is impossible to translate this 'the way of the desert of the sea of reeds', as often happens (*hammidbār* does not occur here, nor can it occur, in the construct state). Of course it is possible that the second part is simply an attempt to explain the first, which was thought to be incongruous. Eissfeldt 1932 wanted to remedy what he thought to be a corrupt text by proposing two readings: *derek hammidbār* and *derek yam sūp*, i.e. 'in the direction of the desert' and 'in the direction of the Sea of Reeds'. He supposes, however, that here this last reference really must be to the Gulf of Aqaba, and not the lagoon. In that case the route would be that which millennia later was to be followed by the pilgrims going to Mecca, the *darb el-ḥajj*, parallel to the horizontal co-ordinates 940/920; this is also the proposal accepted by Haran. However, it can easily be objected that in that case the expression *yam sūp*, which is hardly a frequent one, would be being used here with two different topographical meanings.

7.9.1.4 We can only come to one conclusion on the basis of what I have said so far: the first part of the exodus follows an itinerary of which some stages are known but not others. It seems sufficiently certain that the author thought that the event should be located in an area either in the eastern Delta or, more probably, in Lake Sirbonis. There was probably no other evidence even at that time, and Noth[42] seems to be right in concluding that here we have essentially rationalizing attempts to give a precise historical and topographical context for the miracle, a feature which is clearly absent from the original tradition.

7.9.2 The stage after the miracle, from the Sea to Kadesh, is full of names of places touched on during the journey; however, they are all, without exception, unknown.

Bibliography

V.Fritz, *Israel in der Wüste*, Marburg 1970; G.W.Coats, 'The Wilderness Itinerary', *CBQ* 34, 1972, 135-72; also Davies 1979 and Har-El cited above at 7.9.

7.9.2.1 The attempts to identify the individual stages of the first phase in the journey through the desert can be considered failures, not only because of the vagueness of the data offered by the Bible but also because they always want to see the journey as a route which leads from the place of the miracle to Mount Sinai, a route which is said to coincide with the route to the turquoise mines. This argument cannot be sustained, first of all because the destination was not the present-day Sinai, though that would have made possible the route often indicated in atlases of the Bible, but the oasis of Kadesh, present-day *ʿein el-qudeirat* (coord.098-006), near to which, about six miles south-south-east, there is still an *ʿein qudeis* which has preserved the name;[43] and secondly, because such a route would have been well guarded. At this point another fundamental objection arises: if Ramses II had really been the Pharaoh of the exodus, the fugitives would have been venturing into a territory which was under Egyptian rule rather than escaping it (oral communication by G.Garbini).

7.9.2.2 Moreover, it is certainly in the region of Kadesh that we must look for the Massah and Meribah of Ex.17.3-7 and Num.20.1, 13-14, where the two places are identified by means of an onomastic ideology (cf. also the combination *mᵉrîbat qādēš* in Num.27.14; Deut.32.52; Ezek.47.19; 48.58). It therefore seems clear that here we have a single complex of oases, all interconnected. Moreover, on the basis of Num.27.14, where Kadesh is located in the Desert of Sin, Noth[44] asked whether the various designations of this desert, which seem to denote various regions into which it is divided, are not in reality phonetic variants of the same designation for a single region: *sīnai, sīn* and *ṣīn* (this last term is still attested in Arabic, as *arḍ* or *wādī eṣ-ṣīnī*). So the differentiation between them would be the product of a late and artificial process aimed at giving each major stage a different name: from the place of the miracle to Kadesh *sīn*, from Kadesh to Sinai *sīnay*, from Kadesh onwards *ṣīn*. At all events, one thing seems certain: the first part of the journey through the desert goes from the Sea of Reeds directly to Kadesh and not elsewhere, so it is along this route that the various stages must be sought.[45]

7.9.2.3 However, the reality seems to be perhaps even simpler. There is only one itinerary, with an interruption in the middle: from the Sea of Reeds to Kadesh, and from there to the Promised Land. The pilgrimage to Sinai with the promulgation of the Torah there has now been inserted into it. It should in fact be noted that this last motive appears independent, at least in origin, from that of the journey across the desert and from the exodus generally; it could have taken place in any other locality or region and on any other occasion, all the more so since, as we shall see in the next section, it is difficult, if not impossible, to locate the holy mountain.

7.9.3 *Mount Sinai*. In the biblical tradition the promulgation of the Torah on the holy mountain is presented as a self-contained episode, all contained in the section between Exodus 19 and Numbers 10. This interrupts the present account of the migration from the Sea to Canaan via Kadesh, an account which is full of stereotyped themes: lack of water, the manna and the quails (Ex.16.13-36; Num.11.7-9); the institution of tribunals (Ex.18, a late text) and their functioning (Num.11.16); the leave-taking of Moses by his wife's relatives: his father-in-law (Ex.18.27) and his brother-in-law (Num.10.29);[46] finally, here and there we find the theme of the murmuring in the desert and nostalgia for Egypt. So it is only reasonable to see the Sinai narrative as a section interpolated into the present context, which as a result is divided into two parts.

7.9.3.1 However, as is well known, the Sinai pericope, too, is anything but a unity and indeed is one of the most complex sections in the Hebrew Bible. So the apparent unity should not deceive us.

Bibliography

W.Beyerlin, *The Origins and History of the Oldest Sinaitic Traditions*, Oxford 1965; Jörg Jeremias, *Theophanie. Geschichte einer alttestamentlichen Gattung*, WMANT 33, Neukirchen 1965, 7ff., 38ff.; H.Gese, 'Τὸ δὲ Ἁγὰρ Σινὰ ὄρος ἐστὶν ἐν τῇ Ἀραβίᾳ (Gal.4.25)', in *Das ferne und nahe*

Wort – FS L.Rost, Berlin 1967, 81-94, *GS*, 49-62; G.W.Coats, *Rebellion in the Wilderness*, Nashville 1968; K.H.Walkenhorst, *Der Sinai*, Bonn 1969; G.I.Davies, 'Hagar, el Hagra and the Location of Mount Sinai', *VT* 22, 1972, 152-63; B.Zuber, *Vier Studien zu den Ursprüngen Israels*, Freiburg CH 1976, 15ff.; G.I.Davies, 'The Significance of Deuteronomy 1, 2 for the Location of Mount Horeb', *PEQ* 111, 1979, 87-101; E.Zenger, *Israel am Sinai*, Altenberg 1982; M.Har-El (above 7.8); for archaeological problems and problems relating to the history of Israel cf. B.Rothenberg, 'An Archaeological Survey of South Sinai', *PEQ* 102, 1970, 4-29; M.Weinfeld, 'The Tribal League at Sinai', in *Ancient Israelite Religion – FS F.M.Cross*, Philadelphia 1987, 303-14; M.Görg, 'Der Sinai – (der Berg) des Erzgebietes', *BN* 54, 1990, 12-18.

7.9.3.2 We cannot be concerned here with the problem of the literary structure of the pericope, for which I must refer readers to the *Introductions* to the Old Testament and the commentaries. It is sufficient to note that it is possible to distinguish between pre-exilic material (though this does not seem necessarily connected with the sacred mountain), material of a Deuteronomic or Deuteronomistic type, and finally material from the P redaction.

7.9.3.3 Here we shall essentially be concerned with the geographical and topographical problem,[47] a problem which can be summed up as follows: we do not even know where the sacred mountain was located in the ancient traditions, assuming that the authors were in fact interested in a location and did not simply consider it a mythical entity.

7.9.3.3.1 The tradition which locates Sinai in the southern part of the peninsula of that name is relatively recent: it goes back only to the fourth century CE.[48] Here we have a group of mountains culminating in two peaks, *jebel musa* (7293 feet, coord. 778-048) and *jebel qaṭarīn* (8456 feet, coord. 771-047) a few miles apart: Justinian had the convent of St Katherine built at their feet in the fourth century CE.[49]

7.9.3.3.2 However, other locations have been authoritatively proposed in addition to the traditional location: in the neighbourhood of Kadesh, which would limit the interpolation in the route to the promulgation of the Torah, avoiding a special journey; in northern Arabia, where a tradition reported by St Paul in Gal.4.25 also locates it (here some extinct volcanoes suggest that the phenomena which accompany the theophany could be identified with an eruption[50]); and this location leads to the region of *tebūk*, once a station on the Hegiaz railway, dismantled during the First World War and then abandoned. It is interesting that some texts which are certainly pre-exilic, and in some instances very old, point precisely in this direction. These include Deut.33.2 (where there is the parallelism Sinai – *har'pār'ān* – *śeʿīr*); Judg.5.4-5; Hab.3.3 (with the parallelism Sinai – *har pār'ān* – *teman*, this last a place near Petra): in both cases we have to do with the region of Edom, specifically north Arabia.

7.9.3.3.3 However, though things may seem clear, a number of difficulties remain. For example, is it possible to state that here we have the recollection of events connected with terrifying natural phenomena like eruptions or earthquakes, or should we not rather think of a literary genre which is well attested elsewhere in the Bible, that of the 'theophany'? Its characteristics seem to be constant, even in passages in which possible eruptions are not mentioned at all (cf. Gen.15.17; II Sam.22//Ps 18.8-9); only in Isa.6.1ff. do we hear of anything like an earthquake. Scholars are rightly more inclined towards the second of these alternatives.[51]

7.9.3.3.4 To these difficulties is added another, which is obvious even to the reader who does not know Hebrew: the J tradition consistently uses Sinai, but E, Dtn and Dtr use 'Horeb', while other designations appear in the texts cited in 7.9.3.3.2. Now in different languages it is normal for there to be a number of names for the same feature (for example Cervino/Cervin and the Matterhorn in the Alps), but this variety is inexplicable in the context of the same language and a tradition which must go back to the same archetype. The actual location of Sinai is completely unknown to the Hebrew tradition, so it has never considered this mountain a holy place.

7.9.3.3.5 Finally, a recent attempt thinks in terms of a place situated in the central Negeb, where there is a *har qarqōm* (coord. 967-125),[52] the location of an open-air sanctuary in antiquity and in the Middle Bronze Age; the proposal has in its favour the fact that it puts Sinai about forty miles as the crow flies from Kadesh, so that it could be reached from there in a few days' journey. Otherwise, this seems improbable.

7.9.3.3.6 To sum up, the tradition which identifies Mount Sinai with the present-day Mount Sinai in the south of the peninsula of the same name is relatively late: it dates from about 1500 years after the events; moreover it is a tradition which is unknown in Judaism and grew up in a Christian context. On the other hand, these objections are not insurmountable: place names, especially those of sanctuaries, tend to be retained over a long period, especially in cases like this, where the name is closely connected with the name of the wilderness (above 7.9.2.2). However, we might ask whether here, too, we do not have a later attempt to historicize the events of the sacred history by giving them a location.

7.9.4 Certainly if we want to try to identify at least some of the places mentioned in the itinerary of the exodus, our best bet would be to include those places which still exist today in the Arabic nomenclature of the region. Here I follow the proposals of Aharoni**,[53] who makes these parallels the main argument for the identification of the biblical

Sinai with the Sinai of tradition, situated in the south of the peninsula of the same name. However, this does not say much: we have the Hebrew *pā'rān*, corresponding to the Byzantine φαράν and the Arabic *wādī fir'ān* (Deut.1.1, coord. 018-791; the Hebrew *yoṭbātāh*, corresponding to the Byzantine ιωτάβη, Arabic *ṭabah* (Num.33.3f.; Deut.10.7; coord. 879-139), on the frontier a few miles south of Eilat, disputed until recently; *ḥᵃṣērōt*, corresponding to the Arabic *'ein ḥaḍra* (Num.11.35; 12.16; 33.17f.; Deut.1.1, coord. 098-814). Here too it should be noted that not only do we have few names, but the identification of the places is rather dubious, so that even Aharoni seems to have a basically precarious position.

7.9.5 From Kadesh to the Promised Land we have what for the tradition is the third stage of the journey through the desert; the itinerary would then be followed through Moab to Midian, i.e. through Transjordan. It is here that the contacts with the king of Moab and the Midianites begin (Num.22-25; 31).

However, the main difficulty for these contacts consists in the fact that the populations of the Transjordan did not settle in the region before the twelfth century, indeed perhaps not before the eleventh century or even later. This is also a difficulty for those who accept the substantial historicity of these episodes. We shall return to this in more detail below (7.11).

7.9.6 It follows from these considerations that in the present state of research it is impossible to reconstruct an itinerary for the exodus through the peninsula of Sinai: the only fixed point is the oasis of Kadesh; a probable point is that of the miracle at the Sea of Reeds.

7.9.7 Numbers 33.1-49, a text which the majority of scholars do not attribute to any of the sources of the Pentateuch, though it is probably to be assigned to P (Cortese 1972), was studied in detail by Noth in 1940, and given a new and interesting explanation. Noth's theories have now been accepted by Kallai.

Bibliography

M.Noth, 'Der Wallfahrtsweg zum Sinai', *PJB* 36, 1940, 5-20, *ABLAK*, 55-74; R.de Vaux, 'L'itinéraire des Israélites de Cadès aux Plaines de Moab', in *Hommages à M.A.Dupont-Sommer*, Paris 1971, 331-342; G.W.Coats (above 7.9.2); B.Mazar, 'The Exodus and the Conquest', in *WHJP* III, 1971, 69-79; E.Cortese, *La terra di Canaan nella storia sacerdotale del Pentateuco*, Brescia 1972; M.Haran, 'Exodus' (above 7.9); Z.Kallai, 'The Wandering Traditions from Kadesh Barnea to Canaan: A Study in Biblical Historiography', *JJS* 33, 1982, 176-84; M.Har-El, *The Sinay Journeys* (above 7.9), 230ff. and 252ff.; J.M.Miller, 'The Israelite Journey through (around) Moab and Moabite Toponymy', JBL 108, 1989, 577-95.

7.9.7.1 The starting point is the superscription of this text, 33.1: 'These are the stages (*mas*ᵉ*ē*, the construct of a term which is not found in the absolute, root *nāsaʿ*, 'travel') of the people of Israel, when they left Egypt'. This text is meant to present to the reader a summary of the route covered from Raamses (v.2) to the 'plains of Moab' (v.49), the region of Transjordan opposite Jericho, present-day *ġōr el-kafrīn* (coord.202/10 – 140/44). That this list is late is evident from the fact that it combines the various narratives of the sources of Exodus and Numbers, also including information drawn from Deuteronomy. This would suggest that the author had the complete text of the Pentateuch in front of him. It is also interesting to note that almost twice as many place names are included in the list as appear in the other books of the Pentateuch.[54] Noth concludes from his examination that here we have a text based on an autonomous source which could evidently be arrived at independently of the texts indicated in the other sources. He also notes how by reversing the second part of the list we arrive at what he calls the pilgrimage route from Canaan to Sinai, a route which had many stages in common with the traditional route of the exodus.

7.9.7.2 However, closer examination indicates that the situation is more complex than that described by Noth. First of all, ch.33 is a late text with a long history behind it, something which, moreover, Noth himself readily accepts. Furthermore, there is no mention of the journey to and from Sinai, a feature which is not explained adequately. Nor is it clear why the route of a pilgrimage should have passed through Transjordan, first to turn eastwards and then bend southwards and westwards (v.41) in the direction of Arad (coord. 162-076 or 152-069, cf. also 8.2.6).

7.9.7.3 The Elijah traditions talk of the flight of the prophet towards Mount Horeb (I Kings 1.19), and it is said that Beersheba was one of the stages. The route is said to have taken 'forty days and forty nights' (19.8), but this is a round number, equivalent in Hebrew to 'many'. It is not in fact obvious that Elijah really made a pilgrimage; the texts speak of a flight, and moreover the itinerary was different from that of Num.33, so it does not appear possible to link the two texts.

7.10 Moses

The exodus from Egypt, the journey through the wilderness and the promulgation of the Torah on Mount Sinai are all features which the biblical tradition connects inextricably with the figure of Moses. He embodies a number of features in a single person: the founder of a religion, the legislator, the prophet, the believer who is severely punished in the few cases where his faith has diminished. It is not surprising that there is a vast bibliography on someone who seems to be a key figure in the origins of Israel and its religion; here I can only give a selection from it.

Bibliography

G.von Rad, *Moses*, London 1960; H.Cazelles, 'Moïse', *SDB* V, 1957, 1308-37; M.Buber, *Moses*, New York 1946; R.Smend, *Das Mosebild von H.Ewald bis M.Noth*, Tübingen 1959; E.Osswald, *Das Bild des Mose*, Berlin 1962 (both with annotated bibliographies); K.Koch, 'Der Tod des Religionsstifters', *KuD* 8, 1962, 100-23; F.Baumgärtel, *KuD* 9, 1963, 223-33; A.H.J.Gunneweg, 'Moses in Midian', *ZTK* 61, 1964, 1-9; H.Schmid, *Moses. Überlieferung und Geschichte*, BZAW 110, Berlin 1968; G.Widengren, 'What do we know about Moses?', in *Proclamation and Presence (FS G.Henton Davies)*, ed. J.I.Durham and J.R.Porter, London and Richmond, Va 1970, 21-47; E.F.Campbell Jr, 'Moses and the Foundation of Israel', *Int* 19, 1975, 141-54 (especially on the discussion between Noth and Bright); for a presentation of the theories of W.F.Albright cf. id., 'Moses in Historical and Theological Perspective', in *Magnalia Dei... Essays in Memoriam G.E.Wright*, Garden City, NY 1976, 10-31; J.B.Geyer, 'The Joseph and Moses Narratives: Folk Tale and History', *JSOT* 15, 1980, 51-6, and the response by T.L.Thompson, 'History and Tradition', ibid., 57-61; G.Sauer, 'Vom Exoduserleben zur Landnahme', *ZTK* 80, 1983, 26-32. For Moses as prophet see L.Perlitt, 'Mose als Prophet', *EvTh* 31, 1971, 579-88. Cf. also G.W.Coats, *Moses, Heroic Man, Man of God*, Sheffield 1988; G.Garbini, 'Le serpent d'airain et Moïse', *ZAW* 100, 1988, 264-7; E.Aurelius, *Der Fürbitter im Alten Testament*, Lund 1988, 99; A.Scharf, *Moses und Israel in Konflikt: eine redaktionsgeschichtliche Studie zu den Wüstenerzählungen*, Freiburg im Breisgau 1990; J.Siebert-Hummes, 'Die Geburtsgeschichte des Mose innerhalb des Erzählzusammenhangs von Exodus 1 und 2', *VT* 42, 1992, 398-403 (which I was unable to use). For the various interpretations of his person cf. Donner* I, 1984, 110-12.

7.10.1 Moses appears as the key figure who unites and interprets the events narrated in the last books of the Pentateuch: the liberation of 'Israel' from slavery in Egypt, the journey through the wilderness towards the promised land, and Israel's constitution as a religious community around the Torah given on Sinai.

7.10.2 We have seen above (7.1.3) that Moses' name is Egyptian in origin, even if now it does not have the usual theophoric element; we have also seen how the account of his birth has its roots in the popular traditions of the ancient Near East and especially those of Mesopotamia (7.6.3), whereas we would tend to expect an Egyptian tradition; we have also examined the problem of his meetings with the Pharaoh (7.7.3.1). Only one conclusion can be drawn from what has been said: these texts are in any case very complex at a literary level and often highly improbable on a historical level. So it is not surprising that von Rad and Noth[55] expressed their doubts whether the texts are an adequate basis for a historical reconstruction of the most important events and can therefore help towards a biography of Moses. Koch 1962 went so far as to even deny the existence of Moses as a historical figure, and Garbini in his recent study sees him as an Egyptian who will have joined forces with the Kenites, from where he will have made the brazen serpent (*uraeus*) on the occasion of the plagues which struck Israel at the time of David (II Sam.24); he may even have been the one who introduced the worship of YHWH to the southern tribes.

7.10.3 We can see reasons for an attitude which in the United States has often been called 'nihilistic' (cf. further 7.10.5) as soon as we consider not only the complexity and the late dating of the traditions which have come down to us, but also the mentions of Moses in texts outside the Pentateuch. In fact, given the importance of Moses in the Pentateuch and especially in the narratives of the exodus and the journey through the wilderness, we would expect him to be mentioned frequently right through the Bible, rather as happens in the New Testament with the figure of Jesus of Nazareth. In the New Testament, episodes from the life of Jesus are narrated in the Synoptic Gospels, commented on in the Fourth Gospel, and are the object of continuous reflections and references in Acts, the Epistles and Revelation. However, we do not find anything like this with Moses in the Hebrew Bible: the narrative texts outside the Pentateuch in which Moses is mentioned can be counted on the fingers of one hand and are for the most part Deuteronomistic (Josh.9.24; 24.5; I Sam.12.6,8; I Kings 8.53); the Psalms in which he appears are all exilic or post-exilic (77.21: 90.1, only the title; 103.7: 105.26; 106.16, 23, 32). There are only a few certainly pre-exilic texts which mention Moses: Judg.1.16; 4.11 (with a somewhat obscure reference to 'father-in-law' or 'son-in-law', perhaps meant to be a generic designation, 'kinsman of Moses'[56]); II Kings 18.4, where king Hezekiah has the relic of the 'bronze serpent' (cf. Num.21.4-9) removed from the temple in the course of one of his religious reforms (below 12.2.1). And in the prophetic books we find the same phenomenon: there are only three texts which mention Moses: Micah 6.4 (late); Jer.15.1 (probably Deuteronomistic) and Isa. 63.11-12 (exilic or post-exilic).

7.10.4 So it would seem that only with the Babylonian exile did the figure of Moses acquire the importance that the Jewish tradition attributes to it, whereas the earlier references are sparse and general. It can be deduced from this that for a long time his figure was not considered very important and that, as Noth pointed out fifty years ago, it was certainly not central.[57] In other words, only with Deuteronomy and Dtr does the figure of Moses seem to have begun to assume a pre-eminent position in the biblical tradition!

7.10.5 The thesis put forward by Noth is that only in Dtn and Dtr did the traditions of Moses undergo a first and final development, thus becoming what he calls 'the great bond' which combines the most disparate documents in a single text, the guideline through the most diverse episodes. However, this did not happen before Dtn and P; in the traditions that we can still recognize as being very early, e.g. Ex.24.1-2, 9-11, the figure of Moses appears clearly alongside the 'elders of Israel', and these are traditions which are more authentically primitive and certainly representative for the people, whom Moses is meant to replace. However, for Noth, Moses seems to have begun to assume his own place in the tradition in the route from Kadesh to the plains of Moab, especially during the journey in Transjordan.

7.10.6 The validity of these arguments has been challenged from 1956 onwards (and indeed down to the present day) by Bright (for whom cf. above 3.5.2.3), one of the most distinguished disciples of Albright in the United States.[58] In the first of the two volumes cited above he works with examples taken from the history of the American War of Independence. Around this, and especially in local folklore, a series of stories have grown up which can be readily compared with those about the exodus and the journey through the wilderness. However, apart from the fact that the heroes of the War of Independence moved in a precise historical context, so that for most of the time it is possible to distinguish between history and popular tradition, even Bright arrives at a conclusion which must seem disconcerting to those who want to follow his proposals: 'The trouble is that one cannot by direct argument prove Noth wrong... But neither can Noth prove himself right. We move in a realm where we can no longer lay hold of objective evidence; we can only contradict one another. But the burden of proof is definitely on Noth!' Thus even Bright is forced to admit the inadequacy of the sources for a historical reconstruction of the persons and events involved, even if, like Noth, he accepts the substantial historicity of the figure of Moses. On the other hand, it is obvious that once it is admitted that there are no adequate proofs, it is also impossible to speak of a 'burden of proof' which lies on someone.

7.10.7 So if we want to begin from the proposition that the figure of Moses is substantially historical, we are basically confronted with a problem rather like that of Romulus in the earliest history of Rome. The only difference is of course that, given the character of the religion of Israel, Moses was not taken up into heaven or divinized; nor do we have a tradition which sees him lynched by the senators. We have only a few features which can be used by the historian.

7.10.7.1 The contacts with the Midianites, the people of Moses' father-in-law.

7.10.7.2 The introduction of the cult of YHWH (Ex.3 [E] and 6 [P]).

7.10.7.3 The theme of Moses' foreign wife, the daughter of the Midianite priest (Ex.2.16ff.), cf. the independent tradition in Judg.1.16; 4.11 (cf. nn.47, 56 above). In Num.12.1, however, Moses has another wife, this time from Kush, classical *Aethiopia*, now the Sudan: some scholars think that this is still the same woman.

7.10.7.4 Local features connected with the journey from Kadesh onwards.

7.10.7.5 A tradition about the tomb of Moses, though its location is not mentioned, so that it remains unknown (Deut.34.6). Is this a motive connected with his assumption into heaven?

7.10.7.6 Other features pointed out by Garbini (above 7.10.2), though these are more problematical.

7.10.8 There is even a dispute over the figure of Moses as the founder of the religion of Israel. Noth[59] hesitated to assign him this role, whereas Bright[60] observes: 'Events like those of the Exodus and Sinai call for the presence of a great personality. And a unique faith like that of Israel demands, calls for, a founder, just like Christianity or Islam. To deny this role to Moses would oblige us to postulate the presence of another person with the same name!' Now if we look at the end of this quotation, which is clearly sarcastic, we find that the basis of the argument in fact begs the question. It seems more reasonable to keep within the limits of descriptive statements, as e.g. those of Osswald,[61] who limits herself to indicating the 'decisive role played by Moses' in the events described.

7.10.9 Starting from the central position which Moses and the events of the exodus have had in Jewish worship and piety from time immemorial, it is legitimate to ask what can be said about his person, given the impossibility of any historical demonstration. One response could be that this is a kind of prophetic parable which is meant to develop the theme of the exodus from the Babylonian captivity. This is an explanation which is also accepted by moderately conservative scholars like W.H.Schmidt.[62] The figure of Moses, which has become central only with Dtn and Dtr, in his functions as the founder of the religion, legislator and prophet, then appears as the 'type' of the great post-exilic figure within the so-called theocracy, a subject which we shall discuss in more detail below (13.9.3).

7.11 Moses and Midian

The last part of the journey, for the most part through Transjordan, presents the reader with incidents which happened to 'Israel' in its first contacts with the king of Moab and the Midianites (Num.22-25.31). I alluded to them briefly above (7.9.5).

7.11.1 On the historical level the main difficulty lies in the fact that archaeological evidence indicates that the settlement of the peoples of Transjordan cannot have taken place before the twelfth century BCE and probably not before the eleventh or even shortly afterwards. That would compel us to date the events described long after the thirteenth century, the date generally accepted for the exodus.

7.11.2 Here again we have an example of what Bright[63] has adequately described in the following words: 'The evidence is ambiguous (and incomplete), so that we cannot come to any certain conclusions.' The same thing holds for the places indicated, which are often difficult to identify, while even the traditions 'are often difficult to harmonize'. Hence we can ask whether such 'traditions' should be harmonized. Should they not rather be evaluated as they are? The details for the most part reappear under the theme of the 'settlement', so I shall discuss them in the next chapter (8.2.11).

8

The Settlement in Canaan

8.1 Were Israel and Judah originally foreigners?

The biblical tradition seems at first sight to be unanimous in affirming that Israel and Judah are not indigenous to the land of Canaan, but arrived there from abroad, and that they conquered it by means of wars in which divine intervention was the decisive element. This conception seems absolutely dominant in the biblical tradition and is adopted as an element of the proof of the foreign origin of the tribes and hence of their immigration: what people indeed would confess that they had originally been alien to the land that they considered their own country and to which they claimed inalienable rights?

However, this conception, even if it is predominant, is not the only one: in Chronicles, according to Japhet 1979 (see below), we seem to have the theory that Israel and Judah had always lived in their own land.

8.1.2 The first argument is certainly illuminating, even if not decisive: what was in fact more logical than for the community of the post-exilic restoration to base itself on a prehistoric event which was seen as the divine gift *par excellence*? Only the authors of Chronicles, for whom the problem no longer existed in practice, could ignore it!

Bibliography

A.Alt, 'The Settlement of the Israelites in Palestine', in *Essays on Old Testament History and Religion*, Oxford 1966, 133-69; id., 'Erwägungen über die Landnahme der Israeliten in Palästina' (1939), *KS* 1, 126-75; 'Josua' (1936), *KS* I, 176-92; 'Israel', *RGG* III (²1929), 439ff.; ³1959, 936ff.; W.F.Albright, 'The Israelite Conquest of Canaan in the Light of Archaeology', *BASOR* 74, 1939, 11-22; R.de Vaux, 'Israel, Histoire d'', *SDB* IV, 1949, 758f.; H.H.Rowley, 'From Joseph to Joshua, London ²1951; Y.Kaufmann, *The Biblical Account of the Conquest of Palestine*, Jerusalem ²1953; G.E.Mendenhall, 'The Hebrew Conquest of Palestine',

BA 25, 1952, 66-87; J.A.Soggin, 'La conquista israelitica della Palestina nei secoli XIII e XII a C. e le scoperte archeologiche', *Prot* 17, 1962, 193-208, ET in *OTOS*, 11-30; M.Weinfeld, 'The Period of the Conquest and of the Judges', *VT* 17, 1967, 93-113; P.W.Lapp, 'The Conquest of Palestine in the Light of Archaeology', *Concordia Theological Monthly* 38, 1967, 283-300; M.Weippert, *The Settlement of the Israelite Tribes in Palestine*, 1971, 1-15; S.Yeivin, *The Israelite Conquest of Canaan*, Leiden and Istanbul 1971 (cf. my review in *OA* 13, 1974, 75-8); H.J.Franken, *CAH* II,2, ³1975, 331ff.; G.Wallis, 'Die Sesshaftwerdung Altisraels...', *ZAW* 83, 1971; G.W.Coats, 'Conquest Traditions on the Wilderness Theme', *JBL* 95, 1976, 177-90; Y.Aharoni, 'Nothing Early and Nothing Late – Re-Writing Israel's Conquest', *BA* 39, 1976, 55-76; J.M.Miller, 'Archaeology and the Israelite Conquest of Canaan: Some Methodological Observations', *PEQ* 109, 1977, 87-93; S.Yeivin, 'On the Number of the Israelite Tribes', *EI* 14, 1978, 37f. (Hebrew, with an English summary); A.J.Hauser, 'Israel's Conquest of Palestine: A Peasant's Rebellion?', *JSOT* 7, 1978, 2-19, and the response by T.L.Thompson, 'Historical Notes on "Israel's Conquest of Palestine: A Peasants' Rebellion" ', ibid., 10-17; M.Weippert, 'The Israelite "Conquest" and the Evidence from Transjordan', in *Symposia... ASOR*, Cambridge, Mass. 1979, 15-34; A.Malamat, 'Israelite Conduct of War according to the Biblical Tradition', ibid., 35-55; S.Japhet, 'Conquest and Settlement in Chronicles', *JBL* 98, 1979, 205-18; N.K.Gottwald, *The Tribes*, passim; J.A.Soggin, 'I testi vetero-testamentari sulla conquista della Palestina', *RiBib* 28, 1980, 45-57; A.Rolla, 'La conquista di Canaan e l'archeologia palestinese', 89-96; S.Loffreda, 'L'insediamento israelitico nel Negev alla luce dei recenti scavi', *BeO* 22, 1980, 254-63; V.Fritz, 'Die kulturgeschichtliche Bedeutung der früheisenzeitlichen Siedlung auf dem ḫirbet el-msas und das Problem der Landnahme', *ZDPV* 96, 1980, 121-35, ET *BASOR* 241, 1981, 61-73; B.Mazar, 'The Early Israelite Settlement in the Hill Country', ibid., 75-85; A.G.Auld, *Joshua, Moses and the Land*, Edinburgh 1980; Z.Kallai, 'Territorial Patterns. Biblical Historiography and Scribal Tradition – A Programmatic Survey', *ZAW* 93, 1982, 427-32; H.D.Lance, *The Old Testament and the Archaeologist*, Philadelphia 1981; B.S.J.Isserlin, 'The Israelite Conquest of Canaan. A Comparative View of the Arguments Applicable', *PEQ* 115, 1983; A.Schoors, 'The Israelite Conquest: Textual Evidence in the Archaeological Argument', in E.Lipiński (ed.), *The Land of Israel*, Louvain 1985, 77-92; S.Herrmann, 'Basic Factors of Israelite Settlement in Canaan', in A.Biran (ed.), *Biblical Archaeology Today*, Jerusalem 1985, 47-53; J.Sanmartin Ascaso, 'Geschichte und Erzählung im Alten Orient, I, Die Landnahme Israels', *UF* 17, 1985, 235-82; J.A.Callaway, 'A New Perspective on the Hill Country Settlement in Canaan in the Iron Age I', in *Palestine in the Bronze and Iron Ages. Papers... Olga Tufnell*, London 1985, 31-49; V.Fritz,

'Conquest or Settlement? The Settlement of Nomadic Tribes in the Negeb Highlands in the 11th Century BC', in M.Heltzer and É.Lipiński (eds.), *Society and Economy in the Eastern Mediterranean (c.1500-1000 BC)*, Louvain 1988, 313-40; I.Finkelstein, *The Archaeology of the Israelite Settlement*, Jerusalem 1988; W.Thiel, 'Vom revolutionären zum evolutionären Israel?', *TLZ* 13, 1988, 401-10; M.Weinfeld, 'Historical Facts behind the Israelite Settlement Pattern', *VT* 38, 1988, 324-56; C.Hauer, 'From Alt to Anthropology: The Rise of the Israelite State', *JSOT* 36, 1986, 3-15; J.A.Callaway in Shanks* 1988, 324-56; H.Weippert** 1989, 267ff., 365ff., 393ff.; P.Kaswalder, 'I nuovi dati archeologici e le origini d'Israele', *LA-SBF* 38, 1988, 211-26; S.Herrmann, *Israels Frühgeschichte im Spannungsfeld neuer Hypothesen*, Rheinisch-Westfälische Akademie der Wissenschaften, 1988; S.Kreuzer, *Die Frühgeschichte Israels in Bekenntnis und Verkündigung des Alten Testament*, Berlin 1989; K.W.Whitelam, 'Israel's Traditions of Origin. Reclaiming the Land', *JSOT* 44, 1989, 19-42; V.Fritz, 'Die Landnahme der israelitischen Stämme in Kanaan', *ZDPV* 106, 1990, 63-77.

Particular problems: G.-L.Prato, 'Le origini dell'antico Israele nell'analisi socio-religiosa di N.K.Gottwald', *Gr* 62, 1981, 553-61; F.S.Frick, *The Formation of the State in Ancient Israel*, Sheffield 1985; R.B.Coote and K.W.Whitelam, *The Emergence of Early Israel in Historical Perspective*, Sheffield 1986; L.W.Stager, 'Highland Village Life in Palestine Some Three Thousand Years Ago', *The Oriental Institute Notes and News* 69, Chicago 1981, 1ff.; id., 'Archaeology of the Family in Ancient Israel', *BASOR* 260, 1985, 1-35. For Jericho see my 'Gerico – anatomia d'una conquista', *Prot* 29, 1974, 194-213 (French *RHPR* 57, 1977, 1-17) and 'The Conquest of Jericho through Battle', *EI* 16, 1982, 215*-17*.

8.1.3 There are many accounts of the settlement in the Bible, which I would like to list briefly here. Those which present the settlement as a military 'conquest' are particularly interesting. We shall be returning to this topic in more detail later.

8.1.3.1 The best-known account is certainly that in Josh.1-12. This is clearly a highly idealized and ideological text, to a large extent developed in terms of theology and the cult. In it all twelve tribes, including those settled in Transjordan, conquer the country together.

8.1.3.2 A second account, which now appears as a continuation of the previous one, appears in Judg.1: in it the settlement, also seen here as a 'conquest', appears as a series of attempts by individual tribes and groups.

8.1.3.3 Then there are some fragmentary texts, often understood as accounts of settlement: the expedition of Simeon and Levi against Shechem (Gen.34); the exploration of the southern hill-country under the command of Caleb (Num.13-14; Deut.1.22-23); the expedition against Arad and other places in the Negeb (Num.21.1-3); the conquest by Dan of its own territory in the north (Judg.17-18; cf. Josh 19.47). Moreover, importance has always been attached to those places which were not conquered (Judg.1.27-35, with parallel fragments in Josh.15.63; 16.9ff.; 17.11-18; these are texts which until recently were thought to be very old).

8.1.3.4 One special feature can be found in Josh.8.30-36 and 23; 24; in them 'Israel' finds itself settled in the region of Shechem without any problems with the local population.

8.1.3.5 As I indicated earlier (above 4.4.2.2), II Sam.5.6-9 gives us information about the conquest of Jerusalem by David, while according to I Kings 9.16f., Solomon obtains the destroyed places of Gezer (above 6.5.6) as dowry for the Egyptian princess who is his wife. The problem of the settlement of the tribes in Transjordan (Num.33-34) seems particularly complex.

8.2 The individual traditions in detail

We have a series of notes which are not always easy to co-ordinate; some of them are contradictory, if we leave out what we can call the official version, Joshua 1-12. And it is the very complexity of these accounts which raises the question whether the first part of Joshua was not meant to overcome difficulties and contradictions by means of a new unitary account.

8.2.1 According to the first account, the 'conquest' was a large-scale operation in line with the scheme begun by the traditions of the exodus; like Moses in the desert, Joshua his successor (Josh.1.1) led the people in this phase of the operation. However, a look at its course clearly shows that this is conceived more as a cultic procession than as a military operation: at its head goes the ark, escorted by the tribes, just as had happened in the desert. Only in the case of Jericho do there seem to be traces of an earlier version, which envisaged a military conquest (Soggin 1982). The tribes are said to have crossed the Jordan coming from the 'plains of Moab' (above 7.9.7.1, Num.36.13; Deut.34.1), a region which is also called *šiṭṭīm*, 'acacias', though we cannot establish whether this is an alternative designation or the name of a district or locality (cf. Num.25.1; Josh.2.1; 3.1). The crossing of the river takes place in the region of Jericho, the present-day *tell-es sulṭān* (coord.192-142), a few hundred yards north of the modern city.

The tribes which had obtained territory in Transjordan (Reuben, Gad and the eastern part of Manasseh, below 8.2.11.13) are said to have made their own contribution to the expedition, to help their 'brothers' (Josh.1.12ff.), returning to their own territory after the conquest (Gen.22.1ff.). so the reader is clearly faced with what I have called (above 3.1.7.4) the unitary ideology of the one people of God, an ideology which flourished essentially in post-exilic Judah at the time of the hierocracy.

8.2.2 However, an examination of the geography and topography of Josh.1-12 immediately brings out a remarkable fact: with only four exceptions (7.6, a marginal text; 8.30-35, a totally Deuteronomistic text which is set in Shechem; 10.15ff., where we are in the southern highlands; and 11.1-15, where we are in Upper Galilee and the problem of the itinerary followed is left open, or we have yet another formerly independent tradition of the conquest), the texts refer exclusively to the territory of the tribe of Benjamin, one of the least extensive in tribal geography. And this still holds despite the objections made by Kaufmann 1953. Gilgal (near Jericho, the precise location is unknown) is a Benjaminite sanctuary, and it is from there that all the expeditions leave; all the ceremonies and all the rites connected with the crossing of the Jordan, which is accompanied by a miracle in every way similar to that at the crossing of the Sea of Reeds (above 7.8) take place here; and it is again in the sphere of this sanctuary that the processions connected by the texts with the fall of Jericho also take place. The importance of Gilgal is emphasized by mention of it in texts not connected with the 'conquest': in I Sam.11.1ff. it is said to have been an important sanctuary in the period at the very start of the monarchy, when Saul, a Benjaminite, was chosen as king (above 4.3). It still appears in the early prophetic period (cf. Hos.9.15; Amos 5.5). These observations automatically raise the question whether the sanctuary of Gilgal was not originally the area in which the first elements of the tradition of the unitary 'conquest' arose and were handed down, so that they became the official version of events. This is a question which, given the present state of research, must remain unanswered.

By contrast, the account which appears in Judg.1.1-2.5 knows of a 'conquest' by individual groups and tribes, and has therefore seemed to many scholars to be closer to the events. Moreover it too speaks of a military conquest, from the sanctuary of Gilgal. But what constitutes the introduction to the 'body' of the book of Judges (1.1-2.5) is not a unitary work: the whole section is held together by the fact that Israel leaves from Gilgal, a feature which seems more literary than historical.

Bibliography

The commentaries on Judges; also A.G.Auld, 'Judges I and History: A Reconsideration', *VT* 25, 1975, 261-85; N.H.Rösel, 'Die Überleitungen vom Josua ins Richterbuch', *VT* 30, 1980, 342-50; J.Van Seters, *In Search of History*, New Haven and London 1983, 337-42; R.Smend, 'Das uneroberte Land', in H.Strecker (ed.), *Das Land Israel in biblischer*

Zeit. Jerusalem Symposium 1981, Göttingen 1983, 91-102, *GS* II, 217-28; K.D.Schunck, 'Falsche Richter im Richterbuch', in *Zur Aktualität des Alten Testaments – FS Georg Sauer zum 65.Geburstag*, Frankfurt am Main 1992, 364-70.

The protagonists of the beginning of the chapter are Simeon and Judah (vv.1-21) and the associated groups in the south; in vv.22-26, however, we have the 'house of Joseph' in the central hill-country; the chapter ends with a mention of the territories not conquered (vv.27-35) and a note on the territory of the Edomites (v.36).

8.2.3.1 In the text Judah and Simeon are presented in the act of 'conquering' their own territory, now including that of Caleb (below 8.2.5), which seems to indicate that here we are already in a later stage of the tradition. We hear nothing of the other tribes in this context. The conquests of Judah, however, are limited to the hill-country; in the plain (and the cities of Gaza, Askelon and Ekron, which later belonged to the Philistine Pentapolis, above 4.4.1.4, are mentioned, though we hear nothing of the Pentapolis itself), Judah and Simeon did not succeed in gaining the upper hand. It is difficult to say whether the texts preserve the memory of the situation before the arrival of the Philistines, or whether this is simply a repetition of the scheme used for the tribes of the centre and north; the latter seems to be more probable, given that in the south there were no fertile and densely populated plains that would have been worth the trouble of conquest. In any case we cannot obtain any certain information from the texts, and even the mention of 'chariots of iron' (this, of course, means chariots plated and armed with this metal, v.18) seems to be a feature of the literary genre rather than the memory of a past reality.

8.2.3.2 To begin with, the tribes of the central hill-country are presented under the collective name 'Joseph', i.e. Ephraim and Manasseh, but Bethel, the place which is conquered, belongs to the former of the two tribes. The terms in the narrative seem generic, from the mention of Joseph to that of the city founded by the fugitive traitor to whose collaboration Joshua owed the possibility of entering the city without striking a blow. The traitor referred to here founds another city in the 'country of the Hittites' (for this term, cf. above 2.7.1). Excavations carried out in this place, usually identified with the Arab village of *beitīn* (coord.172-148), have not made any appreciable contribution towards solving the problem.[1]

8.2.3.3 The list of the places which the tribes of Benjamin, Manasseh, Ephraim, Asher and Naphtali did not succeed in conquering during the settlement (the case of Dan is less clear, since the name of this tribe seems to have been added to the list at a later stage) was deemed very important until a few years ago because it was considered to be very old. As we have seen (above 4.5.2), the period of their incorporation into Israel (in whatever way this happened) is usually connected with the Davidic empire (cf.1.28ff.). However, fundamental doubts have recently been indicated (by Smend 1983) about the antiquity of this list, too, the tendentiously pro-Judahite character of which has always been recognized. Moreover this corresponds to what is known independently through excavations: the Canaanite city states continued to survive in the territories of the plains and the coast for a further period of time.

8.2.3.4 The conclusion of this section (2.1-5) probably belongs to the latest stratum of Dtr and seems to be the aetiological legend of an unknown sanctuary which the LXX connects with that of Bethel. The text is especially a reflection on the disobedience of the people, a feature for which the mention of the sanctuary is only a pretext; it has little or nothing to do with the conquest.[2]

8.2.3.5 The problem of the relationship of this prologue to Judges with the end of Joshua has been tackled once more and, I believe, resolved in the study by Rösel 1980. He adopts and develops a theory once put forward by Eissfeldt, arguing that Josh.24 is continued in Judg.1.1ff.; Josh.23 in Judg.2.6ff.

8.2.4 The account in Gen.34, where Simeon and Levi attack Shechem, has often been regarded as an attempt at conquest, This is an organic and self-contained narrative like the Joseph story, in which a search for sources has not produced any results.[3] For some scholars it is the recollection of an ancient enterprise which could have turned out badly.

Bibliography

M.Noth, *Pentateuchal Traditions*, 86f.; G. von Rad, *Genesis*, OTL, London and Philadelphia 1972, 329ff.; C.Westermann, *Genesis I*, Minneapolis 1985 and London 1986, ad loc.; J.A.Soggin, *Genesi II*, Genoa (in preparation), ad loc. *Monographs*: S.Lehming, 'Überlieferungsgeschichte von Genesis 34', *ZAW* 70, 1958, 228-50; A. de Pury, 'Genèse XXXIV et l'histoire', *RB* 76, 1969, 1-49; W.T.In der Smitten, 'Genesis 34 – Ausdruck der Volksmeinung?', *BO* 30, 1973, 7-9; F.C.Fensham, 'Gen.XXXIV and Mari', *JNWSL* 4, 1975, 87-90; W.Kevers, 'Étude littéraire de Genèse XXXIV', *RB* 87, 1980, 38-86; Soggin, 'I testi' (above 8.1.2), 47-50; B.J.Diebner, 'Gen 34 und Dinas Rolle bei der Definition "Israel"', *DBAT* 19, 1984, 59-76; E.Blum, *Die Komposition der Vätergeschichte*, Neukirchen/Vluyn 1984, 210-16; M.M.Caspi, ' "And His Soul Clave to Dinah" (Gen.34)', *AJBI* 11, 1985, 16-53; J.A.Soggin, 'Genesis Kapitel 34: Eros und Thanatos', in *FS E.Nielsen*, SVT XX 1993.

8.2.4.1 The story of the attack by two of the patriarchs on Shechem in a period which is not defined but is connected with the traditions of the time of Jacob, when his sons were already grown up, is a typical family narrative like that of Joseph. Jacob's only daughter, Dinah (cf. Gen.30.21), has been abducted and raped by the eponymous hero of the city of Shechem, son of Hamor; the population of the place is said to be 'Hivite', an ethnic group which the tradition associates with the Horites, with whom they are sometimes confused (LXX in fact translates the term ὁ Χορραῖος).[4] The text presents this population as 'uncircumcised', a designation often used to denote populations of Indo-European origin. Two other texts which deal with this locality, Josh 24.32 and Judg.9.28, present Shechem under the title Hamorite, literally 'asinine'.

8.2.4.2 However, the Shechemites offer the family reparatory marriage, and with this in mind the father of the abductor presents a formal request for marriage to Jacob, a figure who has a low profile in the narrative and thus could have been completely absent. The family of the abductor are aware of being in the wrong and are prepared to concede any form of indemnity provided that the treaty goes forward: 'Ask of me ever so much as marriage present and gift, and I will give according as you say to me; only give me the maiden to be my wife' (v.12). However, for the brothers of Dinah these proposals, too, and not just the abduction and the rape, constitute an insult; moreover it is possible that two concepts of family honour are opposed in the mind of the narrator: the rigorous attitude typical of populations which are not yet sedentary, like the Jacob group, and the lax Canaanite and city attitude for which it is possible to imagine some sort of transaction, a form of compromise, in any situation.

8.2.4.3 The honour of their sister is thus at stake here, and a compromise does not seem possible to the brothers. But since non-sedentary populations were not in a position to make a frontal attack on a fortified city, far less lay siege to it (and the excavations made at Shechem, present-day *tell balāṭa*, coord. 176-179, have shown substantial walls), Simeon and Levi resort to a stratagem: they lay down as a condition for the agreement that the Shechemites, too, should be circumcised. And the Shechemites, also attracted by the evident benefit of having a new and well-to-do population within their borders (vv.21-23), accede to the request. But while they are suffering from the after-effects of the operation, Simeon and Levi attack them treacherously; they plunder and destroy the place, killing the inhabitants. And in the song in Gen.49.5-7 there appears a note which makes the warlike character of the two groups one of the factors which later led to the dispersion. So it is not surprising that the two texts have been connected, though more recent studies (de Vaux*, II, 526ff.) tend to minimize the relationship. The fact remains that in the historical period nothing of the two tribes remains but the names.

8.2.4.4 What is it possible to say about a text like this? In the first place it is noted that an event which should be evaluated with eminently political criteria has been seen in an exclusively family perspective, with a framework of love and death, of marriage treaties and betrayal, in other words a framework which would seem to exclude the political character of the account. Obviously that does not rule out the possibility that underlying the narrative there can be the recollection of some expedition against the locality on the part of the forebears of Israel and Judah. And it in fact proves to have been destroyed at least three times during the second millennium BCE: at the end of the eighteenth century, in the middle of the sixteenth century and at the end of the twelfth century; however, there is nothing in these discoveries to suggest any connection with our texts. Moreover, the element of circumcision as a *conditio sine qua non* for the initiation of marriage relationships is much more reminiscent of the conversions to Judaism during the Hellenistic and Roman period (see also 14.7.4.6) than as a characteristic feature of the prehistory of Israel. Here the text evidently presupposes a knowledge of Gen.17 (P) which puts it in the post-exilic period: circumcision has now become one of the distinctive features of Judaism over against the other peoples, and a Hebrew girl could be given as a wife only to one who had been circumcised, in other words one who either belonged to the people of God or had been converted to it. Some scholars (e.g. de Pury 1969) have tried to connect the episode with the attacks of *ḫapīru* groups (above 6.6.3.1) which are attested in the el-ʿAmarna archive (above 2.8.1), but this attempt seems rather improbable. In addition to the theme of circumcision the texts present other disconcerting elements: Shechem and Hamor are not attested as personal names either in the Bible or outside it, and whereas in the texts cited from Joshua and Judges the term *'anšē ḥᵃmōr* is perfectly acceptable as a gentilic name, here the two names make no sense. It is clear that the definitions of political and ethnic elements are at least confused and stem from a misunderstanding of the information contained in ancient texts. So here we have a late text which has nothing to do with the settlement in Canaan.

8.2.5 Numbers 13–14 and Deuteronomy 1.22-23 speak of an expedition coming from the south.

Bibliography

M.Noth, *Pentateuchal Traditions*, 130ff.; *Numbers*, OTL, London and Philadelphia 1968, ad loc.; F.Stolz, *Jahwes und Israels Kriege*, Zurich 1972, 69-72; E.Cortese, *La terra di Canaan nella tradizione sacerdotale del*

Pentateuco, Brescia 1972, 27-35; Soggin, 'I testi...' (above 8.1.2), 50f.; L.Perlitt, *Riesen im Alten Testament*, Göttingen 1990, 35ff., 38ff.

In their present form the texts set out to give an account of a reconnaissance mission sent by Moses from the region of Kadesh, where 'Israel' was at the time, to the land of Canaan. The orders received are: 'Go up into the Negeb; then go up into the hill-country and see what the land is, and whether the people who inhabit it are strong or weak...' (vv.17f.). So the exploration is aimed at a reconnaissance of the southern sector of Canaan, i.e. the northern Negeb and the southern hill-country, though v.21 seems to list places situated in the extreme north of the country, on the frontier of the Davidic empire. And since in connection with Hebron the text mentions the three 'giants' living there (14.22, see Perlitt 1990), whereas Caleb appears as the only one who offers a positive relationship (13.30), there is a link with Josh. 14.5-15/Judg.1.10-15 (cf. Josh.15.13-20). So since the texts in Joshua and Judges speak of the 'conquest' of Hebron by Caleb, a group later absorbed into Judah, which also incorporated its traditions about the conquest, it seems reasonable to suppose that Num.13-14 also originally referred to the same episode. Of course later, in the economy of the theory of a pan-Israelite 'conquest' (above 8.1.3.1-2), the invasion had to be launched through Gilgal and Jericho, and could not be made independently from the south. As a result the theme of conquest is turned into one of exploration, and it is here that Caleb behaves valiantly, receiving his reward in due time.

8.2.6 Numbers 21.1-13 (cf. also Judg.1.17), however, speaks of an expedition against Arad and other places situated in the eastern Negeb (coord.152-069, or 162-076, the identification is controversial). It ends with a defeat of the Canaanites near a place which is then called, aetiologically, Hormah, 'the ban'. The text does not indicate lasting consequences, though there is no reason to doubt a victory, even if limited to the local level. It would not be strange for the note to be mutilated and partly suppressed because it clashed with the official version.

8.2.7 Judges 17-18 speaks of the settlement of the tribes of Dan in their own territory in the extreme north of the country; there is also an allusion to this in Josh.19.47.

Bibliography

The commentaries on Judges; also M.Rose, *Deuteronomist und Jahwist*, ATANT 67, Zurich 1981, 147ff.

8.2.7.1 The migration of Dan towards the north was caused by circumstances for which the texts do not give an adequate explanation, just as they do not indicate precisely where Dan had lived before the migration. However, a reasonable explanation can be proposed, even if it is conjectural: Dan was settled in a region in the centre and south, but because of the arrival of the Philistines its position there became increasingly problematical. It is even possible that the epic-grotesque stories about Samson have preserved, even if in a totally distorted way, the memory of the first struggles that the group had against the invaders (Judg.13-16).[5]

8.2.7.2 However, the purpose of this account is not historical either; it is polemic against the sanctuary of Dan, present-day *tell el-qādī* (coord. 211-294), whose sacred image is said to have been stolen from an Ephraimite who in turn had made it from precious metal which was the proceeds of a theft. And that is the case despite the proud claim of this priesthood to have descended directly from Moses, without Aaron as intermediary (Judg.18.30f., cf. the inverted *nun* which is meant to turn *mōšēh* [Moses] into *mᵉnaššēh* [Manasseh]). However – though this should not surprise us – there is no reference to the 'golden calf' which according to I Kings 12.29 Jeroboam I had placed in the sanctuary of Dan after the break-up of the personal union (below 10.4).

8.2.7.3 At all events, the redaction of this passage was certainly later than the invasion of the region by Tiglath-pileser III of Assyria (cf. II Kings 15.29 and the Assyrian annals in *ANET*, 283b; *TUAT* I, 373, cf. below 11.2.9), which took place in 733-732 BCE. The texts regard the invasion as a well-deserved punishment for the misdemeanours which had been perpetrated in the sanctuary from time immemorial. On the other hand, the redaction seems to be earlier than that of Dtr, since here the sin of the Danites is not the 'sin of Jeroboam', i.e. placing the 'calf' in the sanctuary. This perspective, which we might call edifying, limits the use of the texts as sources for the historian, all the more so as it also reproduces the pattern typical of the narratives of the exodus and the 'conquest'.[6]

8.2.8 One large section, Judg.1.21,27-35 with the parallels indicated in Josh.15.63; 16.10; 17.11-13, 14-18, has already been examined (above 8.1.3.3, 8.2.3.3).

8.2.8.1 It is important to note that the antiquity of the list, which was accepted almost without question until a few years ago, has recently been put in question with arguments of great weight. The places mentioned all have a common characteristic; without exception they are on the plains: the plain of Jezreel and the plains of the central and northern coasts. This is a region which the el-ʿAmarna archive shows to have been densely populated and sub-divided into dozens of small city-states. Again during the last years of the second millennium BCE, under the brief and contested reign of Eshbaʿal, son of Saul, it is said that the young king had control of Gilead in Transjordan: Ephraim, Manasseh and Benjamin; and perhaps also Asher and the place Jezreel (present-day *zer'in*, coord. 181-218).

8.2.8.2 The same places appear later inserted into Solomon's system of districts (cf. above 5.8.1-2) and some of them were even restored by him and fortified (above 5.1.2.4-5). So they were incorporated into the empire in the time of David (above 4.5.2), 'when Israel became powerful' (Judg.1.18; Josh.17.13). It is probable that this was achieved peacefully, by means of treaties.

8.2.9 Shechem, capital of the northern region of the hill-country (as is Nablus to the present day) appears in Israelite hands in Josh.8.30-35, clearly a Deuteronomistic text, and in chs.23 (late Dtr) and 24 (revised by Dtr). However, we do not have any information about how this occupation took place, even if all the signs are that it took place peacefully. We have seen (above 8.2.4) that the episode narrated in Gen.34 cannot be connected with this event.

Bibliography

The commentaries on Joshua; Soggin, 'I testi' (above 8.1.2); R.Smend, 'Josua 23', in *Probleme biblischer Theologie – FS G.von Rad*, Munich 1971, 501-4; E.Otto, *Jakob in Sichem*, Stuttgart 1979. An attempt to attribute the texts to P can be found in J.Vink, 'The Date and Origin of the Priestly Code in the Old Testament', *OTS* 15, 1969, 1-144: 63ff. Relations between Shechem and Gilgal are discussed by O.Eissfeldt, 'Gilgal or Shechem?', in *Proclamation and Presence (FS G.Henton Davies)*, London and Atlanta 1970, 90-101.

8.2.9.1 Only in Josh.24 do we find material which could be earlier than Dtr, and it is doubtful whether the other two texts are anything more than a Deuteronomistic composition.

8.2.9.2 Relationships between Israel and the population of the region of Shechem seem always to have been good, and to have included not only business dealings but also marriages, if we can accept what is said in Judg.8.29-31; 9.1ff. The second of these texts, however, suggests a deterioration in these relationships, though only for a short period, followed by the destruction of the place.

8.2.9.3 The implicit indication that Israel made a peaceful settlement in the area, with the full agreement of the local population, is interesting, particularly as it contrasts with the official version of the 'conquest', which excludes friendly relations with the Canaanites and rather argues for their expulsion: furthermore it is silent about the central and northern hill country.

8.2.10 I have already dealt with the problems connected with the occupation of Jerusalem (I Sam.5.1ff.) and the gift of Gezer by Solomon's Egyptian father-in-law (I Kings 9.15; cf. 4.4.1.2 and 5.6.6 respectively).

8.2.11 The problem of the settlement of Israel and Judah in Transjordan is particularly complex, and can only partially be resolved; that is also because of the changing fortunes of those involved in this settlement (above 7.11).

Bibliography

N.Glueck, 'Explorations in Eastern Palestine, I-IV', *AASOR* 14, 1934; 15, 1935; 18/19, 1939; 25/28, 1951 (the classic surface exploration of the region); M.Noth, 'Das Land Gilead als Siedlungsgebiet israelitischer Sippen', *PJB* 37, 1941, 50-101; 'Israelitische Stämme zwischen Ammon und Moab', *ZAW* 60, 1944, 11-57; 'Die Nachbarn der israelitischen Stämme im Ostjordanland', *BBLAK* (= *ZDPV* 68, 1946-51), 1-50; 'Gilead und Gad', *ZDPV* 75, 1959, 14-73 (all collected in *ABLAK*, 347-90, 391-433, 434-75, 489-543); id., *Josua*, HAT I, 6, Tübingen ²1953, 78-83 (these are now all classical studies of the topography of the region); M.Wüst, *Untersuchungen zu den siedlungsgeographischen Texten des Alten Testaments, I, Ostjordanland*, Wiesbaden 1975; A.G.Auld, *Joshua, Moses and the Land*, Edinburgh 1980, 2ff. (among other things a critique and completion of Wüst's monumental work, 1975); M.Weippert, 'The Period of the "Conquest"' (above 8.1.2); Z.Kallai, 'Conquest and Settlement of Transjordan', *ZDPV* 99, 1983, 110-18; J.F.A.Sawyer and D.J.A.Clines (ed.), *Midian, Moab and Edom*, JSOT-SS 24, Sheffield 1983 (on arguments based on archaeology); K.A.D.Smelik, 'Een vuur gaat uit van Chesbon', *Amsterdams Cahiers* 5, 1984, 61-109; R.G.Boling, *The Early Biblical Community in Transjordan*, Sheffield 1987; W.G.Dever, 'The Contribution of Archaeology to the Study of Canaanite and Early Israelite Religion', in *Ancient Israelite Religion, Essays... F.M.Cross*, Philadelphia 1987, 209-47; L.G.Heer, 'Tripartite Pillared Buildings and the Market Place in Iron Age Palestine', *BASOR* 272, 1988, 47-67; Z.Gal, 'The Late Bronze Age in Galilee', ibid., 79-84; H.-C.Schmitt, 'Das Hesbonlied Num.21, 27aβb-30 und die Geschichte der Stadt Hesbon', *ZDPV* 104, 1988, 26-43; S.Timm, *Moab zwischen den Mächten*, Wiesbaden 1989, 61-96; E.A.Knauf, 'Hesbon, Sihonstadt', *ZDPV* 106, 1990 [1991], 135-44.

8.2.11.1 This time the complexity of the problem does not stem only from the nature of the sources. It also has an objective basis in the discontinuity of the Israelite settlement in the region during the first half of the first millennium BCE. The relevant biblical texts are Num.32.1ff.//Deut.3.12-20; Josh.1.12-18; 13.9-22; 22.1ff. Another complicating factor is that all the settlements in the south seem to be late.

8.2.11.2 The tribes concerned are Reuben, a group which has left no appreciable traces in the historical period (it is mentioned only in one early text, Judg.5.15-16, while in Gen.49.3f. it seems to have lost its importance; in Deut.33.6 it even seems to be in process of extinction). In Judg.3.1ff. its territory has some obscure connection with the northern part of Moab, but this is an area which Israelites populated only in a precarious way, following an immigration from the west. Under David, and down to the end of the ninth century BCE, the region remained in the possession of Israel, but at the end of the period it succeeded in regaining its independence,[7] as is also attested by the stele of king Mesha (cf. below 10.10.12). It is reported on this inscription that the 'men of Gad' had dwelt in the region of ʿaṭṭarōt (present-day ḥirbet ʿaṭṭārus, coord. 213-109) 'from time immemorial' (mʿlm), line 10. This information is confirmed by Num.32.34f. and is therefore to be preferred to the attempt to locate Gad in Gilead, in the northern region of the modern Hashemite kingdom of Jordan. According to the same stele the Gadites were subjected to the ban and exterminated in honour of Chemosh, the national God of Moab. As is evident, there is little or no room for a group called Reuben.

8.2.11.3 We know virtually nothing about the eastern part of Manasseh, which perhaps immigrated into the region after the difficulties it encountered in settling west of the Jordan. At all events, the members of this group seem to have been the main victims of the Aramaean wars during the ninth century and at the beginning of the eighth (cf. Amos 1.3-5, 13-15; 6.13f.;[8] cf. below, 10.9,3-4).

8.2.11.4 Numbers 21.21-31 mentions struggles between 'Israel' and Sihon, king of Heshbon (present-day ḥesbān, coord. 226-134) and the conquest of Jazer in Moab (v.24; this is perhaps present-day ḥirbet eṣ-ṣar, coord. 228-150),[9] in Moab. This could be ancient tradition; however, the key text, v.30, is corrupt and cannot be restored, which complicates our understanding of the passage. Still, recently it has been argued (by Schmitt 1988, cf. Timm 1989) that this text, too, is the product 'of an interpretative process of the exilic/post-exilic period'.

8.2.11.5 We find a qualitative difference in the episode of Og, king of Bashan, 'the last of the Rephaim', an original, mythical population of ancient Canaan associated with the spirits of the dead (to which the rood rāpāʾ refers, particularly in Ugaritic).[10] The episode 'aims to legitimate the claim of the eastern part of the tribe of Manasseh to a region which the Israelites in fact had never possessed'.[11]

8.2.12 None of these traditions, which for the most part are to be dated centuries after the events which they seek to describe, provides any probable or even just hypothetical framework. However, a study of some of the tribal sayings in Gen.49.1-27; Deut.33.1-29 and Judg.5.14-18 could prove more interesting. Important work here has been begun by Donner* I, 1984, 130-145.[12] It is in fact possible that ancient traditions have been preserved here.

8.3 The settlement according to the biblical sources

If we leave aside Joshua 1-12, the settlement of Israel and Judah towards the end of the second millennium BCE presents itself as follows:

8.3.1 We immediately become aware of the fragmentary character of the Israelite occupation of the region. Precisely this feature shows that Judges 1-2 cannot originally have been the continuation of Josh.23-24, which is what the present redaction means us to believe. So what we have here is not the individual tribes going to take possession of the territories which have already been conquered and then assigned to each of them by lot (cf. Josh.1-2; 13-21), but, as I have already indicated (above 8.2.3), a version of the facts which originally set out to be an alternative. Granted, the information given in Judg.1 differs widely in historical value (the list in 1.21,27-35 was until recently thought to be very old, perhaps going back to a public document of some sort, but, as we have seen, this proposal too has now been put in question). What picture, then, emerges from the information that we are given about the settlement?

8.3.2. In the earliest period, 'Israel' had no access to the plains dominated by the city-states and had to resort to the hill-country.

8.3.3 The settlement took place, at least initially, in sparsely populated or uninhabited regions. The steppes, the scrub and the woodland were well suited to the extensive rearing of cattle, especially for sheep and goats. This is the form of production that we find the brothers of Joseph engaged in (Gen.37.12-17). They even seem to follow a fixed itinerary, so that Joseph does not have much difficulty in finding them; and in Gen.34.23, which in itself is a late text, we can detect a positive attitude of the inhabitants towards these groups. The areas in question were unsuited to intensive agriculture, given that the water supply came essentially from the winter rains and was stored in cisterns.[13] That also explains why the plateaux and the steppes were almost never populated by settled inhabitants (above 2.4.3),[14] except where water existed. Moreover the increasingly widespread use of iron made it possible to fell trees and to introduce new techniques of agriculture and building.

8.3.4 The following regions are interesting in this connection:

8.3.4.1 The southern hill-country with Hebron as its capital.

8.3.4.2 The central hill-country, beginning north of Jerusalem and ending at its last northern spurs before the plain of Jezreel, including the Gilboa chain and the village of Jezreel (above 8.2.8.1);

8.3.4.3 Finally Upper Galilee, the region around Hazor (*tell el-qēdāh*, coord. 203-269) and the mountains of the region.

8.3.4.4 However, we do not know whether these regions of the country could communicate with one another and if so to what extent. They were cut off from the south by the enclave of the city-state of Jerusalem and its territory. (Those who made the journey from Jerusalem to Bethlehem between 1949 and 1967 will know the difficulties of a journey which, following the direct route along the watershed, takes two or three hours on foot.) The centre was divided from the north by the much more powerful plain of Jezreel, dotted with city states.

8.3.5 A final problem is posed by two institutions: the 'levitical cities' and the 'cities of refuge'. It is not in fact easy to find a precise place for them, not only in the context of the settlement but also in the historical and sociological setting generally.

Bibliography

J.Wellhausen, *Prolegomena to the History of Israel* (1886), ET reissued New York 1957, 159ff.; M.Löhr, *Das Asylwesen im Alten Testament*, Halle 1930; W.F.Albright, 'The List of Levitical Cities', in *Louis Ginzberg Jubilee Volume...*, New York 1945, I, 49-73; M.Noth, *Das Buch Josua*, HAT I,7, Tübingen 1953, 100ff.; A.Alt, 'Festungen und Levitenorte im Lande Juda', *KS* II, 306-15; Y.Kaufmann, *The Biblical Account of the Conquest of Palestine*, Jerusalem 1953; B.Mazar, 'The Cities of the Priests and the Levites', *VT* 7, 1957, 193-205; M.Haran, 'Studies in the Account of the Levitical Cities', *JBL* 80, 1961, 45-54, 156-65; A.Cody, *A History of Old Testament Priesthood*, AnBibl 35, Rome 1969, 159ff.; R.de Vaux, *Ancient Israel*, 366f.; T.N.D.Mettinger, *Solomonic State Officials*, CB-OTS 5, Lund 1971, 97ff.; Aharoni**, *The Land*; J.L.Peterson, *A Topographical Surface Survey of the Levitical Cities of Joshua 21 and I Chronicles 6*, Diss.Chicago Institute for Advanced Theological Studies and Seabury-Western Theological Seminary, Evanston, Ill. 1977; J.de.Vaulx, 'Refuge, villes de', *SDB* IX, 1979, 1495-8; A.G.Auld, 'Cities of Refuge in Israelite Tradition', *JSOT* 10, 1978, 26-40; id., 'The Levitical Cities – Texts and History', *ZAW* 91, 1979, 194-206; id., *Joshua, Moses and the Land*, Edinburgh 1980, 79ff.; Z.Kallai, 'The System of Levitic Cities; A Historical-Geographical Study in Biblical Historiography', *Zion* 45, 1980, 13-34 (Hebrew, with an English summary); id., *Historical Geography of the Bible*, Jerusalem 1986, 447-76; R.G.Boling, 'Levitical Cities: Archaeology and Texts', in *Biblical and Related Studies...Samuel Iwry*, Winona Lake, Ind. 1986, 23-32; E.Cortese, 'Gios.21 e Giud.1 (TM o LXX?) e l'"abottonatura" del

"Tetrateuco" con l'opera deuteronomistica', *RiBib* 33, 1985, 376-94; E.Ben-Zvi, 'The List of the Levitical Cities', *JSOT* 54, 1992, 77-106. Also the commentaries on Joshua and Chronicles.

8.3.5.1 The levitical cities are listed in Josh.21.1-42; cf. Num.35.1-8; I Chron.6.39-66. This is a list of forty-eight places assigned to the Levites as grazing land. The idea behind this is that because the tribe of Levi, from which the Levites are made to descend, did not receive a tribal territory of its own, its descendants were given a territory which was considered equivalent, on the produce of which they had to live. Numbers 35.1-8 indicates that each of these cities was to be surrounded by territory forming a square of 2000 cubits (rather over 1,000 metres) on all sides.

8.3.5.2 The cities of refuge appear in Josh.20.1ff., cf. Num.35.9-34 and Deut.19.1-13; they were meant to serve as sanctuary for those who had killed someone unlawfully and were pursued in vendettas by the families of their victims – hence the name. The cities of refuge, seven in number, are all also levitical cities, which suggests that there is some sort of relationship between the two institutions.

8.3.5.3 The Israeli scholar Y.Kaufmann (1953) argued that each of these two institutions (according to a theory which he applied to the whole concept of the settlement) was a utopian project dating from the time of the 'conquest'. Without fixing a particular date, the studies of Haran 1961 and similarly Auld 1978 see the lists as a system of 'priestly' geography/topography, but this implies a late date, with a series of utopian elements (Haran was a pupil of Kaufmann's); however, it cannot be ruled out *a priori* that the Levites will already have settled first in the places in question. The position of de Vaux* II, 1978 is similar: for him the list reflects utopian concepts, but could be based on ancient documents and reflect a real situation.

8.3.5.4 According to other scholars, however, like Löhr 1930, Albright 1945, Mazar 1957, Mettinger 1971, Aharoni, *The Land***, 1979, and Kallai 1980 and 1986, the two institutions will have emerged at the time of the united monarchy, while Ben-Zvi 1982 proposes a date shortly before king Josiah. Others, though, like Alt 1952, Noth 1953 and Cody 1969, consider that the two institutions came into being much later: in the post-exilic period or, at the earliest, the time of king Josiah (below 12.4.1), but in no way earlier.

8.3.5.5 In this flurry of contradictory opinions (a sign of the obscure character of the evidence), it should be pointed out that Wellhausen* 1886 already drew attention to the artificial character of these two institutions: where would it in fact have been possible, in an essentially mountainous region, to trace out squares measuring 1000 yards on each side? Consequently the results of J.L.Peterson's 1977 surface study carried out in connetion with his PhD thesis are particularly interesting. In 1971 he carried out surface examinations on seventy-one out of a total of seventy-six *tells* (only two in Syria, one in Lebanon and two in Jordan were not examined because of *force majeure*) from the Bronze Age and two from the Iron Age. These made it possible to establish that few, less than half, were places already attested as occupied in the tenth century, few were attested in the ninth century and the majority did not appear at all before the eighth century. In other words, here we have a relatively certain *terminus a quo*; it is only relative, because later discoveries following excavations could change the partial results of the research in one way or another. Clearly a place could not be a levitical city or a city of refuge before its foundation. And since the assignation of a locality presupposes its existence at a certain time, assuming that the institution of levitical cities really existed, it could not be older than the reign of Hezekiah (below 12.2); the date of the reign of Josiah seems reasonable.

8.4 Results

All this is confirmation of the majority of the theories proposed by Alt from 1925 onwards;[15] according to these, in reality, at least in its first phases, the 'conquest' will have been the product of essential peaceful settlement in the most distant and least populated territories of the city states in the hill-country, a settlement which often came about with the consent of the local population.[16] Only later, in the time of Saul and especially that of David, i.e. towards the end of the second millennium and the beginning of the first, could military operations have begun, and these will have been directed principally against the Philistines living in the south-western area.

8.4.1 Moreover, this form of peaceful settlement has happened regularly throughout the region, in Egypt, Mesopotamia, Syria and Canaan. Only with the Arab conquest in the seventh century CE do we have a notable exception, as was already pointed out about thirty years ago by Moscati:[17] by contrast, we have to talk in terms of 'a periodical infiltration of groups in the predominantly peaceful form demonstrated by ethnology'. 'There is no indication of a violent invasion at one particular time...' That is the case with the Amorites in Mesopotamia during the first half of the second millennium, with the Hyksos in Egypt (above 7.3.1), with the ancestors of Israel and Judah in Canaan, and with the populations of Transjordan and the Aramaeans in Syria.

8.4.2 If we leave aside Josh.1-12 and Judg.1, the biblical sources agree with this basic view of events. The process must have begun soon after the el-ʿAmarna period and ended with that of David, with the incorporation of Jerusalem and the other city-states into the empire, and with Solomon and the incorporation of Gezer. In the light of this reconstruction of events the mention of 'Israel' on the stele of Pharaoh Merenptah from the end of the thirteenth century (above, 3.6.7.6) also takes on new significance: in fact an ethnic entity called 'Israel' already existed in the north of the country, but it was not yet a nation, and it is impossible to establish its size, composition and territory.

8.4.3 A variant of Alt's theory has been put forward by de Vaux* II, 523-680, which attempts to reconcile Alt's proposals with those of Albright.[18] First of all, de Vaux uses the term *'installation'* ('settlement') instead of *'Landnahme'* ('conquest', a technical term for the occupation of Iceland by Scandinavians) which is dear to German scholars. This is because it is more neutral and better fitted to the way in which things happened: he goes on to distinguish four regions, each with a distinctive type of settlement.[19]

8.4.3.1 A first region is the south, and comprises the tribes of Judah, Simeon and Levi and the groups of Caleb, Othniel, Jerah and the Kenites, all of whom were later absorbed into Judah in circumstances which are unknown to us. The settlement of these groups will have taken place from Kadesh and northern Arabia. The ancestors of these groups would have been in Egypt, but would have left before Moses. The settlement in question was essentially peaceful, except around Hebron, which was populated by Canaanites.

8.4.3.2 A second region is Transjordan and includes Reuben, Gad and Manasseh/Machir, this last arriving at a later stage; this group too will have left from Kadesh and have been led by Moses.

8.4.3.3 A third group populated the central hill-country: Benjamin and Joseph (i.e. Ephraim and Manasseh); this settlement, too, was also essentially peaceful and took place under the leadership of Joshua.

8.4.3.4 A fourth region is Galilee, populated by the groups of Asher, Napthali, Zebulon and Issachar; these had inhabited the region from time immemorial without ever having been in Egypt. Asher and Zebulon ended up by being employed as manual workers in the region, whereas Issachar will originally have been part of Zebulon. In the battle of Meron (Josh.11.1ff.), they are said to have defeated Jabin king of Hazor, occupying and destroying the place.

8.4.3.5 It therefore seems doubtful whether this synthesis actually works: according to the theories of Albright and his disciples, the central region, which is that mentioned chiefly in the book of Joshua, was the scene of the main encounters. Moreover, de Vaux, too, always rejected the connection between the destruction evident from excavations and the Israelite settlement, which is the basic argument put forward by Albright and his school. De Vaux also attaches disproportionate importance to the biblical sources with a view to a reconstruction of events: I need not stress their problematical character again here.

8.5 'Sociological' theories of the settlement

One of the great merits of those theories about the settlement which define themselves as sociological, first proposed by the North American scholar G.E.Mendenhall and then developed by his pupil N.K.Gottwald, is to have established that the settlement is to be seen as a phenomenon which happened essentially within Canaan, with little or no participation on the part of alien elements. With this theory the two scholars stand in marked contrast to both Alt and Noth in Europe and Albright and Bright in the United States.

Bibliography

G.E.Mendenhall, 'The Hebrew Conquest of Palestine', *BA* 25, 1962, 66-87; id., *The Tenth Generation*, Baltimore 1973, ch.VII; J.A.Soggin, 'La conquista israelitica' (above, 8.1.2), 208; M.Weippert, *The Settlement*, 55-62; M.Liverani, 'Introduction' to *La Siria nell'età del bronzo*, Rome 1969, 3-14: 8ff.; the articles by Hauser, Thompson and Rolla cited in 8.1.2 above; Gottwald, *The Tribes*, passim; my review of Gottwald in *Bibl* 62, 1981, 583-90.

8.5.1 Mendenhall's study, presented modestly in a non-specialist review, was heavily criticized to begin with. But any criticism,[20] however legitimate, should not obscure one evident datum: Mendenhall, recently followed by Gottwald (author of a monumental, if rhetorical and repetitive volume on the question), in fact puts forward with absolutely valid evidence an alternative version both to the traditional theory of an invasion from outside and a conquest, and to the theory of a gradual penetration into peripheral regions which were sparsely inhabited. So this is an original position which requires to be included in the discussion; that of a revolt in the rural areas; and this new theory finds the others deficient.

8.5.2 Mendenhall finds particularly problematical some inferences which are often made from the division of Israel into tribes, e.g. that this division presupposes that the people of God had a semi-nomadic origin. He rightly points out that divisions into tribes are also to be found in ancient Greece and ancient Rome, and that down to the present day there are still Arab villages in Syria/Palestine with this structure which show no traces of any kind of original nomadism. This example of Arab villages is interesting: here too there is a widespread practice of migrant grazing, spreading out from the village as a base. Mendenhall rightly points out that the tribal organization serves to indicate a group awareness, what Anglo-Saxon sociologists call the 'in-group'; and in the ancient Near East, too, this structure was connected on an economic and productive level with grazing, along with regular transhumance. So Mendenhall denies that there will have been any antagonism between sedentary populations and semi-nomadic peoples; this is a creation of scholars. The antagonism between the urban nucleus of the city state, the seat of political and economic power which, though not productive, controlled the wealth of the region, and the rural villages which, while producing the greater part of the wealth, had no control of it, seems much more real because it is based on economic and political factors like exploitation and oppression (cf.2.8.3). This contrast often leads to the rebellion of the rural group and its secession from the capital, a course of action which places it outside the law. For Mendenhall, this last position corresponds to the legal status of the *ḫapīru* (above 6.6.3), a category with which some scholars in the past have wanted to identify Israel in the making.

8.5.3 In fact, Mendenhall goes on, the letters from the el-ʿAmarna archive indicate frequent rebellions against the constituted authority of the various city-states nominally subject to the Pharaoh; in some cases these lead to the expulsion of the sovereign and other authorities; sometimes, in extreme cases, to the destruction of the city. Now according to Mendenhall the Israelite settlement will have been the product of revolts of this kind. The leading elements in the countryside, reinforced by groups coming from the wilderness, will have regrouped in a relationship of alliance (Hebrew *bᵉrīt*) between the various groups and with the one who was then to become the God of Israel. The group coming from the wilderness, which will have experienced the power of God in the events of the exodus, will have offered the rebels a unifying ideological element in the new faith.

8.5.4 Mendenhall's basic concept was then developed by Gottwald in 1979. He added virtually nothing new except the theory of a 'conversion' to Yahwism on the part of the rebels (cf. above, 6.7.1, n.46). In this way the rebels, having obtained their liberty, will have become 'Israel',[21] and their new faith will have been the product of their new social reality, again according to the Marxist theories enunciated by Gottwald, to the effect that Yahwism is the symbol of the Israelite social and economic revolution.[22]

8.5.5 If Mendenhall's and Gottwald's proposals proved historically acceptable, they would resolve a series of problems.

8.5.5.1 First of all there is the problem of the evident ethnic and linguistic continuity throughout the region during the transition from the end of the Bronze Age to the beginning of the Iron Age.[23] This continuity is difficult to explain if, with the biblical tradition, we assume another people to have invaded the region and to have taken the place of the native inhabitants. If we were dealing with substantially new settlements, this continuity could not manifest itself without some form of explanation for it.

8.5.5.2 Again, there is the problem of the command, often given in the biblical texts, to destroy the cities and their inhabitants, while nothing of this kind is said about the villages; this could possibly be the recollection of political conflict between the city state and the rural area.

8.5.5.3 There is the problem of the survival of the majority of the Canaanite population and its religion down to Josiah's reform.

8.5.5.4 There is the problem of the term *'ibrīm*, 'Hebrews', as applied to ancient Israel by its adversaries (cf. above 6.6.3.4-5).[24]

8.5.6 However, there are also many aspects which these proposals leave uncertain, and these are aspects which are qualitatively and quantitatively more serious:

8.5.6.1 First of all, Israel and Judah were always aware of not originally having been native to Canaan, but of having come there from abroad (above, 8.1). Of course this aspect is expressed in theological rather than historical and ethnic categories, but many scholars give it a real foundation.[25] This is an aspect for which an adequate explanation needs to be found.

8.5.6.2 Furthermore, as we have seen above (2.8.3), the conflicts arose within the city state rather than stemming from the relationship of exploitation between the main city and the countryside. They developed specifically within the power-structures of this very urban nucleus, between the palace and the assembly of nobles: we have also seen that there is no case in which the term *ḫabīru* is identified with an ethnic group (above 6.6.3.4-5); it is always connected with groups of outlaws, in accordance with the theory of Landsberger 1930, developed by Liverani 1965.

8.5.6.3 Again, while the patriarchs generally appear as breeders of herds of small cattle, they are never connected with villages. Yet the patriarchal traditions (and not those of the liberation experienced during the exodus and settlement) are the ones which provide Israel with the 'ideological foundation for the possession of the fertile land east and west of the Jordan'.[26]

8.5.6.4 Finally, the reference made by Mendenhall and particularly by Gottwald to the *ḫapīru* and to the 'God of the fathers' seems more a case of an explanation of *obscura per obscuriora* than a clarification. As to the concept of the 'covenant' which is supposed to have cemented the alliance of the groups among themselves and with their new God, we have now known for more than a decade that the term *bᵉrīt* and the concept which it expresses do not appear before Dtn and Dtr;[27] this is a feature of which Mendenhall could not yet have been aware, but Gottwald certainly should not have ignored it.

8.5.6.5 However, the most serious question raised by the two authors is that of an extremely conservative use of the texts. The texts are given a burden of proof which they simply cannot bear, and more than a century of textual and literary criticism has passed without leaving any trace on their writings.

8.5.6.6 Again, at an archaeological level there is so far no support for the theory of a revolt in the country and the origin of an 'egalitarian' society (to use Gottwald's expression) which is supposed to have arisen from it.

8.5.6.7 Nor is there the least proof that there was a monotheistic faith in Israel before the formation of the state: nothing is known of this (Dever 1987), nor is it in any way probable.

8.5.6.8 Finally it must be remembered that if we have always to speak of 'Israel' and 'Judah' as two distinct political entities, while we may retain the term 'tribe', we must not forget that this is a traditional translation of the Hebrew terms *šēbeṭ* and *maṭṭeh*: the sociological significance of these terms is unclear and they are attested in relatively late texts.[28]

8.5.6.9 Finally, a last topographical feature: as we saw earlier (above, 8.2.9.2-3), in central and northern Canaan the settlement seems to have taken place without a blow being struck, nor do we hear anything of a possible incorporation of the city states of the plain into the empire by means of military campaigns. Consequently we have to postulate a series of agreements with the local populations and the authorities. That also seems possible for Shechem and perhaps also for Gibeon, where Josh.9, a text which has now been distorted for apologetic ends, has retained the recollection of an original alliance between the cities and the 'invaders'. II Samuel 21.1-14 speaks independently of the violation of this treaty by Saul: hence David assuages the wrath of the Gibeonites by handing over to them the sons of Saul for justice to be done. Instances of this kind may have been much more frequent than the texts are disposed to admit, even if the theological concept of the covenant seems very much later.

8.6 Conclusions

To conclude, it can therefore be noted that a large part of Alt's proposals are still valid today. However, they need to be modified in the following way:

8.6.1 We are not dealing with groups of semi-nomads engaged in transhumance, but with groups which have a past history in the cities (cf. below, 8.7 and Appendix I by D.Conrad), thus originating from the territories of the city-state.

8.6.2 So this is not a settlement of populations from outside, but a movement of populations within. In this sense, if we rule out the theory of a revolt from the countryside, the proposals of Mendenhall and Gottwald prove correct.

8.7 Archaeology

From the end of the last century, Palestine has been the scene of innumerable campaigns of archaeological excavations, far more so than any other area in the world. At least in the early days, these campaigns often set out to prove the historical truth of what was said in the Bible, just as some years earlier there had been attempts to demonstrate the scientific truth of the biblical view in the sphere of the natural sciences (this was indeed the aim of the expedition of the 'Beagle', with Charles Darwin on board, though it was Darwin himself, with his intellectual honesty, who recognized the impossibility of such an approach, with the result that the expedition demonstrated precisely the opposite to what its sponsors had hoped for). Other organizations wanted, more modestly, to illustrate the biblical text, an aim which is stated, for example, in the original statutes of the British Palestine Exploration Fund.[29] However, the presence, at least to begin with, of sometimes confused intentions, and the failure to define aims has not prevented biblical archaeology from refining its techniques, progressively abandoning all claims of an apologetic kind, and rightly adopting the generally accepted methodology of archaeological research. This has happened to such an extent that it is now becoming clear that we should no longer talk of 'biblical archaeology' or 'Old Testament archaeology', but rather of Palestinian archaeology or the archaeology of Syria and Palestine, thus covering the whole region on both sides of the Jordan and as far as the boundaries with Turkey and Iraq. This is a basic problem which we cannot discuss here, but it shows the direction that archaeological studies have been taking for more than a decade. Meanwhile the methods and techniques of excavation have been perfected to such an extent that it is possible to date very clearly and precisely the various strata of a *tell* ('hill of ruins' in Arabic and Hebrew; in Turkish and kindred languages *tepé*) by means of an exact classification of finds of pottery, an indestructible material which cannot be modified chemically. It is impossible (and unnecessary) here to give the reader a synopsis of the excavations and discoveries which have been made so far, or even the general results: I shall simply try to provide some information about the best attested of them and draw some trustworthy conclusions.

Bibliography

W.F.Albright, *The Israelite Conquest* (above 8.1): id., *The Archaeology of Palestine*, Harmondsworth ⁴1960; id., *Archaeology and the Religion of Israel*, Baltimore ³1963; J.A.Soggin, 'Ancient Biblical Traditions and Modern Archaeological Discoveries', *BA* 23, 1960, 95-100; 'La conquista israelitica' (above, 8.12); H.J.Franken and C.H.Franken-Battershill, *A Primer of Old Testament Archaeology*, Leiden 1963; P.W.Lapp, 'The Conquest of Palestine' (above 8.1.2); A.v.R.Sauer, 'The Meaning of Archaeology for the Exegetical Task', *Concordia Theological Monthly* 1, 1960, 519-41; H.H.Schmid, *Die Steine und das Wort*, Zurich 1975; M.Weippert, *The Settlement*, ch.IV; H.J.Franken, *CAH* II. 2 ³1975, 331ff.; id., 'The Problem of Identification in Biblical Archaeology', *PEQ* 108, 1976, 3-11; J.M.Miller, 'Archaeology and the Israelite Conquest of Canaan: Some Methodological Observations', *PEQ* 109, 1977, 87-93; K.M.Kenyon, *Archaeology in the Holy Land*, London ⁴1979; F.Crüsemann, 'Alttestamentliche Exegese und Archäologie', *ZAW* 91, 1979, 177-93; A.Rolla, 'La conquista' (above 8.1.2); V.Fritz, 'Die kulturhistorische Bedeutung...' (above 8.1.2); S.Loffreda, 'L'insediamento' (above, 8.1.2); V.Fritz, 'Bibelwissenschaft I.Altes Testament I,1, Archäologie', *TRE* VI, 1980, 316-45; H.D.Lance, *The Old Testament and the Archaeologist*, Philadelphia 1980; W.G.Dever, 'The Impact of the "New Archaeology" on Syro-Palestinian Archaeology', *BASOR* 242, 1981, 15-29; G.W.Ramsey, *The Quest for the Historical Israel*, Atlanta 1981 and London 1982; Y.Aharoni, *The Archaeology of the Land of Israel*, London and Philadelphia 1982; P.J.King, 'The Contribution of Archaeology to Biblical Studies', *CBQ* 45, 1983, 1-16: J.M.Miller, 'Site Identification: A Problem Area in Contemporary Biblical Scholarship', *ZDPV* 99, 1983, 119-29; B.S.J.Isserlin, 'The Israelite Conquest of Canaan. A Comparative Review of the Arguments Applicable', *PEQ* 115, 1983, 85-94 (with bibliography: he defends the credibility of an armed conquest); A.Mazar, *Archaeology of the Land of the Bible*, New York 1990; D.N.Pienaar, 'A Critical Evaluation of Certain Leading Concepts in Biblical Archaeology', *JNWSL* 16, 1990, 141-51; G.W.Ahlström, 'The Origins of Israel in Palestine', *ScandJOT* 5.2, 1991, 19-34; A.Frendo, 'Five Recent Books on the Emergence of Ancient Israel', *PEQ* 124, 1992, 144-51. For a detailed study of the archaeological question see Appendix I (below, 383-93).

8.7.1 A first basic recommendation constantly made by professional archaeologists to the 'non-professionals', and often repeated, is that they should take the utmost care in evaluating discoveries and especially in connecting them with the texts and in drawing historical conclusions from them, precisely because this process might suggest that they were objective. The reason for this is that when archaeology does not produce epigraphical discoveries or is not supported by relevant historical texts, it is not only an exact science to the degree that it is practised professionally by competent people, but also a mute science. Two examples must suffice.

8.7.1.1 When a place in Palestine seems to have been destroyed, let us say, between the thirteenth and the twelfth century BCE (a date fixed by pottery finds), how do we go about identifying its original name with certainty or even with sufficient probability? (We have to do that if we are to connect it with any ancient texts that may be at our disposal if this name does not emerge from the finds.) Granted, it is possible that the original name of the place has been retained in the modern Arabic name, but it may also happen that this has been transferred to other places nearby. Thus the present-day *'anāta* (coord.175-136) retains the name of the biblical *'anātōt* (Anathoth), the home of the prophet Jeremiah, but the original biblical place is to be located on *rāś el-harrūbe* (coord. 174-135), in its immediate vicinity. So in this case, to excavate under the place whose name corresponds to that in the Bible, in the expectation of finding remains of the ancient place, would lead nowhere.

8.7.1.2 A different example: the Syrian locality of *tell mardiḫ* has been conclusively identified with ancient Ebla of the cuneiform texts, thanks only to the discovery in the second half of the 1960s of an inscription dedicated to a king of Ebla;[30] this identification was then confirmed some years later by the discovery of the library and archives. (For this set of problems cf. Franken 1975 and Miller 1976, 1983.)

8.7.1.3 Now it is a well-known fact that Palestine has produced little epigraphical material worth noting, while its humid winter climate has prevented the conservation of papyrus and parchment texts. It is no coincidence that the writings of *wādī dalīye* and Qumran (below 14.1 and 14.12.4), the former from the second half of the first millennium BCE and the latter from around the end of the first millennium BCE and the beginning of the first millennium CE, were found in the desert regions of the lower valley of the Jordan and the northern shore of the Dead Sea.[31]

8.7.2 So today scholars have at their disposal a vast collection of archaeological discoveries, the fruit of more than a century of intense excavations.[32] However, this is material which for most of the time is difficult to relate to the biblical texts, despite the initially optimistic evaluations, especially in the United States and in Israel, by scholars ranged round the person of W.F.Albright (cf. above 6.5.7-8). I have already referred to their problematical nature many times. As de Vaux* II, 484, has observed: 'There are no pure archaeological facts as such, but only interpreted facts.'

8.7.3 One of the facts that we may consider to have been established over the last quarter of a century is that the transition from the last phase of the Bronze Age to the first period of the Iron Age in Syria and Palestine was not characterized by any breaks in continuity worth noting, at least in those regions which had been populated for a long time. The only truly new element is provided by Philistine pottery, from the beginning of the twelfth century BCE. Its style can easily be connected with that of the Aegean world. Moreover, and I have stressed this often, there are no relevant traces of the settlement of a new population in the region, alongside or in place of the indigenous population (Miller 1977). On the other hand, the transition from the Bronze Age to the Iron Age is characterized by considerable turbulence, and rapid changes accompanied by numerous cases of destruction throughout the region, not only in Palestine.

8.7.3.1 Now it would be legitimate to affirm that such a situation provided the most favourable circumstances first for the settlement of, and later for the seizing of power by, a foreign population. However, it seems illegitimate to identify the disturbances and the destruction in question with the settlement of the ancestors of Israel and Judah, all the more so since, as we have seen, the Bible itself excludes quite a number of places from the 'conquest' in the strict sense (Judg.1.21,27-36 and parallels), while in another instance it explicitly affirms that with the exception of the *tell* of Hazor, the places 'situated on their *tell*' (Josh.11.13) were not destroyed (cf. above 8.2.3).

8.7.3.2 So the reality presented by the biblical texts appears to be much more modest, as Miller has indicated. Only four places are said to have been destroyed: Sepath/Hormah (probably *ḥirbet em-mšāš*, Hebrew *tell māśōś*, coord. 146-069), Jericho (*tell es-sulṭān*, coord. 192-142), Ai (*et-tell*, coord.174-168) and Hazor (*tell el-qēdaḥ*, coord. 203-269), the second and third in circumstances which we shall consider later (below 8.7.4.2).

8.7.3.3 So the situation seems much more complex than a superficial examination of the texts might suggest; however, such an examination today is influenced by the unitary view of the 'conquest' as it appears in Josh.1-12. In reality the places excavated in the course of the last half century (since techniques have been refined) almost all present a series of problems which I want to examine briefly here.

8.7.4 Some sites that have been excavated in fact prove to have been destroyed in the transitional period between the Bronze Age and the Iron Age but others not; these have not yet been identified with any places mentioned in the Bible.

8.7.4.1 Thus we have *tell el ḥeṣi* (coord.124-106), which some scholars identify with Eglon, and *tell er-rabūd* (coord.151-093), perhaps Debir, which proves not even to have been destroyed during this period; *tell bēt mirsim* (coord.141-096), which Albright thought to have been Debir, an identification now generally abandoned, has not been even hypothetically identified. It does not follow from the texts that Bethel, present-day *beitīn* (coord. 172-148), was in fact destroyed, and to say that the destruction is implicit in the texts begs the question. The same goes for Lachish, *tell ed-duweir* (coord.135-108).

8.7.4.2 Other places explicitly mentioned in the accounts of the 'conquest' as conquered and destroyed were not even inhabited in the period which we are considering: Hormah (cf. above 8.7.3.2), Jericho and Ai; and the same goes for Arad (coord. 152-069 or 162-076); Gibeon, present day *ej-jīb*, coord.167-139; Yarmuth, probably *ḥirbet el-jarmūk* (coord.147-124). Another locality, *tell deir-ʿalla*, probably the ancient Succoth (coord.208-178), however, seems certainly to have been destroyed, but by an earthquake and not in military operations, a little after 1200 BCE.

8.7.5 Again, as I have already stressed on several occasions, Palestine is not the only region where there is evidence of destruction of this kind at this time. Syria, too, proves to have had considerable disturbances, and the ensuing destruction is generally attributed to the 'sea peoples' (above 4.4), with whom the Philistines are connected. Moreover Pharaoh Merneptah (above 3.6.7.5) claims to have 'plundered Canaan with every evil', a statement which is followed by a list of the places involved. If the information is historically trustworthy, this was probably in an attempt to regain Egyptian control over the region.

8.7.6 The situation is different, however, in the areas which were originally sparsely inhabited: the hill-country and the steppes. Here we find considerable traces of settlement by new populations, living in unfortified villages (in the northern Negeb). All this can be explained on the ecological level by the discovery of a new mortar for sealing cisterns and making them impermeable; the discovery made possible extensive grazing where originally the breeders of sheep and goats were at best transient. As we have seen, the hypothesis of a conquest by a foreign people is not only unsupported by any objective data but does not even prove necessary, and the theory put forward by Alt and Moscati of a peaceful infiltration seems the most probable.

8.7.7 There remains, then, just one case in which it could be argued that there was a correspondence between the biblical texts and archaeological discoveries, in that the reader is confronted with a destruction which can be verified: Josh.11.1-13 and the case of Hazor narrated there. Jericho and Ai prove to have been abandoned at that period, and at best they had tiny, insignificant populations. Moreover there is nothing historical about the texts which speak of their destruction: the account of the fall of Jericho took place by means of a liturgical celebration with processions,[33] and in the case of Ai we have a dissertation on the value of obedience to the word of God and a threat of punishment which will fall upon those who are rash enough to disobey.

8.7.8 That makes all the more hasty and probably imprudent the hypothesis put forward by Albright in the United States from the 1930s onwards and accepted, though with some criticisms and not without perplexity, by his disciples Bright[34] and Wright, that the destructions and the other signs of disturbance which mark the passage from the Bronze Age to the Iron Age illustrate, even if they do not prove, e.g. the claim in Josh.1-12 of a large-scale military conquest by all Israel. (Albright was fond of using the term 'external evidence' produced by the excavations and considered to be objective, as opposed to the 'internal evidence' of the texts, thought to be more susceptible to the subjective evaluation of scholars.) So far, and clearly we cannot go into the details here of a debate from the now distant years of the 1940s, 1950s and 1960s,[35] the only place which could validly be incorporated into this theory is, as we have just seen, Hazor, which as the excavations suggest, was destroyed at the end of the thirteenth century BCE. However, even in this most particularly favourable case this is not the only possible explanation, but only one of many in the context of the information at our disposal.[36]

8.7.9 What remains to be achieved (and here Mendenhall and Gottwald are certainly right, though cf. already Liverani 1980 and Dever 1981 and the so-called 'new archaeology' in the United States) is what we might call a 'sociological' and 'economic' reclassification of the discoveries. In the absence of political, economic and historical texts, archaeology can provide evidence of ethnic and sociological changes which have taken place; it can give first-hand information about the economy, about demography, states of health, production, the consumption of food, the possession and use of domestic animals, the inhabitants of a particular place, and thus allow synchronous and diachronous comparisons with other areas. This is work which for the most part is still to be done and will take at least a generation, if not more; it should be embarked on as a matter of principle when new excavations are planned. So far archaeologists have been chiefly interested in chronological problems, in an attempt to reconstruct the history of a place; but the fact that such attempts have produced very inconsistent results suggest that we should try another approach, in which in all probability new discoveries can be made.

8.7.10 And it is specifically here (cf. also Appendix I below) that archaeology is in the process of demonstrating a substantial change in the transition from the last phase of the Bronze Age to the first phase of the Iron Age (thirteenth to twelfth centuries BCE): the mosaic of city states in the plains and the largely uninhabited hill-country was supplemented and partly replaced by hundreds of agricultural and pastoral settlements, with little or no fortification. Whether there is any relationship between these groups and the ancestors of Israel and Judah and if so what, is a whole area to be studied.

8.8 The formation of the tribes

One of the facts that we may take to have been established by modern biblical and Near Eastern scholars is that, as far as we can trace their history, the tribes of Israel were constituted as such in Canaan, and therefore after the settlement of those groups which came to make them up.

8.8.1 We do not have the slightest bit of information about the nature and details of this process, as Liverani wrote at the beginning of the 1980s; however, increasing probability seems to be attached to the hypothesis that this was a process which can be explained in terms of movements within the area of Canaan and was predominantly peaceful, i.e. practically without the foreign elements resorting to war. In fact there are no traces of such foreign elements before the settlement of the Philistines, nor are there any signs of violent change. What does seem disconcerting is, as I have already indicated (above 8.5.6.8), that the texts which use the terms šebet and matteh ('tribe') are almost all late, Dtr and afterwards, as has recently been demonstrated by Auld.[37] So here too there arises the well-founded suspicion that this is a reconstruction of ancient Israel as it was seen in the post-exilic period. Here some information at any rate may be regarded as virtually certain.

8.8.2 We know of the existence of a 'mountain of Judah', the hill-country which extends from Jerusalem southwards until it reaches the northern Negeb, and of a 'desert of Judah', the region which descends from the northern Negeb towards the Dead Sea (cf. Josh.11.21; 20.7; 21.11 and II Chron.27.4; Judg.1.16 and Ps.64.1). This is interesting because we know that the first term includes Hebron, a place which the texts themselves claim originally not to have been inhabited by Judahites (above 8.2.5). Terms like 'Bethlehem in Judah' (Judg.17.7; cf. Micah 5.1) thus indicate the region rather than the tribe.

8.8.3 A 'mountain of Ephraim' appears in the hill-country (Josh.20.7; 21.1; I Kings 4.8), where the name is one of Solomon's districts, and other passages. It probably included the greater part of the central hill-country. For Ephraim ('eprayim) also note the apparent dual termination, frequent in place names. Benjamin also appears as a district in I Kings 4.18.

8.8.4 A 'mountain of Naphtali' appears in Galilee (Josh 20.7; I Kings 4.15, where it is a district of Solomon). We find various other localities called after this tribe, e.g. Kedesh-naphtali in Judg.4.5. In I Kings 4.16 Asher and Issachar also appear as districts of Solomon.

8.8.5 So it seems reasonably certain that at least some tribal names are directly derived from the name of the regions in which the tribes were formed, and are names which are continued in those of Solomon's districts (above 5.8). The opposite does not happen, as the reader of the texts might suppose. If there are still some uncertainties, this is only because the names in question so far appeared in extra-biblical texts of the second millennium BCE.

8.8.6 By contrast, it seems that Dan did give its name to the territory which it occupied; the relevant texts in fact indicate that its capital originally had another name, Laish or Leshem (Josh.19.47; Judg.17-18).

8.9 The unifying element

Another problem which has interested scholars now for more than seventy years is that of the common element which united the tribes of Israel once they had settled in their territories, the north under the name of 'Israel' (which later became a synonym for the whole nation) or with the alternative nomenclature 'house of Joseph', and the south as 'Judah'. We have seen (above 4.1.1) that the two groups were originally almost certainly two distinct entities. And it is here that we come up against the hypothesis of the 'tribal league', also, but wrongly, called the 'amphictony'. This is a feature brought out for the first time by Max Weber* 1921 (above 3.5.1.3), passim, who spoke of a 'confederacy' of tribes, and following him by other scholars after the end of the First World War.[38] This view was presented in its definitive form by Noth in his second and rightly famous work. The theory, developed by Noth in his later contributions and especially in *1959, was never more than a hypothesis; nevertheless, it has held the field for more than thirty-five years and still enjoys quite a few often qualified supporters; however, most of its elements have proved to be increasingly problematic.

Bibliography

M.Noth, *Das System der zwölf Stämme Israels*, BWANT IV, 1, Stuttgart 1930; *Pentateuchal Traditions*, passim; and other later writings by him; A.Alt, *Die Staatenbildung der Israeliten in Palästina*, Leipzig 1930 = *KS* II, 1-65; G.Buccellati, *Cities and Nations...*; R.Smend, 'Zur Frage nach der altisraelitischen Amphiktyonie', *EvTh* 31, 1971, 613-30; this has, however, been disputed by G.Fohrer, 'Altes Testament – "Amphiktyonie" und "Bund" ', *TLZ* 91, 1966, 801-16, 893-405; id.,

Studien, BZAW 115, Berlin 1969, 84-119; A.D.H.Mayes, *Israel in the Period of the Judges*, SBT II, 29, London 1974, and in Hayes-Miller*, 297-308; R.de Vaux*, II, 695-716; G.Fohrer, *Theologische Grundstrukturen des Alten Testaments*, Berlin 1972, 21ff.; J.Weingreen, 'The Theory of the Amphictyony in Pre-Monarchial (sic!) Israel', *JANESCU* 5, 1973, 427-33; H.Weippert, 'Das geographische System der Stämme Israels', *VT* 23, 1973, 76-89; N.Kamiki, 'Reconsideration of the Twelve-Tribe System of Israel', *AJBI* 2, 1976, 29-59 (with synoptic tables); N.P.Lemche, 'The Greek "Amphictyony" – Could it be a Prototype for the Israelite Society in the Period of the Judges?', *JSOT* 4, 1977, 48-59; C.H.J.de Geus, *The Tribes of Israel*, Assen 1976; O.Bächli, *Amphiktyonie im Alten Testament*, Basel 1977; F.Crüsemann, *Der Widerstand gegen das Königtum*, WMANT 45, Neukirchen 1978, 10-28; C.Meyers, 'Of Seasons and Soldiers: A Topographical Appraisal of the Premonarchical Tribes of Galilee', *BASOR* 252, 1983, 47-59; N.P.Lemche, 'Israel in the Period of the Judges. The Tribal League in Recent Research', *ST* 38, 1984, 1-28; N.K.Gottwald, 'The Participation of Free Agrarians in the Introduction of the Monarchy to Ancient Israel', *Semeia* 37, 1986, 77-106; A.G.Auld, 'Tribal Terminology in Joshua and Judges', in *Le origini d'Israele – Convegno dell'Accademia nazionale dei Lincei*, Rome 1987, 87-98; S.Herrmann, 'Was bleibt von der Jahwe Amphiktyonie?', *TZ* 48, 1992, 304-14.

8.9.1 As I have already indicated on many occasions, the biblical tradition which claims to be normative presents for the period of the 'conquest' and that immediately following the image of an 'Israel' which operates as a single group, by means of a union which seems principally based on a common faith in YHWH. The theory reappears, as we shall see in the next chapter, in connection with the period of the Judges. In both cases its historicity seems problematical.

8.9.2 This confession of the unitary character of 'Israel' has its negative counterpart in its division into what has traditionally been translated by the term 'tribes', Hebrew *šēbeṭ* and, more rarely, *maṭṭeh*. Both mean 'staff' or 'rod', or simply objects which have that shape; again, they are virtually synonymous. I have briefly indicated (above, 8.5.6.8) the sociological problems raised by such a translation and also the scarcity of ancient texts in which the two terms appear (above 8.8.1).

8.9.3 One thing is relatively certain: in Israel and in Judah the 'tribe' was composed of people who boasted a common ancestor: the eponymous hero of the group, in this case a son of Jacob. The members of a tribe thus accept one another as kindred in the broadest sense of the term. However, we also know that genealogical concepts of this kind do not reflect so much a fact as a status symbol (above 6.5.2.1). St

Paul regarded himself as a member of the tribe of Benjamin when one could no longer speak of the tribe in any way in the social sense of the term, and it was something of which he was proud (Rom.11.1; Phil.3.5).

8.9.4 *The 'tribal' league.* The most interesting attempt to combine the biblical tradition with the information obtained from modern historical and sociological research is certainly that made by Noth in 1930; he never abandoned it, but planned to put it forward again in a revised form. Even shortly before his premature death in 1968 he thought that he could present an updated version of his hypothesis,[39] despite the doubts about its legitimacy which had been formulated by many scholars.

8.9.4.1 The analogy which Noth put forward and developed systematically, after others, as we have seen, had made similar proposals, took its starting point from the ancient Hellenic and Italian amphictyonies. These were unions of intrinsically autonomous groups around the cult of a common sanctuary, i.e. something like sacral alliances. And it is precisely this element which Noth also detected in the lists of the tribes in the Old Testament: lists of the male children of Jacob in Gen.29-30; lists of tribes as they appear in Num.1; 26. In these lists the names of the members could vary, but the number twelve remained constant, as that of the sons of Jacob. Noth made another important distinction: the lists which indicate that Levi was stil a tribe were earlier, and the lists in which Levi either does not appear or appears only as a priestly caste, without a particular tribal territory, were later. In Gen.49.5ff. Levi still appears as a tribe, whereas in Deut.33.8ff. it now exercises only priestly functions.

8.9.4.2 The main parallel in the West is provided by the amphictyonies of Apollo at Delphi and by Demeter at Phyle; these were composed of tribes as opposed to the city states. Then there are also Etruscan and Italic amphictyonies. However, we also find similar structures among people bordering on Israel (cf. Gen.22.20-24; 25.2,13-16; 36.10-14, also characterized by a number of members which remains constant).

8.9.4.3 For Noth, the real history of Israel begins with the birth of the tribal league, and that is why he regards the narratives which precede it as 'traditions of the league' (above 3.5.2.2). His proposal was followed by Buccellati 1967, while Malamat (*Die Frühgeschichte*, 1983) arrived at similar results beginning from different presuppositions.

8.9.4.4 As far as we know, a characteristic of all the amphictyonic regimes was a union of the tribes or groups around the common sanctuary by means of an alliance: each group was then responsible for maintaining the sanctuary for one month a year. Moreover, each member was obliged to provide adequate representation whenever the assembly discussed matters of mutual interest. Again, the central sanctuary seems to have formed a first step in the direction of unity, this time no longer conceived only in religious but also in political terms.

8.9.4.5 According to Noth (and the theme was soon taken up again by von Rad, for whom what for Noth had only been a working hypothesis seems to have become a proven thesis),[40] the Israelite amphictyony will have been founded in the circumstances described by a text which in its essential elements was thought to be old: Joshua 24. Here the 'house of Joseph', the last group to arrive in Canaan, persuaded the other tribes who were already there to accept the worship of the common God YHWH, thus giving rise to the league and forming the central sanctuary at Shechem. In it the representatives of the tribes mentioned in Num.1.5-15 and which bore the title *nāśî'* (literally 'prince') met at more or less regular intervals.

8.9.4.6 The most important object present in the cult was the ark (above 4.2.1.2), probably the central shrine in the strict sense (though its location could change). This explains why from time to time we find the ark at different sanctuaries.

8.9.4.7 One of the functions of the league – and here we find its political relevance – was that of arbitrating in any disputes which might arise among its members; these thus renounced any form of war among themselves. We have an example in Judg.19-21; here the tribes proceed to punish Benjamin, which is guilty of having refused to hand over to the tribunal of the league the perpetrators of a particularly savage crime. The nearest phenomenological parallel, even if it comes from much later, is that of the Amphissaean war, when a member of a Greek amphictyony was punished for refusing to hand over those who had committed sacrilege. The war, fought in 339 BCE, led to the punishment and expulsion of the guilty party.

8.9.4.8 The so-called 'minor judges' will have been the officials of the league, charged with implementing common projects.

8.9.4.9 However, the days of the league were numbered once it proved inadequate to cope with the concentrated attacks of the Philistines and the peoples of the East. Then it had to yield to the monarchy. However, the monarchy too had inherited a number of features of the league: for example, in its early years the precarious status of the sovereign who had no dynasty, but was clearly dependent on something like a charisma (in the sense given to the term by Weber) rather than on clearly constituted institutions. As I have argued in the past,[41] to begin with the monarchy was rather like the institution of the dictatorship in the Roman Republic, a position which arose from temporary needs which more democratic forms of government could not cope with adequately. From this institution, transformed into a dictatorship for life, was to arise a return to monarchy by means of rule.

8.9.5 Noth's proposal, always meant as a hypothesis, had and still has marked advantages.

8.9.5.1 It based biblical tradition and modern research on a single complex. This also explains why the theory was accepted virtually *en bloc*, almost without criticism or exception; even Albright in the United States and his pupils, otherwise so critical of Alt and Noth,[42] accepted it unconditionally, putting particular stress on the aspect of the covenant which was the uniting feature (above 8.5).[43]

8.9.5.2 Again, it was, and still is, apparently a brilliant solution to the historical problems of a period about which we otherwise know little or nothing.

8.9.5.3 It also provided a reasonable explanation of the origin of the earliest sources of the Pentateuch and the Deuteronomistic history,[44] and perhaps even of the milieu in which Deuteronomy came to be formed and therefore also of the origins of Josiah's reform (below 12.4.2).[45]

8.9.5.4 It also gave a clear indication of where we should seek the origin of Israelite worship, of its struggle against Canaanite religion, the concept of the covenant and monotheistic faith.

8.9.5.5 For Buccellati, again,[46] the league was the institution which allowed the transition from the settlement to the state, and was thus in a certain way already a state in embryo.

8.9.6 However, in recent decades the disadvantages of the proposals have also become increasingly clear.

8.9.6.1 First of all, the very concept of the 'amphictyony', which is already an obscure term for the classical world, as Lemche 1977 has recently pointed out, presupposes that the members reside around the sanctuary, and that is also indicated by the etymology of the term. Now in Israel such a topographical element is not present, and while the existence of such a sanctuary as a centre for assembling has often been postulated (for example by those who identified it with the ark, an object which would have been moved from one sanctuary to another before the foundation of the Jerusalem temple), it has never been demonstrated, nor in the present state of the sources does such a demonstration seem possible. It does not even seem probable as a working hypothesis. Rather, the Hebrew Bible stresses the constant number of members (but even this did not always happen, cf. below 8.9.6.3ff.), a feature which seems to be of secondary importance in the Greek and Italian amphictyonies. For this reason Buccellati, who defends the concept of the tribal league,[47] proposes that the term amphictyony should be dropped because it is inappropriate. That would leave only the parallel in the phenomenological field, which is certainly essential.

8.9.6.2 The distinction between the lists of tribes, depending on whether Levi is mentioned as a tribe or as a priestly caste, is valid on the level of the history of the traditions, but not in historical terms. Moreover, as is well known, Num.1 and 26 are not ancient texts but belong to P and reflect later priestly adaptations which generally favour Judah and its position after the exile. Again, the problem of Levi as a tribe or as a priesthood is particularly complex, and there are reasons for asserting that the levitical priesthood has nothing to do with the tribe of Levi, assuming that this ever existed in history. The biblical tradition which seeks to explain the transition from ethnic group to priestly caste makes more sense if it is understood as a later rationalization rather than as a recollection in the tradition of real events.

8.9.6.3 Nor does the number twelve, which, as has often been observed, in fact denotes totality and completeness rather than an actual figure, appear as consistently as Noth would like: the Song of Deborah (Judg.5), the earliest elements of which cannot be dated earlier than the ninth century BCE,[48] mentions only ten tribes, and the list certainly lacks the whole of the south (Judah and Simeon) and probably also Gad (if this is not to be identified with Gilead) and Manasseh (provided that it is not identified with Machir) and of course Levi. If we leave out the south, we have fewer than twelve tribes, and if we include it we have more. Noth and those in favour of the hypothesis never adequately faced this problem raised by the Song, a document which is earlier than the others.

8.9.6.4 Another of Noth's theories is that the figure of king Saul (above 4.3) is little different from those of the judges who were his immediate predecessors;[49] however, there is a fundamental shift between these latter and the first king, with a clear break in continuity with the past.

8.9.6.5 Finally, there seems to be no justification for the speculations which took place in the 1950s and 1960s about the instruments and officials of the league, which would have given the league a truly bureaucratic organization.

8.9.7 Some final conclusions follow from this.

8.9.7.1 In a later period Israel (or better, Judah in the post-exilic period) saw and reconstructed its own structures in prehistoric times in terms of a tribal league. In some cases the texts have been forced in order to include Judah as well, but the whole of the south seems absent from the earliest text, Judg.5, so it seems evident that the memory of the league (assuming that it is possible to call it that) is based on different and sometimes contradictory traditions.

8.9.7.2 On the other hand, the hypothesis of a tribal league does not appear manifestly absurd or necessarily anachronistic; so much so that Buccellati considers it the organ through which the transition was made from the settlement of the individual tribes to the constitution of the state. A scholar like Rudolf Smend, who is certainly no conservative, rightly indicated that to rule out the theory of the league would leave us with virtually no information about a period which the tradition of Israel has always considered formative and therefore basic to the history or rather the prehistory of the people (similarly Donner*, I, 146ff.). Another recent study, that of Crüsemann, has also pointed out that a reappraisal of the hypothesis which led to its rejection would leave an effective void in the earliest history of Israel, a void which he tries to fill by comparing Israel in the period before the state with the so-called 'segmentary' societies in non-Islamic black Africa;[50] I have already pointed out (above 4.8) that these were groups which originally were not directed by any central authority, and therefore had an essentially centrifugal tendency; constrained to provide themselves later with central instruments of government only under the pressure of external threats.

8.9.7.3 However, there is no way of verifying this theory either. The theory of the tribal league has a good part of the biblical tradition in its favour; the latter, by contrast, is based on comparisons which are distant both chronologically and geographically. The recent study by Meyers thus accepts the existence of a tribal league, but only within the sphere of Galilee.

8.9.7.4 As I already indicated at the beginning of this study, the theory of a prehistoric tribal league, a kind of theocratic government around a central sanctuary which is defined in only vague terms, corresponds much more closely to the post-exilic situation, when the one central sanctuary is now the sole reality. So it only seems logical that the concept of the tribal league should have been taken up again, revised and reformulated at this particular period. However, in the present state of research we have no information which has even the slightest element of probability about whether such a league ever really existed in history.

The Time of the Judges

9.1 *Judges* – suffetes

In the historical scheme which underlies the Hebrew Bible, the book of Judges follows the narratives of the conquest. The theme which the work seeks to present to its readers is that of the consolidation of the settlement and the defence of the territory obtained against enemies both within (the Canaanite city states) and without (neighbouring peoples, usually raiders). The Philistines do not appear anywhere, so we could possibly presuppose the existence of traditions prior to their settlement in the region; however, it would also be possible to defend the thesis of a particularly precise redaction, intent on avoiding anachronisms, unlike what happens, for example, in the patriarchal narratives (above 6.1.7).

Bibliography

Cf. J.A.Soggin, *Judges*, OTL, London and Philadelphia 1987, for all points of detail. Also D.W.Gooding, 'The Composition of the Book of Judges', *EI* 16, 1982, 70*-9*; M.Tsevat, 'The Old Testament Stories and their Hittite Analogue', *JAOS* 103, 1983, 321-6; C.Schäfer-Lichtenberger, *Stadt und Eidgenossenschaft* (see ch.8, n.18), 226-7; N.P.Lemche, *Early Israel*, Leiden 1985, Part II, ch.5; A.Bartelmus, 'Forschungen zum Richterbuch seit Martin Noth', *TR* 56, 1991, 221-59.

9.1.1 The title of the book might deceive the reader unfamiliar with the meaning of the term *šōpēt* in the Western Semitic world: the judges of Israel are in fact virtually never involved in activities of a forensic type; only once is it said that Deborah was acting in the context of a court of law (Judg.4.4f.), but that happens before her call to what the text terms the judgeship! On the contrary, the functions of the judges always seem to be connected in some way with the government of the tribes; at least, that is the case with those who for convenience are called 'major' judges: these always function as leaders in a political or military context.

9.1.2 Other judges are traditionally called 'minor' judges; the texts hand down only brief notes about them which are anecdotal and typical of folklore, though they are embellished with figures which bear every appearance of being precise; however, it is not said precisely what the functions of the minor judges were and why this information has been handed down. Some years ago[1] I tried to explain these features with the hypothesis that their functions were similar to those of the 'eponymi' in the Punic world, i.e. that they were connected with dating, so that we could suppose that, as at Carthage, dating would be done by phrases like 'in the year of the judge (or the judges) x and y...', but here we cannot do more than guess.

9.1.3 However, as I have just said, unless the reader has been forewarned, the traditional translation 'judges' does not provide an adequate framework for the reality, even if it is as old as the LXX rendering Κριταί. The Hebrew term *šōpēt*, plural *šōpᵉtīm*, in fact also appears in Phoenician and Punic and was transcribed as *suffetes* by the Roman historians of the Punic War, where it denotes the chief magistrates of the Carthaginians. This connection of the root with the supreme magistrature already appears among the Western Semitic semi-nomads of whom there is evidence at Mari on the Euphrates in the eighteenth century BCE (for the head of the group), in Ugarit and also in Hebrew, though there it is already an archaism. In other words, in the reconstructions which Judah made of its own past before the formation of the state the members of the tribal league elected a leader with full powers in case of great danger; his task was to coordinate communal forces to confront the danger. The conferring of full powers evidently signified that the tribes renounced their own autonomy and independence, though only for a certain time.

9.1.4 Moreover, according to some scholars, it was precisely from the roots of this institution that the monarchy came into being, with Saul as a transitional figure (above 8.9.4.9; 8.9.6.4). However, we have seen (above 8.9.6) how problematical this reconstruction of events is: obviously what Judah thought to be its own past and that of Israel was one thing, and what we can (or rather most of the time cannot, because we do not have adequate sources) reconstruct of it with scientific critical historical methods is another.

9.1.5 The narratives which originally formed the nucleus of the book have also been subjected to a Deuteronomistic redaction which has provided it with an introduction and an epilogue, both meant to be a key for reading each individual episode; finally, a new revision has sought to find charismatic features in the 'major' judges, in that they are endowed with the 'spirit of YHWH'. This definition is clearly not meant to be understood in the significance that it was later to acquire in the primitive Christian church, far less in the modern religious movements which apply this term to themselves, but in the meaning that it has in Max Weber.[2] The following texts are involved: Judg.3.1; 6.34; 11.29; 13.25; 14.6,19; 15.14, all of which say that the 'spirit of YHWH' comes upon the person of one of the judges. With this explanation the redactors mean to remove the human element from the action of the judges in order to attribute everything to an extraordinary intervention by God. So rather than it being the assembly of the league which tests, recognizes and then nominates its own leaders, these are invested with power directly by God. Evidently – and this applies both to the Deuteronomistic introductions and to the epilogues – the charismatic explanation is not a traditional memory of a past era but a theological explanation of what will originally have been a purely secular fact: that some allied groups will have chosen a common leader in particularly difficult situations.

9.1.6 This revision of the concept of the judgeship fits in well with the central thesis of the 'body' of the book (2.6-16.31): in each individual episode the Deuteronomistic introduction explains, in terms of retribution, first the sin and the punishment of the people and then, following its cry of grief and its penitence, the divine response in the person of the charismatic figure; the conclusion of each episode then gives chronological information in stereotyped figures and a note on the peace which finally prevails in the region.

9.2 Chronology

Chronology is one of the major difficulties with which scholars are confronted, here as in all the narratives of the prehistory of Israel and even in some details about the historical period. I have dealt with the question in detail in my commentary and above 3.7, so it is enough here just to present a summary of the issue.

Bibliography

Soggin, *Judges*, Introduction; W.Brueggemann, 'Social Criticism and Social Vision in the Deuteronomic Formula of the Judges', in *Die Botschaft und die Boten – Festschrift für Hans-Walter Wolff*, Neukirchen/ Vluyn 1981, 101-14.

9.2.1 The chronology of the book of Judges is essentially expressed in the Deuteronomistic epilogues, most of the time in stereotyped figures (the number forty, its multiples or divisions, as usually happens in the Deuteronomistic history) or in figures which are quoted out of context. The former go with the historical and theological reconstruction undertaken by Dtn and Dtr to explain to the generations of the exile and the return the reasons for the deportation first of Israel and then of Judah, for the fall of the ruling house (in 587-86 or in the last quarter of the century, cf. below 11.3 and 12.6) and the loss of political independence. These were real national tragedies which seemed to annul all the divine promises of the past and instead to support the theory that the God of Israel had been defeated by the conquerors. The Deuteronomistic history argues that it was not the weakness of YHWH which had allowed all this to happen; on the contrary, it was his power, which had not hesitated to inflict on his own people their well-deserved punishment: God wanted to punish the people for its unfaithfulness and that of its rulers, a phenomenon which could already be seen in its prehistory. And the episodes reported in Judges are the first elements in this theological doctrine of history.[3]

9.2.2 Now if it is no longer possible to reconstruct a chronology of Israel prior to the constitution of the state, we can at least try to see in what way and on what criteria the material handed down to us has been collected. In my commentary I first of all give the chronological information which appears in Judges and then try to make a systematic reconstruction of the way in which it fits into the general context of the chronology from the patriarchs to the first kings.[4] And here it is possible to note the existence of an organic and co-ordinated system with very little left out, even if this system is ideological rather than objective.

9.3 The first 'judges'

The present narrative puts the various figures in a chronological sequence. However, we shall see (below 9.10) that since they operate in relatively restricted territories, we cannot exclude the possibility that originally two or more worked contemporaneously. This is a feature which is now obscured by the pan-Israelite theory of the tribal league.

9.3.1 A first enemy, mentioned in 3.7-11, bears the name Cushan-rishathaim and is confronted by the judge Othniel. Despite attempts to identify the former of these figures, the narrative does not seem to have any foundation in the history of the ancient Near East. The first name has every appearance of being a nickname, meaning 'the little negro with the twofold sin'.

9.3.2 The episode of Eglon and the judge Ehud (3.12-30) seems more important.

9.3.2.1 The content of the account smacks of the Grand Guignol, with elements of a scatological humour which is rather heavy for our taste. Here too the name of the invading king could be a caricature: 'little calf'.

9.3.2.2 However, its topography is not very precise: Jericho is not mentioned by name but is paraphrased as the 'City of Palms' (v.13), perhaps to make the story fit with the destruction in Josh.6. The same thing also happens at the ethnic level; as well as the Moabites, the Amelekites and the Ammonites are both mentioned in the same verse. The description of the figures is often lacking in incisiveness: the enemy appears ridiculous and clumsy; he is fat and stupid, with a ridiculous name. The very features which make the account historically suspect are its main literary characteristic.

9.3.2.3 So it is difficult to recover any historical or political information from the narrative, for example whether at any given period of its history, and certainly close to the time of its settlement, Moab had tried to advance westwards so as also to take in the territory west of the Jordan around Jericho, and to what extent it had taken possession of the territory in Transjordan which the biblical tradition attributes to Reuben (above 8.2.11).

9.3.2.4 On the other hand, once the Deuteronomistic introduction and conclusion is eliminated, we have an almost complete narrative, perhaps lacking only a few elements at the beginning and rather more at the end. It is difficult to say how far Ehud could be considered the main character of a heroic narrative; at present the preponderance of humorous features suggests that we should be cautious.

9.3.3 Shamgar ben Anath is another unknown person: it is not even easy to establish whether the name of the Canaanite deity (above 2.4.6) indicates descent from her or, more probably, the fact that the person came from one of the many places which had this as part of a composite name. Shamgar is interesting beause it is with him that we have the first mention of the Philistines, whom he defeated, as enemies of Israel. The reference could be to a Canaanite alliance with Israel to fight the common enemy, just as later we find a Canaanite coalition, probably headed by a Philistine, to fight against Israel (chs.4-5, below 9.4.4.1). However, we cannot establish any more precise details; even the etymology of the name is uncertain: some scholars think it is of Hurrian derivation, others suggest a Canaanite figure. So the figure described in 3.31 is problematical on the historical level.

9.4 The battle on the plain

The battle fought on the plain of Jezreel between Israel and a Canaanite coalition composed of members who are not mentioned by name, under a certain Sisera, is an episode the importance of which cannot be mistaken, both for its political implications and for the deductions that can be made from it for the ancient history of Israel. It is described in Judg.4-5.

Bibliography

J.A.Soggin, 'Il canto di Debora, Giudici cap. V', *ANLR* VIII. 32, 1977, 97-112; G.Garbini, 'Il cantico di Debora', *PP* 178, 1978, 5-31; J.A.Soggin, *Judges*, ad loc.; 'Bemerkungen zum Deboralied', *TLZ* 106, 1981, 625-39; 'Amalek und Ephraim, Richter 5, 14', *ZDPV* 98, 1982, 58-62; D.F.Murray, 'Narrative Structures and Techniques in the Deborah-Barak Story (Judges IV 4-22)', *SVT* 30, 1979, 155-89; A.J.Hauser, 'Judges 5: Parataxis in Hebrew Poetry', *JBL* 99, 1980, 23-41; C.Grottanelli, 'L'inno a Hermes e il canto di Debora: due facce di un tema mitico', *RSO* 56, 1982 [1985], 27-37; B.Halpern, 'The Resourceful Israelite Historian; The Song of Deborah and Israelite Historiography', *HTR* 76, 1983, 379-201; A.Caquot, 'Les tribus d'Israël dans le Cantique de Debora (Juges 5, 13-17)', *Sem* 36, 1986, 47-70; C.Grottanelli, 'The Story of Deborah and Barak – A Comparative Approach', *SMSR* 53, 1987, 145-62; L.E.Axelson, *The Lord Rose from Seir*, Lund 1987, 51ff.; L.E.Stager, 'Archaeology, Ecology and Social History. Background Themes to the Song of Deborah', *SVT* 49, 1988, 221-4; J.Gray, 'Israel in the Song of Deborah', in *Ascribe to the Lord. Essays in Memory of P.C.Craigie*, Sheffield 1988, 421-55; H.D.Neef, 'Der Sieg Deboras und Baraks über Sisera', *ZAW* 101, 1989, 28-49; L.A.Stager, 'The Song of Deborah – Why Some Tribes Answered the Call and Others Did Not', *BAR* 15, 1, 1989, 51-64; A.Brenner, 'A Triangle and a Rhombus Structure: A Proposed Integrative Reading of Judges IV and V', *VT* 40, 1990, 129-38; N.Na'aman, 'Literary and Topographical Notes on the Battle of Kishon', ibid., 423-36; V.H.Matthews, 'Hospitality and Hostility in Judges 4', *BTB* 21, 119, 13-21.

9.4.1 For the details here, too, the reader must consult the works listed. The following features are worth noting.

9.4.1.1 Although chs.4-5 obviously refer to the same event, they differ in their lists of the groups involved in the battle. In 4.6, 10 only the tribes of Zebulon and Naphtali are mentioned, whereas in 5.14ff., in addition to them we have Ephraim, Benjamin, Machir (perhaps = Manasseh) and Issachar; Reuben, Gilead (perhaps = Gad), Dan and Asher did not respond to the summons. So in ch.5 we have a total of twelve tribes, with the absence of the whole of the south and of Levi.

9.4.1.2 But the topography of the battle also varies from one version to another. 4.6 refers to the environs of Mount Tabor (coord.137-232), on the south-eastern border of the first two tribes mentioned; however, 5.19 speaks of the neighbourhood of Taanach (coord. 171-214), situated about thirty miles further south-west as the crow flies, not an insignificant distance to cover on foot or in a war chariot.

9.4.1.3 In 4.14 an attempt is made to give the combat the character of an episode in a holy war, and so the battle proper is described in relatively pale terms; however, in ch.5 the battle is described in epic and heroic tones.

9.4.1.4 Thus the episode is narrated twice, but with marked differences, and it is not possible to say which of the two accounts reflects the earliest tradition. As a text the song is evidently earlier (even if it is not as early as most scholars have thought), but matters are not in fact so sure at the level of tradition.

9.4.2 In 5.6-8 we have some useful information about the reason for the battle, that is, if we accept the translation that I have suggested in the studies cited above on the basis of an attempt to restore this difficult text. If it is the case that before the battle 'the traders had ceased, and those who went on journeys chose devious routes', and the leaders of Israel were inactive, it is evident that the purpose of the battle (and probably of the war of which it was only one episode, though we hear nothing of that) was to re-establish the communications between the tribes of the central hill-country and those of Galilee which had been broken off, communications which went through the plain and therefore through the unoccupied territories of the city-states.

9.4.3 The details of the killing of Sisera also vary from one version to another (cf.4.21 and 5.26), but in this case it is possible that the first text misunderstood the second, which is very difficult and full of archaic and poetic expressions.

9.4.4 Something else which is far from clear is the general historical context: 4.2 speaks of Jabin of Hazor, who bears the improbable title 'king of Canaan', and the same name also appears in Josh.11.1ff. This would seem to be the same person, but how this works out on the historical level is impossible to clarify. Again, the two texts lack all indications of chronology, so that it is difficult to find even an approximate date for the battle. The majority of scholars propose a date around 1125 BCE, but without giving any substantial reason. However, attention should be drawn to the proposal made by A.D.H. Mayes at the end of the 1960s and reinforced in the 1970s,[5] that the battle should be removed from this indeterminate context and located in the context of the struggles between Israel and the Philistines.

9.4.4.1 The starting point for this proposal is the name of the leader, Sisera, which is certainly not Semitic and probably Luvian in origin, i.e. from an area in Asia Minor. In that case it would be possible to connect him with the 'sea peoples' (above 4.4.1) and to see the adversary of Israel as a Canaanite coalition headed by a Philistine.

9.4.4.2 If that is so, however, it would seem reasonable to put the battle shortly before the one narrated in I Sam.4, i.e. in the last decades of the second millennium BCE, and about a century after the date just mentioned. I Samuel 4 relates how Israel suffered a heavy defeat at the hand of the Philistines in which even the ark was captured by the enemy; this marked the beginning of the process which in a short time was to lead Israel to become a monarchical state (above 4.3).

9.4.4.3 In other words, Israel will originally have won a considerable victory over the coalition, not so much by any intrinsic superiority as by an unforeseen factor (above 2.4.2): a heavy summer downpour, something which is very rare in the region, and which was immediately understood as a sign of divine aid. This will have hindered any manoeuvres of the Canaanite and Philistine war chariots, turning the battlefield into a bog. There was no alternative for the chariot teams than to flee on foot, only to be overtaken and exterminated by the Israelites or the semi-nomadic groups which circulated in the region (cf. the killing of Sisera by Jael, 4.15ff.; 5.20ff.). This is the only possible explanation for the flight of the defeated enemy on foot, when the use of their war chariots would have given them an evident advantage. It is not surprising that the event was considered a miracle in Israel.

9.4.4.4 However, as I have indicated, the Israelite success must have been short-lived: communications between the centre and the north seem to have been re-established, but the Canaanites and Philistines soon recovered (above 4.3). The battle on the heights of Gilboa in which Saul and three of his sons lost their lives (above 4.3.5) and the army of Israel was completely defeated also shows that it is highly probable that there were good relations between the city-states and the Philistines, relations which made it possible for the latter to move through the territories of the former and obtain provisions from them. This allowed them to attack Israel at the most opportune times and places. Only with David (above 4.4) did the situation come to an end, in circumstances which are not all clear.

9.5 Gideon

Chapters 6-8 speak of the actions of Gideon against marauding Midianites and their allies from Transjordan who invaded the territory of Israel to destroy its crops and steal its cattle.

Bibliography

J.A.Soggin, *Judges*, ad loc.; A.G.Auld, 'Gideon: Hacking at the Heart of the Old Testament', *VT* 39, 1989, 257-67.

9.5.1 The Gideon traditions are not at all an easy complex for anyone attempting to analyse them, and for details the reader must consult the commentaries and monographs. The main problem is posed by the variety of themes and motives they contain, sometimes extraneous and at times only very loosely connected with the main narrative. There are also obvious contradictions, signs of continual revisions and re-readings. At all events, Auld's recent study has made it probable that this is a 'late biblical narrative', in which an ancient story may perhaps be being retold.

9.5.2 A first extraneous element inserted into the narrative is that of the foundation of the Israelite sanctuary of Ophrah, the location of which is uncertain (perhaps *eṭ-ṭayībe*, coord. 192-223 or *ʿaffūlāh*, coord. 177-233)[6] in 6.11-24. This is a tradition which is probably earlier than Dtr, since Josiah's reform (below 12.4.2) eliminated this very kind of sanctuary; moreover, the text is interested only in Gideon's clearly anti-Canaanite position, and thus seems to close an eye to the rest.

9.5.3 Gideon appears here as a hero of the struggle against the Canaanite cults, in that he desecrates and demolishes the local sanctuary of Baʿal (6.25-32, above 2.4.7). This could be an ancient feature, though not earlier than the time of Elijah and Elisha, when the first struggles against the religion of Canaan seem to have begun, in favour of the uniqueness of the national God YHWH (below 1.10.7). However, in the present economy of narrative there is only a series of trials and acts of purification and propitiation which qualify Gideon before God and before men as a hero of the faith.

9.5.4 The account is further complicated by the fact that the author has two names, Gideon and Jerubbaal, the second of which is important for the episode of Abimelech which follows (ch.9). This name is said to have been given him after the struggle against syncretism, with a popular etymology which is philologically incorrect.

9.5.5 The battle against the Midianites and their allies is described only after we have heard of a series of hesitations and postponements. However, literary and theological factors rather than any other will have prompted the delay in the time of attack.

9.5.5.1 First of all there is the need to connect the pan-Israelite thesis with the received tradition according to which the battle was fought only by Gideon and his 300 Abiezrites (7.1-8);

9.5.5.2 Secondly, there is the desire to give the glory only to God and not to the bravery, astuteness and other capacities of men. Once these problems have been resolved by means of another literary artifice, the attack can finally begin.

9.5.6 In 7.16-22 Gideon uses a stratagem which leads the Midianites, seized with panic, to kill each other; the survivors flee in terror.

9.5.6.1 The starting points for the operation are on the one hand the spring of Harod (in present-day Hebrew *ʿēn ḥārōd*, in Arabic *ʿein jālūd*, coord. 184-217), above which Gideon had pitched his camp, and on the other the hill of Moreh (probably *jebel nebī-dāḥi*, coord.184-225), on the northern spurs of the central hill-country, with the Midianite camp at its foot. The topographical indications are not always precise, not least because the text is corrupt here and there; what is proposed here is based on a restoration of the text.

9.5.6.2 The defeated enemy is pursued across Cisjordan and Transjordan; its leaders are killed. The text seems to indicate a campaign which covers a great deal of ground, if it is possible to identify the Karkor of 8.10 with *qarqār* near Petra (coord. 205-020) or even with *qaraqīr* in the *wādī sirḥān* in the northern Hegiaz, on the great caravan route. At the end of the enterprise, returning home in victory, Gideon refuses the honours offered him, especially the crown (8.22-32).

9.5.6.3 It is difficult to make a historical assessment of Gideon's enterprises. It is interesting to see how the text itself rules out the official pan-Israelite theory (7.1ff.) and reduces the battle and the expedition to a purely local episode, limited to the groups residing in the region, i.e. to those mainly affected by the raids. Moreover, there should be no difficulty in accepting that certain Israelite groups which had just settled will have had problems with other populations (here presented as groups of bandits coming from Transjordan) who claimed traditional rights of transhumance and grazing; these rights will have perhaps been put in doubt by the settlement of a new population. And since this was a problem of subsistence, it is not surprising that a life-and-death struggle should have developed. At all events, the episode has been handed down in a tone which is remarkably different from what must have been that of the original.

9.6 Abimelech at Shechem

Judges 9, the story of Abimelech, king of Shechem, takes the reader into a totally different context. To begin with, the protagonist has nothing to do with the judges, but is the ruler of a Canaanite city state for which there is also evidence outside the Bible, especially in the el-ʿAmarna letters; moreover he never held any position in 'Israel'.

Bibliography

J.A.Soggin, 'Bemerkungen zur alttestamentlichen Topographie Sichems, mit besonderen Bezug auf Jdc 9', *ZDPV* 83, 1967, 183-98; 'Il regno di Abimelek in Sichem ("Giudici" IX)', in *Studi in onore di Edoardo Volterra*, Milan 1972, 161-89; V.Fritz, 'Abimelech und Sichem in Jdc IX', *VT* 32, 1982, 129-44; N.H.Rösel, 'Überlegungen zu "Abimelek und Sichem in Jdc IX" ', *VT* 33, 1983, 500-3; E.F.Campbell, 'Judges 9 and Biblical Archeology', in *'The Word of the Lord Shall Go Forth'* – *Essays in Honor of D.N.Freedman*, Philadelphia 1983, 263-71; T.A.Boogaart, 'Stone for Stone: Retribution in the Story of Abimelek and Shechem', *JSOT*

32, 1985, 45-56; N.Na'aman, 'Migdal, Shechem and the House of El Berith', *Zion* 51, 1986, 259-80 (in Hebrew, with English summary); J.A.Soggin, 'The *migdal* Temple, *migdāl šᵉkem* Judg 9 and the Artifact on Mount Ebal', in M.Augustin and K.D.Schunck (eds.), *Wünsche Jerusalem Frieden*, Frankfurt am Main 1988, 115-19.

9.6.1 The redactors of the book of Judges inserted the episode of Abimelech at this point because Gideon, identified with Jerubba'al (above 9.5.4), was indicated as the father of the hero of the narrative. The transition to ch.9 now takes place in 8.29, a text which connected Gideon/Jerubba'al with the place Shechem, present-day *tell balāṭa* (coord.176-179), an eastern suburb of Nablus, through the figure of the anonymous Shechemite *pīlegeš* of Jerubba'al. The term *pīlegeš* is usually translated 'concubine', but is certainly to be connected with a superior form of concubine, since the woman was considered to be a legitimate wife and the union in fact conveyed special rights on descendants.[7] This kind of connection between individuals and narratives of different kinds appears in all the literature of the ancient Near East and is almost always secondary.

9.6.2 Abimelech is said to become king of the city state by means of a plot in which, with the complicity of the notables of Shechem (above 2.8.3), he is said to have succeeded in eliminating the seventy sons of Gideon-Jerubba'al, his half-brothers,[8] thus ascending the throne.

9.6.3 So this story stands out from the others in the book by virtue of its essentially political theme: here we have the description of a plot which leads to the coronation of a new sovereign, an assembly which has the right to establish who is to become the new king (the presumption is clearly that the throne is vacant and that there are no immediate legitimate successors), and a series of rebellions against the new king, in the last of which the king is killed. The scene of the episode is the city-state of Shechem: its protagonists are on the one hand the new assembly which seems to have quite precise powers in the constitutional sphere, for example that of nominating or deposing a ruler. For this reason it is possible that the original nucleus of the story goes back to an ancient chronicle of events which gives us at least a brief glimpse into the order of a Canaanite city-state at the time of the Israelite settlement just before.[9] However, this tradition now seems to have substantial novellistic features and to have been elaborated by a fairly discreet Deuteronomistic revision, to which we probably owe the transmission of this important text.[10]

9.6.4 Having obtained power in this way, the king is then said to have antagonized the city assembly for reasons at which we can now only guess; the break is followed by open rebellion. Verse 22 gives us the only chronological information of the narrative: the reign is said to have lasted only three years. In any case, the king seems to have succeeded in quelling the rebellion by means of two expeditions which left the city in ruins (vv.30-41, 42-45).

9.6.5 The king is then said to have fallen, crushed to death during the siege of a suburb of Shechem called the Tower of Shechem (*migdāl šᵉkem*, vv.46ff.), which is certainly to be distinguished from the capital, as I have argued from 1967 onwards.[11] Now, after the campaigns of excavation on Mount Ebal north of Nablus (coord.177-182) from 1982 onwards, this place should probably be identified with a complex discovered there, consisting of an enclosed area containing a temple-tower (*migdāl*) dating from the beginning of the Iron Age.

9.6.6 The excavations carried out by the American Drew-McCormick and ASOR expedition in the 1950s and 1960s attest the destruction of the place towards the end of the twelfth century BCE;[12] and we must seriously take into account the possibility that this was the one described in the present chapter.

9.7 Jephthah

With Jephthah, the reader is taken for the first time in the book of Judges into northern Transjordan, according to the biblical tradition the scene of battles between Israelites and Ammonites. The texts are in Judg.10.6-12.6 and have Jephthah as their main character.

Bibliography

J.A.Soggin, *Judges*, ad loc.; H.(N.)Rösel, 'Jephta und das Problem der Richter', *Bibl* 61, 1980, 251-5; J.A.Soggin, 'Il galaadita Jefte, Giudici XI, 1-11', *Hen* 1, 1979, 332-6; D.Marcus, *Jephthah and His Vow*, Lubbock, Texas 1986.

9.7.1 A first difficulty for anyone studying these texts is that the places mentioned at the beginning (10.17) have not yet been identified in the present state of research.[13] *ṭōb*, mentioned in 11.3, is sometimes identified with *eṭ-ṭayibe* in Transjordan (coord.266-218).

9.7.2 Not only are the topographical details vague, but the story has an anecdotal character; it is rather like a fairy tale. The hero, who has been driven out of the family because he is illegitimate (10.1-3), is later recalled and nominated commander of the troops of Israel. However, the Deuteronomistic prologue (10.6-16) contains reflections of a theological kind, and they occasionally appear elsewhere, though never in relation to the figure of the hero. The narrative contains no names of any of the Ammonites involved, in contrast to the accounts e.g. in I Sam.11.1ff.; II Sam.10.1ff.; Jer.40.14.

9.7.3 The way in which Jephthah is introduced seems rather contradictory: at one time he acts with great circumspection, and at another we see him throwing caution to the winds.

9.7.3.1 He acts with circumspection when in 11.12-18 he enters into direct negotiations with the Ammonites, with the aim of settling the dispute with them peacefully. However, the text which describes the negotiations is a composition which essentially reflects Deut.2 and the last chapters of Numbers, features of which it tends to combine without noting the contradictions that ensue.[14] Theological reflection clearly predominates over the narrative element, evidently the product of consideration of the text of P, so that it is probably later than P. That, too, makes it difficult to detect anything other than generalized historical, geographical and topographical features in this section which are not just general; the whole passage seems to be an edifying romance rather than a narrative with a historical basis.

9.7.3.2 By contrast, Jephthah throws caution to the winds when in 11.29-40 he vows to sacrifice the first person to come out of his house to meet him on his return. As we know, this fate befalls his only daughter, whose name is never given. Here the narrator's interest evidently lies on the one hand in the family drama and on the other in the custom of lamenting the unfortunate girl, rather than in details connected with the history and topography of the events.

9.7.3.3 We also hear of the battle and the victory only in 11.33; here, too, there are problems. It is impossible to infer anything beyond the probability that the battle will have been fought in the region of Rabbath Ammon, present-day Amman (coord.238-151), capital of the Hashemite Kingdom of Jordan.[15]

9.7.3.4 The story of Jephthah ends with an episode of civil war between Ephraim and Jephthah's group in which the latter group are victorious. However, there are many obvious parallels with Judg.8.1-3, and while in Judges 8 the account fits closely with the facts narrated, that is not the case here.

9.7.4 It does not make much sense to raise the question of historicity in cases like this, given that the traditions which describe them do not even seem to be ancient.

9.8 Samson

The legends which have grown up around the person of Samson take the reader into yet another context. Chapters 13-16 are devoted to them.

Bibliography

J.A.Soggin, *Judges*, ad loc.; J.C.Exum, 'Promise and Fulfillment: Narrative Art in Judges', *JBL* 99, 1980, 43-59; 'Aspects of Symmetry and Balance in the Samson Saga', *JSOT* 19, 1981, 3-29; D.Grimm, 'Der Name der Gottesboten in Richter 13', *Bib* 62, 1981, 92-98; R.Wenning, 'Der siebenlockige Samson', *BN* 17, 1982, 43-55; R.Mayer Opificius, 'Simson, der sechslockige Held?', *UF* 14, 1982, 149-51; O.Margalith, 'Samson's Foxes', *VT* 35, 1985, 224-9; K.F.D.Römheld, 'Jdc 13 – Von den Quellen der Kraft', *ZAW* 104, 1992, 28-52.

The territory in which the events described take place is what we have seen (above 8.2.7.1) to be a problematical region, west of Benjamin. Samson himself always has grotesque, Pantagruelesque features, and hardly ever seems to perform any of the functions which the other narratives connect with the functions of judge. The chronology is also confused (cf.13.1 with 16.31). Nor is there any mention of the fact that the hero is supposed to have commanded troops, and there is also a complete absence of the pan-Israelite approach which we have seen to be characteristic of the other episodes. So the whole complex gives the impression of being an artificial construction[16] rather than going back to ancient traditions; that makes the material of little importance for the historian.

9.9 The war against Benjamin

An episode which now appears as an appendix to the book is that of the war between the tribal league and Benjamin, which was guilty of having refused to hand over the perpetrators of a particularly violent crime.[17]

Bibliography

S.Springer, *Neuinterpretationen im Alten Testament*, Stuttgart 1979, 19ff.; J.A.Soggin, *Judges*, ad loc.; H.-W.Jüngling, *Richter 19 E in – Plädoyer für das Königtum*, Rome 1981; S.Niditch, 'The "Sodomite" Theme in Judges 19-20: Family, Community and Social Disintegration', *CBQ* 44, 1982, 365-78; W.J.Dumbrell, ' "In Those Days There Was No King in Israel: Every Man Did What Was Right in His Own Eyes" ', *JSOT* 25, 1983, 23-33; S.Lasine, 'Guest and Host in Judges 19: Lot's Hospitality in an Inverted World', *JSOT* 29, 1984, 37-39; E.J.Revell, 'The Battle with Benjamin (Judges XX.29-48) and Hebrew Narrative Techniques', *VT* 35, 1985, 517-33.

9.9.1 At first sight the narrative of the ban on Benjamin appears to be a unity, an aspect which seems to go beyond the anecdotal character of some of its episodes. However, closer inspection seems to reveal at least one major contradiction: the pro-monarchical formula in 19.1; 21.25, which already appears in the preceding episode (17.6; 18.1), takes as its starting point the story of the violence suffered by the Levite and his concubine (like that of the violence perpetrated by the Danites in the previous narrative) to imply that under a monarchical regime, the guardian of law and order, such things no longer happened, nor would they happen in the future; indeed, it was precisely because of the absence of this central authority that it was possible for such things to have happened in the past. While this thesis is compatible with the story of the migration of the Danites, in the present episode it comes up against the fact that there was the tribal league, whose organs are presented as watching zealously over order and public morality, not hesitating to resort to extreme coercive measures where necessary. In other words, on the one hand the organs of the tribal league appear quite capable of ensuring that life is lived according to the civil rules, while on the other there is an appeal to the existence of a central institution to guarantee the same things!

9.9.2 There are also some other minor discrepancies in the text: the disproportion between the crime committed and the punishment, between the number of the guilty ones and those who have to pay for the crime with their life; the incongruity between the proceedings of a political kind, culminating in the civil war against Benjamin, and the eminently domestic question of the crime against the levite and his concubine (*pîlegeš*, for the meaning of which cf. above 9.6.1) caused by a group of hooligans; again there is an evident parallel between 19.22-28 and Gen.19, though in the latter case the theme is developed coherently, and the same goes for the woman cut in pieces which were than sent to the tribes, a theme which recalls I Sam.11.6. There, however, the gesture is again in its proper place and the invitation connected with it is clear: here its function seems doubtful. So the themes developed in Judg.19-21 seem to be partly secondary, a sign of the artificial character of the account.

9.9.3 On the other hand, underlying the narrative there could be the recollection of a civil war (developed to adapt it to different purposes) which really took place. Benjamin was in fact a group famous for its bravery and its belligerence (Gen.29.27; Deut.33.12; cf. Judg.5.14), but, as a look at a map clearly shows, it was wedged between Ephraim and Judah, so that it could not expand in any way. It might therefore have developed a degree of aggressiveness towards its neighbours and have been semi-destroyed in the attempt to expand its own territory.[18] In that case the origin of the narrative will have been an event of an essentially political character, translated by the tradition into individualistic and family categories of crime and punishment and later into praise of the order and security provided by the monarchy, and then, after its fall, by the tribal league to which the post-exilic hierocracy appealed.

9.9.4 Another feature which might reflect the memory of real situations is that of the relations between Benjamin and Jabesh in Gilead (21.1-14). In I Sam.11.1ff. the messengers from the besieged town go straight to the tribe of Benjamin and are met there by Saul (here it should be noted how the concept of the tribal league seems to be absent); and it is the Jabeshites who give burial to the mutilated bodies of Saul and Jonathan (I Sam.31.11-13). These are features which make plausible the hypothesis of a very close relationship between the city of Jabesh and the tribe of Benjamin. We do not know precisely where the place might have been: *tell el-maqlūb* (coord.214-201) has been proposed, near which *wādī jabiš* has preserved the name of the place to the present day: this is a tributary on the east of the Jordan (coord.209-201).

9.10 Conclusions

To conclude this chapter on the judges and to look back on the persons and events which the tradition connects with them, one might point out:

9.10.1 The tradition now presents each judge as a leader of the troops of 'all Israel', with the sole exceptions of Jephthah and especially of Samson.

9.10.2 The people who are nominated judge come from different tribes, as though there had been a kind of rotation between the individual groups, and each of them in turn was responsible for providing a nomination for the supreme magistrature. The concept is evidently artificial: we need only imagine an emergency in which a judge had to be nominated immediately to see how impossible it would have been to organize the designation with rotation as a criterion.

9.10.3 In any case, even if this is the basic theory of the text, not only does this seem unnecessary to describe the origin of the institution; it does not even appear to be the most logical explanation, provided always we accept its historicity and do not want to consider the whole thing as the product of a later ideology.

9.10.4 The concept that one individual, a kind of dictator like those in the Roman Republic, exercised supreme command over 'all Israel' even temporarily, is based on the Deuteronomistic concept of the tribal league in which Israel and Judah are said to have been already united in the period prior to the foundation of the state. However, I have indicated the impossibility of a union of this kind (above 4.1.1.1) before the empire of David and Solomon, and therefore the problematical character of the league and the institutions connected with it. So even if the texts now present the judges in a chronological succession, this is in no way necessary, and the possibility that two or more judges were contemporaries should not be excluded, even if we can no longer grasp the detail. Thus the episode of Ehud, for example, could have taken place more or less contemporaneously with that of Gideon, and that of Jephthah could have begun before the others ended, even while Abimelech was ruling over Shechem. The conventional chronology of Dtr and the fact that every judge operated in a different territory makes this suggestion possible.

9.10.5 It is virtually impossible to make any assured statements about the so-called 'minor' judges. For an explanation of their functions, which for the most part escape us, cf. above, 9.1.2.

PART THREE

The Divided Kingdoms

The Two Kingdoms to the Time of the Assyrian Invasions

10.1 The dissolution of the empire

The empire of David and Solomon did not last long; even if the complex that Solomon left to his heir seemed powerful and splendid from outside (if we disregard the loss of some peripheral areas, above 5.6.5 and 5.7), the reality was that this was a state economically on the verge of collapse, with many sectors of the population, especially in the North, oppressed and exploited (Noth* 1959, 226). On the death of Solomon the empire will have needed a ruler endowed with more than usual capacities. However, Rehoboam, the son of Solomon designated to succeed him, proved incapable of confronting a situation which, while certainly very difficult objectively, was not desperate. So the united kingdom collapsed, leaving traces only in the memory and the imagination of posterity, its place being taken by two second-rate statelets (Bright* 1981, 229). The ancient dualism between Israel and Judah (above 4.1.1) had never really been overcome, but was only kept down artificially.

10.1.1 The texts provide a relative chronology from the rupture of the personal union onwards. The years of the reign of the ruler of one of the two states are calculated synchronously on the basis of those of the parallel ruler of the other kingdom. However, this causes considerable difficulties in points of detail: only in rare cases do we know the absolute chronology (cf. Appendix II below by H.Tadmor), nor is it clear whether different calendars and different systems of dating were used in the two nations, or whether there may have been regencies, calculated as if one were dealing with true kings, so that the regent appears truly to have reigned – which led to some superimpositions; or if the reign of a sovereign who was regarded as legitimate had been calculated in relation to the years in which there was also a

usurper. Finally, we cannot exclude the possibility that some information has been handed down erroneously or not transmitted at all
(there are examples in Laato 1986, cited in 10.1.2).

10.1.2 However, the question also appears complex at a textual level:
the Massoretic text, that of the LXX and the writings of Josephus often
have different figures.[1] Still, despite these negative factors, the figures
at our disposal are relatively certain, with discrepancies rarely exceed-
ing a decade in the most doubtful cases.

Bibliography

J.Begrich, *Die Chronologie der Könige von Israel und Juda*, Tübingen
1929; A.Jepsen and R.Hanhart, *Untersuchungen zur israelitisch-jüdischen
Chronologie*, Berlin 1964; J.Finegan, *Handbook of Biblical Chronology*,
Princeton [2]1964; H.Tadmor, 'Kronologia', *EBB* IV, 1962, 245-310: 301ff.
(in Hebrew), and 'The Chronology of the First Temple Period', below,
Appendix II; E.R.Thiele, *The Mysterious Numbers of the Hebrew Kings*,
Grand Rapids, Michigan [3]1983; A.Laato, 'New Viewpoints on the
Chronology of the Kings of Judah and Israel', *ZAW* 98, 1986, 210-21;
K.T.Andersen, 'Noch einmal die Chronologie der Könige Israels und
Judas', *SJOT* 3.1, 1989, 1-45; J.H.Hayes and P.K.Hooker, *A New
Chronology for the Kings of Israel and Judah and Its Implications for Biblical
History and Literature*, Atlanta 1988. Synoptic tables are also often
provided in the various *Histories*: Jagersma*; Gunneweg*; Vermeylen*,
93; and also Soggin, *Introduction*, in the Appendix. For an examination
of the figures in the various recensions cf. J.D.Shenkel, *Chronology and
Recensional Development of Kings*, Cambridge, Mass. 1968; R.Kessler,
Staat und Gesellschaft im vorexilischen Juda, Leiden 1992; D.B.Redford,
Egypt, Canaan and Israel in Ancient Times, Princeton, NJ 1992 (which I
was unable to use). The awareness of the problem is an old one, cf. the
rabbinic tractate *Seder 'Olam Rabbah*, from the end of the third century
CE (above 3.7.1).

10.1.3 From the death of Solomon, calculated at either 926 or 922, the
two states lived side by side, sometimes as enemies, at other times
bound by alliances, until the fall of the North in 722-720 (below 11.3).
This dualism was to continue in the post-exilic and New Testament
periods in the hostility between the Judahites and the Samaritans and
is still attested in the earliest rabbinic writings.

Bibliography

A.Alt, 'Das Königtum in den Reichen Israel und Juda', *VT* 1, 1953, 2-
22 = *KS* II, 116-34; A.Malamat, 'Kingship and Council in Israel and
Sumer: A Parallel', *JNES* 22, 1963, 247-53; id., 'Organs of Statecraft in

the Israelite Monarchy', *BA* 28, 1965, 34-65; J.A.Soggin, *Das Königtum*, 90ff.; G.Buccellati, *Cities and Nations*; J.Debus, *Die Sünde Jeroboams*, FRLANT 93, Göttingen 1967; D.W.Gooding, 'The Septuagint's Rival Version of Jeroboam's Rise to Power', *VT* 17, 1967, 173-9; id., 'Jeroboam's Rise to Power - A Rejoinder', *JBL* 91, 1972, 529-33; H.Seebass, 'Zur Königserhebung Jeroboams I', *VT* 17, 1967, 325-33; J.Conrad, *Die junge Generation im Alten Testament*, Berlin 1970; S.Herrmann, 'Geschichte Israels - Möglichkeiten und Grenzen ihrer Darstellung', *TLZ* 94, 69, 644-5; R.W.Klein, 'Jeroboam's Rise to Power', *JBL* 89, 1970, 217f.; É.Lipiński, 'Le récit I rois XII 1-19', *VT* 24, 1974, 430-7; J.Trebolle Barrero, *Salomón y Jeroboán*, Salamanca 1980; M.Weinfeld, 'The Council of the "Elders" to Rehoboam and its Implications', *Maarav* 3.1, 1982, 27-53; R.L.Cohn, 'Literary Technique in the Jerobeam Narrative', *ZAW* 97, 1985, 23-35; G.E.Gerbrandt, *Kingship according to the Deuteronomistic History*, Atlanta 1986; A.Catastini, 'I Re 13,1-10 e la redazione delle tradizioni su Geroboamo I', *Egitto e Vicino Oriente* 10, 1987, 109-21; J.T.Walsh, 'The Content of I Kings XIII', *VT* 39, 1989, 355-70. For an examination of the texts see the commentaries, especially J.A.Montgomery and H.S.Gehman, *Kings*, ICC, 1951; M.Noth, BK IX.1, 1968; J.Gray, OTL, ²1970. The theory of B.J.Diebner in his review in *DBAT* 20, 1984, 192-208: 202 that the information about the separation really relates to what happened much later between the Judahites and the Samaritans (an event which he puts in the second century BCE, but cf. below 14.4), seems to me too forced.

10.1.3.1 The biblical sources which describe the break in the personal union or, from their perspective, the secession of the North which came about on the death of Solomon, appear almost exclusively in I Kings 12; 13; 14; they therefore belong to the Deuteronomistic history. When we take into account the unconditionally pro-Judah bias in this work, it is no surprise that, after a few attempts at understanding, the action of the northern tribes is presented as politically wrong and theologically sinful. Despite this manifestly partisan attitude, however, the history is ready to recognize that the requests made by the North were originally legitimate, attributing a major part of the responsibility for the process which led to the break to the political ineptitude and immaturity in human relations of the king designate, Rehoboam (although he was forty-one years old, I Kings 14.21). Again, according to the Deuteronomistic theory, the will of God himself underlies the event (cf. below, 10.1.3.6.5). One element which emerges clearly from the account of the negotiations, the problems in which we shall be occupied with shortly, is what must have been the situation of the North, especially under Solomon. This would have been contrary, as we have seen (above 5.6.5), to the triumphalistic notes which have been abundantly furnished by the court chroniclers and subsequent celebrations.

10.1.3.2 The biblical texts on which the historian can draw are: I Kings 12.1-19, a markedly romanticized chronicle of the events which led to the break in the negotiations which has been successively amplified (as was demonstrated independently by Trebolle 1980 and Catastini 1987): the parallel text of Chronicles does not provide any variants worth noting. Then I Kings 11.29-40; 12.21-24; 14.1-18, a series of prophetic legends connected with the event and probably reported by DtrP (below 10.1.3.10); finally I Kings 12.25-31; 14.21-31, which some would want to consider extracts from the annals of the kings of Israel and Judah (for the problems of which cf. above, 3.2.2), though now enlarged by Deuteronomistic comments which seek to offer a key to reading the text.

10.1.3.3 The situation gets complicated as soon as the historian examines the LXX version and the work of Josephus, especially *Antt.* VIII, 212. On the one hand the LXX has a long insertion in Codex A at 12.24 (numbered *a* to *z*, which presupposes a Hebrew archetype [Trebolle]), while on the other it does not make Jeroboam play a part from the beginning of the Shechem assembly, something which, however, happens in the Hebrew text (v.3). In the LXX Jeroboam simply returns home on hearing of the death of Solomon, and appears at Shechem only when the negotiations have reached deadlock (v.20), in response to a specific invitation from the assembly. For Josephus the assembly will even have had him called from Egypt, bringing the two contenders into confrontation with each other. It is not possible to point out other features in the context of the present book: for those the reader should consult Trebolle 1980, Cohn 1985 and Catastini 1987. One thing seems clear: the tradition has grown over the centuries, whereas LXX probably offers the version closest to events. It does in fact seem utterly improbable that Jeroboam had been present from the beginning of the negotiations with Rehoboam. Finally, as has been demonstrated by Catastini 1987, ch.13 is ideologically close to Chronicles.

10.1.3.4 The accession of Rehoboam to the throne does not seem to have caused problems worth noting in Jerusalem: not only was the South closely tied to the house of David, a bond which was to last until the exile of 587-6 and perhaps until the end of the sixth century, despite occasional difficulties; the South also seems to have been subjected to less onerous impositions which were not therefore resented as they were in the North. Finally, its territory, for the most part composed of steppe and hill-country, was an eminently poor region with little to offer. The situation in Israel was very different: first of all it seems that the North had maintained the right to approve or reject the candidate for the monarchy; secondly, it seems to have wanted to make use of this prerogative, all the more since, thirdly, there were valid reasons for complaint, something moreover that the texts implicitly recognize. So the sources have no doubt that the immediate reason for the break in the union was the senseless behaviour of the monarch designate.

10.1.3.5 And in fact if there was little to exploit in the South, the situation of Israel was substantially different. Crossed by the great lines of communication, with substantial means of production in the spheres of agriculture, cattle rearing and crafts, especially on the plains belonging to the city-states, the North had precisely those features which almost call for exploitation. However, it seems improbable that there was a 'charismatic' concept of kingship in Israel, a kind of continuation of the activity of the judges (above 9.1.5) as presented by Dtr:[2] the opposite has been demonstrated by O.Buccellati.[3] The North, too, did not lack attempts to found dynasties, and that of Omri (below 10.9.2.3) has rightly remained famous in the ancient Near East. That these dynasties did not last long was for the most part due to a series of circumstances beyond their control, which we shall be examining in due course. Be this as it may, at all events the North was the key area in economic terms and could therefore be exploited; we can probably also deduce from this that at least to begin with it was also more important than the South on the cultural level. Nor would it be rash to claim that Judah succeeded in maintaining itself for around a century and a half after the fall of the North only because of its isolation. At the same time, though, it succeeded in concentrating on itself, its dynasty and the temple of Jerusalem the most vital ideological and theological features of Israel, features which have assured its survival right down to the present day.

10.1.3.6 It is possible to discover some features of considerable interest from the first account, though it is markedly anecdotal, has been successively enlarged and, as I have said, is probably romanticized.

10.1.3.6.1 In the first place, as I have indicated, it seems that in the North the succession to the throne was not automatic: the firstborn son of the dead monarch did not necessarily succeed his father. Rehoboam is said to have had to go in person to Shechem, a place which evidently functioned as the capital of Israel, at least in the administrative sense of the term. There he had to meet 'all Israel', a formula which this time can refer only to the North, assembled to discuss his candidature to the throne. The text does not explain why Rehoboam had to go personally to the assembly instead of summoning it, say, in Jerusalem or in another place of his choice: in II Sam.5.1ff. 'all the tribes of Israel' appear before David in Hebron in the persons of their plenipotentiaries. For this reason basic doubts have been raised about the historicity of the scene (Debus 1967, 28). As for the problem of the improbability of

The Divided Kingdoms

the participation of Jeroboam in the assembly from the start, we have seen that the LXX version is likely to be the nearest to events, while vv.2-3a, 15 and 17 are probably part of the later amplification (Debus, Lipiński, Trebolle and Catastini). However, the narrative does preserve information which is not manifestly unfounded, that Judah and Israel, as in the time of David, each crowned its own sovereign and that in this respect each had remarkable prerogatives and autonomy. Contrary to what I suggested in 1967, it now seems improbable that we can speak of the survival of democratic elements here, especially in the North. And in any case, it is only for Israel that the negotiations come to nothing, despite their laborious course.

10.1.3.6.2 We do not know the composition of the assembly and it is impossible to discover to what point it was already ill-disposed towards Rehoboam from the start and thus resolved to lay down conditions calculated to make the negotiations fail, so that it could then put the blame for the failure on the inexpert and arrogant Rehoboam. Herrmann* 1980, 184f.; Donner* 1977, 384 and *II, 1986, 235ff., are disposed to believe this, and the information according to which Jeroboam returned from Egypt and took part in the assembly suggests that the later tradition thought so too.

10.1.3.6.3 However, if we examine the requests put by the assembly to the candidate, they do not seem either extravagant or provocative: 'Your father made our yoke heavy. Now therefore lighten the hard service of your father and his heavy yoke upon us, and we will be your loyal subjects' (literally, 'we will serve you', 12.4). It appears from these words that the North, and not the South, felt oppressed and exploited. After this the scene changes from the seat of the assembly to the deliberations between the sovereign designate and his counsellors.

10.1.3.6.4 Here the texts present the king designate as being involved with two groups of counsellors: however, it does not seem possible to maintain the thesis of Malamat 1963 that this was some form of institution with two chambers;[4] rather, we have something much simpler, if we accept the usual explanation. On the one hand there are the older and therefore more expert counsellors, 'who had grown old in the service of Solomon' (Donner* 1977, 384, and II*, 1986, 236ff.); these recommend moderation to the young king. On the other hand are the younger and therefore less expert counsellors, some of them the king's childhood companions (12.8). Lipiński 1974 argued that the 'elders' will have been those of the people, who had already opposed the king in the time of Solomon (this is how the expression *'md 'et pᵉnē NP* should be understood), whereas the 'youths' will have been those in the retinue of the monarch and therefore more ready with their adulation. So the fault of the candidate will have been to have neglected the advice of the representatives of the people in favour of that of his own followers. However, none of these arguments seems probable: the theme of the older sage and the youth who is rebellious and sometimes stupid is a literary theme which can be found in any ancient form of wisdom and often in popular traditions down to the present day, and therefore cannot be taken as historically relevant information.

10.1.3.6.5 Be this as it may, the older men recognize the legitimacy and the moderation of the requests of the assembly and also their formal correctness, and exhort the king to accept these proposals. Contrary to the arguments of Weinfeld 1982, who sees the monarchy as being 'at the service' of the people, it should be emphasized that the expression 'serve' here has the meaning of 'submit', 'accept certain conditions', 'be subject', and derives from the language of international treaties. So v.7 is to be translated: 'If today you submit yourself to this people, accepting its conditions and responding to it with good words, its members will be your subjects for ever!' That is because, as Weinfeld demonstrates on the basis of instances from the ancient Near East, 'to accede to someone's request' is the concrete meaning of the expressions 'speak well', 'respond with good words'. By contrast, the 'young' exhort the candidate not to yield; indeed, they tell him to reply to the assembly in a particularly arrogant and crude way (v.10b uses a downright obscene expression, a paraphrase for the penis, Debus 1967 and Noth 1968). And it is to the young that the candidate yields, precipitating the disaster. This too is a feature which, as the text observes (12.15), is not outside the divine intervention (below 10.1.3.10.1).

10.1.3.7 A first attempt by Rehoboam to settle the dispute (12.18-19) fails, and the candidate only escapes by fleeing from what seems to have been a real attempt on his life. His lieutenant Adoram, the person who under David and Solomon seems to have been in charge of the forced labour (above, 4.7.1.1.7, where he appears as Adoniram), having been ordered by the king to carry on the negotiations, is stoned to death.

10.1.3.8 The result of the failure of the negotiations between the assembly and the future king was thus the break-up of the personal union between Israel and Judah and the re-establishment, in Canaan, of two nations, Israel and Judah, as they had existed before the time of David. Benjamin seems very soon largely to have gone over to David (12.21), following the conflicts which I shall be discussing below (10.6.5). The reasons for this territorial and tribal change are not explained, but they are certainly connected with the fact that Judah could not tolerate a northern frontier which ran only a few hundred yards north of the capital.

10.1.3.9 The texts are unanimous in affirming that Judah never wanted to accept the break-up of the personal union as a *fait accompli*, so that a reunion of the two groups, which the North no longer seems to have wanted, became first the goal of the ruler of Judah and then a feature of the eschatological hope (cf. Isa. 9.2-7 [Hebrew 9.1-6]; Jer.3.1ff.; 23.5-6; Ezek.37.15-22 and other passages).

10.1.3.10 A variety of prophetic legends sprang up at different times around the episode (11.20-40; 12.21-24; 14.1-8, probably deriving from DtrP). It is interesting that in part these seek to attribute to Jeroboam something like a divine election, a feature which moreover stands out from the Deuteronomistic historiography, where the condemnation of the northern cause is total, though the legitimacy of its demands is recognized.

10.1.3.10.1 The legend recorded in the first text is connected with the abortive revolt against Solomon, led by Jeroboam when he was still an official of the empire in charge of forced labour (above 5.7.3, cf. I Kings 11.26-28). According to this narrative, Jeroboam was met on the road by the prophet Ahijah of Shiloh, who invested him with rule over the ten tribes of the North. The sovereignty over these tribes is said to have been taken away from Solomon because of his impiety. However, Dtr is anxious to point out that this investiture was conditional on the obedience of the candidate to the divine commandments. The revolt failed and its leader was forced to flee abroad, to Egypt; from there he returned home on receiving news of the death of Solomon. Indeed, I Kings 12.15 sees the attitude of Rehoboam as a product of divine intervention, thus fulfilling the promise made to Jeroboam during his flight. So according to this stratum of Dtr something seems to have happened rather like what Dtr sees as having happened between David and Saul in I Sam.16.1-13 (above 4.3.3): the kingdom is taken away from the one who had shown himself unworthy of it and given to others more worthy.

10.1.3.10.2 The second of these texts, which seems to be a relatively late composition, shows Rehoboam intent on re-establishing the unity of the empire, if necessary by force. He raises an army and moves against those whom he considers rebels, but is dissuaded from launching the expedition by a divine oracle delivered by the prophet Shemaiah. After that he withdraws his troops and disbands them. The note contained in 14.30, which is almost marginal in its present context, seems more realistic: 'There was continually war between Rehoboam and Jeroboam' – a situation which seems to have lasted during the life of the two monarchs and under their successors Asa of Judah and Baasha of Israel (15.16).

10.1.3.10.3 The third text presents Jeroboam on his sick-bed in the act of sending his own wife to Shiloh, to consult Ahijah. The prophet delivers a divine oracle to the woman: YHWH is angry with Jeroboam because he has been unfaithful: therefore the king must die and his dynasty be exterminated. The kingdom will totter and Israel will have to go into exile, where it will be dispersed. The allusion to the events of the last quarter of the eighth century is obvious (cf. below 11.3).

10.1.3.10.4 These texts show what we might call the ambiguous attitude of the various strata of Dtr towards the northern kingdom. On the one hand they have Jeroboam designated through an oracle and see the new state under divine protection; on the other hand they recognize Jeroboam as a sinner, because of the crime of the separation, but especially because of his religious policy, which we shall be considering in due course. So his destiny, together with that of the kingdom in which this infidelity is perpetuated, can only be disastrous. In this sense, too, DtrP ends up by inserting itself into the general thread of condemnation of the North which marks out the other strata of Dtr.

10.1.3.11 Finally there are two texts which, according to some scholars, could go back to the court annals of Israel and Judah – that is, if we accept the existence of such annals and that they were handed down (above 3.2.2: 12.25-31; 14.21-31).

10.1.3.11.1 The first text begins by speaking of the new fortifications built by Jeroboam at Shechem in the central-northern hill-country (present-day *tell balāṭa*, coord. 176-179), at Penuel in Transjordan (probably *tulul eḍ-ḍāhab*, coord.215-176), and at Tirzah (*tell el-far'āh*, coord. 182–188); he also moved the capital of the kingdom to Tirzah (below 10.4.3).

10.1.3.11.2 The second text speaks of the reign of Rehoboam, describing its sinful character in typically Deuteronomistic categories; it then goes on to describe the Egyptian invasion (below 10.4).

10.2 The worship of the 'golden calf'

Bibliography

M.Weippert, 'Gott und Stier', *ZDPV* 77, 1961, 93-117; M.Aberbach and L.Smolar, 'Aaron, Jeroboam and the Golden Calves', *JBL* 86, 1967, 129-40; J.A.Soggin, 'Der offiziell geförderte Synkretismus im 10.Jahrhundert', *ZAW* 78, 1966, 179-204; H.Donner, 'Hier sind deine Götter, Israel', in *Wort und Geschichte – FS K.Elliger*, AOAT 18, Neukirchen 1973, 45-50; E.T.Mullen, 'The Sin of Jeroboam. A Redactional Assessment', *CBQ* 49, 1987, 212-32.

At Bethel (probably present-day *beitīn*, coord.172-148), a mile or two north of present-day Ramallah, and at Dan (present-day *tell el-qāḍī*, coord. 211-294), in the extreme north, Jeroboam is said to have instituted a schismatic form of cult, expressed by means of the image of a golden bull, disparagingly called a 'calf'. This is the Canaanite image of a bull, the symbol of male sexual potency; here, however, its functions seem to have been to serve as a pedestal for the invisible God of Israel, precisely like the ark in the temple of Jerusalem which served as his throne. That this was the case is evident from the announcement in 12.28b: 'Behold your God, O Israel, who brought you up out of Egypt'. And despite the many authoritative statements to the contrary, it seems that the term *ʾelōhīm*, which the Hebrew renders both in the singular, 'God', and in the plural, 'gods', was intended in the singular and not the plural. The reference is in fact to the same 'golden calf' which the tradition in Ex.32.1ff. has instituted by Aaron in person during the absence of Moses: this story has every appearance of having originally been the cultic legend of the provisions made by Jeroboam in matters of worship. It is interesting that the first verses of Ex.32.1ff. are not in fact polemical: it was only later (vv.7ff.) that the polemic, probably a product of the redaction, came into the text.

10.3 The situation and administration in the annexed territories

The sources say little or nothing about the territories which were annexed or made vassals under David.

10.3.1 Towards the end of the reign of Solomon, it is said, some peripheral elements of the empire had begun to detach themselves, partly probably with Solomon's agreement, partly through rebellions (above 5.6.6.1-2 and 5.7). It is probable that this process of detachment continued throughout the tenth century and the beginning of the ninth. We know from I Kings 15.18-20// II Chron.16.2-6 that for some time Damascus remained bound to Israel by a treaty of alliance, having previously regained its freedom (above 5.7), but that this treaty was later abrogated. We learn from the annals of Shalmaneser III of Assyria (*ANET*, 276ff.; *TUAT* I, 360ff.) that Ammon was again independent in 854 BCE, while the stele of Mesha king of Moab states that the region regained its independence at the end of the ninth century. However, the text implies that Moab had already obtained this independence earlier, then later to lose it briefly again (below 10.8.12). Only Edom seems to have remained dependent on Judah.

10.3.2 The biblical texts say virtually nothing about the administrative measures adopted by Jeroboam (who evidently had to reconstruct a large part of the bureaucratic administration). However, it is possible to deduce from the ostraca discovered at Samaria, from the first half of the eighth century (*KAI*, 183ff.; *SSI* I, 5ff.; *ANET*, 321ff.; *TUAT* I, 248ff.; cf. my *Introduction*, Appendix I.4) that the fiscal system inaugurated by Solomon and based on a division into districts (above 5.8) remained fully in force (Noth* 1959, 194, 237), thus resulting in the paradox that a system first considered unjust because it was oppressive and exploited the people, later proved to be the only practicable one on an administrative level. This happens quite often in history.

10.4 The Egyptian invasion

Bibliography

A.Jirku, *Die ägyptischen Listen palästinischer und syrischer Ortsnamen*, Leipzig 1937; M.Noth, 'Die Shoschenkliste', *ZDPV* 61, 1938, 277-304, *ABLAK* II, 73-93; B.Mazar, 'The Campaign of Pharaoh Shishak to Palestine', *SVT* 4, 1957, 57-66; S.Herrmann, 'Operationen Pharaos Schoschenk I im östlichen Ephraim', *ZDPV* 80, 1963, 55-79; D.B.Redford, 'Studies in the Relationship between Palestine and Egypt during the First Millennium BC: II – The Twenty-Second Dynasty', *JAOS* 93, 1973, 3-17; S.Ahituv, *Canaanite Toponyms in Ancient Egyptian Documents*, Jerusalem 1984, 209f. and passim; Donner* II, 1986, 245ff., 291 n.13; Miller and Hayes* 1988, 245ff.; Garbini*, 1988, 28ff.

The second of the texts to which I referred in the previous section speaks of the reign of Rehoboam in the South, his kinsfolk, his works and his failings, all in the Deuteronomistic style. However, at the end we find a very important note reporting an invasion of the region by Pharaoh Shishak, the Egyptian Shoshenk I (c.943-924), founder of the Twenty-Second 'Libyan' dynasty at the beginning of the reign of Rehoboam (I Kings 14.25-28// II Chron.12.2,9-11).

10.4.1 The expedition is recorded with copious details in a great relief executed on the south wall of a portico attached to the temple of Karnak. According to this inscription it took place in the twenty-first year of his reign, i.e. around 925 BCE (*ANET*, 263f.; Jirku 1937, 47f.; not yet in *TUAT*). It is clear that the expedition must have taken place some time before it was recorded on the relief (the proposal by K.A.Kitchen, above 3.7, to date the event in the twentieth or twenty-first reign of the Pharaoh seems too close to the completion of the artefact). If that is the case, however, there is a marked discrepancy between the biblical dating, which puts the event 'in the fifth year of king Rehoboam' (14.25), i.e. in 922 or 918. However, given the uncertainty which prevails in the Hebrew Bible over dates prior to the eighth century, the Egyptian date seems preferable.

10.4.2 Now in this context Garbini* 1988 has highlighted a disconcerting feature: for want of an absolute chronology, Egyptologists (most recently Kitchen) tend to anchor the chronology of the expedition in the biblical chronology, and the core of this chronology seems to be the assumption that the Pharaoh was contemporary with Rehoboam rather than Solomon. But it is known from I Kings 11.40 that Shoshenk offered political asylum to Jeroboam (Kitchen, 72f.), so Garbini proposes an earlier chronology for the Pharaoh: around 950-929. Even if the traditional chronology is maintained, though, the two kings, Solomon and Shoshenk, were contemporaries for a significant period. The aim of Garbini's proposal is to put the Egyptian invasion not in the fifth year of Rehoboam but in one of the last years of Solomon, thus placing it in the context of the decadence of the empire.

10.4.3 This proposal is not the only attempt to bring some order into the complex situation. The problem is that we do not know why the Pharaoh undertook this campaign. Donner* II, 1986, 246, in fact argues that 'this campaign was not much more than a demonstration of strength, the aim of which was to show that after a long pause Egypt was in process of recovery. Shoshenk I was not in a position to exercise his sovereignty over Palestine in concrete form.' Another possibility, though this must remain purely hypothetical, is that Jeroboam had made promises to the Pharaoh during his stay in Egypt which he subsequently did not keep. Be this as it may, Rehoboam, now firmly installed on the throne in the South, succeeded in averting the danger, whereas Jeroboam I must have been 'in great difficulty' (Donner). In fact we read that Rehoboam succeeded in keeping Egypt away from Judah at the cost of sacrificing a large part of the temple and palace treasure (I Kings 14.26// II Chron.12.9f.). At all events, Judah and Jerusalem do not appear on the Karnak inscription, while the Pharaoh plundered the plain of Jezreel and Transjordan, the economically most important territories in the North. It is not said how Jeroboam reacted. It is possible that following these events the capital of the North was transferred from Shechem to Tirzah, present-day *tell el far'āh* (coord.182-88, cf. Donner* 1977, 389, and 1984*, 245f., above 10.1.3.11.1).

10.4.4 It is important that this is the first Egyptian ruler to whom the Hebrew Bible gives a name: *šošaq* in the Kethib and *šīšāq* in the Qere, and that he is not called 'pharaoh' but 'king of Egypt'.

10.5 Fortifications of Rehoboam

II Chronicles 11.5-10 gives a list of fortifications which Rehoboam is said to have made to protect Judah in the south and the west. According to a large number of scholars this list is ancient, which would mean that Judah was now removed from the major lines of communication: it would moreover have lost the whole of the Negeb including Beer-sheba, the coastal plain, and also the southern part of the northern hill-country. But how old is it? The most adequate solution seems to put it in the period of king Hezekiah, at the end of the eighth century BCE (below 10.13.2), even if a number of scholars suggest an even later date.[5] At all events it seems that Judah succeeded in living a tranquil life, if we leave aside its dispute with Israel.

10.6 Fratricidal wars. Aramaean intervention

Bibliography

A.Dupont-Sommer, *Les Araméens*, Paris 1949, ch.III; M.F.Unger, *Israel and the Aramaeans of Damascus*, London 1957, chs. 5, 10; J.M.Miller, 'Geshur and Aram', *JNES* 28, 1969, 60f. There is an at present hypothetical attempt at a chronology of the ancient Aramaean rulers in F.M.Cross, 'The Stele Dedicated to Melcarth by Ben-Hadad of Damascus', *BASOR* 205, 1972, 36-42, but cf. É.Lipiński's review in *VT* 25, 1975, 553-61; É. Puech, 'L'ivoire inscrit de Arslan Tash et les rois de Damas', *RB* 88, 1981, 544-62; W.T.Pitard, 'The Identity of the Bir-Hadad of the Melqart Stela', *BASOR* 272, 1988, 3-21; A.S.van der Woude, 'Zur Geschichte der Grenze zwischen Juda und Israel', *OTS* 25, 1989, 38-48.

The struggles between the two Hebrew kingdoms are the main feature of the first decades of their existence (above 10.3.10.2).

10.6.1 The war between the two Hebrew kingdoms, often dubbed 'fratricidal', must have lasted around forty years: this was clearly not always all-out war, but more or less latent hostilities. To begin with the North had a series of successes; this should not surprise us if we remember the economic and productive potential of this region, so superior to that of the South (above 10.3.5). Moreover, as we know, the North had incorporated the majority of the Canaanite city states with their economic structures and their armies equipped with war chariots. So instead of seeing the South succeeding in rectifying its own northern frontier, we find the troops of the North advancing south. This state of war continued throughout the reigns of kings Rehoboam (c.922-915 or 926-910), Abijah (c.915-913 or 910-908) and Asa (c.913-873 or 908-868) of Judah and Jeroboam I (c.922-901 or 926-907), Nadab (c.901-900 or 907-906) and Baasha (c.900-877 or 906-883) of Israel. It seems that the troops of Israel even succeeded in penetrating to Ramah (present-day *er-rām*, coord. 172-140), situated about five miles north of Jerusalem (I Kings 15.16f.//II Chron 16.1f.)!

10.6.2 Confronted with a situation which could easily have turned into a catastrophe, Asa, king of Judah, asked for help from the Aramaeans of Damascus who, as we have seen (above 5.7.2 and 10.5), had already detached themselves from the empire under Solomon, but had remained bound to Israel by a treaty. The texts report that Asa sent a delegation to 'Ben-Hadad, son of Tab-rimmon, son of Ḥezion' (I Kings 15.18-20//I Chron 16.2-6), probably Bar-Hadad I (c.900-875 or

885-870: the chronology is purely conjectural and according to some scholars, e.g. Aharoni** 1979, 335, the name could have been merely a title).⁶ Asa succeeded in persuading him, though only by paying a substantial amount of tribute (what remained from the tribute paid to Shoshenk I of Egypt), to break his alliance with Israel, to make common cause with Judah, and to attack Israel in the rear.

10.6.3 The attack must have been a surprise, against a region which remained completely undefended, and the effects were serious: the Aramaeans immediately took possession of three key frontier posts: Abel Beth-maacah (present day *'abil el qamḥ,* coord. 204-296), Ijon (present-day *tell ed-dibbin,* coord. 205-308) and Dan (*tell el-qādī,* coord. 200-252), and moreover of 'all Chinneroth (*ḥirbet el-'oreimeh,* coord. 211-294) and the land of Naphtali', all in all a substantial sector of north-eastern Galilee. According to Aharoni** 1979, 333, I Chron. 2.25 would also allude to Ben-Hadad's campaign: 'But Geshur and Aram took from them Havothjair, Kenath and its villages, sixty towns.' This is the area immediately south of the Jarmuk in Transjordan in northern Gilead, the place that is now called *qanawāt* (coord. 302-241). In other words, Israel's last possessions in Transjordan were also lost, and the Aramaeans succeeded in penetrating deep into Israel's territory.

10.6.4 Thus began the wars between Israel and its neighbours in the north-east, wars which for decades bloodied the frontiers between the two countries and which caused Israel major difficulty. However, the information at our disposal is very sparse, and so it is not possible to establish when and in what conditions the Aramaeans went back to their country. It seems improbable that they did so voluntarily and of their own free will. 'This was the first – and not the last – time that Israel's external enemies were able to turn its domestic disputes to their own advantage' (Gunneweg* ⁶1989, 104).

10.6.5 Compelled to throw his own troops into the breach, Baasha speedily abandoned Ramah, leaving in place the material with which he had intended to fortify it; Asa was able to profit from this, immediately advancing northwards, recapturing Ramah and using the material he found there to fortify Mizpah (*tell en-naṣbeh,* coord.170-143) and Geba of Benjamin (present-day *jiba',* coord.175-141). The excavations on *tell en-naṣbeh* have revealed that the place had originally been a fortress built by the North against the South, which was soon reorientated northwards by means of some improvised adaptations.⁷ From then on, however, the boundary between the North and the South seems to have remained virtually unchanged. According to Alt, followed by Donner,⁸ the territories thus obtained by the South will not have been incorporated into Judah but added to those of the city-state of Jerusalem; this could be the explanation of the note contained in II Kings 12.23, according to which Benjamin went with Judah (above 10.1.3.8). The reality seems to be that here we see a partition of Benjamin: one part went to the South as a result of these wars and the other remained with the North. That also explains how it was possible for king Josiah to be able to desecrate the 'high places' from Geba to Beersheba, whereas in II Chron.11.10 Aijalon (present-day *jālō*, coord.152-138), which in I Kings 4.9 belongs to a district in the North, appears as a fortress of Rehoboam.

10.6.6 At this point there seems to have been peace between Israel and Judah. However, although the South seemed technically to have won the war, there is no need to believe that it succeeded in imposing itself on the North; it had merely obtained a more favourable frontier. It is certainly true that the North, caught between two fires, no longer tried to thrust southwards, but it also seems probable that from then on there was what H.Donner (1977*, 391 and 1986*, 250) does not hesitate to call a 'veiled vassal relationship of Judah towards Israel'.

10.7 Asa and the queen mother

The texts (I Kings 15.9-15//II Chron.14.1-4) also report that Asa introduced a religious reform. However, this is described in the stereotyped terms typical of the Deuteronomistic history and Chronicles, so it is impossible to establish whether it ever took place and, if so, what it comprised. In this way Dtr begins a literary scheme in which a series of reforms in the direction of Deuteronomy and Dtr is set against a series of reforms in the opposite, syncretistic direction: it seems probable that these are literary rather than historical notes.[9] One piece of information is presented almost out of the blue: that Asa had had to depose his own mother (I Kings 15.13-15//II Chron.15.16-19); her position at court is described by the title *gᵉbīrāh*.

Bibliography

G.Molin, 'Die Stellung der *Gᵉbīrā* im Staate Juda', *TZ* 1954, 161-75; H.Donner, 'Art und Herkunft des Amtes der Königinmutter im Alten Testament', in *FS Johannes Friedrich*, Wiesbaden 1959, 105-45; N.E.A.Andreasen, 'The Role of the Queen Mother in Israelite Society', *CBQ* 45, 1983, 179-94; Z.Ben-Barak, 'Status and Right of the Gᵉbīrā', *JBL* 110, 1991, 23-34.

The title, which we could translate literally as 'the lady', was borne by the queen mother. Her functions at the court of Israel and Judah are not clearly described, but if we accept the information we can glean from ancient Near Eastern courts, they were connected with the regency in cases where it was impossible for the candidate to the throne to exercise his rule. We know of another case in which the queen mother brought about a real *coup d'état* (below 10.11): this is the case of queen Athaliah in the South. At all events, Asa succeeded in averting the damage: he deposed the lady on the pretext of some cultic offence which is not more closely defined.

10.8 The dynasty of Omri in Israel

With Omri of Israel we find an attempt to form a dynasty in the North where this had failed earlier. Omri was not able to ascend the throne easily or quickly; he succeeded only after around five years of disorders, proof of the difficulty which sometimes existed in Israel at the institutional level. However, this dynasty too did not last long, even if, as we shall soon see (below 10.9.2.3), it rightly remained famous throughout the ancient Near East.

10.8.1 The reign of Omri was preceded, as I have mentioned, by disorders during which some monarchs ruled for brief periods: Ela (c.877-876 or 883-882); Zimri (c.876 or 882), who was perhaps not of Israelite origin; and finally Tibni (c.876-873 or 882-878). Ela and his family were killed by Zimri; Zimri committed suicide when he was besieged by Omri, commander of the army which was laying siege to Gibbethon (probably present-day *tell-melāt*, coord.137-140), a place south-east of Gezer which seems to have been Philistine. Omri was acclaimed king by the army; as we might put it, in the field (I Kings 16.16). However, another sector of the people (the texts say 'half') chose Tibni instead (I Kings 16.21f.). All these episodes are ignored in Chronicles. The reign of Tibni must have lasted about four years, since Zimri (who reigned only a few days, v.15) became king in the twenty-eighth year of Asa of Judah (v.15), while Omri ascended the throne in his thirty-first year (v.23).

10.8.2 The case of Tibni and his brief reign is more interesting than might appear at first sight.

Bibliography

J.M.Miller, ' "So Tibnī died" (I Kings XVI 22)', *VT* 18, 1968, 392-4; J.A.Soggin, 'Tibni, re d'Israele nella prima metà del IX sec.a.C', *RSO* 47, 1972, 171-6 = *OTOS*, 50-5; É.Puech, 'Athalie, fille d'Achab et la chronologie des rois d'Israël et de Juda', *Salamanticensis* 28, 1981, 117-38: 134ff.

After a series of *coups d'état* accompanied by political assassinations, Tibni is said to have been elected by 'half the people' of Israel (v.21), whereas the other half supported Omri. But, as we have seen, Omri had been acclaimed by the troops, so it seems reasonable to postulate that 'the half' that had chosen him was made up of the army. Despite Puech's argument to the contrary, it seems reasonable to suppose that here we have yet another attempt by the assembly of the North (above 10.1.3.6.1) to nominate its own ruler. The attempt did not succeed, because of the intervention of Omri's troops. And after the killing of Tibni, no one could now oppose Omri's ascent to the throne. The incident seems symptomatic because it is evidence of the increasing complexity of the political situation in the North, and also because it shows how there could be two kings side by side, with the chronology of the first included in that of the second (above 10.1.1-2).

10.8.3 With very few exceptions, the biblical texts have nothing but negative comments to make about Omri and his son Ahab. However, we shall see that this ruler was judged differently by the Assyrian annals (below 10.9.2.3).

Bibliography

A.Jepsen, 'Israel und Damascus', *AfO* 14, 1941-44, 153-72; C.F.Whitley, 'The Deuteronomic Presentation of the House of Omri', *VT* 2, 1952, 137-52; A.Alt, *Der Stadtstaat Samaria*, Leipzig and Berlin 1954 = *KS* III, 258-302; H.J.Katzenstein, 'Who were the Parents of Athaliah?', *IEJ* 5, 1955, 194-7; M.F.Unger, *Israel and the Aramaeans of Damascus*, London 1957; M.Astour, 'Metamorphose de Baal – Les rivalités commerciales au IXme siècle', *Evidences* 10, 1959, 75, 34-40; 77, 54-58; W.W.Hallo, 'From Qarqar to Carchemish', *BA* 23, 1960, 33-61; B.Mazar, 'The Aramaean Empire and its Relations with Israel', *BA* 26, 1962, 97-102; H.L.Ginsberg, 'The Omri-Davidic Alliance and its Consequences', in *Proceedings of the Fourth World Congress of Jewish Studies, Jerusalem 1965*, Jerusalem 1967, I, 91-3; R.de Vaux, 'Tirzah', in D.W.Thomas (ed.), *Archaeology and Old Testament Study*, London 1967, 371-83; É.Lipiński, 'Le Ben Hadad II de la Bible et de l'histoire', in *Proceedings of the Fifth World Congress of Jewish Studies, Jerusalem 1969*, Jerusalem 1973, I, 147-9; H.Donner, 'Adad-nirari III und die Vassalen des Westens', in *Archäologie und Altes Testament – FS Kurt Galling*, Tübingen 1970, 49-58; M.C.Astour, '841 BC: The First Assyrian Invasion of Israel', *JAOS* 91, 1971, 383-9; M.Elat, 'The Campaign of Shalmaneser III against Aram and Israel', *IEJ* 25, 1974, 25-35; H.Tadmor, 'Assyria and the West: The Ninth Century and its Aftermath', in H.Goedicke and J.J.M.Roberts (eds.), *Unity and Diversity*, Baltimore 1975, 36-48; N.Na'aman, 'Two Notes on the Monolith Inscription of Shalmaneser III from Kurkh', *TA* 3, 1976, 89-106; J.A.Brinkman, 'A Further Note on the Date of the Battle of Qarqar and Neo-Assyrian Chronology', *JCS* 30, 1978, 173-5; S.Timm, *Die Dynastie Omri – Quellen und Untersuchungen zur Geschichte Israels im*

9.*Jahrhundert vor Christus*, FRLANT 124, Göttingen 1982; C.Schäfer-Lichtenberger, *Stadt und Eidgenossenschaft*, BZAW 156, Berlin 1983, 9.3.1, 9.3.2; Y.Minokami, *Die Revolution des Jehu*, Göttingen 1988; L.E.Stager, 'Shemer's Estate', *BASOR* 277-278, 1990, 93-107. For a list of the main fortified places in the time of the dynasty of Omri cf. D.N.Pienaar, 'The Role of Fortified Cities in the Northern Kingdom during the Reign of the Omride Dynasty', *JNWSL* 9, 1981, 151-7. For the Samaria excavations cf. J.W.Crowfoot et al., *Samaria-Sebaste I-III*, London 1938-57; J.B.Hennessy, 'Excavations at Samaria-Sebaste, 1968', *Levant* 2, 1970, 1-21.

10.8.4 Omri (c.876-869 or 878-871) – the name is perhaps not even Israelite (Gunneweg* ⁶1989, 104ff.) – must have been immediately confronted with a series of grave problems at home and abroad, which had remained in suspense for some years.

10.8.4.1 At home there was a need to re-establish public order after about five years of *coups d'état*, proscriptions and civil war.

10.8.4.2 Abroad, it was necessary to put an end as quickly as possible to the long conflict with Judah, something which does not seem to have been difficult. The alliance concluded between Israel and Judah is attested, among other things, by the marriage celebrated between Athaliah, the daughter (or, probably better, the niece, cf. below 10.13) of Omri (II Kings 8.26//II Chron.22.2) with Joram of Judah, an event to which we shall return in due course. A solution also had to be found to the war with the Aramaeans, which was perhaps the chief threat posed to the kingdom, since the war with Judah had now been dormant for some years. As I have indicated above (10.8.3-4), we know very little of the Aramaean kingdom. At all events it seems improbable that this war will have continued under the reigns of Omri and Ahab: perhaps the Aramaeans had achieved their aims; perhaps, too, the growing Assyrian pressure on their eastern frontier made some caution necessary; this pressure did not yet pose a threat to Israel. Anyway, it seems that the war was not pursued with the same vigour as before, and perhaps it was even broken off.

10.8.5 *The foundation of Samaria*. However, Omri has gone down in history for his foundation of a new capital, Samaria (Hebrew *šōmᵉrōn*), in the sixth year of his reign (I Kings 16.24ff.), i.e. around 871 or 873, on a hill which had hitherto been uninhabited. Its ruins can now be found beside the Arab village of *sebastiye* (coord.168-187). The region took one of its designations, Samaria, from the Hebrew name; in the Assyrian annals it appears as *samerīna*. In the post-exilic period Samaria continued to be used for the Persian province and its inhabitants and passed from there to the Samaritans, the Jewish sect which still exists today (below, 14.4). The excavations carried out on the *tell* of Tirzah and Samaria confirm the main outlines of this chronology.

10.8.5.1 The king's aims in founding a new capital are not indicated in the sources and therefore seem anything but clear. A current theory is that of Donner* 1977, 407ff., and 1986, 256f., esp.n.34: on the basis of a study by Alt in 1954, Donner argues that Shemer, indicated as the landowner who sold the land to Omri, will have been a Canaanite, so that here we have a transaction under Canaanite law. However, this theory seems doubtful (cf. Timm, 143ff.), if not improbable: first of all the name is not necesarily Canaanite, since it is given to a Levite in I Chron.6.31; 7.34, while *šimrīt* appears in I Chron. 24.26 as the name of a Moabite woman; nor does it seem that conclusions can be drawn from an act of buying and selling, i.e. under private law, as to the ethnic derivation of the seller (Timm); finally, as Schäfer-Lichtenberger, 396ff., rightly observes, to talk about 'Canaanite law' only makes matters more obscure, since we know literally nothing about it!

10.8.5.2 The theory put forward by Alt and Donner then goes on to argue that the city will have been given a status similar to that of Jerusalem from the time of David onwards, except that it was never a real city-state (as we have seen, above 4.6.7.2-3, Schäfer-Lichtenberger, following Buccellati, rejects this theory even in the case of Jerusalem). So Samaria will have been the capital belonging to the dynasty, as a city-state, and not to the nation as such; and it was because of this status that Ahab built a temple in it, dedicated moreover to Ba'al and not to YHWH (I Kings 16.32). Here too, then, we would have a kind of personal union between the Canaanite population, with Samaria as the capital, which moreover played a role of primary importance on the territorial and economic level, and the Israelite population, which will have had another capital, Jezreel (now the abandoned Arab village of *zer'in*, coord. 181-218). We hear of this latter place, which must have taken the place of Tirzah, destroyed shortly before by Zimri (I Kings 16.18), later, in the traditions about Elijah (I Kings 21) and Jehu (II Kings 9-10). However, this theory, too, seems weak and improbable: we know nothing of a second capital for Judah, so that the example does not fit, nor do we hear that Jezreel was ever a second capital; it appears only as a residence of the ruling house in certain periods of the year (cf. recently Schäfer-Lichtenberger, ibid.).

10.8.5.3 So on closer analysis this theory too proves invalid: the reality is that we know nothing of the reasons why Omri built the new capital, nor anything about its legal status.

10.8.6 It is also said of the dynasty of Omri that it was particularly concerned to cultivate the alliance with the Phoenicians, relations which perhaps began as early as under David and certainly under Solomon (above, 4.4.2.4; 5.6). The marriage of the crown prince Ahab to a princess daughter of Ittoba'al of Tyre (with Josephus, *Antt.* VIII, 324, and not 'king of the Sidonians', as I Kings 16.32 suggests), called by the improbable name of Jezebel, was the natural seal on this alliance.

10.8.7 The traditions about Ahab now seem to have been combined with those of two prophets who are presented as his inexorable adversaries: Elijah (I Kings 17; 18; 19; 21; II Kings 1.2-17) and Elisha (I Kings 19; II Kings 2.1-25; 3.4-8, 15; 13.14-21). Another two narratives, I Kings 20; 22, seem to be independent of Deuteronomy and to have as their theme the Aramaean wars in which he is said to have engaged. The texts also hand down an account of Jehu's revolt (II Kings 9.1-10.27) and finally scattered notes here and there in the text, according to some scholars drawn from court annals. There are therefore many difficulties in obtaining relatively certain information: the two prophetic narratives are essentially interested in their own heroes and their struggles against their enemies; among the latter, the king and the queen occupy a privileged position. The two chapters on the Aramaean wars seem originally to have been independent of the figure of Ahab and to have been added to his history only at a later stage (Donner* 1977, 400).

Bibliography

A.Alt, 'Das Gottesurteil auf dem Karmel', *FS Georg Beer*, Stuttgart 1935, 1-18 = *KS* II, 135-9; K.Galling, 'Der Gott Karmel und die Ächtung der fremden Götter', in *Geschichte und Altes Testament – FS Albrecht Alt*, Tübingen 1953, 105-26; O.Eissfeldt, *Der Gott Karmel*, Berlin 1953; H.H.Rowley, 'Elijah on Mount Carmel', *BJRL* 43, 1960-61, 190-219 = *Men of God*, London 1963, 37-65; K.Baltzer, 'Naboths Weinberg (I.Kön.21)...', *WuD* 8, 1965, 73-8; F.I.Andersen, 'The Socio-Juridical Background of the Naboth Incident', *JBL* 85, 1966, 46-57; J.M.Miller, 'The Elisha Cycle and the Accounts of the Omride Wars', *JBL* 85, 1966, 441-54; id., 'The Fall of the House of Ahab', *VT* 17, 1967, 307-24; 'The Rest of the Acts of Jehoachaz (I Kings 20.22,1-38)', *ZAW* 80, 1968, 337-42; O.H.Steck, *Überlieferung und Zeitgeschichte in den Elia-Erzählungen*, WMANT 26; G.Fohrer, *Elia*, ATANT 53, Zurich ²1968; H.-C.Schmitt, *Elisa...*, Gütersloh 1972; P.Welten, 'Naboths Weinberg (I Kön.2)', *EvTh* 33, 1973, 18-32; J.A.Soggin, 'Jezabel, oder die fremde Frau', in *Mélanges bibliques et orientaux en l'honneur de M.Henri Cazelles*, AOAT 212, Kevelaer 1981, 453-9; H.Weippert, 'Ahab el Campeador?', *Bib* 69, 1988, 457-79; M.Cogan and H.Tadmor, *II Kings*, New York 1988; A.J.Hauser and R.Gregory, *Elijah*, JSOT-SS 85, Sheffield 1990; C.T.Begg, 'The Chronicler's Non-Mentioning of Elisha', *BN* 45, 1988, 7-11; C.Schäfer-Lichtenberger, ' "Josua" und "Elischa" – eine biblische Argumentation zur Begründung der Autorität des Nachfolgers', *ZAW* 101, 1989, 198-223;

W.Thiel, 'Jahwe und Prophet in der Elisa-Tradition', in *Alttestamentlicher Glaube und biblische Theologie – FS H.D.Preuss*, Tübingen 1992, 93-103.

10.8.7.1 Once we manage to strip off from them all the folklore and material relating to the history of religion, the legends about the prophets Elijah and Elisha reveal a situation of marked tension between certain Israelite groups, with the cult that they practised, and the Israelite court, which pursued its own religious policy. It is not easy to prove whether there really was such a conflict, or whether it is the product of later narrators; at all events it appears rather improbable that it had ethnic origins, like a conflict between Israelites and Canaanites (as happens to some degree in any multi-ethnic state): assuming that such a differentiation ever really existed, at this time it must have become politically insignificant. What could serve as a working hypothesis, though, is that with Elijah and Elisha there began a conscious and coherent attempt at a separation of the typically Israelite religious element from that of Canaan, with which it had been associated up to that point in complete osmosis. These attempts would then have been developed and completed by the prophets from the eighth century onwards. However, this, and especially the attack on the Canaanite fertility cults, put in danger the very economic foundations of the kingdom, based on the fertility of the fields, flocks and herds.

10.8.7.2 Moreover, as I have already often observed, it is not easy to grasp the content and the rites of religion in Israel and Judah in the pre-exilic period generally and in the ninth century in particular. The Deuteronomistic history presents the problem in terms of syncretism, as if a religion which was originally pure and uncorrupt, revealed on Sinai, had come to be corrupted by contact with the Canaanites and as a result of the sin of Israel.

However, from the little that it is possible to discover from the sources and also on the basis of the historical and religious parallels at our disposal, it is probable that the process went in the opposite direction: first a religion in Israel and Judah which was little if at all different from that in Canaan; then the formation of groups, probably led by the prophets, who began to proclaim the uniqueness and exclusivity of the national God YHWH to the point that, around the time of the exile, their groups succeeded in prevailing over the others. It is possible to verify this thesis through the assertion of I Kings 19.18 that only seven thousand people (evidently a round number) had remained in Israel (i.e. in the North) who had not compromised themselves in some way with the Canaanite religion.

10.8.8 The legends about the prophets Elijah and Elisha have handed down, with all the obvious limitations of this genre of literature, some of the salient features of these struggles.

10.8.8.1 They begin with the long drought described in I Kings 17.1ff. (above 2.4.2), which according to the hagiographer was due to a kind of challenge between the prophet and his disciples and the priests of Ba'al as to whether it was YHWH or the Canaanite deity who gave the rain and thus the fertility of the soil. As we know, the dispute was resolved in favour of YHWH (I Kings 18), in the divine judgment on Mount Carmel (the location of *muḥrāqa*, coord. 158-231, today the site of the small Carmelite convent on the north-east side of the mountain chain, has a good claim to be the right one). The narrative could have preserved the recollection, however distant and pale, of the change of sovereignty over Carmel from Tyre to Israel, following the treaty made by Omri with Ittoba'al, and sealed by the marriage of the crown prince Ahab to the princess of Tyre (Donner* 1977, 403 and 1986, 261).

10.8.8.2 Another episode, this time not religious, but with important social dimensions, is that of Naboth's vineyard (I Kings 21). In its present form this story has been considerably amplified by novellistic elements; it deals with an issue which to some scholars has seemed to be the clash between the Israelite land law and that of Canaan, in that the former had come into conflict with the claims of the crown. A comparison with II Kings 9.21, where the field does not seem to have been incorporated into the crown property, shows the kind of additions which have been made here. It is difficult to establish whether the recollections of some real event underlie the story: in itself the story could very well have been one of a great many put into circulation with the aim of discrediting Ahab and his wife, and the evident parallel with another similar episode, that of the prophet Nathan and David after David's adultery with Bathsheba and the killing of her husband (II Sam.11.2-12.15, above 4.2.4.1), where the king is converted after listening to the invective and escapes the divine judgment (as also happens here, I Kings 21.27ff.), makes this hypothesis highly probable. Moreover, as we saw above (10.8.5.1), we know nothing of Canaanite law, whether relating to property or not, nor is it possible to check whether the obvious reference made in I Kings 21.4 to Lev.25.23-31 is only an anachronism of the later redactor or could amount to proof that a norm of this kind was already in effect in the ninth century BCE: however, this latter possibility seems remote.

10.8.9 As I have indicated, Ahab's Aramaean wars (I Kings 20; 22) present the reader with complex chronological problems. Almost all scholars now tend to see these incidents as episodes in which the person of the monarch involved was originally anonymous, and which will only at a later stage have been supplemented by the insertion of the names of Ahab and his Judahite counterpart Jehoshaphat (for whom cf. below, 10.12; Jepsen 1941-44; Miller 1966 and Donner* 1977, 400, and 1984, 250). That is because the Assyrian annals indicate that under the dynasty of Omri the relationships between Israel and the Aramaeans improved to such a point that there was a real coalition against the Assyrians; that virtually rules out their interruption on the local level, as a result of wars (below 10.8.10).

10.8.9.1 The two narratives describe a battle near Aphek (probably the present-day *fiq*, coord.216-242), east of Lake Tiberias on the ascent to the Golan Heights, followed by an Israelite victory over the Aramaeans, who shortly beforehand had laid siege to Samaria (I Kings 20), and is a defeat of Israel at Ramoth Gilead (present-day *tell ramīt*, also east of the lake).

10.8.9.2 However, the second narrative is not so much interested in political and military history as in a theological problem: that of true and false prophecy and how to distinguish one from the other. We know that this problem was very much alive around the time of the Babylonian exile (below 12.6.2); it is also concerned with prophetic inspiration.

10.8.9.3 The first text could in fact refer to Israelite victories following which the Aramaeans were forced to abandon Israelite territory which they had conquered at one time (above 10.8) and to sue for peace, but that must have happened before the reign of Ahab; moreover he was not mortally wounded in battle, as I Kings 23.35//II Chron.18.34 asserts, but according to I Kings 22.39-40 died peacefully in his own bed (but cf. against this H.Tadmor, Appendix II below, 4).

10.8.10 With the dynasty of Omri Israel thus entered the scene of the major international politics of the time, especially those of Assyria.

10.8.10.1 Asshur-nasir-pal II (c.884-868), acting with decisiveness and skill, succeeded in reaching the Mediterranean and subjecting the Aramaeans and the Phoenicians. In the annals of Shalmaneser III (c.858-824), Omri is mentioned for the first time. One might say that Shalmaneser specialized in campaigns westwards, towards Syria and Canaan, so much so that we hear of at least of six of them, in the sixth, tenth, eleventh, fourteenth, eighteenth and twenty-first years of his reign (cf. the texts in *ANET*, 278-80 and *TUAT* I, 360-7). The period is that of Omri, Ahab and their immediate successors.

10.8.10.2 The same annals speak of a battle fought between the Assyrians and a coalition of Syro-Canaanite kings formed by Hadadezer of Damascus (Accadian Hadad-idri, probably Ben/Bar Hadad II, c.870-842 or 875-843, though these dates are conjectural, cf. above 10.8.2), Irḥuleni of Hamath and 'Ahab the Israelite'. The battle took place at Karkar (present-day *ḫirbet qerqūr*) on the Orontes, in 853, a date confirmed by Brinkman's 1978 study. The Assyrians claim to have won this battle, and that is not improbable; however, we cannot trace any political or territorial advantage from this victory. Shalmaneser III claims to have fought against the same alliance in 849, 848 and 845, and all this makes probable the theory that Omri and Ahab succeeded in establishing friendly relations with the Aramaeans, at least while the danger lasted. However, we know of this battle only through the Assyrian annals; the Hebrew Bible is completely silent about it.

10.8.11 The person mainly responsible for Ahab's religious policy, which the biblical texts condemn severely, is said to have been queen Jezebel, the Tyrian princess given to him as a wife (above 10.8.6). However, her very name is perplexing: *'īzebel* means 'without glory' and was therefore hardly suitable as anyone's name. Her constitutional (if we can use this term) prerogatives are also suspect; they seem to have been almost limitless. She interferes directly in affairs of state worship, carries on intrigues to the illicit advantage of the crown, and has those faithful to YHWH persecuted and sometimes killed. Is it possible that she is simply a literary figure, connected with an anonymous Phoenician wife of Ahab who, because she was a foreigner and therefore not an Israelite by religion, was considered guilty of all kinds of malpractices? That is possible. At all events, even if it is said of Ahab that he built a temple dedicated to Baal at Samaria (above 10.10.5.2), one good indication that he must have remained Israelite by religion is that he gave theophoric names with YHWH to his two sons, Ahaziah and Joram.

10.8.12 Ahab was succeeded to the throne by these two sons, first by Ahaziah (I Kings 22.52-54) and then, when he died heirless, by Ahaziah's brother Joram or Jehoram (II Kings 3.1ff.; 8.16-24). They reigned respectively from 850-849 or 852-851 and 849-842 or 851-845. Both were mediocre; we hear nothing of the former and in connection with the latter are told only that he lost the war against Moab begun under his father and specially listed on the stele of king Mesha. The Israelite version of the campaign appears in II Kings 3.

Bibliography

J.A.Soggin, *Introduction*, Appendix I.3 (and bibliography); G.A.Rendsburg, 'A Reconstruction of Moabite-Israelite History', *JANESCU* 13, 1981, 67-73; S.Timm, *Die Dynastie Omris*, Göttingen 1982, 158-80; J.R.Bartlett, 'The "United" Campaign against Moab in 2 Kings 3:4-27', in J.F.A.Sawyer and D.J.A.Clines (ed.), *Midian, Moab and Edom*, Sheffield 1983, 135-46; Donner* 1986, 273f.; Garbini* 1988, 33-7; Miller and Hayes* 1986, 280-4; K.A.D.Smelik, 'The Literary Structure of King Mesha's Inscription', *JSOT* 46, 1990, 21-30; A.Lemaire, 'La stèle de Mésha et l'histoire de l'ancien Israël', in *Storia e tradizioni di Israele, scritti in onore di J.A.Soggin*, Brescia 1991, 143-69; B.C.Jones, 'In Search of Kir

Hareseth. A Case Study in Site Identification', *JSOT* 52, 1991, 3-24. For the topography see Aharoni** 1979 and the map there.

10.8.12.1 This is a war of liberation the course and result of which are listed on the stele of king Mesha, which was discovered at the end of the last century. The stele records that Dibon (present-day *dībān*, coord.224-101), the birthplace and/or residence of the king, was in their hands already before the revolt (line 2); as I have indicated above (8.2.11.2), line 10 tells us that 'the men of Gad lived from time immemorial in the region of "Atarot" '. In the text Omri appears as the one who reconquers the region, and there is also mention of his 'son', though no name is mentioned.

10.8.12.2 The biblical text (II Kings 3) states that under Joram Israel was forced to abandon the siege of Kir-heres (also called Kir-hareseth, usually identified with present-day *el-kerak*, coord. 217-066; for the problem of identification cf. Jones 1991), followed by a human sacrifice offered by the king on the fortifications (II Kings 3.26-27 is to be translated thus and not otherwise), a way of indicating that Israel had been defeated and forced to retreat.

10.8.12.3 There are various inaccuracies in the biblical text, as Garbini* has rightly observed; however, the same may also be said of the stele. This in fact does not say at what time Omri 'oppressed Moab' (lines 4-5), nor does it give the name of the 'son of Omri': is this Ahab, or is the term used in a broad sense and so could it also denote Joram, Omri's grandson (lines 7-8)? Moreover, the figure 'forty years', which in biblical Hebrew is a round figure, appears in line 8, whereas in line 11 there is mention of the 'king of Israel' but with no name, unless of course the text intends a generic statement, 'the kings of Israel from time immemorial'.

The two versions seem to agree on the fact that Moab succeeded in regaining its own independence.

10.8.13 The silence of the stele of Mesha on Joram, the sparseness of the information, and at any rate the brevity of his reign and his passive character, have led one scholar[10] to conclude that he and the king of Judah with the same name (below 10.12.1) were the same person, so that Israel and Judah would have been united, albeit briefly, in this period. We do not have enough information to confirm this theory, but if nothing else, it shows the difficulties caused by the various cases of homonymy and affinity between the two ruling houses.

10.8.14 II Kings 6.8-23 speaks of yet another Aramaean war. The protagonists are anonymous, but the mention of the places and of the prophet Elisha is precise enough. According to vv.24-31 the Aramaeans even besieged Samaria. Is this the same episode as that in I Kings 20 (above 10.10.9.1)?

10.9 Jehu's coup d'état

According to the biblical sources, the dynasty of Omri was overthrown by a *coup d'état* arranged by a certain Jehu, commander of the northern army, who then ascended the throne. There is an interesting note that the disorders arose out of the prophetic groups with Elijah and Elisha at their head (I Kings 19.15-18; II Kings 9.1-10), and were connected with similar movements in Damascus, where a certain Hazael ascended the throne in place of king Ben/Bar Hadad (III?, c. 845?-843?). King Joram and the queen mother were killed in the *coup d'état*, as also was Ahaziah of Judah, who was in Israel as a guest (II Kings 9-10).

10.9.1 From the historical point of view the first impression given by the note is one of total absurdity: it in fact seems impossible that a *coup d'état* which took place in Damascus could have been connected with a movement similar to the prophetic movements in Israel: all the more so since Hazael later caused Israel great difficulties (below 10.13.5). On the other hand there can be no doubt that Hazael succeeded in gaining power; this is confirmed by an Assyrian inscription (*ANET*, 280; *TUAT* I, 366) and the figure is called 'son of no one', a typical title for a usurper (*ANET*, 280; *TUAT* I, 365), which could only represent a confirmation of the *coup d'état*.

10.9.2 Is it possible to know more? In this connection Astour 1969 and 1971 (above 10.8.7) has presented the following hypothetical reconstruction of events, from which a completely new historical and political context appears. According to this, the main place should not be given to the contrast between the prophets and the court, but to a completely successful Assyrian attempt to undermine the coalition between Israel and Aram from within, substituting kings who were its mediators with rulers who were friendly to Assyria in a series of *coups d'état*. These are the lines of Astour's 1971 proposal.

10.9.2.1 Hosea 10.14 mentions a certain Shalman, whom most scholars identify with Shalmanezer III (down to the present, Cogan and Tadmor 1988, 121 n.10). As I have indicated, Shalmaneser III led an expedition to the west in 841. In the course of the expedition he laid siege to Damascus without succeeding in capturing it, and destroyed various places east of the Jordan, among which Hosea mentions Beth-arbel, often identified with present-day Irbid in Jordan (coord.229-218).

10.9.2.2 From here, according to the Assyrian annals (*ANET*, 280; *TUAT* I, 367), in the eighteenth year of his reign he moved to 'the mountains of *ba 'li ra'si*, a cape which projects into the sea'. According to Astour this would be Carmel, the border between Israel and Tyre (above 10.8.8.1), indeed, according to Aharoni** this identification is certain; Noth 1959*, 248 thinks rather of Lebanon, perhaps of Tyre (cf. also Donner* 1986, 280). Meanwhile, however, the rest of the inscription has been found. It reads: '... which projects into the sea and is in front of Tyre' (*TUAT* I, ibid., not yet in *ANET*). This excludes Carmel and indicates rather the *rās en-naqūra/rō'š hanniqrā'*, coord.160-178, the present-day frontier on the sea between Israel and Lebanon (cf. Cogan and Tadmor 1988, 121 n.119). Moreover, if the Assyrian king only touched on the territory of Israel before arriving there, this argument becomes irrelevant for Astour's theory.

10.9.2.3 According to Astour the two *coups d'état*, that in Israel and that in Damascus, should be attributed to the machinations of pro-Assyrian groups, which succeeded in eliminating the Omrids in Israel and the ruling dynasty in Damascus, the heart of the resistance to Assyria. In this case a connection between the two movements should not be ruled out and would appear less absurd than might seem at first sight. Astour sees a proof of this theory in the homage paid to Shalmaneser III by an Israelite delegation headed by Jehu himself, called 'king of the country of Omri' (probably better than 'son of Omri'[11]), a tribute also paid involuntarily to what had been a great dynasty, though this is not recognized by the biblical texts. The episode has been immortalized in the 'black obelisk' of Shalmaneser III, where it has been adequately illustrated: the new king of Israel appears prostrate, face to the ground, before his lord (*ANEP*, 355; the stele is in the British Museum in London).

10.9.2.4 However, Donner* 1986, 280 n.82, has subjected this proposal to a harsh if somewhat general criticism: 'The concept... has no historical probability; it is based on a problematical chronology and works with untenable interpretations of the texts' (similarly Cogan and Tadmor 1988). But the main objection to Astour's proposal seems to me to be that the Assyrians sometimes state that Hazael fought against them, and was defeated (*ANET*, 280; *TUAT* I, 336f.), which does not fit well with the concept of a ruler put on the throne by a pro-Assyrian party. Rather, it favours the thesis that Jehu too had attempted to continue the anti-Assyrian policy of the Omrids, which would also explain his title in the Assyrian records. As for Damascus, the Assyrian texts do not always seem to be well informed about who in fact was reigning, Hadad-ezer (Ben/Bar Hadad) or Hazael.[12]

10.9.3 At all events, the alliance between Israel and the Aramaeans of Damascus, which was the main feature of the foreign policy of the house of Omri, seems to have been terminated. In this new context Hazael was now the enemy *par excellence*, and he appears in this role not only in II Kings 11ff. but also in prophetic texts like Amos 1.3-5 and Isa.9.1. It is only logical to suppose that the Israelite settlements in northern Transjordan were the prime objective of the Aramaeans, and it seems that Israel lost almost all of them (II Kings 10.32-33, a text which moreover seems to exaggerate what happened to the South). In

12.18-19 the Aramaeans possibly appear as allies of the Philistines (below 10.13.5) and are only kept away from Jerusalem with difficulty, by the payment of a heavy fine.

10.9.4 From then on for some years the existence of the two Hebrew kingdoms continued 'in the shadow of the struggles for power in Syria' (Herrmann*, 234). The Aramaean wars must have led to substantial losses for Israel and Judah in men, material, and goods, all the more so as they usually ended with an Aramaean victory. Only once do we have an indication of a Hebrew victory, in II Kings 13.4-5, 22, where Jehoahaz of Israel (c.815-801 or 818-802) and his son Joash (c.801-786 or 802-787) appear as victors first over Hazael and then over his son Ben/Bar Hadad (III or IV, 806?-776?), indicated in the Assyrian annals only with his Aramaic title *mari'*, 'lord' (*ANET*, 282; *TUAT* I, 368).

10.9.5 However, better times also came for Israel. At the end of the ninth century the Assyrians under Adad-nirari III (c.810-783) marched westwards at least four times, in 806, 805, 803 and 797 BCE (*ANET*, 281f.; *TUAT* I, 367f.), and probably in the course of the last campaign forced Damascus first to submit and soon afterwards to accept Assyrian sovereignty (the stele of *tell er-rīmāt*, *TUAT* I, 368).[13] Joash of Israel is also named, as a 'Samaritan'. With the elimination of the enemy in the north-east, the Aramaean threat ceased; but the Assyrians were now perilously near to Israel itself.

10.10 The situation in the South

If the situation in the North was difficult, it was not easy in Judah either, even if its greater isolation, its clearer boundaries and the much greater stability of the dynasty of David avoided constant conflict abroad and at home prevented a series of *coups d'état* (for an isolated case cf. below 10.13).

Bibliography

W.F.Albright, 'The Judicial Reform of Jehoshaphat', in *Alexander Marx Jubilee Volume*, New York 1950, 61-82; W.Rudolph, 'Die Einheitlichkeit der Erzählung vom Sturz der Athalja (2 Kön.11)', in *FS Alfred Bertholet*, Tübingen 1950, 473-8; A.Alt, 'Bemerkungen zu einigen judäischen Ortslisten des Alten Testaments', *BBLAK* (*ZDPV* 68, 1949-51), 193-210 = *KS* II, 289, 305; M.Liverani, 'L'histoire de Joas', *VT* 24, 1974, 438-53; W.Shea, 'Adad-nirari III and Jehoash of Israel', *JCS* 30, 1978, 101-13; H.-D.Hoffmann, *Reform und Reformen*, ATANT 66, Zurich 1980, 93ff.; É.Puech, 'Athalie, fille d'Achab et la chronologie des rois d'Israël et de Juda', *Salamanticensis* 28, 1981, 117-38. Cf. also H.Tadmor, above III.9; C.Levin, *Der Sturz der Königin Atalja*, SBS 105, Stuttgart 1982; J.Trebolle

Barrero, 'La coronación de Joás (2 Re 11)', *Estbib* 41, 1983, 5-16 (these last two studies do not take account of Liverani 1974); G.N.Knoppers, 'Reform and Regression: The Chronicler's Presentation of Jehoshaphat', *Bib* 72, 1991, 500-24. For the 'people of the land' cf. E.Würthwein, *Der ʿam hāʾāreṣ im Alten Testament*, BWANT IV, 17, Stuttgart 1936; J.Soggin, 'Der judäische ʿam hāʾāreṣ und das Königreich im Juda', *VT* 13, 1963, 187-95; R.de Vaux, 'Le sens de l'expression "peuple du pays" dans l'Ancien Testament et le rôle politique du peuple en Israël', *RA* 58, 1964, 167-72; E.W.Nicholson, 'The Meaning of the Expression ʿm hʾrṣ in the Old Testament', *JSS* 10, 1965, 56-66; S.Talmon, 'The Judaean ʿam hāʾāreṣ in Historical Perspective', in *Proceedings of the Fourth World Congress of Jewish Studies, Jerusalem 1965*, Jerusalem 1967, I, 71-6; C.Schäfer-Lichtenberger, *Stadt und Eidgenossenschaft im Alten Testament*, BZAW 156, Berlin 1983, 391ff.

Only the biblical texts which form part of the Deuteronomistic and Chronistic history provide material for reconstructing the period of the kingdom of Judah which extends from the end of the tenth century to the middle of the eighth century BCE. We saw above (10.8) how, after a series of defeats, the war between Israel and Judah, aimed at giving Judah a northern frontier which could be defended strategically, ended in victory for Judah; however, this victory was achieved by persuading the Aramaeans to attack Israel in the rear. Mizpah, the present-day *tell en-naṣbeh* (coord.170-143), at first a bastion of the North against the South, was transformed by king Asa into a bastion of the South against the North. From then on the frontier remained virtually static, and although peace was not officially made, it became an established fact, especially in the period of the dynasty of Omri, during the reign of Jehoshaphat of Judah (c.873-849 or 868-847), under whom peace was also made officially. However, given the predominance of the North, Judah soon found itself involved in the military enterprises of Israel: the Aramaean wars (I Kings 22.2-4, but cf.above 10.10.9; and II Kings 8.28; 9.14, but cf. above, 10.11). In II Kings 3.4 Judah appears alongside Israel in the war against rebellious Moab (above 10.10.12). The relations between Israel and Judah were sealed by the marriage of Joram, son of Jehoshapat of Judah, and Athaliah, sister, or more probably daughter (thus already Noth* 1959, 236, and now Puech 1981 and Donner* 1986, 251), of Ahab of Israel. We have already looked (above 10.10.13) at the problem of relations between the two Jorams.

10.10.1.1 Very little is known about Jehoshaphat, nor is much reported of his two successors Joram (c.849-842 or 847-845) and Ahaziah (also bearing the same name as the northern king, c. 842 or 845: II Kings 8.16-19 and 8.25-28// II Chron. 22.1-6 respectively). The latter is said to have been mortally wounded during Jehu's revolt, while staying with

Joram of Israel (II Kings 9.27-29). He had already lost Edom, which had rebelled (II Kings 8.20-24//II Chron 21.8-10), succeeding with some difficulty in extricating his troops from encirclement by the enemy by means of a hasty flight. In I Kings 22.41-51// II Chron.20.21-31 it is reported that on the basis of an agreement with Ahaziah king of Israel (above 10.10.5.2) he tried to establish trade on the Red Sea, but apparently without success.

10.10.1.2 The texts also report that Jehoshaphat attempted a religious reform (I Kings 22.47), probably directed against Canaanite religion; however, the whole passage is expressed in terms typical of the Deuteronomistic history, so that it is difficult to say what, if anything, really happened. Moreover II Chron.17.1-9 and 19.1-11 report that he initiated a reform of public administration, the cult and the army, and, according to a 1950 study by Albright, also reformed the legal system. However, here too it is impossible to establish whether or not the Chronicler was using ancient traditions, so that it is again impossible to discover precisely what happened (Donner* 1977, 391 and 1984, 251 n.19). For a similar case cf. 10.9 above.

10.11 Athaliah

The killing of Ahaziah after a short reign, in the course of Jehu's revolt in the North, left the throne of David vacant. The legitimate successor was Joash, the infant son of the dead king, but because of his age, he needed a regent.

10.11.1 According to the general practice in the region (above 10.7), the queen mother Athaliah became regent. She exploited the position of strength which her new position automatically gave her by eliminating all the heirs to the throne of David. According to the account in II Kings 11//II Chron.22.9-23.21, only this Joash, son of Ahaziah and therefore grandson of Athaliah, succeeded in escaping. He was rescued by an aunt, sister to the dead king, who is said to have hidden him in the temple. It does not appear from the narrative why Athaliah had wanted to eliminate those who after all were her own sons and grandsons, nor what ultimate aim she had in mind. The usurper reigned for about six years (c.842-837 or 845-840) without realizing the existence of Joash. However, one sabbath at the end of this period the priest Jehoiada summoned the temple guard, armed them, and occupied the sanctuary. After producing the boy, he anointed him king and had him acclaimed by the army and the 'people of the land'. The queen, who had meanwhile arrived at the temple, was arrested, led to the palace and killed there. In this way the Davidic dynasty was saved and the legitimate succession maintained without the continuity being broken.

10.11.2 However, Liverani's classic 1974 study has brought out a more complex situation. On the basis of biblical and especially Near Eastern parallels, he shows the 'theatrical' character of the narrative and its scenes, the way in which it is centred on the small heir to the throne, whose legitimate election to the throne is meant to annul the earlier usurpation. But the scene appears historically improbable, given that the theme is frequent in popular traditions. In the ancient Near East the best known case is that of Idrimi of Alalakh, who also emerged 'from nowhere' to claim the rule over the city-state which is said to have been his by right. In the Hebrew Bible there is a similar case in Judg.9.5b-15 where Jotham, 'the youngest of the sons' of Jerubbaal, also escapes the killing of his family and delivers an exhortation to the rebellious people of Shechem (above 9.6), but without claiming the throne. So in reality it would seem that the Davidic dynasty was similarly interrupted and artificially reconstituted only at a later stage by means of a boy chosen by the priesthood and the sister of the dead king to be opposed to Athaliah, and acclaimed both by the army and by the 'people of the land'. Obviously these could not recognize the boy, who had first been hidden and had then grown up, so the text confronts the reader with a real coronation. However, this is the only case known, so that as an exception it proves the rule of the institutional continuity in Judah. Moreover, the continuity of the dynasty was effectively preserved, even if only legally and formally.

10.11.3 In all these events a group called in Hebrew ʿam hā-ʾāreṣ (literally the 'people of the land') appears on the scene for the first time. Much later (cf. below 13.12.3.1) the term was to denote the ignorant masses, illiterate, incapable of study and therefore of observing the Torah. However, in the pre-exilic period the expression seems to have denoted something like a landed aristocracy, a group descended from the ancient usufructuaries of the tribal lands and therefore economically independent; in the Deuteronomistic history this group in Judah seems to have backed the Davidic dynasty to the hilt, though it does not seem to have had any function at an institutional level (Schäfer-Lichtenberger 1983). The Deuteronomistic historian recognizes the character of this group as bearers of the traditional Yahwistic faith and in this capacity often contrasts it with the population of Jerusalem, still seen as Canaanite, and with the court and its intrigues.

10.11.4 We know little of what happened after the accession of Joash to the throne. Given his youth, it is probable that he had a tutor-regent and that this was the priest Jehoiada, as is explicitly stated by II Chron.24.2-3, 15-22 (Donner* 1977, 384, and 1986, 254f.). Indeed, Chronicles closely connects the initial piety of the young man with the fact that the priest was his guardian: when Jehoiada died, Joash is said to have ceased to profess his faith. II Kings 12.1-22//II Chronicles 24.1-

16, 23-27 gives an account of his reign. The texts present him, among other things, as a supporter of the restoration of the temple, financed by offerings which were collected in a special coffer. The sums needed for the restoration and maintenance of the temple were taken from it and given to the builders.

10.11.5 The texts set in this period an attack by the Aramaeans under Hazael of Damascus against Jerusalem, which was only avoided by the payment of a large indemnity (II Kings 12.18ff.). The Aramaeans are said to have occupied Gath, a Philistine locality, perhaps by agreement with the Philistines (cf. above 10.11.3). However, we know little of the event and therefore find it hard to understand.

10.11.6 Joash fell victim to an assassination (II Kings 12.21-22), but the succession was assured by his son Amaziah (II Kings 14.1ff., c.800-783 or 801-787). The texts report a victory by him over the Edomites in a 'valley of Salt' which is otherwise unknown (this term suggests that it should be located near to the Dead Sea, II Kings 14.7); in the course of this operation he is said to have captured Sela (this is not the present-day Petra, as is often claimed, but rather *es-selaʿ*, coord.205-020). That was probably an ephemeral success, which did not change the political structure of the region in any way.

10.11.7 The texts also report that Amaziah lost a battle against Joash of Israel near Beth-shemesh (present-day *tell er-rumeileh*, coord.147-128); he is said to have been taken prisoner and brought to Jerusalem, where the Israelites demolished part of the walls and sacked the temple (II Kings 14.8-14//II Chron.25.17-25). However, the whole episode seems suspect (Donner* 1977, 395, and 1986, 255), all the more so since it is difficult to know where to put it, if we consider the peace which had now reigned between the two nations for many years.

Amaziah, too, was assassinated in the course of a palace conspiracy, at Lachish (*tell ed-duweir*, coord. 135-108), where he had taken refuge (II Kings 14.19-21//II Chron. 25.25-28). However, the 'people of the land' were on their guard, and put his son on the throne. The new king is listed with a double name, Uzziah and Azariah.

10.12 Jeroboam II

Bibliography

J.Briend, 'Jéroboam II, sauveur d'Israël', in *Mélanges... H.Cazelles*, Kevelaer and Neukirchen/Vluyn 1981, 41-9; É.Lipiński, 'Jéroboam II et la Syrie', in *Storia e tradizioni di Israele – Scritti in onore di J.A.Soggin*, Brescia 1991, 171-6.

It was Jeroboam II (c.786-746 or 787-747) of Israel who profited fully from the elimination of Damascus from the political scene. He succeeded in reconquering all of Transjordan that had traditionally belonged to Israel, from the Dead Sea to *lᵉbō ḥāmāt* (present-day *lebwe*, coord. 277-397), also including *qarnayim* in the east (present-day *tell ʿaštāra*, coord. 247-249), as is indicated by II Kings 14.25 and Amos 6.13.[14] However, the passage which states that he even succeeded in occupying Damascus (14.28) is textually uncertain and historically improbable (Lipiński 1991). The times of Jeroboam II must have also brought economic prosperity, even if, to judge from Amos's invective, the riches were now spread very unevenly between the various social classes. As a result of this, the description of Jeroboam II, himself a notable monarch, in the biblical texts is a negative one.

10.13 Uzziah/Azariah of Judah

Uzziah or Azariah of Judah (c.783-742 or 787-736 BCE) was only a little younger than his contemporary Jeroboam II of Israel; the chronology of this period is controversial.

Bibliography

H.Tadmor, 'Azriya of Yaudi', *ScrHier* 8, 1961, 232-71; J.A.Soggin, 'Das Erdbeben von Amos 1,1 und die Chronologie der Könige Ussia und Jotham von Juda', *ZAW* 82, 1970, 117-21; id., *The Prophet Amos*, London 1987, 3f., 108f.; M.Weippert, 'Menahem von Israel und seine Zeitgenossen in einer Steleninschrift des assyrischen Königs Tiglatpileser III. aus dem Iran', *ZDPV* 89, 1973, 26-53; N.Na'aman, 'Sennacherib's "Letter to God" on his Campaign to Judah', *BASOR* 214, 1974, 25-39; A.Zeron, 'Die Anmassung des Königs Ussia im Lichte von Jesajas Berufung', *TA* 1977, 65-8; R.Borger and H.Tadmor, 'Zwei Beiträge zur alttestamentlichen Wissenschaft aufgrund der Inschriften Tiglatpilesers III', *ZAW* 94, 1982, 244-51; R.Gelio, 'Fonti mesopotamiche relative al territorio palestinese (1000-500 a.c.)', *RiBib* 32, 1984, 121-51: 135-38; Donner* 1986, 256f., 305f.; Garbini* 1988, 38-43.

10.13.1 The now classic study of Tadmor seemed to have put forward a satisfactory solution to the question of the double name of the monarch (the two roots do not have the same meaning), a unique case in Israel and Judah: the two roots *ʿāzaz* and *ʿāzar* were seen as converging in the confession of faith in the one, omnipotent God (however, this proposal is clearly rejected by Garbini*, 38f.). Furthermore, according to Tadmor's thesis we would have a mention of the monarch in a fragment of the annals of Tiglath-pileser III, though only the last part appears there: ...*ya-u KUR ya-u-di*, a text which from the beginning of the century has generally been completed with *Iaz-ri-ya-u*, thus producing 'Azariah of the country of Judah' (thus *ANET*, 282f.; according to *TUAT* I, 370f., doubtful). However, this reading, which is virtually accepted by everyone, was not without difficulty; Donner* 1986, 305, observes that the monarch, already seriously ill (below 10.15.4), would have to be imagined at the head of a coalition, which seems improbable. Na'aman's 1974 study has cast doubt on its correctness, and therefore the identification of the person mentioned with Azariah: the fragment in question does not to relate to Tiglath-pileser III but to Sennacherib, i.e more than a century later, and the name is to be completed as *ha-za-ki-ya-u*, i.e. Hezekiah and not Azariah. In fact we know that Hezekiah took part in a coalition against Assyria (below 12.2.3). So it is clear that the problem has changed in the last decade (Gelio 1984, 814). The question becomes even more complicated if one takes into account, as Garbini suggests, two seals that certainly come from the North, which mention a 'king Uzziah' of the North. Azariah would then possibly also have been king of Israel with the name of Uzziah, and because of this important enough to be mentioned explicitly in the Assyrian annals.[15] For Garbini this rules out the proposals of Na'aman and Gelio, and a possible late date of the fragment is therefore unimportant.

10.13.2 Be this as it may, in the reign of Uzziah/Azariah relatively good conditions seem to have been restored in Judah (II Kings 15.1-7// II Chron.26.1-23). The southern frontier was again extended as far as the Red Sea: II Kings 14.22 speaks of the conquest and restoration of the port of Eilat, to be identified with present-day Aqaba in Jordan (coord.150-882), or with a place south of the present-day Eilat, in the region of the *jazirat al-far'ūn* (coord. 133-871). According to Chronicles, moreover, he fought against the Philistines and in Transjordan. Some fortresses are sometimes dated to this period, assuming that the note in II Chron 11.5-10 is trustworthy (cf. above, 10.7).[16] These fortresses (the southernmost of which is Kadesh-barnea, the present-day *'ein el-qudeirat*, coord.096-006) were provided with agricultural settlements which operated with methods of dry farming that are partly effective even today. Uzziah is also said to have strengthened the fortifications of Jerusalem (II Chron.26.11-15). The text of Chronicles also states that he fought succesfully against the Arabs, the Meunites (not the Μιναῖοι of the Hellenistic period in southern Arabia but a tribe situated near present-day Petra, coord.020-225, and *ma'an*, coord.952-220) and the Ammonites (cf. I Chron.4.41 and II Chron.26.7, Borger and Tadmor 1982).

10.13.3 The relations beween Azariah/Uzziah and Jeroboam were very good indeed. The boundaries of the two nations were very close to those traditionally attributed to the empire of David and Solomon, so that Garbini* 1988 thinks that the commercial enterprises in the Red Sea could have taken place not so much in the time of Solomon as under these two kings (above 6.6.1.3 and n.8 there).

10.13.4 Again according to the texts, Uzziah/Azariah was smitten at the end of his life with a disease which is often translated as 'leprosy', so that he was put into isolation; however, not all the details are clear (II Kings 15.1//II Chron.26.16-21). This is not, however, leprosy proper (Hansen's disease) but a skin disease which was contagious but not fatal.[17] The Hebrew term ṣāraʿat is also used in connection with fabrics and leather (i.e. to denote some form of mould) and with walls (a kind of saltpetre). This made the king incapable of taking any further part in affairs of state, so the regency was entrusted to his son Jotham. Chronicles, followed by Josephus, *Antt.* IX, 222-7, adds that this was a divine judgment on a sacrilegious offering made by the sovereign in the temple, an episode which Josephus associates with a violent earthquake that took place about 760 BCE. This is the same earthquake referred to in Amos 1.1 and some centuries later in Zech.14.5, that seems to have produced the valley which now separates the Mount of Olives from Mount Scopus. However, while the synchronism between the king's illness and the earthquake seems historically acceptable, the Chronicles narrative, taken up by Josephus, presupposes the vision of Isa.6.1ff., as Zeron 1977 has demonstrated, so that it is obviously an artificial construction. The king, incapacitated, was confined 'in the house of isolation to the day of his death' (II Kings 15.5//II Chron.26.21): that is how the expression *bēt ḥopšīt* is generally interpreted. The second term of this phrase is composed of a root which normally denotes liberty, but in Ugaritic (*WUS* 1071) the term is also used to denote the underworld; thus an incurable disease appeared to be the antechamber of death.

10.13.5 The note about the regency of Jotham is particularly interesting for the study of the chronology of the kings of Israel and Judah, which is difficult in this period because of the confusion of the sources. The king remained king in effect, except for the impediment which prevented him from attending to affairs of state; the chronology of Uzziah/Azariah and that of Jotham are thus superimposed for a certain period. It is probable that Jotham was regent until the death of his father, when the succession passed to him. According to the first of the two chronologies that I cite (that of the American Schools), that regency would have lasted from around 750 to around 742; in the second (that of Begrich and Jepsen), however, Uzziah would in fact have survived Jotham, so Jotham's successor, Jehoahaz or Ahaz (c.735-715 or 736-729/725), would have been regent, though only for a short time. This is one example of the difficulties which face scholars in the chronological sphere.

10.13.6 'In the year king Uzziah died', according to Isa.6.1, Isaiah had his vision. Just before and after this period, the great prophets of the Hebrew Bible appear.[18]

11

The Assyrian Invasions

11.1 The Assyrian imperial power

The Assyrian armies which after the *coups d'état* in Israel and Damascus invaded Aram, Israel and the Phoenician city-states, forcing them to pay tribute (above 10.9), now became the dominant feature of the second half of the eighth century BCE and the beginning of the seventh. And while at the time of the dynasty of Omri it had been possible for the statelets of the region to contain, if not to repel, the threat of the great Eastern empire (above 10.8.10.2) by means of a series of coalitions which had proved sufficient for the purpose, the occupation of the throne of Israel and Damascus by less gifted rulers who perhaps, according to one hypothesis (above 10.9.2.1-4), were even pro-Assyrian, destroyed a century of balance which had been laboriously achieved among the nations of the region, albeit with the purely negative aim of resisting invasion; indeed, according to the sources the ancient hostilities between Israel and the Aramaeans began again. This in fact made the way free for the Assyrian armies to move westwards. Now, when resistance was offered at all, it tended to be local, and in one case the Assyrian intervention was even requested (below 11.2.8). At the same time the region became the theatre of encounters which were often only diplomatic, but sometimes also military, between whatever Mesopotamian power was in the ascendant and Egypt, a power which never seems to have renounced its sovereignty over Canaan and Sinai (above 1.5). Moreover, first for Assyria, later for Babylon and finally for Persia Canaan was the launching pad for an attack on Egypt, while for Egypt it was an advance defensive post.

Bibliography

R.H.Pfeiffer, 'Assyria and Israel', *RSO* 32, 1957, 145-50; W.W.Hallo, 'From Qarqar to Carchemish', *BA* 23, 1960, 33-61; D.B.Redford, 'Studies in the Relations between Palestine and Egypt during the First Millennium BC: II. The Twenty-Second Dynasty', *JAOS* 93, 1973, 3-17; B.Oded, 'The Historical Background of the Syro-Ephraimite War Reconsidered', *CBQ* 34, 1972, 153-65; id., 'The Phoenician Cities and the Assyrian Empire in the Time of Tiglat-Pileser III', *ZDPV* 38, 1974, 38-49; H.Tadmor, 'Assyria and the West: The Ninth Century and its Aftermath', in H.Goedicke and J.J.M.Roberts (eds.), *Unity and Diversity*, Baltimore 1975, 36-48; H.Barth, *Israel und das Assyrerreich in den nicht-jesajanischen Texten des Proto-Jesaja*, Hamburg theological dissertation 1974; id., *Die Jesaja-Worte in der Josiazeit*, WMANT 48, Neukirchen 1977; H.Cazelles, 'Problèmes de la guerre syro-ephraim-ite', *EI* 14, 1978, 70*-8*; H.Spieckermann, *Juda unter Assur in der Sargonidenzeit*, FRLANT 129, Göttingen 1982. For the prophets of Israel and Judah in this period cf. H.Donner, *Israel unter den Völkern*, SVT XI, Leiden 1964. For Assyria, its policy and its army cf. e.g. W.von Soden, 'Die Assyrer und der Krieg', *Iraq* 25, 1963, 131-44; H.W.F.Saggs, 'Assyrian Warfare in the Sargonide Period', ibid., 145-54; E.Vogt, 'Die Text Tiglat-Pilesers III über die Eroberung Palästinas', *Bibl* 45, 1964, 348-54; M.Cogan, *Imperialism and Religion. Assyria, Judah and Israel in the Eighth and Seventh Centuries BCE*, Pittsburgh 1971; J.W.McKay, *Religion in Judah under the Assyrians*, SBT II 26, London 1973; H.Tadmor and M.Cogan, 'Ahaz and Tiglath-Pileser in the Book of Kings: Historio-graphic Considerations', *Bibl* 60, 1979, 491-508; R.Borger and H.Tad-mor, 'Zwei Beiträge zur alttestamentlichen Wissenschaft aufgrund der Inschriften Tiglatpilesers III', *ZAW* 94, 1982, 224-51; F.Malbran-Labat, *L'armée et l'organisation militaire de l'Assyrie*, Paris 1982; N.Na'aman, 'Chronology and History of the Late Assyrian Empire (631-619)', *ZA* 81, 1991, 243-67. For the Assyrian names in the Hebrew Bible cf. A.R.Millard, 'Assyrian Royal Names in Biblical Hebrew', *JSS* 21, 1976, 1-14. See also Donner* 1986, 287-303; Miller and Hayes* 1986, 316-23.

11.1.1 The Assyrian expeditions very quickly led to the incorporation into the empire first of the Aramaean kingdoms and the Phoenician cities and then, bit by bit, of Israel. In addition the kingdom of Judah was made a vassal first of Assyria and then, after the brief reign of Josiah (below 12.4), of Babylon with the catastrophe of 587/6; finally, as we shall also see (below 13.6.4.3), it seems that for some decades Judah became a vassal of Persia before being made a province directly administered by the empire.

11.1.2 Babylon had been the cultural centre of Mesopotamia from time immemorial. However, it was Assyria, a region situated on the upper Tigris, which controlled the destinies of the region and of adjacent territories for centuries: from the last years of the second millennium BCE to the end of the seventh century. Its seizure of power was gradual, but led to 'an empire of a completely different type, an unparalleled power structure' (Donner *1977, 416, and 1986, 293) in ancient history. Assyria's main characteristics were, first, that it maintained a permanent and professional army equipped not only with war chariots but also with mounted cavalry, a novelty of the period, and secondly that it had a complete lack of scruples which led it to perpetrate all kinds of atrocities which terrorized people into submitting: it sacked cities and wrought destruction which left little behind in an enemy country, followed by heavy tributes which drew off the little that had been left. Isaiah 5.26-29 illustrates on the one hand the efficiency and capability of this army and on the other how it could be compared with a horde of savage beasts. Of course it is open to question whether and to what extent this reputation for cruelty was based on fact, on events which actually happened, or whether it was not rather the result of skilful propaganda aimed at discouraging any resistance from the start (von Soden 1963 and Saggs 1963), thus making the enemy more malleable and easier to deal with.

11.1.3 Babylon was the only nation to which the Assyrians seem to have shown some respect. Assyria recognized its intellectual debt to Babylon and the Babylonian contribution to civilization generally, so although Babylon had submitted under Tiglath-pileser III, it was allowed a degree of autonomy by means of a form of personal union, even if the governor was always an Assyrian of royal blood. However, this situation, with privileges extending up to a certain point, did not prevent the Assyrians from dealing extremely harshly with their *alma mater* where they thought it necessary.

11.1.4 At the end of the previous chapter (10.13.1) I referred to Tiglath-pileser III (c.745-272), who ascended the throne under the name of *pūlu*, transcribed in Hebrew as *pūl* (II Kings 15.19ff.). He was to 'lead the neo-Assyrian empire to the height of its power, bringing it to perfection on a systematic and conceptual, if not a territorial, level' (Donner* 1977, 418 and 1986, 296). At home, Tiglath-pileser reformed the structure of the state, changing the great provinces, which were difficult to administer, into smaller, more manageable districts. Towards neighbouring nations he inaugurated 'a new imperialistic foreign policy, the effectiveness of which cannot be emphasized strongly enough' (Donner*, ibid.).

11.1.5 Donner* 1977, 418 and 1986, 297ff. has succeeded in indicating the successive stages of the incorporation of a nation into the empire.

11.1.5.1 First of all a vassal relationship of the traditional type was established with the nation in question, following the model practised by the Assyrian kings up till then: limited sovereignty, a foreign policy completely dependent on that of Assyria, and the exaction of heavy tribute.

11.1.5.2 At the first sign of rebellion, there was direct military intervention, with the nomination of a pro-Assyrian ruler, possibly belonging to the ruling dynasty in order to give him authority. This operation was often combined with drastic changes of frontier, followed by the incorporation of the new territory thus obtained into the empire; alternatively, the land was ceded to loyal vassals. With all this went a marked increase in the tribute exacted.

11.1.5.3 At the first sign of any form of opposition, however small, there was again decisive military intervention, this time definitive, followed by the deposition of the ruler responsible and his replacement by an Assyrian governor. The remaining territory was incorporated into the empire, and the leading class was deported so as to leave the country leaderless. New ethnic groups were imported.

11.1.5.4 Finally, an interesting characteristic of the system was its flexibility; it was not applied in a punctilious or dogmatic way, but was adapted to the particular circumstances. That made it especially effective.

11.1.6 Assyria achieved its greatest expansion in the reign of Esarhaddon (680-669), who in the course of three campaigns succeeded in subjecting a large part of Egypt. However, this was the splendour preceding decline; even under Asshur-bani-pal (669-627), the Sardanapalus of Greek legend, to whom we owe the library which has handed down the majority of Mesopotamian literature, we see Assyria now occupied with predominantly defensive wars. In 655, under Psammetichus I (663-609), the founder of the Twenty-Sixth Dynasty, Egypt regained its independence; between 652 and 648 there was a campaign against Babylon from which Assyria emerged victorious but much weakened. On the death of this literate and wise king it was only a question of a few years before the empire collapsed completely.

11.1.7 Here one might point out the intrinsic weakness of all these empires, a feature which often led to their rapid decline (by lasting for several centuries Assyria was an exception). They were all made up of a multitude of nations which had been subjected in a more or less violent and brutal way, were inhabited by different populations and had one thing in common: hostility towards the dominant power, so that they were basically centrifugal. And the very mass of peoples who had to be controlled, coupled with the extension of these empires which had grown up in a completely inorganic way, and the difficulties and slowness of communications, made them virtually ungovernable after a time: their administration was increasingly inefficient, slow and muddled. More and more resources had to be devoted to repression, with a consequent waste of men and means and the destruction of riches.

11.2 The 'Syro-Ephraimite' war

At the time of Tiglath-pileser III the biblical texts speak of a war which traditionally, from Martin Luther onwards, has been called the 'Syro-Ephraimite war', although in reality it also involved the kingdom of Judah. What happened can be reconstructed from various Assyrian inscriptions (*ANET*, 282-4; *TUAT* I, 370ff.), 'although much basic material, details and chronology remains controversial' (Donner* 1986, 307ff.). At all events the episode seems to have been totally local and secondary.

Bibliography

A.Alt, 'Hosea 5,8-6,6. Ein Krieg und seine Folgen in prophetischer Beleuchtung', *NKZ* 30, 1919, 537-68 = *KS* II, 163-87; id., 'Das System der assyrischen Provinzen auf dem Boden des Reiches Israel', *ZDPV* 83, 1929, 220-42 = *KS* II, 188-205; J.Begrich, 'Der syrisch-ephraimitische Krieg und seine weltpolitische Zusammenhänge', *ZDMG* 83, 1929, 213-37 = *GS*, 99-120; H.Donner, *Israel unter den Völkern*, SVT XI, Leiden 1964; E.Vogt, 'Die Texte Tiglat-Pileser III über die Eroberung Palästinas', *Bibl* 45, 1964, 348-54; E.M.Good, 'Hosea 5:8-6.6: An Alternative to Alt', *JBL* 85, 1966, 173-81; P.R.Ackroyd, 'Historians and Prophets', *SEÅ* 33, 1968, 18-54; Oded, 'Historical Background' (above 11.1); L.D.Levine, 'Menahem and Tiglath-pileser – A New Synchronism', *BASOR* 206, 1972, 40-2; M.Weippert, 'Menahem von Israel und seine Zeitgenossen in einer Steleninschrift des Assyrischen Königs Tiglathpileser III. aus dem Iran', *ZDPV* 89, 1973, 26-53; A.Vanel, 'Tabe'el en Is VII 6 et le roi Tubail de Tyr', *SVT* 26, 1974, 17-24; N.Na'aman, 'Sennacherib's "Letter to God" ' (above 10.15); W.H.Shea, 'Menahem and Tiglath Pileser III', *JNES* 37, 1978, 43-9; W.Dietrich, *Jesaja und die Politik*, Munich 1976; Herrmann* 1980, 246-8; E.Asurmendi, *La guerra siro-efraimita*, Valencia 1982; M.E.W.Thompson, *Situation and Theology*, Sheffield 1982; R.Bickert, 'König Ahas und der Prophet Jesaja. Ein Beitrag zum Problem des syro-ephraimitischen Kriegs', *ZAW* 99, 1987, 361-83; H.Cazelles, 'La guerre syro-éphraimite dans le contexte de la politique internationale', in *Storia e tradizioni di Israele – Scritti in onore di J.A.Soggin*, Brescia 1991, 31-48.

11.2.1 The war may have been the consequence of an extreme attempt to revive the anti-Assyrian alliance which had proved to be such a good thing about a century before: its primary aim, to contain the Assyrian expansion, had been completely successful. Many texts inform us about events, even if the information which they offer is always insufficient and often contradictory (Donner*, 1977, 430 and 1986, 306f.); the Assyrian texts do not tell us very much; the biblical texts are to be found in II Kings 16; Isa.7.1-7; 8.1-15; 10.27; 17.1-11; Hos.5.1ff.; 5.8-6.6; 8.7-10. I have already indicated (above 10.15.5) the chronological difficulties relating to this era, especially in connection with the death of Uzziah/Azariah and the regency of Jotham; to these must be added the problems of the death of Ahaz and therefore of Hezekiah's accession to the throne (II Kings 16.20; 18.1). That explains the marked discrepancies between the two chronologies which I am using. Finally, as the recent study by Bickert 1987 indicates, there are many indications that the war in question never took place!

11.2.2 In Israel the death of Jeroboam II (746 or 747 BCE) was followed by the accession to the throne of his son Zechariah (c.746-5 or 747), who was killed by a certain Shallum (c.745 or 747, II Kings 15.8-12, 13-16). Shallum was in turn eliminated by a certain Menahem (c.745-738 or 747-738), a citizen of the former capital Tirzah. Menahem succeeded in pacifying the kingdom by using very strong repressive measures (15.16); this presupposes that he had control over the army. However, Tiglath-pileser (*pūl*) invaded the country (15.18b-20), having subjected and annexed Hamath in central Syria (present day *ḥama*, coord.312-503), and Menahem, together with the other rulers of the region, hastened to send a substantial tribute (a thousand talents of silver according to II Kings, cf. *ANET*, 283; *TUAT* I, 371) as a sign of submission. Israel was thus in the first stage of submission (above 11.1.5.1).

11.2.3 The Assyrian annals mention Menahem explicitly together with the king of Damascus, whose name is transcribed as *rahyanū*, the biblical Rezin,[1] also in the first stage of submission: he appears on an Assyrian stele discovered in Iran.[2] The biblical sources state that Menahem obtained the money by taxing landowners at fifty shekels a head, so that if the ordinary talent amounted to 3,000 shekels (the royal talent, used for paying tribute, amounted to 3,600 shekels), there must have been a good 60,000 of these landowners (Noth* 1959, 282 n.2; Donner* 1977, 424 and 1986, 304f.).[3] This rather high figure is an obvious sign of prosperity and moreover, if reliable, is one of the few economic data we have at our disposal.

11.2.4 Tiglath-pileser seems to have been satisfied by the tribute and the submission he had obtained without striking a blow, and Israel could enjoy some years of peace. However, in 734 the Assyrians reappeared in the region for a campaign against the Philistines,[4] especially against Gaza, whose king took refuge in Egypt. Later he returned from there to be pardoned, but this was an exceptional case. The Assyrians very soon reached the frontier with Egypt and established themselves there; this is the traditional 'Brook of Egypt', present-day *wādī el 'ariš*, the frontier between the two regions from time immemorial. With this move the Assyrians were able to prevent the Egyptians from sending help to the rebels, and preventing the rebels from making any contact with Egypt. The expedition does not seem to have had any consequences for Israel, nor are we told that Tiglath-pileser annexed any territory; some scholars think that the Assyrian province of *dū'ru*, the coastal region around Dor (present-day *hirbet el-burj*, coord.142-224), which was Philistine in origin (above 4.4.1.5), was annexed on this occasion. However, our knowledge about this is virtually nil.

11.2.5 In Israel, political chaos again reigned: Pekahiah, son of Menahem (c.738-737 or 737-736, II Kings 15.23-26) held the throne only for a few months and was deposed by Pekah, son of Remaliah (c.737-732 or 735-732, II Kings 15.27-31), who ascended the throne.

11.2.6 So in 738 Assyria had again reduced Israel and Damascus to the state of vassals in the first phase. Very soon Rezin of Damascus and Pekah of Israel thought of forming another anti-Assyrian coalition (we do not know exactly when), probably watching the way in which the Assyrians could rush around the region as they wanted. However, the necessary condition for this co-operation was the neutralization of the garrisons left along the frontier with Egypt, so that its rear was covered: for this the collaboration of Judah in the alliance seemed indispensable; only in this way would the other rulers of the region, who were hesitating, join in the alliance.

11.2.6.1 Ahaz of Judah did not want to accept this proposal, though we are not told why. Still, the reason is not difficult to guess: first of all, he was not a vassal of Assyria and therefore not burdened by tribute like his northern neighbours; nor did he feel threatened in any way. Again, having observed from close quarters what had happened at Gaza, he probably saw that the chances of success for an alliance of this kind were very remote.

11.2.6.2 Of course an attitude of this kind could only appear to the other allies as a betrayal, since it made the coalition weak in its southern sector; so it seems that the two kings, of Damascus and Israel, tried something like a *coup d'état* in Judah in order to replace the ruler in power with a king favourable to their own plans. The choice fell on an Aramaean called 'the son of Tabeel'. We have no precise information about this person, and even the reading of the name is uncertain (the Massoretic *ṭabᵉ'al* means 'good for nothing' and cannot be real; it is corrected according to Neh.4.7 and LXX); however, it is supposed that this was a highborn family in Transjordan, perhaps related to the royal house of Judah; hence, according to some scholars,[5] he might have been an ancestor of the family of the Tobiads (cf. below 13.8.3.2), which was to make things so difficult for those returning from exile (Neh.2.19ff.) and later for the faithful of Judah before the Maccabaean revolt (below 14.7.4.8). This thesis, proposed for the first time by the

Israeli archaeologist B.Mazar, was developed independently in 1972 by the Israeli B.Oded, who argued that Israel and Damascus certainly did not march on Jerusalem just to force Judah to join in the alliance against Assyria; rather, their aim will have been to reconquer the Israelite territories in Transjordan that Judah had been occupying little by little, profiting from the internal difficulties of Israel (cf. II Kings 15.37, which reports the beginning of hostilities at the time of Jotham, and especially II Chron 27.5-6, which speaks of Jotham's victories over the Ammonites). Of course Oded's thesis presupposes that the two texts are historically trustworthy, something which scholars generally do not accept. Clearly the two theories are not incompatibile, though there is no definitive proof: an attempt to recapture certain Israelite territories in Transjordan occupied by Judah could fit in perfectly with a plan to put another king, favourable to the anti-Assyrian alliance, on the throne of Judah.

11.2.7 So the two armies are said to have marched on Jerusalem (II Kings 16.5-18; Isa.7.1-7; cf. Hos.5.8ff) According to the explanation given by Alt 1919, not superseded by the counter-proposal of Good 1966, this was in order to lay siege to it, and to begin with they seem to have made good progress. Isaiah 7.1ff., which is certainly a late text, describes in humorous tones the panic which seized the court and the government. The situation was all the more threatening since in the South the Edomites had reconquered the port of Eilat (above 10.15.2), driving out the Judahites (emended text, read '^{e}dōm for '^{a}rām, a confusion between res and dalet, and delete 'r^eṣīn' (Rezin), with all the commmentaries, as a gloss on '^{a}rām). Moreover, according to II Chron.28.18, the Philistines had made a deep penetration into the south-west of Judaea.

11.2.8 Ahaz and his counsellors seem completely to have lost their heads: despite the advice to the contrary which the tradition attributes to the prophet Isaiah and to a prophecy which exhorted him to keep calm, Ahaz took a decision which set in motion a dynamic that was to shape the history of Judah for about a century: he asked help from Assyria, offering his own submission and sending a substantial amount of tribute (II Kings 16.7). Indeed, he did more: he went in person to Damascus to make his submission and as a sign of particular devotion seems to have introduced into the temple of Jerusalem an altar modelled on the Assyrian altar he had seen at Damascus. That seems all the more serious in that that this apparently did not happen at the instigation of Tiglath-pileser, a ruler who never imposed his religion on his vassals (Cogan 1971, McKay 1973; however, see the different theory of Spieckermann 1982, 322f.; for the problem cf. Donner* 1986, 332). Thus Judah will have become a vassal of Assyria on its own initiative.

11.2.9 The coalition between Israel and Damascus, attacked in the rear by the might of Assyria, had to withdraw its troops from the south with great speed and throw them against the attacker, so even if Jerusalem was ever besieged, it was no longer in any danger. Damascus succeeded in resisting until 732, when it was conquered and transformed into an Assyrian province. Israel lost all its territory in Transjordan and a good part of Galilee; its ruling class was deported. So the kingdom was reduced to the central hill-country.

11.2.10 Once more the kingdom of Israel lapsed into chaos. Pekah was killed in a plot by a certain Hoshea (*hōšēaʿ*), not to be confused with the prophet of the same name (II Kings 15.30), who was immediately confirmed in office by Tiglath-pileser III as a vassal: in this way Israel started to suffer the second phase of subjection.

11.2.11 That was the tragic end to the 'Syro-Ephraimite' war. Thus far the thesis presented in the biblical tradition (II Kings 16.5-9; Isa.7.1-9). However, the recent study by Bickert has raised a series of problems in connection with it. Bickert points out that there is insufficient evidence to indicate that this war ever took place, nor do we do know anything for certain about the plans that it is said to have produced; moreover scholars have not taken sufficient account of the studies of Oded and Hermann. Something of this sort happened, but it does not seem to have gone beyond the intentions and the project, and the catastrophe which struck Damascus and Israel had nothing to do with this war. Isaiah 7.1ff is notoriously a late text, more interested in the theme of faith than in the facts, while the interest of II Kings 16 is principally in the altar which Ahaz is said to have put in the temple and only secondarily in other features. But see Cazelles 1991, who produces notable arguments in defence of the historicity of the war.

11.3 The end of the kingdom of Israel

Hoshea reigned from about 732 to 724 (II Kings 17.1-4), to begin with a loyal vassal of Assyria, always punctual in his payment of tribute (*ANET*, 283f.; *TUAT* I, 378, cf. Borger and Tadmor 1982).

Bibliography

H.Tadmor 1958; A.Trebolle Barrera, 'La caída de Samaria', *Salamanticense* 28, 1981, 137-52; S.Talmon, 'Polemics and Apology in Biblical Historiography, 1 Kings 17, 24-41', in R.E.Friedman (ed.), *The Creation of Sacred Literature*, Berkeley, Ca 1981; A.van der Kooij, 'Zur Exégèse von II Reg 17.2', *ZAW* 96, 1984, 109-112; B.E.J.H.Becking, *De ondergang van Samaria*, Diss.theol. Utrecht 1985; R.A.Viviano, 'I Kings 17. A Rhetorical and Form Critical Analysis', *CBQ* 49, 1987, 548-59; J.Scharbert, *Zwangsumsiedlungen in Vorderasien zwischen dem 10. und dem 6. Jahrhundert v.Chr. nach altorientalischen und biblischen Quellen*, Munich

1986; M.Brettler, 'Ideology, History and Theology in 2 Kings XVII 7-23', *VT* 39, 1989, 268-82; S.Timm, 'Die Eroberung Israels (Samarias) 722 v.Chr aus assyrisch-babylonischer Sicht', *WO* 20/21, 1989-90, 62-82; B.Becking, *The Fall of Samaria*, Leiden 1992.

On Samaria under the Assyrians cf.A.Alt, 'Das System der assyrischen Provinzen auf dem Boden des Reiches Israel', *ZDPV* 52, 1929, 220-42 = *KS* II, 188-205.

11.3.1 Having been a loyal vassal for some time, Hoshea decided to rebel against Assyria, where in the meantime Shalmaneser V (c.726-722) had come to the throne; indeed, following a practice which is well attested in the ancient Near East, Hoshea could well have rebelled precisely at the time of Shalmaneser's succession to the throne. He refused to go on paying tribute and entered into direct negotiations with Egypt, an action which at all events was forbidden to a vassal (above 11.1.5.1). However, the project was premature: the situation in Egypt was again chaotic, as the Twenty-Fifth Ethiopian Dynasty was laboriously rising to power and attempting, though as yet without success, to reunite its own territory. So it is possible that Hoshea will have had dealings with one of the leading rulers in the Delta, though we do not know who. II Kings 17.4 mentions a certain So, who for some scholars is a king and for others a general,[6] but perhaps this is simply (Donner* 1977, 433, and 1986, 314) the Hebrew transcription of the Egyptian *nśw.t*, generically 'king'.

11.3.2 We do not know what prompted Hoshea to take this imprudent action: the tribute was certainly heavy, but he was taking on an enemy at the zenith of its political, economic and military power, and no crisis seems to have been looming on its horizon. However, there are indications that the situation was not as tranquil as it seems: if we can go by what Josephus, *Antt.* IX, 283ff., tells us, it was in a state of upheaval, so that Hoshea will simply have been uniting the rebels (Miller and Hayes* 1986, 334ff.).

11.3.3 Assyria intervened without hesitation. A last attempt at submission on the part of Hoshea was rejected, because at the same time Israel was pursuing negotiations with Egypt. Shalmaneser took Hoshea prisoner, possibly during his attempt to submit, and occupied the capital Samaria (II Kings 17.5-6; 18.9-11).[7] Shortly afterwards, on the occasion of the accession of Sargon II (721-705), a rebellion broke out in the context of a greater revolt in the region, but the new ruler had no difficulty in suppressing it (*ANET*, 284; *TUAT* I, 379, below 12.2.3.1); this is the most recent reconstruction of events made by Timm 1989-90. Part of the ruling class was deported and replaced by foreign elements; the territory of what had once been the kingdom of Israel became an Assyrian province under the name of *samerīna*, the first time

that this term does not denote the capital, but the country (Donner*
1986, 315).

11.3.4 Little or nothing is known of the later fate of the region: all we
know is that still under Esarhaddon, according to Ezra 4.2, and then
under Assur-bani-pal (Ezra 4.10), other foreigners were settled in the
region (Alt 1929; Donner* 1986, 316); according to II Kings 17.7-41, a
text which seeks to explain the tragedy in terms of the Deuteronomistic
theology (and which Cogan and Tadmor 1988 rightly call 'a sermon on
the fall of the northern kingdom'), a considerable part of the population
will have been replaced by foreign elements who practised a syncretistic
religion: YHWH will have been worshipped along with other deities.
This note is not to be taken literally, as its literary genre indicates; it
anticipates the anti-Samaritan polemic of the post-exilic period, which
we shall be considering below (14.4): there is more information in
Cogan and Tadmor 1988, 210f.

It emerges from the Assyrian texts that the capital was rebuilt and
became the seat of the Assyrian governor (*ANET*, 284f.; *TUAT* I, 378f.).

12

The Kingdom of Judah to the End of the Babylonian Exile

12.1 The last century and a half

The surviving kingdom of Judah, politically and economically the less important of the Hebrew states, as we saw earlier (10.3.5), far from the main lines of communication and the sea, continued its own existence for less than a century and a half, in the shadow of the conflicts between the great powers: first as a vassal of Assyria, a condition from which it never succeeded in freeing itself, then as a vassal of Egypt and finally of Babylon. Attempts to steer a middle course between the great powers which were characteristic of the politics of Judah in this period only led to continued defeats and finally to the fall of the kingdom with a loss of political independence (recovered only for about a century between the second and first centuries BCE under the Hasmonaeans and their successors, below 14.11), the destruction of the temple and of the capital and the deportation of a skilled part of its population, first in 597/6 and then in 587/6. Some of the deportees succeeded in returning home after the fall of Babylon (after 539/8) and rebuilt the capital and temple, re-establishing a very reduced autonomous province of Judaea under the sovereignty of Persia, as we shall see below (13.6.4.3). On the other hand it was recognized that the political room for efficient political manoeuvring was very small.

Bibliography

D.J.Wiseman, *Chronicles of Chaldaean Kings*, London 1956; H.Tadmor, 'The Campaigns of Sargon II of Asshur: A Chronological-Historical Study', *JCS* 12, 1958, 22-40, 77-100; W.W.Hallo, 'From Qarqar to Carchemish', *BA* 23, 1964, 33-61; N.K.Gottwald, *All the Kingdoms of the Earth*, New York 1964; M.Broshi, 'The Expansion of Jerusalem in the Reigns of Hezekiah and Manasseh', *IEJ* 24, 1974, 21-6; E.Stern, 'Israel at the Close of the Monarchy', *BA* 38, 1975, 26-54; A.K.Grayson, *Assyrian and Babylonian Chronicles*, Locust Valley 1975; J.Scharbert, *Zwangsumsiedlungen in Vorderasien zwischen dem 10. und dem 6.Jahrhundert v.Chr. nach altorientalischen und biblischen Quellen*, Munich 1988.

12.1.1 In the last quarter of the eighth century BCE Judah had remained one of the few nations in the region which were still independent, a survivor of the Assyrian invasions. A vassal of the empire in the first phase of subjection (above 11.1.5.1), by way of compensation it had no enemies in the North, though the fact that the territories of the North now belonged first to Assyria and later to Babylon ruled out any attempt at reconquest. On the other hand, Judah could now consider itself the sole heir of Israelite tradition and worship, as well as of the Davidic ideology and state. Moreover it is generally accepted (though there is very little relevant evidence) that it was in this period, immediately after the fall of the northern kingdom, that a good deal of the material which had originated and been transmitted there, like the E source of the Pentateuch, the earliest sections of Deuteronomy, the original parts of the prophets Hosea and Amos, had been transferred to the South to be incorporated in what was later to become the Hebrew Bible. As we have seen (above 10.3.9), in the ideology of the Deuteronomistic history the South had never accepted the separation of the North from the united kingdom; now, to a much greater extent, it could regard itself as the representative of 'all Israel'; the liberation of the North remained one of its tasks even if, as we have seen, it was difficult to accomplish immediately: there was no room for a third great power between Mesopotamia and Egypt.

12.1.2 After the end of the Assyrian empire, the position of Judah as a buffer state between Babylon and Egypt (newly independent from 655, cf. above 11.1.6) was difficult but not desperate. That both empires needed the region, either as a bulwark for defence or as a forward base for attack, provided skilled diplomats with a number of possibilities of playing off one contender against another. It was certainly a dangerous game, but the prize was well worth the risks involved: the retention of political independence and sovereignty, limited though this may have been. However, as we shall see, none of this could be achieved, and the end-result was the destruction of Judah as an independent political entity (below 12.6).

12.1.3 As sources, we again have the Deuteronomistic texts of II Kings 18-25 and the parallels in II Chron.28-36; we also find parallels in Isa.36-39 and in Jer.52. Other important sources are first the Assyrian annals and then the Babylonian chronicles (*ANET*, 287ff., 560ff.; *TUAT* I, 287ff., 401ff.; for the latter cf. also D.J.Wiseman 1956).

12.1.4 Finally, it is interesting to note how, throughout the ancient

Near East, the seventh century BCE was a period of cultural and religious revival. I have already mentioned (above 11.6) the work of Asshur-bani-pal, to whose collection we owe the survival of most of the Mesopotamian literature that has come down to us: similar collections were made later in Babylon by Nebuchadnezzar II (c.605-561), a ruler with whom we shall be dealing in more detail below (12.5.4). In Egypt, too, under the Twenty-Fifth and especially the Twenty-Sixth dynasties, we can see attempts at collecting ancient material.[1] Something of this kind also seems to have happened in Phoenicia, if we accept the testimony of a certain Philo of Byblos, though this is often at second or even at third hand. Philo quotes Sanchuniaton, who is said to have lived in the seventh century. Now the beginnings of the movement which led to king Josiah's reform in Judah, accompanied by the re-editing and preservation of texts from the tradition of Israel and what we are accustomed to call the 'Deuteronomist', have sometimes[2] been connected with not dissimilar intentions in Judah.

12.2 King Hezekiah

The figure of king Hezekiah (Hebrew *ḥizqīyāhū*, c.715-687 or 728/ 25-700, or better, according to H.Tadmor, 727/26-700) immediately confronts the reader with a chronological problem, as can clearly be seen from the difference between the various systems of calculation. The sources in II Kings 18.4-8 tell us that under him three important events took place: a religious reform, a war with the Philistines and finally some anti-Assyrian revolts, ending in defeat.

In the Deuteronomistic history and Chronicles Hezekiah, along with Josiah, is considered one of the greatest kings that Judah ever had; however, a political judgment which took into account the results he obtained rather than his intentions and his religious faith would certainly have to be much more severe: Hezekiah left the country divided and in almost total ruin apart from the capital, which, moreover, suffered the after-effects of a long siege. This situation could not fail to have repercussions on the religion of Judah as well, regardless of Hezekiah's attempts at reform.

Bibliography

A.Alt, 'Neue assyrische Nachrichten über Palästina', *ZDPV* 67, 1945, 128-46 = *KS* II, 226-41; H.H.Rowley, 'Hezekiah's Reform and Rebellion', *BJRL* 44, 1961-62, 395-431 = *Men of God*, London 1963, 98-132; J.A.Brinkman, 'Merodach Baladan II', in *Studies... A.L.Oppenheim*, Chicago 1964, 6-53; F.J.Moriarty, 'The Chronicler's Account of Hezekiah's Reform', *CBQ* 27, 1965, 399-406; E.van Leeuwen, 'Sanchérib devant Jérusalem', *OTS* 14, 1965, 145-71; S.H.Horn, 'Did Sennacherib Campaign Once or Twice against Hezekiah?', *AUSS* 4, 1966, 1-28; I.L.Honor, *Sennacherib's Invasion of Palestine*, New York 1966; B.S. Childs, *Isaiah and the Assyrian Crisis*, SBT II 3, London 1967; O.Kaiser, 'Die Verkündigung des Propheten Jesaja im Jahre 701', *ZAW* 81, 1969, 304-15; P.Welten, 'Die Königs-Stempel. Ein Beitrag zur Militärpolitik Judas unter Hiskia', in *Wort und Geschichte – FS K.Elliger*, Kevelaer and Neukirchen/Vluyn 1973, 199-208 = *Gesammelte Aufsätze* II, 88-103; L.D.Levine, 'The Second Campaign of Sennacherib', *JNES* 32, 1973, 312-17; H.G.M.Williamson, *Israel in the Books of Chronicles*, Cambridge 1977; B.Otzen, 'Israel under the Assyrians – Reflections on Imperial Policy in Palestine', *ASTI* 11, 1978, 96-110; A.K.Jenkins, 'Hezekiah's Reform and Deuteronomic Tradition', *HTR* 72, 1979, 23-43; H.-D.Hoffmann, *Reform und Reformen*, ATANT 66, Zurich 1980; G.Garbini, 'Il bilinguismo dei Giudei', *Vicino Oriente* 3, 1981, 209-23; K.A.D.Smelik, ' "Zeg toch tot Hiskia"; een voorbeeld van prophetische geschiedenis-schrijving', *Amsterdamse Cahiers* 2, 1981, 50-67; H.Tadmor and M.Cogan, 'Hezekiah's Fourteenth Year: The King's Illness and the Babylonian Embassy', *EI* 16, 1982, 198-201 (in Hebrew, summary in English); M.Hutter, *Hiskia. König von Juda*, Graz 1982, and 'Überlegung-en zu Sanheribs Palästinafeldzug im Jahre 701 BCE', *BN* 19, 1982, 24-30; A.Catastini, 'Il quattordicesimo anno del regno di Ezechia (II re 18:13)', *Hen* 4, 1982, 257-63; id., 'Le varianti greche di II Re 18-20', *Egitto e Vicino Oriente* 5, 1982, 75-91; S.Norin, 'An Important Kennicott Reading in 2 Kings XVIII 3', *VT* 32, 1982, 337f.; H.Tadmor, 'Rab-Saris or Rab-Shakeh in 2 Kings 18', in *'The Word of the Lord Shall Go Forth...' Essays D.N.Freedman*, Winona Lake, Ind. 1983, 279-85; S.de Jong, 'Hiskia en Zedekia', *Amsterdamse Cahiers* 5, 1984, 135-46; J.A.Brinkman, *Prelude to Empire. Babylonian Society and Politics, 747-626 BC*, Philadelphia 1984, 57-60; H.Tadmor, 'Sennacherib's Campaign to Judah. Historical and Historiographical Considerations', *Zion* 50, 1985, 65-80 (in Hebrew with an English summary); A.R.Millard, 'Sennacherib's Attack on Hezekiah', *TynB* 36, 1985, 61-77; W.Brueggemann, 'II Kings 18-19: The Legitimation of Sectarian Hermeneutics', *HorBibTh* 7.1, 1985, 1-42; W.H.Shea, 'Sennacherib's Second Palestinian Campaign', *JBL* 104, 1985, 401-18; R.Liwak, 'Die Rettung Jerusalems im Jahr 701 v.Chr. Zum Verhältnis und Verständnis historischer und theologischer Aussagen', *ZTK* 83, 1986, 137-66; D.N.Fewell, 'Sennacherib's Defeat: Words at War in 2 Kings 18:13 – 19:37', *JSOT* 34, 1986, 79-90; A.van der Kooij, 'Das assyrische Heer vor den Mauern Jerusalems im Jahre 701 v.Chr.', *ZDPV* 102, 1986, 98-109; C.T.Begg, '2 Kings 10:12-19 as Element of the Deuteronomic History', *CBQ* 48, 1986, 27-38; F.J.Gonçalves, *L'expédition de Sennachérib en Palestine dans la littérature hébraïque ancienne*, Louvain la Neuve 1986; E.Vogt, *Der Aufstand Hiskias und die Belagerung Jerusalems, 701 v.Chr.*, Rome 1986; A.Laato, 'Hezekiah and the Assyrian Crisis in 701 BC', *SJOT* 1, 2, 1987, 7-21; L.K.Handy, 'Hezekiah's Unlikely Reform', *ZAW* 100, 1988, 11-15; M.Cogan and H.Tadmor, *II Kings*, AB, New York 1988, ad loc.; P.E.Dion, 'Sennacherib's Expedition to Palestine', *EeR* 20, 1989, 5-25; C.T.Begg, 'Hezekiah's Display: Another Parallel', *BN* 41, 1988, 7ff.; G.Garbini[*] 1988, 44-7; L.Camp, *Hiskija und Hiskijabild*, Altenberg 1990; S.Mittmann, 'Hiskia und die Philister', *JNWSL* 16,1990, 91-106. For the biblical text cf. H.M.Orlinsky, 'The Kings-Isaiah Recension of the Hezekiah Story', *JQR* 30, 1939-40, 33-9; the commentaries on the books and the articles by Catastini 1982, Norin 1982 and Dion 1989 cited above. For the death of Sennacherib, see S.Parpola, 'The Murder of Sanherib', in B.Alster (ed.), *Death in Mesopotamia*, Copenhagen 1980, 171-82.

12.2.1 According to II Kings 18.3-4, Hezekiah began his career with a religious reform: he suppressed the 'high places', demolished all kinds of sanctuaries, pagan and syncretistic, and destroyed the relic of the bronze serpent which the tradition traced back to Moses (Num.21.6-9, above 7.10.3). The text of II Chron. 29-31 describes this reform in much more detail: the king is said to have restored and purified the temple, offered sacrifices, especially of expiation, celebrated the passover in the temple (according to Haag 1973 only the feast of unleavened bread) and reformed the cult. There is an interesting note that the North, which had recently been occupied by the Assyrians, was also involved in this reform (II Chron.30.1). According to Williamson 1977, 119ff., however, the Chronicler will have had the inauguration of the temple of Solomon in mind. It is difficult to verify this information, which has every appearance of being a projection of later attempts on the past in order to give them greater authority. For other scholars[3] these are themes which anticipate the reform of king Josiah, making it the final phase of a process begun just under a century before (below 12.4.2). Yet others, however, are more cautious: details of a reform as presented in II Kings, formulated as it is in Deuteronomistic terms, seem doubtful; it is more probable that the writer wanted to concentrate religious life on the temple of Jerusalem, making it, if not the only sanctuary, at least the principal sanctuary for the South as for the North, a first step towards a restoration of the Davidic empire. For Spieckermann 1983, 174ff., however, this is a totally artificial construction, following the scheme of an alternation between pious and reforming rulers and wicked rulers formulated by Hoffmann 1980 (similarly Handy 1988).[4] In any case, the reforming activity attributed to Hezekiah makes it possible that he should be identified with the Emmanuel (Hebrew *ʿimmanū'ēl*) announced in the late text Isa.7.14-15, where a devout and pious king is to succeed the wicked Ahaz who is on the throne. As we know, this prophecy was to be reinterpreted in messianic terms by the New Testament and applied in the infancy narratives to the birth of Christ (Matt.1.23).

12.2.2 II Kings 18.8 says that Hezekiah defeated the Philistines as far as Gaza, thus succeeding in incorporating into the kingdom some territories lost at the time of Ahaz (II Chron. 28.18, above 11.2.7). According to some scholars it is possible that I Chron.4.34-43, which describes the expansion of Simeon, in fact refers to this particular episode (but in that case it is necessary to read *gĕrār* with the LXX instead of *gĕdōr* in v.39, a confusion between *daleth* and *res*, cf. Oded in Hayes-Miller* 1977, 444f.). The notice seems to be confirmed in the Assyrian annals (*ANET* 287; *TUAT* I, 389, where it is reported that the population and the nobles of Ekron (above 4.4.1.4) deposed their ruler and handed him over to 'Hezekiah the Judahite'; and from Sennacherib's 'letter to the deity' it emerges that Hezekiah occupied a royal Philistine city, profiting from the campaigns of Tiglath-pileser III and Sargon II (above 11.2 and 11.31.1)[5] to fight and subject the traditional enemy, which had now been weakened. Mittmann 1990 has demonstrated that this campaign was probably a political mistake on the part of the king, which rebounded against him.

12.2.3 However, the problem of the campaigns of Sargon II (a king who came to the throne following a *coup d'état*) and Sennacherib (c.704-681) in Canaan and the attitude of Hezekiah to Assyria on these occasions seems much more complex, also because of the confusion in chronological information.

12.2.3.1 There is no doubt that, at least to begin with, Hezekiah had continued the pro-Assyrian policy of his father Ahaz (above, 11.2.8). A first anti-Assyrian coalition, formed in about 720 by some city-states of the region, supported by Egypt and also including what was left of the Aramaean kingdom of Hamath and the Philistine kingdom of Gaza, together with the subject peoples of Samaria (above 11.3.3), does not seem to have included Judah in its ranks – if this is how we are to interpret the silence of the Assyrian sources (*ANET*, 285; *TUAT* I, 378ff.) and the lack of biblical texts, with perhaps the exception of Isa.14.28-32. The forces of the coalition were defeated and the few remaining independent nations were attacked (details in Donner* 1986, 313). The repression seems to have been harsh everywhere.

12.2.3.2 However, Hezekiah's attitude was different in the course of the rebellion of 713-711, when under the leadership of the Philistine city of Azotus (*'ašdōd*, coord.117-129, above 4.4.1.4), other Philistine cities, Edom and Moab in Transjordan and perhaps Babylon in Mesopotamia itself rebelled against Assyria. This time, too, the rebels were supported by Egypt, where from about 716 the Twenty-Fifth 'Ethiopian'

Dynasty had reigned, perhaps already under the Pharaoh Shabako (his dates are uncertain, perhaps 716-702). Two texts, Isa.20-16 (on the occasion of the occupation of Ashdod) and 18.1-8 (on the occasion of sending a delegation to Egypt), seem to refer to this revolt. However, the Philistine cities were occupied and annexed, though the other members of the coalition, including Judah, succeeded in avoiding the worst by withdrawing in time.

12.2.3.3 In 705, on the death of Sargon II, his successor Sennacherib found the empire in revolt and had a long struggle to secure the throne. This time Hezekiah seems to have taken the initiative in the region; indeed the coalition forces handed over to him the king of Ekron, a Philistine city which had not wanted to participate in the alliance (above 12.2.2, *ANET*, 287f.; *TUAT* I, 289ff.). The coalition also relied on Egyptian help, despite the contrary view that the biblical tradition attributes to the prophet Isaiah (30.1-5; 31.1-3). But this Egyptian help, too, did not arrive. According to II Kings 20.12-19//Isa.39.1-8//II Chron 32.25-39 (the last is the best text) Hezekiah even entered into negotiations with Merodach-Baladan (Marduk-apal-iddina, c.721-710 and 704-703) of Babylon who had declared his independence, proposing an alliance with him. However, at this point scholars are divided: according to Brinkman 1984 this will have happened at the end of the last period, i.e. around 704-3, but according to Cogan and Tadmor 1988 it will have been at the end of the first period, around 713-11. Is it possible that there was a second rebellion by Babylon towards the end of the century? Be this as it may, Babylon rebelled against Assyria at least once, in 713-11 or 704-3, and declared its own independence, and with that a large part of the Near East was in revolt. However, Sennacherib quickly succeeded in taming the Babylonian revolt and then turned westwards, defeating first the Philistines and then an Egyptian army in the battle of *altāqu*, Hebrew *'eltᵉqē*, perhaps present-day *tell eš-šallāf*, coord.128-144, finally to attack Judah from the south (*ANET*, 287f.; *TUAT* I, 388f.). Only Lachish (probably present-day *tell ed-duweir*, coord.135-108) and Jerusalem succeeded in resisting. Lachish soon fell (see the famous reliefs of the siege and the destruction of Lachish in the British Museum in London, *ANEP*, 327ff.), but Jerusalem, its fortifications and its water system (II Kings 20.20; II Chron.32.1-4; Isa.22.9b; cf. Sir.48.17⁶) had been restored and reinforced shortly beforehand, resisted succesfully; Isa.1.4-9 shows the consequences of the siege.

12.2.3.4 However, the account of the siege which appears in the texts II Kings 18;19//Isa.36.2-22; 37.1-7//II Chron.32.1ff. (with the notable exception of the annalistic-style text II Kings 18.13-16, Cogan and Tadmor 1988) is certainly much later than the events, so that it can be used only minimally to reconstruct them. De Jong 1984 has suggested that the true addressees of the narrative were the exiles, from 587-6 onwards, while Garbini 1981 proposed an even later date, as did Catastini 1982; recently, Cogan and Tadmor have also associated themselves with this position.

12.2.3.5 There is a variety of information about the outcome of the campaign, often contradictory. According to II Kings 18.17ff.// Isa.36-39//II Chron.32.1-19, the city was saved at the last moment by a miracle (Childs 1967, Garbini 1981); in the annals of Sennacherib (*ANET*, 288; *TUAT* I, 389), we read: 'As to Hezekiah, the Judahite, he did not submit to my yoke. I laid siege to forty-six of his strong cities, walled forts and to the countless small villages in their vicinity, and conquered (them) by means of well-stamped (earth-)ramps, and battering-rams brought (this) near (to the walls) (Combined with) the attack by foot soldiers, (using) mines, breaches as well as sapper work... Himself I made a prisoner in Jerusalem, his royal residence, like a bird in a cage.'

However, the Assyrian annals, too, say nothing about a conquest of the city. It is probable that Sennacherib was content to receive substantial tribute from Hezekiah, as the annals report (*ANET*, 288; *TUAT* I, 390): 'Hezekiah... deserted by his irregular and elite troops, did send me, later, to Nineveh, a tribute.' He then goes on to describe the tribute in detail: his description differs only in some points from that given in II Kings 18.13-16. However, the fact that Sennacherib was now at Nineveh and that the emissaries of Hezekiah could reach him there shows that he had lifted the siege. That leads us to suspect that other factors, probably political, had led him to raise the siege and return home and accept the tribute of the rebel Hezekiah. In the present state of research it is impossible to determine what these factors were. So the capital Jerusalem succeeded in surviving unscathed what had clearly been the catastrophe of the nation, which was virtually destroyed. Isaiah 22.1-14 therefore protests against a victory song sung by the people of Jerusalem when the siege was lifted.

12.2.3.6 The apparent contradiction between the notice which speaks of the miraculous deliverance of Jerusalem and that about the tribute paid by Hezekiah and accepted by the besieger has led some modern scholars to postulate two campaigns by Sennacherib, which the redactors later confused. The first could have ended in 701 with the tribute and the submission of Hezekiah; the second would have ended in 688 with the miraculous liberation.[7] This is an explanation which would resolve almost all the problems, but it comes up against insurmountable difficulties: the first is that the annals speak of just one campaign against Judah, that of 701; the second is that chronological difficulties then arise with the person of the Pharaoh mentioned in the narrative (something which moreover is accepted by Bright* 1981, 309, who is one of the supporters of the hypothesis of two campaigns); there are other features in the studies by Hutter 1982 and Cogan and Tadmor 1988, 248ff. It seems much more likely that the sudden and unexpected acceptance by Sennacherib of the tribute and Hezekiah's submission were transformed by the later legendary narrative into a miraculous divine intervention (thus already Noth* 1959, 268 n.3).

12.2.3.7 On the other hand, caution is needed over rationalizing explanations, the best-known of which is that of a plague which broke out among the besiegers[8] (a proposal based on information reported by Herodotus II, 141, that the camp was invaded by rats, who devoured everything made of leather: in fact these will have been bearers of bubonic plague), or historical ones: the Assyrians will have left in haste because of the outbreak of new disorders in Babylon. All these explanations leave things as they are once it is accepted that the narrative is the product of a later theological interpretation of a fact which is otherwise inexplicable.

12.2.3.8 According to II Kings 19.37//Isa.37.38, Sennacherib was killed by two of his sons in a temple. The information is in part confirmed by the annals (*ANET*, 288f.; *TUAT* I, 391f.; for details cf. Parpola 1982).

12.3 Manasseh and Amon kings of Judah

In the decades between the Assyrian invasions and Josiah's reform we find two kings on the throne of David, Manasseh and Amon, both of whom the Deuteronomistic historiography condemns as wicked and impious.

Bibliography

L.W.Fuller, *The Historical and Religious Significance of the Reign of Manasseh*, Leipzig 1912: A.Malamat, 'The Historical Background of the Assassination of Amon, King of Judah', *IEJ* 3, 1953, 26-9; E.L.Ehrlich, 'Der Aufenthalt des Königs Manasse in Babylon', *TZ* 21, 1965, 281-6; E.Nielsen, 'Political Conditions and Cultural Development in Israel and Judah during the Reign of Manasseh', in *Proceedings of the Fourth World Congress of Jewish Studies, Jerusalem 1965*, Jerusalem 1967, I, 103-6; J.W.McKay, *Religion in Judah under the Assyrians* (above, 11.1); H.Spieckermann, *Juda unter Assur in der Sargonidenzeit*, FRLANT 129, Göttingen 1982, 160ff., 307ff.; M.Broshi, 'Expansion of Jerusalem' (above 12.1); M.Cogan, *Imperialism and Religion* (above 11.1); E.Ben-Zvi, 'The Account of the Reign of Manasseh in II Reg 21,1-18 and the Redactional History of the Book of Kings', *ZAW* 103, 1991, 355-75; W.M.Schniedewind, 'The Source Citations of Manasseh: King Manasseh in History and Homily', *VT* 41, 1991, 450-61.

12.3.1 The legacy left by king Hezekiah, who is described by the biblical texts as having been just and pious, was a bitter one. With the exception of the capital, the country was completely in ruins, the economy was devastated, and its territory was markedly reduced and to a large extent under foreign occupation. This legacy was passed on to his son and successor Manasseh (c.687-642). According to the biblical texts he reigned for fifty-five years (II Kings 21.1-18//II Chron.33.1-20), though this figure must be somewhat reduced since he cannot have reigned longer than around forty-five. However, that is still a long reign. According to the sources he acceded to the throne at the age of twelve, which made a regency or some other form of safeguarding the exercise of affairs of state indispensable: this will have lasted for just under a decade. So it will have been under this provisional form of government that those provisions in the political and religious sphere must have taken shape which the biblical history is unanimous in condemning. In Manasseh's reign, Canaanite and syncretistic cults are said to have flourished as never before, even in the temple of Jerusalem, while again under him, 'innocent blood' is supposed to have been copiously shed (II Kings 21.16). The texts do not indicate what they are alluding to, but the tone of the account suggests that, as in the time of Ahab of Israel (above 10.10.8), those faithful to YHWH were cruelly persecuted.

12.3.2 II Chronicles 33.11-17 adds another episode to Manasseh's biography, this time an edifying one: he is said to have been taken to Babylon (sic!) by the Assyrians after the failure of a rebellion and there to have undergone a crisis of faith, followed by a conversion to orthodox Judaism. Following these events, after his return to Jerusalem he is said to have purified the temple from the foreign objects that he himself had put in them. This theme proved popular: a deutero-canonical writing, the Prayer of Manasseh (which was not included in the Roman Catholic canon),[9] reports a prayer which he pronounced on this occasion. This time, too, the reality seems more prosaic. This is a pious legend which seeks to explain how it was possible for a wicked king to have been able to reign for such a long time.

According to the annals of Esarhaddon (*ANET*, 291; *TUAT* I, 397), Manasseh was always a loyal vassal; later, under Assur-bani-pal (*ANET*, 294; *TUAT* I, 397), he made a journey to Nineveh, the capital of Assyria, to deliver the tribute in person, and there he appears on a list of kings who did the same thing. This event must have been repeated periodically, so that it is not possible to speak of a deportation.

12.3.3 Despite the scarcity of information, it is possible to provide quite a clear framework for the reign of Manasseh. Judah was now in what we have seen to be (above 11.1.5.2) the second phase of subjection; it was thus still in a situation of vassalage, in which the rulers had a certain freedom of action, though quite minimal. The Assyrian sources state that Hezekiah had been deprived of a large part of his territory, which was distributed to allied nations and loyal vassals of the empire, especially the Philistines; all that he had left was little more than the territory of the city-state of Jerusalem. Thus it seems that there was a Philistine garrison under Assyrian command at Lachish (coord.135-108; Donner* 1986, 327 n.46, with bibliography, even states that 'the old... kingdom of Judah had ceased to exist because of the territorial provisions of Sennacherib'). It is no wonder that in such circumstances Manasseh had attempted to arrive at an agreement with his adversary. This was crowned with success: in fact it seems that later a large part of Judah was restored to him, though we do not know on what conditions and in what circumstances. Be this as it may, the country was economically ruined and some important cities continued to be unoccupied.

12.3.4 A little later, with the conquest of Egypt, Assyria achieved its maximum territorial extension (above 11.1.6): in 671 Esarhaddon defeated the Pharaoh Tirhakah and occupied Memphis; in 667 Esarhaddon's son Asshur-bani-pal overcame him. However, Egyptian resistance never diminished and, despite the death of Tirhakah, the Assyrians had once again to march southwards, even conquering Thebes; this episode must have made a great impression in Judah as well, as witnessed by the mention of the fact in Nahum 3.8-10. In circumstances like these Manasseh had no room for manoeuvre, and no responsible politician could have thought of rebellion or even of resistance.

12.3.5 According to II Kings 21.12-26//II Chron 33.21-25, Amon, Manasseh's son (c.642-640), must have followed in his father's footsteps. He was assassinated in a palace revolt (*'abdē 'āmōn*) perhaps organized by anti-Assyrian groups (Malamat 1953), but the 'people of the land' (above 1.13.3) punished the assassins and put his eight-year-old son on the throne in his place. This son was regarded by the Deuteronomistic history as the best king since David.

12.4 King Josiah

With the accession of Josiah to the throne (c.640-609 or 639-609, or, better, according to H.Tadmor, 639/38-609) the Deuteronomistic historians present the reforming king *par excellence*. As such he was capable of crystallizing in political options the faithfulness to the God of Israel of the various groups which were headed by the prophets. Such groups will have found their fullest expression in the book of Deuteronomy and later in the Deuteronomistic history.

Bibliography

A.Alt, 'Judas Gaue unter Josia', *PJB* 21, 1925, 100-16 = *KS* II, 276-88;
H.L.Ginsberg, 'Judah and the Transjordan States from 734-582 BC', in
Alexander Marx Jubilee Volume, New York 1950, 347-68; F.M.Cross and
D.N.Freedman, 'Josiah's Revolt against Assyria', *JNES* 12, 1953, 56-8;
D.J.Wiseman, *Chronicles* (above 12.1); A.Jepsen, 'Die Reform des Josia',
in *FS F.Baumgärtel*, Erlangen 1959, 97-108; F.M.Cross and D.N.Freed-
man, 'Epigraphic Notes on the Hebrew Documents of the Eighth-
Sixth Centuries BC', *BASOR* 165, 1962, 34-46; E.W.Nicholson, 'The
Centralization of the Cult in Deuteronomy', *VT* 13, 1963, 380-9; M.Wein-
feld, 'Cult Centralization in Israel in the Light of a Neo-Babylonian
Analogy', *JNES* 2, 1964, 202-12; H.Tadmor, 'Philistia under Assyrian
Rule', *BA* 29, 1966, 86-102; H.Cazelles, 'Sophonie, Jérémie et les Scytes
en Palestine', *JNES* 23, 1964, 202-12; E.W.Nicholson, *Deuteronomy
and Tradition*, Oxford 1967; S.Loersch, *Das Deuteronomium und seine
Deutungen*, Stuttgart 1967; S.B.Frost, 'The Death of Josiah: A Conspiracy
of Silence', *JBL* 87, 1968, 369-82; P.Welten, *Die Königs-Stempel. Ein
Beitrag zur Militärpolitik Judas unter Hiskia und Josia*, ADPV, Wiesbaden
1969; E.Nielsen, 'Political Conditions' (above 12.3); M.Weinfeld, *Deuteronomy and the Deuteronomistic School*, London 1972; H.D.Lance, 'The
Royal Stamps and the Kingdom of Josiah', *HTR* 64, 1972, 315-32;
R.P.Vaggione, 'Over All Asia? The Extent of the Scythian Domination
in Herodotus', *JBL* 92, 1973, 523-30; W.E.Claburn, 'The Fiscal Basis of
Josiah's Reform', ibid., 11-22; A.Malamat, 'Josiah's Bid for Armaged-
don', *JANESCU* 5, 1973, 267-78; E.Würthwein, 'Das josianische Reform
und das Deuteronomium', *ZTK* 73, 1976, 395-423; W.Dietrich, 'Josiah
und das Gesetzbuch', *VT* 27, 1977, 13-35; M.Rose, 'Bemerkungen zum
historischen Fundament des Josia-Bildes in II Reg.22f.', *ZAW* 89, 1977,
50-63; G.S.Ogden, 'The Northern Extent of Josiah's Reforms', *AustBR*
26, 1978, 26-34; H.-D.Hoffmann, *Reform und Reformen*, ATANT 66,
Zurich 1980, 169ff.; H.G.M.Williamson, 'The Death of Josiah and the
Continuing Development of the Deuteronomic History', *VT* 32, 1982,
242-8; M.Delcor, 'Reflexions sur la Pâque du temps de Josias d'après II
Rois 23, 21-23', *Hen* 4, 1982, 205-19; H-D.Preuss, *Deuteronomium*,
Darmstadt 1982; H.Spieckermann, *Juda unter Assur in der Sargonidenzeit*,
FRLANT 129, Göttingen 1982; B.J.Diebner and C.Nauerth, 'Die Inven-
tion des *sfr twrh* in 2 Kön 22 – Struktur, Intention und Funktion
von Auffindungslegenden', *DBAT* 18, 1984, 95-118; D.L.Christensen,
'Zephaniah 2:4-15: A Theological Base for Josiah's Program of Political
Expansion', *CBQ* 46, 1984, 669-82; Y.Suzuki, 'Deuteronomic Refor-
mation in View of the Centralization of the Administration of Justice',
AJBI 13, 1987, 22-58; C.T.Begg, 'The Death of Josiah in Chronicles:
Another View', *VT* 37, 1987, 1-8; H.G.M.Williamson, 'Reliving the

Death of Josiah. A Reply to C.T.Begg', ibid., 9-15; N.Lohfink, 'The Cult Reform of Josiah of Judah: 2 Kings 22-23 as a Source for the History of Israelite Religion', in *Ancient Israelite Religion. Essays... F.M.Cross*, Philadelphia 1987, 459-75; C.T.Begg, 'The Death of Josiah – Josephus and the Bible', *ETL* 64, 1988, 157-63; M.Cogan and H.Tadmor, *II Kings*, New York 1988; I.Eph'al and J.Naveh, 'Hazael's Booty Inscriptions', *IEJ* 39, 1989, 192-200; E.Talstra, 'De hervorming van Josia, of de kunst van het beeldstormen', *GThT* 88, 1988, 143-61; P.Tagliacarne, *'Keiner war wie er' – Untersuchungen zur Struktur von 2 Könige 22-23*, St Ottilien 1989; K.Koch, 'Gefüge und Herkunft des Berichts über die Kultreformen des Königs Josia', in *Alttestamentlicher Glaube und Biblische Theologie – FS H.D.Preuss*, Stuttgart 1992, 80-92; G.N.Knoppers, ' "There Was None Like Him". Incomparability in the Book of Kings', *CBQ* 54, 1992, 411-31.

12.4.1 *Politics*. According to the biblical sources, Josiah not only presided over a religious reform but also sought to restore the Davidic empire, profiting from the decadence of the Assyrian empire (below 12.4.1.1). He achieved this by reconquering territories which had once belonged to the kingdom of Israel (above 11.3); such an enterprise, according to II Chron.34.6, was also largely successful. However, it is impossible to check these assertions (Ogden 1978); a similar thesis was also put forward by Dtr (Lemche* 1988, 169ff.), but this has been put in doubt with good reasons by Spieckermann 1982, 112ff., 150ff.: for the latter this will have been a fantasy, since Josiah lacked the troops for an enterprise of this kind. This also explains his defeat near Megiddo. In the archaeological sphere, too, there is no trace of this conquest. On the other hand, the fact that Pharaoh Necho II encountered Josiah (in battle? below 12.4.6.1) near Megiddo would suggest that at least part of the North had been occupied.

12.4.1.1 The Assyrian empire was in a phase of progressive disintegration, and the territories belonging to the North had thus become a kind of no man's land. In 625 the capital Nineveh had been besieged for the first time by the Medes under Cyaxares (625-585, *ANET*, 303ff.; not in *TUAT*), while Babylon, under Napo-polassar (625-605), had regained its independence. Tribes from the northern territories (according to Herodotus I, 102, the Scythians and groups called *umman manda*) pillaged the region, interrupting communications (details in Cogan and Tadmor 1988, 282ff. and Na'aman 1991). Under the concentric attack of the Medes, the Babylonian tribes from the north, and Egypt under Psammetichus I (664-610), Assyria was soon reduced to a rump. The *coup de grâce* was delivered in 612, when the capital fell under the attack of the Medes and the Babylonians. Nahum 2.1; 3.19 (cf. my

Introduction, ch.22.1) refer to these events (details in Donner* 1986, 339ff.).

12.4.1.2 However, the various excavations made in territories peripheral to Judah show that the country enlarged its boundaries southwards, and the discovery of the ostraca of Tell 'Arad and of Greek pottery here attest the presence of Greek mercenaries, probably in the service of Egypt, but paid by Judah (above 1.5.2); these must have been groups similar to those later described by Xenophon in the *Anabasis*.

12.4.1.3 Finally, the expansion of the kingdom is confirmed by the list of twelve provinces in Josh.15.21-63. Alt in 1925 dated this to the time of king Josiah, and that still seems to be the best explanation of these texts. Jerusalem, too, was considerably enlarged at this period (cf. Broshi 1974 and Aharoni** 1979, ch.V).

12.4.2 *The life of Josiah and his religious reform*. For the life of Josiah see II Kings 22-23; II Chron. 34.1-35.19.

12.4.2.1 Although the two texts refer to the same events and thus have many features in common, they show significant differences on important questions. Their main interest is certainly in the cult and its reforms, a feature which II Kings connects with the discovery in the temple, during the work of maintenance and restoration, of a scroll of the Torah which was hidden there. It should be noted that the book is given the definite article, *sēper hattōrāh*, 'the book' and not 'a book'. The reader of II Kings is given the impression that very little time elapsed between the discovery of the book and the reform, and that the first event was the direct cause of the second, both taking place in the eighteenth year of this king's reign. What II Chronicles tells us seems different (though Spieckermann attaches minimal credibility to it): the two sources agree on the fact that Josiah ascended the throne at the age of eight, which would again necessitate a regency since he had not attained his majority. However, Chronicles puts the conversion of the monarch in the eighth year of his reign and the beginning of the reform in the twelfth year, i.e. all still within the period of the regency; moreover, for Chronicles the reform is not limited to 'Judah and Jerusalem' but will have extended 'to the cities of Manasseh, Ephraim, and Simeon, and as far as Naphtali, in their ruins round about' (the last term is uncertain and is usually read on the basis of the Qere, 34.5-6). However, II Kings 23.19 speaks of 'all the cities of Samaria': this is the first time in the Hebrew Bible that this name denotes the region and not the city.

12.4.2.2 According to Chronicles the reform did not have anything to do with the finding of the book, which took place at the end of the process, but should be seen in the wider context of the reconquest of the North and, in the South, of the territories lost to the Philistines during the Assyrian invasions, i.e. Simeon.

12.4.3 Compared with its predecessors, Josiah's reform was characterized by its radicalism and its rapidity (Lohfink 1987, 467ff.): any alternative and any form of compromise seem to have been excluded *a priori*, at least on a programmatic level. Any kind of Canaanite cult or practice, any kind of syncretism, had to be suppressed; the cult had to be centralized on the sanctuary in Jerusalem, suitably purified of the objects, persons and practices connected with the Canaanite world. And all this was to be followed by the total destruction of the local sanctuaries outside the temple along with their cults, everything taking place in a very short time. Obviously a programme of this kind would have come up against resistance and so clearly would have been difficult to implement; nor is it surprising that it could not be implemented everywhere with the same zeal (Oded in Hayes and Miller* 1977, 460ff.). It is not surprising that there were a number of sanctuaries which escaped destruction.[10] It is also probable that the whole process took some time, and that it was not possible to implement it in compulsory stages. So Oded (ibid.) seems to be right in concluding that the reform, although sponsored by the court and supported without reservations by the prophets, by those elements of the population who were more mature in religious matters, and by the Jerusalem priesthood, took considerably longer than the sources would have us believe. Thus for example (below 13.11.6) we can see that a few centuries later relations between the Jewish community of Elephantine in Egypt and the priesthood of the temple were constant and cordial; this is a disconcerting fact given the principles expounded in the reform.

12.4.4 For the content of the book the reader should see the *Introductions to the Old Testament* (in mine, ch.9.2,7), noting that in the ancient world, both East and West, it was by no means rare to back up the authority and the prestige of a work or to justify unusual measures by means of a miraculous discovery. That also explains why in the past the whole narrative has often been defined as a 'pious fraud' (against this thesis see Spieckermann 1982, 158ff.; cf. Cogan and Tadmor 1988, 294f.). Nor does it seem possible to establish whether parts of the books already existed beforehand (this is improbable, even if it is often argued for, since Deuteronomy, largely identified with the book which was found, gives the impression of being artificial, and obviously arose in circles connected with the temple and the court (cf. Soggin, *Introduction*, and Diebner and Nauerth 1984). Finally, if we remember that the study which is most often quoted (that of Hoffmann 1980) has noted the alternation of pious and therefore reforming rulers with impious rulers who annulled their reforms, the note about the discovery could belong precisely to this literary topos. And in his thesis at the Pontifical Biblical Institute in Rome, unfinished because of his premature death, F.Foresti[11] indicated with convincing arguments that the demand for this centraliz-ation of the cult could not have arisen before the exile, indeed, that it emerged specifically within the community of exiles.

12.4.5 It is also difficult, if not impossible, to establish whether the list of objects and persons removed from the temple and the practices which were abolished (II Kings 23.4-15//II Chron.34.3-5) are based on trustworthy documents or at least traditions, or whether this is simply polemic without real content. I have indicated above (10.10.7) what it is possible to reconstruct of the religion of Israel and Judah in the pre-exilic period, and that makes it probable that such objects and such persons were in fact present in the temple and that certain rites were practised there.

12.4.6 A small Assyrian nucleus survived in the region of Carchemish (present-day *jerāblus* on the Upper Euphrates), and an Egyptian expeditionary force under the command of Pharaoh Necho II (609-594), the successor of Psammetichus I, tried to bring it aid. This has paradoxical features, but it was in the interest of Egypt that there should be two nations in Mesopotamia rather than one united empire, a development which would again have represented a danger for Egypt. The biblical texts relating to this episode are II Chron.35.20-26, which reads 'Necho... went to fight at Carchemish...', while II Kings 23.29 specifically states *'al melek 'assūr*, 'against the king of Assyria'. This is clearly wrong; it is corrected on the basis of the Babylonian Chronicle and by Josephus, *Antt.* X, 75, who rightly reads, '...the Egyptian army, which had come *to his aid*'.

12.4.6.1 However, to reach northern Syria the Pharaoh had to cross the territories of the former kingdom of Israel, which the text indicates had been reconquered by Josiah. And in the attempt to bar Necho's passage Josiah was defeated (?) near Megiddo and killed. But given the present state of the sources it is impossible to establish what really happened, so much so that Frost 1968 even speaks of censorship. II Kings 23.29 states that 'Necho killed him at Megiddo as soon as he saw him'; II Chron. 35.20-25 and similarly Josephus speak of a delegation first sent by Necho to Josiah, calling on him to submit, perhaps in the context of the negotiations through which he was attempting to obtain passage (Williamson 1982, but cf. the discussion between him and Begg 1987). This request will have been refused. Josiah was mortally wounded (in battle?) and taken to Jerusalem, where he died soon afterwards (Donner* 1986, 356ff.).

12.4.6.2 However, it is not even certain whether the battle took place,[12] since the texts do not mention it explicitly; there are scholars who believe that Necho succeeded in taking Josiah prisoner and killed him as soon as it became clear that he did not intend to submit.

12.5 Twilight

The last years of the kingdom of Judah, which Malamat 1975 rightly calls 'the twilight of Judah', were characterized by two kings, Jehoiakim (c.609-598) and Jehoiachin (c.597), and a regent, Zedekiah (597-587/86), all of somewhat mediocre stature. The chief events were the two sieges of the capital, the first followed by a deportation of the nobility, the second by the destruction of the temple and by other deportations. We do not know 'as much as we would like to know' (Donner* 1986, 371) about this period. In 587 or 586 (for the year cf. below 12.6.6) the nation virtually ceased to exist, even if, as we shall see, some scholars maintain with weighty arguments that the extinction was not total (also below 12.7.6). Independence was regained only in the second century (165-163 BCE, below 14.9), to be lost again in 63, when Judaea was occupied by Pompey, for about two millennia, until the foundation of the State of Israel.

Bibliography

M.David, 'The Manumission of Slaves under Zedekiah', *OTS* 5, 1948, 63-79; M.Noth, 'The Jerusalem Catastrophe of 587 BC and its Significance for Israel', in *The Laws in the Pentateuch*, Edinburgh 1966, 260-80; D.J.Wiseman, *Chronicles* (above, 12.1); H.Tadmor, 'Chronology of the Last Kings of Judah', *JNES* 15, 1956, 222-30; M.Greenberg, 'Ezekiel 17 and the Policy of Psammetichus II', *JBL* 76, 1957, 676-97; M.Noth, 'Die Einnahme von Jerusalem im Jahre 597 BC', *ZDPV* 74, 1958, 135-57 = *ABLAK* I, 111-32; M.Tsevat, 'The Neo-Assyrian and Neo-Babylonian Vassal Oaths and the Prophet Ezekiel', *JBL* 78, 1959, 199-204; G.Larsson, 'When did the Babylonian Captivity Begin?', *JTS* 18, 1967, 417-23; A.Malamat, 'The Last Kings of Judah and the Fall of Jerusalem', *IEJ* 18, 1968, 137-56; K.S.Freedy and D.B.Redford, 'The Dates in Ezekiel in Relation to Biblical, Babylonian and Egyptian Sources', *JAOS* 90, 1970, 462-85; J.M.Myers, 'Edom and Judah in the Sixth-Fifth Centuries BC', in *Near Eastern Studies... W.F.Albright*, Baltimore 1971, 377-92; S.S.Weinberg, 'Post-exilic Palestine: An Archaeological Report', *IASHP* 4, 1971, 78-97; H.Cazelles, 'Le roi Yoyakin et le Serviteur du Seigneur', in *Proceedings of the Fifth World Congress of Jewish Studies, Jerusalem 1969*, Jerusalem 1973, I, 121-6; E.Kutsch, 'Das Jahr der Katastrophe: 587 v.Chr.', *Bibl* 55, 1974, 520-45; A.Malamat, 'The Twilight of Judah: In the Egyptian-Babylonian Maelstrom', *SVT* 28, 1975, 123-45; E.Stern, 'Israel at the Close of the Monarchy: An Archaeological Survey', *BA* 38, 1975, 26-54; A.R.Green, 'The Fate of Joiakim', *AUSS* 20, 1982, 103-9: A.Schenker, 'Nebuchadnezzars Metamorphose – vom Unterjocher zum Gottesknecht', *RB* 89, 1982, 498-527; H.Cazelles, '587 ou 586?', in *'The Word of the Lord Shall Go Forth': Essays in Honor of D.N.Freedman*,

Winona Lake, Ind. 1983, 427-35; S.de Jong, 'Hiskia en Zedekia', *Amsterdamse Cahiers* 5, 1984, 135-46; U.Worschech, 'War Nebukadnezzar im Jahre 605 vor Jerusalem?', *BN* 36, 1987, 57-60; A.Malamat, 'The Kingdom of Judah between Egypt and Babylon...', in *Text and Context... Studies for F.C.Fensham*, Sheffield 1988; id., 'The Last Years of the Kingdom of Judah', in *Archeology and Biblical Interpretation – Essays in Memory of D.G.Rose*, Atlanta, GA 1987, 287-314. For the problem of the succession of Josiah cf. Garbini* 1988, 47-51. On Babylon: D.J.Wiseman, *Nebuchadrezzar and Babylon*, London 1985; L.Cagni, 'Le fonti mesopotamiche dei periodi neobabilonese, achemenide e seleucida', *RiBib* 34, 1986, 1-53: 15ff. For the ostraca of Tell Arad cf. Y.Aharoni (ed.), *Arad Inscriptions*, Jerusalem 1975 (in Hebrew) and 1981 (English); bibliography in Soggin, *Introduction*, Appendix I.10.

12.5.1 According to the Deuteronomistic history the death of Josiah ruined the plans of those who had hoped for a reform of belief and the cult along monotheistic lines, on the basis of the message of the prophets; it also dashed the hopes of those who thought that Judah could exploit the hostility between Egypt and Mesopotamia politically, to its own advantage. With the death of Josiah, Judah had gone over to being a vassal of Egypt, for whom it was a northern bulwark; later it became a vassal of Babylon, whose southern advance post it was. And any attempt to lean now on one and now on the other failed. Whatever plans it had, the room for manoeuvre became increasingly small.

12.5.2 Meanwhile Necho II had gone on to Carchemish to bring his own plans to completion, and the 'people of the land' had crowned a son of Josiah king: his name was Jehoahaz (II Kings 23.30//II Chron 36.1), but in Jeremiah and I Chron.3.15 he is called Shallum (in III Ezra 1.32, however, he appears as Jehoiakin[13]). But the Pharaoh deposed him after he had reigned for a few months and replaced him with another son of the dead king, Eliakim, who, as a sign of obeisance to Necho, changed his name to Jehoiakim (II Kings 23.31-34//II Chron.36.3-4, cf. also Jer.22.10-12 and Ezek.19.4).

12.5.3 The new ruler is presented in the biblical history as a tyrant; he is said to have taxed the people heavily and to have been utterly tied to Egypt (II Kings 23.36-24.7; II Chron.36.5-8, cf.also Jer.22.13-19). On the other hand it seems that under him Judah succeeded in regaining the territories which it had under Manasseh (above 12.3.2). The serious fiscal measures are easily explained by the need to fulfil the demands imposed on him by victorious Egypt. However, Jer. 7 and 26 show the risks to anyone who dared to criticize government policy.

12.5.4 Judah remained a vassal of Egypt until 605, when Nebuchadnezzar II (605-561), written in Jeremiah more precisely as Nebuchadrezzar, Babylonian *nabū-kudurri-uṣur*), son of Nabo-polassar, defeated the Egyptians at Carchemish, thus forcing them to withdraw from Syria and Canaan. The battle, which is referred to in Jer.46.2, was followed by a period of Babylonian domination over the region. Judah also automatically fell under this, as is indicated by the Deuteronomistic text Jer.25.1ff.; the episode described in 36.1ff. will have taken place on this occasion (cf. also II Kings 24.1ff. and II Chron.36.5-8). In a letter sent to the Pharaoh by a certain *'ādōn*, probably a Philistine ruler of Ashkelon or Ekron (*TUAT* I, 633f.), and also to other rulers of the region,[14] and discovered at Saqqara in Egypt, the sender exhorts the Pharaoh to hasten to come to their help; but this time, too, no Egyptian aid was given and Ashkelon was destroyed, an event to which Jer.47.5-7 alludes.

12.5.5 *The first siege and first conquest of Jerusalem.* Jehoiakim remained a faithful vassal of Babylon until 601/600, when Necho again invaded Judah from the south, and succeeded in occupying Gaza (*ANET*, 563; *TUAT* I, 403; Wiseman, 70f.).[15] The king seems almost immediately to have sided with Egypt, despite the advice which the biblical tradition attributes to the prophet Jeremiah. Nebuchadnezzar left with a Babylonian expeditionary force, which was joined by Ammonite, Edomite and Moabite allies, in 598, and laid siege to Jerusalem. Jehoiakim died during the siege, we do not know in what circumstances, and his son Jehoiakim (also called Jeconiah) succeeded to the throne (II Kings 24.8-17//II Chron 36.9-10). The new king seems to have surrendered almost immediately to the Babylonians on the second of the month of Adar (15-16 March 597) according to the information in the Babylonian chronicles (while it does not mention the name of the king it substantially confirms the facts, *ANET*, 564; *TUAT* I, 403ff.; Wiseman, 66-73); the king, barely enthroned, was deported to Babylon, but was given favourable treatment there (II Kings 25.27-30; *ANET*, 308).[16] Nebuchadnezzar nominated another son of Josiah, Mattaniah, in his place, changing his name to Zedekiah. So the information given in Dan.1.1 is chronologically incorrect. The Babylonians deported part of the ruling class; those deported also included the prophet Ezekiel. The figures vary: II Kings 24.14 speaks of 10,000, 24.16 of 8,000, while Jer.52.28 gives 3,023; for other information see below 12.6.7. So it is not possible (nor very relevant) to establish how many people were deported (Malamat 1975). Judah entered the second stage of vassalage (Donner* 1986, 373).

12.6 The last year – the last king

Zedekiah's situation was anything but easy. On the one hand the legitimate king was still alive, though he was prevented from exercising his powers, so Zedekiah was in fact only a kind of regent, with limited authority. Consequently Ezek.1.2 counts the years from the date of Jehoiachin's deportation, while Jer.28.4 shows that he was expected to return at any moment, probably on the basis of prophecies which have not come down to us. On the other hand the country was divided into factions: the pro-Egyptian faction which sought to continue the political line begun by Jehoiakim, and the pro-Babylonian faction, begun by Jehoiachin, which accepted the sovereignty of Babylon; the latter was also supported by the prophet Jeremiah. Moreover it emerges from the texts that Zedekiah, as well as not having the authority, did not even have the strength of character and clarity of ideas which would have been necessary in such difficult conditions. Thus according to Jer.37-38, on the one hand he continuously consulted the prophet Jeremiah even when Jeremiah was in prison, and saved his life; on the other he was incapable of saving the prophet from ill-treatment, nor could he impose his own line, which largely coincided with that of Jeremiah, on the factions.

12.6.1 In 594/3 Zedekiah tried to form an anti-Babylonian coalition along with other rulers in the region, strongly opposed by Jeremiah (chs.27-28, but in Jer.27.1 read ṣidqīyāhū, Zedekiah, for yōyāqīm, Jehoiakim!). Egypt again seems to have been behind the coalition; under Psammetichus II (593-589) it was trying to regain a footing in Asia. For reasons unknown to us the plans came to nothing, and the king submitted, sending a delegation to Babylon (Jer.29.3; 51.59).

12.6.2 The attempt was repeated in 589/588, and this time again Egypt, under Hophra, the son of Psammetichus II (Hebrew ḥoprāh, Greek Ἀπρίες, 589-570), seems to have been involved in the enterprise. The third Lachish ostracon (*ANET*, 322; *TUAT* I, 621; *KAI*, 193) mentions the passage through the stronghold of a delegation on its way to Egypt; cf. also Josephus, *Contra Apionem* I, 21, who reports that Tyre also joined the revolt, while according to Ezek.21.24-25 Ammon too will have participated in it. Edom also seems to have taken part, though with little enthusiasm; indeed it was so unenthusiastic that as soon as it saw how things were turning out it joined the winning side (below 12.5.6). However, as Oded rightly notes in Hayes and Miller* 1977, 472, 'Nebuchadnezzar was at that moment at the height of his power and it would have taken more than a coalition of two or three kings to remove the power of Babylon from Phoenicia and Judaea.' Internal divisions also continued in Judah: on the one hand was the pro-Egyptian party, supported by the army and those prophets who announced the inviolability of Zion and the imminent return of the exiles (called 'false' prophets in Jer.5.12 and 14.13, cf. chs.7 and 26 and 28.1ff.), and on the other the group, including Jeremiah, which counselled submission to Babylon. In a moment of euphoria the

'Hebrew' slaves (for the term cf. above 6.6.3.1-5) were emancipated (Jer.34.8-22) in the hope of making the army stronger; however, as soon as the immediate danger was over the owners seem to have gone back on their word. Jeremiah denounces them for this (David 1948, Malamat 1968, 152).

12.6.3 *The second siege and destruction of Jerusalem.* This time Nebuchadnezzar struck without hesitation (II Kings 25.1ff.// Jer.52.1ff.; II Chron. 36.1; Jer.39.1-14). Probably in December 587 (the ninth year of Zedekiah's reign) or 586 (but, as we shall soon see, the chronology is uncertain) Jerusalem was besieged, and in August 587 or 586 it was captured, having received no help from the Egyptian alliance on which Judah had again counted and to which Jer.37.5,11; Ezek.17; 29-32; cf. Lam.4.17, allude: the Egyptian troops were defeated by the Babylonians before they could reach Jerusalem. There are more or less hidden allusions to these events in some prophetic texts, but they pose a complex problem because the texts are often too general (cf. Greenberg 1957, Tsevat 1969, Freedy and Redford 1970 and Myers 1971, who only give a synopsis).

12.6.4 Again, as at the time of the Assyrian invasions, the enemy first went south and then turned northwards. So there were first sieges of Lachish (coord.135-108), cf. the fourth ostracon (*ANET*, 324; *TUAT* I, 622; *KAI*, no.194), and then of Azekah (*tell ez-zakarīye*, coord.144-123). In this context the imprisonment of Jeremiah becomes understandable; as a supporter of the pro-Babylonian party (the Deuteronomistic redaction has even made the prophet call Nebuchadnezzar, 'servant, minister of YHWH', *'ebed yhwh'*, 25.9; 27.6; 43.10), he was naturally suspected of treachery; and when he tried to leave the capital to go to one of his properties (Jer.37.11-15) he was arrested, accused of treachery and dealings with the enemy (crimes which in wartime carry the death penalty), and imprisoned.

12.6.5 After a siege lasting eighteen months, the Babylonians succeeded in making a breach in the walls of Jerusalem; they captured the city and plundered it: the temple was burned and the fortifications were dismantled. Various places in Judah suffered a similar fate. The sacred vessels were carried to Babylon and the king was taken prisoner after a vain attempt to flee (Jer.39.2; 52.6; II Kings 25.3-7). The Babylonians blinded him after killing his kinsfolk; then they transported him to Babylon, where we lose track of him. The Edomites seem to have taken considerable advantage of this state of things: they succeeded in settling in the Negeb and were able to take part in the plundering (cf. Ezek.25.12-14; Obad.19; Lam.4.21; Ps.137.7).

12.6.6 However, the precise year of these events has not yet been established (Gunneweg* 1989, 124f.), because the sources are imprecise: II Kings 25.8 and others have the nineteenth year of Nebuchadnezzar, whereas Jer.52.29 speaks of the eighteenth year; and the corresponding section of the Babylonian Chronicle has not yet been found. To attribute this divergence to different chronological calculations, as some scholars attempt, does not match the complexity of the problems, since both texts originate from Judah and both presuppose the same calendar. Scholars fluctuate between 587 (Kutsch 1974; Bright* 1981, 330; Aharoni, *Archaeology*, 407) and 586 (Malamat 1968, with a detailed discussion, 1975 and 1987, Freedy and Redford 1970 and Tadmor 1976 and 1979), but it is impossible to come to a final decision (Oded in Hayes and Miller* 1977, 473ff.).

12.6.7 This time, too, part of the ruling class and some craftsmen were deported: Jer.52.28-30 speaks of 832 people, and later (below 12.7.72) there is mention of another 745. If these figures are correct (and they seem more credible than those mentioned above, 12.5.5), this was quite a modest quantity. In accordance with the Babylonian system, which differed from the Assyrian (above 11.1.5.3), a governor was nominated who was drawn from the local nobility. His name was Gedaliah (Jer.40.7; II Kings 25.22ff.); he was probably the son of the Ahikam who years before had protected and probably saved Jeremiah (26.24). A seal which reads 'Gedaliah, superintendent at the palace'[17] suggests that he must already have been a high official. He lived at Mizpah (coord.170-143, cf. above 10.8.5). Moreover the Babylonians began an interesting project of colonization by means of local elements from the population; they distributed the lands of those who had been deported to what today we would call the sub-proletariat of the city and the country (Jer.39.10; II Kings 25.12//Jer.52.16; cf. Ezek.33.21-27). By this method the Babylonians created a class of small landowners who were not imported from abroad and whose rights were not based on inheritance or purchase but on the intervention of the occupying power; they owed everything to it and were therefore unconditionally loyal. This policy inevitably created major problems during the restoration, when the deportees who returned home reclaimed their own lands, or an adequate indemnity for them (below 13.9.8).

12.7 Judah during the exile

The destruction of Jerusalem, its fortifications and temple, followed by the deportation of the most prominent members of the population, led to about half a century of eclipse for Judah in its own territory. In exile in Babylon what now considered itself to be the élite of the population continued its life in a conscious form. This is what is usually called the 'exilic period'.

Bibliography

A.Alt, 'Die Rolle Samarias bei der Enstehung des Judentums', in *FS Otto Procksch*, Leipzig 1934, 5-28 = *KS* II, 316-37; J.N.Wilkie, 'Nabonidus and the Later Jewish Exiles', *JTS* NS 2, 1951, 36-44; G.Cardascia, *Les Archives de Murasu*, Paris 1951; H.L.Ginsberg, 'Judah and the Transjordan States from 734 to 582 BC', in *Alexander Marx Jubilee Volume*, New York 1950, 347-68; C.F.Whitley, *The Exilic Age*, London 1957; E.Janssen, *Juda in der Exilszeit*, FRLANT 69, Göttingen 1956; D.W.Thomas, 'The Sixth Century BC: A Creative Epoch in the History of Israel', *JSS* 6, 1961, 33-46; P.R.Ackroyd, *Exile and Restoration*, London and Philadelphia 1968; E.Zwenger, 'Die deuteronomistische Interpretation der Rehabilitation Jojachins', *BZ* 12, 1968, 16-30; S.S.Weinberg, *Pre-exilic Palestine* (above 12.5); L.Perlitt, 'Anklage und Freispruch Gottes', *ZTK* 69, 1972, 290-303; M.D.Coogan, 'Life in the Diaspora; Jews at Nippur in the Fifth Century BC', *BA* 37, 1974, 6-12; P.R.Ackroyd, 'An Interpretation of the Babylonian Exile', *JTS* 29, 1975, 171-80; M.D.Coogan, *West Semitic Personal Names in the Murasu Documents*, HSM 7, Cambridge, Mass. 1976; R.Zadok, *The Jews in Babylon during the Chaldaean and Persian Periods*, Tel Aviv 1976 (in Hebrew); id., 'Notes on the Early History of the Israelites and Judaeans in Mesopotamia', *Or* 15, 1982, 391-3; R.W.Klein, *Israel in Exile*, Philadelphia 1979; E.Stern, *CHJ* I, 1984, 70-87; I.Eph'al, 'On the Political and Social Organization of the Jews in the Babylonian Exile', in *XXI Deutscher Orientalistentag 1987*, Wiesbaden 1983, 106-112; C.R.Seitz, 'The Crisis of Interpretation over the Meaning and Purpose of the Exile', *SVT* 35, 1985, 78-97; W.Herrmann, 'Das Aufleben des Mythos unter den Judäern während des Babylonischen Zeitalters', *BN* 40, 1987, 97-129; Donner* 1986, 383ff. and Garbini* 1988, 192 n.5 (with bibliography); G.Mayer, 'Zur jüdischen Geschichte', *TR* 55, 1990, 1-20; and T.L.Thompson, *Early History of the Israelite People*, Leiden 1992, 348ff. (I was able to use only parts of this important work).

12.7.1 Those who were deported seem to have considered themselves to be the better part of Judah, the 'elect remnant' announced by the prophets,[18] or were considered such by exilic and post-exilic historiography, especially the Deuteronomistic history. They were moreover the ruling class and the craftsman, and therefore more educated and theologically more advanced. Furthermore, these were the ones who collected and edited what had been salvaged of the traditions of their people. It is probable that the most important part of the Deuteronomistic history and probably also Deuteronomy were composed in this setting.

12.7.2 Contrary to Assyrian practice, the Babylonians did not disperse those whom they deported in an attempt to liquidate them ethnically and politically, but settled them in compact groups, especially in the southern region of the country, near to the 'great canal', the watercourse which brought the waters of the Euphrates close to Babylon. This canal passed by Nippur and re-entered the Euphrates near to Uruk (Hebrew *'erek*, present-day Arab *wārkā*). In Hebrew it is called *nᵉhar kᵉbār*, a transcription of the Accadian *nārukabāru*, probably to be identified with the modern *saṭṭ en-nīl* near Nippur (cf. Ezek.1.1ff. and Jer.29.5ff.; Ezra 2.59//Neh.7.61 mention other places). The place called Tell Abib in Hebrew is probably the distortion of an unknown Accadian name. In this region the exiles could meet freely, buy land, build houses and communicate with the homeland. Thus the first nucleus of the Hebrew Diaspora came into being.

12.7.3 All this presupposes that those who had been deported enjoyed relative freedom; and thanks to their situation they soon achieved a degree of prosperity. In the archives of the bank of Murashu and Sons discovered in Nippur in the course of the excavations carried out by the University of Pennsylvania towards the end of the last century (though these date from the fifth century), among the bank's clients we find many Jewish names, recognizable as such because they have YHWH as an element in them: this is a sign that after little more than a century the sitaution of some of those who had been deported was even prosperous; and according to some scholars (most recently Garbini* 1988, with bibliography) even the bank called Casa Egibi will have been Jewish – this is perhaps a corruption of a name composed with the root *'āqab*. So to talk of 'deportation' or 'exile' is appropriate, but to use terms like 'captivity' does not fit the reality of the facts.

12.7.4 Despite this, the exile was always felt by the biblical tradition to be one of the great fundamental breaks in the long history of the people, one of the worst catastrophes:[19] not only was it the end of political independence, but the dynasty which divine oracles had once said would last for ever had collapsed, and with it the underlying ideology of the people of Judah. For this reason the prophets of the exilic period, first Jeremiah and then Ezekiel, tried to keep alive among the people the hope of a restoration in their homeland. Indeed, Ezekiel 40-48 is simply a large-scale and detailed programme for the rebuilding of the temple, the restoration of its worship and the reconstitution of the state. However, the head of the state was no longer to bear the title *melek*, 'king', but only *nāśī'*, 'prince', and was to be subject to the demands of the cult.[20] Here we have the first signs of what would later be the 'hierocracy' - though this must be dated later than it was a few years ago (below 14.7.4.8). At all events, after the attempt by Zerubbabel to re-establish the dynasty (below ch. 13, n.19), the figure of the prince disappears and we have only that of the governor.

12.7.5 It is probable that during the exile the practice of circumcision, sabbath observance and the organic system of dietary laws became particularly important: they were visible signs by which even foreigners could recognize membership of the people of God (Noth* 1959, 297). For other scholars, however, this matter is controversial, and we shall be returning to it later (below 13.11.5); the institution of the synagogue will have taken shape and developed during this period. Be this as it may, it is certain that through the exiles Judah was subjected to a strong Babylonian influence; it adopted the Mesopotamian calendar (the months of which are still used today). People took Babylonian names, as we can clearly see from the leaders of the restoration; the influence of Aramaic was also very important, and it rapidly became the *lingua franca* of the region. The square script was adopted, which is still in use today, in place of the Phoenician script; Aramaic rapidly took the place of Hebrew in everyday life; and Hebrew was now increasingly limited to matters that were closely connected with the cult and with theological discussion.[21]

12.7.6 The situation of those who had remained in the homeland seems to have been difficult, probably more difficult than that of the exiles, even if many of them had been favoured by the distribution of land made by the Babylonians (above 12.6.7). A negative factor to set against that was the destruction of social and economic structures in which those who had benefitted could have expressed themselves and developed.

Bibliography

G.Buccellati, 'Gli Israeliti di Palestina al tempo dell'esilio', *BeO* 2, 1965, 199-210; H.-P.Müller, 'Phönizien und Juda in exilisch-nachexilischer Zeit', *WO* 6, 1970-71, 189-204 and the works cited above, 12.7, by Ginsberg 1950, Janssen 1956, Whitley 1957, Ackroyd 1968 and Thompson 1992.

Also at home, and here certainly more than elsewhere, there was the trauma of the destruction of the sanctuary and the capital and the fall of the ruling house and of the state. Lamentations 1-2; 4-5 shows that these were difficult things to bear, and to the present day the ninth of the month Ab (July-August), the anniversary of the destruction of the temple in 587/6 and in 70 CE, has remained a day of national mourning.

12.7.7 Gedaliah immediately began a programme of reconstruction, inviting those who had survived the catastrophe and the exile to repopulate the cities and to resume everyday activities, thus eliminating at least the most obvious damage.

12.7.7.1 Gedaliah's legal position does not seem completely clear from the sources: was he the governor nominated by the Babylonians for the province of Judaea, as II Kings 25.22//Jer.40.7ff. would seem to indicate, or was he simply the person in charge of Jewish affairs in a larger province, the Samaria of the Assyrian period, to which Judah will have been attached? In that case he would have been simply an official dependent on the governor of Samaria, as Alt argued in 1934 (below 13.6.4.3) and Aharoni** 1979, 409 has argued more recently. King Jehoiachin was still alive, so that, as we shall see (below 12.9), a case of vassalage and therefore of limited independence certainly cannot be excluded. However, it is impossible to make any precise statement and, given the doubts, it is better to keep to the texts and to opt for the first possibility, not least since, in the light of most recent studies, that seems to have been the position in the Persian period.

12.7.7.2 The governorship of Gedaliah, who will probably have helped the region to recover economically and to give itself provisional administrative and economic structures, did not last long. Gedaliah was kiled by a certain Ishmael, son of Nethaniah son of Elishama, a member of the royal family (II Kings 25.25ff.; Jer.40.11-41.10). Ishmael had gathered around him a group of ultra-nationalist supporters, according to Jer.40.14 at the instigation of Baalis, king of Ammon. As a consequence of this action it seems that in 582 Nebuchadnezzar carried out a last deportation of 745 people (Jer.52.30). The rebels took refuge in Egypt and seem to have taken the prophet Jeremiah with them (chs.42-43).

12.7.7.3 We do not know much about Transjordan either. According to Josephus, *Antt. X*, 181f., in the eighteenth year of his reign (i.e. in 582) Nebuchadnezzar liquidated the kingdoms of Moab and Ammon, his former allies. This was the same year in which there was a further deportation of Judahites, as we have seen in the previous section, so it is possible that the two things were connected. The Babylonian inscription of *naḥr el-kalb* (*ANET*, 307; *TUAT* I, 405) probably refers to this event.

12.8 Judah during the Babylonian occupation

When we read the biblical texts and the Babylonian annals we get the impression that the whole country had been reduced to a heap of ruins, that very few of its inhabitants had survived, and that these were to be found particularly among the poorest, who had benefitted from the distributions of land; moreover, of the few who remained some had deliberately chosen exile on the death of Gedaliah. Archaeological excavations also testify to very heavy destruction, so much so that Albright[22] could assert that 'archaeologically speaking, the country was a *tabula rasa'* and that no more than around 20,000 inhabitants could have been left behind. At most there is evidence for only a few poor rural communities.

12.8.1 However, all this is only partly true. Clearly the economic, political and demographic structures of the country had been severely damaged, the state apparatus only functioned in a minimal way and in some areas must have ceased to exist; however, we must be careful about making too sweeping generalizations, not least because the Babylonian expedition had not affected all the regions. Ezekiel 33.24 clearly speaks of 'those living in these ruins in the country of Israel', indicating that many people were left, while Jer.41.5 mentions a pilgrimage to the temple of Jerusalem by the inhabitants of Shechem, Shiloh and Samaria, i.e. the inhabitants of the territory of the former northern kingdom, the reoccupation of which had been king Josiah's goal. That makes it reasonable to suppose that the temple, too, was not completely destroyed and that some form of worship, however minimal, must have been practised there. After all, the interest of Babylon was in restoring a normal situation in Judaea and destroying it only as a potential Egyptian military base, as a bridgehead for Egypt, and therefore in dismantling the fortifications. That clearly caused the destruction of other buildings, but left quite a few structures operative, especially those that the Babylonians had not reached. (This is rightly stressed by Thompson 1992.)

12.8.2 That is also because the spiritual centre had been transferred to the exiles in Babylon, a development illustrated vividly by Ezekiel 10 with the image of the 'glory of YHWH' abandoning the temple. In other words, the information that we have on these events has been shaped by Babylonian Judaism.

12.9 Jehoiachin pardoned

Finally, the texts tell us about the pardon granted to king Jehoiachin 'in the thirty-second year after he had been deported', by Evil-Merodach (*amel marduk*, 562-560) 'in the year of his accession to the throne' (thus rightly Cogan and Tadmor 1988, 328ff. and others; II Kings 25.27-30//Jer.52.31-34). This event has often been loaded with theological connotations, a feature which Cogan and Tadmor regard with scepticism; however, what is indicated is that even if he did not return home, he without doubt remained the legitimate ruler of Judah, a vassal of Babylon.

PART FOUR

Under the Empires of East and West

13

Under the Persian Empire

13.1 The fall of Babylon

The rule of Babylon lasted less than a century. After the death of Nebuchadnezzar II (605-561), who did not extend its frontiers further, it began to decline rapidly.

Bibliography

A.Alt, 'Die Rolle Samarias bei der Entstehung des Judentums', in *FS Otto Procksch zum 60.Geburtstag*, Leipzig 1934, 5-28; id., 'Zur Geschichte der Grenzen zwischen Judäa und Samaria', *PJB* 31, 1935, 94-111, both in *KS* II, 316-37 and 346-62; O.Lenze, *Die Satrapieneinteilung in Syrien und im Zweistromlande von 520-320*, Halle 1935; R.de Vaux, 'The Decrees of Cyrus and Darius on the Rebuilding of the Temple', in *The Bible and the Ancient Near East*, London and Garden City, NY 1971, 63-96; K.Galling, 'Der Tempelschatz nach Berichten und Urkunden im Buch Ezra', *ZDPV* 60, 1937, 177-83; id., *Studien zur Geschichte Israels im persischen Zeitalter*, Tübingen 1964; E.Bickerman, 'The Edict of Cyrus in Ezra 1', *JBL* 65, 1946, 249-75; W.Rudolph, *Esra und Nehemiah*, HAT I, 20, Tübingen 1959: S.A.Cook, 'The Age of Zerubbabel', in *Studies in Old Testament Prophecy...T.H.Robinson*, Edinburgh 1950, 19-36; F.I.Andersen, 'Who Built the Second Temple?' *AusBR* 6, 1958, 1-35; J.M.Myers, *Ezra-Nehemiah*, AB 14, Garden City, NY 1965; A.Dietrich, G.Widengren and F.M.Heichelheim, *Orientalische Geschichte von Kyros bis Mohammed*, Leiden 1966; A.Gelston, 'The Foundations of the Second Temple', *VI* 16, 1966, 232-5; A.A.Akarya, 'The Chronology of the Return from the Babylonian Captivity', *Tarbiz* 37, 1967-68, 329-37 (in Hebrew, English summary); C.G.Tuland, 'Josephus *Antiquities* Book XI', *AUSS* 16, 1966, 232-5; P.R.Ackroyd, *Exile and Restoration*, OTL, London and Philadelphia 1968; R.Mayer, 'Das Achämenidische Weltreich und seine Bedeutung in der politischen und religiösen Geschichte des alten Orients', *BZ* NF 12, 1968, 1-16; W.Zimmerli, 'Planungen für den Wiederaufbau nach der Katastrophe von 587', *VT* 18, 1968, 229-55 =

GA II, 156-91; F.M.Cross, 'Papyri from the Fourth Century BC from Daliyeh', in D.N.Freedman and J.C.Greenfield (eds.), *New Directions in Biblical Archaeology*, Garden City, NY 1969, 45-69; A.F.Rainey, 'The Satrapy "Beyond the River" ', *Demographic Notes on the History of the Past-Exilic Community in Judah in the Citizen-Temple Community*. Sheffield 1992, *AJBI* 1, 1969, 51-78; P.R.Berger, 'Zu den Namen *ššbṣr* und *šn'ṣr*", *ZAW* 83, 1971, 98-100; S.S.Weinberg, 'Postexilic Palestine. An Archaeological Report', *IASHP* 4, 1971, 78-97; J.P.Weinberg, *Demographic Notes on the History of the Post-Exilic Community in Judah in the Citizen-Temple Community*, Sheffield 1992; H.Kreissig, *Die sozialökonomische Situation in Juda zur Achämenidenzeit*, Berlin 1973; K.-M.Beyse, *Zerubbabel und die Königserwartungen der Propheten Haggai und Sacharja*, Berlin and Stuttgart 1972; W.T.In der Smitten, 'Historische Probleme zum Kyrosedikt und zum Jerusalemer Tempelbau von 515', *Persica* 6, 1974, 167-78; F.M.Cross, 'A Reconstruction of the Judaean Restoration', *JBL* 94, 1975, 4-18, and *Int* 29, 1975, 187-201 (without the final table); P.W. and N.Lapp, 'Discoveries in Wādī ed-Dalīyeh', *AASOR* 41, 1976; W.S.McCullough, *The History and Literature of the Palestinian Jews from Cyrus to Herod*, Toronto 1976; D.E.Gowan, *Bridge between the Testaments: A Reappraisal of Judaism from the Exile to the Birth of Christianity*, Pittsburgh 1976; S.Talmon, 'Ezra and Nehemiah (Books and Men)', *IDB-SV* 1976, 317-28; N.Avigad, 'Bullae and Seals from a Post-Exilic Judaean Archive', *Qedem* 4, 1976; G.Widengren* 1977, ch.IX; A.H.J.Gunneweg, 'Zur Interpretation der Bücher Esra-Nehemia', *SVT* 32, 1981, 146-61; id., 'Die aramäische und hebräische Erzählung über die nachexilische Restauration – Ein Vergleich', *ZAW* 94, 1982, 299-302; S.Japhet, 'Sheshbazzar and Zerubbabel – Against the Background of the Historical and Religious Tendencies of Ezra-Nehemiah', *ZAW* 94, 1982, 66-98, and 95, 1983, 218-29; E.M.Laperrousaz, 'Le régime théocratique juïf a-t-il commencé à l'époque perse ou seulement à l'époque hellénistique?', *Sem* 32, 1982, 93-6; W.Schottroff, 'Zur Sozialgeschichte Israels in der Perserzeit', *VuF* 27.1, 1982, 46-68; B.Reicke, *The New Testament Era*, London 1969; E.Stern, *Material Culture in the Land of the Bible in the Persian Period, 538-332 BC*, Jerusalem and Warminster 1982; A.Kuhrt, 'The Cyrus Cylinder and Achaemenid Imperial Policy', *JSOT* 25, 1983, 83-97; P.E.Dion, '*ššbṣr* and *ssnwry*', *ZAW* 95, 1983, 111f.; E.Eph'al, 'On the Political and Social Organization of the Jews in the Babylonian Exile', *ZDMG* 133, 1983, Suppl.5, 106-12; P.Frei and K.Koch, *Reichsidee und Reichsorganisation im Perserreich*, Freiburg im Breisgau 1984; L.Cagni, 'History, Administration and Culture of Achaemenid Mesopotamia', in T.Mikasa (eds.), *Monarchies and Socio-religious Traditions in the Ancient Near East*, Wiesbaden 1984, 55-62; P.R.Ackroyd, 'Historical Problems of the Early Achaemenidean Period', *Or* 20, 1984, 1-15; W.D.Davies and L.Finkelstein (ed.), *The Cambridge History of Judaism*, I, 1984; II,

1989; A.H.J.Gunneweg, *Esra, Nehemia* (2 vols.), Gütersloh 1985, 1987; L.Cagni (above 12.5), 55ff.; J.W.Betlyon, 'The Provincial Government of Persian Period Judaea and the Yehud Coins', *JBL* 104, 1986, 633-42; J.Lust, 'The Identification of Zerubbabel with Sheshbazzar', *ETL* 63, 1987, 91-5; E.M.Meyers, 'The Persian Period and the Judaean Restoration', in *Ancient Israelite Religion. Essays... F.M.Cross*, Philadelphia 1987, 509-21; T.Petit, 'L'évolution sémantique des termes hébreux et araméens *pḥh* et *sgn* et accadiens *paḥātu* et *saknu*', *JBL* 107, 1988, 53-67; P.-A.Beaulieu, *The Reign of Nabonidus, King of Babylon (556-539 BC)*, New Haven CN 1989; H.G.M.Williamson, 'The Governors of Judah under the Persians', *TynB* 39, 1988, 59-82; M.Saebø, 'The Relation of Sheshbazzar and Zerubbabel Reconsidered', *SEÅ* 54, 1989, 168-77; P.Sacchi, 'L'esilio e la fine della monarchia davidica', *Hen* 11, 1989, 131-48; E.Blum, *Studien zur Komposition des Pentateuch*, Berlin 1990, 333ff. and 345ff.; F.Bianchi, 'Zorobabele re di Giuda', *Hen* 13, 1991, 133-50; P.R.Davies (ed.), *Second Temple Studies. The Persian Period*, Sheffield 1992; K.Hoglund, *Achaemenid Administration in Israel and Judah*, Atlanta, Ga 1992; E.Nodet, *Essay sur les origines du Judaisme*, Paris 1992. For the completion of this chapter I owe much to the doctoral dissertation of my pupil F.Bianchi, which I hope will soon be published. For the history of this period see Sacchi* 1976. For relations between Ezra and Nehemiah, III Ezra and Josephus, cf. H.G.M.Williamson, *Israel in the Books of Chronicles*, Cambridge 1977 (with bibliography) and Garbini* 1988, ch.13. For the legal situation of the Judahites see M.Meissner, *Die Achämenidenkönige und das Judentum*, Berlin 1938, 6-32.

13.1.1 After the death of Nebuchanezzar, which was followed by seven years of disorder which saw three rulers alternating, Nabonidus (*nabū-nā'id*, 555-539) ascended the throne. The sources, which are prejudiced against him, present him as an eccentric, little interested in affairs of state but zealous in his interventions in the cult and in his private piety: he was a devotee of Sin, the moon god, whose sanctuaries he had restored throughout the country. Where possible he strengthened that cult, favouring its development in every way. This activity antagonized the all-powerful priesthood of the national god Marduk. For ten years Nabonidus is even said to have withdrawn to northern Arabia, leaving the government in the hands of Belshazzar as his regent: Belshazzar is the main character in the legends related in Dan.5.1-6.1. In fact Nabonidus seems to have wanted to strengthen the southern frontier with his presence and even to extend it.

13.1.2 However, abroad, the Babylonian empire was confronted with the growing power of the kingdom of Media, which shortly beforehand had played so great a part as its ally in the fall of Assyria (above 12.4.1.1). Media was extending slowly but surely westwards, incorporating not only the Assyrian territory conquered at the end of the seventh century but also Armenia and eastern Asia Minor. To the south-east it had subjected the Persians, a nation governed by the dynasty of the Achaemenids, the ancient rulers of Elam.

13.1.3 Thus in place of the kingdom of Media there arose a much greater and more powerful empire, whose brilliant and dynamic ruler Cyrus II (559-530) of the Achaemenid dynasty had overthrown Astyages, son of the Cyaxares who had conquered Assyria and with the support of the Median nobility had ascended the throne of Media and Persia. He continued the expansionist policy of Media, both westwards and eastwards. In vain Nabonidus allied himself with Lydia and with Egypt: now it was no longer possible to halt the advance of the Medes and Persians. Thus at the beginning of the second half of the sixth century BCE Cyrus conquered the western part of Asia Minor and Lydia whose king, Croesus, has gone down in Greek legend for his conspicuous, albeit useless, riches; to the east Cyrus conquered what remained of eastern Persia. In this way Babylon was clamped in an enormous pincer movement which extended from the south-east to the north-west: the Persians moreover had the strategic advantage of occupying territory situated in the hill-country and the mountains, from which they dominated the plains of Mesopotamia (Donner* 1986, 391ff.).

13.1.4 This is the period in which the message of the anonymous biblical prophet conventionally called Deutero-Isaiah is usually set. He proclaimed to the deported Judahites, in the context of a clearly monotheistic and universalistic message, that YHWH the God of Israel was the Lord of the universe and of history, who exercised lordship over all things and had raised up Cyrus, king of Persia, his 'anointed' (Hebrew *māšîaḥ*) as liberator of the people in exile (44.28; 45.1). This message was then expanded in a baroque way by Josephus, *Antt.* XI, 5, who remarked that Cyrus had even read and meditated on the prophet Isaiah! Liberation was in any case imminent because the fall of Babylon was near (47.1).

13.1.5 Cyrus's attack on Babylon was only a few years in coming. In 539 the army of Nabonidus was defeated in the battle of Ophis on the Tigris and a little later Cyrus entered the Babylonian capital, where he was welcomed in triumph.[1] Soon he also took the crown of Babylon, so that Syria and Palestine automatically became part of his kingdom. In 525 his successor Cambyses (530-522) also occupied Egypt, giving the Persian empire an extent comparable to that of Assyria at the beginning of the seventh century.

13.2 Persian domestic policy

Bibliography

Cf. on 13.1. Also S.McEvenue, 'The Political Structure in Judah from Cyrus to Nehemiah', *CBQ* 43, 1981, 353-64; L.Cagni, articles in 12.5 and 13.1; J.W.Betlyon, ibid.; P.D.Hanson, 'Israelite Religion in the Early Postexilic Period', in *Ancient Israelite Religion. Essays... F.M.Cross*, Philadelphia 1987, 485-507, and the relevant articles in *CHJ* I, 1984; S.Herrmann, 'Israels Frühgeschichte im Spannungsfeld neuer Hypothesen', *Studien zur Ethnogenese* 2, 1988, 43-95: 43f. n.1.

The kings of Media and Persia adopted a completely new policy towards their subject peoples, especially in comparison with that of Assyria, and also with that of Babylon. There were no more deportations of enemies to distant lands, no more attempts to shatter the ethnic and political structure of subject populations (and the resulting confrontation with ever new attempts at resistance on their part), but an attitude of considerable respect. This was probably not so much an expression of what Noth* 1959, 302, has called 'benevolent tolerance' in the modern sense of this expression (cf. also Donner*, 1986, 393f.) as a matter of practicality and economy, seeing that the power remained formally in the hands of the court and its officials and was not delegated: it was simpler, and indeed cost less, to obtain the spontaneous collaboration of their subjects at a local level than to have to impose their sovereignty by force. The 'Cyrus Cylinder' (*ANET*, 316; *TUAT* I, 407ff.) speaks explicitly of this new policy without mentioning the Judahites.

13.2.1 One evident sign of this new attitude appears in the royal inscriptions. Traditionally composed only in the language of the conqueror, they now appear in a trilingual version, in Persian, Elamite and Babylonian, and are written in Babylonian cuneiform.

13.2.2 The government seems to have been even more liberal in its official correspondence and public acts: here too other languages were allowed, and in Syria-Canaan and Egypt Aramaic now dominated, a development to which I have already alluded (12.7.5). Aramaic is a Western Semitic language attested in inscriptions from the ninth century onwards and introduced into the region by the Aramaean migration at the end of the second millennium. Disseminated by traders, it had already become a kind of *lingua franca* in the region at the end of the seventh century, as is evident from the letter of *'ādōn*, a Philistine ruler, shortly before the exile (above 12.5.4). It seems that towards the second half of the sixth century Aramaic now rapidly took the place of the various Canaanite dialects and Hebrew. As we have seen (ibid.), Hebrew was destined to remain predominantly the language of the temple, the cult and religious discourse generally, even if it was never to become completely extinct as a spoken language (cf. the texts of Qumran and Ecclesasticus, and later the Mishnah).[2] Thus a new phase of Aramaic began, usually called 'imperial Aramaic'.

13.3 Persian religious policy

Thus the attitude of the Persians towards their subjects was very liberal for this period, though we must be cautious (as Donner* 1986, 393f. rightly observes) in using modern concepts like tolerance and liberalism. At all events there was no longer any pressure from above, and the decrees which limited freedom of religion and worship were annulled; the statues of the gods and the sacred vessels which had been taken from the temples and carried off to Babylon were restored to the cults of the countries from which they had come. Cyrus's successor Cambyses also followed the same line throughout the empire and in Egypt, which had just been conquered, although he was a much more authoritarian and less tolerant ruler, not averse to repressive actions and sometimes unnecessary cruelty (Josephus, *Antt.* XI, 26, even calls him 'evil by nature'). The policy of Darius I Hystaspes (522-486) again proved liberal (cf. below 13.6).

13.3.1 Chief among the sources for the study of this period are the biblical books of Ezra and Nehemiah, though the problem here is the same as that for Chronicles generally;[3] we also have the books of the prophets Haggai, Zechariah 1-8, Trito-Isaiah (chs.56-66) and Malachi.[4] Another important text is the pseudepigraphical book III (I) Ezra,[5] probably the source of Josephus *Antiquities* XI, and in part parallel to II Chronicles 33 – Ezra 10 and Nehemiah 7.73-8.18. Finally, we have the papyri from the Jewish military colony of Elephantine,[6] on the Upper Nile in Egypt, from the end of the fifth century, with important information on the religious and administrative life of the colony and on the Jerusalem priesthood (cf. below 13.11.6).

13.3.2 These sources indicate that Cyrus issued an edict which authorized the Judahites to return home and to rebuild the temple of Jerusalem. There are two versions of this:

13.3.2.1 Ezra 5.6-6.12, a text transmitted in Aramaic in the context of a correspondence between the Persian court and the satrapy of 'Transeuphrates', the capital of which was Damascus.[7] The problem is of course whether this correspondence, and therefore the edict contained in it, is authentic. The problem is not a new one; it was already being debated towards the end of the last century between Wellhausen and Meyer. Nowadays a majority of scholars argue for the authenticity of these writings, including Bickermann 1946, Cross 1975 and Talmon 1976, 321; however, Gunneweg* 1984, 150, already raised basic doubts and denied their authenticity in his 1985 commentary, 100ff. Moreover many contemporary scholars are against the authenticity, since there are too many discrepancies in the text: thus for example the sequence of the kings of Persia is confused, while features which according to Haggai and Zechariah relate to the time of Darius I are dated to the period of Xerxes and Artaxerxes I, i.e. more than half a century later. That suggests a late redaction which was not always competent, even if three fragments of Ezra yet to be dated (second to first century BCE) have been found at Qumran (4Q 117, chs.4-5). It seems obvious that notices of this kind should be denied any 'authentic historicity' (Gunneweg 1985, 85ff.). So Kaiser[8] has taken over the harsh judgment pronounced by Hölscher in 1923: this is a 'gross falsification', the product of the narrator. The authenticity of the decree has recently been defended by Herrmann 1988, as it is by many Iranologists, who stress the stylistic similarity with Persian edicts of the time (oral communication by Gherardo Gnoli).

13.3.2.2 The second version of the decree appears in Ezra 1.2-4 and is certainly apocryphal, though Bickermann 1946 defended its authenticity. On the most favourable interpretation this is a paraphrase of the decree made by the author in his own words.

13.3.2.3 Be this as it may, it appears highly unlikely that in the first year of his reign (Ezra 5.13, i.e. in 539/8, if we understand this to mean, as would seem obvious, his reign over Babylon) Cyrus was occupied specifically with a remote and tiny corner of his empire, a region which he had never visited. On the other hand it seems possible that the edict may go back to a standardized formula into which the official responsible entered at various points the country and the people to which it referred; in that case the text about Judaea and its inhabitants would simply be the expression of the imperial policy in a particular case. However, that applies only for the first version of the decree. In any case it is clear that it is within the sphere of Cyrus's policy towards the deported nations, a policy which authorized them to return to their own countries, rebuild their destroyed sanctuaries and reconstruct their cults, that we must look for the first ferments of restoration on the part of the first to be repatriated.

13.3.2.4 However, those who returned cannot have been numerous: the country, which had been unpopulated and partly destroyed for decades, could not take in large quantities of people in a short time; moreover, many of those deported did not in fact return 'because they did not want to abandon their possessions' (Josephus, *Antt.* XI, 8). To that must be added the interesting though little known theory of Akarya 1968 (cf. also Donner* 1986, 209ff. and Miller and Hayes* 1987, 446) that the first return will not have taken place under Cyrus but about twenty years later, at the end of the reign of Cambyses or even under Darius I, since the texts say nothing about an earlier repatriation.

13.4 Jewish officials in Persian service

Bibliography

As on 13.1

The texts also report that a certain Sheshbazzar was commissioned by the Persian court to restore the sacred vessels which had been taken away from the temple by Nebuchadnezzar (Ezra 5.15, cf. 1.8, 11).

13.4.1 We know only the name of this figure and nothing else; moreover we do not even know the name in a clear form: it is reported in different forms by the LXX, by III Ezra and by Josephus. It is clearly Babylonian, but since it seems improbable that a Babylonian would have been entrusted with such a mission by the Persian administration it seems likely that he was one of the deported Judahites. Albright,[9] followed by Myers 1965, Cross 1975, Avigad 1976 and Aharoni** 1979, always argued that this Sheshbazzar is the same person as the grandson of Jehoiakim called Shenazzar (*šenᵉ'aṣār*) in I Chron.3.17, who appears as Σαναβάσσας in III Ezra and Σαναβάσσας in Josephus: the two last names derive from the transcription of a Babylonian name (though not attested) *sin-ab-uṣur* or, perhaps better (according to Herrmann* 1980, 304), *šamaš-apla-uṣur*.

If this suggestion is accepted as a working hypothesis, the official in question becomes an uncle of Zerubbabel and most of the problems are resolved; however, Berger 1971 challenges this. For him the first name, as I have pointed out, is not attested anywhere in its Babylonian form, whereas the second would have to be transcribed differently in Hebrew. Dion 1983, who follows Berger, and now Donner* 1986, 410 n.21, also differ. Donner considers such an identification a 'castle in the air'. Another proposal has been recently made by Saebø 1989 (cf. Lust 1987): Sheshbazzar is to be identified with Zerubbabel.

13.4.2 Moreover Sheshbazzar is given the title *peḥah*, usually translated 'satrap', though so far the meaning of the term is not certain (cf. below 13.6.4.3).[10]

13.4.3 Since it is not clear what *peḥah* means, it is impossible to establish what position Sheshbazzar had in the Persian bureaucracy. Was he, for example, governor or prefect of the more or less autonomous province of Judaea? Or was Judah dependent on the satrapy of 'Transeuphrates' through Samaria and Damascus? It could also be that Sheshbazzar was entrusted only with returning the temple vessels to their legitimate owners and that his title refers to functions which he performed elsewhere. According to the discoveries published by Avigad in 1976 (below 13.6.5) the first proposal seems preferable, but as yet the problem is far from being resolved. Donner* 1986, 411 (with bibliography) simply defines Sheshbazzar's title as 'commissioner in charge of the return'.

13.4.4 It is not even possible to prove the authenticity of the list of vessels restored to the temple of Jerusalem (Ezra 1.7-11) or of the first to return home (Ezra 2.1-70//Neh.7.6-72).

13.5 Those who returned

Be this as it may, it seems clear that all these events and the stimulus produced by them did not lead to more than the return of a small group of those who had been deported and the restoration of the foundations of the temple (Ezra 3.6ff.; 5.16ff.; Zech.4.9; cf. Hagg.1.1-11).

13.5.1 The sources credit the beginning of the rebuilding to Sheshbazzar or to Zerubbabel without deciding in favour of one or the other; it is possible, therefore, for the two sometimes to be confused, as happens in Josephus, *Antt.* XI, 13. Some scholars in fact want to identify the two (cf. above 13.4.1 and the discussion in Talmon 1976, 319f.). However, in the light of what I have said it is more probable that Sheshbazzar began the work and was then replaced by Zerubbabel, who managed to conclude it. In this connection it should be noted that the semantically similar roots *bānāh* and *yāsad*, which normally mean 'build' and 'lay the foundations', can also simply mean 'restore' (above 5.1.3.5, Andersen 1958 and Gelston 1966), so that they do not necessarily indicate a new construction.

13.5.2 However, the sources state that the work did not go forward as it should have done and give a plausible explanation for this: on the one hand an economic crisis, aggravated by drought and a plague of locusts, and on the other difficulties with the local population (Ezra 3.3; Josephus, *Antt.* XI, 114 anachronistically calls them 'Samaritans', or by that did he simply mean the inhabitants of Samaria?). Perhaps, more simply, the reference could be to that part of the population which had not been deported and which had received land from Nebuchadnezzar. They offered their help to those who had returned, and met with a refusal (Ezra 4.1ff.).

13.5.3 Other difficulties arose in the wake of the disorders which broke out on the death of Cambyses. These disorders did not directly affect Judaea (Aharoni**, 412, below 13.6), but they probably made caution desirable (Noth* 1959, 280); perhaps the rebuilding of the temple complex was premature – technically, economically and politically.

13.6 Disorders in the empire

When Cambyses died in 522 without leaving a direct heir to the throne, disorders broke out all over the empire. These were interpreted by the prophets Haggai and Zechariah as signs of the forthcoming establishment of the kingdom of God.

13.6.1 The succession passed to Darius, son of Hystaspes, from another branch of the Achaemenids, a group which was well integrated into the court of Cambyses but had yet to be recognized. Such recognition was never without problems in the ancient Near East. So first of all Darius had to deal with rebellions throughout the empire.

13.6.2 After about a year of hard and not always victorious struggles, Darius succeeded in overcoming his enemies, thus assuring, towards the end of 521, his uncontested right to ascend the throne. His enterprises have been listed on the rock of Beḥistūn in Persia, near the truck route from Baghdad to Teheran (*ANEP*, no.249; text in *TUAT* I, 419-50); the text is translated into various languages, including Aramaic.

13.6.3 These events must have shaken the empire to its foundations during 522/21; as I have indicated, they also made a strong impression in Judaea, indeed it was thought that the 'day of YHWH', already announced in Amos 5.18,[11] and the end of the world, followed by the inauguration of the kingdom of God, were imminent. So it seemed vital and particularly urgent to prepare to receive the Lord who was about to arrive. And what could be better than to restore the temple in a definitive way, so that YHWH had an adequate dwelling, a place where he could reside, in whatever way that might be conceived? The prophet Haggai tells us about the beginning of the disorders, Zechariah about their end.[12]

13.6.3.1 With Haggai, we find ourselves at the beginning of the year 521/20, i.e. shortly after the consolidation of the empire or when the disorders were already in their final phase. However, the news does not yet seem to have arrived at Jerusalem, among those who had returned, so their expectation of the imminent end of the world remained unchanged. Haggai exhorts the people first to rebuild the partially ruined sanctuary, thus bringing to completion the enterprise begun with the laying of the foundations. The kingdom of God was indeed on the way.

13.6.3.2 In Proto-Zechariah the situation seems to be different: the first vision (1.7ff.) shows that the people of Judah were now disheartened because everything was peaceful, the revolutions had finished and the cataclysms which were to herald the imminent end had not taken place. However, according to the prophet, the rebuilding had to continue, though under other auspices: the cult had to be re-established fully, because the judgment on the nations, though postponed, was imminent.

13.6.4 Ezra 3-5, Haggai and Zechariah give important information about the composition and the functioning of the first community of those who had returned from Babylon, around the year 520.

13.6.4.1 The priesthood now seems to belong exclusively to 'the priests the levites, the sons of Zadok', according to the rules laid down in Ezek.44.15: a tradition reported in I Chron 6.34ff. gives Zadok a genealogy going back to Aaron. It is always difficult to talk in terms of truth and falsehood in connection with documents of this sort, but it seems evident that this genealogy uses elements of that of Abiathar, who was deposed and exiled by Solomon (above 4.7.1 and 5.2); compare also the figure of the High Priest, mention of whom in the pre-exilic period seems to be anachronistic, since such functions were largely exercised by the king (above 5.2.2.5).

13.6.4.2 Alongside the High Priest there also appears the representative of secular power, 'the prince', Hebrew *nāśī*, mentioned in Ezek.45.7ff. (cf. above 12.7.4). Joshua and Zerubbabel respectively appear to be discharging these functions; the latter was the last member of the house of David, and probably returned with one of the first groups to go back. His name, *zᵉrubbābel* in Hebrew and *zēr-babīli* in Babylonian, is clearly Mesopotamian, like that of Sheshbazzar.

13.6.4.3 However, as with Sheshbazzar, it is impossible to establish the precise functions and thus the powers of Zerubbabel, who is also called *peḥah*, a term which, as we have seen, is usually translated 'satrap'. This is a function attested for the first time in Assyria, but it can indicate a range of officials up to governor. After an exhaustive examination of the texts, Petit 1988 (above 13.1) argues that the value of the title and thus the degree of the official are established by mentioning the territory over which he had been set: if this was important, he was also the 'satrap'. According to Josephus, *Antt.* XI, 32, Zerubbabel will have been a favourite of Darius I, in which case he would have been directly accountable to the king, thus by-passing the hierarchy which ran through the governor of Samaria and the satrapy of 'Transeuphrates'; however, that leaves the problem of his functions unresolved. Was he the official in charge of the rebuilding of the temple (thus Galling 1937 and Donner* 1986, 410)[13] or the commissioner in charge of resettling those who had returned (thus Sacchi* 1976)? If we can use the material published by Avigad in 1976 (below 13.6.5), this question too could be resolved satisfactorily. However, the recent studies by Sacchi 1989 and Bianchi 1990 have argued, with points which deserve the closest attention, that Zerubbabel was in fact the last king of Judah, a vassal of Persia. That would satisfactorily resolve the problem of his functions.

13.6.4.4 But Zerubbabel suddenly disappears, and it is impossible to determine what happened to him. He could simply have returned to court, his mission accomplished; others, however (there is a discussion in Bright* 1981, 371), think that he was quietly eliminated to avoid the rise of a new form of Judahite nationalism around the figure of the last member of the house of David. This last suggestion is not to be ruled out *a priori*, though there is no proof of it;[14] indeed, it should be noted that the two explanations are not mutually exclusive. And the proposal by Sacchi and Bianchi, mentioned above, remains, arguing that the Jerusalem priesthood will have eliminated the last king of the house of David, perhaps because he was not sufficiently attentive to their requests.

Be this as it may, Zech.6.9-15, a text which Sacchi* 1976, 32, has rightly called 'a very early and deliberate correction',[15] mentions 'two crowns', one evidently originally destined for the high priest and the other for Zerubbabel, while according to the present texts Joshua has to wear them both.

13.6.4.5 Anyway, no member of the house of David was ever again called to function as satrap. It is easy to document this: I Chron.3.19-24 presents a succession of members of the house of David down to around the last quarter of the fifth century; and the names inscribed on seals and coins published by Avigad (provided that this is credible documentation, cf. 13.6.5 below) would allow us to trace the names of the governors (among whom, however, Ezra and Nehemiah do not appear!) down to the third quarter of the fourth century BCE. No member of the house of David appears among them.[16] Nor can we discover whether the governors had or at least continued to bear the title *nāśī* (cf. Ezek.45.7ff.); however, this seems improbable, since for the prophet this title was destined only for a member of the house of David. If all this seems plausible, the dualism between High Priest and governor must have lasted until the end of the Persian period, i.e. to the beginning of the third century, contrary to what hitherto was maintained almost unanimously (Sacchi* 1976, 32 and 47); indeed Laperrousaz 1982 argues that what Josephus calls a 'theocracy' (but it is better to talk of a 'hierocracy') would not have begun until the Macedonian conquest, i.e. around a century and a half later (cf. below 14.7.4.10).

13.6.5 The time has now come to examine the documentation published by Avigad in 1976 and already mentioned several times. If it proved reliable, it would enable us to resolve a number of problems relating to this troubled period. However, its credibility proves problematical.

13.6.5.1 This material, consisting of seals and stamps on amphorae and *bullae* on ceramics, is thought to provide the names of the governors

appointed by the Persians who bore the Aramaic title *phw'*, corresponding to the Hebrew *peḥah* (it seems that a proposal by F.M.Cross to read
phr', the 'vessel', no longer needs to be taken into consideration).
However, there are also many seals inscribed with *yhwd*, i.e. *yᵉhūd*.
That would correspond to the title borne by Ezra and Nehemiah: *peḥah*
and *hattiršātā'*, the latter, attested only in Ezra 2.63; Neh.7.65, 60 and
8.9, a Persian title: the region is also often called *mᵉdīnāh*, Aramaic
mᵉdīnātā', which would indicate an autonomous administrative territory. That would cause problems for the suggestion made by Alt in
1934 and accepted by the majority of scholars,[17] that Judah will in
practice have been annexed to Samaria and that Sheshbazzar and
Zerubbabel will only have been charged with a special mission, while
Nehemiah alone will have been governor. Now in the documentation
published by Avigad, all appear as governors, as satraps, and the title
paḥat yᵉhūdāh attributed to Zerubbabel would thus seem quite legitimate,
even if the territory under his jurisdiction was very small, as Bright*
1981, 383ff., points out (Williamson 1988 differs).

13.6.5.2 However, the authenticity and thus the credibility of this
material has been challenged by Garbini[18] with arguments worth
noting, and also by other scholars. To go by the script, the discoveries
date from two different periods, one of which is too early and the other
too late for them to provide information relating to the sixth, fifth and
fourth centuries, and they have to be divided into three different
groups; nor does the editor report the circumstances in which what he
calls an 'archive' was discovered. The Israeli E.Stern, probably one of
the greatest experts on Judaism in the early post-exilic period, and
J.D.Purvis, also consider this material problematical, both independently of Garbini, though they do not go into details; again it should
be noted, as already indicated, that neither Ezra nor Nehemiah appear
among the governors, a fact which could support their authenticity.

13.6.5.3 After more than fifteen years there should be some clarification of these problems, which the majority of scholars (e.g. Ackroyd
in *CHJ* I, 157; Donner* 1986; H.Weippert** 1988, 722) have simply
ignored, so that this material, which is so important if it should prove
authentic, can be made avaailable for scholars to use.

13.6.6 Be this as it may, on 13 Adar of the sixth year of Darius (i.e.
12 March 515), the rebuilding of the temple was completed. Jewish
scholars therefore call the post-exilic period down to 70 CE 'the period
of the second temple'.

13.7 Ezra and Nehemiah

We have virtually no certain information about the rebuilding and
inauguration of the temple in 515, though the discoveries published

by Avigad in 1976 and other texts allow us to reconstruct the genealogies of the High Priest, the house of David and the Persian governors of Judaea and Samaria down to the end of the fifth century, and for some even later.

Bibliography

A.van Hoonacker, 'Néhémie et Esdras: une nouvelle hypothèse sur la chronologie de l'époque de la restauration', *Le Muséon* 9, 1890, 151-84, 316-53, 389-401; C.C.Torrey, *Ezra Studies*, Chicago 1910; A.Alt, 'Die Rolle Samarias' (13.1 above); M.Noth, *The Chronicler's History* (1943), JSOT-SS 50, Sheffield 1987; H.Cazelles, 'La mission d'Esdras', *VT* 4, 1954, 113-40; J.Morgenstern, 'Jerusalem – 485 BC', *HUCA* 37, 1966, 1-28; B.Mazar, 'The Tobiads', *IEJ* 7, 1957, 137-45, 229-38; A.Pavlovský, 'Die Chronologie der Tätigkeit Esdras – Versuch einer Lösung', *Bibl* 38, 1957, 275-305, 428-56; S.Mowinckel, *Studien zu dem Buche Ezra-Nehemia*, three vols, Oslo 1964-65; K.Galling, *Studien* (above 13.1); C.R.North, 'Civil Authority in Ezra', in *Studi in onore di Edoardo Volterra*, Milan 1972, VI, 377-404; W.T.In der Smitten, 'Nehemias Parteigänger', *BO* 29, 1972, 155-7; id., *Esra, Quellen, Überlieferung und Geschichte*, Assen 1973; C.G.Tuland, 'Ezra-Nehemiah or Nehemiah-Ezra?', *AUSS* 12, 1974, 47-62; F.M.Cross, 'Reconstruction...' (above 13.1); S.Talmon, ibid; Sacchi*, ch.III; W.Vischer, 'Nehemia, Sonderbeauftragter und Statthalter des Königs', in *Probleme biblischer Theologie. FS Gerhard von Rad*, Munich 1971, 603-10; R.W.Klein, 'Ezra and Nehemiah in Recent Studies', in *Magnalia Dei... Essays G.E.Wright*, Garden City, NY 1976, 361-76; N.Avigad, 'Bullae and Seals' (above, 13.1); A.H.J.Gunneweg, 'Zur Interpretation der Bücher Esra-Nehemia', *SVT* 32, 1981, 146-61, and the commentaries cited above; also R.Zadok, 'Remarks on Ezra and Nehemiah', *ZAW* 94, 1982, 296-9; D.J.A.Clines, *Ezra, Nehemiah and Esther*, Grand Rapids, Michigan and London 1984; H.G.M.Williamson, *Ezra and Nehemiah*, Sheffield 1987; K.Baltzer, 'Liberation from Debt Slavery after the Exile in Second Isaiah and Nehemiah', in *Ancient Israelite Religion. Essays... F.M.Cross*, Philadelphia 1987, 477-85; T.Cohn-Eskenazi, *In an Age of Prose. A Literary Approach to Ezra-Nehemiah*, Atlanta 1988; J.Blenkinsopp, *Ezra-Nehemiah*, OTL, London and Philadelphia 1988; R.Masor, 'Some Chronistic Themes in the "Speeches" in Ezra and Nehemiah', *ExpT* 102, 1989-90, 72-6. For the Samaria papyri cf. P.W.and N.L.Lapp, 'Discoveries in the Wadi ed-Daliye', *AASOR* 41, 1974, 1ff.

13.7.1 During the first quarter of the fifth century BCE something very serious must have happened in Jerusalem: a new, though partial destruction, even if it did not affect the temple. Morgenstern 1956ff., following H.Winckler, even talks of a 'catastrophe' which took place in 586-5.

13.7.1.1 The information appears in a message sent to Nehemiah from Jerusalem to Susa, capital of Persia, in the month of Chislev (November-December) in the twentieth year of king Artaxerxes I Longimanus (446-23, i.e. in 445 BCE), which is reported in an amplified form by Josephus, *Antt.* XI, 159ff. Elephantine papyrus Cowley no.30,[19] dated in the year 408, indicates that he was the ruler at the time and not others of the same name (Artaxerxes II Mnemon, 404-360, and Artaxerxes III Ochus, 360-338), or even Xerxes I (486-464), as Josephus always calls him. The papyrus mentions the sons of Sanballat 'governor of Samaria', certainly the opponent of Nehemiah (2.10,19 and elsewhere).

13.7.1.2 In the so-called 'Samaria papyri', discovered in the 1960s in *wādī ed-dalīye*, only two of which have so far been published, the dynasty of the Sanballatids appears, down to the end of the Persian era (Cross 1975, Talmon 1976).

13.7.2 The message which arrived at Susa said: 'The survivors there in the province who escaped exile are in great trouble and shame; the wall of Jerusalem is broken down, and its gates are destroyed by fire' (Neh.1.1-3). It is not known precisely what happened; however, it is certain that the text cannot be a generalized reference to the ruins left by the Babylonians more than a century before and not yet rebuilt, because that would be quite notorious. There seems, rather, to have been some recent happening, and this is confirmed by the reaction which the text attributes to Nehemiah (Neh.2.1-2). Again, the damage must have been relatively modest if Nehemiah could have repaired it in less than two months (fifty-two days, Neh.6.15). There could have been a new attack by some of the surrounding peoples or even an outbreak of conflict between those who had returned and claimed their land back and those who, having remained in the country, had been given the land by the Babylonians and did not intend to hand it over. In any case, as Sacchi* 1976, 42, rightly observes, since we have no information at all, the event must have been of secondary importance. One suitable context would be the rebellion by Egypt on the death of Darius I in 483 (Aharoni** 1979, 412) and the revolts which followed, all of which took place during the Persian expeditions against Greece. However, it is impossible to say more without the discovery of new material.

13.7.3 In the book of the prophet Malachi,[20] probably composed shortly before Nehemiah's mission, we find a series of cases of what the most orthodox tradition of the Judahite faith could regard as neglect or even prevarication on ethical and cultic issues; this was one more reason for someone to take matters in hand. The fact remains that

Nehemiah felt the need to investigate matters at first hand, and succeeded in persuading the king to send him on an official mission.

13.8. Nehemiah's first mission

So in the year 445 Nehemiah arrived in Judaea for the first time, on a mission for king Artaxerxes 1.

13.8.1 However, it is not clear whether this was an attempt by the Persian court to restore some order in a region which was important as a base against an often rebellious Egypt, or whether this was a direct intervention by the Babylonian Jewish Diaspora, which was much more strict and less accommodating to the local populations than that of Judah (thus Sacchi* 1976, 39f.); the two possibilities are not mutually exclusive, though it is again suspicious that at a time of crisis the great king should be more or less directly occupied with the problems of a small group situated in a marginal region.

13.8.2 The biblical texts are cautious about giving Nehemiah any official commission.

13.8.2.1 In Neh.5.14 he appears with the title *peḥām*, an unknown term which could be a corruption of *peḥāh*, the word which appears in 12.26. Thus North 1972 argued that he had no official commission.

13.8.2.2 However, according to the documentation published by Avigad in 1976 (above 13.6.5) there would be a possibility that Nehemiah would have been a satrap, even if he is not mentioned in the documents (above 13.6.4.3).

13.8.2.3 According to the sources, he will have remained at Jerusalem for twelve years, i.e. until the end of 433 (5.12; 13.6). In the present state of research there is no reason to doubt this chronology.

13.8.3 A commission of this kind, whether it was official or not, which in any case had extraordinary powers and had been conferred directly by the ruler on someone who at court had only been a page (though an important one, so important that Sacchi* 1976 even makes him 'a powerful minister of the emperor'), in fact by-passed the authority of the satrapy of 'Transeuphrates' and of the local governors. So we can understand how these governors should have been first obstructive and then hostile, clearly being accustomed to deal with lesser people.

13.8.3.1 Nehemiah 2.10 mentions Sanballat the Horonite, whom a letter from Elephantine (cited above, 13.7.1.1-2) explicitly calls governor of Samaria. He was probably a Yahwist by religion, since his sons had theophoric names with YHWH as an element.

13.8.3.2 Then we also find a certain 'Tobias the Ammonite slave', again with a Yahwistic name (though it is probably better to understand the term *'ebed* as 'official' or perhaps even as 'minister', rather than as 'slave' in a derogatory sense).[21]

18.8.3.3 The obstructiveness of the local authorities is therefore understandable, though we should rule out the theory in the text that this was essentially due to the fact that at last 'someone had come to seek the welfare of the children of Israel'; cf.also 2.19; 6.1-6, where the two figures mentioned are joined by a certain 'Geshem the Arab'. Some scholars want to identify Geshem with the father of a certain *qyn*, king of Kedar, the owner of a silver cup with an inscription mentioning both of them, and which is certainly earlier than 400 BCE.[22] Hostile reactions do not seem to have been slow in coming: Ezra 4.11 speaks of a letter sent to Artaxerxes, who accused the Judahites of subversion; this was followed by the injunction to Nehemiah to suspend all work. By all accounts Nehemiah (2.11-15) had already inspected the walls with a view to rebuilding them.

13.9 Ezra's mission

The problem of Ezra's mission seems much more complex; in the present state of research there cannot be said to be any satisfactory proposal (there is a good presentation of the problems in Bright* 1981, 391-402) which does not resort to radical negative solutions.[23]

Bibliography

A.van Hoonacker, 'Néhémie et Esdras' (above 13.7); H.H.Schaeder, *Esra der Schreiber*, Tübingen 1930; H.Cazelles, 'La mission d'Esdras', *VT* 4, 1954, 213-40; U.Kellermann, 'Erwägungen zum Esragesetz', *ZAW* 80, 1968, 373-85; K.F.Pohlmann, *Studien zum Dritten Esra*, Göttingen 1970; S.Mowinckel, *Studien* (above, 13.1); K.Koch, 'Esra and the Origins of Judaism', *JSS* 19, 1974, 173-97; G.Widengren, in J.H.Hayes and J.M.Miller* 1977, 514ff.; C.Houtman, 'Esra and the Law', *OTS* 21, 1981, 91-115; B.-Z.Wacholder, *The Dawn of Qumran. The Sectarian Torah and the Teacher of Righteousness*, Cincinnati 1963; H.G.M.Williamson, 'The Composition of Ezra I-VI', *JTS* NS 33, 1983, 1-30; R.Rendtorff, 'Esra und das Gesetz', *ZAW* 96, 1984, 165-84; cf. the bibliography to 13.1.

13.9.1 In Ezra 7.12 we read that Ezra, for whom 7.1-5 provides a genealogy which goes back to Aaron and whom 7.6 describes as a 'priest... scribe of the Torah of the God of heaven', had come to Judaea along with a group of ex-deportees, again with a direct commission from Artaxerxes. However, while this direct relationship with the ruler appears probable in the case of Nehemiah, who is described as a page in the personal service of the king, the situation is different with Ezra.

The text says only that '... the hand of YHWH, his God, was with him, so that he granted all that he desired' (7.6). This text provides an explanation of Ezra's successes which is clearly the product of later theological reflection, while leaving obscure the dynamics through which the commission was conferred on him. At all events, it is clear that the sources have in mind Artaxerxes I, so that the mission will have begun in 458.

13.9.2 However, what we might call the traditional chronology according to which Ezra will have arrived in Jerusalem about thirteen years before Nehemiah (and their synchronism, called for by Neh.12.36, though this is a text which many scholars consider an interpolation, and a co-ordination of their work would be necessary or at least probable) comes up against such difficulties that Talmon 1976 has called them 'disconcerting'.

13.9.2.1 This is not the place for discussing the problem of the chronology of Ezra in detail; for that the reader should consult the *Introductions* to the Old Testament (mine, ch.43.3). It is enough to point out that the traditional theory is still supported today by Rainey (in Aharoni** 1979, 423 n.105), Kellermann and Cross. Nowadays the majority of scholars opt for an arrival of Ezra after Nehemiah, in which case Artaxerxes would be Artaxerxes II Mnemon, 404-360, and the seventh year would be 398.[24] A third proposal was formulated in 1957 by A.Pavlovský: Ezra will have come to Jerusalem not in the seventh but in the thirty-seventh year of Artaxerxes, in 428: Pavlovský arrives at this result by presupposing an error in the text. However, there is nothing in the text in favour of his theory, and so it has found no support.[25]

13.9.2.2 But what are the difficulties with the traditional thesis? First of all there is nothing in the book of Nehemiah to suggest that Ezra had already been at work. Indeed, the dates given would seem to exclude this, and also the co-ordination of their work.

13.9.2.3 Even less clear are the relations which Ezra is supposed to have had with the governor in office on his arrival, who was probably, according to the documentation in Avigad 1976, a certain *'aḥzay*. Ezra (and indeed Nehemiah) could certainly be inserted between the governors mentioned in the list (as Talmon 1976, 327, does, though only in parenthesis), but this would be illegitimate interference in texts which are already problematical, not to mention the fact that in that case the invective of Neh.5.15 which accuses 'the governors who were before me' of having oppressed the people, exacting from them unjust taxes, would apply to Ezra as well!

13.9.2.4 So the situation seems to exclude, rather than presuppose, the fact that Ezra and Nehemiah coincided and therefore worked together, though it should be recognized that this is essentially an argument from silence. Moreover Talmon 1976, 320, rightly points out that Haggai and Zechariah were contemporaries and worked in the same city but without ever referring to each other in their texts.

13.9.2.5 Again, in Ezra 10.6 Ezra spent the night fasting, at the house of a certain Johanan ben Eliashib; however, in Neh.12.22-33 Eliashib appears as a contemporary of Nehemiah and has a grandson by the name of Johanan. But this argument, too, is inconclusive in itself: it has been attacked by Cross 1975, 9ff., who argues that there will have been an Eliashib I, father of Johanan I, a contemporary of Ezra, and an Eliashib II, father of Johanan II, a contemporary of Nehemiah. One of the two pairs, father and son, will have been omitted by haplography, which often happens in connection with 'papponomy', the practice of giving sons the names of their paternal grandfathers. This theory is unconditionally supported by Rainey, in Aharoni**, *The Land*, 423 n.105, but is severely criticized for its defects on the textual critical side and because of an error of fact by Widengren in Hayes and Miller* 1977, 505ff. (though he recognizes its 'persuasive and attractive character', 509) and by Bright* 1981, 402.

13.9.2.6 In 1890 the Belgian scholar A.van Hoonacker of the University of Louvain suggested that the solution to the various problems lay in accepting that Ezra will not have arrived in Jerusalem already in the reign of Artaxerxes I but in that of Artaxerxes II (404-358), so that the seventh year would have fallen in 398. The abuses which appear in the Elephantine papyri would then have been those which Ezra tried to eliminate (Fohrer* 1982, 214ff.). This theory has been adopted by a great many scholars;[26] a few of them have even suggested Artaxerxes III (360-338), i.e. in 354.

13.9.2.7 So it would seem that despite everything there are also a number of features in favour of the traditional theory according to which Ezra will have come to Jerusalem before Nehemiah; they include the opinion of the redactors of the two books and the chronology that they present. On the other hand, there are so many problematical features that it must be considered at least doubtful and therefore hardly viable.

13.9.3 In the face of these problems the question arises whether it is possible to discover anything about Ezra in historical terms. There have been scholars in the past, as there are in the present, who ask whether Ezra ever existed, or whether he is a creation of middle Judaism. A first suggestion in this latter direction was made by E.Renan in 1893,[27] who was followed shortly afterwards by C.C.Torrey in 1896 (in definitive form in 1910);[28] the theory was presented again a few years later by G.Hölscher in 1922[29] and it has been recently taken up again by Garbini* 1988, ch.13 (who gives further bibliography). The figure of Ezra will have been a creation of the author or the redactors of the two books, with the aim of legitimating what they considered to be the right composition and organization and the true faith of the new community. This comprised a prohibition against marrying non-Jewish wives (Ezra 9.1-10.17, below 15.10.9), the imposition of the Torah as a personal obligation on every member of the community (Neh.8.1-9), and its approval as a law by the state. In that case the book of Ezra would have to be dated some centuries later, which would explain the not inconsiderable number of inaccuracies in its chronology in general and of the Persian period in particular. According to Garbini, Ezra's reform will not have taken place in the fifth century but in the second, and will have been carried out by the high priest Alkimus around 159, in accordance with what is said in I Macc.9.54-56 and partly described in III (I) Ezra. On this occasion the figure of Ezra the scribe will have been created as the new Moses, and again according to Garbini this will be the context in which 'Judaism' in the strictest sense of the term came into being. Moreover, the name Ezra will simply be the Hebrew-Aramaic form of the Greek Alkimos, 'the courageous', 'the hero' (cf. below 14.7.10).

13.9.4 Finally, Ezra is unknown to Sir.49.13, which mentions only Nehemiah, a silence which has given rise to a rash of proposals.[30]

13.9.5 This radical solution to a problem the complexity and intricacy of which is beyond question, is certainly based on arguments worth considering. However, it remains to be demonstrated whether these can sustain the heavy weight that they have to bear, namely to eliminate completely a considerable and important part of the tradition. At all events it is clear that 'the narrative... [must be] understood primarily as a theological interpretation of the mission of Ezra and not used for any form of historical reconstruction' (O.Kaiser, *Einleitung in das Alte Testament*, [5]1984, 181).

13.9.6 Be this as it may, it seems that towards the end of the fifth century BCE, after a catastrophe the nature of which we cannot determine but which had taken place a few years before, the community of Jerusalem and neighbouring Judaea underwent a rigoristic reform, the leading light behind which was someone sent by the Babylonian diaspora, Nehemiah. Nehemiah was against any form of compromise in the sphere of faith and any integration with the other peoples in everyday life (Neh.10.29, Sacchi* 1976, 38ff., who also points out, 44, that Neh.10 is probably based on contemporary documents). The reform also affected public worship and everyday conduct as well as faith.

13.9.7 It seems that this reform gave new stimuli to national life: under the leadership of Nehemiah the walls of the capital were rebuilt (Neh.2.11-3.32), despite the hostility to the project on the part of the local authorities (above 13.8.3.3). The texts mention Sanballat the

Horonite, Tobias the Ammonite, and the Ammonite and Philistine populations (Neh.3.33-4.17). For this reason the enterprise had to be brought to a conclusion by armed labourers (4.10ff.). The city was then repopulated by the settling of new inhabitants from the countryside (7.4-5; 11.1-2). At the end of the work the new walls could be inaugurated with a solemn religous rite (12.27ff.).

13.9.8 To give the population a fresh start, without any kind of burdens or debts, Nehemiah ordered a general remission of debts (Neh.5.1-13). This text does not seem to refer so much to ordinary debts, for example those that the farmer could contract for seed and repay some months later after the harvest: it seems to refer to a more important question. As we saw above (12.6.7), the Babylonians had redistributed the lands of those who had been deported among the population which remained. As a conjectural explanation I would like to suggest that the provision brought to an official conclusion all the law suits which had arisen over the land which the exiles reclaimed (this suggestion was already made, implicitly, by Noth* 1959, 326f.). A conflict of this kind, which risked becoming permanent, threatened the very existence of the tiny community; it will have been ended by allowing the properties to remain with those who had cultivated them for more than a century.

13.9.9 Another feature which is historically important is that at the end of the so-called edict of Artaxerxes (Ezra 7.12ff., though its authenticity is open to doubts similar to those about the edict of Cyrus, above 13.2.3), there is an important assertion: the Torah becomes the law of the state in Judaea and the norms codified in it are applied by means of the intervention of the civil authority. This very soon gave rise to the rendering of *tōrāh* with the Greek νόμος (below 14.12.5.6). Prayers and sacrifices were offered in the temple 'for the life of the king' at state expense (Ezra 6.10); the people of Judah paid taxes direct like the other populations (if this is how we are to understand Neh.9.37) and sometimes extraordinary tribute, which on one occasion was punitive (Josephus, *Antt.* XI, 297ff.).

13.10 Nehemiah's second mission

What motives prompted Nehemiah to return to Judaea in 432 BCE? We have no precise information.

13.10.1 One reason could have been that the high priest Eliashib was pursuing an autonomous policy, aimed not at separation from but rather at accommodation with other governors in the region. He was, as the texts say, 'close to Tobias', an expression which probably means that he was related to him. He was also related to Sanballat, since one of his grandsons had married a daughter of Sanballat (Neh.13.28). He had then allowed Tobias to use a room in the temple precinct – we do not know on what grounds and for what purpose (below 14.4.1).

13.10.2 Other reasons for Nehemiah's return could have been abuses which he had not succeeded in eliminating during his first stay: priests who neglected their functions (13.10; cf. Mal.1.6ff.); tithes which were not paid or were paid inadequately (13.12ff.; cf. Mal.3.6ff.); failure to observe the sabbath (13.15ff.); and marriages with foreign women (13.23; cf. Mal.2.10ff), an abuse which, as we have seen, did not stop even at the family of the High Priest.[31]

13.11 The rise, role and powers of the priesthood

The centralization of worship in the Jerusalem temple, which according to Deuteronomy took place at the beginning of the last quarter of the seventh century BCE under Josiah (above 12.4.2), and the emergence in the post-exilic period of the figure of the High Priest, surrounded by the Zadokite priesthood, are the main characteristic elements of the religion of Judah in this period. Some of its distinguishing features can be deduced from the P source of the Pentateuch; others appear later in the work of the Chronicler.

13.11.1 Despite the presence for about 200 years and perhaps more of a civil governor who was by nationality a Judaean, down to the Macedonian period, if we accept Avigad's documentation (indeed in the first decades even of a vassal king of the empire who, according to some scholars, cf. above 13.6.4.4, was then deposed in circumstances which we cannot ascertain; the only exception, the Persian Bagoas at the time of the Elephantine papyri, confirms the rule), the prestige and influence of religious power seem to have grown rapidly. On the one hand, in fact the governor represented first Persia and the other occupying powers, and was accountable for his mandate only to the court which had nominated him. On the other, the temple was now the only place in which Judah could still exercise any form of self-government, limited though it was; in this respect too it was helped by what I have called the 'tolerance' (above 13.2) of the empire in political and religious matters.

13.11.2 However, the temple had also assumed considerable importance in the economic sphere because of the tribute which it received regularly from the diaspora (the so-called 'obol') and the exercise of functions which we might regard as those of a bank (below 14.7.1.4). So there is nothing strange in the fact that the religious authorities came to acquire increasing importance alongside the civil government (and, if the suggestion is a valid one, the monarch for the first few decades of the empire), not only in matters of cult and belief but also in everyday life.

We are told little about the cult and its character at this period so we can only go by deductions and inferences.

13.11.2.1 The process of the renewal of the cult, which according to the Deuteronomistic history began under Josiah and perhaps already under Hezekiah, was pursued in a radical way in the post-exilic period. The originally agricultural character of the traditional festivals, clearly Canaanite in origin, was rapidly eliminated and replaced by what has often been called their 'historicization', i.e. their connection with events in the sacred history of the people, which they thus helped to celebrate.

13.11.2.2 Here the Babylonian exile, unanimously interpreted as divine judgment, was one of the key points of reference for the interpretation of Judah's past (Noth 1959*, 340f.). With it went a great fear of violating the divine commandments and a constant desire for purity before God. That is sufficient explanation of the importance which the rites of purification and expiation took on in this period: chief among them was the great 'Day of Atonement', *yōm kippūr*, celebrated on 10 Tishri (September-October; Lev.23.27-32; 25.9ff.; but cf. the much earlier text Lev.16).

13.11.2.3 Until recently[32] one often came across the theory that Ezra had brought the P source of the Pentateuch to Judaea from Susa. The foundation for this was Ezra 7.12, 14: '...according to the law of your God which is in your hand' (the edict, for which cf. above 13.9.9, is addressed to Ezra in the second person). It was precisely in this period that the Pentateuch was finished on the basis of P. However, the first of the two proposals is untenable: the expression quoted does not in fact mean that Ezra had actually brought a document, far less one that could be identified with part of the Pentateuch (Noth* 1959, 335; Kellerman 1968, 374f.). The same perplexity applies to the proposal that the document was a version of Deuteronomy (Cazelles 1956; Sacchi* 1976, 44). The second proposal seems more probable, even if there is no proof of it; indeed, it would not be strange for the Aramaic expression *dātā' dī-'elāh šemaiyā'*, 'the law of the God of heaven', to denote the now completed Pentateuch, the first element of the canon and the most important element in the Hebrew Bible in the making.

13.11.2.4 However, a new possibility should be explored: that the so-called law of Ezra is more or less identical with the 'Temple Scroll' (11 Q 19-20) found at Qumran. This is a conclusion arrived at independently by Houtman in 1981 and Wacholder in 1983, both quoted with approval by Garbini* 1988.

13.11.2.5 In this way the Pentateuch, as a norm for faith and everyday life, for meditation, study and to be put into practice, and at the same time, in the circumstances we have considered (above 13.9.9), the law of the state for the territory of Judah, will have started on its canonical career which was soon to make it holy scripture *par excellence* for the Judahites and for the Samaritans (for the latter cf. below 14.4).

13.11.3 All this happened in what had become a very small territory. To the north the frontier ran near Bethel (coord.172-148) and Baal-hazor (present-day *tell ʿaṣur*, coord.177-153); eastwards it extended to the Jordan and the Dead Sea, including En-gedi (coord.187-097); southwards it extended to Beth-sur (*ḥirbet eṭ-ṭubīqe*, coord. 159-110); westwards it ran to Azekah (*tell zakariye*, coord.144-123), Gezer (coord.142-140) and Ono (coord.137-159), cf. Aharoni** 1979, map 34.

13.11.4 However, 'Israel' extended far beyond these wretched bounds. A large part of Canaan was inhabited by people loyal to Jerusalem, with the sole exception of Samaria. So the capital was not only the main city of an insignificant province of the empire (assuming that this is what it was), but also the seat of the temple and therefore of the cult. It was the focal point of the vast and rich Babylonian Diaspora which sent it men and financial means (cf. Zech.6.9-10), though on the other hand it did not hesitate to intervene, as in the case of Nehemiah, in what might otherwise have been thought to be internal matters of the Judahite community.

13.11.5 Given the distance between the centres of the Diaspora and many places in the Holy Land from the Jerusalem sanctuary, the decentralization of the cult became increasingly necessary, since it was impossible to ask people living in Mesopotamia, Egypt and Persia periodically to make the long, expensive and risky journey. The solution was found in the creation of what in the Greek world came to be called the synagogue.

Bibliography

P.Lifschitz, *Donateurs et fondateurs dans les synagogues juïves*, Cahiers RB 7, Paris 1967; L.I.R(abinowitz), 'Synagogue', *EncJud* 15, 1971, 579-84; K.Hruby, *Die Synagoge – Geschichtliche Entwicklungen einer Institution*, Zurich 1971; J.Swetnam, 'Why Was Jeremiah's New Covenant New?', *SVT* 26, 1974, 111-15; E.M.Meyers, 'Synagogue', *IDB-SV*, 1976, 842-4; F.Hüttenmeister and K.Galling, 'Synagoge', *BRL* ²1977, 327-32; H.Shanks, *Judaism in Stone*, New York 1979; J.C.Griffith, 'Egypt and the Rise of the Synagogue', *JTS* NS 37, 1987, 1-15; L.L.Grabbe, 'Synagogues in pre-70 Palestine: A Re-Assessment', *JTS* NS 49, 1988, 401-10.

13.11.5.1 It is possible to argue that this institution arose in the period betwen the edict of Cyrus and the governorship of Nehemiah. In Hebrew it is called *bēt kᵉnesset*, literally 'house of meeting', in Greek συναγωγή: it served for communal prayer, study and the communal reading of the scriptures and other writings, for singing and as a centre of social activity.

13.11.5.2 We do not know for certain when and where the first synagogue was founded; however, we know that the institution spread rapidly wherever there was a Jewish nucleus, i.e. also, as we have seen, in places distant from the Holy Land. Rabinowitz 1971 found an indication of its foundation in the mention of the 'small sanctuary' of Ezek.11.16 (my translation, but the text is uncertain and some scholars correct it, or at any rate understand it differently), while according to Swetnam 1974 there is already an allusion to the synagogue in Jer.31.31ff. At all events, synagogues certainly existed in the first century BCE, and one in Egypt even seems to go back to the third century BCE (Shanks 1979), so it appears certain that the synagogue is already attested long before the destruction of the temple in 70 CE, which means that it grew up independently of this.

13.11.6 We are relatively well informed on one sector of the Diaspora, though this is a small and untypical group: the Jewish military colony and community of Elephantine, situated on the island of the same name near the present-day border between Egypt and the Sudan, at the level of the First Cataract and the Aswan Dam.

Bibliography

A.E.Cowley, *Aramaic Papyri of the Fifth Century BC*, Oxford 1923; E.G.Kraeling, *The Brooklyn Aramaic Papyri*, New York 1953; B.Porten, *Archives from Elephantine*, Berkeley 1968. Cf. also G.Widengren*, 532-5; Fohrer*, 212ff.; R.Contini, 'I documenti aramaici dell'Egitto persiano e tolemaico', *RiBib* 34, 1986, 73-109: 83ff., 93ff.; cf. also Widengren in Hayes and Miller* 1977, 523-5, and my *Introduction*, Appendix II 1-2 (bibliography). For the general problem of the military colonies in Egypt cf. A.Temerev, 'Social Organization in Egyptian Military Settlements of the Sixth-Fourth Centuries BCE: *dgl* and *m't*', in *'The Word of the Lord Shall Go Forth.' Essays... D.N.Freedman*, Winona Lake, Ind. 1983, 523-5.

13.11.6.1 It is not possible to establish for certain when, in what circumstances, for what purposes and by whom this Jewish military colony was founded: a first possibility would be the Persian occupation under Cambyses, i.e. around 525 BCE (above 13.3); on the other hand there must already have been Judahites on the island before that, with their own temple, since in Papyrus Cowley 30, line 13, the priests who are reporting to Jerusalem state that 'our fathers in the time of the kings of Egypt built this temple in the fortress of Jeb [= Elephantine]', so that Cambyses must have found it there at the time of the conquest (M.Smith in *CHJ* I, 219). A large part of the archive of the colony and the community has been preserved: the earliest letter dates from 495, the latest from 398, and it is probable that the colony disappeared soon afterwards, probably in one of the many revolts against Persia.

13.11.6.2 A first characteristic of the cult of the community is thus the presence of a temple of its own in which complete worship was carried out, including sacrifices, as at Jerusalem. A second characteristic is that beliefs seem to have been polytheistic or at least syncretistic: alongside the God of Israel, whose name is always written *yhw*, two other deities appear to whom worship is offered: *'anat bēt-'ēl* and *'asīm bēt-'ēl*; the latter may perhaps be mentioned in Amos 8.14 in the form *'asmah** (in the construct, *'ašmat*).[33] So the community does not seem to have been affected either by Josiah's reform or by that of Nehemiah. A connection with the North, suggested by the relationship of the deity with Bethel, seems to be ruled out, since the correspondence is exclusively with the Jerusalem temple authorities.

13.11.6.3 Another characteristic is that, contrary to all the logic of later Judahite orthodoxy, the relations with the Jerusalem priesthood were frequent and cordial. Fohrer* 1982, 224ff., takes seriously into account the possibility that one of the tasks of Ezra (or better, I would suggest, of the second mission of Nehemiah, above 13.10) was to put an end to this kind of 'abuse'.

13.12 The end of the Persian empire

Bibliography

O.Kaiser, 'Zwischen den Fronten – Palästina in den Auseinandersetzung zwischen Perserreich und Ägypten in den ersten Hälfte des 4.Jahrhunderts', in *FS J.Ziegler*, Würzburg 1972, II, 197-206.

The Persian empire lasted just over two centuries; the expeditions against Greece which ended in the defeat of the Persians by sea and land dealt a heavy blow to the political and military power of the empire and led to a series of revolts. These were almost continuous in Egypt, and the country succeeded in gaining its liberty for long periods; others broke out among the Phoenician cities, which had nevertheless provided the fleets for the expedition against the Greeks. Finally, there were also conflicts between the satraps themselves, the most serious of which occurred between the years 369 and 360. Artaxerxes III Ochus (358-339), a capable and decisive ruler, managed to take over the reigns of power: in 345 he subjected the Phoenician cities, in 341 he reconquered Egypt and was able to provide some reinforcement for the tottering power of Persia. However, this was only for a short time:

he was assassinated, and with his death the recovery ended. Now the end was only a few years in coming.

14

Under the Macedonians and Diadochi

14.1 The Macedonian empire

In the battle of Issus, near to present-day Alexandretta, in 333, Alexander, son of Philip II of Macedon, who went down in history with the title 'the Great', defeated the Persian army of Darius III Codomannus (335-332); in 332 he occupied Syria and Canaan on his march towards Egypt. Tyre resisted him for a good seven months, Gaza for two. In Canaan the (future?) Samaritans gave Alexander a good welcome; Josephus (*Antt.* XI, 325ff.) tells us that Jerusalem first resisted in the name of loyalty to the Persians, but was then miraculously saved, and the High Priest submitted. On his return from Egypt Alexander was able to pass undisturbed through the region on his way to Mesopotamia, where in 332 he defeated the survivors of the Persian army at Gaugamela, near Arbela. Samaria, whose capital was the seat of the satrapy, rebelled against him later, in 331 (C.Rufus, in Stern I, 448ff.), and in the course of this revolt groups of nobles will have fled from Samaria and taken refuge in the Jordan valley: to them are usually attributed the papyri of *wādī dalīye* (F.M.Cross, oral communication, cf. above 13.7.1.2). Samaria will have been punished by the settlement of a Macedonian colony.

Bibliography

F.-M.Abel, *Histoire de la Palestine depuis la conquête d'Alexandre jusqu'à l'invasion arabe*, Paris 1952; V.Tcherikover, *Hellenistic Civilization and the Jews*, Jerusalem 1959; O.Plöger, *Theocracy and Eschatology*, Oxford 1968; S.K.Eddy, *The King is Dead*, University of Nebraska 1961; S.Zeitlin, *The Rise and Fall of the Judaean State*, Philadelphia I, 1962; II, 1967; III, 1978; E.Bickerman, *From Ezra to the Last of the Maccabees – Foundations of Post-Biblical Judaism*, New York 1962; D.S.Russell, *The Jews from Alexander to Herod*, London 1967; O.H.Steck, 'Das Problem theologischer Strömungen in nachexilischer Zeit', *EvTh* 28, 1968, 445-58; M.Smith, *Palestinian*

Parties and Politics that Shaped the Old Testament, New York 1971, London
²1987; O.Plöger, *Aus der Spätzeit des Alten Testaments*, Göttingen 1971;
G.F.Delling, 'Perspektiven der Erforschung des Hellenistischen Juden-
tums', *HUCA* 45, 1974, 133-76; O.Kaiser, 'Judentum und Hellenismus',
VuF 27.1, 1982, 68-88; M.Hengel, *Judaism and Hellenism*, London and
Philadelphia 1974; T.Fischer, *Seleukiden und Makkabäer*, Bochum 1980;
P.Schäfer, *Die Juden in der Antike – Geschichte des Judentums von Alexander
dem Grossen bis zur arabischen Eroberung Palästinas*, Tübingen 1982;
C.Saulnier and C.Perrot, *Histoire d'Israël III: De la conquête d'Alexandre à
la destruction du Temple (331 a.C. – 135 a.D)*, Paris 1985; S.J.D.Cohen,
From the Maccabees to the Mishnah, Philadelphia 1987; T.Fischer, 'Has-
monaeans and Seleucids. Aspects of War and Policy in the Second and
First Centuries BCE', in *Greece and Rome in Eretz Israel*, ed.A.Kasher,
U.Rappaport, G.Fuks, Jerusalem 1990, 3-20; D.Gera, 'On the Credibility
of the History of the Tobiads', ibid., 21-39; J.Mélèze-Modrzjewski,
'L'image du Juïf dans la Pensée Grecque vers 300 avant nôtre ère', ibid.,
105-18; J.S.McLaren, *Power and Politics in Palestine. The Jews and the
Governing of their Land 100 BC – AD 70*, Sheffield 1991; G.Boccaccini,
Middle Judaism, Minneapolis 1991. For chronology see R.Hanhart, *Zur
Zeitrechnung des I und II Makkabäerbuches*, Berlin 1964; K.Matthiae,
*Chronologische Übersichten und Karten zur spätjüdischen und urchristlichen
Zeit*, Berlin and Stuttgart 1978; T.Fischer, *Seleukiden und Makkabäer*,
Bochum 1980. For Zech.9.1-8, cf. K.Elliger, 'Ein Zeugnis der jüdische
Gemeinde im Alexanderjahr 332 BC', *ZAW* 62, 1949-50, 63-115 (not in
GS); H.Delcor, 'Les allusions à Alexandre le Grand dans Zach.IX.1-8',
VT I, 1951, 110-24. For the Zeno papyri, cf. V.Tcherikover and A.Fuks,
Corpus Papyrorum Judaicorum I, Cambridge, Mass. 1957; they are not
included in M.Stern, *Authors*, I-II. For the political and religious
movements, their thought and their doctrines, cf. H.G.Kippenberg,
Religion und Klassenbildung im antiken Judentum, Göttingen 1978, chs.5,
6, 7; C.Thoma, *Christliche Theologie des Judentums*, Aschaffenburg 1978;
G.Delling, 'Alexander der Grosse als Bekenner des jüdischen Glaub-
ens', *JSJ* 12, 1981, 1-51. For the most important classical texts in
translation cf. R.S.Baghall and P.Derow (eds.), *Greek Historical Documents – The Hellenistic Period*, Atlanta, Ga 1981.

14.1.1 The Macedonian conquest differed notably from previous
conquests in which an eastern power subjected others in the same
region: in this latter case it all remained, as it were, in the family.
However, with the conquest by a Hellenistic power the West erupted
into the region, bringing with it completely new customs and a
substantially different view of the universe. Thus began a process of
Hellenization, which was pursued under the Diadochi, Rome and
Byzantium and was interrupted only by the Islamic conquest in the

seventh century CE. So we may rightly talk of the end of one era and the beginning of another. The period in which the whole of the vast region of the East seems to have been culturally autonomous and intact was at an end, and it began progressively to be Westernized. However, this process initially came up against heavy resistance, not only in Judaea. Yet Judaism too was profoundly affected by it, as is evident from the fact that in the second revolt (below 15.8) in the second century BCE, the ultra-nationalist movement of Bar Kochba also used Greek in its own correspondence.

14.1.2 There is virtually nothing about this period, which we must regard as very important, in the proto- and deutero-canonical writings of the Old Testament: Chronicles does not go beyond the Persian period except in genealogies; Maccabees considers it only in the broadest of terms. So the historian is exclusively dependent on Josephus, and book XII of his *Antiquities* deals with the period only in summary form. Some elements are provided by classical authors, and their texts have been collected in M.Stern's monumental anthology (1974-1984). Just one prophetic text, Zech.9.1-8, could allude to the passage of Alexander the Great through the region, according to the studies of Elliger 1950 and Delcor 1951.

14.1.3 We know from Josephus, *Antt.* XI, 337, that Alexander continued the religious policy begun by the Persians. Judaea and Samaria were left alone and their inhabitants were allowed to live according to the Torah; it is also probable that this continued to be the law of the state.

14.1.4 We do not know what happened to the civil governor introduced by the Persians. According to Avigad's documentation (above 13.6.5.1), the last governor will have been a certain *yḥzqyh*, i.e. *yᵉḥezqīyāh* in Massoretic vocalization, who will have been in office around 330, and therefore a contemporary of the High Priest Onias I. According to these documents, the governorship will have been maintained during the Macedonian period, so that the transition from one regime to another took place without disturbances. However, we do not know what happened later, even if it is probable that the institution was maintained. It is probable that the Tobiads of Transjordan (above 13.8.3.2 and below 14.7.4.8) succeeded in holding the governorship over the course of several generations, until the High Priest Onias III expelled them from the country (below 14.7.4.10); in any case, as I have already indicated (above 13.11), with the importance assumed by the temple the High Priest and the religious authority associated with him acquired increasing prestige and power, in fact being on an equal footing with the civil power.

14.2 The disintegration of Alexander's empire

Alexander died unexpectedly in 323, leaving open the problem of the succession. He had two sons, one legitimate and the other illegitimate, but both of them were minors, so this made a regency necessary. Alexander's generals assumed responsibility for this, each of them meanwhile having become a governor of a region of the empire. They came to be called 'Diadochi', Greek 'successors', a term which adequately reflects the *de facto* situation. One of them was assigned the European territories, Macedonia, Greece and Thrace; another Egypt; a third Asia Minor; and a fourth Babylonia, Syria and Canaan. Syria and Canaan were contested between Babylonia and Egypt, repeating a pattern which had now lasted for millennia.

14.2.1 The death of the two sons of Alexander in 310 and 309 (they were probably assassinated) left things as they were, legitimating the *de facto* power of the Diadochi. Each of them held on to what he had and founded a dynasty, at the same time seeking to enlarge his own territories.

14.2.2 Almost immediately Canaan came under the dominion of the Ptolemies-Lagids of Egypt. Ptolemy, the ex-governor of Egypt with a seat at Alexandria, the city founded by Alexandria on the shore of the Mediterranean west of the Delta, suddenly occupied Canaan and Phoenicia, taking them from the Seleucids of Mesopotamia. This operation caused him some difficulties with the other Diadochi, but the Ptolemies succeeded in retaining control of the region. Jerusalem was occupied in 312. Information about the fate of the Judahite community is, again, unknown; we only know that according to Josephus, *Antt.* XII, 7, many inhabitants of Jerusalem were deported to Alexandria; furthermore the Alexandrian Diaspora grew rapidly as a result of constant immigration from the mother country. Relations between the Jews of Alexandria and the Ptolemies were always good, and it is under Ptolemy II Philadelphus (285-246) that legend puts the Greek translation of the so-called Septuagint (so named after the number of scholars, seventy, who are said to have taken part in it).[1] This translation is an obvious example of the degree of Hellenization reached by the Jewish community at least in Alexandria, and of its assimilation at the linguistic level; this development was also furthered by the incorporation of not a few 'proselytes' (literally 'those who have joined'), people who had never been Hebrew or Aramaic speakers (below 14.7.4.6).

14.2.3 As far as we can see, under the government of the Ptolemies-Lagids the region enjoyed considerable prosperity, even if this was offset by heavy taxation. We get some information about the period from the 'Zeno papyri', the report of an Egyptian official who had travelled through Canaan and Transjordan between 260 and 258 BCE, i.e. during the reign of Ptolemy II, which has been partially preserved. Zeno does not seem to have had contacts with the religious authorities, but only with Tobias, who was the civil governor (Josephus, *Antt.* XII, 160). He belonged to a famous house, one of whose members is mentioned in Zech.6.9-15 among those sent to Judaea from Babylon around 520-515 (above 13.6.4.4), and another among the adversaries of Nehemiah (above 13.8.3.2); and according to B.Mazar's proposal (above 11.2.6.2), one of his forebears will even have been the Tabeel whom Isa.7.6 (emended text) mentions as the opponent of Ahaz.

In the present state of research it is not yet possible to reconstruct a succession of the Tobiads.

14.3 Under the Seleucids of Syria

At the beginning of the second century BCE, after a series of hostile encounters, Syria and Canaan passed from the Ptolemies-Lagids to the Seleucids of Syria, a dynasty founded in 312 by Seleucus I Monophthalmos, called Nicanor.

14.3.1 Under Antiochus III the Great (232-187), an ally of Philip V of Macedonia and a friend of Hannibal, to whom he gave sanctuary at his court after the battle of Zama (202 BCE), the Seleucid empire extended as far as Asia Minor and the Ionian cities there. This soon led to conflict with Rome. Before that, however, in 198 Antiochus had been able to occupy Syria and Judaea, defeating Ptolemy V Epiphanes at the battle of Panaea (or Panaeum, present-day *bānyas*, coord.215-295, the New Testament's Caesarea Philippi).

14.3.2 The conflict with Rome, whose power Antiochus had underestimated, ended at the battle of Magnesia (between Sardis and Smyrna, 190 BCE) with a disastrous defeat.

14.3.2.1 Antiochus was forced to sue for peace and could obtain it only on very harsh terms: he had to abandon all Asia Minor and the Greek cities, pay a heavy fine, give hostages to Rome including his own sons Antiochus and Demetrius, send war elephants and the fleet, and extradite Hannibal (who, however, succeeded in escaping). Antiochus was killed during an attempt to sack a temple, with the aim of obtaining the money needed to pay Rome.

14.3.2.2 The payments to Rome and the constant indebtedness which resulted from them are a basic factor for anyone who wants to understand the Seleucid policy towards the Jewish community in the next decades.

14.3.3 The transition to Seleucid lordship does not seem initially to have caused problems for the Jewish community; it is even probable that to begin with the community was delighted to be liberated from the excessive fiscal demands of the Ptolemies, though as a result the mother country was cut off from the Egyptian Diaspora. Moreover initially the Seleucids seem to have been well disposed to the Jews and Josephus, *Antt.* XII, 138-44, also mentions some edicts of Antiochus III which benefitted the community of Judah.

14.3.4 Antiochus III was succeeded by his son Seleucus IV Philopator (187-179). The new ruler does not seem to have been a brilliant man, but he was not without ability, and was able at least partly to extricate himself from the difficult situation he inherited from his father. However, he too was constrained by the debts from the war with Rome and tried to remedy this by taking money from various sources, including the temple of Jerusalem. In other respects, it seems that he was quite friendly to the community in Judah: Josephus, *Antt.* XII, 119ff., reports that he contributed to the expenses of the temple cult from his personal funds. He also succeeded in ransoming some of the hostages that his father had had to leave in Rome, including his brother Antiochus; however, the other brother, Demetrius, had to remain in Rome (below 14.10.5). Seleucus was assassinated by his minister Heliodorus and the succession passed to Antiochus, who was on his way back from Rome.

14.4 The Samaritans

Josephus (*Antt.*XI, 304ff.) connects the Samaritan schism with the rigoristic measures of Nehemiah.

Bibliography

H.H.Rowley, 'The Samaritan Schism in Legend and History', in *Israel's Prophetic Heritage – FS J.Muilenburg*, New York and London 1962, 208-22; id., 'Sanballat and the Samaritan Temple', *BJRL* 38, 1955-56, 166-98 = *Men of God*, London 1963, 246-76; J.Macdonald, *The Theology of the Samaritans*, London 1964; G.E.Wright, 'The Samaritans at Shechem', in *Shechem*, New York 1965, 170-89; F.M.Cross, 'Aspects of Samaritan and Jewish History in Persian and Hellenistic Times', *HTR* 59, 1966, 201-11; J.D.Purvis, *The Samaritan Pentateuch and the Origins of the Samaritan Sect*, Cambridge, Mass. 1968; P.Sacchi, 'Studi samaritani', *RSLR* 5, 1969, 413-40; M.Smith, *Palestinian Parties* (see 14.1 above), 148-92; H.G.Kippenberg, *Garizim und Synagoge. Traditionsgeschichtliche Untersuchungen zur samaritanischen Religion der aramäischen Periode*, Berlin 1971; A.L(oewenstamm), 'Samaritans', *EncJud* 14, 1971, 725-57; R.J.Coggins, *Samaritans and Jews. The Origins of the Samaritans Reconsidered*, Oxford 1975; F.M.Cross, 'Papyri from the Fourth Century' (above 13.1); J.D.Purvis, 'Samaritans', *IDB* SV, 1976, 770f.; S.Talmon, 'Ezra and Nehemiah' (above, 13.1); H.Tadmor, 'Some Aspects of the History of

Samaria during the Biblical Period', *The Jerusalem Cathedra* 3, 1983, 1-11; R.Egger, *Josephus Flavius und die Samaritaner*, Fribourg CH 1986; J.Hausmann, *Israels Rest*, Stuttgart 1987, 5-23; M.Cogan, ' "For We, Like You, Worship Your God" ', *VT* 38, 1988, 286-92; A.D.Crown (ed.), *The Samaritans*, Tübingen 1989; in this volume especially M.Mor, 'The Persian, Hellenistic and Hasmonaean Periods', 1-18; N.Schur, *History of the Samaritans*, Frankfurt am Main 1989, ²1992; U.Rappaport, 'The Samaritans in the Hellenistic Period', *Zion* 55, 1990, 373-96 (in Hebrew, with an English summary); A.D.Crown, 'Manuscripts, Cast-Type and Samaritan Palaeography', *BJRL* 72, 1990, 87-130; R.T.Anderson, 'The Elusive Samaritan Temple', *BA* 57, 1991, 104-7; F.Dexinger and R.Pummer, *Die Samaritaner*, Darmstadt 1992.

14.4.1 A certain Manasseh, brother of the High Priest Jaddua mentioned in Neh.12.11,22, contemporary of the governor Bagoas (the only governor, as we have seen, who was probably not a Judahite, but a Persian), who is also mentioned in the Elephantine letters (above 13.11.6) and thus lived towards the end of the fifth cenrury, had married a non-Jewish woman against his brother's will. This case is similar to that mentioned in Neh.13.28, where one of the sons of the high priest Jehoiada had married a daughter of Sanballat, the governor of Samaria (above 13.8.3.1 – for some authors, including Sacchi*, ch.IV, the similarity is so great that this is one and the same case); other instances of mixed marriages appear in Josephus, *Antt.* XI, 312. Now Manasseh is said to have taken refuge in Samaria with Sanballat, probably the second of that name, and therefore the grandson of Nehemiah's opponent, in order to escape the rigours of Jerusalem orthodoxy. Here I am following the chronology of Talmon 1976 and not that of Cross 1975, 5ff.; Cross puts the episode in the time of Sanballat III, who died around 332 BCE, i.e. at the time of the Macedonian conquest.

14.4.2 In this way there will have emerged in Samaria a Jewish community with a Zadokite priest, which was located in Shechem. According to Sacchi* 1976, 54f., Ezra will have maintained relations with this group over a certain period, relations which were quickly broken off because of the incompatibility of the respective positions.

14.4.3 Now we cannot *a priori* exclude the possibility that a new community emerged in the wake of a conflict between the rigorists of Jerusalem and the community in Samaria, which was less rigorist, and this can serve as a working hypothesis (Purvis 1976). Nor can we exclude the possibility that the North became a focal point for all those who were generally discontented with the way things were going in Jerusalem. That is all the more likely since the North was inhabited by a population with a Yahwistic faith, who not unjustly regarded themselves as the heirs of the ancient kingdom of Israel. So there was what we might nowadays call grass-roots support for a possible policy of religious independence from Jerusalem. Moreover the Samaritan traditions preserved to the present day tend essentially to mention Ezra and his provisions as the reason for separation on the religious plane (Widengren* 1977, 511). On the other hand, credible though this hypothesis may be, it must be remembered how different the two groups were at an ethnic, political and religious level, as I indicated at the beginning of this study (above 1.1.1, cf. 3.7.1.4).

14.4.4 From a political point of view there was some hostility towards the Judahites on the part of the Sanballatids, the governors of Samaria on behalf of the Persians, especially after the measures taken by Nehemiah (and by Ezra, above 13.8.3, 13.9.6), and that must have meant that the authorities were at least neutral towards the separation, if not in favour. If to this we add the evident political skill of the Sanballatids, who managed to keep the governorship of Samaria within the family for at least six generations known to us (and perhaps for more), we have a complete picture of the situation.

14.4.5 So following the reforms of Nehemiah (and Ezra) Judaea shut itself up in a substantial orthodoxy; however, it was precisely this which proved capable of preserving what were to become the fundamental values of Judaism, those basic features which have allowed it to survive over the millennia. Something different seems to have happened with the Samaritans.

14.4.5.1 First of all we must clarify a philological point. Sacchi* 1971, ch.IV, has connected the name with the root *šāmar*, 'observe (a law)', hence the ancient pronunciation *šāmārīm*, 'the observant'; the term evidently led itself to confusion with *šōmᵉrōn*, 'Samaria'.

14.4.5.2 However, the Samaritan community, born out of a desire for liberty and openness, found itself, equally paradoxically, in a conservative role. Attached to a traditional religious attitude which seems to have been only superficially affected by Josiah's reform and therefore 'at an early stage of religious development' (Widengren* 1977), it remained open to almost all the pressures and customs of popular piety.

14.4.5.3 It is no longer possible to establish when and in what circumstances the break came about. Indeed, as Coggins 1975, 164, points out, followed by Widengren* 1977, relationships between the two groups were only broken off at a much later stage.

14.4.5.4 Certainly the building of a temple on Mount Gerizim (present-day *jebel eṭ-ṭūr*, south of present-day Nablus, coord. 176-179) involved the community in a *de facto* break with Jerusalem, as it was an obvious alternative to the sanctuary of Zion. And there is an approximate date for this building: the Persians always favoured the

Jerusalem cult, so it is likely that it was authorized later, in the Macedonian period.

14.4.5.5 On the other hand, this matter of the alternative sanctuary must not be considered basic, since we know from the example of the Elephantine temple (above 13.11.6) that the Jerusalem priesthood did not take its own claims to exclusiveness too seriously; however, it should be noted that the priests of Elephantine maintained frequent and cordial contacts with those of Jerusalem, whose superiority they implicitly recognized. The opposite happened with the Samaritans.

14.4.6 If the Samaritan temple on Gerizim was built at the beginning of the Macedonian period, the largely legendary accounts reported by Josephus, *Antt.* XI, 321-4 (Noth* 1959, 319, against Bright* 1981, 409ff.), take on weight: according to these the Samaritans immediately submitted to Alexander the Great (above 14.1.3), receiving authorization from him to build their own sanctuary, whereas Jerusalem is said initially to have vacillated, invoking its loyalty to the Persians (Josephus, *Antt.* XI, 325f.). In this way Jerusalem will have obtained nothing more than the simple confirmation of its own previous status. Be this as it may, the existence of a Samaritan temple on Gerizim is attested in the first half of the second century BCE (cf. II Macc.6.2), where it is mentioned along with that of Jerusalem; moreover, this text suggests that the temple had already been there for some time, so it does not seem too risky to date its construction to the beginning of the Macedonian period.

14.4.7 Later, Jerusalem always considered the community and the cult of the Samaritans to be illegitimate. When Chronicles,[2] like the Deuteronomistic history work before it, speaks of 'Israel', it always means the South *and* the North, which it considers ideally united and would like to see united in practice. The text of Chronicles is not generally polemical towards the Samaritans, contrary to what one would expect and often hears (cf. Hausmann 1987). In its theology the Jerusalem temple certainly stands at the centre of the spiritual history of the people and the Northern kingdom, which is considered a forebear of the Samaritans and is not once given a favourable mention. The Deuteronomistic history, and especially DtrN in II Kings 17.24-41, regards the population of the North as the product of an ethnic mix, practising a syncretistic cult (above 11.3.4); however, there is no proof that this was how things really were, so the text must be taken to be purely polemical. Moreover II Kings 17 is not the only text to speak of the forebears of the Samaritans: according to Ezra 4.1-5 they (or better, their ancestors) offered help in the rebuilding to those who returned from Babylon since they worshipped the same God; and according to II Chron.30 they will even have celebrated the Passover together in Judah under Hezekiah (above 12.2.1). Hence not all the judgments of the Samaritans and their forebears made by the Hebrew Bible are equally negative (Cogan 1988). The New Testament again seems polemical; in the answer which Jesus gives to the Samaritan woman in John 4.22 he states: 'You worship what you do not know; we worship what we know, for salvation is from the Jews.' This clearly implies the illegitimacy of the Samaritan cult, even if the discourse immediately gives clear signs of going beyond such a polemical position.

14.4.8 Down the millennia the Samaritans have formed a particularly important group, a real alternative community to that first of Judah and then of orthodox Judaism. A certain decadence begins with the Islamic conquest from the seventh century onwards. But its acceptance only of the Pentateuch, the one canonical biblical text at the time of separation, left the movement outside the prophetic message and that of the other biblical books; the exclusion from the great debates which troubled but also purified Judaism and constantly brought it up to date, fixed the Samaritans in an archaic form of piety. This attitude also appears from the fact that even today they still use an archaic form of writing, derived from the Phoenician, not because it is more practical, but simply because it is traditional.

14.4.9 The Samaritans survive today in the persons of a few thousand individuals around Nablus, overlooked by their sacred mountain Gerizim, in territory administered by the Israeli army since 1967, and at Holon, a south-eastern suburb of Tel Aviv.

14.5 Apocalyptic

The late Persian period and the beginning of the Macedonian period saw the progressive exhaustion, followed by the extinction, of what was one of the most characteristic and creative movements in ancient Judaism, prophecy. In its place, and for some time parallel to it, there appeared another movement, basically esoteric and speculative in content, apocalyptic.[3]

Bibliography

Translations of the texts can be found in E.Kautzsch, *Die Apokryphen und Pseudepigraphen des Alten Testaments*, Tübingen 1900; R.H.Charles, *The Apocrypha and Pseudepigrapha of the Old Testament*, Oxford 1913; P.Riesler, *Altjüdisches Schrifttum ausserhalb der Bibel*, Augsburg 1928; W.H.Kümmel (ed.), *Jüdische Schriften aus hellenistisch-römischer Zeit*, Gütersloh 1973ff.; J.H.Charlesworth (ed.), *The Old Testament Pseudepigrapha*, Garden City, NY and London 1983-85 (two vols.).

On apocalyptic: E.Schürer, *Geschichte des israelitisch-jüdischen Volkes im Zeitalter Jesu Christi*, Leipzig 1910 (a classic work, updated in a completely new edition by G.Vermes, F.Millar and M.Black, *The History of the Jewish People in the Age of Jesus Christ*, Edinburgh 1973-87; H.H.Rowley, *The Relevance of Apocalyptic*, London 1947; O.Plöger, *Theocracy and Eschatology* (see 14.1); D.S.Russell, *The Method and Message of Jewish Apocalyptic*, London 1964; R.H.Charles, *Eschatology*, reprinted New York 1963; W.Bousset, *Die Religion des Judentum*, third edition ed. H. and E.Lohse, Tübingen 1966; P.von der Osten-Sacken, *Die Apokalyptik in ihrem Verhältnis zur Prophetie und zur Weisheit*, Munich 1969; J.M.Schmidt, *Die jüdische Apokalyptik*, Neukirchen/Vluyn 1969; J.Schreiner, *Alttestamentlich-jüdische Apokalyptik*, Gütersloh 1970; L.Rost, *Judaism outside the Hebrew Canon: An Introduction to the Documents*, Nashville 1976; H.Gese, 'Anfang und Ende der Apokalyptik, dargestellt am Sacharjabuch', *ZTK* 70, 1973, 20-49 = *Vom Sinai zum Sion*, Munich ²1983, 202-30; W.C.van Unnik (ed.), *La littérature juive entre Tenach et Mishna*, Leiden 1974; P.D.Hanson, *The Dawn of Apocalyptic*, Philadelphia 1975; J.A.Soggin, 'Profezia ed apocalittica nel Giudaesimo postesilico', *RiBib* 30, 1982, 161-73; C.Rowland, *The Open Heaven*, London 1982; P.Sacchi, 'Riflessioni sull'essenza dell'apocalittica', *Hen* 5, 1983, 33-62; G.Boccaccini, 'E Daniele un testo apocalittico?', *Hen* 9, 1987, 267-302; D.E.Gowan, *Eschatology in the Old Testament*, Philadelphia 1987; P.Sacchi, 'Esquisse du développement du messianisme juif a la lumière du texte qumranien 11Q Melch', *ZAW* 100 (1988 supplement), 202-14; H.Hellholm (ed.), *Apocalypticism in the Mediterranean World and the Near East*, Tübingen ²1989; P.Sacchi, *L'apocalittica giudaica e la sua storia*, Brescia 1990; I.Shatzman, *The Armies of the Hasmonaeans and Herod. From Hellenistic to Roman Framework*, Tübingen 1991; L.L.Grabbe, 'Maccabean Chronology', *JBL* 110, 1991, 59-74. The theology and the pertinent texts have now been re-examined by G.Boccaccini, *Middle Judaism*, Minneapolis 1991.

14.5.1 Those who returned from the Babylonian exile had been helped, comforted and even rebuked, first by the prophets Haggai and Zechariah, then by the anonymous prophet called Trito-Isaiah shortly afterwards, and finally, just before the arrival of Nehemiah and Ezra, by another anonymous figure known as Malachi. Two other prophets, Joel and the anonymous Deutero-Zechariah (as we saw above, 14.1.2, Zech.9.1-8 perhaps bears witness to the coming of Alexander the Great), preached in a period we cannot date precisely but which was probably around the end of the fourth century BCE. We know of no prophet after this period, and the quality of post-exilic prophecy is generally regarded as being notably inferior to that of its pre-exilic predecessors. That is also because the loss of political independence left little room for a preaching which had often had a political and social content. The New Testament then knows of new prophets, the greatest of whom is said to be John the Baptist.

14.5.2 Parallel to the progressive extinction of prophecy, however, there arose a new movement which derived directly from it, even if it can be considered something of an illegitimate child, apocalyptic. Its texts are to be found for the most part in the pseudepigraphical books (so called because they are often attributed to figures from the prehistory and history of Israel who certainly cannot have composed them); they never came to form part of the Hebrew canon, apart from the book of Daniel (though its apocalyptic character has recently been denied in a study by Boccaccini 1987), and brief sections here and there in the other prophets.

14.5.3 Apocalyptic has much in common with prophecy: faith in the God of Israel as Lord of history who is guiding it to its end and completion, who elects Israel as his instrument to pursue his own plans in this history; the election of the people of God seen not as a privilege but as a responsibility; the certainty that the exile in Babylon was the divine judgment *par excellence* on the unfaithfulness of the people, quite apart from other judgments to come.

14.5.4 However, there are also many basic differences, so that apocalyptic really is a bastard child. In apocalyptic the message is secret, entrusted to someone who receives the revelation and is to publish it only 'in the last times'. So the apocalyptists are not preachers, witnesses, whereas the prophets were precisely that; rather, the apocalypses are repositories of revealed truths to be kept hidden. Election appears as something established from time immemorial and as an individual gift, not accessible to the many. And all the discourse on the end of time and the catastrophes which will usher in the kingdom of God is ahistorical, atemporal discourse, which makes relevant use of mythical material. Moreover, doctrines make an appearance which were previously absent, like the doctrine of hereditary original sin, which was to have so much importance in the primitive church. Finally, there is a strong intellectualist approach, a highly speculative way of advancing the discussions, to such a degree that a scholar like von Rad[4] wanted to derive apocalyptic from biblical wisdom, or at least connect it closely with wisdom.

14.5.5 The catastrophes of the years 70 and 135 CE (below 15.5 and 15.8) finally discredited apocalyptic: instead of bringing the kingdom of God to a purified community, the sufferings, though interpreted eschatologically, had brought destruction and dispersion. So it was easy for the orthodoxy of rabbinic Judaism to extinguish most of the traces of apocalyptic: only a few survive in the rabbinic writings and some in those of the New Testament. The millenarians in sectarian Christian groups had more success.

14.6 Antiochus IV Epiphanes

Antiochus IV (175-164), brother of the dead Seleucus IV and a former hostage at Rome, ascended the throne. He took the title Epiphanes, 'God revealed'; we do not know whether he meant it to convey just that or whether it was merely a piece of rhetoric. However, it could easily seem provocative in the sphere of orthodox and apocalyptic Judaism. Like his father Antiochus III he seems to have been a brilliant man, endowed with remarkable skills, even if these must have been mitigated by forms of extravagance (he loved pomp and satisfied this love by spending a good deal badly) and fickleness (he is said to have flitted from one philosophical school to another). However, these problems (shared moreover by other Hellenistic rulers) were certainly not the ones which disturbed his reign.

14.6.1 He was soon in conflict with Egypt which, as from time immemorial, laid claim to Syria and Judaea; this last region had been effectively under its sovereignty up to the beginning of the second century BCE (above 14.3.1).

14.6.1.1 The clash rapidly degenerated into open conflict and in 169 Antiochus invaded Egypt, profiting from the preoccupation of Rome, which was caught up in a war with Perseus of Macedonia. He succeeded in occupying the Delta, but aware of the impossibility of keeping the whole vast country under his control, contented himself with supporting Ptolemy VI, who was in combat with his brother, later to become Ptolemy VII. In this way he hoped to settle a ruler favourable to himself on Egypt. However, the plan failed: the two brothers made common cause against the invader.

14.6.1.2 The next year, in 168, Antiochus thought that he would invade Egypt again. However, Rome, which had brought its war against Perseus to a victorious conclusion, instructed Antiochus, through its legate, to withdraw immediately and unconditionally. As well as suffering damage from the interrupted campaign, Antiochus thus had the added humiliation of being forced to recognize that to all intents and purposes a Roman legate had greater powers than he did. We might ask whether the attitude of Rome, while hardly correct on the level of protocol, was not deliberate: Rome clearly wanted to humiliate Antiochus.

14.6.2 Precluded from expanding southwards or westwards, Antiochus IV turned eastwards, to Armenia and Persia, ruled over by the Parthians; there he died in 164/3, according to I Macc.6.8ff. and II Macc.9.5ff., after a serious illness and no longer completely sane. This is also confirmed by classical authors (Prato 1989, cf. on 14.7).

14.7 Antiochus IV and Judaism

The policy of Antiochus towards his Jewish subjects has become the classical example of religious persecution in antiquity, with its martyrs, its heroes and the malicious persecutor. In Jewish apocalyptic literature Antiochus appears as the personification of the attack of the forces of evil on the 'righteous' (cf. Dan.7.25); in primitive Christian thought he appears as the type of the Antichrist.

Bibliography

E.Schürer, *Geschichte des jüdischen Volkes in Zeitalter Jesu Christi*, Leipzig ⁵1920, brought up to date and revised as *The History of the Jewish People in the Age of Jesus Christ (175 BC – AD 135)* (see 14.5); J.Bonsirven, *Palestinian Judaism in the Time of Jesus Christ*, New York 1964; E.Bickermann, *Der Gott der Makkabäer – Untersuchungen über Sinn und Ursprung der makkabäischen Erhebung*, Berlin 1937; id., *From Ezra to the Last of the Maccabees*, New York 1949; H.H.Rowley, 'Menelaus and the Abomination of Desolation', in *Studia Orientalia Joanni Pedersen...dicata*, Copenhagen 1953, 303-15; M.Delcor, 'Le temple d'Onias en Égypte', *RB* 75, 1968, 188-203; Tcherikover, *Hellenistic Civilization and the Jews* (see 14.1); A.Giovannini and H.Müller, 'Die Beziehungen zwischen Rom und den Juden im 2.Jhdt v.Chr.', *Museum Helveticum* 28, 1971, 156-71; R.Hanhart, 'Zum Wesen der makedonisch-hellenistischen Zeit', in *FS J.Ziegler*, Würzburg 1972, I, 49-58; M.Hengel, *Judaism and Hellenism*, London and Philadelphia 1974; id., *Jews, Greeks and Barbarians*, London and Philadelphia 1980; Y.Tsafrir, 'The Location of the Seleucid Akra in Jerusalem', in Y.Yadin (ed.), *Jerusalem Revealed*, Jerusalem 1975, 85-9 (with a discussion of the locality): O.Mørkholm, *Antiochus IV of Syria*, Copenhagen 1976; J.A.Soggin, *I manoscritti del Mar Morto*, Rome 1978; B.Heininger, 'Der böse Antiochus', *BZ* 33, 1989, 43-59; cf. also the commentaries on I Maccabees. For relations between the Maccabees and Rome cf. W.Wirgin, 'Judah Maccabee's Embassy to Rome and the Jewish-Roman Treaty', *PEQ* 101, 1969, 15-20; T.Liebmann-Frankfort, 'Rome et le conflict judéo-syrien (164-161 avant nouvelle ère)', *L'antiquité classique* 38, 1969, 101-20; T.Fischer, 'Zu den Beziehungen zwischen Rom und den Juden im 2 Jhr.v.Chr.', *ZAW* 86, 1974, 90-3; D.Timpe, 'Der römische Vertrag mit den Juden von 161 v.Chr.', *Chiron* 4, 1974, 133-52; D.Flusser, 'The Kingdom of Rome in the Eyes of the Hasmonaeans and as Seen by the Essenes', *Zion* 48, 1983, 149-76 (Hebrew, summary in English). See also K.Bringmann, 'Hellenistische Reform und religiöse Verfolgung in Judäa. Eine Untersuchung zur jüdisch-hellenistischen Geschichte', *AGWG.PH*, 1983, 120-40; R.Abos Padilla, *Plädoyer für Antiochus IV Epiphanes*, Frankfurt am Main 1984; V.Keil, 'Onias III – Märtyrer oder Tempelgründer?', *ZAW* 97, 1985,

221-33; E.Nodet, 'La dédicace, les Maccabées et le Messie', *RB* 93, 1986, 321-75; D.J.Harrington, *The Maccabean Revolt: Anatomy of a Biblical Revolution*, Wilmington, Del 1988; G.-L.Prato, 'La persecuzione religiosa nell'ermeneutica maccabaica: l'Ellenismo come paganesimo', *Ricerche storico-bibliche* 1, 1989, 99-122; B.Bar-Kochva, *Judas Maccabaeus*, Cambridge 1989. Also the commentaries on I-II Maccabees.

14.7.1 Now while I would not want to deny or even to diminish the importance of the religious factor in the persecution of the people of Judah by Antiochus IV, scholars have to rid themselves of the presupposition that this factor was the only or even the predominant one, as a superficial examination of the sources might suggest. As far as we can see, political and economic factors are far more important than they might seem at first sight.

14.7.1.1 These features appear especially in the religious sphere, where Judah was special. For an up-to-date survey of the various attempts at an explanation cf. Prato 1989. In fact we know of marked tensions within Judaism in the social sphere: those existing between on the one hand the priestly class concentrated on the temple and the upper classes which they headed, and on the other the middle classes, whose position the Pharisees were soon to express, are well known (above 14.12.3). Then there was a class of lowly people, equivalent to the modern proletariat, to which the so-called ʿam-hā-ʾāreṣ belonged (below 15.4.3).

So it would be interesting to examine the whole revolt from the perspective of a class struggle, a struggle which found its expression in religious categories.

14.7.1.2 I have just indicated a first factor, by nature eminently political: with the Seleucid conquest of Judaea, the Jerusalem community found itself cut off from its Diaspora in Egypt and especially from that in Alexandria (above 13.2), whose relations with the Ptolemies of Egypt had always been good. But once the break between the Ptolemies and the Seleucids had been formalized, with the wars that followed, relations between the Jerusalem community and that of Alexandria automatically became suspect.

14.7.1.3 A further element of tension appears in the economic sphere: the Seleucid attempt by various means to appropriate sums belonging to the Jerusalem temple treasure. These were not just sheer attempts at theft, as one might suppose, the more serious because they were also sacrilege: already under Seleucus IV, a ruler who was well disposed towards the Jewish community (above 14.3.4), an attempt was made in this direction; these were essentially economic measures, spurred on by the heavy war debt that Antiochus III had incurred with Rome and that he needed to pay. The economic situation of Antiochus IV was not only no better; rather, it was worse because of the expenses of his abortive campaign against Egypt. So rather than deliberate sacrilegious acts or persecutions of the Jewish faith, what we have here is the attitude that Antiochus had about any temple (cf. Polybius 30.46ff., in Noth* 1959, 364), since temples were the repositories of substantial riches.

14.7.1.4 The temple of Jerusalem also had considerable capital. It was an important, if not the most important, centre of economic power in the country, and among other things performed the functions which banks, savings banks and pawnbrokers do today. So what formally appeared as sacrilege was simply a kind of compulsory loan, an expedient, like so many others, to replenish the depleted state coffers.

14.7.2 The first attempt to appropriate money belonging to the temple, with which we shall be occupied in more detail later (below 14.7.4.8), met with resistance from the High Priest Onias III and the mass of the people. They feared not only the consequences of the sacrilege but also losing the money deposited there (cf. II Macc.3, which also reports a compelling miracle). However, what we seem to have here is more the licence, the excess of power, of an official than a policy of persecution.

14.7.3 Nevertheless, with the accession to the throne of Antiochus IV, the feelings of the court towards the Jewish community, which at first, as we have seen, had been benevolent, seem to have changed progressively for the worse. This is clear from the following:

14.7.3.1 Under Antiochus IV an organic and coherent policy of Hellenization began, applied by force where persuasion proved insufficient.

14.7.3.2 However, this new policy did not grow up in a void: it was based on the work of a pro-Hellenistic party of which a certain Jason (probably a Hellenized form of Joshua) was a member. Jason was the brother of the High Priest Onias III, but for a long time was at odds with him. And Jason, with the aim of securing support from the court for his own candidature as High Priest, did not hesitate to promise Antiochus substantial sums for state funds, to be paid from the temple treasure (II Macc.4.8); he also guaranteed his own collaboration in the work of Hellenization.

14.7.3.3 A detailed examination of the sources reveals a disconcerting fact: the pressure exercised by this group was a basic element in the political approach adopted by Antiochus. In other words, as we shall also see, it is reasonable to suppose that without the support and the offer of money from the pro-Hellenists of Jerusalem, Antiochus would have behaved in a more discreet, more moderate, more cautious way (Bickermann 1937, Hengel 1974 and Bright* 1981, 419). Only the certainty of having a qualified Jewish group on his side prompted the king to take extreme measures.

14.7.3.4 Another factor has been brought out by Sacchi* 1976, 96ff.: 'It is difficult to believe that Antiochus intended a religious persecution'; he simply wanted to ensure the military security of Jerusalem, a place which was strategically important in view of the clash with Egypt.

14.7.3.5 Both Menelaus (below 14.8.1) and the Hellenists hoped to be able to eliminate not so much Judaism generally, of which they regarded themselves as an integral part, as the rigoristic Judaism produced by the reform of Nehemiah and Ezra.

14.7.3.6 This is confirmed by an interesting proposal from Tcherikover 1959, 191, 196, according to which the revolt will have begun before the persecution proper and will primarily have been directed not against the state but against the Hellenists who supported it (Schäfer in Hayes and Miller* 1977, 562ff.). In other words, to begin with this will have just been a conflict within the Jewish community, between the traditionalist faction and the pro-Hellenist faction, though it soon degenerated, following the support given by the army to the latter, into a struggle for national liberation (Sacchi* 1976, 106).

14.7.4 A project like that of enforcing Hellenization upon a country might seem quite absurd to the modern reader, all the more so since in this way Hellenism, which was open in cultural and religious matters, ended up contradicting itself.

14.7.4.1 Again an examination of the data confronts the reader with situations more complex than the theories which might be produced about them. In the East, as in the confrontations with Rome, Hellenism presented itself as the culture *par excellence*, and therefore as an alternative to traditional culture. This was the problem faced by all the peoples of the region, and not just Judaism. However, Judaism, with its monotheistic belief, did not fit well with the polytheistic schemes that applied to the other nations, which were much more flexible in this respect.

14.7.4.2 Moreover the Greeks had an attitude of superiority towards other peoples which they did not even try to hide. The generic term they used for them was 'barbarians', a term whch was not necessarily offensive in origin, at least intentionally; rather, it was ironic and onomatopeic. Little by little, however, it became increasingly charged with connotations more like those which we attach to it today. It was a derogatory epithet: the barbarian is someone who speaks an incomprehensible language, has different and disconcerting customs, eats strange and often repugnant food, does not rule according to just laws, and is ignorant of art and other forms of culture. Again, over against the 'barbarians' the Greek language was presented as the universal language *par excellence*, and philosophy and religion also appeared universal, the latter discounting any local variants: finally, literature and science, jurisprudence and music were also universal. All this was expressed in new meeting places: gymnasia, circuses, baths, philosophical schools and new monumental cities.

14.7.4.3 Despite all this, in Greece and in Rome, little was known about the East and conceptions were often fantastic: virtually nothing was known about the Jews at all.[5] And in any case it was difficult to respect someone whom one did not know or knew only in a partial and often erroneous way, and who was felt, generally, to be on a lower cultural level.

14.7.4.4 From an Israelite point of view the problem was posed in the following terms. Formerly Israel had undergone violent experiences like oppressions and deportations generally; however, these had been interpreted as a trial or punishment on the part of God, so they had not affected the faith; on the contrary, they had strengthened it. The religion of those who had persecuted Israel had not had any importance for the people of God. By contrast, Hellenism presented itself as an alternative world-view, in the face of which it was necessary to make choices: either to remain a Jew or to embrace the new way of living and thinking, thus imperilling the faith. The Hellenists among the Jews thought that they could do both, while remaining within the bounds of good faith; according to the orthodox they had in fact chosen Hellenism and denied Judaism.

14.7.4.5 On the opposite side, then, stood the austere Jewish faith, aniconic in worship and therefore little interested in the decorative arts. From Deutero-Isaiah onwards it was also universalistic (see above 13.1.4), though through the mediation of the concept of the people of God. It was endowed with social institutions which were unique in antiquity, like the sabbath rest and the emancipation after six years service of those who had been enslaved for debt. And it had an ethical level which cannot fail to appear remarkable even to the most knowing modern reader; its justice may not have been very subtle, if one likes to put it that way, nor very theoretical, but it was effective and almost completely lacking in cruel punishments or punishments which offended human dignity. All this was clearly opposed to a society which behind its impeccable façade had marked elements of corruption: its cruel spectacles, its often sadistic punishments, the parasitism of its upper classes, its wealth based on the exploitation of paid and slave workers, and its great estates.

14.7.4.6 Not only did that happen, but Judaism went over, as it were, to the counter-attack; among those groups from which the Pharisees would emerge later it adopted a markedly missionary attitude. This zeal also appears from a critical saying about the Pharisees attributed to Jesus: '.. you traverse sea and land to make a single proselyte'

(Matt.23.15). Here it remains open whether the logion is meant to refer to proselytism in general or to attempts to get new members for the sect; the term 'proselyte' as it appears in the original suggests the former alternative; at any rate this practice is thought to be relatively ancient.

14.7.4.7 However, while it is easy to criticize the corruption of the Hellenistic world behind its fine façade, the atmosphere surrouding some of the Jewish ruling classes, gathered round the Zadokite priesthood of the Jerusalem temple, left much to be desired, even if it appears that the corruption was limited to a few sectors – those who were the most enthusiastic supporters of Hellenism. Already under Seleucus IV the situation had reached such a point that Sacchi* 1976, 93f., can speak of symptoms of decay.

14.7.4.8 II Maccabees 3.4 reports that '…a man named Simon, of the tribe (here the term stands for 'priestly class') of Bilga,[6] in being made captain (προστάτης) of the temple', clashed with the High Priest Onias III over a question connected with the administration of the markets. This apparently trivial motive in fact cloaks a struggle for power: Simon was connected with the Tobiads, the family which had had a kind of hereditary governorship of the region, first under the Ptolemies (with whom they continued to have connections) and then the Seleucids. Having failed to get anywhere with Onias, Simon went to Tarsus, to the governor general. He told him that there were enormous riches in the Jerusalem temple, far too much for the needs of the cult and therefore probably the fruit of corrupt dealings. He suggested that he might offer adequate recompense if he were made High Priest in place of Onias. However, an inspectorate sent to Jerusalem to check on the accuracy of the denunciation and if possible to remove some of the treasure was confronted by Onias with arguments which were hard to refute: the temple held deposits belonging to widows and orphans and also funds deposited by Hyrcanus the Tobiad, which therefore probably belonged to the public administration. So these sums could not be touched. The attempt to make an inventory anyway, with a view to future proceedings, came up against such resistance from the priests and the population, accompanied by a miracle, that the inspector called a halt to his attempt (above 14.7.1.3).

14.7.4.9 Clearly it is impossible to talk, yet, of a persecution: there had been a straightforward denunciation on the part of a senior official, and the governor responsible had ordered a check to see whether or not there were irregularities in administration. Having established that the accusations were unfounded, the official responsible registered the denunciation, but in all good faith tried to list the goods in question; only in this last respect does he seem to have gone to extremes. However, this move too was immediately abandoned when it came up against resistance from the interested parties. On the other hand, as Sacchi* 1976 and others have rightly seen, Simon's action in offering a payment to the authorities to obtain the High Priesthood began what was soon to become the usual practice:; an attempt to obtain office not through the competent Jewish organs but by state intervention, promising sums taken from the temple treasure, again to cope with the financial difficulties of the empire.

14.7.4.10 This is probably the time in which we are also to put the expulsion from Jerusalem of the Tobiads, the civil governors of Judaea as well as Transjordan. The result of this action was that the High Priest became the only person endowed with authority in Judaea (Josephus, *War* I, 31), so that it is from then on that the theocracy, or better the hierocracy proper, begins.

14.7.5 On the promise of a much more substantial offering than that made by Simon, Jason (above 14.7.3.2) obtained the nomination to the High Priesthood and the deposition of Onias III, which was also to come about with the collaboration of the Tobiads who had been expelled (II Macc.4.7). Among the various promises made was one that a gymnasium and an ephebate would be established in Jerusalem. The deposition of Onias III by the political authorities in 175/174 was an unprecedented intervention by the authorities in an internal matter relating to the Jewish cult; Onias was exiled to the region of Antioch and his place was taken by Jason. Jason immediately introduced the two institutions mentioned above; some of the priests were interested in them, and they neglected their duties simply so that they could take an active part (4.11ff.). Some participants in the games are said to have gone so far as to have had plastic surgery in order to hide their circumcision (I Macc.1.15; *Antt.* XII, 241; cf. II Macc.4.16, which speaks quite generally of 'awkward situations'). II Maccabees 4.18ff reports that on another occasion Jason sent through intermediaries a contribution from temple funds to the sacrifices offered to pagan deities in connection with the games at Tyre.

14.8 Antiochus IV and the High Priests

It seems that Antiochus IV passed through Jerusalem for the first time during a journey in the region, perhaps on his return from Egypt in 169; however, the chronology of these events is confused (cf. below 14.9.1-2). He was received with all the honours (II Macc.4.21f.), but his stay was too brief for him to be able to take account of the situation personally.

14.8.1 Jason, three years after his nomination to be High Priest, sent a certain Menelaus to the king (according to Josephus, Menelaus is a Hellenization of Onias; however, perhaps Menahem would be better).

Menelaus was a brother of the Simon (above 14.7.4.8) who for the first time set in motion the process by which the High Priest was nominated by the political authorities. If the reading proposed above (n.5) for II Macc.3.4 is correct, Simon and Menelaus were therefore of priestly stock, contrary to what is sometimes asserted (cf. Widengren in Hayes and Miller* 1977, 582, and Soggin 1978, 71), if not Zadokites in the strict sense. However Menelaus, instead of carrying out his mission, offered the king a large sum of money for himself to be proclaimed High Priest in place of Jason (II Macc.4.23ff.). The plan, in which the Tobiads also seem to have played a major part, was aimed at eliminating the last representative of the dynasty of Onias III; it succeeded completely: Jason was forced to hide (II Macc.4.23ff.) and thus the line of Zadokite High Priests was broken. However, Menelaus does not seem to have been able to keep the promises he made to the king; II Macc.4.27f. merely states the fact without giving any explanations. There could have been a variety of reasons, for example that he had promised more than he could reasonably fulfil, since it was not possible to make unlimited payments from the temple treasury. But another plausible motive appears in II Macc.4.28ff.: here it is stated that a royal official had been installed on the 'acropolis' (probably the temple complex), who received the taxes directly, so that they no longer passed through the temple treasury; and this official seems to have caused a number of difficulties for Menelaus.

14.8.2 At the same time Onias, from exile, did not cease his campaign against Menelaus, whose malpractices and abuses he stigmatized. Menelaus took advantage of the absence of the king, who was on a military campaign, to persuade the regent of the kingdom to have Onias killed (II Macc.4.30ff.). His murder must have taken place in 171/70 and was also thought unprecedented: there seems to be a reference to it in Dan.9.26, 'After the sixty-two weeks an "anointed" one shall be cut off, without there being any fault in him' (emended text), and 11.22, 'Finally, the prince of the covenant shall be killed' (this text too is uncertain). However, Antiochus seems to have been taken by surprise and even angered by the act: II Maccabees indicates that he punished the regent of the kingdom by stripping him of office and executing him. Perhaps this was because the crime went beyond his plans, or perhaps it was also because he was holding Onias in reserve to blackmail Menelaus, a plan which Onias's assassination ruined.

14.8.3 Thus far the tradition. But in this case, too, prudence is called for: the study by V.Keil (1985, cf. already M.Delcor 1968) takes up a theory of Josephus (*War* I, 13-15 and VII, 420-32, but in *Antt.* XIII, 62 and XX, 235f. he again puts forward the traditional thesis) that Onias III will not have been killed near Damascus (which is what II Macc.4.30-38 indicates) but will have fled to Egypt, where he built a temple at

Leontopolis (north of Memphis, present-day *tell el-yehudīye*). To conceal this action, which was somewhat unorthodox by later criteria, the fictitious figure of Onias IV will have been invented as the founder of the temple in question. For this see again the commentary by Stern, *Authors* I, 405ff., though he defends the tradition.

14.9 Definitive break

Relations between the court and the Judahite community continued to get worse, though it is impossible because of the disorder in the chronology to produce a diachronic outline of events. What I shall say here is therefore purely conjectural in this respect. We know about most of the events in some detail, since they are reported in I Macc.1.20-23; II Macc.5.1-26; Dan.11.28-31; Josephus, *War* I, 31ff. and *Antt*. XII, 239-50; however, for the reasons indicated it is impossible to establish their precise sequence and therefore their correlation (there is an important discussion by Schäfer, in Hayes and Miller* 1977, 564-8).

14.9.1 A first event, the forerunner of later conflicts, was the discovery that there had been some sacrilegious thefts in the temple in 169, i.e during Antiochus's first campaign in Egypt (above 14.6.1.1). Lysimachus, brother of Menelaus, was thought by popular opinion to be the thief, and the people seized him and killed him (II Macc.4.39ff.). Thus far there should have been no problems, since the death penalty was usually called for in cases of sacrilege; however, the elders of Jerusalem sent an account of things to Antiochus, who was in Tyre, and also accused Menelaus of complicity. Thereupon, Menelaus sent a large sum of money to the king, with the result that he absolved Menelaus of blame and sentenced the members of the delegation to death (II Macc.4.43ff.).

14.9.2 During the second campaign in Egypt in 168 (above 14.6.1.2), ruined shortly afterwards because of the intervention of Rome, there was a sudden rumour that the king was dead (II Macc.5.1ff.), accompanied by various miracles and apocalyptic signs. Jason immediately came out of hiding (above 14.8.1) and attacked Menelaus and his supporters with about a thousand men. This undertaking was at first crowned with success and was followed by the killing of many collaborationists, but then it failed and Jason had to flee again. The texts, which do not show much sympathy for him, make him wander from city to city as far as Arabia, where he is said to have been assassinated.

14.9.3 Although it was directed exclusively against Jews and not against Syria, the rebellion gave Antiochus the pretext for direct intervention. He wanted to regard this as an act of high treason in time of war. And with the troops returning from Egypt he besieged and conquered Jerusalem, venting on its inhabitants the anger and sense of frustration brought about by the Roman insult to him. He killed those he believed to be hostile and, competently assisted by Menelaus, occupied and sacked the temple thoroughly (I Macc.1.21ff.; II Macc. 5.15ff.). He then returned to Antioch, leaving a garrison in Jerusalem with orders to finish the matter off.

14.9.4 In the next year, 167, he issued a series of decrees aimed at the compulsory Hellenization of Judaea, and sent an army under the command of a certain Apollonius to implement his orders (I Macc.1.29; II Macc.5.24). They reconquered Jerusalem by means of a stratagem (first they came in friendship and then entered the defenceless city on the sabbath), plundered it, and killed or sold into slavery a number of its inhabitants. They partly dismantled the walls, and with the materials thus obtained built a fortress, the Acra. The location of this fortress is uncertain (perhaps it was to the north of the temple on the site later to be occupied by the 'Antonia', below 15.2.6, as claimed by some earlier modern scholars – but in that case where? In the Kidron valley? There is a discussion by Schäfer, in Hayes and Miller* 1977, 554ff.). At all events it seems that it must have been located close to the temple, the complex it was aimed at controlling. A garrison was posted in the fortress, made up of pagan soldiers (I Macc.1.33f. says 'sinners, outlaws'); the city was now under military occupation.

14.9.5 Soon afterwards, once the military problems had been resolved, officials arrived in Judaea charged with supervising the implementation of Hellenization and ensuring that everyone made the compulsory sacrifice to the new deities. They worked in groups and controlled the whole country. The temple was desecrated and transformed into a sanctuary dedicated to Zeus Olympius, whose image the Jews called the 'abomination of desolation' (Hebrew *šiqqūṣ mᵉšōmēm*, an allusion to *baʿal šāmēm*, the Canaanite deity identified with Zeus Olympios (cf.I Macc.1.54; Deut.9.27; 11.31; 12.11; and, in the New Testament, Mark 13.14 par.). The operation took place on 15 December 167, and on 25 December sacrifices were offered to the Sol Invictus, the unconquered sun, whose resurrection was celebrated on that day – the deity perhaps being identified with Antiochus IV himself. All forms of Jewish worship were done away with (in any case they could not have been held in desecrated places); not only was public worship abolished but also all private, domestic practice: the observance of the sabbath and the Jewish feasts and the practice of circumcision; violations of the new laws carried the death penalty, and many scrolls of sacred books were destroyed. The privileges which the community had enjoyed during the Persian period were abolished. The fate of the Samaritans was similar: their temple on Mount Gerizim was desecrated and dedicated to Zeus Xenios. So it seems clear that they had to endure the same fate as the Judahites.

14.9.6 Many Jews did not actively oppose these measures and even gave in to the enticements, pressures and threats. Others, however, resisted, and some, when up against it, chose martyrdom rather than 'lead an infamous existence' (II Macc.6.18-19). This text and 7.1ff. tell two stories of Judahites who chose death rather than contaminate themselves: Eleazar, the 'doctor of the law', and the anonymous mother who was tortured to death after her seven sons had suffered the same fate, all, the sources tell us, in the presence (somewhat improbably) of Antiochus himself. Hebrews 11.35ff. in the New Testament probably alludes to the two episodes.

14.9.7 Yet others chose to take to the scrubland in the uninhabited areas of the country (I Macc.2.29ff.), and here and there acts of open resistance to the king's regulations began. Early on, the resistance had to decide whether or not to observe the rigid sabbath laws (II Macc.2.39-41), since the Syrians took advantage of this observance to attack and kill them. It was decided that armed defence in cases of this kind was one of those necessities which allowed practising Jews to violate the sabbath rest (below 14.12.5.3). Organized resistance was soon to grow from these barely organized groups.

14.9.8 According to I Macc.2.29, quoted above, those who took to the scrubland included 'many who … went down to the wilderness to dwell there, they, their sons, their wives and their cattle'. As far as we know, this note refers to two categories of people, those who were content to escape the persecution, trying only to live a life in accordance with their faith, e.g. those who were to become the Qumran sect (below 14.12.4),[7] and those who hastened to take arms against the oppressor whenever there was a favourable opportunity.

14.9.9 'Triumphant Hellenism made the mistake, not uncommon to victors, of underestimating its foe. Victorious in its chief objectives, the cities, Hellenism failed to pay sufficient attention to the desert, partly because of the greater difficulty which this would involve, and partly because its importance was not properly understood' (Ricciotti* II, 236). This is a mistake often made by all occupying forces: to believe that the control of some key localities is enough to have the whole country in hand. However, then the resistance comes out of the scrub, soon involving the cities and ultimately occupying them. And in this instance there were abundant regions suitable for partisan war: the territories on the eastern side of the hill-country dropping down towards the Jordan valley and the Dead Sea, and then the valley of the Jordan itself and the Dead Sea. And the areas on the borders between the hill-country and the Shephelah (above 2.3.8) offered good opportunities for those who wanted to wage a guerrilla war. The resistance simply defined themselves with a significant name, the 'pious', the 'faithful' (Hebrew *ḥassīdīm*, transcribed into Greek as Ἀσιδαῖοι; their emphasis was on loyalty to the covenant and the norms contained in it. Now it was enough for the various groups to unite and for a large part of the active Jewish population to be involved in organized resistance.

14.9.10 The occasion arose very soon. The priestly family of the Hasmonaeans, the descendants of a certain Jehoiarib, mentioned in I Chron.9.10; 24.7, had established themselves at Modein (coord.148-148), a place on the edge of the Shephelah, at the latitude of present-day Ramla. Their leader was an old man, Mattathiah, who had left Jerusalem, where he could no longer exercise his ministry. He lived with his five sons, Jonathan, Simon, Judas (surnamed Maccabaeus, probably 'hammer' or 'hammerer', *Antt.* XII, 365ff.), Eleazar and Jonathan. One day, according to I Macc.2.15ff., in 167/166, probably during the summer, since all the action takes place in the open air, 'the king's officers who were enforcing the apostasy came to the city of Modein to make them offer sacrifice'. According to the text, a number of people submitted, while others, gathered around Mattathiah, kept apart. They repeatedly refused the demands of the royal officials, and when Mattathiah saw a Jew in the process of offering sacrifice, he killed him; then he also killed the royal official and destroyed the altar. Thereupon 'he and his sons fled to the hills and left all that they had in the city' (I Macc.2.28).

14.9.11 The priest and his sons (who continued his work after him) immediately became a focal point for those who hitherto had chosen forms of passive resistance and also those who were already active. Mattathiah died the next year and Judas was appointed in his place.

14.10 The Hasmonaean campaigns

This is not the place to follow in detail the campaigns of the Hasmonaeans, their victories and their defeats, to the point at which they achieved their aims after almost thirty years of fighting. For these details see the careful analyses of Ricciotti* 1932, II, 283ff.; Noth* 1959, 359ff.; and Schäfer in Hayes and Miller* 1977, 585-96, who also deals with the problem of the sources. Here I shall give only the broad outlines of events, emphasizing some essential points.

14.10.1 To begin with, the Jews were able to achieve a series of victories which, while certainly not decisive, were sufficient to show them that it was possible to resist and defeat the enemy; moreover they provided the resistance with the arms that they needed – they took them from the enemy. In this way Judas succeeded in gaining possession of a large part of Judaea. One reason for his success was that Antiochus IV, engaged in the war in the East, could not throw all his forces into the fight against the rebels. Nevertheless his troops remained superior to the rebels in quality, quantity and equipment; however, the rebels were more mobile, knew the ground perfectly, and had the advantage of being on the attack. Moreover they had a far superior motivation: all their victories were interpreted as a sign of divine favour.

14.10.2 The campaign culminated in the capture of all of Jerusalem but the Acra, where the surviving troops of Antiochus and the collaborators took refuge. Judas immediately devoted himself to the restoration and the purification of the temple, where he installed Zadokite priests who had not compromised themselves with the regime. He removed from it anything that had come into contact with the pagan cult, including the altar of sacrifice, which was totally rebuilt. On 25 Chislev (November/ December) 164, about three years after its desecration, the temple was solemnly rededicated (an event still celebrated at the feast of Hanukkah, 'dedication') and protected by the installation of a small garrison.

14.10.3 The death of Antiochus IV in the East (above 14.6.2) in the spring of 164/3 liberated Israel from its declared enemy, but not from the laws which he had promulgated nor from the garrison which remained in the Acra; moreover the Seleucid policy outside Judaea remained unchanged. To alter this state of affairs Judas launched a series of military campaigns especially in those regions inhabited by Jews faithful to Jerusalem, in Galilee and Transjordan. Unable to hold on to these regions because of his indequate resoures, he evacuated the Jewish population to Judaea. Then he turned southwards, occupying Idumaea, which had been settled by the Edomites (above 12.6.5), and moving towards Philistine territory. His aim was not to occupy this territory but to discourage any attempt at aggression by these traditional enemies of Judah. Then he laid siege to the Acra, whose garrison sought aid from Antiochus IV's successor, Antiochus V Eupator (164-161). Antiochus V was still in the tutelage of his guardian, the general Lysias, who had nominated himself regent of the kingdom, ignoring the wishes of Antiochus IV, who had nominated a certain Philip.

14.10.4 Lysias and Antiochus V attacked Judaea from the south with the troops which in the meantime had been freed for action at the end of the eastern campaign. The Syrians now had overwhelming superiority, and Judas Maccabaeus was defeated in a series of encounters; he was forced to lift the siege of the Acra. In the battle of *bēt z^ekaryāh* (the present-day *el-ʿazar*, about six miles south-west of Jerusalem, coord.118-163), his army was defeated, not least because of the use of war elephants. The capital was besieged and encircled, and provisions soon began to run out.

14.10.5 However, catastrophe was avoided by an unforeseen event: Philip, the royal tutor and regent designate of Antiochus IV, but ignored by Lysias and Antiochus V, arrived at Antioch with an army to take power in the name of his protégé, and Lysias and Antiochus had to send troops to Syria. So they offered honourable and acceptable terms of peace to Judas Maccabaeus: among other things he was guaranteed complete freedom of conscience and worship. Judas had no other choice than to accept; moreover, the aim of the rebellion seemed to have been achieved. Meanwhile Menelaus had been killed on the orders of Lysias and Antiochus, probably in connection with the negotiations. So the High Priesthood remained vacant.

14.10.6 But meanwhile another figure had appeared in Antioch, having also decided to come into the limelight: this was Demetrius, the other son of Antiochus III, who was also a possible contender for the throne. He had once been sent as a hostage to Rome and had never been ransomed (above 14.3.2.1 and 14.3.4). He had succeeded in escaping, perhaps with the complicity of the Roman authorities, who were always hostile to the Seleucids, in order to create difficulties for Antiochus V (Gunneweg* 1989, 166ff.). On his arrival home, he succeeded in having both Lysias and Antiochus V killed by the troops, and had himself crowned as Demetrius I Soter (161-150).

14.10.7 Immediately, representatives of the Hellenistic Jewish party came to him to ask for the post of High Priest to be given to their candidate. This was a certain Alcimus (perhaps a Hellenization of the Hebrew Eliakim). They managed to convince the king, the nomination took place, and the new High Priest went to Jerusalem accompanied by a Syrian army under the command of a certain Bacchides.

14.10.8 This new situation led to a division among the Hasidim. Some, the branch which we could call the doves, thought that the essential aim of the rebellion, the re-establishment of freedom of religion and worship, had now been achieved; after all, the country had now been under foreign domination for centuries without that having caused any inconvenience worth noting; the Hellenists also put forward similar arguments, though for different reasons. However, the supporters of the Hasmonaeans, whom we could call the hawks, did not agree; if all was peaceful and their aims had been achieved, why had Alcimus come with an army? As Ricciotti* 1932, II, 244, saw well, it was naive to think that orthodox Jews and Hellenists, Hasidim and collaborators, members of the resistance and Seleucid troops, could suddenly 'live together in Jerusalem, side by side, without disturbing each other'. That would not have been easy even without the army: its presence clearly destroyed what little trust there could still be. Alcimus, too, soon found himself in difficulties, though we do not know precisely why. Resorting to repression, he had several dozen orthodox Jews killed by the Syrian troops: moreover he constantly intrigued at court against the Jews who were faithful to the law.

14.10.9 In I Macc.9.54-56 it is reported that in 160 Alcimus had the wall in the inner court of the temple demolished.[8] This cannot have been the wall which separated the Jews from the pagans, so that we could think of a reform within Judaism. The episode is understood by Garbini* 1988, 163ff., as a reform which will have eliminated the existing differences between the priesthood and the laity and, again in his view, will have been what is described in detail in the pseudepigraphical III Ezra 8-9. It will have been projected back on the fifth century and attributed to Ezra, a figure created *ad hoc* on this occasion (above 13.9.3). The wall in question was never rebuilt, even under Herod. According to Garbini this reform followed a line also attested in Chronicles and later accepted by the Pharisees, but rejected both by the Hasidim and by the Zadokites. As a result of these events some of the latter will have gone into the desert, founding the community of Qumran on the north-western bank of the Dead Sea (below 14.12.4). The proposal is an interesting one and deserves attention; however, it is doubtful whether the texts produced by Garbini can support the weight of such an important thesis, not least because it seems extremely doubtful that a figure as doubtful as that of Alcimus could have introduced such an important reform which was later accepted by the Pharisees.

14.10.10 The events mentioned above resulted in the Hellenists gaining the upper hand, if only for a short time, while the Hasmonaeans and their allies again had to take to the hills. Demetrius sent an army in support of Bacchides, but it was defeated, so that the king felt again compelled to intervene in force. The Jews were finally heavily defeated in the battle of Elasa, a place which has not been identified, and Judas fell in the battle. Jonathan was elected as his successor. The fighting continued with varying results, often with victories for the Hasmonaeans; however, these were only local ones, and there were no longer any great hopes of final victory: the enemy was too strong. Be this as it may, the death of Alcimus in 159 robbed Bacchides of a person and an institution to protect and aid. The post of High Priest remained vacant, this time for seven years.

14.10.11 Shortly before his death it seems that Judas Maccabaeus had entered into negotiations with Rome, the traditional enemy of the Seleucids. This did not bring any immediate advantages, but it put the revolt in a wider context of international politics.

14.10.12 As had already happened once in the past, salvation came unexpectedly to the Judahites from internal disensions among the Seleucids.

14.10.12.1 In 153 a war broke out between Demetrius and Alexander Balas (150-145), a pretender to the Seleucid throne who claimed to be the natural son of Antiochus IV, whom he resembled. He was also the son-in-law of Ptolemy VI Philometor of Egypt, who gave him unconditional support. Bacchides was immediately summoned home, while Demetrius offered Jonathan peace on favourable terms. The Syrians withdrew almost everywhere, leaving only a garrison on the Acra and at Beth-zur (above 13.11.3).

14.10.12.2 However, Alexander Balas also courted the favours of Jonathan and gave him the post of High Priest, though he was not of Zadokite stock. In the course of the autumn festival of 152 Jonathan was consecrated and installed in the temple.

14.10.12.3 Alexander Balas achieved complete victory over Demetrius and in fact made Jonathan governor. Jonathan thus combined both civil and religious power in his own person, a somewhat unorthodox development, but in practical terms remarkably effective, especially in view of what was to happen.

14.10.13 The alliance between the two continued for some time. In 147 Demetrius, son of Demetrius I, rebelled and tried to seize the throne; Jonathan took advantage of this to lay siege to the Acra and occupy a large part of Samaria.

14.10.14 Demetrius proved victorious and was crowned as Demetrius II Nicator (145-138, 129-125); Jonathan could expect the worst, but was able to defend his cause with such skill that he obtained not only confirmation of his own personal position but also the ancient privileges accorded to Jewish worship and moreover the concession of substantial tax exemptions for the Jewish community. He was also assigned three districts of Samaria whose population had remained faithful to Jerusalem and had not gone over to the Samaritans. However, he had to raise the siege of the Acra.

14.10.15 Still, Jonathan's political skill proved to be his downfall (Noth* 1959, 378): when Demetrius refused to withdraw from the Acra and Beth-zur, Jonathan allied himself with yet another pretender to the throne, this time a certain Antiochus son of Alexander Balas, who was supported by the general Diodotus Trypho; in reality, Trypho wanted the throne for himself and used the young prince as a cover. The general, a good politician, immediately took account of Jonathan's power and therefore thought that he should eliminate him; he succeeded without too much difficulty, having him imprisoned by a stratagem and then killed in 143. However, before that, Jonathan had already renewed negotiations with Rome, and had begun others with Sparta.

14.10.16 The Hasmonaeans chose Simon, brother of Judas and Jonathan, who renewed contact with Demetrius II. Demetrius, who needed help from the Judahites to liquidate his rival and Trypho, granted the country *de facto* independence. In the middle of 141 Simon finally succeeded in seizing the Acra and extending the frontiers of Judaea in a number of campaigns. He also continued the contacts with Rome and Sparta (in I Macc.12; 14; 15 and *Antt.* XIV, 143 there is documentation of these transactions, though there is some controvesy over its authenticity). He too obtained nomination as High Priest; the anomaly of his position was regularized in 140, when the line of Onias III (whose son had been declared unworthy to succeed because he had founded a temple in Egypt, but cf. 14.8.3 above!) was declared defunct. However, despite the fact that it exercised civil power *de facto*, the monarchy was never recognized, since the expectation was of a descendant of the house of David. In that respect, legally speaking, he was a usurper.

14.10.17 In 139 Demetrius became the prisoner of Mithridates, king of Pontus, and his brother Antiochus VII Sidetes (138-129) became regent of the kingdom (I Macc.14.1-3; *Antt.* XIII, 184ff.).

14.10.18 Simon died in 134, assassinated at Jericho by his son-in law along with two of his sons. Some scholars suspect that this happened at the instigation of Antiochus VII, the regent of Demetrius II, who was a prisoner (I Macc.16.11-24).

14.11 The Hasmonaean kings

With John Hyrcanus (134-104) a real Hasmonaean dynasty began. As the years went by, its members proved increasingly tyrannical, with marked symptoms of decadence, thus moving away from what had been the ideals of its founders. Again scholars are forced to make use almost exclusively of material provided by Josephus and classical authors, since there is no biblical information nor any credible Jewish tradition about individuals and events.

14.11.1 John Hyrcanus was the third son of Simeon; he escaped the massacre in which his father and brothers died because he had not gone to Jericho with them. He too resumed contacts with Rome, and *Antt.* XIII, 259-66; XIV, 247-255 also contain documentation on them, though this is controversial. At the beginning of his reign John had to face an invasion from Antiochus VII who, after some victories, succeeded in laying siege to Jerusalem. Since the previous year had been a year of jubilee, in which no work had been done on the land and therefore there was no harvest, the countryside and especially the besieged capital soon found themselves in difficulties over food supplies. John was very soon forced to yield, but Antiochus offered him acceptable terms; at all events, the country again came under Seleucid sovereignty. However, the Seleucids soon resumed fighting against the Parthians and were heavily defeated. Antiochus VII died in 129 and Demetrius II, who had meanwhile been released from prison, returned to the throne. He was assassinated in 125.

14.11.2 Thus freed from the tutelage of the Syrians, John dedicated the rest of his life to the aggrandisement of his own country. He conquered Samaria and destroyed the temple on Mount Gerizim (above 14.4.5.4-6), and in 108 conquered the capital Samaria. He later forced the Idumaeans, who had left their own country in Transjordan east of the Dead Sea and in 587-6 had settled in the Negeb (above 12.6.5), to convert to Judaism and be circumcised. John had originally been a disciple of the Pharisees (below 14.12.3), but later went over to the Sadducees, probably because the former criticized the concentration of civil and religious power in the hands of the same person, and also because of his cruelty, more characteristic of a Hellenistic ruler than a Jewish priest (*Antt.* XIII, 288ff.). These accusations were not without foundation, when we remember that John planned formally to assume the title of king. Finally, some of his administrative arrangements, like the employment of pagan mercenaries in his service, were incompatible with the Jewish faith.

14.11.3 Aristobulus I (104-103) succeeded John. He had his mother, who was to have been regent, and his brother Antigonus, assassinated. His other brothers, among them Alexander Jannaeus, were imprisoned. He was such a supporter of Hellenism that he changed his original name, Judas, into one which did not even have any assonance with it; Josephus (*Antt.* XIII, 318) therefore calls him 'Philhellene'. Again according to Josephus, *War* I, 78ff.; *Antt.* XIII, 311, remorse hastened his end. He too used force to convert non-Jews, this time the Ituraeans, the inhabitants of either northern Galilee or the southern Lebanon.

14.11.4 Aristobulus was succeeded by his brother Alexander Jannaeus (103-76), who had previously been imprisoned for a period.

Bibliography

C.Rabin, 'Alexander Jannaeus and the Pharisees', *JJS* 7, 1966, 3-11; M.Delcor, 'L'éloge des Romains d'après I Mc 8', *Hen* 13, 1991, 19-28.

Alexander resumed the expansionist policy of his father. He too was hostile to the Pharisees, probably for the same reasons; they even reached the point of calling for Syrian intervention. And the Syrians came, under the command of their king Demetrius III Eucarius (94-88), defeating the troops of Alexander near Shechem. The Pharisees, however, seeing that Demetrius aimed at re-establishing Seleucid supremacy over Judaea, gave up the alliance and Demetrius returned home. The actions of the Pharisees certainly saved the country, but they were left without protection. The repression by Alexander was very harsh (*Antt.* XIII, 377-382): Josephus in fact reports that several hundred of them were crucified and their families were killed before their eyes. This was the first time that such punishment was meted out by Jews to other Jews and did not fail to cause consternation among the people, a number of whom again took to the hills. The event is probably referred to in the Dead Sea Scrolls *pesher* on Nahum 2.12f., (4QpNah = 4Q169, 1.1f.): '[...] *trws*, king of Greece, who sought, on the counsel of those who seek smooth things, to enter Jerusalem [lacuna...]'; it then continues: '[lacuna...] concerns the furious young lion [lacuna...] on those who seek smooth things and hangs men alive, a thing *never done formerly* in Israel. Because of a man hanged alive on [the] tree, it is written' (a reference to Deut.21.22f. follows).

Now the first name, incomplete because of a lacuna, is generally completed as *dmy-trws*, i.e. Demetrius, while 'those who seek smooth things' are the Pharisees, who were also enemies of the Dead Sea sect; the 'furious young lion' is clearly Alexander, who first 'hung men alive' (Soggin 1978, 102f.). The whole passage is eloquent testimony to the impression that the episode must have made. In reality Alexander was only 'the lowest type of Hellenistic soldier', as Ricciotti, II, 292, rightly points out, going from one war to the next and obtaining results which can only be considered modest compared with the means expended. At all events he kept the territory he received and in Transjordan succeeded in enlarging it at the expense of the Nabataeans. He died of an illness probably also contracted because of his dissolute life.

14.11.5 Alexander was succeeded by his widow Alexandra Salome (76-67); before he died, Alexander proposed that peace should be made with the Pharisees (*Antt.* XIII, 403) because they enjoyed so much popular support. This he did, and Josephus *Antt.* XIII, 187 says that on his death they mourned him as a 'just king'. His conversion is reported in the Talmud, bQidd 23a.

14.11.6 Alexander left two sons: the idle Hyrcanus II, the older son, and Aristobulus, skilful and enterprising. Hyrcanus became High Priest, and Aristobulus commander of the army. On the death of Alexandra, Hyrcanus came to the throne, but after three months he abdicated in favour of his brother Aristobulus (67-63).

14.11.7 The kingdom might have seemed solid from the outside, but it was very soon disturbed by a serious conflict: Antipater, the governor of Idumaea, rebelled, aided by the Nabataeans of southern Transjordan (their capital, Petra, coord. 210-120, is still justly famous). In exchange for their support he promised them the restoration of the territory taken from then by Alexander Jannaeus. Antipater tried to enlist Hyrcanus in his cause, inciting him among other things to revoke his abdication. He gained some military successes and laid siege to Jerusalem. However, underlying the conflict there was also the contention between the Pharisees and the Sadducees: the former were supporters of Hyrcanus and the latter of Aristobulus. With military operations at a stalemate, both sides appealed to Rome, which in 64/

63 had annexed Syria (in Qumran the Romans appear as *kittīm*), and Rome decided in favour of Aristobulus, ordering the others to withdraw.

14.11.8 However, Hyrcanus decided to appeal directly to Pompey, who had arrived in Damascus in 63. At the same time a delegation also arrived from Jerusalem, which asked the Romans to put an end to the rule of the corrupt and incompetent Hasmonaeans. The delegation proposed what we might call a 'hierocratic' solution: politically the country would be under the sovereignty of Rome, but internally it would be governed by the temple priesthood.

14.11.9 Pompey was favourably disposed towards Aristobulus, but Aristobulus left him, taking refuge in his own fortress; then he too sought peace. He obtained it, but on harsh conditions: he had to hand over his fortresses and the capital to Rome. He refused to hand over the capital and it was besieged; it fell after three months, in 63. The Romans penetrated the temple and Pompey himself entered the Holy of Holies, which only the High Priest could enter, and then only once a year; understandably, this caused consternation among the faithful. Pompey found nothing in the Holy of Holies: Tacitus, *Hist.* V, 9 (Stern, *Authors* II, no.281) says that Pompey found there *nulla intus deum effigie, vacuam sedem et inania arcana* ('no divine image, but only an empty place and no sacred objects').

14.11.10 Hyrcanus was nominated High Priest and 'ethnarch': he had to renounce the title of king. Aristobulus had to follow Pompey's triumph to Rome. However, the real victor in the contest seems to have been the skilful Antipater, of whose family we shall hear more later (below 15.1.1). From then on, in fact, the country was under the dominion of Rome, though it was sometimes governed by rulers who thought themselves more or less independent.

14.12 Judaea: groups and thought

At the end of the first millennium BCE, Judaism, which had undergone Josiah's and Nehemiah's reforms, and had been refined by the sufferings of exile, foreign occupation and the struggle with Hellenism, began to show clear signs of those characteristics which have distinguished it down the millennia, to the present day.

14.12.1 Not all the characteristics which distinguish it today are clearly present. Modern Judaism was shaped by a further tragedy: the destruction in 70 CE, in the course of the first revolt (67-74 CE), of the temple, one of its basic features, the centralized seat of worship and piety. As Simeon I the Just put it around 300 BCE, 'For three things the world exists: the *torah*, the cult (in the temple) and the good works of the righteous' (Mishnah, *Aboth* I.2). Jews prayed in the direction of the temple (Dan.6.11; cf. I Kings 8.44, 48, a late text) and went to Jerusalem on pilgrimage (Tob.1,6; cf. also the Gospels). For those who lived in the land the temple was still, as we have seen (above 14.7.1.4), a centre of economic and political power. However, if we leave aside the presence of the temple, in this period some basic elements of the thought and practice which were to characterize Judaism in the following millennia began to take shape. The one real difficulty lies in the unorganized nature of the sources and their sparseness.

14.12.2 *The Sadducees.* In the temple, ministry was exercised by priests descended from Zadok (above 13.11), called in Greek Σαδδουκαῖοι, hence our Sadducees. They are also well attested, as we know, in the New Testament.

Bibliography

A.C.Sundberg, 'Sadducees', *IDB* IV, 1962, 160-2; K.Schubert, *Die jüdische Religionsparteien im neutestamentlichen Zeitalter*, SBS, 1970, 48ff.; J.Le Moyne, *Les Sadducéens*, Paris 1972; E.Bammel, 'Sadduzäer und Sadokiten', *ETL* 55, 1979, 105-15; A.J.Saldarini, *Pharisees, Scribes and Sadducees in Palestinian Society*, Wilmington, Del. 1988; E.Main, 'Les Sadducéens vus par Flavius Josèphe', *RB* 97, 1990, 161-206; E.Main, 'Les Sadducéens vus par Flavius Josèphe', *RB* 97, 1990, 161-206; G.Stemberger, *Pharisäer, Sadduzäer, Essener*, Stuttgart 1991; G.Boccaccini, *Middle Judaism*, Minneapolis 1991.

14.12.2.1 Characteristic of the Sadducees was on the one hand their strongly traditionalist approach to the faith, common in any conservative religious group. On the other hand, however, they were ready to make considerable concessions on a practical level, with an openness which could arrive at compromises with contemporary authorities and currents, e.g., as we have seen, Hellenism, sometimes beyond anything called for to achieve security (above 14.7.3.2). However, perhaps this presentation, which is that of I and II Maccabees, is too partisan, and we should think rather of a continuation of the line of the opponents of the adversaries of Nehemiah (above 13.9.7, cf. Sacchi* 1976, 96ff.), a line which sought agreement rather than confrontation with the local population, so that today we would call the Sadducees liberals.

14.12.2.2 Be this as it may, it seems certain that some Sadducees went beyond a general openness, adopting customs, beliefs and practices from the surrounding pagan world, and allowed the nomination to the post of High Priest to be delegated to the court, which favoured the best offer rather than the most worthy person. However, that should not blind us to another equally evident fact: that the phenomena of corruption affected only a few, and not all, sectors of the Sadducean priesthood. Some of its members voluntarily exiled themselves from Jerusalem simply to be able to live out their own faith without compromise, though at considerable economic and personal sacrifice, once it had become impossible for them to exercise their ministry in the desecrated temple (above 14.9.5).

14.12.2.3 At any rate, it is often possible to find Sadducees active in relations with the occupying power of the day: first the Seleucids, then the members of the Hasmonaean dynasty and finally the Romans. Nor does it seem to be a coincidence that in the course of the trial of Jesus one of the few features that can be attested with some certainty is the relationship between the Sanhedrin and the Roman procurator Pilate, a relationship which, while being far from cordial, presupposes close and regular collaboration (below 15.3.1).

14.12.2.4 In the sphere of faith, the traditionalism of the Sadducees led them to reject almost all the doctrines which were not attested, or were only scantily attested, in the Hebrew Bible: they rejected the resurrection of the dead, which only appears in a few passages which are all certainly late (Isa.26.14; Dan.12.2-4, cf. II Macc.12.44ff.; cf. also various passages in the New Testament). They also rejected the development of angelology and demonology, characteristic of Judaism between the Testaments and especially of apocalyptic.

14.12.2.5 With the destruction of the temple in 70 CE the Sadducees lost both their own function and the economic basis of their existence as a social class, so their ministry came to an end. Down to the present day, the fact that the temple has not been rebuilt has prevented the rise in Israel of a class of priests, though various functions in synagogue worship are reserved for their descendants (recognizable by names like Cohen and Levi and various derivatives), and some restrictions are imposed on them by the law.

14.12.3 *The Pharisees*. The problem of the origin of the Pharisees appears far more complex: it seems that at least in part they were heirs of the movement of the Hasidim (above 14.9.8) and that they were already in existence at the time of Jonathan Maccabaeus (160-143, *Antt.* XIII, 171), making a final break from the Hasidim at the time of John Hyrcanus I (134-104, *Antt.* XIII, 288).

Bibliography

W.Beilner, 'Der Ursprung des Pharisäertums', *BZ* 3, 1959, 235-51; C.Roth, 'The Pharisees in the Jewish Revolution of 66-73', *JSS* 7, 1962, 63-80; L.Finkelstein, *The Pharisees*, Philadelphia ³1962; A.Michel and J.Le Moyne, 'Pharisiens', *SDB* VII, 1966, 1022-115; K.Schubert, *Die jüdischen Religionsparteien...*, 22-47; J.Neusner, *The Rabbinic Traditions about the Pharisees before 70* (3 vols), Leiden 1971; M.Man(soor), 'Pharisees', *EncJud* XIII, 1971, 363-6; E.Rivkin, 'Pharisees', *IDB-SV*, 1976, 657-63; H.-F.Weiss, 'Pharisaismus und Hellenismus', *OLZ* 74, 1979, 421-33; A.I.Baumgarten, 'The Name of the Pharisees', *JBL* 102, 1983, 411-28; 'Josephus and Hippolytus on the Pharisees', *HUCA* 55, 1984, 1-25; A.Saldarini, *Pharisees* (above 14.12.2); G.Stemberger, *Pharisäer* (ibid.); K.G.C.Newport, 'The Pharisees in Judaism Prior to AD 70', *AUSS* 29, 1991, 127-37; G.Boccaccini, *Middle Judaism* (see above).

14.12.3.1 It seems that the name derives from the Hebrew *p^{e}rūšīm*, the 'separated ones': the Pharisees consciously distanced themselves from the ignorant and rough masses, the *'am hā-'āreṣ*, an expression which, contrary to the meaning that it had in the monarchical period (above 10.13.3), now took on what was clearly a negative significance: ignorant, boorish, illiterate and therefore incapable of studying the Torah and practising the commandments.

14.12.3.2 The characteristic feature of the piety of the Pharisees was their zealous observance of the Torah (below 14.12.5.2-3), an observance over which they would not accept compromise of any kind. They therefore followed directly in the shadow of Nehemiah and Ezra (Beilner 1959; Sacchi* 1976, 96ff.), rejecting all contact with pagans except those who were on the way to conversion. The commandments had to be observed punctiliously – the apostle Paul himself (Phil.3.5-6) recalls his own Pharisaic origins and the zeal with which he had observed the various rules in the past.

14.12.3.3 However, they were far more pragmatic at a doctrinal level. At least to begin with, they did not reject dialogue with the apocalyptists (above 14.5), though they rejected a good deal of apocalyptic belief: for the Pharisees, eschatology consisted especially in the observance of the commandments, because only sin delayed the coming of the kingdom of God (Mishnah, *Aboth* III, 15). And they were also open to new doctrines: the resurrection of the dead followed by a universal judgment, the development of angelology and demonology, all features which to a large extent came from apocalyptic, entered and formed part of their belief.

14.12.3.4 Alongside the written Torah the Pharisees produced an oral Torah which collected the summaries of discussions, interpretations and updatings of the biblical tradition with a view to the new situation in which they were to be applied. These were the elements which in the second century CE came to be codified in the Mishnah and, later, in the Talmudic tractates and commentaries. Jesus is probably referring to their position when he criticizes them because they annul the Torah by means of their tradition (Matt.5.13 par.).

14.12.3.5 Precisely because of their rigour, but also because of their openness, the Pharisees were followed and respected by the people; indeed, it seems that they became the natural spiritual and civil leaders, especially when the catastrophes of 67-70 and 132-135 CE destroyed the priesthood as a social class and institution and discredited apocalyptic. It was in fact the Pharisees who gave to Judaism at the time of the destruction of the temple both the canon of the Hebrew Bible and that traditional collection of exegetical and ethical norms which allowed it to be updated for later reading. Only thanks to them, one might say, did Israel succeed in surviving almost two millennia of Diaspora.

14.12.3.6 The norms which the Pharisees presented to the people could be summed up in one basic principle: not only the priesthood of the temple but the whole of the people of God must be 'holy', since according to Ex.19.6 all Israel, and not just its elite, is called to be a 'kingdom of priests – a holy nation' (Neusner 1971, 671). Or, to put it in the words of a Talmudic text: 'While the temple existed it was the altar which atoned for Israel; now the table of any man atones for it' (bBer 55a, an allusion to the increasing importance that dietary laws were assuming).

14.12.3.7 The refusal of the Pharisees to talk with pagans could lead to positions of intransigence. On the other hand, the Pharisees always rejected any form of zealotism (Roth 1962); they were generally pacifists, though some of them never refused to participate in war once it had broken out. In the context of the Hasidim, therefore, they were among those who wanted to end hostilities once religious liberty had been attained (above 14.9.8). However, that is in no way a sign of weakness or lack of interest in what was happening around them: their courageous attitude towards the Hasmonaean rulers accompanied with remarkable patriotism led them to martyrdom (above 14.11.2-4), simply in order to safeguard what they considered to be the norm of conduct for the people of God.

14.12.3.8 Moreover they believed in a form of free will, which they did not find difficult to reconcile with the absolute sovereignty and foreknowledge of God. In all probability the origin of the dualistic doctrine of human nature in which a good impulse (Hebrew *yēṣer ṭōb*) and an 'evil impulse' (Hebrew *yēṣer raʿ*) are constantly in conflict originated with the Pharisees. In their view, however, human beings could help the good impulse to fight the evil impulse by means of the study and the practice of the Torah (Sifre Deut.45,103).

14.12.3.9 It therefore seems impossible to accept in a historical context the basically negative judgment which the New Testament seems to want to pass on the Pharisees and which has come down from them in Western languages to present-day terminology: that they were hypocrites, in that they feigned a piety which they did not have, simply to maintain their control over people's consciences. This is a judgment which first of all reflects the polemic among Jewish groups of the time, and was only later used by the primitive church in a generally anti-Jewish way. Thus the Qumran sectarians were markedly anti-Pharisaic, calling them 'those who seek falsehood' (above 14.11.4 and below 14.12.4.2), while elsewhere they appear as 'masters of hypocrisy'. For the sectarians of Qumran the explanation of the phenomenon is easy: they accused them of ethical laxity and saw their hypocrisy in the fact that they demanded a great deal, but then contented themselves with a less radical observance of the commandments than was required by the sect. Thus, for example, in the question of divorce, the Damascus Document of the sect (CD IV, 20ff.) takes the wording of Gen.1.27 literally and affirms the unconditional indissolubillity of marriage; virtually the same position is taken by Jesus (Mark 10.2-9; Matt.19.3-8 – and in his footsteps even today by those Christian churches which reject the remarriage of divorced persons). However, the Pharisees were much more pragmatic, to such a degree that at least two schools developed among them, one more strict and the other less so. The anti-Pharisaic polemic in the New Testament is therefore to be seen, at least in origin, as the result of discussions, debates and probably also polemic between the Pharisees and their opponents, the Sadducees, the Essenes and soon also the primitive Christian church.

14.12.3.10 Close to the Pharisees, if not immediately identical with them, were the so-called 'scribes', the 'doctors' or 'masters of the Law', of whom little is known.

14.12.4 *The Essenes*. Another group has been found only since the discovery of the Dead Sea Scrolls from 1947 on: its members are generally identified with the Essenes.

Bibliography

It is possible to give only a very small selection from a bibliography which has now reached enormous proportions.

Editiones principes: M.Burrows (ed.), *The Dead Sea Scrolls of St Mark's Monastery*, New Haven, CN 1950, II.2, 1951; E.L.Sukenik (ed.), *The Dead Sea Scrolls of the Hebrew University*, Jerusalem 1955; N.Avigad and Y.Yadin (ed.), *A Genesis Apocryphon*, Jerusalem 1956; A.S.van der Woude (ed.), *Le Targum de la grotte XI de Qumrân*, Leiden 1971; N.Sokoloff (ed.), *The Targum of Job from Qumran Cave XI*, Ramat Gan 1974; Y.Yadin (ed.), *The Temple Scroll*, Jerusalem 1977 (in Hebrew) and 1983 (in English). The lesser texts have been published with various editors in the collection *Discoveries in the Judaean Desert*, Oxford 1955ff.

Translations: J.Maier, *Die Texte vom Toten Meer*, Basel and Munich

1960; E.Lohse, *Die Texte aus Qumran*, Munich 1964, Darmstadt ²1971; F.Michelini-Tocci, *I manoscritti del mar Morto*, Bari 1967; L.Moraldi, I *manoscritti di Qumran*, Turin 1971, ²1983; B.Jongeling et al., *Aramaic Texts from Qumran*, Leiden 1976; G.Vermes and M.D.Goodman (ed.), *The Essenes according to the Classical Sources*, Sheffield 1979; G.Vermes, *The Dead Sea Scrolls in English*, Harmondsworth ³1987.

Bibliographies: W.Baumgartner, 'Der palästinensische Handschriftenfund', *TE* 19, 1951, 97-154; S.Wagner, *Die Essener in der wissenschaftlichen Discussion*, Berlin 1960; A.S.van der Woude, 'Fünfzehn Jahre Qumranforschung (1974-1988)', *TR* 54, 1989, 221-61. There is a complete catalogue of the writings so far known, in F.García Martínez, 'Lista de MSS procedentes de Qumrân', *Hen* 11, 1989, 149-232, followed by L.Rosso Ubigli, ibid., 233-269. *Monographs*: K.Elliger, *Studien zum Habakuk-Kommentar vom Toten Meer*, Tübingen 1953; H.Bardtke, *Die Handschriftenfunde am Toten Meer*, Berlin 1953-1962; J.Hempel, *Die Texte von Qumran in der heutigen Forschung*, NHWG.PH 1962, 281-374; J.Maier and K.Schubert, *Die Qumran-Essener*, Basel and Munich 1973; J.A.Soggin, *I manoscritti del Mar Morto*, Rome 1978 (with bibliography); P.R.Davies, 'The Story of Qumran', *BA* 51, 1988, 203-7; S.Talmon, *The World of Qumran from Within*, Jerusalem 1989; G.Boccaccini, *Middle Judaism*, Minneapolis 1991; D.Dunant, *The Dead Sea Scrolls*, Leiden 1992; E.Tov (ed.), *The Dead Sea Scrolls on Microfiche*, Leiden 1992. M.Baigent and R.Leigh, *The Dead Sea Scrolls Deception*, London 1991, is a polemical treatment in journalistic style.

14.12.4.1 Because of the withdrawal of the members of the sect from public life and what the majority of scholars regard as the monastic existence at least of the group which formed their nucleus, we formerly knew only the little that Josephus and shortly afterwards Philo of Alexandria and some classical authors report about them. Their accounts are often coloured by moralistic and edifying reflections, aimed at making the community exemplary for its virtue. The Essenes lived in a community which practised celibacy, in a 'monastery' at *ḥirbet qumrān*, on the north-western shore of the Dead Sea (coord.194-128). Other members, who did not practise celibacy, continued to live in their ordinary places of residence, though they made regular pilgrimages to Qumran. It is only through the discoveries of their writings, which took place in often romantic circumstances from 1947 onwards, that it has been possible to form an image, though only partial, of the group.

14.12.4.2 Their founder, who is not otherwise known, bears the title *mōreh ṣedeq*, 'Teacher of Righteousness' or, probably better, 'Righteous Teacher'; he seems to have been killed in obscure circumstances.

14.12.4.3 The origin of the group is to be sought among those

Sadducees who chose to join the Hasidim because their way of life had been compromised by Hellenism. The date of this is usually put at the middle of the second century BCE, i.e. in the time of Alexander Balas (150-145) and Jonathan Maccabaeus (160-143). Their Sadducean origin, combined with their rigorism, would explain their opposition to the Pharisees (above 10.3.2; 11.3.6). They, too, essentially seem to have been pacifists, although they developed a marked aggressiveness in their doctrines and the way in which they expressed them (final apocalyptic struggles between the 'sons of light' and the 'sons of darkness'). For other details see the works listed above and especially Soggin 1978.

14.12.4.4 It is not always easy to make a detailed reconstruction of the doctrines of the group, not only because not all the sources have yet been published but also because of a cryptic language, addressed to the members of the group and not always comprehensible to the modern reader. In my 1978 study I attempted to classify the doctrines of the group into those which derive directly from the Hebrew Bible and those which are variants of these or originate from other sources.

14.12.4.4.1 A series of doctrines of the group can be derived from the Bible, though often the formulation of them tends to be more severe.

Scripture and especially the Torah stand at the centre of the piety of the group, a feature which it shares with other sectors of Judaism. However, the 'Teacher' is considered the principal interpreter of scripture, and his exegesis is the norm for the community (cf. 1QS VI.6; 1QpHab VII.1, commentary on Hab.2.3). But the exegesis is turned into a way of seeing references to the 'Teacher' and the group in the ancient texts; sometimes the original text is amplified by interpolations which end up by substantially modifying its original meaning. Thus for example 1QS II,2-4 offers an amplified version of the priestly blessing in Num. 6.24-26, which I quote with the original biblical text in italics:

May he bless you with all good things
and keep you from all evil;
and *lighten* your heart with discernment of life,
and *be gracious to you* with eternal knowledge
and lift up his countenance benignly *upon you*
for eternal *peace*.

Problems of faith and everyday life are regulated in accordance with the biblical commandments. Concepts like that of the divine covenant, a covenant which the community relates exclusively to itself (indeed, the group defines itself as 'the community of the new covenant') are still central; this appears particularly in the Damascus Document, CD VI.19; VIII.21; XIX.34; XX.12, but probably also in 1Q pHab II.3; so too are marriage, circumcision and observance of the law. This last is practised in a particularly rigorous way. In CD XI.13-17 it is said: 'No man shall assist a beast to give birth on the Sabbath day. And if it should fall into a cistern or pit, he shall not lift it out on the sabbath... No man shall take a living person out, but should he fall into water or fire, let him be pulled out with the aid of a ladder or rope or some such tool...' As we know, the New Testament differs (Matt.12.11; Luke 14.5, cf. below 14.12.5.3-4).

The Holy Spirit is the divine gift which gives strength to observe the commandments. 1QH VII 6-7 declares: 'I thank you, O Lord, because you have upheld me by your strength. You have shed your holy Spirit upon me that I may not stumble.' But here a shift of accent should be noted: the Spirit produces wisdom rather than prophecy and charismatic gifts, so that Hempel 1962, 349, can rightly speak of an 'intellectualization of piety'. Even if the reconstrution of past history is done mainly in the category of sin before God, that does not so much happen as a confession of sin as in an intellectualistic way (cf. above, the paraphrase of the Aaronic blessing). In any case, only a radical change by the people towards the Torah of Moses provides a remedy.

In eschatology, too, the group has its own doctrines, though these are for the most part taken from the Bible. The end of time will be later than was announced by the prophets. Like other groups, the group apparently expected two Messiahs on the basis of Zech.4.11-4, where mention is made of 'two anointed', one with political and the other with religious functions. IQS IX.11 in fact speaks of the 'Anointed of Aaron and Israel'. Compared with apocalyptic, the eschatology of the group is quite moderate, while the angelology seems very developed, as in other contemporary writings.

14.12.4.4.2 However, it is not only the Bible which serves as a source for the doctrine of the group; other material appears which is alien to the Bible, though we cannot always identify its origins. Thus the universe is understood as a battlefield between 'light' and 'darkness', and the 'sons of light', identified with the sectarians, are engaged in struggle to the end of time with the 'sons of darkness' (the others); but with divine aid they will emerge from the battle victorious. The concept of 'sons of light' is also known to the New Testament, but without the motive of the final struggle (cf. Luke 16.8; Eph.5.8 and I Thess.5.5; cf. also the contrast between 'light' and 'darkness' in the Fourth Gospel and the Johannine tradition). However, two spirits are in combat even within the human person (1QS IV.16ff.), probably an anticipation of the rabbinic doctrine of the two dispositions (above 14.1.3.8), though only formally so; in fact there is no cosmic dualism among the rabbis, and human beings are given means of defending themselves against evil. On the other hand there is no profession by the group of any kind of dualism of a metaphysical kind according to the Iranian scheme: God remains unique and helps the 'light' to obtain the final and inevitable victory. Therefore the doctrine does not seem to have much in common either with Iranian dualism or with later Jewish and Christian Gnosticism, which identifies the good element in human beings with the spirit, and the bad with the flesh.

Finally, the calendar used by the community is not biblical; it clearly differs from the traditional Jewish lunar calendar which is still in use today, since it has 336 days. Qumran, along with the groups which composed the books of Jubilees and Henoch, uses, rather, the solar calendar, at that time calculated at 365 days. This is a complex problem which we cannot go into in detail here.

14.12.4.5 All this, however, does not mean that the group was an essentially religious community, and there are authors (cf. recently Davies 1988 and Baigent and Leigh 1991) who accuse scholars of having looked at the group according to criteria which relate only to Christian monasticism (i.e. do not apply before the third and fourth centuries CE), and deny the value of this approach. In this case, too, caution is needed, so as not to approach the group with alien presuppositions.

14.12.4.6 The destruction of the group is generally connected with Titus's expedition against Massada (below 15.5.8). After these events we lose track of the community, though there are some scholars who believe that they find it later in the doctrine and practice of the Jewish sect of the Karaites.

14.12.4.7 The fact that not all of the texts have as yet been published has given rise, since the late 1980s, to discussions which are not without strong polemical tones and which have often turned into personal attacks on scholars. The main arguments can be found in the North American journal *Biblical Archaeology Review* and in Baigent and Leigh 1991 (now in paperback). They make essentially two points; that the scholarly committee in charge of the publication of the scrolls was composed in practice of self-appointed scholars, and that at present some texts are being withheld from publication because they would challenge the Christian faith.

There is some truth to the first argument: the scholars who started to study the scrolls and their doctoral students have kept working on them. But since 1967, when the Israeli Department of Antiquities took over, the team has been considerably broadened, and photographs of the scrolls have been made available on request.

The second argument is simply untrue and plays on the natural curiosity of non-competent readers. Of course it may arouse interest in the scrolls in wider circles, outside the world of specialists, but it will also point it in a wrong direction. So books like that by Baigent and Leigh must be described as nonsense (cf. the review by M.Broshi, *BA* 55, 1992, 107f., who puts it among the 'poor, silly books'). The real problem is the fragmentary state of the scrolls and the heavy damage done to them, which makes their restoration a difficult jig-saw puzzle.

The wider availability of the copies of the original scrolls can certainly be an asset for those who want to study them; on the other hand there is now an acute danger of 'pirate' editions, made by people without the necessary skills and competence.

14.12.5 *Constants in Jewish faith in this period*. Despite all this diversity in the faith and practice of the various groups, it is possible to identify various constants in the Judaism of the time.

14.12.5.1 First of all it is necessary to rid oneself of the prejudice, frequent in traditional Christian circles, that Judaism was doctrinally fossilized and ethically attached to a cold and legalistic observance of the dead letter, unmindful of the real and most important problems – was a Judaism, in short, which had exhausted its own mission and was waiting only to be replaced by a movement which had incorporated its most valid points. This is the view of Judaism which has sometimes been presented by the writings of the primitive church, and it then became the judgment that the Christian tradition handed down on Judaism and its values. Who can forget the mediaeval iconography in which the synagogue is depicted as an ugly, blindfolded, hag while the church is depicted as a beautiful woman with her eyes open? To debunk this image we need only remember the readiness with which thousands of Jews took up arms to defend their faith and their practice of worship, or their readiness for martyrdom, from the time of the Maccabees to that of Bar Kochba; and also the fascination which Judaism has always had for many areas of the pagan world, a fascination which has found tangible expression in many conversions to Judaism. Paradoxically, the New Testament often seems to be behind this negative image; however, as we have seen (above 14.12.3.9), most of the time the New Testament is reflecting internal debates, discussions and polemic within Judaism; at other times, though, we have texts which represent polemic not so much against Judaism as against the demands made by Jewish Christians, who argued that it was necessary to become a Jew before becoming a member of the Christian church. Moreover, the Judaism of the time had a multitude of facets, varying from extreme rigorism to laxity, from exclusivism towards other people to mission and proselytism, from absolute exclusion to openness.

14.12.5.2 And if we leave aside the most rigid groups, like that of Qumran, it is clear that practising Jews did not seem the slightest bit worried about a hard casuistry of precepts and prohibitions, but on the contrary lived out a life based on the certainty of being able to fulfil the divine will and on doing everything possible to fulfil their own mission, accepting the gifts of divine grace and providence (of which the Torah was certainly the main one), trying to respond to them in a less inadequate way, in the certainty that obedience to the divine will was the best way of creating a more just society. And they were ready to accept even martyrdom when their faith came up against, or in any way conflicted with, the demands of other powers, including those of the state. In other words, Judaism seems to have resolved what St Paul saw as the conflict between 'the law' and 'the gospel' by seeing the Torah as first of all, before being law, good news (something that the young Luther was well aware of) in that it made it possible to realize the divine will on earth.

After the example I gave above (14.12.3.9), of marriage and repudiation, I would like to introduce here what is one of the basic features of Jewish faith and practice, sabbath observance.

14.12.5.3 There is no need here to point out that a law which requires the cessation of all activity and thus of production for a seventh part of the week is not only a religious but also a social law: in fact it ensured that everyone, Jew or non-Jew, free or slave, man, woman or animal, had to break off every activity for just over twenty-four hours each week. In basically family and patriarchal enterprises, it was evident that those who did not work on that day also had to eat and otherwise be kept, even if they did not produce anything. And this feature also explains why there were continual attempts to violate this law, attempts to which witness is already borne by the casuistry of the Decalogue (Ex.20.8-11//Deut.5.12-15). As we have seen (above 14.9.7), even the Hasidim originally faced the problem whether they should violate the sabbath to defend themselves against their enemies, or whether it was right to allow themselves to be massacred on that day by those who did not have such scruples (I Macc.2.32-38; cf. II Macc.6.10f.). It is also interesting to note how among the majority of scholars writing on classical antiquity there is a complete lack of understanding of the social as well as the religious nature of the commandment: in fact it often seems to be explained in terms of the congenital laziness of the Jewish people.

14.12.5.4 It is understandable how the matter should have been debated for a long time, and often violently, before it could be resolved by a series of rules. We also find an echo of these debates in the New Testament, the texts of which are obviously to be read on this basis. Mishnah *Yoma* VIII.6 says, '...whenever there is doubt whether life is in danger this overrides the sabbath'. And the following section (VIII.7) quotes the example of a building which has collapsed: if there is even the slightest suspicion that someone might be under the debris it is necessary to go on removing it, even on the sabbath. Similarly, Mishnah

Shabbath V.22 says, 'But if there is any mortal danger, there is nothing which comes before such danger.' Thus it is, for example, quite in order to summon the help of a midwife on the sabbath (*Shab.* VIII.3); to kindle or put out lights for fear of attacks by humans or demons; to help a sick person to rest; but not to economize on oil or wicks (ibid. II.5). And R.Akiba, tortured by the Romans in 132 CE, ruled that it is not lawful to violate the sabbath to do things that could have been done the day before; however, the sabbath has not been violated when there was no such possibility (*Shab.* XIX.1). For 'the sabbath has not been given for you, but you have been given for the sabbath' (Mekilta ad Ex.31.13, cf. Jesus in Mark 2.27). However, the rigorous attitude of the Qumran group seems to have been very different (cf. above 14.12.4.4.1).

14.12.5.5 To speak of legalism in contexts like these clearly does not get to the heart of the question. However, where it is legitimate to use this term is in the attempts, which must have been frequent, to get round this commandment by means of pseudo-legalistic subtleties. Where Jesus seems to have gone beyond his own contemporaries is when he extended the criterion of mortal danger to the healing of a sick person which could in fact have been performed on any other day of the week; this is a criterion which the Hebrew tradition never accepted.

14.1.5.6 A second factor which substantially determines the Jewish faith and piety of this and successive times is Holy Scripture. It is not known whether and to what point it was more or less complete in the form and dimensions in which we know it today; however, it is certain that the Pentateuch was already in existence, and the same can be said of a large part of the Prophets and Psalms. Thus it is also certain that the Torah enjoyed the utmost prestige, the greatest canonicity. The term mainly means not only 'law', as it is often translated, but 'word of God' or 'Holy Scripture', cf. Pss.1.1ff; 19A.1ff.; 37.31; 119.97, etc.

14.12.5.7 A third element is the dietary laws, the practice of which begins to be amply attested (cf. above 14.12.3.6). In Dan.1.8ff. Daniel and his friends, deported to the Babylonian court, take great care not to be contaminated by eating the food put before them at the king's table, and prefer vegetarian food and only water to drink. It is clear that the problem here is not that of eating pure animals, which are suitable as food, and impure animals, which are forbidden food, but of ritual slaughter and ritually pure wine. See also Tob.1.10-12, where all those who have been deported eat local food, while the hero and his family observe the rules for the ritual purity of food; in Judith 10.5 the bread is also pure, and therefore made in accordance with rabbinical rules.

15

Under the Romans

15.1 The civil wars

The beginning of Roman domination in the region coincides with the civil war between Pompey and Caesar, an event which involved Palestine only marginally. At all events, it ushered in an unstable period. The sources are essentially Josephus, *Antt.* XIV-XX (up to 67 CE) and *Jewish War*, though in them, as we have seen, the author is often dominated by the need to make an apologia for the Jewish cause generally and himself in particular. Be this as it may, scholars are generally agreed that when Josephus seems inaccurate, it is more through the omission of facts than by deliberate distortion of them. Some information is also provided by Tacitus in the *Histories* and the *Annals*, sources which are all in M.Stern II, 273-94.

Profiting from the disorders, Aristobulus several times tried to regain the throne, and once even succeeded in escaping from his Roman imprisonment. Finally peace was restored and, with Caesar's victory, Hyrcanus was confirmed High Priest and ethnarch, while Antipater was nominated procurator of Judaea.

Bibliography

A.Momigliano, 'Ricerche sull'organizzazione della Giudea sotto il dominio romano (63 a.C – 70 d.C)', in *ASNSP* III, 3, 1934, 183-221, 347-96; S.Perowne, *The Life and Times of Herod the Great*, London 1956-59; J.Jeremias, *Jerusalem in the Time of Jesus*, London and Philadelphia 1969; E.Lohse, 'Die römische Statthalter in Jerusalem', *ZDPV* 74, 1958, 69-78; M.Hengel, *The Zealots* (1961), Edinburgh 1989; S.Zeitlin, *Rise and Fall of the Judaean State* (above 14.1); W.E.Filmer, 'The Chronology of the Reign of Herod the Great', *JTS* NS 17, 1966, 283-98; S.Sandmel, *Herod: Profile of a Tyrant*, Philadelphia 1967; T.D.Barnes, 'The Date of

Herod's Death', *JTS* 19, NS 1968, 204-9; S.G.F.Brandon, *Jesus and the Zealots*, Manchester 1967; E.M.Smallwood, *The Jews under Roman Rule*, Leiden 1976; A.Schalit, *König Herodes. Der Mann und sein Werk*, Berlin 1969; M.Smith, 'Zealots and Sicarii, their Origin and Relation', *HTR* 64, 1971, 1-19; M.G.Angeli-Bertinelli, *Roma e l'Oriente*, Rome 1979; H.Guevara, *La resistencia contra Roma en la época de Jesús*, Meitingen 1981; J.P.Lémolnon, *Pilate et le gouvernement de la Judée*, Paris 1981; P.G.Antonini, *Processo e condanna di Gesù. Indagine storico-esegetica sulla motivazioni della sentenza*, Turin 1982; E.Bammel and C.F.D.Moule (eds.), *Jesus and the Politics of his Day*, Cambridge 1983; P.M.Bernegger, 'Affirmation of Herod's Death in 4 BC', *JTS* NS 34, 1983, 526-31; M.Goodman, *The Ruling Class of Judaea: The Origins of the Jewish Revolt against Rome, AD 66-70*, Cambridge 1988; E.M.Myers, 'Early Judaism and Christianity in the Light of Archaeology', *BA* 51, 1989, 69-79; D.E.Groh, 'Jews and Christians in Late Roman Palestine', ibid., 80-96; W.Fricke, *Standesrechtlich gekreuzigt*, Frankfurt am Main [4]1988; R.Horlay, 'Bandits, Messiahs and Longshoremen: Popular Unrest in Galilee around the Time of Jesus', SBL Seminar Papers 27, Atlanta Ga 1988, 183-99; K.C.Hanson, 'The Herodians and Mediterranean Kingship', *BTB* 19, 1989, 75-84; E.Gabba, 'The Finances of King Herod', in *Greece and Rome in Eretz Israel*, ed. A.Kasher, U.Rapaport and G.Fuks, Jerusalem 1991, 160-8.

15.1.1 Herod Antipater who, as we have seen, had been the real victor in the context between Hyrcanus and Aristobulus (above 14.11.7), first involved his own sons in the government, putting them in positions of power. Phasael, the older, became commander of the military region of Jerusalem, and restored its fortifications, while Herod, the younger, was given command of the northern region, despite his youth. Both were to distinguish themselves because they were capable and dynamic, especially Herod, who succeeded in ridding Galilee of the bands of robbers which had formed there during the disorders. However, the two were never popular with the people, first of all because they were of foreign origin (the Idumaeans of southern Judaea had been forcibly converted and circumcised by John Hyrcanus, above 14.11.1), and also because they were wilful and violent. Be this as it may, Herod thus entered political life and from then on assumed increasingly important functions.

15.1.2 On the death of Caesar in 44 BCE and the outbreak of the second civil war, Antipater, at first a supporter of Caesar, unexpectedly found himself in the territory controlled by Cassius, who governed Syria. He immediately went over to Cassius' side. However, he was killed in 43 BCE and Herod, after avenging the death of his father, succeeded him to the throne, leapfrogging his older brother. He managed in steering a skilful course between Cassius and Antony, and from the latter obtained for himself and his brother the ethnarcy of Judaea; only the High Priesthood remained to Hyrcanus.

15.2 Herod the king

During the Parthian invasion in 40 BCE, Antigonus, son of Aristobulus, succeeded in regaining his father's throne for a short time and kept it even when the Romans reconquered the country in 39 BCE. However, Herod, who had taken refuge in Rome and had been given the title of king by Antony and Octavian, returned home strengthened by the protection of the two triumvirs and, with the aid of Roman troops, had no difficulty in regaining his own territory, including Jerusalem, which fell after a short siege. Antigonus, who fled to Antioch, was killed by Herod in 37. In the same year Herod married Mariamne, granddaughter of Aristobulus and Hyrcanus and sister of Antigonus, and therefore the last heir to the Hasmonean throne. Thus Herod also acquired a certain dynastic legitimacy. The chronology of his reign is often obscure because of contradictory information; however, P.M.Bernegger 1983 has confirmed 37 BCE as the year of his accession to the throne and 4 BCE as the year of his death.

15.2.1 Herod, whose ability had already been demonstrated on Caesar's death, confirmed his dexterity by manoeuvring skilfully between Antony and Octavian. In relations with Rome his guideline was never to allow himself to be directly involved in the struggle for power, but always to appear beside the victor at the right moment. These tactics did not always succeed; in 32, when the conflict between Antony and Octavian broke out again, he took sides with the former, but did not play an active part in the war. Then, after the battle of Actium in 31, he managed to go over to the other side, making his submission in person to Octavian when the latter was in Rhodes, in 30 BCE. However, before that, he had gone so far as to have Hyrcanus killed and Mariamne and her mother imprisoned, ordering that both should be killed if he did not return from his mission. His self-defence before Octavian was conducted with discretion and skill: he openly confessed that he had taken Antony's side, and succeeded in convincing Octavian not only to confirm him in office but even to entrust him with other territories: among these were Samaria and Peraea, the region to the east of Lake Tiberias.

15.2.2 In 29 he had his mother-in-law and his wife Mariamne killed, and later, in 12/11 BCE, two of his sons by her, Alexander and Aristobulus; shortly before his death he had yet another one, Antipater, killed. The Pharisees and their disciples also suffered harsh persecution under him. He died in 4 BCE.

15.2.3 The Gospel according to Matthew puts shortly before Herod's death the birth of Jesus of Nazareth, whom the primitive church proclaimed after his crucifixion to have risen and to have been the Messiah (Hebrew *māšiªḥ*, Greek Χριστός, 'anointed'; the title first of the kings of Judah and then of the High Priest) expected by Israel, the Davidic king who would free the people of God from its oppressors and inaugurate the kingdom of God on earth. Matthew 2.16-17 connects the birth of Jesus with the so-called 'massacre of the innocents', a legendary incident.

15.2.4 It is possible (and a number of scholars take this seriously into consideration) that psychologically Herod was not completely normal, being disturbed by serious persecution mania and an inferiority complex. This last element seems to have been especially dominant in his relations with Mariamne, whom he loved and hated, and who moreover did everything possible to stress her own royal origins and her husband's plebeian lineage. Persecution mania must have pursued Herod all his life, making him see plots and betrayals everywhere, even among his closest friends.

15.2.5 Extremely skilful in foreign policy, as we have seen, Herod was no less so in governing his own country. A superb administrator, he managed to use state funds for a series of remarkable public works. He had the temple of Jerusalem rebuilt, substantially enlarging it (what is now called the 'western wall' or the 'wailing wall' is simply the supporting wall of the temple mount); and on the north side of this he built a fortress which he called the Antonia, in honour of his first protector. Its remains can now be seen at the beginning of the Via Dolorosa, in the Franciscan Monastery of the Flagellation and the Convent of the Sisters of Notre Dame of Zion. He also built a number of palaces: the Herodion, south-east of Bethlehem (coord.173-119), and Massada[1], near the west shore of the Dead Sea (coord.138-080); there were also others, in Transjordan as well. In honour of Augustus, Herod first restored Samaria, calling it Sebaste, i.e. Augusta, and then had the port of Caesarea built, a few miles south of Mount Carmel (coord.140-212). He had some fortresses constructed and restored the western gate of Jerusalem, giving it three towers called respectively Phasael (in honour of his brother), Mariamne (in honour of his wife) and Hippicus (in honour of a friend), and there he built his own palace. The three towers are still in existence today and have been incorporated into the Turkish fortress at the Jaffa gate, rebuilt, along with the walls, by Suleiman the Magnificent in the sixteenth century. Under Herod's administration the country achieved unprecedented prosperity and had hardly any unemployment or poverty. However, what we might call the 'good government' of Herod was not enough to win him the sympathy of his subjects, who continued to see him as a stranger and, moreover, as a violent and cruel man.

15.3 *The Roman administration*

On the death of Herod, from 4 BCE to 6 CE, the country went through a chaotic decade. Archelaus, a surviving son, reigned for a short time, but the region was the scene of various revolts, either against the Herodians or against the Romans or against both. They were all quelled in blood.

15.3.1 In 6 CE Judaea became directly dependent on Roman administration and was governed, with the brief interregnum of 'king' Agrippa (41-44 CE), son of Aristobulus IV (the second son of Herod and Mariamne, whom Herod had had killed along with his brother Alexander, above 15.2.2), by procurators. Transjordan, Peraea and Galilee continued to remain under Herod's successors.

15.3.2 Direct administration by Rome, the form of government which initially the Judahites themselves had asked for (above 14.11.8), weary as they were of the Hasmonaeans and then of Herod, soon proved very burdensome and was often disturbed by unpleasant developments.

15.3.2.1 From a religious point of view Judaism, which enjoyed the status of a *religio licita*, continued to have its traditional autonomy, and the ethnarch (the title born by the High Priest) had ample powers in the civil sphere as well. Officially Rome respected Jewish worship, and did not interfere in it; however, all too often this was a purely formal respect which did not preserve the Judahites from acts and ceremonies which they considered provocative, like the erection of statues dedicated to the divinized emperor or the parade of military standards, all connected with some deity. A parade of this kind was organized under Pontius Pilate, as Josephus reports (*Antt.* XVIII, 60ff. and *War* II, 175ff.) at the beginning of his governorship in 27 CE. And contrary to the image which the Gospels present of him (as an honest, albeit not very intelligent and courageous bureaucrat, with the air of a philosopher), he was a cruel and rapacious man, one of the worst Roman officials the country ever had (cf. also Luke 13.1ff.).

15.3.2.2 Moreover, the contempt that the Romans had for Jewish faith and worship (cf. also the phrase of Tacitus quoted above, 14.11.9) was hardly disguised. The Roman officials had no direct knowledge of Judaism, nor did they show anything but a negative interest in it. Furthermore, they exercised their functions in an authoritarian and repressive way and were almost always venal and corrupt, more preoccupied with enriching themselves and with their careers than with the public good. The collection of taxes, leased out to private individuals (those whom the Gospels call publicans) and backed up by military force, must have led to all kinds of abuses.

15.3.2.3 It is therefore easy to understand the almost endemic state of rebellion in the region, which politically speaking created a kind of vicious circle: corruption and oppression led to revolts, and these in turn led to repression with even heavier forms of oppression. And, as often happens in situations of this kind, it is not always easy to distinguish between rebellions of a political kind and more or less clear forms of brigandage. At all events we know that, as in the time of the Seleucids, groups again took to the hills, and that new groups of armed resistance began to form. We know of a certain Judah of Galilee, who also appeared in Judaea in 6/7 CE, preaching revolt against the census ordered by the Romans for fiscal reasons. This is the census mentioned in Luke 2.1-5, where it is connected with the governorship of P. Sulpicius Quirinius in Syria. We do not know why Luke.2.1 (there is a discussion by Leaney in Hayes and Miller* 1977, 638-9) puts it a decade earlier, still under Herod. Judah the Galilean is also mentioned by Gamaliel in Acts 5.37. He was killed and the revolt was put down, but out of it grew the Zealots (Aramaic *qanānā'*, root *qinnā'*, 'be jealous of', 'be zealous', 'be pledged to a cause'). Zealots are also attested in the New Testament: in Matt.10.4//Mark 3.18 a Simon wrongly called 'Canaanite' is even one of the Twelve; Luke 6.15, the other parallel passage in the Synoptics, rightly has 'Simon the Zealot'. A later offshoot of the Zealots was the group called Sicarii: armed with a kind of dagger (*sica*), they performed individual acts of terrorism against the Romans and against Jews who were thought to be collaborators. Perhaps the second part of the name of Judas Iscariot himself, the disciple of Jesus who betrayed him, is a distorted form of Sicarius – that would explain the name, which is not otherwise attested. Josephus, *Antt.* XVIII, 1ff., regards the Zealots as a fourth party, along with the Sadducees, the Pharisees and the Essenes, so there must have been many of them, forming a group with its own characteristics. It is possible that Barabbas, the assassin whom Pilate pardoned instad of Jesus at the request of the mob, had in reality been a Zealot or even a Sicarius, and therefore was regarded with sympathy by the people.

15.4 Jesus of Nazareth

We can only deal with the figure of Jesus of Nazareth in passing here. Evaluations of a christological kind in any case belong to the history of the primitive church and of Christian doctrine, rather than to the history of Israel. Nor, for the same reasons, is it possible to give readers a bibliography here.

15.4.1 According to the Gospels, Jesus was accused by the Jewish authorities before the Roman procurator of being a political and social agitator, after a trial before the Sanhedrin which is so full of errors and improbable and sometimes even absurd features that it cannot go back to an authentic tradition. After some hesitation the procurator condemned him to death by crucifixion, and the reason for the sentence, fixed to the cross-beam, bears witness to the subversive character of the imputed blame.[2]

15.4.2 Again according to the Gospels, for a brief time Jesus was an itinerant preacher in Galilee, especially in the region around Lake Tiberias; at least once he went to Jerusalem, there, again according to the Gospels, to present his own messianic claims (however, some passages have what has been called the messianic secret). The very character of the Gospels makes a systematic reconstruction of the content of his message and preaching difficult.[3] In Jerusalem, again according to the Gospels, he was welcomed as Messiah, with a ceremonial which shows marked analogies to the Jewish ceremonial for the Feast of Tabernacles.

15.4.3 It is difficult to say precisely what led to the break between Jesus and almost all the Jewish authorities, first with the Pharisees and then with the Sadducees in the temple. One reason could be that in his preaching he spoke chiefly to the ʿam hā-ʾāreṣ, whom all the others despised for being rough and ignorant and therefore incapable of study and the practice of the Torah (above 14.12.3.1), while in his criticism he did not spare the leading groups; indeed, he aimed his criticism at them.

15.4.4 On the Jewish side, however, very little indeed, almost nothing, is said about Jesus: there is a brief reference in Josephus, *Antt.* XX, 200, while a more detailed text, *Antt.* XVIII, 63f., is regarded by many scholars as a later Christian interpolation with apologetic aims.[4] Nothing appears in the earliest rabbinic writings.[5] So it is reasonable to suppose that the preaching of Jesus, far from having had the impact that the Gospels attribute to it on the Judaism of the time, and that it clearly had in the sphere of the nascent Christian church, passed virtually unobserved, as did everything Jesus did. This was because it was in competition with the activity of other preachers and 'prophets'; moreover, it took place in a peripheral region, inhabited by a mixed Jewish and pagan population, and therefore was hardly noticed by the rabbis and the Hebrew sages of the time. Thus the affirmation implicit in the title of section 34 of Noth's *History*, 'The Rejection of Christ', seems unacceptable on the historical plane, quite apart from being doubtful theology.

15.5 Outbreaks and revolts

The sources abound in lists of incidents between the Romans and the Judaeans, all sparked off by religious issues.

15.5.1 There was one revolt in 41 CE because the Romans tried to put an image of the emperor in the temple; they may well have had no intention of causing offence, far less of provoking the Jews, since this was common practice among pagans. On another occasion, in the course of reprisals against a village near where a Roman patrol had been attacked, the Torah scrolls of a local synagogue were profaned. These instances could be multiplied (cf. Leaney in Hayes and Miller* 1977, 644ff.).

15.5.2 One thing seems certain: given the situation that had come into being, it did not take much for the local revolts to degenerate into a general uprising, of the kind that had happened in the time of Antiochus IV two centuries earlier.

15.5.2.1 The occasion was provided by some actions of the procurator Gessius Florus in 67 CE, who took the sum of seventeen gold talents from the temple. He was probably the most corrupt of the officials sent by Rome. It is therefore possible (as a number of scholars accept) that Gessius deliberately provoked the incidents so as to be able to hide his own misconduct behind the punitive provisions. However, the only source at our disposal is the work of Josephus, who quite clearly favours the Jewish cause: there is very little information from the Roman side, and that would also need to be heard. Still, the corruption of the Roman administrative system is well known, so there is nothing extraordinary about the accusations made against Gessius: what were remarkable were the consequences that they had, not only for Israel but also for Rome. This was the occasion that the Zealots had been waiting for for years.

15.5.2.2 Of course, as at the time of the Maccabees, a revolt of this kind did not begin from a single isolated act, and here too scholars must be careful not to take the religious factor as the main one: the tensions between Jews and non-Jews had already lasted for years, especially in those areas where there was a mixed population. Caesarea, the seat of the Roman procurator, was such a place.

15.5.3. Moreover there were social, economic and political features to which scant attention has so far been paid, but which certainly played a major part in the outbreak of the revolt. I shall try to list the main ones on the basis of most recent studies.

15.5.3.1 Unlike the Seleucids and the Hellenists, the Romans had not succeeded in creating in Judaea a social class which was, if not favourable to them, at least neutral, and which would have also been acceptable to the Jews at the same time (Goodman 1987). If one can trust the Gospels, as is probable in this case, the so-called publicans (above 15.3.2.2) were most hated of all by their compatriots.

15.5.3.2 Again it seems probable, as has been convincingly demonstrated by S.J.D.Cohen in Shanks* 1988, 222ff., that the importance of the Roman provocations in the religious sphere, i.e. the theological element, was not too great at that time; indeed, Cohen goes so far as to deny that there were real provocations in this area by the Romans. However, there were many factors for which the Romans were not to blame or for which they had very little responsibility, including the marked social tensions. For example, at the end of the rebuilding of the temple begun by Herod, 18,000 workers were immediately laid off and at best only found occasional work from then on. We also know of conflicts between the senior and junior clergy in the temple and disorders among the countryfolk in Galilee, which often flared up in looting. There were marked contrasts between the upper classes and the lowest classes of the population; finally, the Zealots issued polemic against the moderate elements, while eschatological hopes of 'final pangs' followed by the establishment of the kingdom of God and other thoughts of this kind contributed to the general uncertainty, precisely as at the time of the Maccabees.

15.5.3.3 At all events, the reaction of Jerusalem to the seizing of the talents by the procurator was not what could be called prudent or administratively correct: the procurator was publicly jeered at and insulted. By way of reprisal he allowed his troops to ransack a particular district, and the troops made full use of his permission, putting a section of the holy city to fire and the sword. Then the procurator demanded that the population should give a triumphal welcome to two cohorts arriving from Caesarea.

15.5.3.4 The High Priest, along with a good many of the Sadducean priests and the Pharisees, urged the people to yield and do what was asked, but when the two cohorts did not respond to the salute of the crowd, the crowd again let fly against the procurator, and the soldiers took up arms.

15.5.3.5 The people of Jerusalem then occupied the temple and cut off communications between it and the Antonia. Exhortations to moderation from the priesthood and king Agrippa II (for whom cf. above 15.3.1)[6] fell on deaf ears: the people would have been disposed to make concessions, but did not intend to submit to Gessius Florus, and there was little or no way of proceeding against him by administrative or judicial means.

15.5.3.6 Meanwhile the Zealots had begun to occupy the various fortresses of Herod, all more or less unguarded; they also captured a considerable amount of arms and equipment. Thus they took possession of the palace fortress of Massada, of Herodion (above 15.1.3), and of other palaces and fortresses in the Jordan valley and in Transjordan. At the same time Eleazar, son of the High Priest, occupied the temple. The sacrifice for the king, begun under Ezra (above 13.9.9), was suspended, and a prohibition was issued against offering sacrifices for aliens.

15.5.3.7 The ruling class in Judaea seems to have been fully aware that it had no chance of winning in an open struggle against Rome; in vain the High Priest, the priests and the Pharisees pointed out that the practice of the sacrifice for the emperor was based on traditions which now went back for centuries, thus seeking to suppress the rebellion from within. The troops sent by Agrippa proved insufficient to quell what had become a general popular revolt. At least this is the thesis put forward by Josephus in his *Jewish War*: only some fanatics and not persons of wealth and culture were responsible for the revolt (thus S.J.D.Cohen in Shanks* 1988, 224ff.).

15.5.3.8 The rebels soon found themselves masters of the situation, having taken possession of the whole capital, including the temple and the Antonia. The definitive break with Rome, that the authorities had tried to avoid with every possible means, was thus sanctioned at a formal level and, as Noth* 1959, 436, points out, 'all that remained now was a struggle to the death'.

15.5.3.9 The High Priest, who had opposed the break with every means at his disposal, was killed, and Herod's palace at the western gate was set on fire. A Roman cohort which had been given a safe conduct to leave the city was massacred. The revolt spread throughout the country and only in cities with an ethnically mixed population – Caesarea, Scythopolis (the ancient Beth-shean), Ptolemais (formerly Acco, Acre) and Ashkelon did the Romans succeed in holding the Jews in check. Disturbances even broke out in Alexandria, in Egypt.

15.5.3.10 That same year C.Cestius Gallus, Roman legate in Syria, seeing that the movement was increasingly taking the characteristics of a general uprising by the Jews against Rome, moved south with a legion. He had no difficulty in occupying all the coastal cities in which the Jews had not been defeated, and moved against Jerusalem, camping nearby on Mount Scopus (coord.173-134, the hill which is a continuation of the Mount of Olives and is today the site of the Hebrew University). However, he immediately saw that his troops would not be enough to lay siege to and reduce a strongly fortified city defended to the last, and therefore he withdrew. But his men were caught in an ambush near Beth-horon (present-day *bēt 'ūr*, coord.160-143) and were defeated; the survivors had to flee, leaving a good deal of their arms and equipment behind on the ground. Thus for the moderates any possibility of negotiations disappeared.

15.5.3.11 The Zealots remained masters of the field, and their leaders began to organize the defence; many of the moderates, now that conflict had broken out, joined the combatants. However, as one can imagine, the organization always left much to be desired. It was impossible to make real soldiers out of the undisciplined Zealots and therefore to organize a trustworthy army; they had no arms, equipment, military institutions, qualified officers and technique; it was impossible to coordinate production and concentrate forces in a region with partly a mixed population which was sometimes more anti-Jewish than anti-Roman. But now there was no going back on the revolt – the bridges had been burned.

15.5.3.12 The country was divided into military districts, and Galilee was put under the command of a certain Joseph son of Mattathiah, later to become the scholar Flavius Josephus. He was a moderate, and had not yet lost hope of arriving at some form of understanding with Rome, given the absolute impossiblity of a victory; because of this pragmatic opportunism he is said to have been the object of various kinds of abuse from the Zealots. In other words, the country had arrived at a kind of polarization of national political life which recalled that existing shortly before the Maccabaean revolt; only then it was a question of Jews loyal to the Torah and Hellenistic Jews, while now it was everyone against Rome. Still, one group, aware of the impossibility of a victory, sought some form of compromise, while the other trusted in its own valour and force of arms.

15.5.4 Unfortunately for the rebels, this division soon degenerated into real internecine struggle during the periods of calm, when it would have been better to try to reinforce their effectiveness or seek a compromise. From the beginning this laid a heavy burden on the rebels, whose possibilities of success were, as we saw, in any case slight.

15.5.5 Given the dimensions that the conflict had now assumed, Nero decided to launch a mass attack. He sent one of his best generals, T.Flavius Vespasianus, who in 43-44 had distinguished himself as commander during the invasion of Britain.

15.5.5.1 Vespasian, operating with skill, soon succeeded in reconquering a large part of the country, especially those regions with mixed populations – Galilee, northern Transjordan, the plain of Esdraelon – so that the rebels saw themselves soon reduced to holding only tiny Judaea.

15.5.5.2 It was on this occasion that Josephus was taken prisoner and went over to the enemy, adopting the name Flavius in honour of his Roman protector.

15.5.5.3 Months of relative calm followed for the rebels. Vespasian temporized, waiting to see what happened in Rome, where after the death of Nero, Galba, Otho and Vitellius followed as emperor in rapid succession, all nominated by their troops. The troops in the East also nominated Vespasian himself as their emperor after Vitellius was killed in 69. Vespasian came to the throne in the summer of 70 and entrusted the command of the army to his son Titus.

15.5.5.4 The rebels had not made use of the months of relative calm; their factions continued to fight one another, armed to the teeth, especially around Jerusalem: Zealots fought against moderates, and partisan bands came out of the wilds to fight the others. So at the time of the final attack the rebels were not only divided but also notably weakened by internecine struggle.

15.5.6 Titus laid siege to the capital in the spring of 70, shortly before the Jewish Passover, with at least four legions and numerous auxiliary troops. He too camped on Mount Scopus. In the face of the imminent danger the internal struggles largely ceased and the final defence of the city began. To show how unprepared the rebels were, it is enough to point out that the public celebration of the Passover took place that year in the usual way, with the presence of thousands of pilgrims. In the besieged and overpopulated city, hermetically sealed by the circumvallation of the besiegers, the food situation soon became critical and not long afterwards desperate: Josephus narrates a series of horrifying episodes, all caused by the famine. At all events, the defenders succeeded in maintaining discipline in the city, though only by resorting to very harsh measures.

15.5.7 The work of the besiegers was very difficult, as it had been in earlier instances. On the east, south and west the walls of Jerusalem formed a complex that jutted out over the drop to the valleys of Kidron and Gehenna, so that the city could be taken by assault only from the north. And on this side three successive walls had been built, the innermost one connected with the Antonia. However, these problems were not new to the besiegers. With their advanced siege tactics they succeeded in taking the three walls one after the other. Then, in July, they captured the Antonia, and in August, the temple complex, which went up in flames in the fighting (against the express order of Titus, Josephus says, but now it was no longer possible to hold back the soldiers; however, this note is part of Josephus' general approach to his work, namely that Vespasian and Titus waged war as perfect gentlemen and even had mercy on the poor Jews, dominated by fanatics, cf. S.J.D.Cohen in Shanks* 1988, ibid.). The rest of the city was completely razed to the ground, except for what remained of Herod's palace (above 15.5.3.7), and part of the eastern fortifications where the Roman troops were quartered.

15.5.8 The various fortresses which still resisted were reduced one after the other; the last, Massada, fell only in 74 (earlier it was thought to have fallen in 73)[7] after a long and desperate resistance by those under siege, according to Josephus culminating in a collective suicide (though there is no trace of this in the excavations). It was probably during this phase of the campaign that the Qumran community was also destroyed (above 14.14.4).

15.5.9 Tacitus and Josephus provide the following information about the catastrophe: more than 600,000 Jews will have been killed in the military operations, about twenty-five per cent of the population, and many others will have been taken prisoner and sold as slaves. So it would seem possible that something like half the Jewish population had been eliminated. The Arch of Titus in the Forum at Rome gives a picture of the triumph of the future emperor in which there is a reproduction of the candelabrum captured from the temple.

15.6 Judaism after the catastrophe

Despite the seriousness of events, the Romans do not seem to have nurtured any particular animosity towards Judaism as a religion at a political level; evidently it was enough for them to have put down the revolt and established conditions which made it impossible for it to be repeated.

Bibliography

J.Neusner, *Life of Yohanan ben Zakkai*, Leiden ²1970; id., *Development of a Legend: Studies on the Traditions concerning Yohanan ben Zakkai*, Leiden 1970; id., *From Politics to Piety*, Leiden 1973; Neusner*, 663-77; id., 'The Formation of Rabbinic Judaism: Yavne (Jamnia) from AD 70 to 100', in H.Temporini (ed.), *Aufstieg und Niedergang der römischen Welt*, 19.II, Berlin 1979, 3-42; id., *The Mishnah before 70*, Atlanta, Ga 1987. For the so-called Synod of Jamnia cf. P.Schäfer, 'Die sogenannte Synode von Jabne. Zur Trennung von Juden und Christen im ersten/zweiten Jahrhundert n.Chr.', *Judaica* 31, 1975, 54-64, 116-26, now in *Studien zur Geschichte und Theologie des rabbinischen Judentums*, Leiden 1978, 45-64.

15.6.1 The Romans allowed Judaism to continue as a *religio licita*, probably in the hope that it would be a focal point for the more moderate element. So they did not oppose a Pharisee, Johanan ben Zakkai, who had been arrested and taken to Titus' camp in romantic circumstances, largely legendary, when he set up a house for study in the locality of Jabneh, Greek Jamnia (coord.126-141).

15.6.2 With the destruction of the temple, the Sadducean priesthood had largely lost its own role and means of subsistence (above 14.12.2.5); moreover a large number of its members had lost their lives during the destruction of the sanctuary. The Qumran sectarians had been dispersed, and the first Christians are reported to have sought refuge for some time at Pella in Transjordan (present-day *tabāqat fāḥl*, coord. 206-207), though this note lacks any historical foundation.[8]

15.6.2.1 Thus only the Pharisees remained. Because they were not tied to official structures, although they had suffered severe losses, their organization had remained intact. At Jabneh they immediately began on the work of reorganizing the community in the Holy Land. Very soon the school of Jabneh, which collected together the best tradition and the most qualified people it could, was also recognized by the Diaspora. 'From politics to piety' is the effective description which Neusner gave of this development in 1973: from a political perspective Israel had certainly been destroyed, but it remained as the bearer of a faith and a practice.

15.6.2.2 Johanan and his followers succeeded in overcoming the shock and the disorientation among the survivors, feelings which are quite comprehensible after the crisis. The temple, which in the past had too often also been the centre of intrigue and collaboration with the occupying forces, had lost much of its prestige even before the catastrophe; that explains why there was no thought of rebuilding it, though that had been a priority for those returning from exile in Babylon in the second half of the sixth century (above 13.6.3.1-2). In this way the doctrines and life-style of the Pharisees (above 14.12.3) became what we are accustomed to call normative Judaism, which has governed Israel for almost two millennia in a Diaspora which very soon extended from the Yemen, Iraq and Persia to the Baltic, from Russia to Spain and Great Britain, and then to America, South Africa and Australia. And it is in this context (though we have no precise information) that the canon of the Hebrew Bible was to emerge and the oral Torah began to be collected. Thus began the great exegetical works and commentaries. But all this now belongs to another, later phase of the history of Israel.

15.7 Imperial province

Once the revolt had been quelled, the region became an imperial Roman province. Temple worship was not resumed, nor was the temple rebuilt; the obol destined for it was instead sent to the sanctuary of Jupiter Capitolinus, for Israel evidently a measure which was politically provocative and religiously sacrilegious. What was really a tax on being a Jew was only abolished under Nerva (96-98 CE).

Bibliography

S.M.Baron, *A Social and Religious History of the Jews*, II.2, New York 1952, 89-122, 368-77; Noth* 1959, 448-54; S.Perowne, *Hadrian*, London

1980, esp. 149ff.; A.Fuks, 'Aspects of the Jewish Revolt in AD 115-117', *Journal of Roman Studies* 51, 1961, 98-104; J.A.Fitzmyer, 'The Bar Kochba Period', in *The Bible in Current Catholic Thought – Gruentaner Memorial Volume*, New York 1962, 133-68 = *Essays on the Semitic Background of the New Testament*, London 1971, 305-54; H.Mantel, 'The Causes of the Bar Kochba Revolt', *JQR* 58, 1987-8, 224-42, 274-96; Y.Yadin, *Bar Kochba*, London and New York 1971; J.Neusner*, 863ff.; P.Schäfer, *Der Bar Kokhba Aufstand. Studien zum zweiten jüdischen Krieg gegen Rom*, Tübingen 1981; A.Kloner, 'Underground Hiding Complexes from the Bar Kochba War in the Judaean Shephelah', *BA* 46, 1983, 210-21; A.Applebaum, 'The Second Jewish Revolt (AD 131-135)', *PEQ* 116, 1984, 35-41; B.Isaac and A.Oppenheimer, 'The Revolt of Bar Kokhba', *JJS* 36, 1985, 33-60; M.Mor, 'The Bar Kochba Revolt and Non-Jewish Participants', ibid., 200-9; D.Goodblatt, 'A Contribution to the Prosopography of the Second Revolt', *JJS* 38, 1987, 38-55; T.D.Barnes, 'Trajan and the Jews', *JJS* 40, 1989, 145-62.

The sources are almost completely silent about events between the first and second revolts: Josephus's work ends with the first revolt. It is therefore difficult to establish the causes of the second Jewish revolt in 132, more than sixty years after the destruction of the second temple. This is recognized by all scholars.

15.7.1 One explanation put forward by some scholars is that there were those in Judah who, as the seventieth anniversary of the destruction of the sanctuary drew near, began to think of an imminent end of the age and thus of the end of pagan rule over the Holy Land. The figure derives from an allegorical explanation of Jer.12.51 and 29.10 and the speculations contained in Dan.9.1ff., and other apocalyptic writings of the time.

15.7.2 However, important as this theological explanation may be for giving the ideological background, it seems more probable that it should be combined with economic, social and political factors, as at the time of the first revolt. Factors which the Jews regarded as a provocation were thus combined with expectations of an apocalyptic and zealot time, in which the war was simply the beginning of the catstrophes which announced the imminent end of the age and the coming of the messianic kingdom. At all events, we know from two apocalyptic and pseudepigraphical books, Syriac Baruch and IV Esdras, that the destruction of the temple had caused on the one hand serious collective disturbances and on the other a great longing to establish temple worship at any cost.[9]

15.7.3 However, leaving aside all these elements, we shall not be far from the truth if we postulate that the political and economic causes which also underlay the second revolt were more or less the same: it is unimaginable that the Roman administration, avaricious and corrupt as it was, should suddenly have become solicitous, generous and honest, all the more so since the emperors of the Flavian dynasty – Vespasian (69-79), Titus and Domitian (81-96) – are hardly likely to have been better disposed towards Israel after the bloody campaign. Only under Nerva did the situation begin to improve, as I have indicated. But clearly there were still a number of factors which, given the right moment, could have precipitated events.

15.7.4 One example of how the Jews could be harried is given by a well known text of Suetonius, *Domitian*.12.2 (Stern II, no.320), from the end of the first century CE: '*Praeter coeteros Judaicus fiscus acerbissime actus est; ad quem deferebantur qui vel[ut] inprofessi Judaicam viverent vitam, vel dissimulata origine imposita genti tributa non pependissent. Interfuisse me adolescentulum memini, cum a procuratore frequentissimoque concilio inspicentur nonagenarius senex, an circumsectus esset* ('quite apart from the other taxes which were imposed upon the Jews with the utmost severity, both those who without confessing their Jewish faith openly lived as Jews, and those who hid their own origin and did not pay the taxes with which their people was burdened, were severely punished. I remember having been present in my youth when a nonagenarian was examined by the procurator, and moreover in a crowded hall, to establish whether he had been circumcised'). Episodes of this kind certainly did not calm things down.

15.7.5 The scant information we have indicates that in the first decades of the second century CE disorders broke out in the Jewish Diaspora. Various rebellions took place in the year 115, rebellions which, even if not directly connected with the events of 132-135, show that that things were coming to the boil.

15.7.6 Under Trajan (98-117), during an expedition against the Parthians, a revolt broke out in 115 among the Jews of Cyrene, Alexandria and Cyprus and even Mesopotamia, i.e. almost on the Roman front line. We have no direct information about the cause, though it is known that disorders were always frequent in places with mixed populations. A.Fuks, who in 1961 made a precise analysis of the movements based on the most recent papyrological discoveries, points out that the revolts were always brutal in character, with the extermination of the populations, leaving scorched earth behind, especially in Cyrenaica, Cyprus and Egypt; in Mesopotamia, on the other hand, the revolt seems to have come about with the approval of the local population. Trajan did not hesitate to crush all these revolts, but the fact that this took him some years and that the repression continued under Hadrian shows that the struggle, and therefore the repression, must have been very harsh. We do not know whether the rebellion extended to Judaea, but we do know that Lusius Quietus, who had just crushed the revolt in Mesopotamia, was soon afterwards nominated governor of Judaea. If this is a coincidence, it would be a remarkable one: was this perhaps to re-establish order here too? This is what Noth* 1959, 449, supposes.

15.8 The last revolt

The last great revolt in the Holy Land broke out under Hadrian (117-138); from the little we know, its dimensions were similar to that of 67-74. The remaining information on its origins is partly contradictory; it is in Dio Cassius 69.12-13 (Stern II, no.440) and Eusebius, HE 4.6 (Noth* 1959, 449).

15.8.1 According to Dio, the Jews rebelled because of the foundation by Hadrian of Aelia Capitolina on the ruins of Jerusalem and the inauguration there of a sanctuary dedicated to Jupiter Capitolinus, and took up arms.

15.8.2 However, according to other sources the revolt broke out because a law promulgated by Hadrian had identified circumcision with castration, a practice forbidden by Roman law, though we do not know from when. Moreover a few years later, under Antoninus Pius (138-161), circumcision was again allowed as a legitimate exception to the law on castration, together with other Jewish practices prohibited after the second revolt.

15.8.3 The two pieces of information only seem contradictory: both fit perfectly into the context of the period. Hadrian travelled to the East in 130-131, and during his travels inaugurated some new cities. He certainly went to Gerasa (present-day Jerash, coord.198-238) in Transjordan, still famous for its magnificant ruins. We do not know whether he also went to Jerusalem, though this seems likely; at all events, a mere plan of this kind, even if it were not carried out, would have been enough to create considerable tension among the survivors of Palestinian Judaism. As to the prohibition of circumcision, that clearly affected all the peoples of the Roman empire who practised it, and not just Israel, so it can hardly be considered a measure just against the Jews: in fact, however, it was a heavy blow to Israel's faith and practice, in which circumcision was (and still is) a basic and distinctive feature.

15.8.4 So in both cases there were marked elements of tension: the desecration of holy places and intolerable interference in internal matters of faith. In the past, at the time of the Maccabees and the first revolt, both these things had contributed to the outbreak of rebellion, and so they did now.

15.8.4.1 A certain Simon *ben kōsībā'* soon emerged as the leader of the rebellion ; he was acclaimed by his followers as *bar kōkbā'*, 'son of the star', understood messianically according to Num 24.16: '…a star arises from Jacob'. Later the rabbis caricatured the name as *bar kōzība'*, 'son of the lie', i.e. 'liar'. Here we find a true charismatic as the term is used by Max Weber (above 9.2): his authority was in fact recognized by all without the internecine struggles which had characterized the first revolt (above 15.5.4). Even the venerable Rabbi Akiba, who had originally opposed the revolt, was convinced and fascinated (jTaʿan, 68d.).

15.8.4.2 Meanwhile Hadrian had returned to Rome. To begin with, he does not seem to have been very concerned about the revolt. So it was easy for the rebels initially to gain considerable successes: they recaptured Jerusalem and succeeded in liberating a large part of the country. Simon governed this from the ancient capital, minting his own coinage. Every series of coins was characterized by a cipher denoting 'the year of the liberation of Israel'. Moreover, he must have restored temple worship, since on one of the coins a priest with the name of Eleazar appears; according to some scholars he will also have begun to rebuild the temple.

15.8.4.3 However, this time again, once Rome had decided to make a serious intervention, the struggle soon proved hopeless, though the rebels adopted more guerrilla tactics, avoiding combat in the open. The Romans, skilfully led by Julius Severus, who had distinguished himself in Britain, where he had been governor, arrived in the country with overwhelming force and decided to follow similar tactics: the rebel strongholds were besieged one after the other and the defenders overcome by hunger and thirst.

15.8.4.4 We know of the sieges of *bēt ṭer*, present-day *ḫirbet el-jehūd* ('ruin of the Judaeans', coord.162-166), near the Arab village of *bittīr* (the last station, no longer in use, before Jerusalem on the railway line); the place fell after a heroic resistance to the last, overcome by hunger and thirst, with the help of the usual siege techniques. It was probably here that Simon perished.

15.8.5 The last rebels took refuge in the complex of caves above the *wādī murabbaʿat*, in Hebrew *nahal ḥeber* (coord.182-093), which flows down to the Dead Sea, hoping that they would be able to continue their guerrilla warfare from there. However, in this desert region they were soon blockaded and reduced by hunger and thirst. Archaeological discoveries now in the Museum of Israel in Jerusalem (the region and especially the caves were excavated in 1960-61) show that the majority of the resistance preferred death to capture.

15.9 Consequences

Again the Jewish population had been subjected to a trial of the utmost severity; there are reports of about 850,000 dead (Fohrer* 1982, 230).

Many teachers were also killed, those who had been laboriously trying to reconstruct Judaism on the ruins of the first revolt; they included R.Akiba, who was tortured by the Romans despite his venerable age.

15.9.1 Jerusalem was made a colony and called Aelia Capitolina; it was rebuilt with all the urban characteristics of a Roman city (visible today in the *cardo* excavations, on the north-west side of the Jewish Quarter): Jews were forbidden to enter it. The celebration of Jewish ceremonies was also forbidden, as were the practice of circumcision and the production or possession of scrolls of the Torah. This time, then, as opposed to 70-73, we have a series of measures which were aimed against Judaism as a religion.

15.9.2 The traditional name Judaea was replaced with that of Palaestina, from the name of the Philistines who had lived in the south-west of it. As Noth* 1959, 406, rightly observes, the surviving Jews had become strangers in their own homeland, just as they were strangers in the regions of the Diaspora.

15.10 Diaspora

That brings to an end the biblical and immediately post-biblical period of the history of Israel. However, as we know, this history does not stop there, though some scholars would like from this point (or even earlier) to talk of Judaism in the strict sense.

15.10.1 In the Diaspora, which now also included the desecrated Holy Land, Israel continued not only to survive but also to develop and flourish. Nevertheless the Holy Land remained the true homeland. The Passover salutation, 'Next year in Jerusalem', probably arose at this time. In the synagogue liturgy there continued to be prayers for rain and harvest in the 'homeland', far or near, connections with which never ceased, not least because in many regions not affected by the war numerous communities continued to exist.[10]

15.10.2 In the Diaspora, consciously or unconsciously, it could be said that Israel followed the exhortation which according to tradition Jeremiah had addressed to his fellow countrymen who had been deported to Babylon in 597: 'Build houses and live in them; plant gardens and eat their produce. Take wives and have sons and daughters; take wives for your sons, and give your daughters in marriage, that they may bear sons and daughters... Seek the welfare of the city where I have sent you into exile, and pray to the Lord on its behalf, for in its welfare you will find your welfare...' (Jer.29.4-9).

Following these guidelines Israel continued and continues to survive over almost two millennia, in the West often the object of discrimination, sometimes of persecutions which in the worst instances were expressed in looting, expulsions and killings. In other regions, especially under Islam at its height, Israel was allowed to develop spiritually and intellectually, often sharing in the exercise of power.

15.10.3 In the Western Diaspora Israel has always sought to reconcile the duties of the good citizen with those imposed by its faith. In periods of tolerance Jews have not only studied their own scriptures but have distinguished themselves as doctors, philosophers, philologists, musicians, grammarians, humanists, astronomers, physicists and bankers; later as psychologists and sociologists. Some of them have even become the counsellors of kings. However, that, along with the foundation of the State in 1948, belongs to another era of the history of Israel.

List of Plates

1. Sinai, Palestine, Jordan, and Arabia with the Red Sea in a modern satellite
   photograph

2. Town gate in unbaked brick from the nineteenth/eighteenth century BCE,
Tell Dan (by courtesy of the Hebrew Union College, Jerusalem)

3. Megiddo. To the right, the ruins of the temple, and to the left an altar from
   the late Canaanite period, end of the Bronze Age (by courtesy of the
   Department of Antiquities and Museums of the State of Israel, Jerusalem)

4. Megiddo, 'Solomon's Stables' reconstruction (by courtesy of the
   Department of Antiquities and Museums of the State of Israel, Jerusalem)

5. Megiddo, 'Solomon's Stables' (by courtesy of the Department of
   Antiquities and Museums of the State of Israel, Jerusalem)

6. Tell Arad during the excavations (by courtesy of the Archaeological Institute of the University of Tel-Aviv)

7. The temple of Tell Arad (by courtesy of the Archaeological Institute of the University of Tel-Aviv)

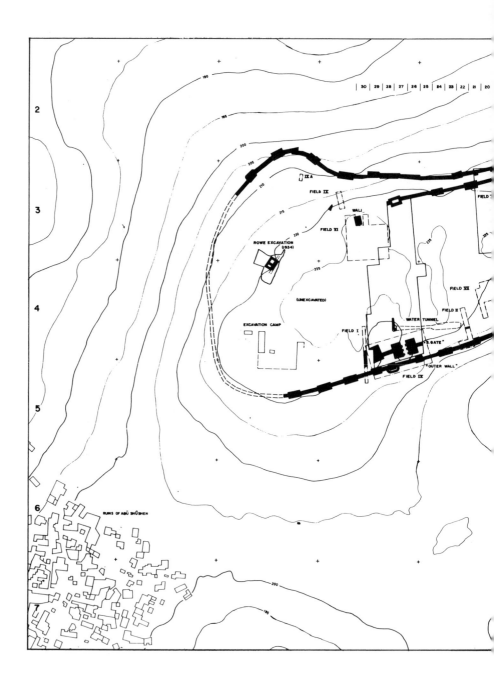

8. Gezer. Plan of the sites of excavations made between 1964

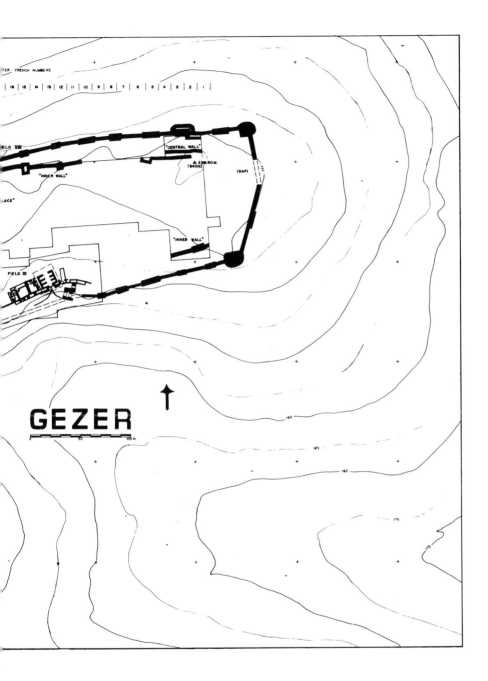

and 1973 (by courtesy of the Hebrew Union College, Jerusalem)

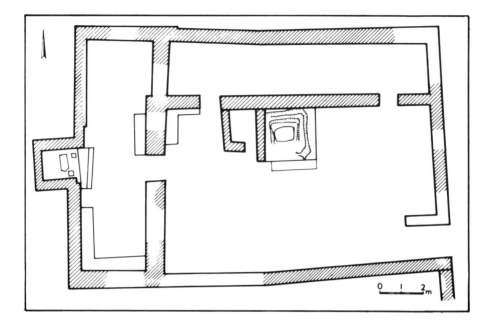

9. Plan of the temple of Tell Arad (by courtesy of the Archaeological Institute of the University of Tel-Aviv)

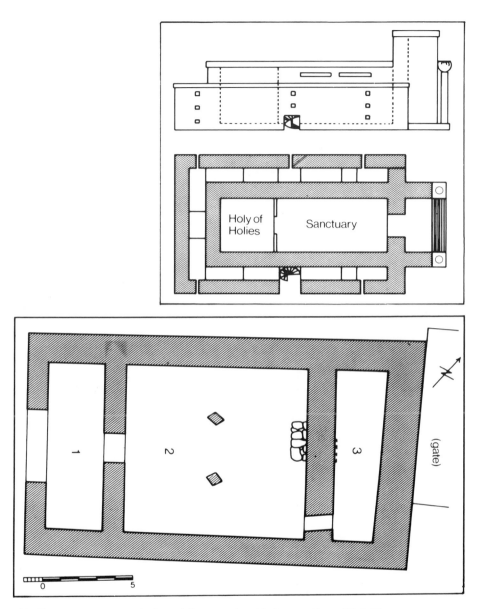

10. Reconstruction and plan of the temple of Solomon (from W.G. Dever, 'Monumental Architecture in Ancient Israel', in T. Ishida (ed.), *Studies in the Period of David and Solomon*, Tokyo 1982, 262-306, fig. 11 – the original is in *IDB* IV, 1962, 537 fig. 7)

11. Schematic plan of 'Temple 7300' of Shechem, MB-IIC (*c.* 1650-1550 BCE) (from W.G. Dever, 'Monumental Architecture in Ancient Israel', in T. Ishida ed., *Studies in the Period of David and Solomon*, Tokyo 1982, 269-306 – the original is in W.G. Dever, *BASOR* 216, 1974, 40 fig. 10)

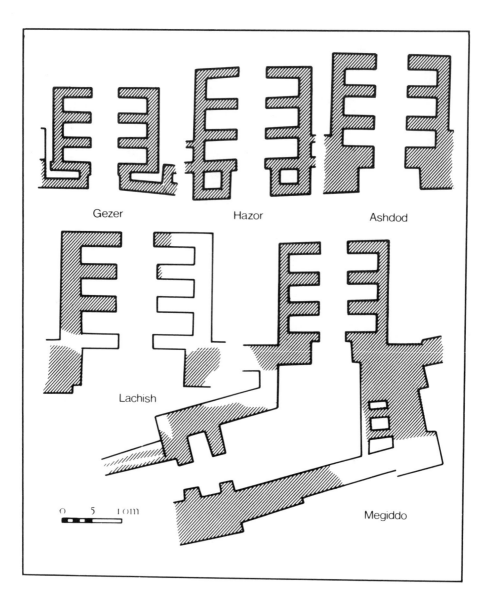

Gezer

Hazor

Ashdod

Lachish

Megiddo

0 5 10m

12. Town gate from the tenth century BCE, the time of the united monarchy (from W.G. Dever, 'Monumental Architecture in Ancient Israel', in T. Ishida, ed., *Studies in the Period of David and Solomon*, Tokyo 1982, 269-306, fig.11)

13. Gate from the time of Solomon, tenth century BCE, looking south-south-eastwards. Note the large drainage channel which runs across the street (by courtesy of the Hebrew Union College, Jerusalem)

14. The *tell* of Beer-sheba during the excavations (by courtesy of the
Archaeological Institute of the University of Tel-Aviv)

15. The western quarter of the *tell* of Beer-sheba, with typical houses from the Israelite period (by courtesy of the Archaeological Institute of the University of Tel-Aviv)

16. The altar with four 'horns' discovered during the excavations on the *tell* of Beer-sheba (by courtesy of the Archaeological Institute of the University of Tel-Aviv)

17. Remains of the northern wall of Jerusalem, from the end of the eighth century BCE (by courtesy of the Israel Exploration Society, Jerusalem)

18. Remains of a tower inserted in the northern wall of Jerusalem, from the seventh century BCE. Note on the left hand side the building that uses it as a foundation, which comes from the time of the Maccabees (by courtesy of the Israel Exploration Society, Jerusalem)

APPENDIX 1

An Introduction to the Archaeology of Syria and Palestine on the Basis of the Israelite Settlement

Diethelm Conrad

I. Theory

1. Definitions

The meaning of the term 'archaeology' has shifted in a number of ways between the Greek period and the present day. To begin with, as in Josephus, it denoted the narration of ancient history, i.e. the description of historical developments, including the habits and customs of particular peoples and times. After the Enlightenment, subject-matter like individuals, states and religions of antiquity (and in the case of the Bible, biblical questions) came to be dealt with under this heading. It is only with the rise of an active programme of excavation in the last third of the nineteenth century and during the twentieth century that the term has now come to be understood to refer above all to field archaeology in (Syria and) Palestine. Now as in addition to 'the archaeology of (Syria and) Palestine', terms like 'biblical archaeology' and 'archaeology of the land of Israel' are also used and – especially over the last decade – have become the subject of vigorous discussion, I must first venture a few definitions to clarify matters.

1.1 In content and method, the archaeology of (Syria and) Palestine is a special division of Near Eastern archaeology, limited to the region of Syria and Palestine, i.e. to the sphere in which biblical history ran its course. Because of the historical and cultural contacts between the cultures of Syria and Palestine and the cities and cultures in the north and south of this region, it is of course essential to look beyond its limits, e.g. to Mesopotamian and Egyptian archaeology. However, apart from the coasts, above all in the north-east, Syria comes closer to Mesopotamia than to Palestine, i.e. to a wider horizon, so that in our case it is more accurate to speak simply of Palestinian archaeology or the archaeology of Palestine. Chronologically, Palestinian archaeology extends from the Stone Age (the earliest history) to the present. Numerous scholars are now working to clarify developments here, especially in Israel and Jordan, but also in America and Europe. In principle, the term 'archaeology of the Land of Israel' has the same meaning; it is used especially by Israeli scholars.

1.2 German-speaking scholars in particular still prefer the term 'biblical archaeology'. This, too, is a specialist division of the archaeology of the Near East, the location of which is limited to the sphere of (Syria and) Palestine and the time-span to the second and first millennium BC. Biblical archaeology keeps to a methodically controlled correlation of archaeological finds and written sources (essentially the biblical text).

1.3 Objections are made by each perspective to the other, and also come from a third perspective. Those who favour 'biblical archaeology' over against 'Palestinian archaeology' object that in the latter the correlation of archaeological discoveries and written sources is either not controlled at all or not controlled by an adequate method. Those who favour 'Palestinian archaeology' over against 'biblical archaeology' argue against the limited time-span of the latter. As biblical archaeology often relates only to the Old Testament period, objections to it are made by New Testament scholars. In fact the period between the Testaments and the first centuries of the Christian era should also be included here, as neither Christian nor Byzantine archaeology covers this period (though Palestinian archaeology does!). American scholars also rightly object to the term biblical archaeology because it is associated with a fundamentalist approach according to which biblical archaeology confirms or even proves the historical reliability of the biblical traditions. However, if biblical archaeology is understood in accordance with the definition given in 1.2, this fundamentalist conception can be rejected.

2. *Branches of work*

The scientific discipline of Palestinian or biblical archaeology came into being in the course of the nineteenth century as a result of the growth of historical interest in the land of the Bible as well as in other areas. Three different branches can be established: they were there from the beginning and are not just the result of specialization. These are: surveys, archaeological fieldwork carried out through excavations, and systematic archaeology. One special branch of the subject which has developed in recent years in Palestinian archaeology as elsewhere is marine archaeology, distinctive because of the special technical equipment needed.

2.1 By covering the country systematically and evaluating select pottery finds, surveys discover settlements and how long they lasted, and lead to a history of the settlement of the land (topography) and occasionally to the identificaiton of sites with places known from written sources (toponomy).

2.2. Excavations (often called 'dust' or 'dirt' archaeology) disclose the remains of buildings and enable the collection of artefacts from the daily life of their inhabitants over a period (above all pottery fragments). These are data for a history of settlement and culture, which also has social, economic and religious dimensions.

2.3 By collecting, examining, sorting, classifying and interpreting the facts which are produced by surveys and excavations, systematic archaeology (often also called 'armchair archaeology') attempts to bring these together into a history of the settlement, culture and society of the people of Israel and of earlier and neighbouring cultures, though so far only a beginning has been made on this (in the form of a lexicon).

2.4 Marine archaeology investigates sites on the coast of Palestine, especially submerged harbour installations (Caesarea, Dor, Acco, etc.) and other remains connected with seafaring (e.g. shipwrecks and their cargo).

3. Methods

In the course of the history of the discipline, extending over more than a century, specific methods have been developed for the branches of archaeology mentioned above, each of them appropriate to the work to be carried out. These are widely recognized today and guarantee the scientific character of the discipline. Treatment of the pottery (finds) is particularly important. Catalogues of types and forms are constantly refined and allow the origin and dating of ceramic vessels and their sherds to be determined with increasing accuracy. To this degree pottery is a kind of fossil, providing a chronological guide.

A whole spectrum of methods can be used not only in carrying out archaeological investigation but also in planning it and evaluating it. It should be stressed that nowadays all excavations are done with special attention to stratigraphy. In other words, during excavation the shifting of earth and the levels which together make up a stratum of settlement are carefully noted and described in both the horizontal and the vertical plane. It goes without saying that methods are constantly developed and refined, and techniques from the natural sciences are increasingly being incorporated into them. Such techniques are useful in prospecting (aerial archaeology, electrical and magnetic techniques), dating (dendrochronology, archaeomagnetism, thermo-luminescence and obsidian dating) and in the determination of origins (pollen analysis, palaeo-biology, analysis by röntgen fluorescence, neutron activation and electron microscopes). As these techniques are very expensive, a cost-analysis is very important here. Computers must increasingly be involved in mastering the mass of data which is produced in this way, and also for statistical investigations. Nowadays, sociological methods are used for formulating questions and evaluating and interpreting results, and ethnological data are used for comparisions. However, the discussion over the nature and extent of their use is far from over.

4. The problem of interpretation

All the data produced by surveys and excavation are mute unless they are accompanied by textual discoveries – and this happens only very rarely. That means that the data have to be elucidated and interpreted. Thus our understanding of archaeological data is an understanding of their interpertation and therefore has 'only' the status of a hypothesis. This shows how important methodology is in interpretation, if agreement over results on an objective basis is to be achieved. Consequently the subjective presuppositions of the interpreter, whether historical, cultural or religious, have also to be taken into account. However, it is impossible to put too much stress on the importance of knowledge of the environment of any datum or object to be interpreted. This demonstrates the great importance of geographical knowledge of Palestine in the broadest sense. It includes physical geography, geology, climate (rainfall), flora and fauna, topography, communications (for trade and travel) and historical geography, along with all kinds of written documents: the Bible, texts from surrounding nations, epigraphical texts (inscriptions) on stone, clay, papyrus, leather and so on from Palestine itself. However much the texts may speak for themselves, they, too, need interpretation. This applies above all to biblical texts, as a result of the special circumstances surrounding their origin, collection, transmission and purpose. The interpretation of them is the task of biblical exegesis.

This brief statement already makes it clear that archaeological data and the text of the Bible cannot be brought together directly: each needs to be interpreted. In the process it has emerged that only on very rare occasions do archaeological data shed direct light on the text of the Bible or vice versa. Thus archaeological data (like the text of the Bible) remain independent sources for conditions (and on occasion also events) relevant to the history of culture, society, economics and religion.

5. *Periods in archaeology and cultural history*

The following table may be regarded as a conventional framework for the identification of periods in any discussion of the history of culture in Palestine:

Up to 4000 BCE	Stone Age
Fourth millennium BCE	Chalcolithic Age
3200–1200 BCE	Bronze Age (divided into:)
3200–2200 BCE	Early Bronze Age
2200–1550 BCE	Middle Bronze Age
1550–1200 BCE	Late Bronze Age
1200–535 (330) BCE	Iron Age (divided into:)
1200–1000 BCE	Iron Age I: The Period of the Judges

1000–587 BCE	Iron Age II: The Period of the the Monarchy
587–535 BCE	Iron Age III, also the Babylonian period
535–330 BCE	(often still Iron Age III:) Persian Period
330–65 BCE	Hellenistic Period
65 BCE–324 CE	Roman Period (including Herod, 37 BCE–4 CE)
324–634/40 CE	Byzantine Period

All these periods are further subdivided, depending on cultural changes. This is partly a historical and partly a cultural phenomenon, often connected with changes in technology and society. The individual periods initially represent only a relative chronology, which becomes an absolute chronology only through datable synchronisms. So in this area, too, archaeology is also an auxiliary discipline for historians.

II. Example: The Israelite Settlement

In view of the state of our literary sources, i.e. the text of the Bible, it is still difficult to arrive at a historically accurate picture of the Israelite settlement. So in the present state of research, what can Palestinian archaeology contribute to the clarification of this period, taking into account what I said in I. above? To answer the question we must first look again at the biblical account, previous archaeological evidence and previous models of historical methodology before moving on to more recent archaeological results and their interpretation.

1 The account in Josh.1–12 suggests that the land promised to the Israelites by God was conquered from the east in a rapid expedition with powerful thrusts southwards (e.g. Lachish) and northwards (e.g. Hazor). However, on closer examination we can see that there is very little specific material for this account. Moreover there are other texts, e.g. Judg.1, which contradict both the view of the conquest as an action by all the tribes (here, rather, it is a matter of individual actions) and the extent of the territory conquered.

2 The excavations in Jericho and Ai showed that neither in Jericho nor in Ai did a city exist at the end of the Late Bronze Age, but that both older cities had been destroyed and abandoned long before any possible occupation by the Israelites under Joshua. And whereas Hazor and the Late Bronze Age or the beginning of the Iron Age, so that they may be said

to have been destroyed at this time, this evidence in itself does not indicate who destroyed them, and whether the city concerned was destroyed by military attack, siege or a conflagration; indeed it might have fallen victim to a disaster like a catastrophic fire. Moreover, it should be pointed out that where the traces of destruction can be dated they are distributed over a period of about a century.

3 Because of the uncertain historical facts in the period of the settlement, a historical reconstruction of this era can be made only on the basis of hypothetical models into which these facts fit. The contradictions in the literary sources and the ambivalence of the archaeological evidence and the different judgments passed on it have by now led to very varied models.

W.F.Albright and American scholars following him have been more confident about the biblical text and have seen the results of archaeology as external evidence which confirms the biblical accounts and the military conquest of the country.

A.Alt, M.Noth and numerous German scholars have seen the settlement more as a peaceful process. Israelite groups are said to have infiltrated the sparsely settled areas in the hill-country and valleys remote from the Canaanite city-states and outside their spheres of influence, and formed themselves into tribes there. Their military conflicts with the Canaanite cities only took place as a second stage.

A third model, first put forward by G.Mendenhall in 1962, which has found supporters since then – often in a modified form – argues that a peasant revolt took place in Canaan in which there was an exodus, an emigration of dissatisfied peasants from the social sphere dominated by the Canannite city-states. Some scholars already see Yahwism at work in this connection; they claim that the occurrence of 'Israel' on the Merenptah stele, which is now dated about 1207 BCE, belongs in this wider connection.

4 In the first half of this century the main interest was in investigating the history, the rise and fall, of the great cities known from the Bible; now, however, archaeologists are more interested in regional studies. A whole series of such projects is under way; the investigations are far from being complete. Results have only been published in a few cases, and then they are mostly provisional. However, these are of great significance for the question of the Israelite settlement, as new facts are emerging. Surveys of particular regions, whether complete or still in progress, have shown that the characteristic of the sudden destruction of the Late Bronze Age city is not so important for the cultural change from the Late Bronze Age to the Iron Age; in the meantime there has also been enough evidence of an uninterrupted development from the Late Bronze Age to the Early Iron Age. The real characteristic of cultural change is that the Late Bronze Age is stamped by a political and social system of city states and their material and religious culture. These cities lie on the coast, on the periphery of the great plains and valleys and on the major lines of communication (there are also a few of them in the hill-country). With the beginning of the Iron Age countless new unfortified villages appear, above all in the hill-country.

Of course this great change in the settlement pattern also has political and social significance, And the question is whether it has anything to do with the settlement of Israelite groups.

There is evidence of a hundred such settlements in the central hill-country of Ephraim and Manasseh; these are often arranged in groups around an ecological feature, like a valley, and can also have a common cultic centre, like the 'bull site' (coord.180–201) between Tirzah and Dothan (coord.172–202). The first settlements are found in the north of this area, and seem to have extended from the north-east to the south-west.

This evidence seems to contradict what J.A.Callaway has said to be the result of his investigations of Ai and Raddana (coord.169–146). Both settlements are supposed to have come into being as early as 1220 BC. Cisterns were constructed below the houses before they were built, with sophisticated arrangements to purify the rainwater flowing into them. Paved streets are just one indication that the new settlers had already lived a sedentary life elsewhere, and had a high degree of technical skill, which they could only have acquired on the coastal plain. That would suggest an extension of settlements from west to east. However, it seems that the foundation date of these settlements has to be lowered by more than half a century.

In the hill-country of Judah there are no Late Bronze Age cities apart from Jerusalem and Debir, and the same is true of the Negeb. Thus here the Late Bronze Age settlements are even more sparse than in Ephraim and Manasseh. Countless new villages also came into being in these two areas, in the Negeb first of all from the eleventh century BC. Giloh (coord.167–126) is an example from Judah, but that was abandoned again with the incorproation of Jerusalem under David.

In the valleys of the north (Megiddo and Beth-shean), Canaanite culture extends further into the Iron Age, and only from the tenth century onwards do Israelite settlements appear to any great extent. There are again Early Iron Age settlements in Lower and Upper Galilee, and in Gilead. A special characteristic of these areas is that the earliest settlements occur on the tops of hills, and only later descend to the valleys. Here, too, there are hardly any Late Bronze Age cities.

Virtually all these villages were built in places where hitherto there had been no settlement. There are a few villages on abandoned tells which had been settled in the Middle Bronze or even in the Early Bronze Age (Ai; Arad; Malhata, coord.152–069), but were abandoned for a long time. Finally there is also the transition from the Late Bronze Age city to the Iron Age village (Hazor, also Megiddo).

These villages show a series of common characteristics. The basis of their livelihood is in all cases agriculture and cattle breeding, the latter of both sheep and goats and in some cases of larger animals (oxen, etc.). The villages are usually unfortified, but there are settlements with an outer ring of houses for defence, both from the eleventh century BC in the south (e.g. Tell Masos, with external entrances; Tell es-Seba'; Tell Esdar, coord.147–064) and also in the north (Megiddo; Hurvath 'Abot in Upper Galilee, coord.193–276). It is already possible to see the construction of terraces in villages in the hill-country. In some settlements the earliest stratum is formed by pits; this is the case in Tel Masos, Tell es-Seba' and also Hazor. Most villages are small and had one or two hundred inhabitants. This would perhaps represent a whole extended family or a clan. Tell Masos, with an estimated 1500 inhabitants, is an exception. The recently discovered Hurvath 'Aboth also seems to be larger than usual.

Houses with free-standing pillars in the courtyard but also on and in the walls to strengthen the construction are typical of the architecture of these villages. It used to be assumed that this method of building, together with the plan of a three- or four-room house, was a characteristic of the Israelite method of building. However, possibly there is a Late Bronze Age forerunner of it. A further architectural characteristic of these villages is the numerous silos in open spaces between the houses.

The pottery found in these villages is restricted to a few forms. Cooking pots, storage jars and *pithoi* make up about eighty per cent of all types. Three regions can be distinguished which have a varied repertory of forms: Upper Galilee with connections with Tyre; the central hill-country; and the northern Negeb, but they all link up with earlier traditions of pottery and with the pottery of neighbouring regions. On the whole the pottery is cruder and technically less good. Whether the so-called collared rim jar was really a product of Israelite society (as has been assumed since Albright) has recently been rightly disputed. About 1.70 m high and containing 40–60 litres, the collared-rim *pithoi* are likely to have been used for storing water which had to be brought from springs sometimes between three and six miles from the villages.

Documents wih alphabetic writing have been found in some of these villages, above all the alphabet of Izbet Sartah (coord.146–168). There is a tendency to see this as an expression of an egalitarian society in which the democratization of education has advanced.

The result of this brief account may be said to be that a vigorous activity of settlement can be seen throughout the country at the beginning of the Iron Age. Nothing can yet be said on the basis of archaeological evidence about the origin of these settlers or the ethnic groups to which they belonged. However, we may note that the settlers had previously lived as pasturalists (this term should be preferred to that of nomads) – but within the country: they had not come from outside. The collapse of the Late Bronze Age economic and ecological system with which they were bartering – also in order to complete their diet – forced these people to produce the cereals they needed themselves, and to settle down gradually. The way in which the settlements developed geographically is not clear. All this implies that the 'settlement' was not a unitary process but must have been much more complex. That also means that none of the models of the process of settlement is adequate in itself to explain the process of the settlement, but rather a combination of them all is needed. If we are to achieve further clarification, new investigations must be carried out. It remains amazing how quickly in this new society people could come to worship a common god, YHWH.

Select Bibliography

On 1.1

W.F.Albright, *The Archaeology of Palestine*, Harmondsworth ³1956

K.M.Kenyon, *Archaeology in the Holy Land*, London ²1965

S.M.Paul and W.G.Dever, *Biblical Archaeology*, Jerusalem 1973

H.Donner, *Einführung in die biblische Landes- und Altertumskunde*, Darmstadt 1976

V.Fritz, 'Bibelwissenschaft I. Altes Testament, I/1. Archäologie (Alter Orient und Palästina)', *TRE* VI, 1980, 316–45

Y.Aharoni, *The Archaeology of the Land of Israel*, Philadelphia and London 1982

V.Fritz, *Einführung in die biblische Archäologie*, Darmstadt 1985

A.Mazar, *Archaeology of the Land of the Bible, 10,000–586 BCE*, Anchor Bible Reference Library, New York 1990

Academic Journals

ADAJ	*Annual of the Department of Antiquities of Jordan*
BA	*Biblical Archaeologist*
BASOR	*Bulletin of the American Schools of Oriental Research*
BAR	*Biblical Archaeology Review*
IEJ	*Israel Exploration Journal*
Levant	*Levant, Journal of the British School of Archaeology in Jersualem*
ZDPV	*Zeitschrift des Deutschen Palästina Vereins*

On I.2

1. H.Donner (cf.I.1), 64–72 (and bibliography)

2. M.Avi-Yonah and E.Stern (eds.), *Encyclopedia of Archaeological Excavations in the Holy Land I–IV*, Jerusalem 1975–78

E.K.Vogel, 'Bibliography of the Holy Land Sites'

I, *HUCA* 42, 1971, 1–96

II, *HUCA* 52, 1981, 1–92

Elenchus biblographicus biblicus. Archaeologia biblica

3. K.Galling (ed.), *Biblisches Reallexikon*, Tübingen ²1977

B.Reicke and L.Rost (eds.), *Biblisch-Historisches Handwörterbuch*, Göttingen 1–3, 1963–1966; 4, 1979

H.Weippert, *Palästina in vorhellenistischer Zeit, Handbuch der Archäologie, Vorderasien II/1*, Munich 1988

H.-P.Kuhnen, *Palästina in vorhellenistischer Zeit, Handbuch der Archäologie, Vorderasien II/2, Munich 1990*

4. E.Linder and A.Raban, *Marine Archaeology*, London 1975

On I.3

R.Amiran, *Ancient Pottery of the Holy Land*, Jerusalem 1969

Y.Aharoni, Z.Herzog, M.Kochavi, S.Moshkovitz and A.F.Rainey, 'Methods of Recording and Documenting', in Y.Aharoni (ed.), *Beer-Sheba I*, Tel Aviv 1973, 119–32

W.G.Dever and H.D.Lance (eds.), *A Manual of Field Excavations. Handbook for Field Archaeologists*, Cincinnati, New York, Los Angeles and Jerusalem, 1978

D.Brothwell and E.Higgs (eds.), *Science in Archaeology. A Survey of Progress and Research*, London ²1969

B.Hrouda (ed.), *Methoden der Archäologie. Eine Einführung in ihre naturwissenschaftlichen Techniken*, Munich 1978

P.Ihm, *Statistik in der Archäologie*, Bonn 1978, Archaeo-Physika, Vol.9

F.G.Maier, *Neue Wege in die alte Welt. Methoden der modernen Archäologie*, Hamburg 1977

N.K.Gottwald, *The Tribes of Yahweh. A Sociology of the Religion of Liberated Israel 1250–1050 BCE*, Maryknoll and London 1979

F.Crüsemann, *Der Widerstand gegen das Königtum. Die antiköniglicher Texte des Alten Testaments und der Kampf um den frühen israelitischen Staat*, WMANT 49, Neukirchen-Vluyn 1978

C.Schäfer-Lichtenberger, *Stadt und Eidgenossenschaft im Alten Testament. Eine Auseinandersetzung mit Max Webers Studie 'Das antike Judentum'*, BZAW 156, Berlin and New York 1983

On I.4

F.Crüsemann, 'Alttestamentliche Exegese und Archäologie. Erwägungen angesichts des gegenwärtigen Methodenstreits in der Archäologie Palästinas', *ZAW* 91, 1979, 177–93

E.Noort, *Biblisch-archäologische Hermeneutik und alttestamentliche Exegese*, Kampen Cahiers No.39, Kampen 1979

Y.Aharoni, *The Land of the Bible. A Historical Geography*, Philadelphia and London ²1979

D.Baly, *Geographical Companion to the Bible*, London 1963

J.B.Pritchard (ed.), *Ancient Near Eastern Texts relating to the Old Testament*, Princeton ³1969

J.B.Pritchard (ed.), *The Ancient Near East. Supplementary Texts and Pictures Relating to the Old Testament*, Princeton 1969

O.Kaiser (ed.), *Texte aus der Umwelt des Alten Testaments*, Gütersloh 1982ff.

On II.1–3

V.Fritz, *Israel in der Wüste. Traditionsgeschichtliche Untersuchung der Wüstenüberlieferung des Jahwisten*, Marburg 1970

M.Weippert, *The Settlement of the Israelite Tribes in Palestine*, SBT II 21, London 1971

On II.4

I.Finkelstein (ed.), 'Excavations at Shiloh 1981–1984: Preliminary Report', *TA* 12, 1985, 123–80

– , 'Izbet Sarta. An Early Iron Age Site near Roch Ha'ain, Israel', *BAR* 299, Oxford 1986

– , *The Archaeology of the Israelite Settlement*, Jerusalem 1988

– , 'Following the Pottery Trail: Israel Enters Canaan', *Biblical Archaeology Review* XVII/5, 1991, 28–47

A.Mazar, 'The"Bull Site" – An Iron Age I Open Cult Place', *BASOR* 247, 1982, 27–42

J.Callaway, 'Excavating Ai (et-tell): 1964–1972', *BA* 39, 1976, 18–30

A.Mazar, 'Giloh: An Early Israelite Settlement Site near Jerusalem', *IEJ* 31, 1981, 1–36

Z.Gal, *The Lower Galilee in the Iron Age* (unpublished PhD thesis), Tel Aviv 1982 (in Hebrew)

S.Mittmann, *Beiträge zur Siedlungsgeschichte und Territorialgeschichte des nördlichen Ostjordanlandes*, ADPV, Wiesbaden 1970

V.Fritz and A.Kempinski (eds.), *Ergebnisse der Ausgrabungen auf der Hirbet el Mšāš (Tell Masos) 1972–1975*, ADPV, Wiesbaden 1983

M.M.Ibrahim, 'The Collared Rim Jar of the Early Iron Age', in *Archaeology in the Levant. Festschrift K.M.Kenyon*, ed. R.Moorey and P.Parr, Warminster 1978, 116–26

A.Demsky, 'A Proto-Canaanite Abecedary dating from the Period of the Judges and its Implications for the History of the Alphabet, *TA* 4, 1977, 14–27

APPENDIX 2

The Chronology of the First Temple Period
A Presentation and Evaluation of the Sources

H. Tadmor

A. The Sources and Their Value

1. Chronology and chronography

Dating events according to the regnal years of the current monarch was accepted practice throughout the ancient Near East – in Egypt, Babylonia and Assyria[1] – as well as in Judah and Israel. A unified counting system to be used by every city and county in the state is essential to centralized administration. One can therefore assume that from the very inception of the united monarchy in Israel, especially under the rule of David and Solomon, the foundation was laid for a single reckoning system to be shared by both the civil and the military administration. The reckoning would naturally be made according to regnal years, inasmuch as the system of reckoning by era known in Greece or in Rome[2] was foreign to the people of the ancient Near East until the Hellenistic age.

Ostraca of the monarchic period, such as those from Samaria and Lachish, refer simply to the regnal year, e.g. 'in the ninth year',[3] without mentioning the king's name, as do the Egyptian ostraca from the New Kingdom. In official documents written on parchment or papyrus – which have not survived – details were probably listed in full: the king's name, the regnal year, the month, and the day. The ancient chronographers summarized chronological data in extensive chronographic compositions such as 'Chronicles of the Kings of Judah' or 'Chronicles of the Kings of Israel', which are referred to in the book of Kings. The exact nature of these works remains unclear, but they probably recorded not only the length of each king's reign but also his age upon accession to the throne, the name of his father, and in Judah the name of the queen-mother.

After the division of the united monarchy, the chronographers supplement their extensive compositions with synchronisms. Thus the accession year of a king of Israel was juxtaposed to the regnal year of the contemporary Judaean monarch (henceforth, Judaean synchronism), and the year of accession of a king of Judah was juxtaposed to the regnal year of the contemporary king of Israel (henceforth, Israelite synchronism). Because the chronographers considered the separate Hebrew kingdoms two divisions of a single people, whose histories intertwined, they recorded the chronological data synchronistically. Similarly, in Mesopotamia during the Neo-Assyrian period, the intricate connections between the Assyrian empire and Babylonia gave rise to synchronistic literature, the foremost example of which was the 'Babylonian Chronicle'.[4] This work narrated the main events in Babylonia from the first half of the eighth century onward (dating them by the current Babylonian monarchy) and integrated those Assyrian and Elamite kings directly or indirectly involved in Babylonian affairs. The narration takes the form of a synchronous chronicle.

At the end of the First Commonwealth and especially during the Babylonian exile, chronographers composed extensive chronographic works in which they attempted to forge a full and continuous chronological scheme for the entire monarchic period. The exilic redactor of the book of Kings had at his disposal not only extensive chronographic works but apparently older documents, like chronicles and king-lists.[5]

Since the Northern Kingdom had disappeared a century and a half prior to the redaction of the book of Kings, the Israelite chronicles probably did not survive intact for such an extended period. The redactor was often unable to find required data in the available sources and was therefore compelled to add certain details – such as Israelite synchronisms – on the basis of his own calculations or approximations. Because these calculated dates did not always suit the heterogeneous evidence in the sources, they gave rise to some contradictions (fairly common in the Israelite synchronistic data, but relatively rare in the data about the Israelite regnal years). The Judaean data in the hands of the redactor seem to have been more reliable, so that the number of errors in the transmission of the chronological data is relatively small.

Although it is still debated whether the ancient chronological material used by the redactor of the book of Kings was drawn from a 'canonical' corpus, the details of which had already been harmonized, the numerous inconsistencies in the chronological data in Kings seem to indicate that the redactor drew upon divergent sources, often conflicting. Certain passages derive from ancient chronicles and are incorporated verbatim into the book of Kings. These preserve authentic chronological information with which the editor did not tamper. Finally, there is a certain validity to the conjecture that in a significant number of places there have been scribal errors in transmission. Changes in system of writing numerals, as evidenced in Hebrew epigraphic documents, might over long periods have readily given rise to errors.

2. The history of research

The study of biblical chronology did not start with modern biblical scholarship: struggles with the contradictory dates in the book of Kings are ancient. Thus in several versions of the Septuagint in Kings – the Codex Vaticanus (= version B of the Septuagint) and the Lucianic recension –

traces of a chronological system different from the one in the Masoretic text (= MT) are distinguishable.

It has been suggested that this residue (in particular the synchronisms between Jehoshaphat and his son Jehoram and the Kings of the Omride Dynasty) reflects the *Vorlage* of the Septuagint, which is considered more reliable than the Masoretic Text in matters of chronology.[6] This question, however, is still unsettled. The problems which arise from the Septuagint version are complex and it has been argued that the Masoretic Text is in fact original and to be preferred, the variants in the Septuagint being no more than later attempts to harmonize the contradictory dates in the Septuagint's Hebrew *Vorlage*.[7] Josephus, in his attempt to settle the contradictory dates, suggested a system of his own, different in certain elements from MT.[8] Furthermore, the authors of the rabbinic chronograph *Seder Olam Rabbah* encountered difficulties in reconciling the contradictory biblical data of the MT.[9] So, too, the mediaeval exegetes Rashi, Ibn-Ezra, and Gersonides offered harmonistic attempts to reconcile the obvious contradictions.

From the middle of the nineteenth century on, biblical scholarship has repeatedly delved into the chronological questions of the reigns of the kings of Judah and Israel.[10] The early investigators preferred to use the regnal years rather than synchronisms; twentieth-century scholars tend to prefer synchronisms. Even here the problem has been tackled in several ways, with a general inclination toward the Judaean synchronisms rather than the Israelite.

The fact is that none of the systems thus far suggested – even the most conservative textually – have succeeded in preserving simultaneously both the synchronisms and the regnal year data. Those who try to uphold the maximum number of biblical chronological data are usually forced into far-fetched assumptions about the possibility of long periods of co-regencies or into other conjectures often devoid of scriptural support.

Opinions also vary about how regnal years were reckoned (below, 4). The most extreme conjecture is that the reckoning system was subject to several changes even within the time-span of a single reign.[11] Such an approach is often motivated by a desire to verify and harmonize as many biblical dates as possible.

3. Questions of methodology

The point of departure for the present study is the assumption that the data concerning regnal years in Israel and Judah does not represent the official reckoning current during the king's reign, and here the present author differs from prevalent systems of biblical chronology. We are confronted instead with data that has already been edited – sometimes painstakingly – by the editors of the chronological framework of Kings. Consequently, assessment of this data for a modern chronologist is entirely dependent on a proper evaluation of the methods employed by those ancient chronologists who prepared that framework.

Before undertaking the analysis of the ancient chronologists' *modus operandi* (below, 6), one must clarify a number of questions inherent in any discussion of dating systems: What type of calendar was used in the biblical period? Was the year a solar year, as in Egypt, or was the calendar lunar-solar as in Mesopotamia (in which the solar year, with 365 days, was adjusted to the twelve-month lunar year by the intercalation of a thirteenth month every few years)? On the one hand the term for month *yrḥ* (moon), or *ḥdš* (new), indicates that the basic unit of the biblical calendar was lunar. On the other hand there is no doubt that the major festivals of the year – the Feast of Unleavened Bread in the month of Abib, Pentecost at the time of the wheat harvest, and the Ingathering Festival 'at the turn of the year' (Ex.34.22) – were determined by the seasons and the agricultural cycle. One can conclude therefore that the calendar in biblical Israel was a lunar-solar one. Nonetheless, we do not know how these two elements – the 365-day solar year and 354-day lunar year – were harmonized. Was it by intercalating a month, as in Babylonia, or by adding ten days at the end of every twelve-month cycle, as in Egypt, or by some other method?[12]

4. The reckoning of regnal years

How were the regnal years reckoned and, in particular, how was the year of accession counted?

Let us first define the term 'regnal year'. Does it refer to an actual calendrical year, counted from the day of the king's ascension to the throne (or from the day of coronation) to the corresponding day in the following year? Or does it refer to the nearest calendrical year following accession or coronation, counted from one New Year's day to the next?

In Mesopotamia and Egypt the regnal year generally coincided with the calendar year. During the New Kingdom in Egypt (the Eighteenth to Twentieth Dynasties), however, regnal years were reckoned from the day of the Pharaoh's coronation.[13] While there is no direct evidence as to which of these two methods was used in Judah and Israel, there are clear, although indirect, indications that in the system used by the editors of Kings the regnal years of every king coincided with the calendar year. The advantage of this system was that both the royal chronographers and the king's officials in the various branches of state administration would have no difficulty in determining when a regnal year began, since New Year's Day – whether in the agricultural or cultic calendar – was simultaneously 'the New Year for kings' in the official reckoning.

The question to be answered next is: How did the king count the year in which he ascended the throne?

The two methods of counting a king's initial year in the ancient Near East were 'post-dating' and 'ante-dating'.[14] In the post-dating system the king's first year begins not with his accession to the throne, but with the following New Year. For purposes of chronological reckoning, the part of the year from the day the king was enthroned until the next New Year was not counted for the new king (i.e., it was a 'zero year', since it was reckoned as the remainder of the last year of the previous king).

In the ante-dating system the first year of the king was reckoned from the day the king ascended the throne or sometimes from the day of the official coronation. In this system it was possible for a king who actually reigned a very short time, e.g. only one month – half before the New Year and half after – to be credited with a reign of 'two years', since the first two weeks would be considered the 'first year', and the second two, from New Year's Day on, the 'second year' of the reign. When setting up a continuous chronological scheme we must reduce by one year the total number of regnal years counted according to the ante-dating system, since the last incomplete year of the king's reign must be included in the regnal years of his successor.[15] Otherwise the same calendar year would be credited to both the old and new kings. In the post-dating system, however, the number of a king's official regnal years was identical with the number of years he actually ruled.

The ante-dating system was current in Egypt during the Old and Middle Kingdoms and reappeared at the time of the Twenty-Sixth Dynasty. The post-dating – or as some scholars designate it, 'the accession year' – system was practised only in Babylonia and fell out of use with the rise of the Hellenistic empires. It grew out of the custom of naming each year of a king's reign. In this system the king's accession year had a special term: 'the year of the start of the reign' (in Akkadian, *šanat rēš šarrūti*), his year 1 beginning only with the following New Year, at Nisan.[16] In Assyria, however, years were counted by the names of specially designated eponyms (*limmu*),[17] and hence the question of counting the accession year separately did not usually arise. The Assyrian royal inscriptions, starting from the middle of the ninth century, counted regnal years according to *palû*, 'regnal period, term of office'. But this count, introduced under Babylonian influence, did not always coincide with the count according to regnal years.[18]

Post-dating enjoyed wide use in Syro-Palestine as a result of the spread of Babylonian administrative practices during the Neo-Babylonian and Persian periods. It is mentioned in II Kings 25.27 as the time when Evil-Merodach king of Babylon freed Jehoiachin from prison: *biš^enat molkō*, i.e. during his accession year or *šanat rēš šarrūti* in Babylonian terminology.[19]

For earlier periods, however, it can be assumed that Israel and Judah employed the ante-dating system, since it was both simpler and more natural than the unconventional post-dating. Nevertheless, the chronological data beginning with Manasseh or Amon, kings of Judah, can be suitably explained only by the post-dating system. The uncommon use of post-dating can be accounted for in one of two ways: 1. Amon, or his father Manasseh, introduced the Babylonian post-dating system into Judah; or 2. even though ante-dating was actually used in Judah throughout its history as a kingdom the exilic chronologist edited the data (below, 6), and adjusted the regnal years in the period between Manasseh or Amon and Zedekiah according to the post-dating system (below, B.4).

5. The 'Royal New Year' in the biblical period

A tradition from the Second Temple period (Mishnah *Rosh ha-Shanah* 1.1) distinguished between 'New Year for kings', i.e. the royal New Year, and 'New Year for years', i.e. the calendrical New Year: the former in Nisan and the latter in Tishri. This tradition seems to have reflected the practice of the first century CE. The Hasmoneans, King Herod, and the leaders of the First Revolt against Rome reckoned their years from Nisan, as had apparently been the case in Judah in the biblical period (see below). In the course of the first century CE, however, and especially during the first half of the second century, counting the years from Tishri in matters of economy and religion, prevailed over that of Nisan. Since then 1 Tishri has been the only New Year in the Jewish tradition.[20]

Modern scholarship ever since the end of the nineteenth century has been divided on the question of the start of the year in Judah and Israel in biblical times and the date of the royal New Year. Some hold that only one calendar was used in Israel and Judah, which ran from Nisan to Adar. Others maintain that the oldest calendar in Judah and Israel began in Tishri and that counting from the spring (Nisan) was the result of Assyrian or Babylonian influence. Many believe that the royal New Year in Judah and its counterpart in Israel were half a year apart, but even on this point opinion differs: according to some, the Judaean kings counted from Tishri, and the Israelite kings from Nisan; according to others, they counted from Nisan in Judah, from Tishri in Israel.

The evidence in our sources points to the fact that in ancient Israel there actually were two New Years, the one in the spring – in the first month – and the other in the fall – in the seventh month (in the northern kingdom perhaps in the eighth month; cf. I Kings 12.33). The Gezer calendar, which lists the farmer's yearly agricultural activities, opens with *yrḥw 'sp*, 'the season of ingathering' – the end of Elul Tishri, or the beginning of Marheshvan. The terminology of Ex.23.16, *wᵉhad hā-'āsip bᵉṣēʾt ha-šānā*, and of Ex.34.22, *wᵉhag hā-'āsip tᵉqupat ha-šānā*, presupposes an agricultural year which begins, or ends, with the Festival of the Ingathering in the fall. Other traditions in the Pentateuch (Ex.12.2; Lev.23-24; Num.23.16; 33.35; Deut.16.1) speak of the month of Abib as the first month. In fact, the months in the biblical period are always counted from the spring. The point can be illustrated from Jer.36.22: in the ninth month the king sat in his winter palace in front of a blazing hearth.

At the same time, it can be conjectured that during and after the united monarchy there were several reckoning systems used in different spheres of life; in commerce and agriculture it was customary to count from the fall, while in the cult – especially in the traditions of the Jerusalem priesthood – it was accepted that the year commenced in the spring. The practice of counting the New Year from the spring as in Mesopotamia has always been followed by the people of Israel, whereas the agricultural year, in the autumn, was taken over from the ancient local tradition of pre-conquest Canaan.

We can now return to the question posed at the outset: When did the kings of Judah and Israel reckon the beginning of their regnal years? Although explicit evidence is exceedingly rare, there are a few indications that in Judah the years were counted from the spring. Thus in Jer.46.2, the battle of Carchemish, when the Egyptian army was defeated by the Babylonians, is dated in the fourth year of Jehoiakim (605 BCE, and see below, the table of fixed dates). One can deduce that at the end of the seventh century BCE regnal years began in the first month of spring.[21] Since reckoning customs tend to be extremely conservative, we can safely assume that even prior to Jehoiakim Judaean kings counted from the spring. This would, in turn, correspond with the practice of the Jerusalem priesthood, mentioned above, whose year started in the month of Abib.

On the other hand, we have no data about the regnal New Year in the Northern Kingdom, and there is disagreement among scholars as to whether it was in the spring or the autumn. However, there is indirect evidence that New Year in Judah did not coincide with that in Ephraim; it is to be found in II Kings 15.8,10; Zechariah, who reigned for six months, ascended the throne in the thirty-eighth year of Uzziah of Judah and died in Uzziah's thirty-ninth year. During these six months a new regnal year had therefore commenced in Judah. At the same time, however, no new year had begun in Israel;[22] if it had, Zechariah's six-month reign would have been counted as two years (cf. the brief reigns of Nadab son of Jeroboam I and Elah son of Baasha of Israel). May one conclude that this half-year discrepancy in matters connected with the regnal New Year existed not only in the days of Uzziah and Zechariah but throughout the period of the kingdoms of Judah and Israel? If indeed, as already noted, the kings of Judah counted their years from the spring and if there is a half-year discrepancy, we are forced to conclude that the Ephraimite kings reckoned their regnal years from the autumn (either from the seventh or the eighth month).[23]

6. The editorial method of the ancient chronologist

We turn to the main problem presented at the outset of our discussion (above, 3): What was the *modus operandi* of the ancient chronologist in constructing the chronological framework of the book of Kings? We believe that he must have used the standard procedures employed by Mesopotamian chronologists in respect to the rounding off of years.[24] Since a main interest of this editor was to synchronize the reigns of the kings of Judah and Israel, he was naturally concerned only with the number of full regnal years. If his sources reported that a certain king of Judah reigned x years plus y months (e.g., David in Hebron: seven years and six months, II Sam.5.5), he would have had to delete the number of months in excess of full years (i.e. the last incomplete year), and count only the complete years. Exactly the same practice would be followed by a modern chronologist who sets out to arrange a synchronistic scheme on the basis of regnal data calculated by ante-dating.

The result is that all of the kings of Judah and Israel, whose regnal years have been rounded off by the editor, actually reigned (according to their own count) one year more than is attributed to them in Kings. Consequently, Rehoboam reigned seventeen years and x months and died in the eighteenth year of his reign; and since Rehoboam and Jeroboam ascended their respective thrones in the same year, Rehoboam died in Jeroboam's eighteenth, not his seventeenth, year. This is indeed recorded in the synchronism in I Kings 15.1: 'Now in the eighteenth year of King Jeroboam the son of Nebat, Abijam began to reign over Judah.' Moreover, the assumption that the editor deleted the extra months, leaving the number of complete years, solves two major chronological problems: the ten regnal years of Menahem of Israel and the single year of Ahaziah. According to the synchronisms, Menahem began to reign in the thirty-ninth year of Uzziah, king of Judah, and died in Uzziah's fiftieth year (II Kings 15.17, 23). Hence, Menahem reigned not ten but eleven or even twelve years (counting by the ante-dating system). The best way to preserve both the figure 'ten' and the synchronisms of II Kings would be to assume that Menahem reigned actually ten years plus x months (i.e., eleven years in his own official count) and that the ancient editor, faithful to his method, deleted the extra number of months fixing Menahem's total to ten full years.

The other difficulty solved by the present assumption involves the single regnal year of Ahaziah of Judah. According to the system of ante-dating, if his reign terminated before a New Year, it would have been considered a zero for synchronistic purposes, in which case the chronologist would have reported the exact number of months of that incomplete year. If his reign had extended beyond one New Year – i.e., into his second official year – he would have been credited with two years. We therefore assume that the editor found in his sources that Ahaziah had reigned one year and a few months, but, in keeping with his system of rounding off, he deleted the number of months and credited the king with one year (II Kings 8.26).

What were the sources used by our editor? It stands to reason that the major portion of the material from Judah consisted of official chronicles, or gleanings from them, which lasted both full regnal years and additional months. By contrast, the Israelite material at his disposal was partly original, partly reworked. It would seem that for the period between Jeroboam and the end of the Omride dynasty, only data about complete regnal years reached him. That is to say, in his source the number of regnal years of the Israelite kings had already been rounded off and only whole years were listed. These numbers were somewhat similar: Jeroboam, twenty-two years; Nadab, two years; Baasha, twenty-four years; Elah, two years; Omri, twelve years; Ahab, twenty-two years; Ahaziah, two years; Joram, twelve years. Rounding off numbers according to cycles of 2 + 22 and 12 years, which indeed was rather close to the actual number of regnal years, was resorted to, it seems, as a mnemonic device (or even may have resulted from contamination). Accordingly the editor did not tamper with these numbers, which had already been rounded off, even though each one of them was one year higher than the actual number of regnal years. The Judaean synchronisms for this period fit this assumption. On the other hand, for the period after the rise of Jehu our editor's data seem to have been more exact. Here he consistently kept to his method of rounding off, so that Jehu's twenty-eight years and Jehoash's sixteen years were in fact twenty-eight years + x months and sixteen years + y months, which in the ante-dating system were counted officially as twenty-nine years and seventeen years respectively.

In contrast with his standard working procedure, our chronologist was precise when dealing with the kings who reigned for less than a year. Here his methods were those of the compilers of the Babylonian kinglists:[25] he recorded the actual number of regnal years, months, or even days. Thus, he recorded for Zimri seven days, Zechariah six months, and Shallum one month, giving Jehoahaz and Jehoiachin of Judah three months each. These figures must certainly derive from chronicles or official records and bring us one step closer to the no longer extant chronological sources.

7. Co-regencies

One other principle which guided our chronologist was the assumption that during the entire period of the Israelite monarchy there were no co-regencies: i.e., the heir to the throne serving as regent during his father's lifetime counted this period as part of his own reign. Our sources do point, however, to periods of co-regency: Jotham 'judged the "people of the land"' during the lifetime of Uzziah his father (II Kings 15.5)[26] and Uzziah apparently was regent for fifteen years during the lifetime of his father Amaziah (II Kings 14.17).[27] Whether the chronologist knew about these and other co-regencies but decided to ignore them, or whether he did not know about them at all – as was probably the case – it is clear that the method he chose has created serious discrepancies in the chronological scheme of the book of Kings.

The assumption that there actually were co-regencies in both Judah and Israel – in itself logical and clearly alluded to in the sources – does much to solve a few of the more serious contradictions.[28]

B. Determining the chronological scheme

1. Fixed dates

The chronological scheme of the monarchic age divides naturally into three periods: (a) From Jeroboam until the rebellion of Jehu; (b) From Jehu until the fall of Samaria; (c) From the fall of Samaria until the destruction of the First Temple. Inasmuch as the chronological data from the last period are the most certain, our chronological considerations begin with the late period and then work backwards.[29]

It is only natural that information from extra-biblical sources will provide absolute dates and serve as 'anchor points'. The following table lists twenty external synchronisms for the First Temple period,[30] drawn on the whole from Assyrian and Babylonian sources. The dates are chronologically absolute (in the Julian calendar), since Assyrian and Babylonian chronologies of the first millennium BCE are based on continuous listing of years down to the Hellenistic and Roman periods, verifiable by astronomical reckoning.[31]

TABLE OF DATES

Event	Synchronism*	Year	Biblical Reference
1. Ahab the Israelite participates in the battle of Qarqar as one of twelve kings of Syria	6th year of Shalmaneser III	853 BCE	—
2. Jehu 'the son of Omri' pays tribute to Assyria	18th year of Shalmaneser III	841 BCE	—
3. Jehoash, king of Israel, pays tribute to Adad-nirari III		796 BCE	—
4. Menahem, king of Israel, pays tribute to Pul (Tiglath-pileser III), king of Assyria	8th year of Tiglath-pileser III	738 BCE	II Kings 15.19–20
5. Campaign of Tiglath-pileser III to Philistia. Ahaz (Jehoahaz) pays tribute ot Assyria		734 BCE	—
6. Conquest and exile of the inhabitants of Galilee and Transjordania by Tiglath-pileser III, during the reign of Pekah		733–732 BCE	II Kings 15.26
7. Death of Pekah; Hosea ascends the throne		732 BCE	—
8. Tiglath-pileser II receives tribute from Hoshea during his campaign in Chaldaea	731 BCE	—	
9. 9th year of Hoshea; Hoshea taken captive by Shalmaneser V; siege of Samaria begins		724 BCE	II Kings 17.4–5
10. Capture of Samaria by Shalmaneser V		722 BCE	II Kings 17.6; 18.10
11. Exile of Israelites by Sargon II	2nd year of Sargon	720 BCE	
12. Sargon's campaign to Ashdod	9th–10th years of Sargon	713–712 BCE	Isa. 20.1–2

Event	Synchronism*	Year	Biblical Reference
13. Sennacherib's campaign to Judah	4th year of Sennacherib (his 3rd campaign)	701 BCE	II Kings 18.13:Isa. 36
14. 31st year of Josiah; campaign of Necho; the battle of Megiddo; the reign of Jehoahaz	18th year of Nabopolassar	609 BCE	II Kings 23.29
15. 4th year of Jehoiakim; defeat of Egypt at Carchemish by Nebuchadnezzar	21st year of Nabopolassar	605 BCE	II Chron. 35.20; Jer. 46 (between Nisan and Ab)
16. Capture of Jerusalem by Nebuchadnezzar	7th year of Nebuchadnezzar II	598/7 BCE	
17. Exile of Jehoiachin and of 10,000 men	8th year of Nebuchadnezzar II	597 BCE	II Kings 24.12–14;
18. 10th year of Nebuchadnezzar II	18th year of Nebuchadnezzar II	587 BCE	Jer. 32.1
19. 11th year of Zedekiah; Destruction of the Temple	19th year of Nebuchadnezzar II	7th of Ab, 586 BCE	II Kings 25.8
20. Release of Jehoiachin from prison in 37th year of his captivity	Accession of Evil-merodach	25th or 27th of Adar 561 BCE	Jer. 52.31

* All dates are given in terms of the Assyro-Babylonian year, which began in Nisan (April-May) and ended in Adar (March-April).

2. From the fall of Samaria until the destruction of the First Temple

This is a period of 134½ years, according to the regnal year date for Judaean kings which extends from the sixth year of Hezekiah (inclusive) until the eleventh year of Zedekiah. The half year – three months of Jehoahaz and three months of Jehoiachin – is taken up (in the post-dating system) in the reckoning of complete years, leaving only 134 years. The period is divided into 112 regnal years, from the conquest of Samaria (sixth year of Hezekiah) until the death of Josiah, and twenty-two from the death of Josiah until the destruction of the temple in the eleventh year of Zedekiah.

The dates of the last four kings of Judah – Jehoahaz, Jehoiakim, Jehoiachin and Zedekiah – are determined by the synchronisms between Jehoiakim and Zedekiah and Nebuchadnezzar king of Babylon (see the table above):

Death of Josiah	609
Reign of Jehoahaz and accession of Jehoiakim	609
Reign of Jehoiakim	608/7-598/7
Reign of Jehoiachin and accession of Zedekiah	597

It is difficult to determine the exact date of the destruction of the temple.

The dates 587 and 586[32] have been proposed. Since the corresponding passage in the Babylonian Chronicle which tells of the conquest of Jerusalem and the destruction of the temple is not extant,[33] there is as yet no generally accepted conclusion. The question involves yet another, more difficult, problem: When was the exile of Jehoiachin and when exactly did Zedekiah start counting regnal years – from the spring of 597, the autumn of 597, or only from the spring of 596? The present writer, who adheres to the view that Judah counted the years from the spring, prefers to place the destruction of Jerusalem in 586 in agreement with II Kings 25.8, which synchronizes the eleventh and last year of Zedekiah with the nineteenth year of Nebuchadnezzar (which began 1 Nisan 596). Zedekiah's first year would accordingly begin in Nisan 596, rather than in Nisan 597, immediately after Jehoiachin's exile. The explanation offered for this postponement of one year is that while people were being carried to exile (and no doubt the 10,000 people were carried off *after* 1 Nisan 597), Zedekiah would have refrained from celebrating his accession and hence reckoned his regnal years from the spring of 596. The shortcoming of this suggestion is that it postulated an extremely unusual accession year of 12 plus x months. Therefore one of the following alternatives might be considered: (*a*) that the equation of Zedekiah's eleventh year with Nebuchadnezzar's nineteenth is not reliable (and there is not sufficient reason to assume that), or (*b*) that it was the ancient chronographer who counted Zedekiah's regnal years from (spring) 596 rather than from (spring) 597. In any event, unless additional evidence is unearthed, 586 seems to be a preferable date for the destruction of the Temple.

Since Josiah's death in his thirty-first regnal year has been reckoned at 609 BCE, his first regnal year must have been 639/8 BCE. Between 722 BCE, the date of the fall of Samaria, and 639/8 BCE, the start of Josiah's reign, 83 years elapsed. But the sum of years of Judaean kings from the sixth year of Hezekiah (the year of the conquest of Samaria, according to II Kings 18.9f.) until the first year of Josiah is only 81 years: 24 years of Hezekiah (from his sixth until his twenty-ninth year), fifty-five years of Manasseh, two years of Amon, all according to the post-dating system.

Several solutions to this discrepancy have been suggested:

1. The total number of regnal years of Manasseh and/or of Amon as transmitted by MT is corrupt. Manasseh should be credited with fifty-seven years and/or Amon with four years. All the ancient versions and translations, however, support the figures given in MT.

2. Alternatively it has been suggested[34] that Hezekiah was co-regent during the last two regnal years of his father Ahaz but these two years were not included in his twenty-nine regnal years. The synchronisms which place the start of the siege of Samaria in Hezekiah's fourth year and its destruction in his sixth are numbered from his co-regency. This suggestion raises more difficulties than it solves, especially as it does not accord with placing the death of Ahaz in the year 727, the last year of Tiglath-pileser III (see below, 3).

We propose yet a third solution, in line with our assumption that the ancient editor rounded off years (above, 6): The twenty-nine years of Hezekiah, the fifty-five of Manasseh and the two of Amon represent only the complete regnal years of these kings. Each of them reigned a few additional months which amount, when added together, to two years. Our chronologist deleted, according to his practice, the extra months and recorded only full years.

Another point to be considered is that the regnal years of the last kings of Judah, beginning with Manasseh, were reckoned by post-dating. Was it actually employed during the reign of Manasseh (as a result of Mesopotamian influence?) or did the exilic chronologist apply the post-dating system to the last kings of Judah, starting with Manasseh or Amon? (If so, it would seem that our chronologist had already at his disposal a chronological framework – in the ante-dating system – for the pre-Manasseh period.) For the present, the problem must remain unsolved.

3. From the rebellion of Jehu until the fall of Samaria

If Hezekiah came to the throne in 727/6 BCE, then between this date and the rebellion of Jehu in 842, 115 years would have elapsed. But the total number of regnal years of the kings of Judah and Israel during this period exceeds 115. In Israel the total is 140, a twenty-five year discrepancy, and in Judah 159, a forty-four year discrepancy.

To account for these discrepancies one must assume either that the numbers in MT are corrupt or that some of the kings were co-regents, sharing power and authority during their fathers' liftetime. These possibilities are not mutually exclusive.

Reckoning in both Israel and Judah was done by the antedating system (above, 4). According to our approach the number of regnal years recorded in Kings for this period includes only the number of years allocated to him in Kings (e.g. Jehu died in his twenty-ninth year, Jehoahaz in his eighteenth, Jehoash in his seventeenth, Menahem in his eleventh, etc.).

The absolute date fixed by external synchronism for the end of this period is the fall of Samaria. Even here, however, scholarly opinion is divided. In the past it was customary to accept at face value Sargon's claim in the Khorsabad Annals that he had conquered Samaria and exiled its inhabitants at the beginning of his reign, during his *šanat rēš šarruti*, i.e. between December 722 (or January 721) and April 721. This entry in the Annals is contradicted, however, by a more reliable inscription, according to which Sargon appears not to have undertaken a military campaign before his second year, i.e., not before April 720. The compilers of the royal Annals apparently transferred an event from 720 to 721 in order to open the narrative of Sargon's reign with a great military victory. The biblical reference to the king of Assyria who besieged and conquered Samaria (II Kings 17.5f.) is therefore to Shalmaneser V and should be considered reliable. This tradition is further supported by the Babylonian Chronicle, which states that Shalmaneser V conquered *šamara'in* (the Aramaic form of *šom^erōn*/Samaria).[35]

Another vexing chronological problem concerns the date of the accession year of Hezekiah. According to II Kings 18.10, Hezekiah was in his sixth year at the time of Samaria's fall. Confirming this datum is Isa.14.28: 'In the year that King Ahaz died came this oracle: Rejoice not all Philistia, that the rod which smote you is broken.' Breaking the rod which smote Philistia is probably a reference to the death of Tiglath-pileser III, the only Assyrian king from the days of Ahaz worthy of such an epithet. It appears therefore that Ahaz died and Hezekiah came to power in the same year that Tiglath-pileser died,[36] which according to the Babylonian Chronicle was 12 Tebet 727/6 BCE (27 December 727 or 15 January 726).

On the other hand, the heading in II Kings 18.14 (Isa 36.1) states that: 'In the fourteenth year of Hezekiah, Sennacherib king of Assyria came up against all the fortified cities of Judah and took them.' As this event, reported in detail in Sennacherib's Annals, is fixed beyond any doubt as the year 701 BCE, it follows that Hezekiah's acccession took place in 716/5. This date, however, is contradicted both by Isa.14.28, as explained above, as well as by the series of synchronisms between Hezekiah and Hoshea in II Kings 18.1,9f. A modern biblical chronologist, who prefers to rely upon the date in II Kings 18.13, must reject the authenticity of the synchronisms in II Kings 18.[37] It has therefore been suggested[38] that the heading in II Kings 18.13 (Isa.36.1) belonged originally to the tale about Hezekiah's illness and his miraculous recovery (II Kings 20.1-11; Isa.38.1-8) and was placed in its present position by a later editor, who related all the prophetic stories concerning Isaiah and Hezekiah to the fateful year of Sennacherib's campaign and the miraculous salvation of Jerusalem.

4. From Jeroboam until the rebellion of Jehu

The total number of years of the kings of Israel (from Jeroboam I until Joram son of Ahab) is 98, and those of the kings of Judah (from Rehoboam until Ahaziah son of Jeroboam), 95. Inasmuch as Jeroboam and Rehoboam ascended the throne at the same time and Joram and Ahaziah were both killed during Jehu's rebellion, the number of regnal years for the kings of both Judah and Israel must be equal.

We have assumed (above 6) that the data about regnal years of the Judaean kings, even in this period, include only the complete years, without the months of the incomplete last year, whereas the data for Israelite kings include the incomplete final year. If so, in order to work out the chronological table one must decrease by one the regnal years of each Israelite king.

Two external synchronisms are available: 1. The battle of Qarqar, in which Ahab participated, took place in the sixth year of Shalmaneser III of Assyria (= 865 BCE); 2.Jehu paid tribute to Assyria in the eighteenth year of Shalmaneser III of Assyria (= 841 BCE).

The main crux in the chronology of this period concerns the years 853-

841. If Ahab was killed in the battle against Aram (I Kings 22) after he participated in the battle of Qarqar,[39] then in the thirteen years inclusive between 853 and 841 we must be able to account for the following data for the Northern Kingdom:

x = period of time that Ahab reigned from the battle of Qarqar until his death;

2 regnal years of Ahaziah (actually one calendar year);

12 regnal years of Joram (actually eleven calendar years);

y = period of time from Jehu's rise to power until delivery of tribute to Assyria.

The x figure should include at least a few months, for Ahab was Ben-hadad's ally at Qarqar and it is not likely that Ahab would have attacked his former ally at Ramoth-Gilead so soon after Qarqar. The tribute was certainly paid after Nisan 841 BCE, whereas the rebellion seems to have taken place the previous winter while the king was recuperating from his wounds in the Omride dynasty's winter residency, Jezreel.

In addition to the difficulty of accounting for twelve = x = y years in the short interval between 853 and 841 BCE, there are several contradictions between various synchronisms and the totals of the regnal years.[40]

One might perhaps solve the chronological crux by an emendation: if Jehoram son of Ahab reigned not twelve but only ten years (actually nine full years and a few additional months) we are left with about two years for the period of Ahab's reign, between Qarqar and Ramoth-Gilead, and about a year for the period between Jehu's accession and the payment of tribute to Assyria. Add to this, nine or ten years of Jehoram's reign and we arrive at a total of thirteen years (at most) between 853-841 BCE.

However, no system in biblical chronology proposed so far offers a fully satisfactory solution to the conflicting data in this period, especially that which concerns the reign of Jehoshaphat. Here the Greek versions (above, A.2) preserve somewhat different figures, which according to several scholars should be preferred to those of the Massoretic Text.[41]

5. The united monarchy

The length of Saul's reign is unknown. The passage in I Sam.13.1 ('Saul was one year old when he reigned and ruled over Israel two years') is clearly defective. The original reading must have included a reasonable number in each case: Saul was x years old when he began to reign and he reigned y years and 2 years over Israel. Completion of the number in the tens column is a matter of conjecture.

The information in II Sam.5.4; 11.42 about the reigns of David and Solomon is also very scanty.

David: thirty years old when he
began to reign

	seven years over Judah
	thirty-three years over Israel
Total	forty years.
Solomon:	forty years over Israel
Total	forty years.

The forty-year reigns of David and Solomon seem to be approximate and typological figures. David is reported to have been thirty years old when he assumed power and is said to have reigned forty years and six months (II Sam.5.4), making him seventy years old when he died; this is, in all opinions, a typological number signifying an average life-span (Ps.90.10).[42] Nevertheless, the abundance of stories in Samuel about David's career forces us to assume that he had a lengthy reign of at least several decades. Solomon also reigned for an extended period and his successor reached the throne at the age of forty-one (I Kings 14.21). Therefore, just as the chronographer rounded off the 38/39 year reign of Jehoash king of Judah to forty years,[43] so both David and Solomon were credited with forty years, a typological number commonly used in the Bible to indicate a full generation.[44] Likewise, units of eighty, forty and twenty years expressing two, one, or half generations (Judg.3.11,30; 8.28; 15.20; I Sam.7.2) were employed by the chronographer who narrated the period that preceded the establishment of the monarchy.[45] However, by its very nature, such data originating in oral tradition and important as it may be for genealogical chronology, cannot be subjected to strict chronological enquiry.

CHRONOLOGICAL TABLE
(C = century; *c.* = approximately)

Century BCE	Israel (Judah)		Egypt	Phoenicia and Transjordan
13	Exodus from Egypt (?)		*c.* 1290–1224: Ramses II	
12	End C13–end C12 BCE: Settlement?		*c.* 1223–1211 (1224–1204): Merenptah	
11	*c.* 1020–1000 (1012–1004): Saul *c.* 1000–961 (1004–965): David		*c.* 964–956 (978–959): Siamun *c.* 959–945:	
10	*c.* 961–922 (965–926): Solomon *c.* 922 (926): Division of the empire		Psausennes *c.* 935–914 (945–924): Shishak I	*c.* 976–930 (973–942): Hiram of Tyre
	Kingdom of Israel	**Kingdom of Judah**		
9	*c.* 922–901 (926–907): Jeroboam I *c.* 901–900 (907–906): Nadab *c.* 900–877 (906–889): Baasha *c.* 877–6 (883–2): Elah *c.* 876 (882): Zimri *c.* 876–3 (882–878): Tibni *c.* 873–869 (878–871): Omri *c.* 869–850 (871–852): Ahab *c.* 850–849 (852–1): Ahaziah *c.* 849–42 (851–845): Jehoram *c.* 842–815 (845–818): Jehu	*c.* 922–915 (926–910): Rehoboam *c.* 915–913 (910–908): Abijah *c.* 913–873 (908–868): Asa *c.* 873–849 (868–847): Jehoshaphat *c.* 849–842 (847–845): Joram *c.* 842 (845): Ahaziah		*c.* 891–859 (873–842): Ittobaal of Tyre *c.* 850: Mesha of Moab *c.* 814–813: Foundation of Carthage

Syria	Mesopotamia (Assyria)	Greece	Events
		C12: Trojan War	So-called 'Israel' stele
			c. 1050: battle of Song of Deborah, Judg.5(?)
c. 900–875 (885–870): Bar Hadad I c. 875–843 (870–842): Bar Hadad II (= Hadadezer)			
			C9: Aramaean wars
	c. 858–824: Shalmaneser III		853: battle at Kadesh on the Orantes
c. 845–842: Bar Hadad III?			
c 843–806(?) (841–806): Hazael			841: Jehu pays tribute

Century BCE	Israel	Judah	Egypt	Syria
8	c. 815–801 (818–802): Jehoahaz c. 801–786 (802–787) Joash c 786–746 (787–747): Jeroboam II c. 746–5 (747): Zechariah c. 745 (747): Shallum c. 745–738 (747–738): Menahem c. 738–7 (737–6): Pekahiah c. 737–732 (735–732): Pekah c. 732–724: Hoshea c. 723–2: Fall of Samaria c. 720: End of resistance after 720: Assyrian province	c 842–837 (845–840): Athaliah c. 837–800 (840–801): Jehoash c. 800–783 (801–787): Amaziah c. 783–742 (787–736) Uzziah/ Azariah 750–742 (756–736): Jotham regent c. 735–715 (736–729/726): Ahaz c. 715–686 (728–700): Hezekiah		c. 806–775: Bar Hadad IV (III) = Mari' c?: Rezin of Damascus 732: fall of Damascus
			c. 710/09–696/5: Sabako	
7			c. 690–664: Tirhaka	
	End C7: Josiah reconquers part of the North?	c. 687–642: Manasseh c. 642–640 Amon c. 640 (639)–609: Joiah 609: Jehoahaz 609–598 Jehoiakim	c. 663–609: Psammetichus I 655: independent again 609–594 Necho II	

Mesopotamia (Assyria and Babylon)	Media	Greece	Rome	Events
c. 810–783: Adad-nirari III				
c. 782–773: Shalmaneser IV		c. 776: First Olympiad		796: Joash pays tribute c. 760: Earthquake (Amos 1.1)
		754–3: year 3, VI Olympiad	753: foundation of Rome 753–509: the seven kings	
c. 744–727: Tiglath-Pileser III				738: Menahem pays tribute to Tiglath-Pileser III 734: Syro–Ephraimite war 734: Ahaz pays tribute to Tiglath-Pileser III
726–722: Shalmaneser V 721–705: Sargon II				733–2: Tiglath–Pileser III conquers Galilee and Transjordan 732: Death of Pekah 731: Hoshea pays tribute to Tiglath-Pileser III
704–681: Sennacherib c. 703: Merodach–Baladan of Babylonia 680–69: Esarhaddon 668–27: Asshur-bani-pal 625: First fall of Nineveh 612: Second fall of Nineveh 607–5: Nabopolassar of Babylon	625–585: Cyaxares of Media			724: Siege of Samaria begins 722: Samaria falls to Shalmaneser IV 721: Deportation by Sargon II 713–12: Campaign by Sargon II in south 701: Siege of Jerusalem 609: Battle of Megiddo 605: Battle of Carchemish

Century BCE	Judah	Egypt	Syria
6	598: Jehoiachin 597–587/86: Zedekiah 587/86–539: Babylonian exile	589–570: Hophrah 568–626: Amamis	
5	c. 539/8: Edict of Cyrus 538–521: Sheshbazzar and Zerubbabel 'governors' 521–c. 330: Seven civil governors (Avigad)? c. 485–385: Five Sanballatids known for Samaria	525: occupation by Cambyses	
4	332: Alexander conquers the region c. 300: Simon I high priest 323–198: Under the Ptolemies of Egypt	After 323: Ptolemy Lagids	After 312: Seleucids
3	c. 200: Simon VII high priest	285–246: Ptolemy II Philadelphus	223–187: Antiochus III 187–175: Seleucus IV
2	after 198: Under the Seleucids of Syria ?–175: Onias III high priest 174–171: Jason high priest 171–162: Menelaus high priest 162: Alkimus high priest 165–160: Judas Maccabaeus 160–142: Jonathan Maccabaeus 142–134: Simon Maccabaeus		174–164: Antiochus IV 169: Invasion of Egypt 168: Invasion of Egypt 164–161: Antiochus V 161–150: Demetrius I 153–145: Alexander Balas

Mesopotamia (Assyria)	Media and Persia	Greece	Rome	Events
605–561: Nebuchadnezzar II				597: First fall of Jerusalem, deportation summer 587 or 586; second fall of Jerusalem, destruction and deportation
	559–530: Cyrus II			
555–539: Nabonidus				
	530–522: Cambyses		509: Republic	561: Jehoiachin pardoned
	522–486: Darius I			516 Dedication of temple
		492–490: First and Second Persian wars 431–04: Peloponnesian war		
	355–332: Darius II			333: Battle of Issus 312–198: Conflict between Diadochi
			281–272: Pyrrhic wars 264–241: First Punic War 218–201: Second Punic War 200–197 Second Macedonian War 192–187: War against Antiochus III 171–168: Third Macedonian War 149–146 Third Punic War	LXX translated 167: Desecration of temple 165: Maccabaean revolt 164: Reconsecration of temple c. 125: Qumran monastery founded

Century BCE	Judah (Judaea)
1	134–104: John Hyrcanus
	104–103: Aristobulus
	103–76: Alexander Jannaeus
	76–67: Alexandra Salome
	67–63: Aristobulus II
	63: Pompey intervenes
	37–4: Herod

Century CE	Judaea
1	6: Roman province.
	Zealots
	26: Pilate procurator
	c. 27–30: Ministry of Jesus
	41–44: Agrippa king
	52: Felix procurator
	59?: Festus procurator
	64: Gessius Florus procurator
	66: Beginning of first Jewish revolt
	67: Roman expedition under Vespasian; reconquest of Galilee
	69: Vespasian temporizes
	69: Titus commands the troops
	70: Conquest and destruction of Jerusalem
	74: Massada falls
	115–117: Jewish revolt in various provinces
	132: Second Jewish revolt begins
	135: Revolt finally tamed; *Judaea* now becomes *Palaestina*

Rome

91–88: Social wars
60–53: First triumvirate
49–45: First Civil War
44–30: Second Civil War
43–36: Second triumvirate

14: Augustus dies
14–37: Tiberius emperor
37–41: Caligula emperor
41–54: Claudius emperor
54: Nero emperor

68: Death of Nero
68–69: Galba, Otho and
Vitellius emperors
69–79: Vespasian emperor
79–81: Titus emperor
87–117: Trajan emperor
117–138: Hadrian emperor

Notes

2. The Country

1. This information has been collected, with a commentary, by H.-J.Zobel, 'k^{e}na'an', *TWAT* IV, 224-43.
2. *AHw* I, 479.
3. *Ep. ad Rom. Exp.*, 13, *PL* 35, 2096.
4. Cf. B.Maisler (Mazar), 'Canaan and the Canaanites', *BASOR* 102, 1946, 7-12; S.Moscati, *Predecessori d'Israele*, 67, and 'Sulla Storia del nome Canaan', in *Studia Biblica et Orientalia*, AnBibl 12, Rome 1959, 266-9; M.Noth, *OTW*, 49-52.
5. W.F.Albright, 'The Role of the Canaanites in the History of Civilization', in *Studies in the History of Culture. Waldo H.Leland Volume*, Menasha, Wisc. 1942, 11-50, reprinted in *The Bible and the Ancient Near East. Essays in Honor of William Foxwell Albright*, Garden City and London 1961, 328-62; but cf. the critical comments by G.Garbini, *I Fenici*, ch.1. See also S.Moscati, *Il mondo dei Fenici*, Milan 1966.
6. Noth, 'Geschichte des Namens Palästina', *ZDPV* 62, 1939, 125-44 = *ABLAK* I, 294-308.
7. Cf. the passionate if unconvincing defence of the use of 'Land of Israel' and even of *Eretz* (sic!) *Israel* by A.F.Rainey, the translator of Y.Aharoni, *The Archaeology of the Land of Israel*, Philadelphia and London 1982, XIIIf.
8. For these peoples cf. T.Ishida, 'The Structure and Implications of the List of pre-Israelite Nations', *Bibl* 60, 1979, 461-90; N.K.Gottwald, *The Tribes*, 498-503. For the theme in general cf. the exhaustive articles by A.R.Millard, 'The Canaanites', and M.Liverani, 'The Amorites', both in D.J.Wiseman (ed.), *Peoples of Old Testament Times*, Oxford 1973, 29-52, 100-33. For the Hivites now see O.Margalit, 'The Hivites', *ZAW* 100, 1988, 60-70; for the Girgashites, M.Görg, 'Dor, die Teukrer und die Girgashiter', *BN* 28, 1985, 7-14; for the Perizzites, L.E.Stager, 'Archaeology, Ecology and Social History: Background Themes to the Song of Deborah 7, *VT* 40, 1988, 220-34: 224f., where they are connected with p^{e}rāzōt ('non-fortified villages'), Judg.5.7, and the Hivites with ḥawwōt ('shepherds' settlements'). However, N.Na'aman, 'Canaanites and Perizzites', *BN* 45, 1988, 42-7, is sceptical about these identifications, drawing attention to the late date of all the texts and their often fabulous character.

9. R. de Vaux, 'Les Hurrites de l'histoire et les Horites de la Bible', *RB* 74, 1967, 461-503.

10. M.Liverani, 'Ville et campagne dans le royaume d'Ugarit. Essai d'analyse économique', in *Societies and Languages of the Ancient Near East. Studies in Honour of I.M.Diakonoff*, Warminster 1982, 250-2, provides an interesting example of the ruthless exploitation of the country for the building of the royal palace in the city; cf. also N.P.Lemche, *Ancient Israel*, SVT 37, Leiden 1985, 198ff.

11. The first two can be obtained in specialist libraries and bookshops.

3. Problems, Methodology, Bibliography and Sources

1. A.Kuenen, *De godsdienst van Israël*, I, Haarlem 1869, 32ff. (ET London 1874, 30ff.); B.Stade, *Geschichte des Volkes Israel*, Berlin I, 1885, 16ff.

2. W.F.Albright, 'Historical and Mythical Elements in the Joseph Story', *JBL* 37, 1918, 111-34: 113f. For an example of the way in which the texts can be transformed see the recent study by A.Catastini, *Isaia ed Ezechia*, Rome 1989.

3. Cf. Soggin 1988.

4. Cf. my *Introduction to the Old Testament*, London and Philadelphia ³1989.

5. P.A.H.de Boer, 'Egypt in the Old Testament: Some Aspects of an Ambivalent Assessment', in *Selected Studies in Old Testament Exegesis*, Leiden 1991, 152-67.

6. Cf. R.E.Clements, 'The Prophecies of Isaiah and the Fall of Jerusalem, 587 BC', *VT* 30, 1980, 421-36, and O.Kaiser, *Isaiah 1-12*, OTL, London and Philadelphia ²1983 (cf. my review in *VT* 34, 1984, 496-9).For the exilic and post-exilic redaction of the biblical books cf. J. van Seters, 'Confessional Reformulations in the Exilic Period', *VT* 22, 1972, 448-59, and a conservative author like D.N.Freedman, ' "Son of Man, Can These Bones Live?" ', *Int* 29, 1975, 171-86: 'In the most literal sense of the word the Bible is the product of the exile.' So it is not surprising that for some time now some scholars have called the exilic and post-exilic period the creative period: cf. D.W.Thomas, 'The Sixth Century BC: A Creative Epoch in the History of Israel', *JSS* 6, 1961, 33-46; P.R.Ackroyd, *Exile and Restoration*, London 1968, 143; cf. also R.E.Friedman, *The Exile and Biblical Narrative*, Cambridge, Mass. 1991.

7. K.A.D.Smelik, 'Vertellingen in de Hebreeuwse Bijbel', *Amsterdamse Cahiers* 9, 1988, 8-21.

8. Garbini* 1988 rightly indicates the oddity of the fact that rulers of less importance than those of Israel and Judah have left steles, while nothing is left of the Hebrew ones; he attributes this, of course conjecturally, to a systematic destruction of all the royal inscriptions, cf. Meg.Ta'an., cited in J.A.Fitzmyer, *A Manual of Palestinian Aramaic Texts*, Rome 1978, no.150, 8, p.187: 'On 3 Tishri the mention was eliminated from the sources'; however, the editor suggests a different translation and interpretation.

9. G.Garbini, 'Le fonte citate nel "libro del Re" ', *Hen* 3, 1981, 26-46.

10. Cf. n. 1 above.

11. E.Meyer, *Geschichte des Altertums*, II.2, Stuttgart ²1931, 25ff.; J.A.Montgomery and H.S.Gehman, *The Books of Kings*, Edinburgh 1951, 128ff.; J.M.Sasson, 'On Choosing Models for Recreating Premonarchic History', *JSOT* 21, 1981, 3-24; M.C.Astour, review, *JAOS* 102, 1982, 192-5. Two reviews of my 1984

History also take this line: O.Carena, *BeO* 27, 1985, 113-15; G.L.Prato, *Or* 67, 1986, 143-7, cf. Ackroyd, quoted by C.S.Rodd, review *JTS* 39, 1989, 142.

12. Thus Garbini* 1988, 38.
13. Thus Liverani, review, *OrAnt* 26, 1987, 146-50; T.L.Thompson, *The Origin Tradition of Ancient Israel*, Sheffield, I, 1987, 30ff.; also Coote and Whitelam 1987, 140ff.; Lemche* 1988, 32.
14. Cf. my 1988 study, 259ff.
15. J.A.Soggin, *Das Königtum in Israel*, Berlin 1967, and 'Der Beitrag des Königtums zur israelitischen Religion', *SVT* 23, 1972, 9-26.
16. For Max Weber see now W.Schluchter (ed.), *Max Webers Studie über das Judentum*, Frankfurt am Main 1981; C.Schäfer-Lichtenberger, *Stadt und Eidgenossenschaft im Alten Testament*, Berlin 1983.
17. The care needed even in dealing with texts about the period of the state appears from the analysis by H.Spieckermann, *Juda unter Assur in der Sargonidenzeit*, Göttingen 1982, 277; if this is true of the period of the state, think what must be the situation for prehistory! For the problems see B.J.Diebner and H.Schult, 'Thesen zu nachexilischen Entwürfen der frühen Geschichte Israels im Alten Testament', *DBAT* 10, 1975, 41-7.
18. W.H.Schmidt, 'Die deuteronomistische Redaktion des Amosbuches', *ZAW* 77, 1965, 168-93, and my *The Prophet Amos*, ET London 1987, 17f.
19. Cf. n.6 above.
20. Hayes and Miller* 1977, 1ff.; G.Garbini, *I Fenici*, ch.7, and 1986* is negative about the reliability of the material reported by Josephus.
21. S.Moscati, *I predecessori d'Israele*, Rome 1956, 54ff.; see now H.Engel, 'Die Siegesstele von Marnepta. Kritischer Überblick über die verschiedenen Versuche historischer Auswertung des Schlussabschnittes', *Bib* 60, 1979, 373-99; G.Fecht, 'Die Israelstele, Gestalt und Aussagen'; E.Hornung, 'Die Israelstele des Merenptah', both in *Fontes atque Pontes. Festschrift H.Brunner*, Wiesbaden 1983, 106-38, 224-39; N.H.Rösel, 'Israel – Gedanken zu seinen Anfängen', *BZ*, NF 25, 1984, 76-91; L.E.Stager, 'Mernepta, Israel and the Sea Peoples', *EI* 18, 1985, 56*-64*; and I.Singer, 'Mernepta's Campaign to Canaan and the Egyptian Occupation of the Southern Coastal Plain of Palestine', *BASOR* 269, 1988, 1-10; J.J.Bimson, 'Merenptah's Israel and Recent Theories of Israelite Origins', *JSOT* 48, 1990, 3-19.
22. Bright*, 144ff.; Otto, 80 n.1 and Lemaire*, 18 n.2. At first Eissfeldt argued that the Egyptian *yšr'r* cannot be identified with *yśr'l*, cf. *CAH* II, XXVIa, ²1965; then he accepted their equivalence, *CAH* II.2, ³1975, 318, 544f., without giving an explanation (this was pointed out by J.M.Sasson).
23. For this work cf. H.L.Strack and M.Stemberger, *Introduction to the Talmud and Midrash*, Edinburgh 1991, 354.
24. *Judges*, 10f.

4. David and His Empire

1. B.J.Diebner, review, *DBAT* 20, 1984, 192-208, esp. 198.
2. L.Rost, *Israel bei den Propheten*, Stuttgart 1937; A.Alt, 'Das Königtum in den Reichen Israel und Juda', *VT* 1, 1951, 2-22: 4, *KS* II, 116-34: 117; R. de Vaux, *Ancient Israel*, London 1961, 96-8; and recently É.Lipiński 1985. However, Z.Kallai, 'Judah and Israel – A Study in Israelite Historiography', *IEJ* 28, 1978, 251-61, defends a substantial unity between Israel and Judah.

3. Cf. my *Judges*, OTL, London and Philadelphia 1987, on Judg.1.27-35. This also applies if this text should prove to be late, cf. n.21 below and 4.5.2.

4. For Mesopotamia cf. e.g. A.L.Oppenheim, *Ancient Mesopotamia*, Chicago 1964, 166, and D.J.Wiseman, *CAH* II.2, ³1975, 443ff.; for Egypt see K.A.Kitchen, *The Third Intermediate Period*, 220-35 and J.Cerný, *CAH* II,2, ³1975, 606ff. E.Leach, *Genesis as Myth and Other Essays*, London 1969, 81, is similarly sceptical and speaks in terms of 'myth history', cf. also 'Anthropological Approaches to the Study of the Bible during the Twentieth Century', in E.Leach and D.A.Aycock (eds.), *Structuralist Interpretations of Biblical Myth*, Cambridge 1983, 7-32: 10, where there is talk of Moses, Saul and David; there is no archaeological evidence for the historicity either of the narrative or of events connected with it.

5. For the motif of the person of humble origins raised to supreme office see the basic study by H.Schult, 'Amos 7,15a und die Legitimation des Aussenseiters', in *Probleme biblischer Theologie – Gerhard von Rad zum 70. Geburtstag*, Munich 1971, 462-78, and, for Amos 7.10-17, my *The Prophet Amos*, ad loc.

6. The 'succession narrative' was 'discovered' and examined by L.Rost, *The Succession to the Throne of David* (1926), Sheffield 1982; cf. also R.N.Whybray, *The Succession Narrative*, SBT II 9, London 1968; E.Würthwein, *Die Erzählung von der Thronnachfolge Davids – theologische oder politische Geschichtsschreibung?*, Zurich 1979; T.Ishida, 'Solomon's Succession to the Throne of David – A Political Analysis', in T.Ishida (ed.), *Studies...*, 175-87. For a predominantly aesthetic and literary analysis cf. J.Fokkelman, *King David*, Assen I, 1981; II, 1986; III, 1991; for Vol.1 of this important work see the reviews by F.Langlamet, *RB* 90, 1983, 100-47, and by me, *Hen* 5, 1983, 268-72. For the earliest sections of the 'history' cf. F.Langlamet, 'David le fils de Jesse', *RB* 89, 1982, 5-47.

7. E.Meyer, *Geschichte des Altertums* II.2, Stuttgart 1931, 281-6: 285f.

8. It seems to me improbable that there is a direct relationship between I Sam. 16.13a and I Kings 1.39a, as Mettinger, 207, argues; both texts deal with the 'anointing' of a king and are similar in that they belong to the same literary genre and describe the same action.

9. As is evident from its vocabulary (A.Rofé, oral communication).

10. Perhaps this is a Canaanite population, in the north-western part of the central hill-country, rather than the semi-nomadic group of the same name in the Sinai desert, cf. my 'Amalek and Ephraim, Ri 5,14', *ZDPV* 98, 1982, 58-62.

11. Similar procedures are attested in Assyria, cf. H.Tadmor, 'History and Ideology in the Assyrian Royal Inscriptions', in F.M.Fales (ed.), *Assyrian Royal Inscriptions – New Horizons*, Rome 1981, 13-33, and 'Autobiographical Apology in the Royal Assyrian Literature', in H.Tadmor and M.Weinfeld (ed.), *History, Historiography and Interpretation*, Jerusalem 1983, 36-57.

12. J.H.Hayes, 'Saul: The Unsung Hero of Israelite History', *Trinity University Studies in Religion* 10, 1975, 37-47; D.M.Gunn, *The Fate of King Saul*, Sheffield 1980, passim; W.L.Humphries, 'From Tragic Hero to Villain: A Study of the Figure of Saul and the Development of I Samuel', *JSOT* 22, 1982, 95-117.

13. N.P.Lemche, 'David's Rise', *JSOT* 10, 1978, 2-29, and Schunck 1992.

14. S.Moscati, 'L'archeologia comincia a parlarci dei Filistei', *Il Messagero di Roma*, 12 February 1965.

15. A.Loffreda, 'Ancora sul ṣinnōr di II Sam.5.8', *LA-SBF* 32, 1982, 59-72, and C.Schäfer-Lichtenberger, *Stadt und Eidgenossenschaft*, 385-96.

16. Ibid., the thesis has been taken up and documented at a literary level by Floss 1987.

17. H.Timm, 'Die Ladeerzählung (I Sam.4-5; II Sam.6) und das Kerygma des deuteronomistischen Geschichtswerkes', *EvTh* 29, 1966, 509-26, and A.F.Campbell, *The Ark Narrative*, Missoula, Mont. 1975; cf. again Soggin in Hayes-Miller* 1977, 368.

18. D.Harden, *The Phoenicians*, London ³1963, 51 and 168f., and S.Moscati, *Il Mondo dei Fenici*, Milan 1966, 33-36. Also B.Peckham, 'Israel and Phoenicia', in *Magnalia Dei... Essays... G.E.Wright*, Garden City, NY 1976, 224-47, who rightly observes that despite the apparent abundance of material, 'the history of their relationships remains elusive'.

19. D.J.McCarthy, *Treaty and Covenant*, Rome ²1978, 143 and passim; Noth*, 187f.

20. M.Delcor, 'Les Kerethim et les Cretois', *VT* 28, 1978, 409-22.

21. R.Smend, 'Das uneroberte Land', in G.Strecker (ed.), *Das Land Israel in biblischer Zeit*, Göttingen 1983, 91-102, now in *GS* II, 217-28.

22. A.Alt, 'Jerusalems Aufstieg' (1925), *KS* III, 243-57; 'Die Staatenbildung der Israeliten in Palästina' (1943), *KS* II, 1-65; 'Das Grossreich Davids', *TLZ* 75, 1950, 213-20, *KS* II, 66-89. Cf. also Soggin in Hayes and Miller *1977, 349-56.

23. Simons**, §317; Aharoni**, analytical index s.v.; this thesis now seems to be confirmed by the excavations of E.D.Oren, 'Ziklag – A Biblical City on the Edge of the Negeb', *BA* 45, 1982, 155-66; V.Fritz, 'Der Beitrag der Archäologie zur historischen Topographie am Beispiel von Ziklag', *ZDPV* 106, 1990 [1991], 78-85. G.Buccellati rightly points out that the place is included in the list of the cities of Judah and Simeon (Josh.16.31; 19.5; I Chron.4.30) so that its legal status is evidently different from that of Jerusalem, which is never included in such lists. We shall be discussing this later.

24. J.A.Soggin, *Joshua*, and R.G.Boling, *Joshua*, Garden City, NY 1982, ad loc.

25. A.Alt, 'Der Stadtstaat Samaria' (1954), *KS* III, 258-302.

26. Cf. my study, 'Der offiziell geförderte Synkretismus während des 10.Jahrhunderts', *ZAW* 78, 1966, 179-204, and 'Der Beitrag des Königtums zur alttestamentlichen Religion', *SVT* 23, 1972, 9-26; also in Hayes-Miller* 1977, 361-3. For the division of the reign of David into two periods, one favourable and the other unfavourable, which probably goes back to Dtr, cf. R.A.Carlson, *David. The Chosen King*, Stockholm 1964; the criterion is also applicable to other kings, like Saul and Solomon. For II Sam.7 cf. now A.Caquot, 'Brève explication de la prophétie de Nathan (2 Sam.7.1-17)', in *Mélanges bibliques et orientaux en l'honneur de M.Henri Cazelles*, AOAT 21, Kevelaer 1981, 51-69, and J.Coppens, 'La prophétie de Nathan – sa portée dynastique', in *Von Ugarit nach Kerala – FS J.P.M.van der Ploeg*, ibid., 1982, 91-100 (bibliography).

27. Cf. my 'La religone fenicia nei dati della Bibbia', in *La religione fenici – matrici orientali e sviluppi occidentali*, Rome 1981, 81-90, and 'Appunti per lo studio della religione d'Israele in epoca preesilica', in *Biblische und judaistische Studien – FS Paolo Sacchi*, Bern 1990, 55-63; cf. also M.Smith, *Palestinian Parties and Politics that Shaped the Old Testament*, London ²1987, ch.2; Garbini, *I Fenici*, ch.5; B.Lang (ed.), *Der einzige Gott*, Munich 1981; id., *Monotheism and*

the Prophetic Minority, Sheffield 1983; id., 'Der vergöttlichte König im polytheistischen Israel', in D.Zeller (ed.), *Menschwerdung Gottes – Vergötterung von Mensch*, Fribourg CH 1988, 37-60. For the archaeological problems see W.G.Dever, 'Material Remains and the Cult in Ancient Israel', in *'The Word of the Lord Shall Go Forth...' Essays D.N.Freedman*, Winona Lake, Ind. 1983, 571-87. Cf. finally N.P.Lemche, 'The Development of the Israelite Religion in the Light of Recent Studies on the Early History of Israel', *SVT* 43, 1991, 97-115.

28. J.H.Tigay, 'You Shall Have No Other God', *Israelite Religion in the Hebrew Inscriptions*, Atlanta 1986, but cf. the very critical review by G.I.Davies, *JTS* NS 39, 1989, 143-6. For recent support of the theory that an originally pure religion of Israel was contaminated see D.Kinet, *Baʿal und Yahwe*, Frankfurt am Main and Bern 1977, passim, esp. 209ff., cf. my review, *Prot* 38, 1983, 110.

5. The Empire under Solomon

1. J.Liver, 'The Book of the Acts of Solomon', *Bib* 48, 1967, 75-101, favours the existence of the 'Book of the Acts..'; G.Garbini, *I Fenici*, Ch.VII and *History** 1988, 31f., does not conceal his own scepticism. Contemporary authors do not reject references to manuscripts, cf. U.Eco, *The Name of the Rose*, London and New York 1983. For the birth of Solomon cf. T.Veijola, 'Salomo – der Erstgeborene Bathsebas', *SVT* 30, 1979, 230-50 = *Gesammelte Studien*, Helsinki and Göttingen 1990, 84-105 and T.Ishida, 'The Role of Nathan the Prophet in the Episode of Solomon's Birth', in *Near Eastern Studies... Takahito Mikasa*, Wiesbaden 1991, 135-8. The former considers Solomon to be the couple's first child not to die, the latter sees Solomon as appointed to the succession from childhood.

2. Cf. recently B.J.D(iebner), review of the 1984 English edition of this work, *DBAT* 20, 1984, 192-208: 199; he speaks of a 'legendary and mythical king of peace' of the 'golden age'. This point is also stressed by G.J.Wightman, 'The Myth of Solomon', *BASOR* 277-8, 1990, 5-22, who denies that there is any evidence of his building activities. But see the criticism by W.G.Dever, 'Of Myths and Methods', ibid., 121-30; also M.Görg, 'Zur Darstellung königlicher Baumassnahmen in Israel und Assur', *BN* 59, 1991, 12-17; R.Körner, 'Märchenmotive bei König Salomo (1 Kön 10-11)', *BN* 62, 1992, 25-31.

3. Y.Yadin, 'New Light on Solomon's Megiddo', *BA* 23, 1960, 62-8, and 'Megiddo of the Kings of Israel', *BA* 33, 1970, 66-96; also 'A Note on the Stratification of Israelite Megiddo', *JNES* 32, 1973, 330. Cf. also J.B.Pritchard, 'The Megiddo Stables', in *Near Eastern Archaeology – FS Nelson Glueck*, Garden City, NY 1970, 268-76. Yadin argues that these were indeed stables, but dates the complex much later. For the palace of the time of Solomon cf. the studies by B.Gregori, 'Considerazioni sui palazzi ḫilani nel periodo salomonico a Megiddo', *Vicino Oriente* 5, 1982, 85-110; D.Ussishkin, 'Schumacher's Shrine in Building 338 at Megiddo', *IEJ* 39, 1989, 149-72; and 'Notes on Megiddo, Gezer, Ashdod and Tel Batash in the Tenth to Ninth Centuries', *BASOR* 277-278, 1990, 71-91; G.I.Davies, 'Solomonic Stables After All?', *PEQ* 120, 1988, 130-41, and A.Kempinski, *Megiddo*, Munich 1989.

4. Y.Yadin, *Hazor: The Head of All Those Kingdoms*, London 1972; id., *Hazor, The*

Rediscovery of a Great Citadel of the Bible, London 1975; also Y.Aharoni, 'The Building Activity of David and Solomon', *IEJ* 24, 1974, 13-16; W.G.Dever (ed.), *Gezer*, Jerusalem I, 1970; II, 1974. Also U.Müller, 'Tor', *BRL²*, 1977, 346-8, with five plans, and Z.Herzog, *Das Stadttor in Israel und in den Nachbarländern*, Mainz 1986.

5. Y.Aharoni, "Arad: Its Inscriptions and Temple', *BA* 31, 1968, 2-32: recently, however, doubts have arisen about the Solomonic dating of the artefact (R.K.Amiran, orally).

6. J.A.Soggin, 'The Ark of the Covenant, Jeremiah 3,16', in P.Bogaert (ed.,) *Le livre de Jérémie*, Louvain 1981, 215-21.

7. For this theme cf. J.C.de Moor, *The Seasonal Pattern in the Ugaritic Myth of Ba'lu*, Kevealer and Neukirchen/Vluyn 1971, 60-113. It is not surprising that, given the circumstances, the reutilization of a pre-existing Canaanite temple has also been suggested (cf. K.Rupprecht, *Der Tempel von Jerusalem*, Berlin 1977). However, interesting though this theory is, it does not seem to be sustainable in the light of the sources in our possession, cf. my review in *BO* 36, 1979, 83ff. Nor is it new; it already appears in Josephus, *BJ* 6, 438, where the building of the temple is attributed to Melchizedek, Gen.14.18, though in a clearly rhetorical context (cf. B.Mazar in *The Jerusalem Post Magazine* of 25 March 1983, 6). Another difficulty arises for some in the dimensions of the temple – 33 x 11 metres – for which there are only later parallels in the region. Does the description have the post-exilic temple in mind? Thus P.Sacchi, 'Israele e le culture circonvicine', *RSLR* 19, 1983, 216-28.

8. Cf. R.Schreiden, 'Les enterprises navales du roi Salomon', *AIPh* 13, 1955, 587-90; G.Bunnens, 'Commerce et diplomatie phéniciennes au temps de Hiram Ier de Tyr', *JESHO* 19, 1976, 10-31; for Garbini this information reflects the time of Uzziah and Jeroboam II, below 10.15.3. For the places and the countries, which are almost all unknown, cf. M.Görg, 'Ophir, Tarschisch und Atlantis. Einige Gedanken zur symbolischen Topographie', *BN* 15, 1981, 76-87; Y.Ikeda, 'King Solomon and his Red Sea Trade', in *Near Eastern Studies. Dedicated to.. Takahito Mikasa*, Wiesbaden 1951, 113-38.

9. G.Ryckmans, 'Ophir', *SDB* VI, 1960, 744-61; V.Christides, 'L'énigme d'Ophir', *RB* 77, 1970, 240-7, for a summary of the discussion. The US Geological Survey suggests *mahd ed-dahab*, a place on the sea between Mecca and Medina, still rich in gold-bearing sands, *BA* 39, 1976, 85.

10. For 'peacocks', W.F.Albright, *Archaeology and the Religion of Israel*, Baltimore ³1953, 212 n.16, proposes 'baboons'.

11. For these problems see the basic study by Y.Ikeda, 'Solomon's Trade in Horses and Chariots in Its International Setting', in T.Ishida (ed.), *Studies...*, 1982 (above n.8), 215-378, though it needs to be corrected. For *muṣri* or *miṣrayim*, cf. BHS and the commentaries, and most recently Garbini* 1988, 31. Cf. also Y.Ikeda, 'King Solomon and His Red Sea Trade', in *Near Eastern Studies... Takahito Mikasa*, Wiesbaden 1991, 132-32, which I was unable to use.

12. H.Donner, 'The Interdependence of Internal Affairs and Foreign Policy during the Davidic-Solomonic Period', in T.Ishida (ed.), *Studies...*, 205-14: 207f., notes the existence of a break between vv.13 and 14 and deduces from this that it is not possible to understand the transfer of this territory in terms of payment or compensation for the debts contracted; however, he does not

offer another more adequate explanation, although he accepts that this 'was hardly a triumph for Solomon's foreign policy'.

13. Donner, ibid. In a study which appeared recently, J.K.Kuan, 'Third Kingdoms 5.1 and Israelite-Tyrian Relations during the Reign of Solomon', *JSOT* 46, 1990, 31-46, has produced noteworthy arguments that in the alliance between Solomon and Hiram, too, the latter was the dominant parter.

14. For Solomon's Egyptian father-in-law cf. S.H.Horn, 'Who Was Solomon's Egyptian Father-in-Law?', *BibRes* 12, 1967, 3-7; K.A.Kitchen (3.7), 1973, 235ff.; H.D.Lance, 'Solomon, Siamun and the Double Ax', in *Magnalia Dei..., Essays...G.E.Wright*, Garden City, NY 1976, 209-26: 222. For the problem of these relations cf. A.Malamat, 'A Political Look at the Kingdom of David and Solomon and its Relations with Egypt', in T.Ishida (ed.), *Studies..*, 189-204; 1983, 83; F.Pintore, *Il matrimonio interdinastico nel Vicino Oriente durante i secoli XV-XIII*, Rome 1978, who on p.78 examines the problems briefly; also S.J.D.Cohen, 'Solomon and the Daughter of Pharaoh: Intermarriage, Conversion and the Purity of Women', *JANESCU* 16-17, 1984-85, 23-37; Garbini* 1988, 27f.; Donner* 1984, 218. We know nothing of a campaign in this region by a Pharaoh of the Twenty-First Dynasty, led against anyone.

15. Garbini*, ibid.

16. For this cf. the basic study by A.Alt, 'Israels Gaue unter Salomo (1913)', *KS* II, 76-89; W.F.Albright, 'The Administrative Division of Israel and Judah', *JPOS* 5, 1925, 17-89. An alternative explanation has been put forward by F.Pintore, 'I Dodici intendenti di Salomone', *RSO* 45, 1970, 177-207, who thinks rather that the purpose of the system was to organize staging posts and provisions for royal convoys. The proposal has not been taken up, even though it does not exclude the previous one; however, it is probable that the 'finance officers' also had this responsibility. Two recent studies confirm Alt's theory: Y.Aharoni, 'The Solomonic Districts', *TA* 3, 1976, 1-16; E.Na'aman, 'The District System in the Time of the United Monarchy', *Zion* 48, 1983, 1-20 (in Hebrew, with an English summary).

17. D.B.Redford, 'Studies in the Relations between Palestine and Egypt during the First Millennium BC', *JAOS* 93, 1973, 3-7; 'Studies on the Ancient Palestinian World', in *FS F.V.Winnett*, Toronto 1972, 141-56.

18. Thus F.M.Cross and G.E.Wright, 'The Boundary and Province List of Judah', *JBL* 75, 1966, 202-26; G.E.Wright, 'The Provinces of Solomon (I Kings 4,7-15)', *EI* 8, 1967, 58*-68*; E.Pintore, 'Dodici intendenti' (n.16). See also my *Joshua*, OTL, London and Philadelphia 1972, ad loc., and R.G.Boling, *Joshua*, AB, Garden City, NY 1982. This explains the reticence of Alt, 'Judas Gaue unter Josia' (1925), *KS* II, 276-88.

19. Cf. the Hebrew dictionaries and *AHw*, 619.

20. G.von Rad, 'The Joseph Narrative and Ancient Wisdom', in *The Problem of the Hexateuch and Other Essays*, Edinburgh 1966 reissued London 1975, 48-56: O.Gerleman, *Das Hohelied*, Neukirchen/Vluyn 1963, 77; C.(Bauer) Kayatz, *Studien zu Proverbien 1-9*, Neukirchen-Vluyn 1966, 135ff.; von Rad revised his own theory in *Wisdom in Israel*, London and Nashville 1972, 41ff. A critical re-examination of the problem has been made by R.N.Whybray, 'Wisdom Literature in the Reigns of David and Solomon', in T.Ishida (ed.), *Studies*, 13-26.

21. R.B.Y.Scott, 'Solomon and the Beginnings of Wisdom in Israel', *SVT* 3, 1965, 262-79.
22. R.N.Whybray, *The Intellectual Tradition in the Old Testament*, Berlin 1974, 15-54: F.W.Golka, 'Die israelitische Weisheitsschule oder "des Kaisers neue Kleider" ', *VT* 33, 1983, 257-70. The issues suggested by K.I.Parker, 'Solomon as Philosopher King? The Nexus of Law and Wisdom in I Kings 1-11', *JSOT* 53, 1992, 75-91, seem improbable to me.

6. The Patriarchs

1. R.E.Clements, *Abraham and David*, SBT II, 5, London 1967, and my *Introduction*, ch.8.2.
2. Cf. W.M.Clark in Hayes-Miller* 1977, 120ff.
3. For a late dating of this text cf, J.Ha, *Genesis 15 – A Theological Compendium of Pentateuchal History*, Berlin 1989.
4. Cf. W.J.Martin, ' "Dischronologized" Narrative in the Old Testament', *SVT* 17, 1969, 179-86.
5. P.A.H.de Boer, 'Egypt in the Old Testament: Some Aspects of an Ambivalent Assessment', in *Selected Studies in Old Testament Exegesis*, ed. C.van Duin, Leiden 1991, 152-67.
6. For this 'Amorite migration' cf. e.g. G.Posener, J.Bottéro and K.M.Kenyon, *CAH* I,2, [3]1971, 532-97 and Bright* 1981, 93 (in favour), and M.Liverani, 'The Amorites', in D.J.Wiseman (ed.), *Peoples from Old Testament Times*, Oxford 1973, 100-33 (against, with convincing arguments); cf. also Liverani's notable study 'Un'ipotesi sul nome di Abramo', *Hen* 1, 1979, 9-18.
7. Cf. again G.Garbini, 'I miti delle origini nell'ideologia ebraica', in *Le origini d'Israele – Convegno dell'Accademia nazionale dei Lincei*, Rome 1987, 29-38.
8. Quite different, and often largely fantastic, are the attempts at locating them by the so-called Genesis Apocryphon, cf. J.A.Fitzmyer, *The Genesis Apocryphon*, Rome [2]1971, ad loc.
9. M.Noth, *A History of Pentateuchal Traditions* (1948), ET Garden City, NJ, reissued Chico, Ca 1982, 112f.
10. Ibid.
11. Cf. A.Rofé, 'La composizione di Genesi 24', *BeO* 23, 1981, 161-5, and 'An Enquiry into the Betrothal of Rebeka', in *Die hebräische Bibel und ihre zweifache Nachgeschichte. FS R.Rendtorff zum 65.Geburtstag*, Neukirchen/Vluyn 1990, 27-39.
12. Cf. the annals of Tiglath-pileser I (c.1116-1078), *ANET*, 275; *TUAT* I, 356ff., and J.Dupont-Sommer, *Les Araméens*, Paris 1949, 17f.; de Vaux, *Early History*, I, 180.
13. Noth, *History of Pentateuchal Traditions* (n.8), 95ff.
14. J.Meinhold, 'Die Gattung der Josephsgeschichte und des Estherbuches: Diasporanovelle, I', *ZAW* 87, 1975, 306-24; II, *ZAW* 88, 1976, 72-93; L.Ruppert, 'Zur neueren Diskussion um die Josephsgeschichte der Genesis', *BZ* NF 33, 1989, 92-7. See further my 'Notes on the Joseph Story', to be published in *Studies for G.W.Anderson*, Edinburgh 1993 (with bibliography).
15. For these semi-nomads see the classical study by J.-L.Kupper, *Les nomades en Mésopotamie au temps des rois de Mari*, Paris 1957. It is impossible to go into detail here, cf. A.Malamat, 'Mari and the Bible', *JAOS* 82, 1962, 143-50, and 'Mari', *BA* 34, 1971, 2-22; also de Vaux, *Early History*, I, 1, iii. T.L.Thompson,

Historicity, chs.III-IV, is very critical. See also N.K.Gottwald, *The Tribes of Yahweh*, Maryknoll and London 1979, 437ff., 465ff. The conclusion by M.A.Morrison, 'The Jacob and Laban Narrative in the Light of Near Eastern Sources', *BA* 46, 1983, 155-64, is to be accepted: 'The story of Jacob and Laban does not contain any of those characteristic details which would allow us to identify it with a particular period' (164).

16. Nomadism and semi-nomadism are forms of life bound up with a mode of production; by contrast the migrant arrives at his destination and settles there, ending the migration. Despite the possibility of formal similarities, the two types are thus clearly distinct.

17. Gottwald, *Tribes of Yahweh* (n.14), 308ff.

18. A.Malamat, 'King Lists of the Old Babylonian Period and Biblical Genealogies', *JAOS* 88, 1968, 163-73; M.D.Johnson, *The Purpose of the Biblical Genealogies*, Cambridge 1969, ²1988, 77ff.; R.R.Wilson, 'The Old Testament Genealogies in Recent Research', *JBL* 94, 1975, 169-90, and *Genealogy and History in the Biblical World*, New Haven and London 1977; T.J.Prewitt, 'Kingship Structures and the Genesis Genealogies', *JNES* 40, 1981, 87-98.

19. Thus Diebner 1975.

20. K.Galling, *Die Erwählungstraditionen Israels*, Giessen 1928, 65ff.

21. H.Gunkel, *Die Genesis*, Göttingen ³1910, Introduction; H.Gressmann, 'Saga und Geschichte in den Patriarchenerzählungen', *ZAW* 30, 1910, 1-34; Galling, *Erwählungstraditionen* (n.19), 9.

22. See the comments by Thompson 1974, 3 n.6.

23. E.g. N.Glueck, *The River Jordan*, New York ²1968, 8f. and passim.

24. W.F.Albright, 'The Israelite Conquest of Palestine in the Light of Archaeology', *BASOR* 74, 1939, 11-23; J.Bright, *Ancient Israel in Recent History Writing*, SBT I, 19, London 1956; G.E.Wright, 'Modern Issues in Biblical Studies: History and the Patriarchs', *ExpT* 71, 1959-60, 292-6 (in discussion in the same issue with G.von Rad). There is a summary of the discussion in my 'Ancient Biblical Traditions and Modern Archaeological Discoveries', *BA* 23, 1960, 95-100; R.de Vaux, 'Methods in the Study of Early Hebrew History', in J.P.Hyatt (ed.), *The Bible and Modern Scholarship*, Nashville and New York 1965, 15-29.

25. G.E.Wright, 'What Archaeology Cannot Do', *BA* 74, 1971, 70-6. For an evaluation of Wright's work cf., W.G.Dever, 'Biblical Theology and Biblical Archaeology – An Appreciation of G.Ernest Wright', *HTR* 73, 1980, 1-15.

26. G.von Rad, *Old Testament Theology* I, ET Edinburgh 1962, reissued London 1975, 105ff.

27. J.A.Soggin, 'Teologia dell'Antico Testamento – dopo Gerhard von Rad', *Prot* 39, 1984, 1-17, and 'Geschichte als Glaubensbekenntnis – Geschichte als Gegenstand wissenschaftlicher Forschung', *TLZ* 110, 1985, 161-72.

28. M.Noth, 'Hat die Bibel doch Recht?', in *FS Günther Dehn*, Neukirchen 1957, 7-22; 'Der Beitrag der Archäologie zur Geschichte Israels', *SVT* 7, 1960, 262-82: 269ff., both in *ABLAK* 1, 17-33, 34-51.

29. Proposals made initially by C.H.Gordon, 'Biblical Customs and the Nuzi Tablets', *BA* 3, 1940, 1-12, then taken up by E.A.Speiser, *Genesis*, AB 1, Garden City 1965, passim. For criticism see T.L.Thompson, chs.III, X; J.Van Seters, passim; W.M.Clark, in Hayes-Miller* 1977, 120ff.

30. Thompson, *Historicity*, ch.II.

31. Ibid.

32. M.Noth, *A History of Pentateuchal Traditions*, passim, and reently C.Wester-mann, *Genesis* II, ET Minneapolis 1985 and London 1986, ad loc.

33. L.Woolley, *Excavations at Ur*, London ³1955.

34. Bright*, 1981, 90f. favours this solution; Herrmann*, 49, is uncertain.

35. C.H.Gordon, 'Abraham and the Merchants of Ura', *JNES* 17, 1958, 28-31; id., 'Abraham of Ur', in *Hebrew and Semitic Studies... G.R.Driver*, Oxford 1963, 77-84, thinks in terms of a Hittite locality by the name of Ur(a) attested in Ugarit, north of Harran, but otherwise unknown (*WUS*, 369: *'ar-II* and *'ari*); the same argument has recently been put forward by G.A.Rendsburg (orally); against this, and with valid arguments, H.W.F.Saggs, 'Ur of the Chaldees', *Iraq* 22, 1960, 200-9, and de Vaux, *Early History**, I, 187ff.: Ur is always connected with Babylonia.

36. W.F.Albright, 'New Light on Early Recensions of the Hebrew Bible', *BASOR* 140, 1956, 27-33: 31f.

37. Most recently de Vaux, *Early History*, I, 182-7.

38. Bright*, 1981, 90 is doubtful but favourably inclined; for T.L.Thompson, associations of this kind 'would constitute a serious error in interpretation', 21ff., 87.

39. de Vaux, *Early History**, I, 183, takes this seriously into consideration, but rejects the proposal.

40. Cf. my *Joshua*, 237ff.

41. Again recently W.C.Van Hattem, 'Once Again: Sodom and Gomorra', *BA* 44, 1981, 87-92, who even suggests locating the whole episode in the Late Bronze Age, third phase.

42. An attempt to find a mention of the five cities of the valley in an unspecified text from Ebla, made by P.Matthiae and G.Pettinato at the General Meeting of the American Schools of Oriental Research, St Louis, Mo, 29 September 1976, has meanwhile proved erroneous, though it has often been repeated. For the communication cf. (D.N.Freedman), 'A Letter to the Reader', *BA* 40, 1977, 2-4, and, recently id., 'Ebla and the Old Testament', in T.Ishida (ed.), *Studies...*, 309-55: 328.

43. There is a synopsis in M.Weippert, *Settlement*, 76-9.

44. An interesting comparison between Idrimi of Alalakh, who fled and for some years took refuge among the ḥapīru, and David fleeing before Saul, has been suggested by G.Buccellati, 'Da Saul a Davide', *BeO* I, 1959, 99-128. For Idrimi see the contribution by various authors in *UF* 13, 1981, 199-290; cf. also M.Liverani, 'Farsi habiru', *Vicino Oriente* 2, 1979, 65-77.

45. For the sources cf. M.Weippert, *Settlement*, 72 n.4.

46. N.K.Gottwald, *The Tribes of Yahweh*, Maryknoll and London 1979, 213-19, 401-9.

47. Ibid., analytical index under 'Converts to'.

48. Albright* 1940, 189, and ²1957, 248.

49. A.Alt, *KS* I, 26 n.2; O.Eissfeldt, *KS* III, 363 and 392 n.4; de Vaux, *Early History**, I, 269; A.Lemaire, 'Les Benē Jacob', *RB* 85, 1978, 321-37; D.R.Hillers, 'Paḥad Yiṣḥāq', *JBL* 1972, 90-2 differs; cf. also H.-P.Müller, review, *ZAW* 66, 1976, 309 and *Monotheismus in Israel*, Bonn 1980, 120; M.Malul, 'More on *paḥad iṣḥaq* (Genesis XXXI 42, 53) and the Oath by the Thigh', *VT* 35, 1985, 192-200.

50. P.Garelli, *Les Assyriens en Cappadocie*, Paris 1963, provides an up-to-date treatment of these matters.

51. *ARM* V, Paris 1952, no.20.

52. *KAI* 216, line 22; cf. also 24, line 16 and 25, line 6.

53. Cf. my *Judges*, ad loc. For the problem of the association of the patriarchs with sacred trees and their sanctuaries see M.Liverani, 'La chêne de Shardanu', *VT* 27, 1977, 212-16.

7. Slavery in Egypt and the Exodus. Moses

1. Noth* 1959, 110ff.; A.Alt, *Die Herkunft der Hyksos in neuer Sicht*, Berlin 1954, *KS* III, 72-98; Bright* 1981, 120.

2. Bright*, 121.

3. Cf. my 'I testi vetero-testamentari sulla conquista della Palestina', *RiBib* 28, 1980, 45-57.

4. M.Noth, *Die israelitischen Personennamen...*, Stuttgart 1928, 63. According to the information collected by J.M.Weinstein, 'The Egyptian Empire. A Reassessment', *BASOR* 241, 1981, 1-28: 17ff., in the late Bronze Age and down to the end of the twelfth century BCE this nominal control will have turned into an actual occupation of the territory; that is quite evident from the many buildings of an Egyptian type attested for the period. It makes even more probable the presence of Egyptian names.

5. Aharoni, *The Land*** 1979, 196, wrongly sees here a quotation of the term *ʿprw*.

6. For different reasons, D.B.Redford, 'Exodus I 11', *VT* 13, 1963, 411-18, and J.J.Bimson, *Redating the Exodus and Conquest*, JSOT-SS 5, Sheffield 1978, 36ff. have objected to this identification. W.Helck, 'Ṯkw und die Ramsesstadt', *VT* 15, 1965, 25-48, responds to Redford; for Bimson cf. my review in *VT* 31, 1981, 98f.

7. Rather than from *muškēnu(m)*, 'cities [built with] forced labour', as E.A.Speiser would prefer: 'The *Muškēnum*', *Or* 27, 1958, 19-28 = *Oriental and Biblical Studies*, Philadelphia 1967, 33-43; but cf. *AHw* II, 684.

8. For the details cf. W.H.Schmidt, *Exodus*, Neukirchen/Vluyn 1974ff., 34ff., with bibliography.

9. M.Noth, *A History of Pentateuchal Traditions* (1948), Englewood Cliffs NJ 1972, reprinted Chico, Ca. 1982, 208-13; G.von Rad, *Genesis*, OTL, London and Philadelphia 1972, 347ff.

10. Von Rad, ibid.; cf. also J.L.Crenshaw, 'Method in Determining Wisdom Influence upon "Historical" Literature', *JBL* 88, 1969, 129-42, and Whybray 1968 and Coats 1973 already cited.

11. Cf. the works cited in the preceding note.

12. A.Alt, 'Erwägungen über die Landnahme der Israeliten in Palästina', *PJB* 35, 1939, 8-63: 61 = *KS* 1, 126-75: 173.

13. A.Alt, 'Hyksos' (n.1), 72-98.

14. Thus still T.J.H.James in the title of his contribution to *CAH* II.1, ³1973; in the text, however, he is much more cautious!

15. The problem of the Hyksos' rise to power and subsequent fall cannot be dealt with here. Cf. D.B.Redford, 'The Hyksos Invasion in History and Tradition', *OR* 39, 1970, 1-51, who stresses that these are not strictly alien elements, and B.Couroyer, 'Les Aamon-Hycsós et les Cananéo-Phéniciens', *RB* 81, 1974, 321-54, 481-523. See also N.K.Gottwald, *The Tribes of Yahweh*, Maryknoll and London 1979, 391-4, and the notes to this section, especially

296, 297. In general see the histories by Noth* 1959, 29-32; de Vaux* I, 75-81; Herrmann*, 19f.

16. Cf. the conclusions, 203ff.

17. G.E.Wright, *Biblical Archaeology*, Philadelphia and London ²1962, 54ff.

18. von Rad, *Genesis* (n.9); de Vaux* I, 291-62; and Wright, *Biblical Archaeology* (n.17).

19. Vergote, *Joseph en Égypte*, 135ff., cites other earlier examples. D.B.Redford, 'Hyksos Invasion', rightly observes that the Joseph story is far less well informed on Egypt than appears at first sight; it even seems to reflect the situation in the court of Judah rather than in the court of Pharaoh. As a *terminus ante quem* he suggests the fifth century BCE.

20. Vergote, *Joseph en Égypte*, 135ff., and *HAL* ³, s.v. with bibliography.

21. J.C.Croatto, 'Abrek "intendent" dans Genèse XLI 43', *VT* 16, 1966, 113-15; E.Lipiński, 'From Karatepe to Pyrgi', *RSF* 2, 1974, 45-61: 46. This translation is mentioned with reservations by de Vaux* I, 297f., cf. also W.Herrmann, 'Zu Gen 41.53', *ZAW* 62, 1950, 321. For the problem in general see M.Ellenbogen, *Foreign Words in the Old Testament*, London 1962, 3-5.

22. *AHw* I,3.

23. Cf. Wright, *Biblical Archaeology* (n.17), 56; S.Herrmann, *Israel in Egypt*, SBT II, 27, 25f.

24. J.A.Wilson in *ANET* suggests 'bedouins', but *šws* is better translated 'shepherd', which is what it denotes. For these people cf. R.Giveon, *Les bédouins Shoushou des documents égyptiens*, Leiden 1971.

25. For the material on this region see S.Yeivin, *The Israelite Conquest of Canaan*, Leiden 1971, 243-64 – appendix D.

26. I do not understand the argument by S.Talmon, ' "400 Jahre" oder "vier Generationen" (Gen.15.13-15): geschichtliche Zeitangaben oder literarische Motive?', in *Die hebräische Bibel und ihre zweifache Nachgeschichte. FS R.Rendtorff zum 65.Geburtstag*, Neukirchen/Vluyn 1990, 13-25.

27. Cf. my *Judges*, 10-12, with bibliography.

28. M.Noth, *Die israelitische Personennamen* (n.4), index; W.F.Albright, 'North-West Semitic Names in a List of Egyptian Slaves from the Eighteenth Century BC', *JAOS* 74, 1954, 222-32; Schmidt, *Exodus* (n.8), 42, who takes seriously the possibility that the midwives were Egyptian (19f.).

29. Cf. above, n.5: the text does not say anything about the compulsory character of the work or about the conscription of whole ethnic groups to it.

30. There is a splendid treatment of the problem of the different versions of the same event within the same political organization by M.Liverani, *Prestige and Interest*, Padua 1990.

31. J.Pedersen, 'Passahfest und Passahlegende', *ZAW* 52, 1934, 161-75; E.Otto, 'Erwägungen zum… Ursprung… des Plagenzyklus' (7.7.4); in a similar form R.Rendtorff, *The Problem of the Process of Transmission in the Pentateuch* (1977), Sheffield 1990, 165, and E.Blum, *Studien zur Komposition des Pentateuch*, Berlin 1990. Blum does not mention Pedersen's work in the bibliography.

32. de Vaux* I, 362.

33. For the problems cf. E.Galbiati, *La struttura letteraria dell'Esodo*, Alba 1956, 111-33; U.Cassuto, *A Commentary on the Book of Exodus*, Jerusalem 1967, 92ff.

34. As G.Fohrer, 1954, 75ff., rightly pointed out. Recent examples are K.A.Kitchen, *Ancient Orient and Old Testament*, London 1966, 157; A.Ademollo 1976.

35. M.Noth, *Exodus*, OTL, London and Philadelphia 1962, 102-19.
36. Noth* 1959, 112.
37. For the traditional dating cf. my *Introduction*, 1979, 104f.; for a late dating cf. F.Foresti, 'Composizione e redazione deuteronomistica in Ex.15.1-18', *Lateranum* 48, 1982, 41-69, and my *Introduction*, ³1989, 79.
38. H.Cazelles, 'Moïse', *SDB* V, 1957, 1308-37: 1325, and Aharoni, *The Land***, 199-201, who speaks of places 'all situated in the north-eastern part of the Nile Delta'.
39. Against Noth* 1959, 112, and L.H.Grollenberg, *Atlas of the Bible*, London 1956, map 9.
40. M.Dothan, 'The Exodus in the Light of Archaeological Survey in Lake Sirbonis', in *Proceedings of the Fifth World Congress of Jewish Studies, Jerusalem 1969*, Vol.I, Jerusalem 1973, 18-20 (in Hebrew, with an English summary).
41. G.E.Wright and F.L.Filson, *The Westminster Historical Atlas of the Bible*, Philadelphia and London ²1956, map V, reproduced in Bright* 1981, map III. In both cases the starting point is the eastern region of the Delta.
42. Noth* 1959, 117.
43. Cf. n.40 above.
44. Noth, *Exodus* (n.35), 140.
45. Ibid., 133.
46. The map in Aharoni, *The Land***, 1979, n.13.
47. For the problem cf. my *Judges*, on 1.16.
48. See G.I.Davies, *The Way...* (above 7.9) and M.Har-el, *The Sinay Journeys* (above 7.9), for other suggestions of places and their respective merits, especially the traditional location.
49. Aharoni** 1979, 198, however, favours the traditional location with arguments of substantial weight.
50. Aharoni**, ibid., and de Vaux* I, 426-39.
51. Noth*, 130f.; *Exodus*, 155f.; Bright* 1981, 124, and J.Jeremias, ad loc.
52. E.Anati, *La montagna di Dio: Har Karkom*, Milan 1986 (English NY 1986).
53. Aharoni, *The Land***, 199-201.
54. Noth, 'Wallfahrtsweg' (7.9.7), 6/46; Aharoni, *The Land***, 200f., differs.
55. G.von Rad, 'The Form-critical Problem of the Hexateuch', in *The Problem of the Hexateuch and Other Essays*, Edinburgh 1966, 1ff.; *Old Testament Theology* I, 198ff.; Noth, *Exodus*, ad loc., and 1959*, 136.
56. Cf. my *Judges*, ad loc.
57. Noth* 1959, 135; *Pentateuchal Traditions*, 160; see also Cazelles, 'Moïse' (n.38), 1319.
58. J.Bright, *Early Israel in Recent History Writing*, SBT I 19, London 1956, 19, 52ff. and 105ff.: 109; id. 1981*, 126.
59. Noth*, 136.
60. Ibid. The position of W.Eichrodt, *Theology of the Old Testament*, London and Philadelphia I, 289ff., is similar.
61. E.Osswald, *Mose...*, passim, and 'Moses', in *RGG*³, 1959, IV, 1151.
62. W.H.Schmidt, 'Gott II, AT', in *TRE* XIII, 1984, 608-26: 614ff. For the problem cf. B.J.Diebner, *DBAT* 20, 1984, 192-208: 200f.
63. Bright* 1981, 128f.

8. The Settlement in Canaan

1. But see the alternative identification, supported by good arguments, in Bimson, *Redating the Exodus and Conquest*, 215ff.
2. R.Smend, 'Das Gesetz und die Völker', in *Probleme biblischer Theologie... FS G.von Rad*, Munich 1971, 494-509.
3. G.von Rad and, recently, W.Kevers, cf. the following bibliography.
4. E.A.Speiser, 'Ethnic Movements in the Near East in the Second Millennium', *AASOR* 13, 1932-33, 29ff.; R.T.O'Callaghan, *Aram Naharaim*, Rome 1948, 54 n.8.
5. Cf. Soggin, *Judges*, ad loc.
6. A.Malamat, 'The Danite Migration and the Pan-Israelite Exodus-Conquest: A Biblical Narrative Pattern', *Bib* 51, 1960, 1-16. For the variant in Joshua cf. J.Strange, 'The Inheritance of Dan', *ST* 20, 1966, 120-39.
7. For the stele of Mesha cf. my *Introduction*, 1989, 553ff., and II Kings 1.1; 3.1ff. (below 10.10.12).
8. For these texts cf. my *The Prophet Amos*, London 1987, 2ff., 109ff.
9. Noth*, 1959, 62ff. and Aharoni**, *The Land*, 278 n.55.
10. C.L'Heureux, 'The Ugaritic and Biblical Refaim', *HTR* 67, 1974, 265-74; J.C.de Moor, 'Rāpi'ūma – Rephaim', *ZAW* 88, 1976, 323-45; M.Dietrich – O.Loretz – J.Sanmartin, 'Die ugaritischen Totengeister *rou(m)* und die biblische Rephaim', *UF* 8, 1976, 46-52.
11. de Vaux* 1978, II, 567.
12. Cf. H.Donner, 'The Blessing of Issachar (Gen 49.14-15) as a Source for the Early History of Israel', in *Le origini d'Israele, Convegno dell'Accademia Nazionale dei Lincei*, Rome 1987, 53-63.
13. Cf. Coote and Whitelam, *Emergence of Early Israel* (above, 2.1), ch.2.
14. W.F.Albright, *The Archaeology of Palestine*, Harmondsworth ³1962, 113, 210; R.de Vaux, *Ancient Israel*, London 1961, 240; C.C.McCown, 'Cistern', *IDB* I, 1962, 631; R.D.H(illers), 'Cistern', *EJ* V, 1971, 578f.; S.M.Paul and W.G.Dever, *Biblical Archaeology*, Jerusalem 1973, analytical index, For the problem of the settlement in the hill country see Appendix I below, II.4.
15. They have been opposed, with good arguments, by V.Fritz, 'The Conquest in the Light of Archaeology', in *Proceedings of the Eighth World Congress of Jewish Studies, Jerusalem 1981, 1*, Jerusalem 1982, 15-21, who considers them inadequate: in fact, in the present state of research we know little or nothing of the development of the settlement: cf. A.Alt, 'Settlement', 150ff.; id., 'Erwägungen...', 137ff.
16. For the sociological problems see the study by W.Thiel, 'Die Anfänge von Landwirtschaft und Bodenrecht in der Frühzeit Altisraels', *AOF* 7, 1980, 127-41 (though it is not very up-to-date on American studies).
17. S.Moscati, 'Chi furono i Semiti?', *ANLM* VIII. 8, 1957, 35ff.
18. C.Schäfer-Lichtenberger, *Stadt und Eidgenossenschaft im Alten Testament*, Berlin 1983, 187-90.
19. I suggested something of this kind, though only in a very embryonic form, as early as 1962.
20. W.Thiel, *Die soziale Entwicklung Israels in vorstaatlicher Zeit*, Berlin and Neukirchen 1980, 90ff., who considers this conception a 'fantasy'. For other criticisms cf. ibid., 10. Mendenhall has recently criticized Gottwald's theories, quite harshly, though it is not easy to understand why.

21. Gottwald, *The Tribes*, 555ff. The contrast between the city and the rural world was already pointed out by Weber in 1921; for details see C.Schäfer-Lichtenberger, *Stadt* (n.18), 40ff. Here and there Gottwald recognizes his own debt to Weber, even if Weber never speaks of revolts.
22. Ibid., 700ff.
23. Liverani, *Introduction*, and H.J.Franken, *CAH* II.2, ³1975, 331ff.
24. There is a survey in Weippert, 63-102.
25. Ibid., 102.
26. Ibid., 103.
27. Cf. my introduction, Excursus I, and the bibliography there.
28. C.H.J.de Geus, *The Tribes of Israel*, Assen 1976; O.Bächli, *Amphikytonie im Alten Testament*, Basel 1977; J.W.Rogerson, *Anthropology and the Old Testament*, Oxford 1978, 8-101. The problem is discussed in detail by Gottwald, *Tribes*, passim. Cf. also Auld, above 8.9.
29. 'A Society for the accurate and systematic investigation of the archaeology, topography, geology and physical geography, natural history, manners and customs of the Holy Land, *for biblical illustration*' (my italics).
30. G.Pettinato, P.Matthiae et al., *Missione archeologica italiana in Siria IV*, Rome 1972, 1-37.
31. Cf. my *Introduction*, Appendix II.
32. These can be found in the Rockefeller Museum and the Museum of Israel in Jerusalem; in the Louvre in Paris; and in the British Museum in London, to mention only some of the main collections, as well as many lesser public and private collections.
33. Cf. my 'Gerico – anatomia d'una conquista', *Prot* 29, 1974, 193-23 (French *RHPR* 57, 1977, 1-17).
34. Bright* 1981, 137ff., in a much reduced form.
35. Cf. J.M.Miller, in Hayes-Miller* 1977, ch. IV, 262ff.
36. R.de Vaux, 'A Comprehensive View of the Settlement of the Israelites in Canaan', *Perspective* XII, 1-2, 1971, 23-33, and II*, 658ff.; M.Liverani, review, *OA* 15, 1976, 145-59.
37. Already M.Noth*, 1959, 53-68 and now A.G.Auld, 'Tribal Terminology in Joshua and Judges', in *Le origini d'Israele – Convegno dell'Accademia nazionale dei Lincei*, Rome 1987, 87-98.
38. E.Sellin, *Gilgal*, Leipzig 1917, who speaks of a 'Yahweh coalition' and of 'federation'; Weber* 1921, passim; A.Alt, 'Eine galiläische Ortsliste in Jos.19', *ZAW* 45, 1926, 39-81: 75ff. (not in KS). For the problem as seen by Noth shortly before his death cf. O.Bächli, 'Nachtrag zum Thema Amphiktyonie', *TZ* 28, 1972, 356; de Geus, *Tribes of Israel* (n.28).
39. Bächli, 'Nachtrag' (n.38).
40. G.von Rad, 'Problem', 1ff., and *Studies in Deuteronomy*, SBT I 9, 1953. Both studies have rightly remained famous.
41. Cf. my 'Zur Entwicklung des alttestamentlichen Königtums', *TZ* 15, 1969, 401-18.
42. Bright* 1981, Ch.IV, esp. 162ff.
43. So far G.E.Mendenhall and N.K.Gottwald, *Tribes*, index s.v. 'Covenant'.
44. M.Noth, *History of Pentateuchal Traditions* (ch.6.n.8); *The Deuteronomistic History* (1957), Sheffield ²1991.
45. E.W.Nicholson, *Deuteronomy and Tradition*, Oxford and Philadelphia 1967, 48ff.

46. Buccellati, *Cities and Nations*, 111ff.
47. Ibid.
48. Cf. my *Judges*, ad loc, and 'Bemerkungen zum Deboralied, Richter Kap.5', *TLZ* 106, 1981, 625-39. For the significance of the number twelve cf. de Geus, *Tribes of Israel* (n.28), 117.
49. Buccellati, *Cities and Nations*, 127 and 195-200, who rightly disagrees with my earlier studies.
50. C.Schäfer-Lichtenberger, *Stadt und Eidgenossenschaft* (n.18), 333f., 425f., has recently re-examined the problem of relations between Israel in the period before the state and 'segmentary' societies, cf. earlier F.Crüsemann, *Der Widerstand gegen das Königtum*, Neukirchen 1978, 200-9f., and even earlier A.Malamat, 'Tribal Societies; Biblical Genealogies and African Lineage Systems', *Archives européens de sociologie* 14, 1973, 126-36. This is clearly a line of research worth pursuing, given the many analogies we find between the organizations of the two groups, which are hardly a coincidence, in view of the distances.

9. The Time of the Judges

1. J.A.Soggin, 'Das Amt der "Kleinen Richter" in Israel', *VT* 30, 1980, 245-8.
2. Weber*, 1921, 52ff., 92ff.; *Wirtschaft und Gesellschaft*, Tübingen ⁴1956, I, 140ff., II, 662ff.
3. L.Perlitt, *Bundestheologie im Alten Testament*, WMANT 36, Neukirchen 1969, 7ff., formulated this theory in a now classic way.
4. W.Richter, *Die Bearbeitungen des 'Ritterbuches' in der deuteronomistischen Epoche*, BBB 21, Bonn 1964; and my *Judges*, 8ff., 10ff.
5. A.D.H.Mayes, 'The Historical Context of the Battle against Sisera', *VT* 19, 1969, 353-60; *Israel in the Period of the Judges*, London and Philadelphia 1974, ch.3.
6. This last theory has been proposed by Aharoni**, 1979, 263.
7. See the discussion by H.-W.Jüngling, *Plädoyer für das Königtum*, AnBibl 84, 1981, 80.
8. This is a figure which denotes a sizeable quantity and therefore should not be taken literally, cf. Judg.1.7; II Kings 10.1 and the inscription of Panamuwwa II (*KAI*, 215; *SSI*, II, 14, line 3) from the second half of the eighth century BCE. For the theme cf. F.C.Fensham, 'The Numeral Seventy in the Old Testament and the Family of Jerubbaal, Ahab, Panamuwwa and Athirat', *PEQ* 109, 1977, 113-15.
9. Cf. my 1972 article, which needs substantial revision twenty-five years from the time it was delivered (at the end of the 1960s).
10. Cf. Soggin 1967.
11. The general tendency is to identify the two places, most recently Aharoni** 1979, 264ff., and Fritz. I have explained my position in Soggin 1967 and in *Judges*, ad loc.; cf. recently 1988; Na'aman 1986 has independently reached analogous results. For the character of the artefact cf. my *Genesi 1-11*, Genoa 1991, 279.
12. G.E.Wright, *Shechem. The Biography of a Biblical City*, New York 1965, 101ff., 122, with an exhaustive account of the excavations and a bibliography.
13. There is an attempt in Aharoni** 1979, 265, but without giving the coordinates.

14. For details cf. my *Judges*, ad loc.
15. For details and various attempts at a solution cf. S.Mittman, 'Aroer, Minnith and Abel Keramin', *ZDPV* 85, 1969, 63-75.
16. Thus rightly M.Noth, *Das Buch Josua*, Tübingen ²1953, 14 and on Josh.19.40-29.
17. For Dan's conquest of its own territory cf. above 8.2.7.
18. This is the theory put forward by O.Eissfeldt, 'Der geschichtliche Hintergrund der Erzählung von Gibeas Schandtat (Richter 19-21)', in *FS Georg Beer zum 70.Geburtstag*, Stuttgart 1935, *KS* II, 64-80, and now followed by many scholars. The actual motive is among those that Momigliano has called 'silly causes' for a war, cf. 'Some Observations on the Causes of War in Ancient Historiography' (1958), in *Secondo contributo alla storia degli studi classici*, Rome 1984, 13-27. There is other material in my *Judges*, where I draw attention to the scepticism already expressed by Wellhausen.

10. The Two Kingdoms to the Time of the Assyrian Invasions

1. The genealogies of Genesis pose similar problems to the reader, cf. my *Genesis 1-11*, Genoa 1991, 109, 184f.
2. Thus the basic study by Alt 1951, followed by Soggin 1967 and some others.
3. The contrary has been demonstrated by Buccellati 1967, 195-212.
4. Thus also Soggin 1967, 138; however, meanwhile the matter has proved very doubtful.
5. P.Welten, *Geschichte und Geschichtsdarstellung in den Chronikbüchern*, WMANT 42, Neukirchen 1973, 11-15; V.Fritz, 'The "List of Rehoboam's Fortresses" in 2 Chr.11.5-12 – A Document from the Time of Josiah', *EI* 15, 1981, 46*-53*. The late character of the list had already been pointed out by G.Beyer, 'Beiträge zur Territorialgeschichte von Südwestpalästina im Altertum, I: Das Festungssystem Rehabeams', *ZDPV* 54, 1931, 113-34. For other proposals cf. N.Na'aman, 'Hezekia's Fortified Cities and the LMLK Stamps', *BASOR* 261, 1986, 5-2; Y.Garfinkel, '2 Chr 11.5-10, Fortified City List and the LMLK Stamps', *BASOR* 271, 1988, 69-73; but cf.N.Na'aman, '2 Chronicles 11:5-10 – A Reply to Y.Garfinkel', ibid., 74ff.
6. Cf. the attempts by Cross 1972, 36-42 (but cf. the comments by É.Lipiński, *VT* 25, 1975, 553-61) and Puech 1981, 544-62.
7. G.E.Wright, *Biblical Archaeology*, Philadelphia and London ²1962, 148 (with illustrations), and H.Donner* 1977, 391.
8. Alt, 'Das Königtum' (above 10.1.3), followed by Donner* 1977, 391, and 1986, 250.
9. For this topic see the important but little-quoted work by H.-D.Hoffmann, *Reform und Reformen*, Zurich 1980.
10. J.Strange, 'Joram, King of Israel and Judah', *VT* 25, 1975, 191-201, and Miller and Hayes* 1986, 280-4; Garbini* 1988, ch.3 (i).
11. Cf. H.Tadmor, 'The Historical Inscription of Adad Nirari III', *Iraq* 35, 1973, 141-50: 149. However, Noth* 1959, 247 n.2, suggested 'of the house of Omri'.
12. For the difficulties which also arise on the level of interpreting the biblical data (chronological, geographical and ideological), cf. now E.A.Knauf, 'From History to Interpretation', in D.V.Edelman (ed.), *The Fabric of History*, Sheffield 1991, 26-64, esp. 58ff.

13. S.Page, 'A Stela of Adad Nirari III and Nergal ereš from Tell al Rimah', *Iraq* 30, 1968, 139-63.
14. For further details cf. my 'Amos VI 13-14 und I.3 auf dem Hintergrund der Beziehungen zwischen Israel und Damaskus im 9. und 8.Jahrhundert', in *Near Eastern Studies in Honor of W.F.Albright*, Baltimore and London 1971, 433-41, and my *The Prophet Amos*, London 1987, 1f., 110f..
15. G.Garbini, 'I sigilli del regno d'Israele', *OA* 21, 1982, 163-76 and *1988.
16. Noth* 159, 238 n.4; Donner* 1977, 395, and 1986, 256, seem doubtful, while Aharoni** 1979, 345, is favourable. For the southern frontier cf. C.Meyers, 'Kadesh Barnea: Juda's Last Outpost', *BA* 39, 1976, 148-51.
17. For the so-called 'leprosy' cf. E.V.Hulse, 'The Nature of Biblical Leprosy', *PEQ* 107, 1975, 87-105 (the definitive study on the medical aspects of the disease). For the texts cf. T.Seidl, *Tora für den "Aussatz" Fall*, St Ottilien 1982, and the various encyclopaedias. For the problem in the region cf. J.V.Kinnier-Wilson, 'Leprosy in Ancient Mesopotamia', *RA* 60, 1966, 47-59 and 'Medicine in the Land and Times of the Old Testament', in T.Ishida (ed.), *Studies...*, 337-65: 354 and 363ff.
18. For these prophets see my *Introduction to the Old Testament*, London and Philadelphia ³1989.

11. The Assyrian Invasions

1. The two names could seem different for someone who did not know Hebrew and Aramaic: in reality the guttural in the Accadian *raḥyānu* transcribes the Aramaic *'ayin*, which in Hebrew is represented as *tsade*.
2. *ANET*, 282f. and *TUAT* I, 370f.; cf. also D.J.Wiseman, 'The Historical Inscriptions from Nimrud', *Iraq* 13, 1951, 21-6.
3. Cf. my 'Ancient Israel – An Attempt at a Social and Economic Analysis of the Available Data', in *Text and Context..., Studies.. F.C.Fensham*, Sheffield 1988, 201-8: 202f.
4. Cf. n.2 above.
5. Cf. W.F.Albright, 'The Son of Tabeel (Isaiah 7:6)', *BASOR* 140, 1955, 34f.; B.Mazar, 'The Tobiads', *IEJ* 7, 1957, 137-45, 229-38, a theory accepted by Aharoni** 1979, 370. Levine 1972 mentions a certain Tubail, king of Tyre, who appears in a list of kings made subject by Tiglath-pileser, and on the basis of this list A.Vanel 1975 has suggested that Tabeel should be identified with him; however, this proposal has not met with any following.
6. R.Borger, 'Das Ende des ägyptischen Feldherrn Sib'e' = Sō', *JNES* 19, 1960, 49-53; H.Goedicke, 'The End of "So, King of Egypt" ', *BASOR* 171, 1963, 64-6; E.Krauss, 'Sō, König von Ägypten – Ein Deutungsvorschlag', *MDOG* 110, 1978, 49-54.
7. Tadmor 1958 puts forward the hypothesis that there will have been two Assyrian campaigns against Samaria, the first under Shalmaneser V in 722 and the second under Sargon II in 720; the latter will have succeeded in occupying the city definitively.

12. The Kingdom of Judah to the End of the Babylonian Exile

1. Cf. J.A.Wilson, *The Culture of Ancient Egypt*, Chicago 1951, 294ff.
2. Albright* 1957, 314ff.

3. Y.Aharoni, 'The Horned Altar of Beer Sheba', *BA* 1974, 2-6; Y.Yadin, 'Beer Sheba: The High Place Destroyed by King Josiah', *BASOR* 222, 1976, 5-18.

4. There is an interesting attempt to rescue the historicity of King Hezekiah's reform in Cogan and Tadmor 1988, 219ff.

5. Cf. H.Tadmor, 'Philistia under Assyrian Rule', *BA* 29, 1966, 86-102.

6. For the system of water supply in Jerusalem see now R.Wenning and E.Zenger, 'Die verschiedenen Systeme der Wassernutzung in südlichen Jerusalem und die Bezugnahme darauf in biblischen Texten', *UF* 14, 1982, 279-94 (bib.!). The identification of *tell ed-duweir* with the biblical Lachish has been put in doubt by G.W.Ahlström, 'Tell ed-Duweir: Lachish or Libnah', *PEQ* 15, 1983, 103f.

7. Thus W.F.Albright from the 1930s onwards, cf. 'The History of Palestine and Syria', *JQR* 24, 1933-34, 363-76; id., *The Biblical Period. From Abraham to Ezra*, ²1973; thus still Bright* 1981, 298f. The commentaries by Wildberger and Kaiser show that the texts represent a late stage of the tradition; cf. also Garbini 1981. An extreme attempt to salvage the credibility of the narrative appears in K.A.Kitchen, 'Egypt, the Levant and Assyria in 701 BC', in *Fontes atque Pontes. FS H.Brunner*, Wiesbaden 1983, 143-50. There is a list of those who support a second Assyrian expedition in Bright* 1981, 298 n.4: Nicholson, de Vaux and Horn. In the first 1964 edition of his commentary Gray accepts it, but not in ²1970. S.Timm, *Moab zwischen den Mächten*. Wiesbaden 1989, 355, has recently proposed the year 703/702 instead of 701.

8. Thus again W.von Soden, 'Sanherib vor Jerusalem, 701 v.Chr.', in *Antike und Universalgeschichte. FS E.Strei*, Münster 1972, 43-51: 45, now in *Bibel und alter Orient*, Berlin 1985, 149-57.

9. Cf. my *Introduction*, ch.50; Ehrlich; Bright* 1981, 311; and Oded in Hayes and Miller* 1977, 454f.

10. Y.Aharoni, 'Arad, Its Inscriptions and Temple', *BA* 31, 1968, 2-32, and 'Trial Excavations at the "Solar Shrine" at Lachish', *IEJ* 18, 1968, 157-69; these studies indicate the existence of a temple at Arad dated to the time of Solomon, while there is evidence of temples in Lachish and Elephantine (Egypt) in the post-exilic period; for the latter cf. below 13.11.6.

11. F.Foresti, 'Storia della redazione di Dtn 16,18 – 18,22 e le sue connessioni con l'opera storia deuteronomistica', *Teresianum* 39, 1988, 1-199: 99f., cf. 104ff.

12. Noth* 1959, 278f.; Herrmann*, 271f.; and Gunneweg* 1989, 121f. have doubts.

13. Garbini 1988 rightly notes a remarkable confusion in the texts here.

14. W.H.Shea, 'Adon's Letter and the Babylonian Chronicle', *BASOR* 223, 1976, 61-4; B.Porten, 'The Identity of King Adon', *BA* 44, 1981, 36-52.

15. É.Lipiński, 'The Egypto-Babylonian War in the Winter 601-600', *AION* 32, 1972, 235-41.

16. Jehoiakin lived at court with a personal entourage and was pardoned on the accession to the throne of Nebuchadnezzar's successor (cf. below 12.9). He remained at court as a guest but could not return home. The relevant Babylonian texts were examined by E.Weidner, 'Jojachin, König von Juda, in babylonischen Keilinschrifttexten', in *Mélanges syriens offerts à M.René Dussaud*, Paris 1929, II, 923-35.

17. Cf. S.Moscati, *L'epigrafia ebraica antica*, Rome 1951, 61.

18. This is a late concept in formulation, but probably pre-exilic in its roots, cf.

O.Carena, *Il resto d'Israele*, Bologna 1985; however, J.Hausmann, *Israels Rest*, Stuttgart 1987, is more cautious.

19. Cf. my article 'Profezia ed apocalittica nel Giduaesimo postesilico', *RiBib* 30, 1982, 161-73.
20. W.Zimmerli, 'Planungen für den Wiederaufbau nach der Katastrophe von 587', *VT* 18, 1968, 229-55, *Gesammelte Aufsätze* II, 165-91, and G.G.Macholz, 'Noch einmal: Planungen für den Wiederaufbau nach der Katastrophe von 587', *VT* 19, 1969, 322-52. See also M.Greenberg, 'The Design and Themes of Ezechiel's Program of Restoration', *Int* 38, 1984, 181-208, and S.Niditch, 'Ezechiel 40-48 in a Visionary Context', *CBQ* 48, 1986, 208-24.
21. See my 'Bilinguismo o trilinguismo nell'Ebraismo postesilico', in A.Ceresa-Gastaldo (ed.), *Il bilinguismo degli antichi*, Genoa 1991, 83-94.
22. W.F.Albright, *The Biblical Period* (above n.7), 110 n.180; similarly Weinberg 1971 and K.M.Kenyon, *Jerusalem*, London and New York 1967, 78-107.

13. Under the Persian Empire

1. S.Smith, *Babylonian Historical Texts Relating to the Capture and Downfall of Babylon*, London 1924.
2. J.A.Soggin, 'Bilinguismo o trilinguismo nell'Ebraismo postesilico', in A.Ceresa-Gastaldo (ed.), *Il bilinguismo degli antichi*, Genoa 1991, 83-94.
3. See my *Introduction*, chs 42 and 43, and Williamson.
4. Ibid., chs. 26, 27, 28, 29, 30.
5. Ibid., 53.3; Williamson, and Garbini* 1988, ch.13.
6. Ibid., Appendix II.1-2.
7. I cannot go into details here about the organization of the Persian state and public administration; see A.T.Olmstead, *History of the Persian Empire*, Chicago 1948 (with bibliography), and O.Bucci, 'L'attività legislativa del sovrano achemenide e gli archivi reali persiani', *RIDA* III, 25, 1978, 11-93; it is a pity that this important study treats the biblical texts uncritically.
8. O.Kaiser, *Introduction to the Old Testament*, ET Oxford 1975, 180f., who quotes G.Hölscher, *HSAT* II, Tübingen ⁴1923, 419ff. For 4Q 117 cf. E.Ulrich, 'The Biblical Manuscripts from Qumran, Cave 4. A Progress Report on their Publication', *RQ* 14, 1989, 149-232: 151 and 178; also Blenkinsopp, 1989, 71f. It seems that 4Q117 confirms the Massoretic text against III Ezra.
9. W.F.Albright, 'The Date and Personality of the Chronicler', *JBL* 40, 1921, 104-24: 108ff.; however, the suggestion is earlier and goes back to E.Meyer, *Die Entstehung des Judenthums*, Halle 1896, 77.
10. For the term cf. Alt 1934, 24/333 n.2. How complex the problem is also appears from the recent study by Sacchi 1989; in his view a form of monarchy will have continued to exist in Judaea in the early post-exilic period and Sheshbazzar and Zerubbabel will have been both kings and governors; they will then have been overthrown by a plot arranged by the priesthood, perhaps even after a short civil war (cf. Zech 12), in the reign of Darius I. There is much in favour of the theory; similarly Bianchi 1991.
11. Cf. my *The Prophet Amos*, London 1987, 127ff.
12. Cf. my *Introduction*, chs 26, 27.
13. In III Ezra 2.8 we read that he was προστάης τῆς 'Ιουδαῖ, which Sacchi* 1976 wants to correct to προστάτης τῶν 'Ιουδαῖν, cf. Josephus, *Antt.* 11.31, who

calls him Ἰουδαίων ἡγέμων, while Ezra 6.7 mentions *peḥah yᵉhudaïye*, which is not to be corrected, as is usually done; however, cf. also Sacchi 1989.

14. Olmstead, *History* (n.7), 142; cf. most recently A.S.van der Woude, 'Serubbabel und die messianischen Erwartungen des Propheten Sacharja', *ZAW* 100 (1988 supplement), 138-56, and Sacchi 1989.

15. See my *Introduction*, ch. 27.2-3.

16. P.D.Hanson, *The Dawn of Apocalyptic*, Philadelphia 1975, 348-52, differs; however, he did not yet know the material published by Avigad in 1976.

17. For a criticism cf. already M.Noth 1959*, 321, and M.Smith, *Palestinian Parties and Politics that Shaped the Old Testament*, New York 1971, 193ff. For the reading *pḥr*, 'vassal', which is no longer possible, cf. F.M.Cross, 'Judaean Stamps', *EI* 9, 1969, 20*-7* and Williamson 1988, 71 n.10.

18. For this material cf. G.Garbini, 'Nuovi documenti epigrafici dalla Palestina', *Hen* 1, 1979, 396-400, and 'La "storia d'Israele" ', *Hen* 5, 1983, 243-55; Stern 1982, 245-8, and *CHJ* I, 72; J.D.Purvis in Shanks* 1988, 254 n.33, and recently Blenkinsopp 1989, who points out the uncertain character of the information in question; this was already indicated by McEvenue 1981, 361ff.

19. The papyrus is published in *ANET*, 492, and *TUAT* I, 255.

20. Soggin, *Introduction*, ch.30.

21. W.F.Albright, 'Dedan', in *Geschichte und Altes Testament – FS A.Alt*, Tübingen 1953, 1-12: 4ff. proposed the reading *ṭōbīyāh wᵉʿebed hāʾammōnī*, thus presupposing another Persian governor in Transjordan: this does not seem possible, even if F.M.Cross 1975 considers the proposal 'very attractive'. So Tobias came from a family which worshipped YHWH, and he was governor of Transjordan.

22. Cf. I.Rabinowitz, 'Aramaic Inscriptions of the Fifth Century BCE from a North-Arabian Shrine in Egypt', *JNES* 15, 1956, 1-9, and W.J.Dumbrell, 'The Tell Maskhuta Bowl and the "Kingdom of Qedar in the Persian Period" ', *BASOR* 203, 1971, 133-44.

23. Cf. my *Introduction*, ch.43.3, and Fohrer* 1982, 208ff.

24. Ibid., ch.43, and Widengren in Hayes and Miller* 1977, 535; Fohrer* 1982, 211f.

25. See J.A.Emerton, 'Did Ezra Go to Jerusalem in 428 B.C.?', *JTS* NS 17, 1966, 1-19.

26. There is a list in Soggin, *Introduction*, ch.43.3; cf. also Widengren* 1977, 535; Fohrer* 1982, 211ff.

27. E.Renan, *Histoire du peuple d'Israël*, IV, Paris 1893, 96-106. The expression 'Middle Judaism' was recently created by G.Boccaccini, *Middle Judaism. Jewish Thought 300 BCE to 200 CE*, Minneapolis 1991, and seems appropriate to me.

28. C.C.Torrey, *The Composition and Historical Value of Ezra-Nehemiah*, Giessen 1896, and id., *Ezra Studies*, Chicago 1910.

29. G.Hölscher, *Geschichte der israelitisch-jüdischen Religion*, Giessen 1922.

30. P.Höffken, 'Warum schwieg Jesus Sirach über Esra?', *ZAW* 87, 1975, 184-202: C.T.Begg, 'Ben Sirach's Non-Mention of Ezra', *BN* 42, 1988, 14-18, criticizes both him and Garbini.

31. For an explanation of this prohibition, which should not be understood in an ethnic-racist sense, cf. Soggin, *Introduction*, ch.30.2.

32. Ibid., ch.2.1-2.

33. J.A.Soggin, *The Prophet Amos*, London 1987, 140.

14. Under the Macedonians and Diadochi

1. Cf. Soggin, *Introduction* ch.2.6.
2. Ibid., ch.42.1.
3. Ibid., ch.17.
4. G.von Rad, *Old Testament Theology* II, Edinburgh 1965, reissued London 1975, 301ff.
5. Cf. D.Auscher, 'Les relations entre la Grèce et la Palestine avant la conquête d'Alexandre', *VT* 17, 1967, 8-30, and the classical texts collected by Stern.
6. With the Old Latin and Armenian, according to F.-M.Abel, BJ. The text has 'Benjamin', which is certainly wrong, even if it is the *lectio difficilior*, since he would then have been a lay person. For Bilga as a priestly family cf. I Chron.24.14.
7. Cf. Soggin, 1978, 73ff.
8. Garbini* 1988, 163f.; cf. also Meg Taʿan.8, ed J.A.Fitzmyer, *A Manual of Palestinian Aramaic Texts*, Rome 1978, no.150, pp.181-7 and 248.

15. Under the Romans

1. It is possible that the circular construction at Massada situated on the middle terrace is the tomb of Mariamne, cf. A.Schalit, 'Das Problem des Rundbaus auf der mittleren Terrasse des Nordpalastes des Herodes auf dem Berge Masada', *Theokratia* 2, 1970-2, 45-50.
2. For the trial of Jesus, in addition to the studies cited cf. P.Winter, *On the Trial of Jesus*, Berlin 1961, and P.-G.Antonini, *Processo e condanna di Gesù*, Turin 1982.
3. It is the achievement of Albert Schweitzer, *The Quest of the Historical Jesus*, London 1910, ³1954, to have demonstrated that the Synoptic Gospels, not to mention the other writings in the New Testament, are inadequate as a basis for composing a 'life of Jesus', though attempts are always being made by modern authors who apparently are unfamiliar with Schweitzer's work.
4. There is a recent positive evaluation of this text in G.Vermes, 'The Jesus Notice of Josephus Re-examined', *JJS* 38, 1987, 1-10; Vermes considers it a 'sympathetic neutral stand'.
5. J.Maier, *Jesus von Nazareth in der talmudischen Überlieferung*, Darmstadt 1978; this is at present the definitive study on the question, but for some comments see the review by D.Goldberg, *JQR* 73, 1982-83, 78-86.
6. This is the son of Agrippa I, to whom the Romans, as compensation for the loss of Judaea, which was put back under the administration of the procurators, had granted the territories previously belonging to Herod in Transjordan and Lebanon. However, most of the time he continued to reside in Jerusalem, where he maintained the right to nominate the High Priest.
7. Cf. W.Eck, 'Die Eroberung von Massada und eine neue Inschrift des L.Flavius Silva Nonius Bassus', *ZNW* 60, 1969, 282-9. However, the results of this study were questioned by Reicke 1982, 289 n.24, who suggests Josephus' dating, April 72 (cf. *BJ* 7,409).
8. Cf. S.G.Sowers, 'The Circumstances and Recollection of the Pella Flight', *TZ* 26, 1970, 305-20; A.R.C Leaney, in J.H.Hayes and J.M.Miller* 1977, 659 (with bibliography); G.Lüdemann, 'The Successors of Pre-60 Jerusalem Christianity. A Critical Evaluation of the Pella Tradition', in E.P.Sanders

(ed.), *Jewish and Christian Self-Definition* I, London and Philadelphia 1980, 161-73, and *Opposition to Paul in Jewish Christianity*, Minneapolis 1989, 200-13; J.Verheyden, *De vlucht van de Christenen naar Pella*, Brussels 1988; C.Koester, 'Origin and Significance of the Flight to Pella Tradition', *CBQ* 51, 1989, 90-106. It seems that the note is a fabrication by Eusebius, necessary for his exposition, cf. *HE* 3.5.3-4 and Epiphanius of Salamis, *Panarion* 29.7, 7-8, and *De mensuris* 15.

9. For these two apocalyptic writings cf. the study by W.Harnisch, *Verhängnis und Verheissung der Geschichte*, FRLANT 97, Göttingen 1969.

10. An example of Jewish agricultural settlement with a trustworthy tradition which goes back to a time before the two catastrophes is that of *pᵉqīʿīn*, Arabic *buqʿeiah*, coord 181-261. The Jewish population had to leave during the Arab revolt of 1936, and could not return until a decade later.

Appendix 2: The Chronology of the First Temple Period

1. See *WHJP* IV, 1, 63-101, 260-9.
2. See J. Finegan, *Handbook of Biblical Chronology*, Princeton 1964, 108-223; E. Bickerman, *Chronology of the Ancient World*, London 1968, 70-7; G.E. Samuel, *Greek and Roman Chronology*, Munich 1972, 245-8.
3. See e.g. D. Diringer in O. Tufnell, *Lachish III*, Oxford 1953, 339 (ostracon no. 20); J.C.L. Gibson, *Textbook of Syrian Semitic Inscriptions* I, Oxford 1971, 8f., (Samaria ostraca nos. 1, 2, 6, 10, 19).
4. The Babylonian Chronicle: F. Delitzsch, *Die babylonische Chronik*, Leipzig 1906 (= ASGW, phil-hist. Kl. XXV). For the Synchronistic King List from Ashur cf. A.L. Oppenheim, *ANET*, 272-4. On the Egyptian king lists: A. Gardiner, *Egypt of the Pharaohs*, Oxford 1961, 46-69.
5. A. Jepsen, *Die Quellen des Königsbuches*, Halle a/S 1956, 30ff.; E.R. Thiele, *The Mysterious Numbers of the Hebrew Kings* = (*MNHK²*), Grand Rapids, Mich. 1956, 174-91; S.R. Bin-Nun, *VT* 18, 1968, 414-32.
6. J.M. Miller, *JBL* 86, 1967, 277-88, and especially J.D. Schenkel, *Chronology and Recensional Development in the Greek Text of Kings*, Cambridge, Mass. 1968.
7. D.W. Gooding, *JTS* NS 21, 1970, 118-31; E.R. Thiele, *JBL* 93, 1974, 174-200.
8. Thiele, *MNHK*, 167-203.
9. See in general *JE* XI, cols.147-9; *EJ* XIV, cols. 1091-3 (including bibliography).
10. For a bibliographical survey until 1961, see H. Tadmor, 'Chronology', *Enc.Miqr.* IV, Jerusalem 1962, col.261-4. Additional studies include: D.N. Freedman, in G.E. Wright (ed.), *The Bible and the Ancient Near East. Essays in Honor of W.F. Albright*, 1961, 203-28; C. Schedl, *VT* 12, 1962, 88-119; J. Gray, *I and II Kings*, London 1964, 55-74; A. Jepsen and R. Hanhart, *Untersuchungen zur Israelitischen-jüdischen Chronologie*, BZAW 88, Berlin 1963, 1-47; V. Pavlovsky and E. Vogt, *Biblica* 45, 1964, 321-47; M. Miller, *JBL* 86, 1967, 276-88; A. Jepsen, *VT* 18, 1968, 31-45; W.R. Wifall, *ZAW* 80, 1968, 317-36; S. Yeivin, *M.Zer Kabod Volume*, Jerusalem 1968, 367-81 (in Hebrew).
11. This was suggested by Thiele in *MNHK²*, and more recently by Wifall (above n.10).
12. On the problem of calendar and intercalation in the biblical period, see J.B. Segal, *VT* 7, 1957, 250-307.
13. A. Gardiner, *JEA* 31, 1945, 11-28; id., *Egypt of the Pharoahs*, Oxford 1961, 69-

71. It is quite possible that the Persian court practised a similar custom (cf. E. Bickerman, *Chronology of the Ancient World*, London 1968, 90), which may explain the contradiction between the dates in Neh.1.1 and in Neh.2.1. This would also obviate the necessity of emending the text in Neh.1.1 and in Neh.2.1. For previous suggestions, see Tadmor, *JNES* 15, 1956, 227 n.70, and more recently D.J.A. Clines, *JBL* 93, 1974, 35.

14. For these, as well as for the terms 'accession year' and 'non-accession year', see J. Finegan, *Handbook of Biblical Chronology*, 80-6.

15. Cf. the Egyptian practice in the Hellenistic and Roman periods (e.g. 'the thirtieth year' [of Ptolemy XII], which is year 1 [of Cleopatra VII]); T.C. Skeat, *Mizraim* 6, 1937, 8; see also Finegan, *Handbook*, 80f.

16. This practice originated in Babylon during the Kassite dynasty, in the thirteenth century BCE, but it may in fact have started in the fourteenth century; see also J.A. Brinkman, *WO* 6, 1971, 153. The terms $r^e\check{s}it\ mal^ek\bar{u}t$ and $r^es\bar{\imath}t\ maml^ek\bar{u}t/mamleket$ used for the reigns of Jehoiakim and Zedekiah (Jer.26.1; 27.1; 28.1; 49.34) are not necessarily exact chronological terms like the Babylonian *šanat rēš šarrūti*, but general terms which indicate the initial period of these kings' reigns, whether it was less than a year, a full year, or more than a year. The Akkadian term *rēš šarrūti*, 'the beginning of the reign', occurs in some literary texts without the chronological connotation. See also Tadmor, *INES* 15, 1956, 227 n.17; id., *Studies in Honor of Benno Landsberger*, Chicago 1965, 353. For a variant opinion see N. Sarna, *Hagut Ivrit be-America* 1, Tel Aviv 1972, 121-30 (in Hebrew).

17. A. Ungnad, 'Eponymen', *RLA* II, 412-59.

18. Tadmor, *JCS* 12, 1958, 22-33.

19. See Tadmor, *JNES* 15, 1956, 227; *Enc.Miqr.* IV, cols., 267f. The term $\check{s}^enat\ molk\bar{o}$ (II Kings 25.27) also appears in a Phoenician inscription from the Persian period. Where Aramaic was predominant, the term used was a translation of *sănat rēs šarrūti*: see now F.M. Cross, 'Papyri from the Fourth Century BC from Dālīyeh', *New Directions in Biblical Archaeology*, ed. D.N. Freedman and J.C. Greenfield, Garden City, NY 1969, 44f.

20. M. Steen, *Compendia rerum Judaicarum ad Novum Testamentum*, I/1, Assen 1974, 62-68, and M.D. Herr, ibid., II, 1976, 843-5.

21. *Enc.Miqr.*, cols 265-6. It is possible that Ezekiel counted the years of Jehoiachin's exile from the spring, although the evidence in Ezekiel is not decisive because it could, in part, conform with the autumn reckoning: see A. Malamat, *IEJ* 18, 1968, 146ff.; id., *VTS* 28, 1975, 125-45; K.S. Freedy and D.B. Redford, *JAOS* 90, 1970, 262-74. Further support for the view that the year in Judah started in the spring has recently been brought by D.J.A. Clines, *Australian Journal of Archaeology* 2, 1972, 9-34; id., *JBL* 93, 1974, 22-40.

22. See Tadmor, *Scripta Hierosolymitana* 8, 1961, 259ff.

23. See Talmon, *VT* 8, 1958, 48-74.

24. For details of the methods employed by the Egyptian and Mesopotamian chronographers, see *Enc.Miqr*, cols 271-4.

25. For a somewhat different view, see J.A. Brinkman, *A Political History of Post-Kassite Babylonia*, Rome 1968, 63-7.

26. See *Enc.Miqr.* IV, col.286; VI, col.126.

27. See *Enc.Miqr.*, I, col.439.

28. See especially E.R. Thiele, 'The Question of Coregencies among Hebrew Kings' in *A Stubborn Faith. W.A. Irwin Festschrift*, Dallas 1956, 39-52.

29. The chronological scheme briefly delineated here has been presented in detail in the present writer's article on biblical chronology in *Enc.Miqr.* IV, cols.274-302; cf. bibliography, ibid., cols.309f. and above, n.10.

30. See ibid., cols.255-9, tables 7-9, and accompanying notes. Two new synchronisms have been added: no.3, see A.R. Millard and H. Tadmor, *Iraq* 35, 1973, 57ff., and Tadmor, ibid., 64; no.8 will be published in our *Inscriptions of Tiglath-pileser III, King of Assyria*, The Israel Academy of Sciences and Humanities (forthcoming). Note also the following new studies on synchronism no.4: L.D. Levine, *BASOR* 206, 1972, 40-2; M. Cogan, *JCS* 25, 1973, 96-9. For synchronism no.20, see above, n.19. For the problem of Egyptian synchronisms in the biblical period see K.A. Kitchen, *The Third Intermediate Period in Egypt*, Warminster 1973; id., 'Late Egyptian Chronology and the Hebrew Monarchy', *JANES* 5, 1973 (= T. Gaster Festschrift), 225-33.

31. For Assyrian and Babylonian chronology in the first millennium BCE see G. Smith, *The Assyrian Eponym Canon*, London 1876; F.X. Kugler, *Sternkunde und Sterndienst in Babel*, II/2, Münster in Westfalen 1912, 342-61; R.A. Parker and W.H. Dubberstein, *Babylonian Chronology 626 BC - AD 75*, Providence RI 1956.

32. See A. Malamat, *IEJ* 18, 1968, 135-57; id., *SVT* 28, 1975, 123-45; and *WHJP* IV, 1, ch.X. (Basing himself on a Tishri calendar he arrives at 586 for the destruction date.)

33. D.J. Wiseman, *Chronicles of Chaldaean Kings* (626-556 BC) in the British Museum, London 1956, 72.

34. See J. Lewy, *Die Chronologie der Könige von Israel und Juda*, Giessen 1927, 19f., n.3.

35. For details see Tadmor, *JCS* 12, 1958, 33–40.

36. See J. Begrich, *ZDMG* 83, 1929, 213; 86, 1932, 61. For a fundamentally different view, according to which Hezekiah assumed power in 716/5, see Thiele, *MNHK*², 155-72; id., *VT* 16, 1966, 83-107.

37. E.g. Thiele, above, n.36; W.F. Albright, *BASOR* 100, 1945, 22; also, more recently, J. Gray, *I and II Kings*, OTL, London and Philadelphia ²1970, 58, 74.

38. L.L. Honor, *Sennacherib's Invasion of Palestine*, New York 1926, 70; J. Lewy, *OLZ* 31, 1928, 158f.; Tadmor, *Enc.Miqr.* IV, cols.278f.

39. Jepsen had conjectured that the story of Ahab's death, I Kings 22, should actually be placed in the time of the Jehu dynasty, and that the king who fell in the battle of Ramoth-Gilead (in a war against Ben-Hadad III son of Hazael) was actually an heir of Jehu (A. Jepsen, *AFO* 14, 1942, 154-8). This view has recently been taken up again and developed by Miller, who contends that the king was Jehoahaz son of Jehu (J.M. Miller, *JBL* 85, 1966, 441-5; id., *ZAW* 80, 1968, 337-42). We have not adopted these views mainly because they raise more historical and historiographical problems than they attempt to solve.

40. *Enc.Miqr.* IV, cols.289-94.

41. See most recently J.D. Schenkel, *Chronology and Recensional Department in the Greek Text of Kings*, Cambridge, Mass. 1968, 61-108. But see the critical remarks of E.R. Thiele, *JBL* 93, 1974, 182-90.

42. Cf. A. Orr, *VT* 6, 1956, 304, 360; R. Borger, *JNES* 18, 1958, 74.
43. See *Enc.Miqr*. III, col.481; IV, cols.281f.
44. *Enc.Mirq*. IV, cols.247-51.
45. For a possible Sumerian parallel see T. Jacobsen, *The Sumerian King List*, Chicago 1939, 93 n.145 (Mes-anne-pada and his son A-anne-pada, the two early kings of Ur, reigning forty years each). Assigning forty years to a generation is also common in the Greek chronographic tradition; see G.E. Samuel, *Greek and Roman Chronology*, Munich 1972, 241-6. Cf. also D.W. Prakken, *Studies in Greek Genealogical Chronology*, Lancaster, Penn.1943, 20.

General Index

Index of Biblical References

Index of Modern Scholars